Global Business

In loving memory of my parents,
Gabriël Johannes Hough and
Maria Magdalena Hough

Johan Hough

To Ansa, for unfailing support,
encouragement and inspiration, and
to my children, Sylna and Wilhelm, for
their understanding and devotion

Ernst W. Neuland

Global Business

Environments and Strategies

Managing for Global Competitive Advantage

Editors

JOHAN HOUGH
University of South Africa

ERNST W NEULAND
University of Pretoria

Authors

JOHN DANIELS
University of Richmond, USA

TIM RADEBAUGH
Brigham Young University, USA

RONEL ERWEE
University of Southern Queensland, Australia

UNIVERSITY PRESS

OXFORD
UNIVERSITY PRESS

Great Clarendon Street, Oxford OX2 6DP

Oxford University Press is a department of the University of Oxford.
It furthers the University's objective of excellence in research, scholarship,
and education by publishing worldwide in

Oxford New York

Athens Auckland Bangkok Bogotá Buenos Aires Calcutta
Cape Town Chennai Dar es Salaam Delhi Florence Hong Kong Istanbul
Karachi Kuala Lumpur Madrid Melbourne Mexico City Mumbai
Nairobi Paris São Paulo Singapore Taipei Tokyo Toronto Warsaw

with associated companies in Berlin Ibadan

Oxford is a registered trade mark of Oxford University Press
in the UK and certain other countries

Published in South Africa
by Oxford University Press Southern Africa, Cape Town

Global Business: Environments and Strategies
Managing for Global Competitive Advantage

ISBN 0 19 571852 6

First published 2000

Designer: Mark Standley
Indexer: Sarah Maddox

Published by Oxford University Press Southern Africa
PO Box 12119, N1 City, 7463, Cape Town, South Africa

Set in 10pt on 12pt Photina MT by Compleat Typesetters
Reproduction by Compleat Typesetters
Cover reproduction by The Image Bureau
Printed and bound by Creda Communications,
Eliot Avenue, Eppingdust II, Cape Town

Chapters 3–5 reprinted from J Daniels and L Radebaugh,
International Business, 8th edition (pages 57–187).
© 1995 by Addison-Wesley Publishing, Inc.
Reprinted with permission of Addison-Wesley Longman.

The authors and publishers gratefully acknowledge permission to reproduce
material in this book. Every effort has been made to trace copyright holders, but
where this has proved impossible, the publishers would be grateful for information
which would enable them to amend any omissions in future editions.

Abridged table of contents

Table of contents

About the editors

JOHAN HOUGH obtained the degrees B.Sc. Honours (Agriculture), M.Sc. (Agriculture) and D.Com. from universities in South Africa and graduated from the Faculty Programme in International Business, South Carolina, in the United States. He is Professor of International Business at UNISA, in charge of the graduate and undergraduate courses in International Business. He has lectured in Sweden, Finland and the United States. Johan has been instrumental in the development of strategic alliance profiles and linkages for international and multinational businesses and the establishment of an investment database to attract investment to southern Africa. His areas of expertise include strategic management, international business research, facilitating local and international alliancies and spearheading global competitiveness in southern Africa. He has also received the Ernst Oppenheimer Overseas Research Grant, Foreign Research Bursaries from UNISA and a post-doctoral grant from the HSRC.

ERNST W. NEULAND obtained the B.Sc. Honours and M.Sc. degrees from the University of Stellenbosch, and the BBA (cum laude), MBA and DBA degrees from Potchefstroom University. He is Professor of Management and International Business at the University of Pretoria, where he teaches Strategic Management and International Business Management. His current research interests are in International Business Strategy. During 1980, Ernst spent his sabbatical at the University of Georgia in the United States, and has since presented papers both locally and abroad, notably in Israel, Mexico and the United States. He is a founder member and the first president of the Southern Africa Institute for Management Scientists (SAIMS), of which he currently holds honorary membership. He was also instrumental in establishing the Southern Africa Chapter of the Academy of International Business (AIB) in 1996, and served as Chapter Chairperson for the first term from 1996 to 1998. He currently serves on the editorial boards of the *SBL Research Review* and the *Journal of African Business*, and is involved in in-company management development programmes in International Business.

Acknowledgements

Numerous people deserve our gratitude for their assistance in preparing this book. Firstly, we would like to thank the following people at Oxford University Press who have worked with us on this project: Leanne Martini, senior commissioning editor, Johannesburg; Lisa Compton, editorial manager, Cape Town; and Margaret Greaves, freelance language editor, Cape Town.

Secondly, we would like to thank Addison-Wesley Longman for their contractual permission to use material from the book by John Daniels and Lee Radebaugh entitled *International Business: Operations and environments*, which was extremely helpful in our compilation of Chapters 3 to 5.

The assistance of Mr Willie van den Heever, Mr Bert Coetzer and Ms Eve Frangos of Price Waterhouse Coopers in providing information on international taxation and accounting is greatly appreciated. A word of appreciation also goes to Dr Gideon Nieman of the Department of Business Management at the University of Pretoria for providing information on franchising. The permission granted by the Graduate School of Business Leadership of the University of South Africa to use the research paper by T Mbabvu, *Foreign exchange movements: The Zimbabwean foreign exchange market*, is acknowledged with gratitude. A special word of thanks also goes to graduate students Rian Odendaal, Freda Prinsloo, Dominika Pietzrak, Elouise Barnard, Tanya Jacobs, Hein Mienie, and Arnoud van den Bout in the Department of Business Management at the University of Pretoria. The research studies by these students provided valuable information on the Euro, and the Nando's and Sentrachem cases.

Ernst is also deeply indebted to Stell Kefalas of the University of Georgia for his stimulating thoughts and encouragement over 20 years. It was Stell who originally sparked Ernst's interest in and continual dedication to international business.

Johan wants to thank Zelda for her unfailing motivation and support during the writing of this book.

Lastly, we would like to offer our sincere thanks to our academic colleagues at the University of South Africa and the University of Pretoria for their continued support and understanding.

Preface

Global Business: Environments and strategies is the first academic book on International Business to be published in South Africa. This pioneering work approaches International Business from southern African and global perspectives with the aim of developing the knowledge, insights, fundamental understanding and relevant skills that managers need in order to be successful in vastly different cultural, political, economic and legal environments across the world.

Because of the dramatic changes that have occurred throughout the world during the last two decades in particular, and the continuing trend towards internationalisation and a globalised economy, management education and development in International Business have become imperative if South African firms are to compete successfully in the international arena.

The changes in today's global business environment will gain even greater momentum as the world economy continues to shift from nationalism to regionalism and, increasingly, to globalisation. This means that any country, any enterprise, and any brand of product or service will face unlimited competition when trade barriers and other protective market measures are removed.

In anticipation of these developments, the management of multinational enterprises and other firms involved in international business has to be pro-active. This will generally require knowledge of internal as well as external environments, and the management and leadership skills to utilise environmental information and to capitalise on opportunities in the competitive global arena.

Accordingly, this book focuses on the relevant global business environments and relevant competitive and functional strategies that are of importance to international management and leadership. In our approach to this pioneering work, we acknowledge the existence of the phenomenon of globalisation, as well as the reality of the on-going impact of new factors on the global market place, with changing and increasing demands on international management. New markets have opened, while others are in the process of emerging. Improved technologies, especially in communications and transportation, are continually evolving, and barriers to trade are declining. These factors have all contributed to a major expansion of international trade and investment.

With these demands in mind, we approached the design of this book from the perspective of the need for relevant management education, training and development in the context of South Africa and southern Africa, notwithstanding the underlying theory and universal methodology of International Business on which this book is based.

Practical cases

South African, southern African and international cases on global issues, such as economic integration, changing global mindsets, leadership, finance, marketing, human resources and strategic alliances, add practical value to the theory of International Business. Furthermore, it provides both students and practitioners with a unique opportunity to benefit from local, international and practical business situations.

The framework of the book

This book consists of 12 chapters divided into four parts. In Part I, *Scope and dynamics of global business*, the first chapter deals with an overview of global business. International trade and global economic integration is then discussed in detail in chapter 2. In Part II, *Global business environments*, chapters 3 to 6 discuss the cultural, political, legal, economic and global monetary environments. Part III deals with *Global business leadership and strategies* where chapter 7 focuses on international management and leadership issues and the need for developing global mindsets in multinational enterprises. Chapters 8 to 10 provide the global management context within which functional international business strategies, such as marketing, human resources, and financial management, are conducted. Part IV, *Southern Africa and Africa: international co-operation and future perspectives*, addresses global collaboration and strategic alliances in chapter 11, while some future perspectives on southern Africa as an emerging regional market are discussed in chapter 12.

International business material on CD-ROM

Global Business: environments and strategies benefits from its related CD-ROM on International Business, entitled *Southern Africa: a global vision*. The CD links in the book include contributions by President Thabo Mbeki, Clem Sunter, Trevor Manuel, Chris Stals, Thomas Bata, Alec Erwin, Jeffrey Sachs, André la Grange, Jan de Bruyn and Louise Tager, confirming the importance of this publication for undergraduate students, graduate students and practitioners involved in the challenging field of International Business.

PART I

The scope and dynamics of global business

1 An overview of global business

Key issues

- Global business defined
- Types of international business
- Trends in the internationalisation of business
- Macro-economic determinants of international business
- Growth in global business and foreign investment
- Profile of South African companies involved in international business
- Internationalisation and evolution of multinational enterprises

1.1 Introduction

Rapid technological change and the increasingly global nature of competition are forcing South African firms to distribute their products more widely and quickly, cope with environmental change, and reduce costs.

Successful businesses of the future will treat the entire world as their domain in terms of meeting their supply and demand requirements. In such a globalised market, the domestic company will not be sustainably competitive. Globalisation is not a new concept, but there are relatively new factors that have contributed to its recent prominence, such as the opening of new markets for South African businesses and new communication and transport technology, resulting in a major expansion of international trade and investment.

The 1997, 1998 and 1999 World Competitiveness Reports by the World Economic Forum in Switzerland show a decline in South Africa's competitive position (relative to other newly-industrialised nations), especially in the area of internationalisation. Internationalisation is measured in terms of trade, exports, imports, cross-border investment flows, international alliances and partnerships with foreign firms, protectionism, and export/import diversification. South Africa's level of internationalisation has declined since 1992, while, in terms of partnerships with foreign firms, the country occupies the penultimate competitive position among newly-industrialised nations. Although South Africa's relative competitive position has declined, the country is still rated among the top five emerging markets in the world (see box titled 'Management perspective').

Management perspective: South Africa ranked among top five emerging markets

MORGAN STANLEY, the investment group, rates South Africa in its top five emerging markets in the world, with Hong Kong and Malaysia topping the global list. Stable interest rates in the United States and a moderately weak dollar should ensure a favourable backdrop for emerging markets. 'The top five markets based on low financial vulnerability, good valuations, earnings and liquidity are Hong Kong, Malaysia, India, South Korea and South Africa,' said Ajay Kapur, a strategist at Morgan Stanley. The least favourite emerging markets were Russia, Brazil, Chile, Taiwan and Turkey, he said. There had also been a dramatic reduction in the financial vulnerability of Thailand, South Korea, the Philippines, Indonesia and Malaysia.

SOURCE: *Business Report*, 15 January 1999.

Recent research on the retail financial services sector (Exhibit 1.1) shows the relative importance of globalisation for South Africa's financial institutions over the next five years. About 90% of executives based in South Africa planned international expansion over the next five years, while 87% of the firms in the USA and Canada anticipated the same, compared with European firms, of which only 27% planned international expansion. It is therefore becoming increasingly important for South African enterprises to be aware of the significance of international business issues, the reasons for international relations, environments and factors influencing international business, and events that affect international trade and investment patterns.

With regard to the future trends dominating the financial sector in South Africa, respondents pointed out the emergence of cross-border banking in the wake of the total

Exhibit 1.1: Firms most committed to global expansion

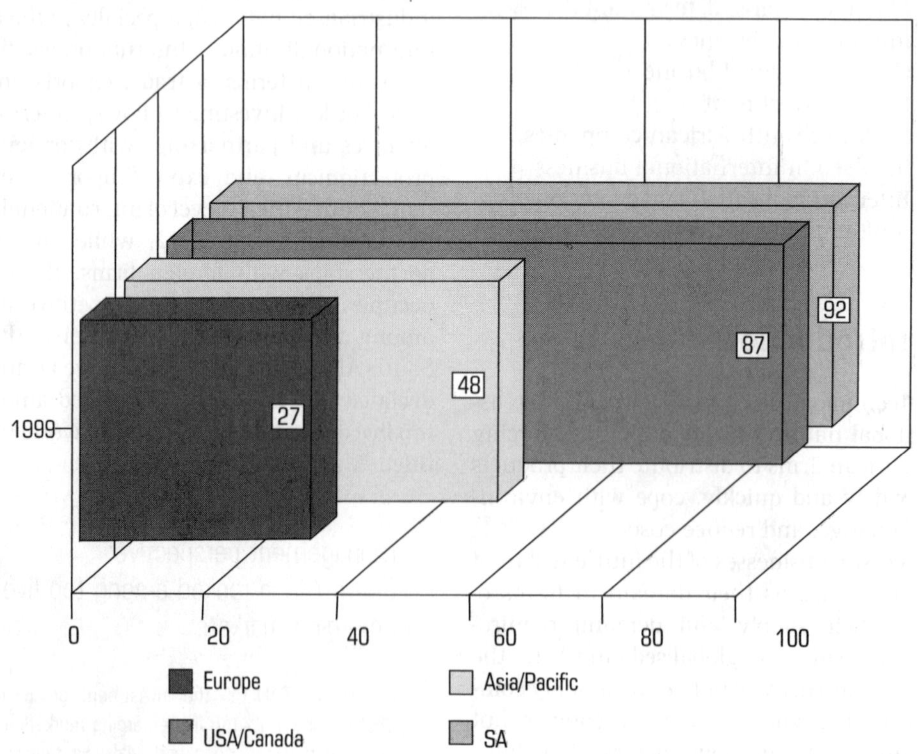

SOURCE: *Business Day,* 25 March 1999, p. 18.

lifting of South Africa's foreign exchange controls.

From a global perspective, international executives expected their firms to increase their presence in China, Asia, Latin America and Eastern Europe. Australia and New Zealand were the only locations where executives expected global business to increase in the next five years.

1.2 Global business defined*

Global business involves all those commercial activities between two or more countries. These commercial activities may be undertaken by private companies with a view to profit-making, or by government organisations, in which case there is generally no profit motive.[1]

Global commercial activities are defined as the movement of resources, goods, services and skills over international borders. The resources involved are raw materials, capital, people, and technology, while goods refer to half-finished and finished products. Services include accounting, advertising, communications, computer services, advisory services, education and training, legal opinions, and banking activities, while skills cover management and technical skills.[2]

It is obvious that there are various reasons for doing international business, that it is influenced by the objectives of international enterprises, and that it also affects the business environment. Take particular note of the interaction between the operations of international enterprises and their external and competitive environments (Exhibit 1.2).

Exhibit 1.2: Interaction between the operations of international enterprises and their external and competitive environments

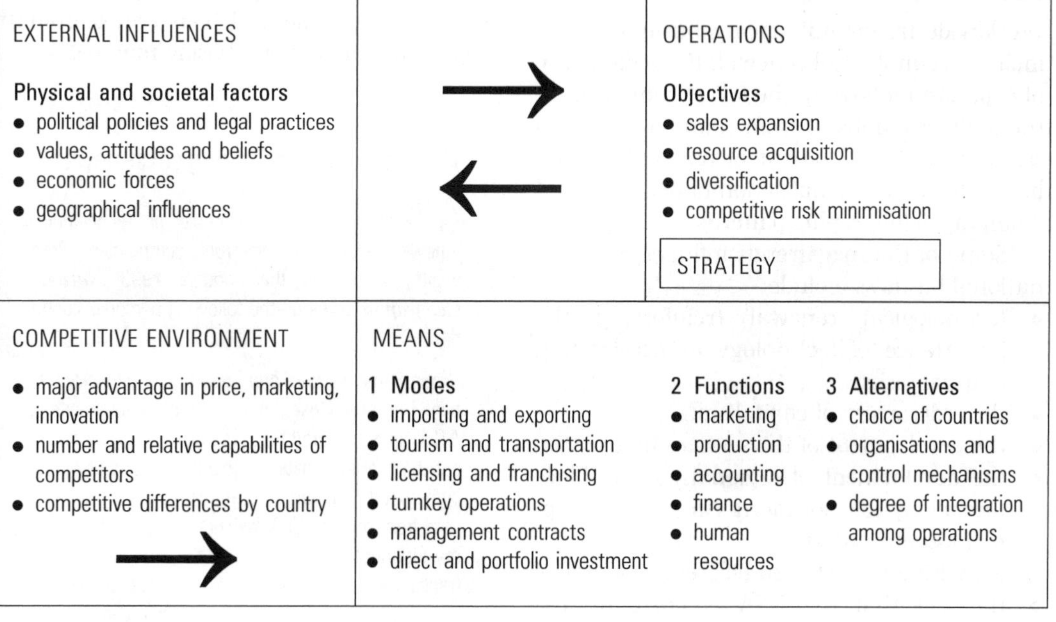

SOURCE: Daniels, J.D. & Radebaugh, L.H. 1998. *International business: environments and operations.* 8th edition. Reading, Mass: Addison Wesley, p. 10.

* "Global business" and "international business" are used interchangeably in this book.

1.3 Types of international business

The following types or modes of international business are identified:[3]

- merchandise exports and imports;
- service exports and imports;
- tourism and transportation;
- use of assets;
- investments, including direct and portfolio investments, licensing, concessions and turn-key investments, co-operative agreements;
- multinational enterprises.

These types of international business are discussed in more detail in Section 9.7.2, where international market entry modes are considered.

1.4 Trends in the internationalisation of business

Worldwide trends influencing business today include technological renewal, the rediscovery of capitalism following the fall of communism, the shift in emphasis from manufacturing to services, the development of regional trading blocs, the internationalisation of business, and changing demographic patterns.

Some of the megatrends influencing international business include:

- technological renewal (reinforcing the importance of technology in accelerating manual tasks);
- the rediscovery of capitalism;
- the development of the services industry;
- the development of regional trading blocs (including the Southern African Development Community);
- increasing ties between different economies;
- the fact that the USA is currently the number one economic force in the world;
- increasing competition among international industries;
- the unstable international political climate;
- changing demographic patterns and the impact of AIDS;
- outsourcing;
- privatisation;
- changing value systems.

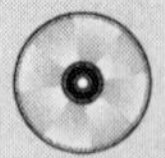

Compact disc

1 President Thabo Mbeki spells out the vision for regional economic integration and success in the Southern African Development Community.

Modern communication media have made it possible to exchange scientific, technical and commercial information rapidly and efficiently. This has facilitated the creation of new markets and increased competition. Modern communication has also accelerated and facilitated purchasing activities, especially in countries like South Africa and Australia, which are remote from the major international purchasing markets.

The impact of technological renewal

An excellent practical example of technological renewal relates to electronic currencies. Peter White, writing in the January 1993 *National Geographic* gives us the following personal illustration:

'I'm in Paris, it's late, and I need money quickly. The bank I go to is closed, of course, but outside sits an ATM, an automated teller machine – and look what can be made to happen, thanks to computers and high-speed telecommunications. I insert my ATM card from my bank in Washington, DC, and punch in my identification number and the amount of 1 500 francs, roughly equivalent to $300. The French bank's computers detect that it's not their card, so my request goes to the CIRRUS system's inter-European switching center in Belgium, which detects that it's not a European card. The electronic message is then transmitted to the global switching center in Detroit, which recognizes that it's from my bank in Washington. The request goes there, and my bank verifies that there is more than $300 in my account and deducts $300 plus a fee of $1,50. Then it's back to Detroit, to Belgium, and to the Paris bank and its ATM – and out comes $300 in French francs. Total elapsed time: 16 seconds.' The impact on trade – and especially international trade – is clear. Technology is (and will become) one of the strategic drivers in this industry.

In the period following the Second World War, rapid and sustained growth in international business operations was one of the most important catalysts for change in the business community throughout the world. The competition that resulted from business expansion in the East, especially in Japan and also in Hong Kong, South Korea, Singapore, and Taiwan, gave rise to far-reaching changes in business environments in the West.

South Africa, by contrast, remained a relatively small participant in international trade and by 2001/2002 its share in the international export market will still be less than 1%. This is probably mainly attributable to a tendency to export only under conditions of surplus production, the limitations resulting from previous foreign sanctions on the South African economy, relatively high inflation, and a prolonged recessionary climate.

In addition, the formation of regional trading blocs, such as the European Union (EU), the North American Free Trade Agreement (NAFTA) between the United States, Canada and Mexico, and the alliance of Pacific Ocean countries, has influenced the proportional value of the international trade for which individual countries are responsible. It has also affected the real growth rate of the countries in the various blocs and the living standard of their citizens.

The topic of regional trading blocs is particularly relevant because South Africa was accepted back into the British Commonwealth in June 1994. At present, the country does not belong to any other major bloc, but this should change in the near future. (South Africa is a conditional member of the Lomé Convention, which came into existence because the French insisted that the EU accept its overseas territories as part of the mainland.) The South African economy has suffered as a result. By contrast, the state of affairs in countries belonging to regional trading blocs is far better. Real economic growth in member countries of the EU, for example, is expected to be about 2,5% in 2000/2001 as a result of significant increases in exports to countries like Malaysia, Thailand and Singapore.

Tasks facing South African enterprises

To attain a higher economic growth rate and improve the standard of living, South African enterprises will have to export more, and relations with the large regional trading blocs will also have to be improved.

South African businesses need to be aware that the commercial activities of the multinational enterprises of the world's leading export countries were an important catalyst for their achievements in the area of economic growth. At the same time the level of activity of these enterprises can be seen as a real and useful indicator of the growth of international business. In fact, we could probably say that, in socio-economic terms, multinational enterprises have expanded their international business to such an extent that they now have a significant influence on economic, social and political developments in the major industrialised countries, and often dominate events in many of the less developed countries.

Multinational enterprises have contributed to the growth in world trade and have helped improve the welfare of the people in the countries involved. These enterprises may, however, also cause political, economic and social problems for their host countries since, in some instances, they find themselves having to develop strategies in accordance with political criteria rather than the profit principle. The southern African experience of multinational enterprises, however, has generally been positive.

There are, of course, various reasons for the considerable growth in international business since the Second World War. The influence of technological developments is one factor we have already mentioned. The expansion and growth of multinational enterprises as a result of improved management skills is another. But there are also several other reasons for the increased internationalisation of business. These are discussed in the next section.

The nine greatest medical technological inventions of all time

1790	First dental drill was invented by John Greenwood
1796	Discovery of vaccines by Edward Jenner
1846	Discovery of anaesthetics by Sir James Simpson
1847	Sterilisation was firstly introduced by Ignaz Semmelweiss to reduce the occurrence of childbed fever
1853	The first practical hypodermic syringe was introduced by Charles Pravaz
1895	X-ray machine was discovered by accident by Wilhelm Roentgen
1928	Antibiotics were discovered by Alexander Fleming
1955	Gregory Pincus invented a convenient and nearly 100% effective contraceptive
1982	The first permanent mechanical heart was implanted in a patient by Dr Barney Clark

SOURCE: Stower, D. 1999. 'The 100 greatest inventions'. *Popular Science*, Vol. 254 (2), pp.10–11.

1.5 Macro-economic determinants of international business

The following macro-economic determinants are helping to shape international business.[4]

1.5.1 Theory of comparative advantage – comparative cost benefits in international trade

The international business operations of enterprises are primarily shaped by the theory of comparative advantage and the relative cost benefits of producing different commodities in different countries. The question that arises is why countries trade with one another rather than each meeting its own needs.

All countries have certain resources in varying quantities and forms, which results in different cost structures and different prices for exploiting these resources and converting them into manufactured products. Because of these differences, one country has a comparative cost benefit over others when it comes to the exploitation of a resource or the manufacturing of a product.

Countries therefore tend to export products with the greatest comparative advantage benefit (or the smallest comparative disadvantage), and to import those with the smallest comparative benefit (or the greatest disadvantage).

Multinational enterprises developed as a result of the principle of comparative advantage, which enables them to benefit from the exploitation of natural resources or manufacturing and distribution possibilities in other countries.

Examples of South African enterprises which have used the comparative cost benefit principle are the Rembrandt group, Anglo American and Liberty Life.

1.5.2 Technological renewal and production expertise

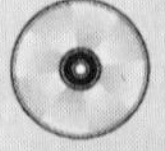

Compact disc

2 Mr Clem Sunter of Anglo American explains his ideas about major global megatrends which will impact on global business for the next 10-20

years, and tells how businesses could move from a lock-in situation to perpetual transition.

Technological renewal makes it possible to expand people's skills. Training and traditional expertise in expanding industries mean that people's skills grow more quickly in some countries than in others. Most technological progress occurs in industrialised countries, and enterprises in these countries therefore have a greater share in trade and investment in the world's manufacturing sector. By increasing the demand for new products and services, technology has a tremendous impact on international business.[5] (The box titled 'The nine greatest medical technological inventions of all time' on p. 8 demonstrates the impact of technology on the medical profession.)

The possession of natural resources is also no longer an exclusive advantage for any specific country because product or process technology can easily be transferred to purpose-built production sites. It is, for instance, sometimes easier – and less costly – to sell or hire advanced skills or expertise, or establish subsidiaries in other markets and begin production abroad, than it is to transport raw materials or manufactured goods from one country to another.

Huge potential in African banks

Global Technology views the financial services sector in Africa as a growth area. Kevin Williams, director of Temenos SA, a Global subsidiary, says there is a shake-up occurring in banking because most countries are deregulating and commercialising. African financial institutions must provide more structured finance that can be monitored and reported to a central authority as countries develop. 'Many are still looking to set up legitimate financial services,' Williams says. Some are opting for the Globus banking system distributed in the region by Temenos.

Another key reason for expected growth, Williams says, is that many African banks, faced with foreign competition, including institutions from South Africa, arrive on their doorsteps. 'If you arrive in many African countries with a semblance of a decent financial offering, you are going to capture large chunks of those markets quickly,' Williams says. With this in mind, and because many African institutions use inefficient systems, they urgently need to upgrade their systems. 'Global is based in Africa, we have a huge infrastructure, and we've got expertise which we've built up over 10 years.'

SOURCE: *Financial Mail*, www.fm.co.za. 'Temenos seeking out new markets', 2 October 1998.

1.5.3 Theories on direct foreign investment

International movements of capital are important macro-economic determinants in the international business community. The general theory of capital flow points to a foundation of direct investment, according to which capital will move from one country to another in reaction to differences in the marginal productivity of capital. In other words, capital will flow from where it is abundant to where it is scarce, or from countries where the rate of return is low to those to where it is high.[6]

It must, however, be pointed out that this theory no longer explains all international movements of capital. There are now considerable movements of capital between the EU, Japan and the United States as large development investments are made in various markets. International speculators in the early 1990s moved massive amounts of capital when various European currencies, including the pound sterling, the Italian lira and the Irish pound, were put under pressure, one after the other, to test the breaking points in the exchange rate system of the EU. Multinational enterprises also often create capital by lending in the host country, rather than transferring capital.

Evidently, the marginal productivity of capital theory is no longer considered sufficient to explain the movement of capital between countries. Other factors, including the role of multinational enterprises, also come into play.

1.5.4 International agreements and institutions

Multinational agreements and organisations have a significant influence on international business activities. Multinational agreements are a result of the realisation that countries are becoming increasingly interdependent and that a measure of consistency and uniformity is necessary to ensure an international flow of goods and services.

Important examples of such agreements are:

1 the multilateral agreements concluded by large regional trading blocs such as the EU and NAFTA, and the Pacific Ocean countries;
2 the General Agreement on Trades and Tariffs (GATT), which has freed up the international movement of trade and reduced trading limitations by means of agreements reached in various rounds of negotiations; and
3 the International Patent and Trade Marks Convention, which creates ownership rights for enterprises that do business internationally.

Among the major international institutions of importance to international business are:

1 the International Monetary Fund (IMF), which helped to change the international exchange rate regulations;
2 the World Bank, the Development Bank of Asia and the Inter-American Development Bank, which provide loans and assistance for approved, government-guaranteed projects; and
3 the International Air Transportation Association (IATA) and various shipping conferences, which regulate international air travel and air and sea transport.

1.5.5 The product life cycle theory and international trade cycles

The product life cycle theory offers an explanation for certain shifts in world trade. It compares world trade and investment with stages in the life cycle of a product and states that the production location of products will shift from one country to another as they move through their life cycle. Thus a new product in the initial stage, or phase one, is typically developed in reaction to an identified need in the market and exported by the country which developed it. Phase two is characterised by increased exports by the innovating country, while competition increases and there is some overseas production. In phase three the product reaches maturity, and there is a drop in exports from the innovating country as production begins in less developed countries where costs are lower. In phase four, the final stage in the product life cycle, the market begins to decline with increased production in less developed countries and the innovating country becoming a net importer of the product.

1.5.6 The oligopoly model

Enterprises operating under oligopolistic conditions (where there are only a small number of sellers) tend to make considerable investments in foreign markets. Such multinational enterprises usually have another common characteristic, namely that they operate on a large scale. One reason for this, at least as far as some industries such as aircraft manufacturing are concerned, is that the scope of the market is limited, and these enterprises have to rely on economies of scale as an important element of competitive advantage.

The oligopoly model helps us to understand the role of the large multinational enterprises in the movement of capital in the international market. The model also helps us to understand why multinational enterprises make large direct investments abroad. It shifts the focus of theories on the international movement of capital to an analysis of the motivation and behaviour of businesses and their role in the movement of international capital.

1.5.7 The international transfer of resources

International business has benefited by the transfer of resources over national borders. These resources include technology, management expertise, capital, labour and natural resources. For example, an important benefit of foreign direct investment (FDI) is that a multinational enterprise (MNE) can learn valuable skills from its exposure to foreign markets and transfer these skills and technologies to the MNE in the home country.

Resources are not equally distributed geographically. The differences in distribution are known as differentials in the demand-supply ratio of resources between countries. The differentials in the distribution of resources create opportunities internationally for multinational enterprises.

These differentials create further opportunities for multinational organisations by creating economic pressure which facilitates the movement of resources between the countries concerned. Measures taken by governments similarly tend to influence the movement of resources.

1.5.8 The balance of payments

The trade balance between countries is reflected in a favourable or unfavourable balance of payments. The growth of developing countries, in particular, depends on their ability to maintain a positive balance of payments. If a country's balance of payments is unfavourable, its economic growth is put under pressure because imports, including the imports of capital goods required for domestic industrial growth, often have to be limited. The alternative is for the shortfall on the balance of payments to be eliminated by a net inflow of foreign capital loans. If it is difficult to obtain such loans, as has been the case with South Africa, the options are either (1) acceptance of a lower economic growth rate, or (2) intensified efforts to increase exports. In the latter instance, it is essential that the government take steps to encourage enterprises to increase their involvement in international business operations.

It is also important to understand South Africa's balance of payments since it forms the framework within which foreign exchange is used for imports and exports and to clear foreign debt. The balance of payments is therefore critically important in the development of international purchasing and settling strategies since it influences the ability to move money across international borders.

1.6 Growth in global business and foreign investment

1.6.1 Growth in global business activities

Worldwide trends influencing international business were explored in Section 1.4. The reasons for the internationalisation of an enterprise's business include expansion of sales, resource acquisition, diversification to minimise competitive risk, saturated markets, and depreciating currencies. Other objectives are achieving low costs in order to strengthen the enterprise's competitive position, and gaining access to natural resources. The political stability of countries which are business partners is another important reason for doing business beyond national borders. The globalisation of markets is discussed in Chapter 9 (Section 9.2).

Besides these tendencies toward greater sales and profits, the following factors have contributed significantly to the positive growth in international business:

- Modern communication media have made it possible to exchange scientific, technical and commercial information rapidly and efficiently. This has facilitated the creation of new markets and increased competition. Modern communication has also accelerated and facilitated purchasing activities, especially in countries like South Africa, Zimbabwe and Botswana, which are remote from the major international purchasing markets.

- Rapid means of international travel and transport without corresponding price hikes have made it possible to control subsidiaries in different parts of the world and visit suppliers in other countries. The lifting of economic sanctions in the early 1990s has, for example, reopened international air routes to South African businesspeople and facilitated access to international selling and purchasing markets and new sourcing opportunities.
- Modern management techniques used by multinational enterprises have channelled new ideas, technology and production processes – and also resources and capital – to wherever they are needed on the world market. The presence in South and southern Africa of numerous multinational enterprises from countries such as Germany, France, the United Kingdom, the United States, Japan, Malaysia, and Singapore, has therefore contributed significantly to the growth of the southern African economy, especially since the early 1990s.
- Private companies have shown that they can adapt to changing circumstances and still exploit overseas markets efficiently and function under foreign governments with their diverse political policies.
- An understanding of the principle of economic expediency has enabled managers to develop foreign markets before their competitors could enter the field. Southern African enterprises are now well placed to expand their business operations on the North African market. The world's capital markets have developed to the point where they are now able to meet the needs of multinational enterprises more efficiently. Under its new political dispensation South Africa has far easier access to these markets.
- International trade has moved away from bilateralism in the direction of multilateralism. Various rounds of GATT negotiations resulted in the establishment of the World Trade Organisation (WTO). These negotiations have helped to liberalise and expand world trade.
- Large foreign aid programmes of the EU, the United States and the former Soviet Union have helped recipient countries expand their share in international trade considerably.
- The diplomatic tension between communist and non-communist countries resulted in greater political and economic co-operation between the non-communist countries and served as an incentive for the operations of multinational countries. The downfall of the communist regimes has opened the door for South Africa to establish commercial ties with countries such as Russia, Poland, Hungary, and Romania.
- Sustained growth in the world's gross product has been the result of the creation of new markets and the expansion of existing ones. South African enterprises should be on the lookout for new markets (including southern Africa) to develop. Botswana is one of the countries where there is a liberal foreign exchange and payments system with no exchange control restrictions on current remittances.

Country perspective: Botswana

Since independence in 1966, Botswana has established itself as one of the few successful multiparty democracies in Sub-Saharan Africa. Elections are held regularly at five-year intervals. Government is also committed to the development and maintenance of a democratic, open and non-racial society.

Botswana has international telecommunications links with the rest of the world and road networks have been established with Zimbabwe, South Africa, Namibia and Zambia. The country's railway system links Botswana with South Africa and Zimbabwe. Regular air services connect Gaborone's Sir Seretse Khama International Airport with the rest of the world.

To encourage investment in Botswana, the government is committed to creating an enabling environment in which the private sector can participate in economic development. There is a liberal foreign exchange and payments system. There are no exchange control restrictions on current remittances. Foreign investors are able to remit their profits and dividends abroad and to make capital investments outside Botswana. There are several specific incentive schemes – all of them geared towards assisting the establishment and growth of new investments.

SOURCE: *Official SADC Trade, Industry and Investment Review.* 1998. Southern African Marketing Co.

1.6.2 Factors influencing foreign investment

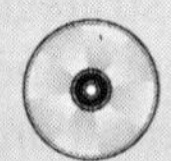

Compact disc

3 The 14 key factors affecting FDI into southern Africa are explained in this CD clip.

Various aspects and conditions should be considered before investing overseas. The following ten factors should be kept in mind specifically before investing internationally.[7]

Political stability. This is identified as the most important factor since violent *coups d'état*, aggressive neighbouring states and terrorism may endanger even the most profitable investments and the lives of personnel. Many enterprises have lost millions of rand because they did not consider these factors.

Economic performance. No investor will invest in a country in which the economic basis is fundamentally weak, unemployment and inflation are spiralling out of control, and the citizens do not have a physical share in the country.

Attitude to investors. Government officials who come into contact with overseas investors must be informed of the employment, investment and other opportunities associated with such investments so that they receive these people favourably and courteously.

Government policy. Government policy on capital transfers to the investor's home country, foreign financing of staff salaries, foreign exchange control, and import protection are factors that affect international business.

Infrastructure. The cost of industrial land, roads, railways, electricity, water and telecommunication may make a country non-competitive and its neighbours may, therefore, be better options.

Labour issues. Factors to be taken into account include entrenched labour relations and collective bargaining practices, labour costs, training of labourers and development opportunities, work ethics, trade unions, availability of professional and technical personnel, and the influence of party politics on employees.

Banking and finance. Various questions can be asked here, for instance:

- Are all the banking and financing instruments necessary for modern international trade available?
- Are there enough banks with international links to perform competitively worldwide?
- What is the cost of capital and how easy is it to gain access to funds?
- Are there branches of international banking groups, or does the state place restrictions on the establishment of such banks?

Government bureaucracy. A positive attitude on the part of the state towards international projects is important because it can accelerate approval and completion of projects and, of course, foreign investment and the creation of new job opportunities.

Business environment. The business environment includes elements such as availability of lawyers, accountants, building contractors, business partners, and so on. Other important aspects are whether local businesspeople have confidence in their country and choose to invest locally or elsewhere because of negative perceptions of local business opportunities.

Quality of life. The quality of schools, medical facilities, housing and security are important considerations for foreign personnel working on international projects or in the subsidiaries of multinational enterprises.

> Crime fears in South Africa add momentum to skills flight
>
> The upward trend in emigration persisted last year, and with crime showing little sign of abating and a recession looming, more people are likely to join the run in the coming year. In 1997-1998 about 3% of low-level workers, 11% of skilled workers and 14% of executives who resigned did so because of emigration, according to the P-E Corporate Services Salary Survey, which covers 750 organisations employing 1,5m people.
>
> 'The main reasons for emigration remain rooted in concerns about safety and security and declining standards of essential services,' says P-E Corporate Services MD Martin Westcott. 'The added threat of job insecurity and possible retrenchment will tip the scales in favour of emigration for many executives considering this option.'
>
> SOURCE: *Financial Mail*, www.fm.co.za, 29 January 1999.

1.7 Profile of South African companies involved in international business

Exhibit 1.3 (p. 15) gives an indication of the number of South African businesses, based on the Standard Industrial Classification (SIC), involved in doing business across borders. These businesses are categorised as importers and exporters.[8]

It is clear from Exhibit 1.3 that most exporters and importers are operating in the manufacturing and wholesale and retail sectors of the South African economy. Another observation is that the number of importers is almost double that of the exporters. For South Africa as an emerging economy, it is important that an export orientation should be encouraged to increase its internationalisation profile and competitive position.

1.8 Internationalisation and evolution of multinational enterprises

1.8.1 Strategies for international commitments in the internationalisation process

Various companies in different industries find themselves at different levels of internationalisation. Different strategies are therefore necessary for companies to operate successfully and to honour international commitments. Exhibit 1.4 (p. 16) gives a picture of some strategies that companies might follow to expand their presence in and exposure to the international markets. These involve following gradual successive steps or phases:

1 passive to active pursuit of opportunities (see A in Exhibit 1.4);
2 internal to external handling of the business (see B in Exhibit 1.4);
3 limited to extensive modes of operations (see C in Exhibit 1.4);
4 few to many locations (see D in Exhibit 1.4);
5 similar to dissimilar environments (see E in Exhibit 1.4).

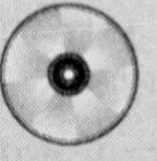

Compact disc

4 Mr Thomas Bata of Bata Shoes in Canada gives a short summary of his business philosophy with regard to southern Africa.

Exhibit 1.3: Number (and percentages of the total) of South African exporters and importers per section

SIC section	Number of exporters	% of total	Number of importers	% of total	Total number
Agriculture	70	2	63	1	133
Mining and quarrying	23	1	14	0	37
Manufacturing	1577	55	2155	45	3732
Electricity and water	1	0	3	0	4
Construction	8	0	50	1	58
Wholesale and retail	1118	39	2238	47	3356
Transport, storage and communication	33	1	94	2	127
Business services	23	1	71	1	94
Personal services	11	1	123	3	134
TOTAL	**2864**	**100%**	**4811**	**100%**	**7675**

SOURCE: *Bureau for Marketing Research*, Unisa, 1999.

The way in which a local enterprise moves through various phases as it begins to develop into a multinational operation is described below (Section 1.8.2).[9]

1.8.2 Evolution of multinational enterprises

Phatak divides the evolution of a local enterprise into a multinational one into the following seven phases, as outlined in Exhibit 1.5 (p. 17).

Phase 1: International (overseas) inquiries

Phase one begins when a company receives an inquiry about one of its products directly from a foreign businessperson or from an independent domestic exporter and/or importer. The company may ignore the inquiry, in which case there is no further evolutionary development. However, if the company responds positively and its product sells at a profit on the foreign market, then the stage is set for more sales of its products abroad, and company executives are likely to become favourably disposed towards the idea. Other inquiries from the foreign buyers are received more enthusiastically, and the company sells its products abroad through a domestic export intermediary. The latter could be an export merchant, an export commission house, a resident buyer (a buyer who is domiciled in the exporting company's home market and represents all types of private or government buyers from abroad), a broker, or a combination export manager (an exporter who serves as the exclusive export department of several non-competing manufacturers).

Exhibit 1.4: Strategies for international commitments in the internationalisation process

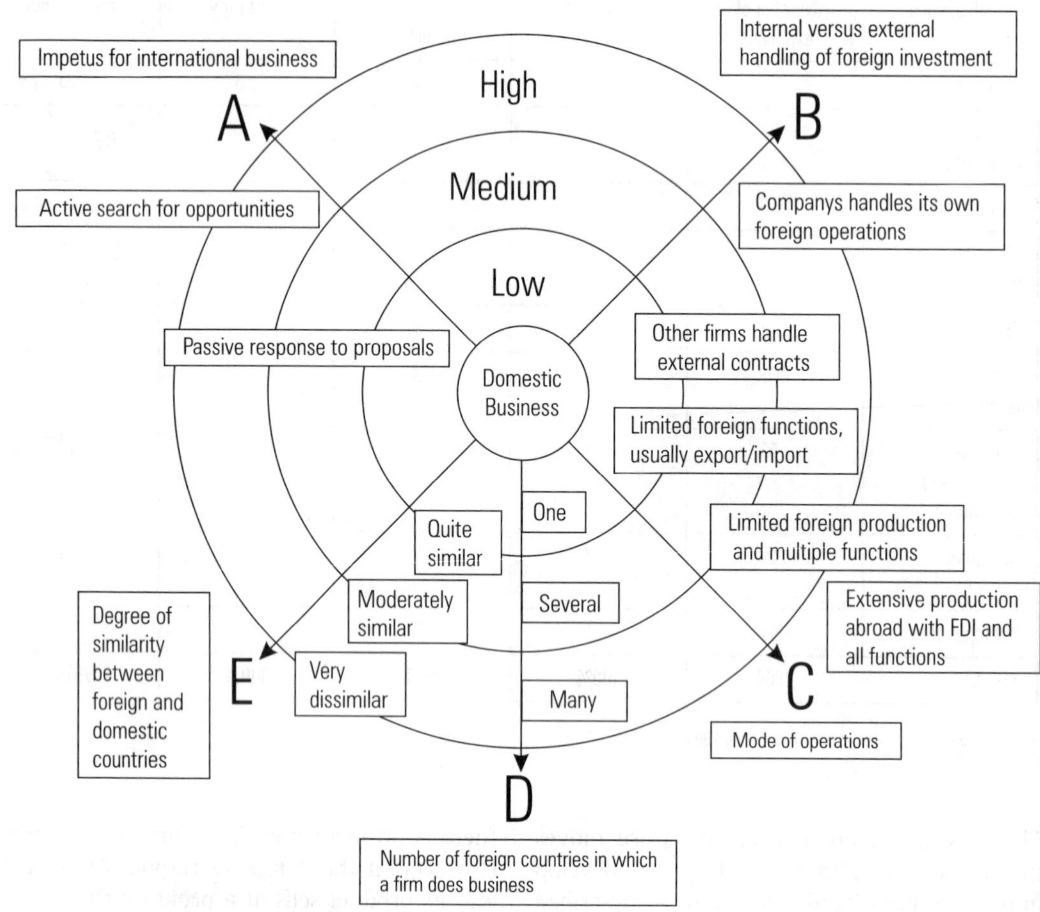

SOURCE: Daniels, J.D. & Radebaugh, L.H. 1998. *International business: environments and operations.* 8th ed. Reading. Mass: Addison Wesley, p. 25.

Phase 2: Export manager

As a company's exports continue to expand and the executives decide that the time is ripe to take export management into their own hands and no longer rely on unsolicited inquiries from abroad, they may decide to assume a proactive rather than a reactive position on exports. An export manager with a small staff is appointed to actively search for foreign markets for the company's products.

Phase 3: Export department and direct overseas sales

As export sales continue their upward surge, the company has difficulty operating with only an export manager and his or her small staff. A fully-fledged export department or division is established at the same level as the domestic sales department. The company then drops the domestic export intermediary and starts to sell directly to importers or buyers located in foreign markets.

Exhibit 1.5: Process by which local companies might develop into a multinational enterprise

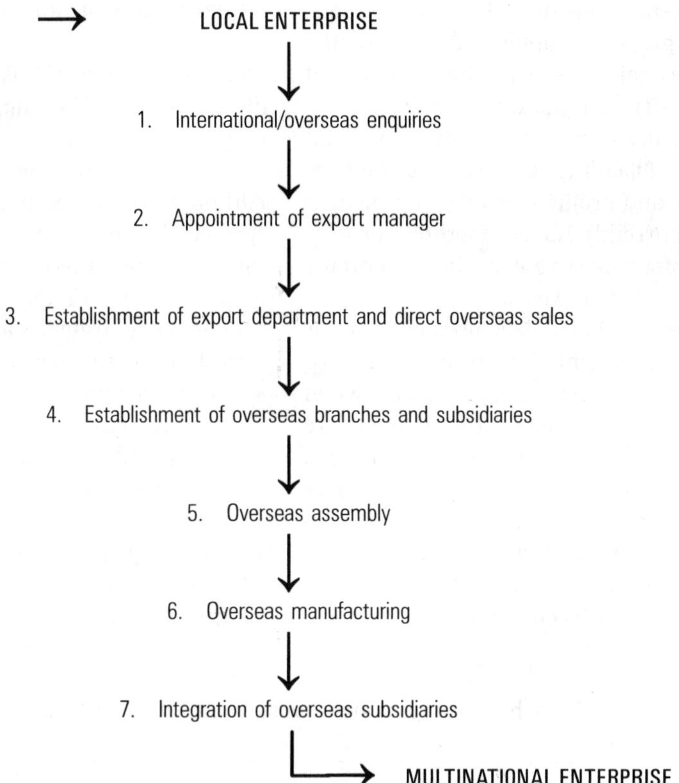

SOURCE: Adapted from Phatak, A.V. 1992. *International dimensions of management*. 3rd ed. Boston: PWS-Kent.

Phase 4: Overseas branches and subsidiaries

Further growth in export sales requires the establishment of sales branches abroad to handle sales and promotional work. A sales branch manager is directly responsible to the home office, and the branch sells directly to intermediaries in the foreign markets. A sales branch gradually evolves into a sales subsidiary, which is incorporated and domiciled in the foreign country and enjoys greater autonomy than previously.

Phase 5: Overseas assembly

Assembly occurs abroad for three major reasons: cheaper shipping costs for unassembled products, lower tariffs, and cheaper labour. The company may begin assembly operations in one or more of the foreign markets if it is more profitable to export the unassembled product rather than the whole product. Often tariffs and transportation costs are lower on unassembled parts and components than on assembled, finished products. For example, the parts of an unassembled television set can be packed in a smaller box than a fully assembled set.

Phase 6: Overseas manufacturing

After the previous stages have been accomplished, the next step is the establishment of production abroad. At this stage the company has a well-developed export programme supported by country market studies, promotion and distribution programmes tailored to the needs of each country market, and research aimed at identifying new foreign markets. Exhibit 1.6 gives a graphical display of the market-entry choices based on the link between product diversity and market complexity.

The company's executives may now begin to experience difficulties in increasing the total sales volume and profits in foreign markets in which they currently have a foothold, or they may find it impossible to enter other potentially lucrative markets via exports.

The above-mentioned difficulties often occur when local governments impose high tariffs or quotas on the import of certain products or when they ban the import totally if the products are being produced locally by a domestic company. In such cases the company executives may decide to penetrate the foreign market by producing the product in the foreign market itself.

Three methods are generally available for commencing foreign production:

(a) contract manufacturing (see Exhibit 1.6);
(b) licensing (see Exhibit 1.6);
(c) direct investment in manufacturing facilities.

Each of these methods has advantages and disadvantages. The appropriate strategy or method will therefore depend on the special circumstances of the company concerned. Although these methods are discussed here specifically to clarify the evolution of the multinational enterprise, they are explored in greater detail in Chapter 9 (Section 9.7), where market entry strategies are considered as part of overall marketing strategy.

- Contract manufacturing. Under a contractual agreement, the foreign producer produces and sells the company's product in the foreign market, but the company continues to promote and distribute it.
- Licensing. In the case of a licensing agreement, the foreign company pays a royalty to the international company for its patents,

Exhibit 1.6: Market entry based on product diversity and market complexity

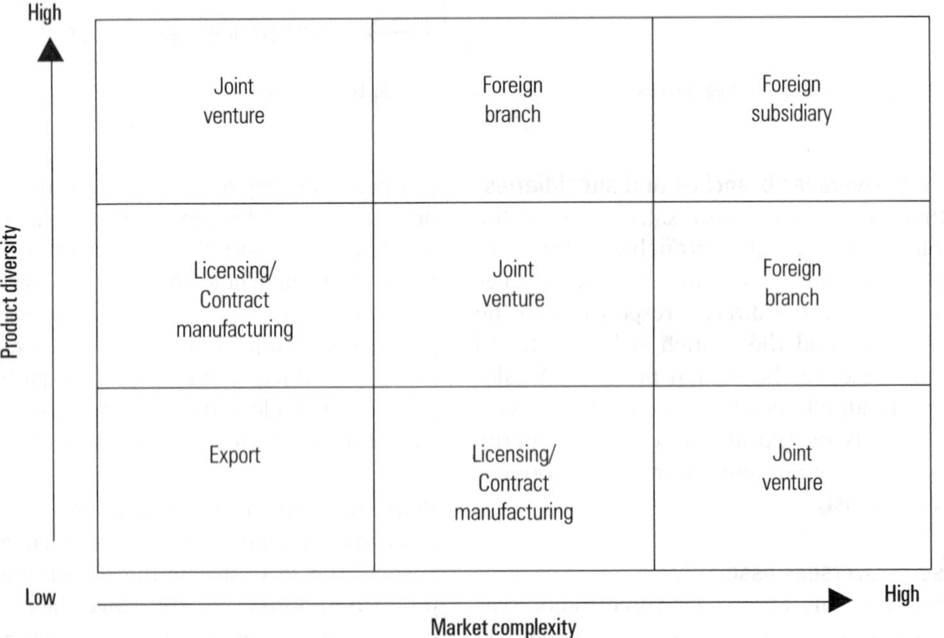

SOURCE: *Business Day*, 'Mastering global business', April 1999.

trademarks and trade secrets. If the company adopts this route to foreign manufacturing, more often than not it finds licensing to be a less than satisfactory approach to penetrating the foreign market. The company's dissatisfaction with licensing may stem from its executives' belief that the foreign licensee is not doing enough to promote sales of the licensed product or that the licensee is not maintaining product quality (thus damaging the reputation and the trademark of the company). There are many other reasons that could cause dissatisfaction with the licensee's performance and with the total licensing arrangement. For the licensor company, then, establishing a manufacturing facility via direct investment becomes an increasingly attractive method for tapping foreign markets.

- Investment in manufacturing. After establishing a manufacturing facility in a foreign market, the company has a total business to manage in a foreign country. It must therefore perform the many business transactions abroad – purchasing, finance, human resource planning and management, manufacturing, marketing, and so on. The company is also obliged to make significant commitments of technical, management and financial resources to the new foreign entity.

Phase 7: Integration of overseas subsidiaries

As the parent company managers decide to integrate the various foreign subsidiaries into one multinational enterprise system, they lose considerable autonomy because strategic decisions are now made by top management at company headquarters. The company's management begins to view the entire world as its theatre of operations; it plans, organises, staffs, and controls its international operations from a global perspective. Strategic decisions such as the following are made after a careful analysis of their worldwide implications:

- In what country should we build our next production facility?
- Throughout the world, where are our markets and from which production centre should they be served?
- From which sources in the world should we borrow capital to finance our current and future operations?
- Where should our research and development laboratories be located? From which countries should we recruit people?

When the management of the company starts thinking and operating in global terms, it has evolved into a truly multinational enterprise.

Not all companies go through each of the seven stages described in the preceding sections. Some companies stop short of complete integration of their domestic and foreign operations, preferring instead to manage them in a decentralised manner without an overall global strategy. Others may choose to co-ordinate the operations of subsidiaries in a certain region of the world, such as Europe, and keep subsidiaries in other regions unattached and semi-autonomous. Still other companies may decide to think globally with respect to only a few of the enterprise's functions. For instance, managers may think in worldwide terms where financial and production issues are concerned, but not for marketing, personnel, purchasing, and research and development. Thus there are different degrees of multinationality when it comes to operating on a multinational scale. Some firms may progress further along the multinational path and become true multinationals, whereas others may choose to end their journey at various milestones along the way.

Should companies use a foreign partner to move into other countries, or go it on their own? This is a key question. The 'International business in practice' box provides an interesting answer from an American company.

International business in practice

When Peter H. Tracy, president of Micropatent, a patent-information service in East Haven, Connecticut, decided he needed an overseas partner to sell MicroPatent's CD-ROMs to foreign subscribers, he devised an unusual two-stage approach. 'I knew we needed to start out with a joint venture, because we were a new company and completely lacked a foreign distribution network. But I also wanted us to be able to quickly bring those international operations in-house, which meant we needed a joint venture with an exit strategy attached.'

Stage one, back in 1989, consisted of negotiating a five-year contract with a British publisher. 'We reserved North American distribution rights for ourselves and gave the British company distribution rights everywhere else.' MicroPatent received a royalty on every overseas sale; by the time the contract expired, last year, royalties had contributed about $1 million to the company's $6 million in annual sales.

Stage two involved MicroPatent's recent assumption of international marketing responsibilities. 'Our British publisher tried to persuade us to extend the contract – which was tempting,' notes Tracy. 'But in recent years, we'd moved into different markets, especially on the Internet, and we believed we'd be better off by ourselves.' The transition worked smoothly because Tracy had planned his company's exit strategy up front. 'We were prepared because we always insisted that our partner give us the name of each new customer it signed up for us. In return, MicroPatent will pay its former partner a reduced royalty for the next three years on any of its customers that stay with us.'

SOURCE: www.inc.com/international. *Inc. Online's Guide to International Business: Making the business of going global a little bit easier*, February 1999.

This is a practical example of a company which used a foreign partner to move into another country. The Asian market is so big and growing so rapidly that MicroPatent would have been better off negotiating two of those arrangements, one with a European partner and one with an Asian company. (www.inc.-com/international).

A manufacturing company in South Africa (Multotec) has also been selected as a case to illustrate the internationalisation process.

1.9 Summary

This chapter introduced the concept of international business. As globalisation increases, many domestic companies will not be sustainably competitive. South African and southern African companies need to be aware of the significance of international business issues, the reasons for international relations, environments and factors influencing international business, and foreign investment patterns.

Various modes of entry or phases are possible for companies to become more globalised and earn more foreign currency through their exports of products, services or skills. There are megatrends which influence the success of these efforts, such as population, technology, formation of strategic alliances, development of the services industry, development of regional trading blocs, and the fact that international industries are becoming increasingly competitive.

There are many reasons for the internationalisation of an enterprise's business: for example, to expand markets and sales, to acquire resources, to diversify, to minimise competitive risk, to expand beyond saturated markets, to lessen the impact of depreciating currencies, to achieve lower costs, to gain access to natural resources, and to take advantage of the political stability of countries where business partners are located.

A local enterprise moves through various phases as it begins to develop into a multinational enterprise, but not all companies go through each of the seven stages of internationalisation described in this chapter. Some companies stop short of complete integration of their domestic and foreign operations by adopting an overall global strategy, preferring instead to manage these operations in a decentralised manner.

Various macro-economic determinants which are helping to shape international business also came under discussion. In the next chapter the focus will be on international trade, international trade issues and the development of major global trading blocs which influence global business today.

Case Study

Multotec Cyclones (Pty) Ltd[10]

Introduction

Multotec is an example of a South African company in the early development stages of internationalisation. Sufficient information could be obtained to analyse the various issues involved in internationalisation in the form of various reports, planning documents and statistics, as well as a personal interview conducted with the managing director. Four questions were asked: Why did the company decide to internationalise? How did the process evolve? What were the implications for the company and how were they managed? How is the subsequent future development of the company visualised?

Multotec: a company profile

The company was targeted because of a clear international commitment and business philosophy as is apparent from its mission statement. It had an annual turnover of R33,5 million for the year ending February 1996, of which 25% was represented by export activities and other international operations. The vision of the managing director is that exports should account for 50% of turnover with the current product range by the year 2000. Multotec makes an excellent case study as an example of a company with an increasing international dimension in business and an emerging global mindset that penetrates the strategy, structure and culture of the organisation.

Multotec Cyclones (Pty) Ltd was started in 1981 and is one of three companies of Multotec Holdings (Pty) Ltd. The other two operating companies in the group are Multotec Manufacturing and Multotec Wear Linings. Multotec Cyclones operates from premises in Gauteng, South Africa, and the following extract from the mission statement was taken from the business's strategic planning document:

> Multotec Cyclones is an innovative company who endeavours to identify and anticipate clients' business needs in the extractive metallurgical and industrial sectors in the southern African and also in selected international markets.

It is apparent from this extract that the company has an international dimension in its operations, and it will become clear that this dimension is to become stronger as part of future strategies. The company operates in the mining industry, more specifically the extractive metallurgical industry, and differentiates itself from competitors by its professional knowledge of the process technology and application of its technologically-advanced quality products and services. Its products are used for the beneficiation or refinement of minerals, and the product range can be categorised as follows:

- Cyclones, i.e. hydrocyclones and dense media cyclones;
- Gravity-concentrated equipment, i.e. spiral and centrifugal;
- Sampling equipment, i.e. dry and slurry sampling;
- Column flotation, i.e. column and interface measuring devices.

Most of the above products are manufactured at the company's plant in Kempton Park, although it makes use of subcontractors for some of the component parts. Its clients comprise almost the whole range of mines in the southern African mining industry.

The staff component consists of 120 people, ranging from engineers to 60 factory workers. The company has a lean structure with an engineering and operations division, and a product-based marketing division. Multotec values integrity and a strong business ethic, is client-orientated, and strives to maintain a competent and professional team of people. The managing director admits that the organisational culture is influenced strongly by the German discipline of the founder of the group. This is balanced by giving full autonomy to each company in the group with decentralised responsibility and decision-making power. This ultimately contributes to the profitability of the company.

Motivation for internationalisation

There were several factors which drew the company into the international arena, of which the visionary leadership and will-power of the managing director were not the least. According to the managing director, the company is still the acknowledged market leader with at least 90% of the market share in the extractive metallurgical industry in South Africa. It therefore has to maintain a constant vigilance, since, in the post-sanction period, other domestic and international entrants will keep challenging its leadership position. In the case of one of its products, the spiral concentrator, the market started to fluctuate considerably during the early 1980s. The company had to bring stability back into the market, and therefore had to reduce its dependence on one market so as to reduce its risk. The domestic market was just no longer large enough, and it was discovered that some foreign markets presented higher profit opportunities than the domestic one and would allow for limited economies of scale.

In the late 1980s the company decided that it had to expand its total market size by looking for new users, new uses and more usage of its products. This could best be achieved by penetrating the international market and, as market leader, it would also become the chief beneficiary of any increased sales in the industry. The motivation for internationalisation can thus be summarised as follows :

- visionary leadership;
- overcapacity in the domestic market;
- opportunities in foreign markets;
- exploitation of core competency, i.e. process technology in the beneficiation of minerals.

The reasons for expanding the business of Multotec were primarily proactive. It became apparent during the interview, though, that certain reactive reasons were also behind the decision. The scenario for economic development and growth in South Africa is not considered to be favourable, and the managing director tried to secure the long-term survival of the company by exploring international markets. The company gained considerable competitive advantage against possible new entrants into the domestic market by building up a world-wide network, and also went through the learning curve of competing in a world-class environment.

The process of internationalisation

The company followed a strategy which Kotler calls a geographical expansion strategy and started selling products in other countries in the mid-1980s. Amid sanctions and severe recessionary conditions, exports reached a high in 1994/95, accounting for 30% of the turnover. Multotec started with selective international markets and applied the following criteria for candidate countries :

- Market attractiveness – the selected market should obviously have intensive mining activities;
- Growth potential – attractive markets for capital sales are preferred;
- Communication – the company decided to minimise the potential problems of inaccuracy, misunderstanding and inefficiency caused by cross-cultural communication and other 'psychic barriers'. They therefore opted initially for markets where English is the primary language medium.

The following five modes or strategies of entry exist when a company decides to enter a particular foreign country:

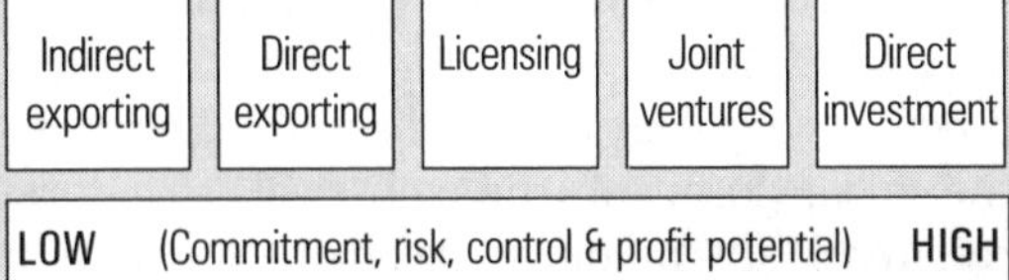

Multotec opted for at least four of the five strategies, and has also made substantial direct investments in at least two companies. Many of these entries were made possible by identifying projects and other opportunities. The company adopted the principle of using local companies to do the marketing in a specific country.

The process of internationalisation that has evolved since the mid-1980s resulted in the following:

- **Multotec Zimbabwe**: The parent owns 100% of the company, and initially made a direct investment of R250 000.
- **Tema Systems, Holland**: Multotec South Africa created a joint venture and share ownership (50%) with this Europe-based company, with an initial direct investment of R500 000. From there they also distribute to Tema BV in the Pacific Rim, and Jordan, as well as other companies in Belgium, France, England, Spain, and Portugal.
- **Tema Systems, USA**: This company is a distributor and sells products on behalf of Multotec to Canada and Mexico, i.e. direct export.
- **CMI, Australia**: The company is a licensee* and also imports from South Africa. It furthermore acts as distributor to New Zealand and New Guinea.
- **Agent, Zambia**: A process engineer acts individually as a foreign-based agent, and the company pays a considerable share of his salary.
- **Other agents** : These are foreign-based companies which sell products on behalf of Multotec all over the world including Iran, Turkey, Brazil, Argentine, Peru, and Chile.

In South Africa direct or personal selling takes place from the head office (also from an agent based in Richards Bay), but in the international market Multotec uses either agents, distributors or licensees for marketing its products. It seems clear that Multotec does not limit its options to one strategy of internationalisation. It follows a dynamic process and seems to have adapted to each particular situation, thereby minimising the risk factor and gaining experience as far as possible. In this regard the research of Barkema et al. has proven clearly that through knowledge of the various modes and ownership structures of foreign entry, companies reduce the cultural barriers. They have also proved that centrifugal expansion patterns are more successful than a random strategy, in other words, firms should gradually expand in cultural space. It is interesting to note that only in the cases of Zimbabwe (fairly easy to control) and Australia (minimum 'cultural distance') were substantial direct investments made. The joint venture with Tema/Multotec Europe provides access to new markets, more resources and a partner with whom to share risk. It is also a flexible way of entering the European market and the managing director is rightfully optimistic about the growth potential in this area.

The impact on organisational structure

The following organisational structures are possible when engaging in international activities:

- an international division structure;
- a regional division structure;

* The following extract taken from the licence agreement between Multotec and CMI Australia reflects the essence of the relationship: 'The licensor (Multotec Cyclones) hereby grants an exclusive license for the currency of this agreement to the licensee (Chemical Mining and Industrial (CMI)) to manufacture, have manufactured, use and sell the products within the territory'.

- a product division structure;
- a functional division structure;
- a matrix structure.

These proposals unfortunately do not provide for the trend of companies organising themselves into networks. Because Multotec is not a multinational with subsidiaries, its relationship with agents, distributors and licensees can only be described as a loose network of interdependent and co-operative entities. In the case of a foreign-owned company or a joint venture, there is a stronger structural relationship. Since no specific structure was presented to the authors, we decided to propose an original model that could be utilised by Multotec to develop a better understanding of its structural relationships with foreign entities. The model is based on a new organisational metaphor called the spherical network (see Miles 1995) and serves as basis for the structural organisation.

According to this metaphor, independent, competent partners rotate around a common expert or knowledge base, i.e. Multotec's distinctive leadership in extractive metallurgical process technology and applications thereof. In the ideal form of the spherical structure, resources are infinitely flexible, i.e. when a particular problem or opportunity confronts the network, the sphere rotates, quickly providing the initiator with a means of accessing the network's entire array of expertise and resources. Multotec's international relationships can be described as a loosely organised spherical network, with diverse partnerships built around a common technology. In an ideal spherical network the principle of network democracy governs, i.e. there is no overall network owner. In the case of Multotec, the

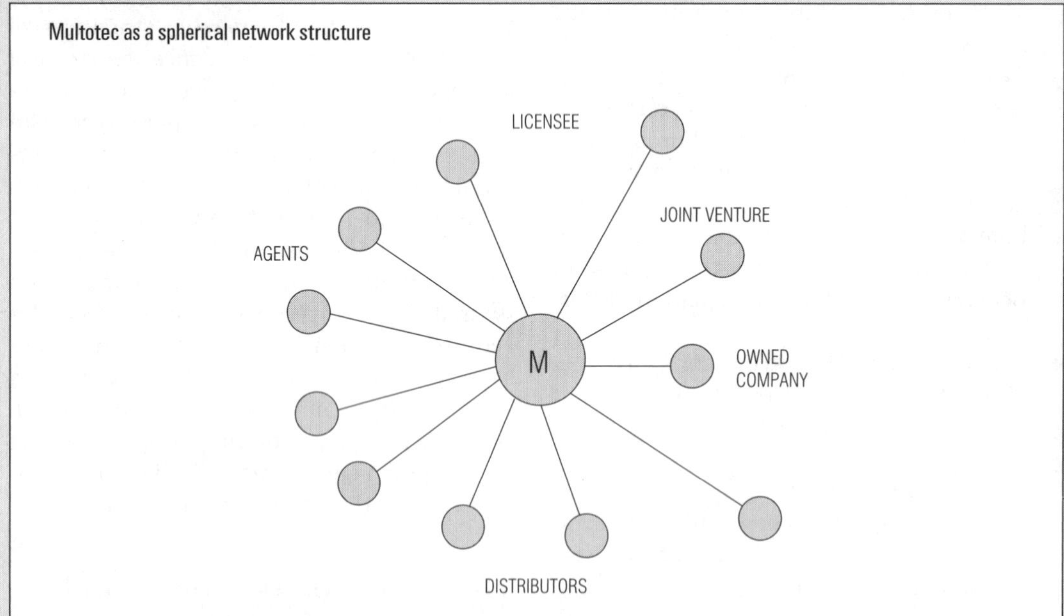

Agents:	No stock, controlled price, independent marketing
Distributors:	Own stock, uncontrolled price
Licence-holders:	Own manufacturing, own stock, uncontrolled price
Joint venture:	Share ownership and control, joint decision-making
Ownership:	Wholly owned and full control

principle of *network autocracy* governs with centralised product technology and quality control. The proposed structure is portrayed in the illustration 'Multotec as a spherical network structure'. Five distinctive relationships are portrayed, and the strength of the structural relationship is reflected by the thickness and texture of the various cords.

The centrifugal power, around which the network develops, ensures authority, stability, quality, and ultimate decision-making on product and technology-related issues. In the case of the wholly-owned company and the joint venture, there may be limited sharing of resources, organisational culture and management styles. The relationship with the licensee is structured according to a licence agreement. Once selected or appointed, agents and distributors operate autonomously.

Managing the relationship: influence and control

According to Percy Barnevik, president and CEO of Asea Brown Boveri (ABB), the only way to structure a complex global organisation is to make it as simple and local as possible. These principles are also the basic approach of Multotec in its dealings with foreign partners. It is important to note that the uniqueness of an industry will always determine the amount of control necessary from headquarters. When you are dealing with patented products and processes and licence agreements, there is, to a large extent, an invisible control mechanism embodied in probation periods and in escape and restraint-of-trade clauses. Nevertheless, Multotec makes use of at least two vital mechanisms to accomplish the control they want, namely data management and managers' management mechanisms. The following passage was taken from one of its strategic documents.

> The following key factors are prescribed for international agents, distributors and licence-holders:
>
> - at least one personal meeting per annum;
> - training by Multotec Cyclones on products for various representatives;
> - visits by senior staff with the representative in the specific country to clients on a yearly basis;
> - presentation of quality seminars or papers on a regular basis in that country;
> - assistance offered with target marketing;
> - inspection of quality on a regular basis; and
> - assistance with production if required.

In addition to the above factors for 'channel management', joint planning sessions are held with foreign agents and regular performance reports are required by headquarters. In the case of joint ventures and owned companies (Zimbabwe and Europe), financial statements must be presented quarterly, and joint decision-making takes place on key strategies. It is therefore clear that Multotec uses the following data management mechanisms for control purposes:

- information systems and feedback;
- measurement systems; and
- strategic planning, especially marketing plans.

One of the most critical success factors for Multotec in the strategic control of partners in the international market is the choice of key managers. The following major criteria are used for managers and companies alike:

- a competent process person with knowledge of the extractive metallurgical field;
- a person with sales experience is preferred;
- the company image must be compatible with Multotec;
- the company must be progressive, reputable, service- and quality-orientated; and
- there must be a cultural match.

The typical managers' mechanisms that can be deduced from these are as follows :

- choice;
- development and training; and
- patterns of socialisation.

The managing director plays an important role in applying the above mechanisms. He is an entrepreneur with a hands-on approach in the development of an international network. In many instances he will intervene personally to resolve conflicts or problems with foreign operations, most of which relate to business ethics and non-performance. Alternatively, a small task force may be sent to deal with such problems.

Although the foreign agents, distributors and licensees of Multotec products might be perceived to be mere outposts, Multotec wants to maintain close relationships with them. Careful screening and selection, induction and orientation, training, intensive communication, and information-sharing, all add to building up this close relationship. The balance between global efficiency and local responsiveness is obtained through the miniature replica structure in the case of agents and distributors, and the rationalised structure in the case of licensees and joint ventures. Multotec, being the innovator of the expert knowledge base, on the one hand simply transposes its process technology from one market to the other. On the other hand, it has to be sensitive to foreign market demands and adopt a balanced approach towards control over its products. This can be described as follows: *'Products made in the subsidiary (licensee or joint venture) under a rationalised structure are made for the parent market as well as the subsidiary market. They are therefore made to parent specifications ... The subsidiary needs parent direction on product specifications because it is not as knowledgeable as the parent.'*

The roles of national managers

Although Multotec's network is loosely structured and does not comply with the criteria for a multinational with subsidiaries and subsequent managerial roles, at least one of the roles and responsibilities is applicable to the individuals with whom Multotec deals in foreign operations. The following can be highlighted:

- The national manager as front-line implementer: The agents or distributors have to adapt their own marketing strategies to Multotec's strategic intent with the focus on a distinctive process technology, and translate this into their domestic mining industry. They have to be entrepreneurial in finding and exploiting market opportunities, and maintain the business ethics that Multotec values.
- Although a great deal of assistance is provided to agents and distributors in terms of training, establishing of structures and support, Multotec's marketing-driven foreign operations require considerable skills and abilities from its partners. The managing director has pointed out that the risks involved in choosing the 'wrong' partner are tremendous. These can jeopardise a company's bona fides and credibility to such an extent that entry into the foreign market becomes impossible. To a large extent, the managing director acts as role model and sets the tone for the management style within the network. He values quality, business ethics, will-power, an open mind and an entrepreneurial approach – aspects which cut across cultural borders. He has grown in the perception that you have to acknowledge cultural differences without becoming paralysed by them.

Implications for strategy, structure and culture

The international dimension of the Multotec mission and operations has made a considerable impact on most aspects of the business. The following were highlighted in an interview with the managing director:

- **Long-term strategy**: Most of the markets targeted for growth of the various products

are foreign-based. Exceptional market share growth is foreseen in Australia, Europe, the USA, Brazil, and the rest of Africa. Exports are seen to account for 50% of the total turnover by the year 2000. An aggressive marketing strategy will therefore be pursued in opening up new foreign markets.
- **Organisational culture**: Although the foreign operations are not overseen by an international department and might be perceived as 'isolated' in terms of the business operations, a cultural shift is taking place within Multotec. Its international operations require extremely consistent product quality, back-up and after-sales service, on-time delivery and process ownership in various parts of the business. There is thus a growing awareness of the competitiveness in the international market and the 'mindset' of staff and workers is changing accordingly.
- **Information and communications systems**: The company had to upgrade its overall communication skills and implemented e-mail facilities recently. This was necessitated by the transfer of sketches, regular reporting, quick reaction to opportunities and 'internal' communication. Additional information had to be included in engineering manuals since engineering standards and product requirements vary from country to country.
- **Product innovation**: Process knowledge about the various products had to be increased, and research and development (R&D) accordingly upgraded. Transfer of technology in the international market became increasingly difficult, and steps had to be taken to facilitate this.
- **Broadening the 'language paradigm'**: The company had to become much more sensitive to the whole array of international languages and the difficulties in translating basic documentation and letters. Portuguese, French, and even Russian translators had to be subcontracted to customise manuals and other specification documents. This obviously helped in opening up the organisational mindset to the global arena.

Multotec has succeeded in opening up its strategy towards becoming an international competitor. It adopted strong leadership, flexible structural organisation and cultural open-mindedness. It also acted fast in setting up support systems and procedures to address the challenges resulting from foreign operations.

Conclusion

Multotec recently qualified as one of the top 100 technology companies in southern Africa. One of their products, the spiral concentrator, is acknowledged as a top 100 product (more than half of the revenue for this product is generated in foreign markets). The managing director recently received an award from the South African Coal Association for his company's contribution to the coal industry. These achievements are largely due to the internationalisation strategies followed by the company. It had to 'weigh' its core competency, i.e. a distinctive process technology, against the best practice and the best markets in the world, before it could be seen to be a top achiever.

This survey has explored the various issues involved when a company develops its international strategies. The managing director of Multotec Cyclones has proven to be something of a business clairvoyant in the group of companies, and forecast the future before the rest. The company has effectively penetrated the foreign markets all over the world, and managed the implications thereof successfully. It has thereby successfully managed the paradigm shift from isolation to internationalisation. It is foreseen by the authors that Multotec will expand its international business still further and even start to follow different modes of entry into the market, given the limits posed by the mining industry.

Questions

1 Why do you think Multotec has used various operating forms for the different foreign markets it has entered?
2 What are the reasons, advantages and disadvantages of Multotec's expanding abroad rather than concentrating its efforts on the South African market?
3 Multotec's earliest foreign thrust was into the southern African market. Do you agree with this expansion priority?
4 Do you think it is possible for managers to develop a 'global mindset'?

Endnotes

1 Daniels, J.D. & Radebaugh, L.H. 1998. *International business: environments and operations.* 8th ed. Reading, Mass: Addison Wesley, p. 9.

2 Czinkota, R.C., Ronkainen, I.A., Moffet, M.H. & Moynihan, E.O. 1998. *Global business.* 2nd ed. New York: Harcourt Brace, p. 7.

3 Daniels & Radebaugh, op. cit., pp. 15–19.

4 See Unisa Advanced Programme in Purchasing Management. 1998. Pretoria.

5 Daniels & Radebaugh, op. cit., p.12.

6 Robock, S.H. & Simmonds, K. 1989. *International business and multinational enterprise.* 4th ed. Boston: Irwin.

7 Jegatesan, J. 1993. 'The best of all possible worlds for investment.' *Sunday Times*, 7 November

8 Importers and exporters register. 1999. Bureau for Market Research. Pretoria:Unisa.

9 Phatak, A.V. 1992. *International dimensions of management.* 3rd ed. Boston: PWS-Kent.

10 We acknowledge the co-operation of Erwee R., University of Southern Queensland, Neethling, H., Roelofse, S., Van der Merwe, L., Venter, L. & Sobalev, D. Graduate School of Management, University of Pretoria. Supplementary material was taken from:

Barkema, H.G., Bell, J.H.J. & Pennings, J.M. 1996. 'Foreign entry, cultural barriers, and learning.' *Strategic Management Journal*, 17, pp. 151–166.

Beamish, A. 1991. *The impact of globalisation: managing parent-subsidiary relations.* New York: Irwin.

Doz, Y.L. & Prahalad, C.K. 1992. 'Headquarters influence and strategic control in MNCs', in Bartlett, C.A. & Ghosal, S. *Transnational Management*, Chapter 5. Homewood: Irwin.

Erwee, R. 1966. 'Strategies for internationalising South African companies', in Smit, E. & Morgan, N.I. *Contemporary issues in strategic management.* Pretoria: Kagiso Publishers, p. 74–109.

Expatriate Profile. 1996. PC programme in the laboratory of the Graduate School of Management, University of Pretoria.

Interview with Mr J.A. Engelbrecht, Managing Director of Multotec Cyclones, on 15 May 1996.

Kotler, P. 1994. *Marketing management: analysis, planning, implementation, and control.* 8th ed. London: Prentice-Hall.

Marketing strategic planning. 1991. A publication of Multotec Cyclones (Pty) Limited, compiled by Engelbrecht, J.A., June.

Miles, R.E. & Snow, C.C. 1995. 'The new network firm: A spherical structure built on a human investment philosophy.' *Organisational Dynamics*, Winter 1995, pp. 5-18. *Multotec Cyclones (Pty) Ltd Quarterly Report – Year ending February 1996*, compiled by Engelbrecht, J.A.

'Roles and responsibilities of the country manager: MNC operations from the national organisation's perspective.' 1985. *HBS Case Services.* 9–385–326. Boston: Harvard Business School.

International trade and economic integration

Key issues

- Globalisation of the world economy
- International trade theories
- Free trade and trade regulation
- Economic integration and major trading blocs
- Implications of regional trading blocs and trade agreements for South African businesses

2.1 **Introduction**

At the heart of the phenomenon of globalisation is a massive experiment in economic restructuring – a process spearheaded by the Western trading powers. This 'gamble' is being executed under the rubric of better living standards for all. But there is no guarantee that this noble goal will be the end product. On the contrary, globalisation may very well exacerbate gaps between rich global blocs and poor regions, which have already become the reality in many parts of the world. Yet the dividend of international 'free' trade is taken as given by the architects of the World Trade Organisation (WTO).

In this chapter we will focus on the globalisation of the world economy and free trade, international trade theories, the WTO, and other major modern trading blocs. A country's 'comparative advantage' is often seen as the only basis for prosperity. South Africa and other countries should therefore strengthen their 'comparative advantage' if they are to survive in this self-help post-Cold War era. This era is one of global economic liberalism. The new liberal orthodoxy insists that liberalisation of markets is the best way to increased prosperity. The rise in Western living standards, proponents believe, should be emulated.

Non-Western states are under pressure to embrace the virtues of liberalisation, competitiveness and the free market. But the record of the free-market gospel is chequered. The last decade has seen unemployment in the Organisation for Economic Co-operation and Development (OECD) countries grow to 35 million, and this does not include the Third World, where millions of people are jobless and still more millions 'underemployed'.

International trade and foreign direct investment are booming in some parts of the world, but certainly not in Africa. For many people the link between trade and prosperity is hard to discern. There is growing unease over the effect of 'global free trade'. Everyone speaks of 'free trade' without emphasising 'fair trade'. Fair trade is a nobler goal, but can global trade be fair as well as free? 'Open, fair and undistorted competition' is the goal of the WTO.

The WTO lacks the power to tell countries how they should craft policy. It hopes that countries will embrace consensus-based trade diplomacy and map out 'mutually beneficial' rules for international trade. It seeks to provide for maximum fairness, openness and transparency. But inevitably, within this anarchic global order, states take advantage of loopholes everywhere and battle to advance their own interests.[1]

At the same time, entirely new areas have opened up for international trade and the level of international investment is at a record high. These networks of global linkages have resulted in the so-called 'global village' or globalisation of the world markets.

2.2 Globalisation of the world economy

Ironically, the economic self-interest of nations is best served, broadly speaking, by playing by the rules and also by pushing for 'fair', not just 'free', trade. A great deal of back-stabbing takes place in global trade. Free trade is not necessarily fair trade – a reality South Africa would have to emphasise in its trade negotiations with the EU and other players. Today the bulk of all international trade and cross-border investment is carried out by a handful of industrialised countries. Yet almost every country has embraced free market capitalism. The WTO has 122 members with 28 more queuing up to be admitted.

As we can detect from the above discussions, something fundamental is taking place in the world economy.[2] The term 'global shift' has been used to describe the core of this change, and we see this internationalisation or globalisation in all the markets of the world (see Chapter 9, Section 9.2). The Asian crisis of the late 1990s, where the negative effect of the collapse of the local currency and stock market reverberated worldwide, is only one example of this global shift where national markets are merging into one huge market-place.[3]

However, we have to ask ourselves if this trend towards one huge 'market-place' has promoted the globalisation of markets and the increase in production. There is plenty of evidence that the lowering of trade barriers has

Exhibit 2.1: The growth of world trade and world output

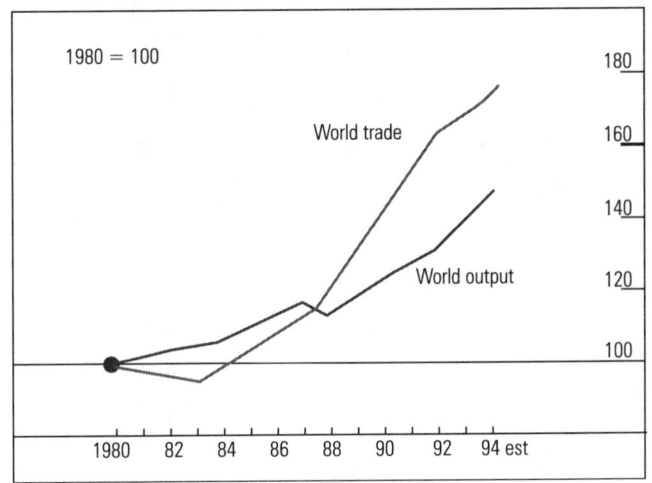

SOURCE: F. Williams, 'World Trade in Goods Jumps 9%,' *Financial Times*, April 4, 1995, p. 22.

facilitated the globalisation of production and thus the world economy. For example, during the last decade the volume of world trade grew faster than the volume of world output.[4]

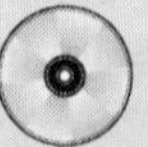

Compact disc

1 Mr Alec Erwin discusses the importance of trade with the SADC countries.

From Exhibit 2.1 (p. 31) we can see that world trade outpaced world output from 1980-1994. Total world output grew by 40% during this period, while total world trade grew by 70%. It is also clear that this gap widened from 1988 onwards.

Exhibit 2.2 gives an indication of the decline in the average tariff rates on manufactured goods from 1913 to 2000.

Average tariff rates have fallen drastically since the 1950s and will approach 3,9% by 2000 if the Uruguay agreement is fully implemented.[5]

2.3 International trade theories

A description of the evolution of the different international trade theories will now be summarised. Exhibit 2.3 (p. 33) provides an overview of the path of this evolution.

2.3.1 The theory of absolute advantage

Adam Smith published *The Wealth of Nations* in 1776, in which he tried to explain the process by which markets and production actually operate in society. He came to the conclusion that the real wealth of a nation lies in the quality of life of its citizens. Adam Smith's contributions were in the areas of absolute advantage and the division of labour. In 1776, people used buttons and pins to keep their clothing in place and therefore pin-making was very important at that time. In analysing the operations of a pin factory employing ten workers, Smith observed that some workers could make one pin per day while others might be able to produce 20 per day. However, the maximum production of the factory would not exceed 200 pins per day. If they were to

Exhibit 2.2: Average tariff rates on manufactured products, percentage of value

	1913	1950	1990	2000*
France	21%	18%	5,9%	3,9%
Germany	20%	26%	5,9%	3,9%
Italy	18%	25%	5,9%	3,9%
Japan	30%	–	5,3%	3,9%
Holland	5%	11%	5,9%	3,9%
Sweden	20%	9%	4,4%	3,9%
Britain	–	23%	5,9%	3,9%
United States	44%	14%	4,8%	3.9%

*Based on full implementation of the Uruguay agreement.

SOURCE: Hill, 1998. *International business: Competing in the global marketplace.* 2nd ed. Washington: Irwin/McGraw-Hill, p. 8.

Exhibit 2.3: The evolution of international trade theory

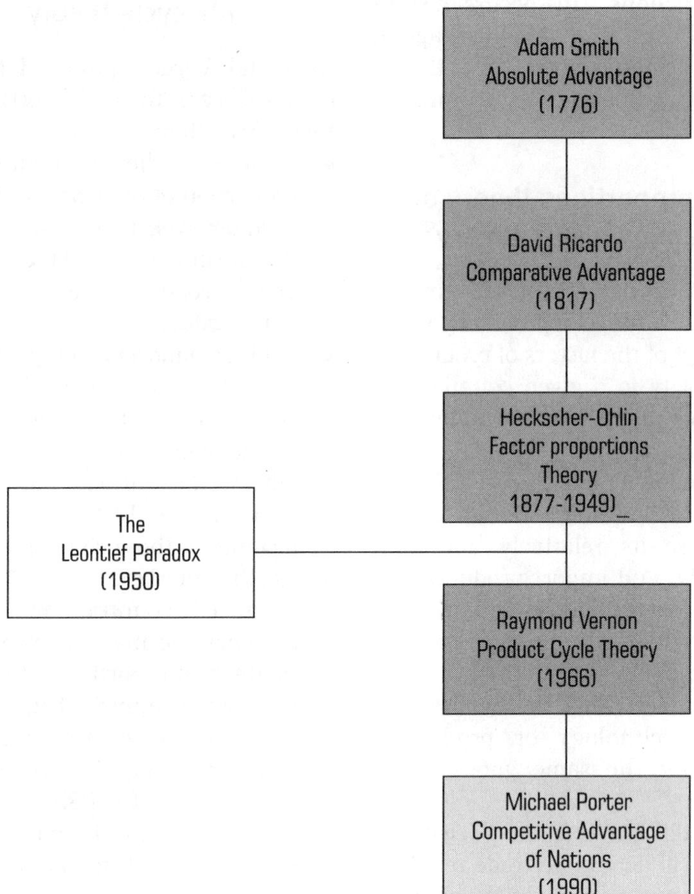

restructure the process in such a way that each worker specialised in performing only one part of the process, they could make as many as 48 000 pins per day!

Smith extended his division of labour in the production process across countries, meaning that each country would specialise in one product for which it was uniquely suited.[6] The English had an absolute advantage in producing textiles, while the French had an absolute advantage in the production of wines. Thus, more would be produced by fewer. Countries could produce more products in total and trade the goods that were cheaper than those produced locally.

2.3.2 The theory of comparative advantage

According to Ricardo's theory (published in 1817 in his book, *Principles of Political Economy*), it makes sense for a country to specialise in the production of those goods that it produces most efficiently, and to buy the goods that it produces less efficiently from other countries, even if it could produce them more efficiently than another country.

The basic message from this theory is that potential world production is greater with unrestricted free trade than it is with restricted trade. Ricardo's theory suggests that consumers in all nations can consume more if there are no trade restrictions. This occurs even in countries that lack an absolute advantage in the production of any good. His theory provides a strong rationale for encouraging free trade.[7]

2.3.3 Factor proportions theory or factor endowments theory[9]

The Heckscher-Ohlin theory of trade expands the comparative advantage approach by introducing the concept of the factors of production and their availability in a given country, e.g. production factors are either abundant or scarce.

The factor endowments theory of trade concludes that a country should export products that use its relatively abundant factors intensively, and import products that use its relatively scarce factors intensively.[8] Factor intensities depend on the state of technology and the current method of manufacturing a product. This theory assumes that the same technology or production would be used for the same goods in all countries.

Thus, it is not differences in the efficiency of production that will determine trade relations between countries – as they did in the classical theory, where it was assumed that technology or labour productivity is different across nations. The factor endowments theory assumes that there are no such differences in productivity between countries.

2.3.4 The Leontief paradox

Wassily Leontief postulated that since the United States was relatively abundant in capital compared with other countries, it would be an exporter of capital-intensive goods. However, he found that exports from the USA were less capital-intensive than the country's imports.[10] Since this result was at variance with the predictions of the theory, it has become known as the Leontief paradox.

2.3.5 Product cycle theory or product life cycle theory[11]

Raymond Vernon proposed the product life cycle theory in the mid-1960s. The core of his theory was that:

- for most of the twentieth century a large proportion of the world's new products has been developed and sold in the USA;
- the size and wealth of the USA market have given producers the incentive to develop new products;
- while demand for a new product is starting to grow in the USA, demand in other advanced countries is limited to high-income groups;
- as demand grows over time in other advanced countries, it becomes feasible for firms in the USA to set up production facilities in those countries;
- as the market in the USA and other advanced countries matures and price becomes the main 'competitor', producers might start exporting to the USA;
- developing countries begin to become more cost-competitive over time, and they will start producing for the other advanced countries and the USA;
- the USA switches from being an exporter of the product to being an importer.

This situation is illustrated in Exhibit 2.4 (p. 35).

2.3.6 Competitive advantage of nations: Porter's diamond model[12]

In 1990 Michael Porter published the results of research that attempted to determine why some nations succeed and others fail in global competitive situations. Porter argued that innovation is the driving and sustaining force of competitiveness. His thesis was that the following four attributes of a nation shape the environment in which local firms compete, and that they either promote or inhibit the creation of innovation or competitive advantage (see Exhibit 2.5 on p. 36).

Exhibit 2.4: Product life cycle theory

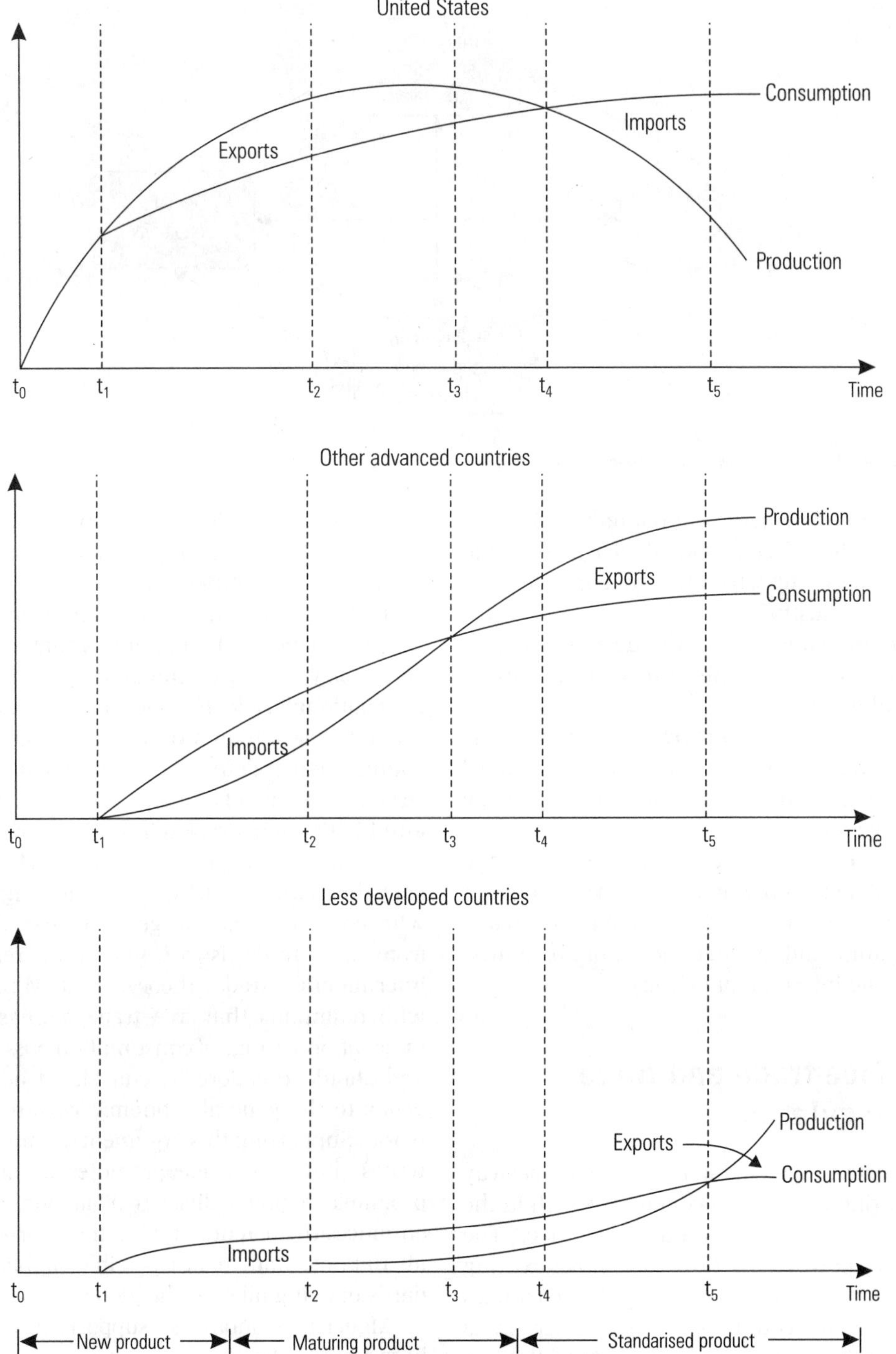

SOURCE: Raymond Vernon, 'International Investment and International Trade in the Product Cycle,' *Quarterly Journal of Economics* (May 1966) 199.

Exhibit 2.5: Porter's diamond model

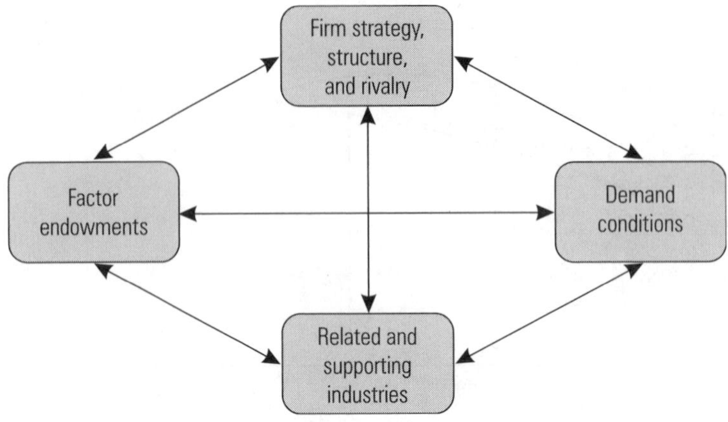

SOURCE: Porter, M.E. 1990. *The comparative advantage of nations.* New York: Free Press, p. 133

- **factor endowments** – a nation's position in production factors like skilled labour and developed infrastructure to compete in a given industry;
- **demand conditions** – the degree of health and competition the firm must face in its local market;
- **related and supporting industries** – the presence or absence of supplier and related industries that are locally and globally competitive;
- **firm strategy, structure and rivalry** – the conditions in the home industry that either hinder or aid the firm's ability to create, organise and manage the nature of domestic and international rivalry.

2.4 Free trade and trade regulation

It is generally agreed that the most suitable way of ensuring worldwide economic growth in the long term is free international trade. The problem, however, is how to remove existing trade barriers without harming the economies of individual countries. This thorny issue always raises cries from opponents to the free trade theory. They favour protectionist policies based on trade barriers, maintaining that this is the best way of improving economic conditions in individual countries.

In his commentary on Adam Smith's *The wealth of nations*, Mill maintains that a *laissez-faire* policy should be the guiding principle in international trade. He favoured free exports to promote the interests of all states, because 'a country which destroys or prevents altogether certain branches of foreign trade . . . (is) thereby annihilating a general gain to the world'.[13]

Among the modern economists who advocate the principle of free trade are Ingram,[14] who confirms that the general asset derived from free trade is an important tenet of international trade theory, and Winters,[15] who maintains that free trade increases the international range of consumption possibilities and should therefore be considered advantageous to the general economic welfare of the world. Supporting this argument, Samuelson[16] writes that 'free trade promotes a mutually profitable regional division of labour, greatly enhances the potential real national product of all nations, and makes possible higher standards of living all over the globe'.

Modern economists support free trade because it:

- increases consumption possibilities;

- is beneficial to general economic well-being;
- promotes higher living standards.

2.4.1 International trade barriers

We must, of course, also be aware of the arguments against free international trade. However, these arguments are usually based on protectionist national economic policies, and are even influenced by non-economic factors such as social, political, moral, or aesthetic environments, with the object of obstructing free trade and thus promoting the national economy of an individual country.

But what exactly are trade barriers and how are they created? Winters[17] divides them into two categories:

1 tariff barriers that are created when governments put financial levies on the import of goods, either in the form of specific taxes or tariffs, or as *ad valorem* tariffs;
2 non-tariff barriers that may be described as all measures, besides tariffs, that may affect international trade through quantitative government restrictions, or price or cost levies.

Tariff barriers are clearly identifiable and thus easy to detect. Non-tariff barriers are less obvious but have an adverse effect on the flow of trade. Exhibit 2.6 (p. 38) clearly shows the difference between tariff and non-tariff barriers as market entry strategies.

Non-tariff barriers usually result from national economic policies designed to protect sectors competing with imports, or to support export sectors. These policies include import quotas, restrictions on public purchases of goods produced on the local market, export restrictions, various levies, production subsidies, income tax concessions on export profits, advance deposit schemes for imports, different exchange rates for different transactions, exchange rate control, and foreign exchange restrictions.

The Board on Tariffs and Trade has developed tariff and non-tariff procedures to protect South African enterprises against overseas competition. An important example is the procedure used by the textile and clothing industries against imports from countries like China and Pakistan by means of 'dumping' countermeasures. These trade measures mean that the transition of the South African economy to greater international competitiveness through free trade will probably be a slow process.[18]

Non-tariff barriers can also include measures such as excessive import documentation requirements, delays with customs procedures, restrictions on advertising and customs evaluation procedures, health requirements, labelling requirements, and taxes on the employment of foreign personnel. Non-tariff barriers may also not aim specifically at protection but adversely influence free trade by affecting the government's expenditure plans, restrictions on toxic materials, regional subsidies, monopolistic policies, variations in the national insurance prescriptions, or the mandatory use of national weights and measures.

2.4.2 The General Agreement on Tariffs and Trade (GATT)

As its name indicates, GATT is not an organisation of member states. It is an agreement to which the participating states subscribe as contracting parties. The principal objective of GATT is mutual tariff reductions between countries. The contracting parties undertake to extend any tariff reductions they may allow one of their trading partners to all other participating countries. This is referred to as the 'most-favoured-nation' (mfn) policy.

When discussing GATT we need to bear in mind the following three points:

1 GATT is an agreement between contracting parties in terms of which they have to extend their most-favoured-nation policy to all the other parties;
2 GATT provides a means of settling trade disputes through reference to the GATT Council; and

Exhibit 2.6: Tariff and non-tariff barriers

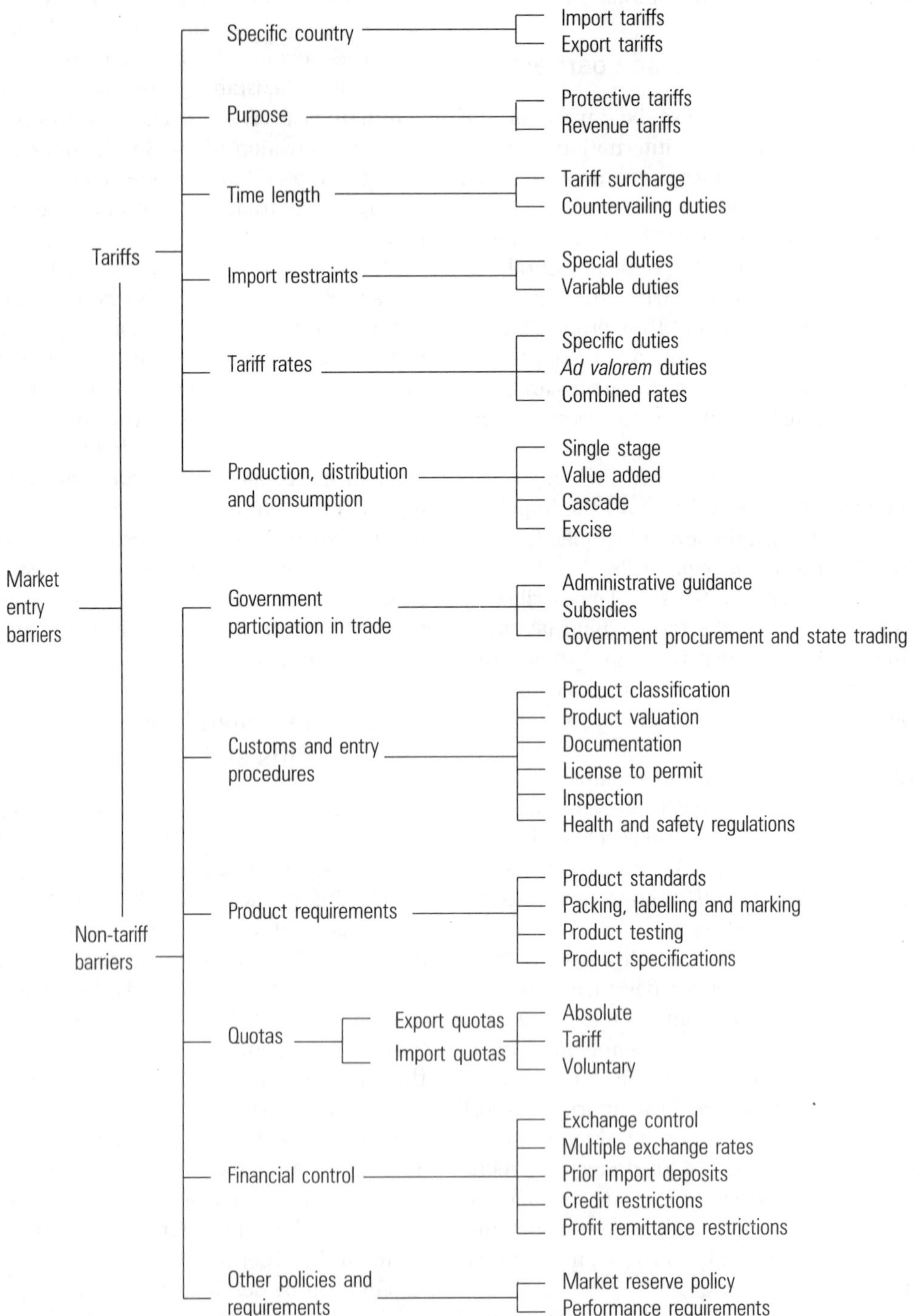

SOURCE: Onkvisit and Shaw (1988) in Doole, I. & Lowe, R. 1999. *International Marketing Strategy*, 2nd ed. London, International Thomson Business Press, p. 48

3 one of the purposes of GATT is to bring about tariff reductions between contracting countries by means of a series of multilateral negotiations known as 'negotiating rounds'.

GATT

- forbids quantitative restrictions in principle
- grants most-favoured-nation rights
- helps to resolve trading differences
- negotiates tariff reductions by means of negotiating rounds

It is also important to be aware that GATT allows certain exceptions to its rules. For example:

1 quantitative restrictions are permitted when temporary balance of trade problems occur; and
2 the creation of a customs union is allowed in spite of the most-favoured-nation clause. The latter exception is particularly important because it made the creation of the EU possible. At the time of writing, South Africa was a member of a customs union comprising Lesotho, Botswana and South Africa.

To date there have been eight major negotiating rounds on tariff reductions. The most recent was the last round or Uruguay Round, which was concluded on 15 December 1993; the agreement was signed on 15 April 1994 and took effect in 1995. The WTO was established in terms of this agreement, known as the Marrakesh Agreement.

It must be pointed out that all the GATT negotiating rounds have had considerable problems with non-tariff barriers. These problems have been felt by the less developed countries in particular. These countries have been prejudiced by:

1 the protectionist agricultural policies of the Western industrialised countries, and
2 the continued protection of manufactured goods such as textiles and clothing.

Although tariffs on these goods are usually low, the level of non-tariff protection is significant.

2.4.3 The World Trade Organisation (WTO)

The WTO is the only international body dealing with the rules of trade between nations. The WTO is GATT plus a great deal more. GATT (the agreement) was small and provisional, and not even recognised in law as an international organisation. It has now been replaced by the WTO. GATT (the agreement) has been amended and incorporated into the new WTO agreements. While GATT deals only with trade in goods, the WTO agreements now cover services and intellectual property as well. They are, in fact, the legal ground-rules for international commerce and trade policy. The agreements have three main objectives:

- to help trade flow as freely as possible;
- to achieve further liberalisation gradually through negotiation;
- to set up an impartial means of settling disputes.

A number of simple fundamental principles run throughout all the WTO agreements.

They are the foundation of the multilateral trading system, and they include non-discrimination ('most-favoured-nation' and 'national' treatment), freer trade, predictable policies, the encouragement of competition, and extra provisions for less-developed countries.

The functions of the WTO are to:

- administer WTO trade agreements;
- act as a forum for trade negotiations;
- handle trade disputes;
- monitor national trade policies;
- give technical assistance and training for developing countries;
- co-operate with other international organisations.

The economic case for an open trading system based upon multilaterally agreed rules is simple enough and rests largely on commercial common sense. There is also evidence to support it. Protectionism leads to bloated, inefficient companies, the possibility of factory closures and job losses. One of the WTO's objectives is to reduce protectionism and accordingly avoid these possible adverse effects.

2.5 Economic integration and major trading blocs

2.5.1 Principle of economic integration

The case for economic integration is based on the fact that unrestricted free trade will allow countries to concentrate on the production of goods and services that they can supply most efficiently. The principle is that greater world production and trade would be possible with fewer trade restrictions. Regional (economic) integration can be seen as an attempt to achieve additional gains from the free flow of goods and services between countries.

2.5.2 Major trading blocs

The most important trading blocs that have come into being since the Second World War are:

(a) the European Union (EU);
(b) the North American Free Trade Agreement (NAFTA);
(c) Latin American economic integration;
(d) ASEAN (Association of South-East Asian Nations) integration;
(e) Southern African Development Community (SADC);
(f) Africa, Caribbean and Pacific Co-operation (ACP countries);
(g) the Cairns group;
(h) Common Market for Eastern and Southern Africa (COMESA);
(i) Indian Ocean Rim Association for Regional Co-operation (IOR-ARC).

These trading blocs or arrangements developed as governments took steps to expand their markets and protect their national industries. A short analysis of these trading blocs will shed some light on their importance for South Africa and southern Africa.

(a) The European Union (EU)

By way of introduction we can say that the EU is the most important example of a trading bloc that we have seen to date. As the world's largest exporter, it is now responsible for ±20% of international trade in comparison with ±13% for the United States and ±12% for Japan. Its internal market is the result of the decisions and actions of independent European governments, which are geographically close neighbours, to eliminate all internal trade barriers and control measures between them. The development of this regional trading bloc has been particularly successful, and the link between the EU and other groupings will be discussed in more detail later in this chapter. (See the Appendix to this chapter on p. 59 for a summary of the SA/EU trade, development and co-operation agreement.)

(b) The North American Free Trade Agreement (NAFTA)

NAFTA was established by the United States and Canada in 1989. Mexico signed the agreement at the end of 1992 and its inclusion was a major step towards an American common market.

The original objective of NAFTA was to eliminate most of the existing trade tariffs between the United States and Canada over a period of 10 years. The agreement is important because:

1 there were considerable trade barriers between the two countries, even though Canada is the USA's largest trading partner; and
2 economists predicted that it would go a long way towards encouraging economic growth, creating job opportunities and increasing personal incomes in both countries.

The success of NAFTA in dealing with contentious issues, such as the trade in services and in agricultural products, heightened expectations that it could serve as a model for the multilateral trade negotiations during the Uruguay Round of GATT which was signed in 1994.

The inclusion of Mexico has, of course, enlarged the trading bloc considerably. NAFTA has been approved by the American Congress and the new, bigger free trade unit began operating at the beginning of 1994.

Mexico gives NAFTA a further 87 million people, but it must be pointed out that about two-fifths of its labour force of 35 million are underemployed. Mexico's inflation rate, which had reached triple figures in the 1980s, dropped to 11% by 1992, and the extensive deregulation strategy, currently in place, is expected to help the Mexican economy grow rapidly with American and Canadian support.

The USA is one of South Africa's largest trading partners. NAFTA is thus a source of concern to the country, since part of the United States' trade and investments may shift to Mexico in the future. Such shifts occur because countries with preferred access to a trading bloc will increase their share in that bloc at the expense of outsiders. This may make purchases by South African companies in NAFTA countries more complicated and more expensive.

Looking at the trade characteristics of NAFTA as a regional trading bloc, we see that:

1 the United States occupies a central geographical position with Canada and Mexico on either side;
2 the three trading partners are geographically close and have direct access to one another;
3 there is excellent geographical mobility with a transport network which includes air, road and sea links;
4 the three countries have enormous natural resources;
5 the United States and Canada have expanded their labour and manufacturing capacity and these skills are being developed in the Mexican market;
6 all three countries have an entrepreneurial culture, although this is less obvious in Mexico than in the other two partners;
7 trading relations are governed by a treaty;
8 although there is no free trade, a joint effort is being made to reduce tariff and non-tariff barriers.

(c) Latin American economic integration

The largest trading bloc in Latin America is called MERCOSUR. It was established in 1988 between Argentina, Brazil, Paraguay, and Uruguay. MERCOSUR facilitated a reduction in tariffs between these countries and increased trade by about 80% between Argentina and Brazil in the late 1980s.[19]

Another customs union that is struggling to get off the ground is the so-called CARICOM agreement that was established in 1973 between the English-speaking Caribbean countries. It is also known as the Caribbean Common Market. However, these governments have not yet established a common external tariff as a step towards economic integration.

(d) ASEAN

The countries of the Association of South-East Asian Nations (ASEAN) group offer new international trade possibilities for South African enterprises. Business strategists should use the information made available by the trade missions of these countries in South Africa or contact the Department of Trade and Industry.

The co-operation between the ASEAN countries is inspired by the necessity for a common approach to economic and trade relations with the rest of the world. To date, however, the results achieved by the ASEAN countries' economic co-operation have been limited.

Looking at the trade characteristics of the ASEAN trading group, we see that:

1 they are geographically widespread;
2 the trading partners nevertheless have direct access to one another;

3 a transport network of air and sea links allows for reasonable geographical mobility;
4 the participating countries have natural resources;
5 they already have diverse labour and manufacturing capacities and these skills are being developed;
6 all the participating countries have an entrepreneurial culture;
7 trade relations are governed by an agreement.

(e) The Southern African Development Community (SADC)

The Southern African Development Community (SADC) represents a significant growing market for American trade and investment in particular, offering an abundant supply of natural resources, a population of 135 million consumers, and a combined GDP of over $150 billion. Interest in the region has also been heightened by southern Africa's political stability and economic growth, privatisation and free market reforms, the introduction of investment incentives, and the reduction of tariffs and other barriers to trade.

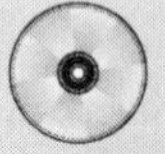

Compact disc

2 Mr Dwayne Gathers of the California Trade Office discusses the progress of trade between the American state of California and southern Africa.

Country focus: Namibia

During the eight years after independence, Namibia has entrenched both political and economic stability, which has been acclaimed throughout the world. Besides its democratic governance and sustenance of political stability, Namibia has positioned itself as a major business and trading partner in the southern African region, through investment in infrastructure development and the introduction of modern and competitive fiscal and incentives regimes.

In the First National Development Plan, which Namibia embarked upon in 1995, the government opted for a strategy that promotes diversified economic growth and assigns a central role to the private sector. The objective is to move the country from being merely a producer of raw material toward an economy where industrial activities and manufacturing should play a significant leading role.

In this context, Namibia has embarked upon the implementation of an Export Processing Zone (EPZ) programme, a country-wide programme aimed at encouraging manufacturing, value-adding, trading, and affiliated activities such as offshore banking. Namibia's rules for investment are, indeed, among the most liberal globally, allowing for 100% foreign ownership, access to all sectors of the economy, very low tax rates or even full tax exemption, and the ability to repatriate all profits and proceeds of sale.

Namibia's investment climate is highly conducive to attracting foreign companies. The country offers a generous range of incentives and low taxation. Foreign investment is seen as crucial in promoting export-led growth. Particular emphasis is being put on manufacturing investment to diversify the economy, removing its reliance on mining and primary sector exports.

SOURCE: *Official SADC Trade, Industry and Investment Review*. 1998. Southern African Marketing Co.

(f) Africa, Caribbean and Pacific Co-operation (ACP countries)

The African, Caribbean and Pacific countries consist of 71 developing countries (including Namibia) which have a special associate relationship with the EU. In terms of this relationship, the ACP countries benefit from tariff-free access to EU markets for nearly all their export products. They also receive a good deal of support, including a guarantee scheme for export profits, which makes concession loans from the EU available should their export profits fall significantly. In exchange, the ACP countries allow EU members certain concessions in their own markets, although this does not include tariff-free access.

The relationship between the EU and the ACP countries is governed by the Lomé Agreement of 1975, which has its origin in France's insistence that the EU accept its overseas territories, because they can essentially be considered part of the mainland. (South Africa has been granted conditional membership in terms of the Lomé Agreement, but this might change in the near future.)

Looking at the trade characteristics of the ACP group, we see that:

1 the ACP countries are not located in a centralised geographical area but are scattered across the entire globe;
2 the geographical accessibility of the trading partners is not ideal;
3 geographical mobility is restricted by distance and often also by poorly organised air, rail, sea and road transport networks;
4 there are considerable natural resources, some of which are not adequately exploited;
5 labour and manufacturing capacities differ to some degree, but are severely underdeveloped;
6 the entrepreneurial culture of many of the trading partners is limited;
7 trade relations are governed by an agreement that emphasises the ACP countries' relationship with the EU, rather than that between the countries themselves;
8 there are free trade benefits within the EU.

It is now important to take a closer look at the Lomé Convention. The Lomé Convention is due to expire in February 2000, after having served as the basic framework for economic co-operation between the EU and 71 ACP countries for the past two decades. The Convention's main objective is to promote economic, cultural and social development of the ACP states.

However, the Lomé model of co-operation can no longer address the expectations of all ACP and EU countries. A large number of ACP states have experienced restrained economic growth accompanied by marginalisation from meaningful international division of labour, although some of them have indeed benefited from the partnership. The EU is moving towards a common market and has established a monetary union and eastward expansion. On the other hand, the global economic outlook has drastically changed under the momentum of trade liberalisation within the WTO.

In view of these changes, parties to the Lomé Convention cannot escape the effects of globalisation of the world economy, in which they are also one of the largest players in terms of their economic influence and geographical coverage. For SADC countries collectively, the Lomé arrangement has been beneficial inasmuch as it helped support domestic prices, provide price protection against loss of industry to South Africa, create a stable and competitive market, stimulate liberalisation and the development of downstream industries, and improve production standards and infrastructure, particularly the abattoirs, which are often better than some abattoirs of the EU.

The EU has become the most important destination for SADC exports because of the Lomé trade provisions. SADC countries direct between 20% to 50% of their exports to the EU, where the margins of preference are superior to all other preferential trade arrangements extended to developing countries by the developed countries.

A number of SADC countries benefit from beef and sugar commodity protocols. The beef protocol, with a total quota of 5 200 tons for six ACP countries (four of these are SADC countries) and an import duty reduction of 92%, has assured the region of a large lucrative market for its beef and thus a source of foreign exchange earnings. The sugar protocol has supported sugar production in the region through the quotas that attract EU-guaranteed prices, which are well above world market rates. However, trade preferences have not justified themselves in terms of production and export diversification, international competitiveness and stimulating economic transformation in the SADC/ACP countries.

It is generally argued in the EU that non-reciprocal trade preferences have not only failed but they have become irrelevant and incompatible with the WTO provisions.

(g) The Cairns group

The Cairns group consists of 15 countries which export mainly agricultural products. The countries are Argentina, Australia, Brazil, Canada, Chile, Colombia, Fiji, Indonesia, Malaysia, New Zealand, Paraguay, the Philippines, Thailand, Uruguay, and South Africa.

During the Uruguay Round of GATT negotiations (South Africa was not part of the Cairns group at that stage), the Cairns group suggested a compromise which, in the long term, would lead to worldwide liberalisation of trade in agricultural products. They requested special rights for developing countries to protect their farmers against foreign competitors. They also asked for an effort to be made to support farmers in keeping food production high so that the populations of these countries could survive for a period of at least 10 years. This was how long it was expected to be before they can reap any benefit from the proposed worldwide liberalisation of agricultural trade.

At the same time the Cairns group also proposed that:

1 export subsidies on agricultural products be frozen and then gradually eliminated;
2 national support policies hampering trade in agricultural products should gradually disappear;
3 import tariffs be reduced to a very low level or eliminated totally;
4 tariffs be used to replace import quotas;
5 health regulations be eliminated where they are used as a cover-up for protectionist policies.

The trading characteristics of the Cairns group may be summarised as follows:

1 The geographical accessibility between the trading partners is not ideal.
2 There are enormous distances between some of the trading partners, and geographical mobility is restricted by a poorly organised network of air, rail and road transport, especially in South America.
3 The countries have considerable natural resources, but the scope of the trading bloc is limited to an agricultural agreement.
4 The countries have diverse labour and manufacturing capacities, but they have to be viewed from the perspective of agriculture.
5 Some of the trading partners have an entrepreneurial culture.
6 The free trade principle is not enforced since the object of the Cairns group is to co-ordinate agricultural policies.

(h) Common Market for Eastern and Southern Africa (COMESA)[20]

The history of COMESA began in December 1994 when it was formed to replace the former Preferential Trade Area (PTA) which had existed since the earlier days of 1981.

COMESA consists of 21 countries, namely Angola, Burundi, Comoros, Democratic Republic of Congo, Djibouti, Egypt, Eritrea, Ethiopia, Kenya, Madagascar, Malawi, Mauritius, Namibia, Rwanda, Seychelles, Sudan, Swaziland, Tanzania, Uganda, Zambia, and Zimbabwe. COMESA (as defined by its Treaty) was established 'as an organisation of free independent sovereign states which have agreed to co-operate in developing their natural and human resources for the good of all their people', and as such it has a wide-ranging series of objectives which necessarily include in their priorities the promotion of peace and security in the region.

However, because of COMESA's economic history and background, its main focus is on the formation of a large economic and trading unit capable of overcoming some of the barriers that are faced by individual states. COMESA's current strategy can thus be summed up in the phrase 'economic prosperity through regional integration'. With its 21 member states, population of over 385 million and annual import bill of around US$32 billion, COMESA forms a major market-place for both internal and external trading. Its area is impressive on the map of the African continent and its achievements to date have been relatively significant.

The COMESA states, in implementing a free trade area, are well on their way to achieving their target of removing all internal trade tariffs and barriers, an exercise which is to be completed by the year 2000. Within four years after that COMESA will have introduced a common external tariff structure to deal with all third party trade and will have considerably simplified all procedures.

Other objectives, which will assist in the achievement of trade promotion, include:

1 Trade liberalisation and customs co-operation, including the introduction of a unified computerised customs network across the region.
2 An improvement in the administration of transport and communications to ease the movement of goods, services and people between the countries.
3 The creation of an enabling environment and legal framework, which will encourage the growth of the private sector, the establishment of a secure investment environment, and the adoption of common sets of standards.
4 The co-ordination of macro-economic and monetary policies throughout the region.

Several institutions have been created to promote sub-regional co-operation and development, namely:

- the COMESA Trade and Development Bank in Kenya;
- the COMESA Clearing House in Zimbabwe;
- the COMESA Association of Commercial Banks in Zimbabwe;
- the COMESA Leather Institute in Ethiopia;
- the COMESA Re-Insurance Company (ZEP-RE) in Kenya.

In addition, a Court of Justice was established under the COMESA Treaty and became formally operational in 1998. Further initiatives exist to promote cross-border initiatives, form a common industrial policy and introduce a monetary co-ordination programme.

COMESA offers its members and partners a wide range of benefits which include:

- a wider, harmonised and more competitive market;
- greater industrial productivity and competitiveness;
- increased agricultural production and food security;
- a more rational exploitation of natural resources;
- more co-ordinated monetary, banking and financial policies;
- more reliable transport and communications infrastructure.

(i) Indian Ocean Rim Association for Regional Co-operation (IOR-ARC)[21]

Current membership includes the 19 member states: Australia, Bangladesh, India, Indonesia, Kenya, Madagascar, Malaysia, Mauritius, Mozambique, Oman, Singapore, South Africa, Sri Lanka, Tanzania, and Yemen.

The charter of the IOR-ARC was adopted at the first ministerial meeting in Mauritius on 6-7 March 1999, when the organisation was formally launched. The charter clearly indicates that the IOR-ARC 'seeks to build and expand understanding and mutually beneficial co-operation through a consensus-based, evolutionary and non-intrusive approach'. The charter is primarily an outward-looking forum for economic dialogue and co-operation, with the following key objectives:

- improved market access through trade liberalisation;
- facilitation of freer and enhanced flows of goods, services and investment throughout the region.

The IOR-ARC is firmly based on the principle of 'open regionalism' as encouraged by the WTO.

The following benefits are proposed for South Africa:

1 Important historical trading ties within the IOR region will be re-established.
2 South Africa is one of the strategic 'triangles' around which the IOR was built and

this will therefore establish the country as a global player in the community of nations.

3 The formation of the IOR will co-ordinate and increase economic co-operation in the fields of trade and investment.

4 The IOR region has enormous potential and offers vast business and investment opportunities over a wide spectrum. In the north-west are various oil-rich countries, with more than 60% of the world's proven oil reserves. In southern Asia there are emerging economies like India, with huge untapped markets. On the south-eastern flank of the IOR are economic success stories like Singapore and Malaysia, and also mineral-rich Australia. The islands of Mauritius and Seychelles are attractive tourist destinations, as is the east coast of Africa, which has huge tourist potential.

5 There are already concrete examples of joint projects such as investment facilitation, trade promotion programmes, upgrading of ports and marine transport, and technological enhancement, which will benefit all the member states of the IOR.

6 Since the Indian Ocean carries a third of the world's oil and a significant percentage of its container cargo, there is much scope for co-operation in maritime matters, including safety of shipping, search and rescue, and environmental impact studies aimed at minimising the risk to the marine environment through oil spills.

2.6 Implications of regional trading blocs and trade agreements for South African businesses

The following eight principles have been identified as criteria for success with regard to regional trading blocs:

1 A trading bloc should be situated in a certain geographical region;
2 Its members should be geographically close and accessible to one another;
3 Geographical mobility based on good transport systems facilitates and supports trade between member countries;
4 Natural resources need to be available;
5 Diverse labour and manufacturing capacities are necessary;
6 An entrepreneurial culture is important;
7 A formal agreement, or a series of more informal agreements, is necessary to structure trade within the trading bloc and with third countries;
8 Internal free trade within the regional trading bloc and also tariff and/or non-tariff barriers against outsiders to protect their internal commercial activities.

The relative importance of the world's primary trading countries discussed in the previous section, and the criteria for success listed above, make it possible to evaluate the future potential of today's large regional trading blocs. Within this framework, certain conclusions will also be drawn about South Africa's position in the world market and the environment in which the country's international purchasing strategies will have to be developed.

The EU meets all eight of the success criteria for trading blocs identified above, and current international trade statistics confirm its position as the world leader. Its share of the international trade is almost 34%, half of which takes place within the EU. In March 1999, South Africa and the EU concluded three years of trade and development negotiations with the signing of an extensive trade, development and co-operation agreement in Brussels. (See Appendix 1 for a summary of this agreement.)

The second major regional trading bloc is NAFTA. With the establishment of NAFTA, the USA, Canada and Mexico have become an important regional trading bloc. NAFTA is also expected to become the basis for closer co-operation with the Cairns group, and with some of the Pacific Rim countries, to form an economic counterweight to the EU.

The future success of these two important regional trading blocs will be heightened by:

- geographical mobility based on their excellent transport capacity;
- the availability of vast natural resources of their own;
- strong manufacturing and entrepreneurial capacities.

By contrast, the ACP countries, for example, are not centrally located in the international trade system, their members are not geographically close, and their transport capacity is not as good as that of the large trading blocs. The ACP countries also have relatively poor manufacturing and entrepreneurial capacities, but, in most instances, have adequate natural resources. Their relative power is anchored in agricultural products but their share in world trade continues to decrease, which also limits their ability to become powerful global trading forces.

In the general international trading pattern, we must once again stress the important role played by GATT in freeing international trade from the many tariff and non-tariff barriers that were introduced after the Second World War.

It should be pointed out that it has become a matter of some urgency that world leaders should resolve the conflict between a world trade system and the development of regional trading blocs such as the EU and NAFTA, which advocate certain protection measures.

We will now consider the implications of the trend toward the formation of regional trading blocs for South Africa, by evaluating some of the country's strengths and weaknesses in the international market.

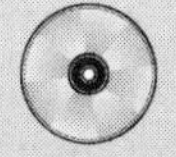

Compact disc

3 Mr Cedric Savage of Tongatt discusses the benefits of the SADC as a trading bloc.

It is necessary, first of all, to point out that the South African economy has traditionally displayed a relatively high degree of 'openness'. The trade figures for various years between 1911 and 1999 show that imports and exports have constituted a substantial portion of the country's total economic activity throughout the period. There is, therefore, a notable tendency to free trade.

It is, however, South Africa's mining and agricultural products that earn the greater part of the foreign currency. The country remains heavily dependent on the successful export of relatively few items, and the composition of exports largely reflects its natural resource endowment. Growth has been slow in the volume of merchandise exports in general, and in the export of manufactured products in particular.

Earlier on, South Africa imported mainly consumer goods. As the mining and then the manufacturing industries developed, more and more capital goods were imported. The content of the country's imports have thus 'hardened' in the sense that the proportion of consumer goods in total declines and it becomes increasingly difficult for the government to take any corrective action that might be required in the field of import restriction, without severely affecting the level of domestic economic activity. In the case of the South African economy, this problem has been compounded by the fact that, in times of economic expansion, it has been coupled with a chronic tendency for imports of goods and services to exceed exports.[22]

While the South African economy shows a fairly strong tendency toward imports, its exports remain focused on mining and agricultural products. It is, therefore, not sufficiently balanced to support a strong individual thrust towards trade expansion on the international scene. The country needs to develop a stronger export culture, as well as more consistent trade practices and better ties with trading partners.

When South Africa left the British Commonwealth in 1958, it in fact cut, for political reasons, an economic tie which in the present international market would have had numerous trade benefits. In addition, South Africa's isolation was heightened by decades of economic sanctions – a period in which the country's economy was exposed to virtually intolerable stress. South Africa's reintroduction into the British Commonwealth is regarded as a step in the right direction.

The future lies in South Africa's arrangements with and membership of large regional trading blocs like the EU, NAFTA, IOR, COMESA, and the Cairns group. In this instance, it was a good strategy to form a partnership with the EU as part of a common market in southern Africa (South Africa is a conditional member of the Lomé Convention).

Such a strategy makes a good deal of economic sense because it would:

- turn South Africa into a major partner in a regional trading bloc in southern Africa;
- take advantage of the fact that there is geographical mobility, based on good transport systems, to make trade possible between members and to support it;
- make it possible to exploit the vast natural resources of the region;
- use South Africa's diverse established labour and manufacturing capacities to help drive the economic activity of southern Africa;
- ensure that South Africa's extensive entrepreneurial culture is used efficiently;
- create the potential for a formal agreement between the countries of southern Africa and consequently for alliances with existing trading blocs such as the ACP countries and the EU;
- promote internal free trade within the regional trading bloc.

A policy of promoting free and fair trade is highly commendable, although the South African government will probably retain, for some time, its existing trade barriers, in accordance with WTO requirements, to encourage job creation and to stimulate the manufacturing sector to follow a labour-intensive growth route. It is also important to focus on increased privatisation of state assets and to become involved with the country's neighbours, especially the SADC countries.

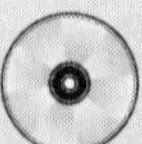

Compact disc

4 Ms Louise Tager of Transnet explains the benefits of privatising Transnet, and also the activities of Transnet in the SADC.

2.7 Summary

Globalisation may very well exacerbate gaps between rich global blocs and poor regions.

Internationalisation or globalisation can be seen in all the markets of the world, and the Asian crisis of the late 1990s is but one of the examples of this global shift, where national markets are merging into one huge marketplace.

Average tariff rates in the major countries of the world have fallen drastically since the 1950s and will approach 3,9% by the year 2000, if the Uruguay agreement is fully implemented.

It is generally agreed that the most suitable way of ensuring worldwide economic growth in the long term is free international trade. The problem is how to remove existing trade barriers without harming the economies of individual countries.

Modern economists support free trade because it increases consumption possibilities, is beneficial to general economic well-being, and leads to higher living standards.

Non-tariff barriers include measures such as excessive import documentation requirements, delays with customs procedures, restrictions on advertising and customs evaluation procedures, health requirements, labelling requirements, and taxes on the employment of foreign personnel, and, together with the better-known tariff barriers, restricts the trend towards trade liberalisation.

GATT precludes quantitative restrictions in principle, grants most-favoured-nation rights, helps to resolve trading differences and negotiates tariff reductions.

The functions of the WTO are to administer its trade agreements, act as forum for trade negotiations, handle trade disputes, monitor national trade policies, give technical assistance and training for developing countries, and co-operate with other international organisations.

The most important trading blocs for African countries that have come into being since the Second World War are the EU, NAFTA, MERCOSUR, CARICOM, ASEAN, SADC, the ACP countries, COMESA, and the IOR-ARC.

The importance of these trading blocs and agreements for South African business justifies careful evaluation of both opportunities and risks by South African enterprises involved in international business.

Case Study

ISCOR Mining[23]

Company profile

Iscor Ltd is a South African listed, integrated minerals and metals company, producing and marketing a range of iron and steel products, associated raw materials and by-products in the local South African and international markets. In 1997 the company was ranked no. 29 in the world on the basis of metric tons crude steel output and no. 7 among industrial companies on the Johannesburg Stock Exchange in terms of market capitalisation. At that time it employed 41 664 people.

Iscor's main mining businesses comprise iron ore, with an activity level of approximately 24,2 million tons (Mt) per annum (of which 15,8 Mt are exported per annum), and coal, with an activity level of approximately 17 Mt per annum (of which 2 Mt are exported per annum). The successful acquisition of mining rights to the copper deposit at Tenke Fungurume in Zaire is an important diversification in the company's mining activities. Other mining activities include dolomite, quartzite and lead-zinc-silver deposits.

Iscor's main metals businesses comprise carbon steel with an annual output of approximately 3,3 Mt of flat steel products, of which 39% was exported in 1996/7. Of the long or profile products, 55% was exported and 38% of the speciality steel products was exported. The addition of the Tenke Fungurume copper deposit in 1996 made Iscor an international player (in terms of both operations and sales) in the metals commodity markets.

Management philosophy

Iscor's mission is to add value for its shareholders. The board of directors considers the following performance areas vital for the company's success:

- management of the cyclicality of its businesses;
- maintenance of a strong balance sheet;
- utilisation of leading-edge technology;
- empowerment of employees to contribute their full potential;
- social, ethical, and environmental compatibility.

The elements of this management philosophy deserve further examination in a global context. First, acknowledgement of the cyclical nature of the business (commodities) and the focus on a strong balance sheet signify deep understanding of the fundamental determinants of survival, profitability and growth in the commodities business. The severe cyclicality of the global stainless steel market, which Iscor is currently penetrating, and of the ferrochrome market, must be taken into account.

Second, the focus on leading-edge production technology means that the company acknowledges that it operates in a high-volume, low-margin business. The most effective operating strategy is, therefore, cost leadership. Leading-edge technology can be acquired in two ways – either through in-house development or agreements to transfer know-how (bench-marking, joint ventures).

Third, and perhaps most important, the focus on empowerment of employees, to enable the latter to contribute to their full potential, suggests an intimate understanding of the social dynamics in the workplace and the culturally diverse South African labour environment. The company seems to possess the required cultural sensitivity to operate effectively and efficiently in a foreign business environment.

Finally, the growing importance of a management philosophy of environmental responsibility at home in the light of a steadily increasing environmental awareness among the South African population, is self-evident.

However, there are international implications as well. Take stainless steel production as an example. First-World consumers of stainless steel are increasingly cutting back on installed capacity because of the carcinogenic nature of components contained in the waste products of the production process. They present a threat because the concept of 'green marketing' is gaining in popularity among First-World consumers. The latter invariably insist on inspection of the manufacturing facilities of prospective suppliers before placing firm orders, to ensure that the threat to the environment is not simply transferred from industrialised nations to developing nations in an irresponsible manner.

Financial profile

International direct investment requires capital which can be sourced either from retained earnings (strong balance sheet), or from investors (new equity, both local and foreign). Market capitalisation on 1 July 1996 amounted to approximately R8 billion. The company has sufficient liquidity to take on the additional market risk of expanded commodity operations, but it should focus on investment opportunities in countries with low labour costs.

Extent of global activities

Iscor's degree of globalisation (both current and future) is summarised in Table 2.1. The company is steadily evolving toward the multinational/transnational phases.

Table 2.1: Iscor's international corporate evolution (bracketed entries indicate direction of development)

	Phase I Domestic	Phase II International	Phase III Multinational	Phase IV Transnational
Primary orientation			Price ①②④	Strategy ①②③④
Competitive strategy			Multinational	(Global) ⑤
Importance of world business			Extremely important	(Dominant)
Product/Service			Standardised ①②	Mass-customised ③
Technology			← Totally different, but shared concepts →	
R&D/Sales			← Currently less than 1%, but set to increase, especially ⑤ →	
Profit margin			Low ①②	Initially high ③
Competitors			Some ①②	Pre-emptive ③
Market			← Relatively large →	
Production location		Very large, concentrated ③	Multinational, least cost ①⑤	
Exports		Growing ①		Imports & exports ③
Structure			← Still very centralised →	

The assessment in Table 2.1 is based on interviews with the CEO, Mr H.J. Smith, in 1996, and on the following ventures:

- Major developments in 1997 were that Macsteel International, the 50% international marketing joint venture which handles all Iscor's steel exports, started trading during January and had already made a contribution to Iscor's profits during the first six-month operating period. Net equity accounted earnings from investments showed little net change. However, a provision of R27 million for losses incurred by Ticor was more than offset by profits earned by Macsteel International. Furthermore, Indo-China Nominees (Pty) Ltd obtained a 5,11% shareholding in Iscor.
- No substantial changes in investments and subsidiaries took place during 1997, except for the structuring of Iscor's international investments under the umbrella of Rocsi Holdings Limited. Rocsi Holdings was capitalised mainly for the funding of the investment in Ticor Limited and the acquisition of the shareholding in Macsteel International.

Motives for internationalisation

With the South African economy on the brink of radical transformation, a paradigm shift in both government and business policies seems to be inevitable to ensure that South African firms will be in a position to internationalise. For this reason, corporations must develop global strategies to be able to stay competitive and succeed.

Although global enterprise is the answer for some companies, global strategic planning is more complex than domestic planning. At least five factors can contribute to this increase in complexity:

1. Multinational enterprises (MNEs) face multiple political, economic, legal, social and cultural environments.
2. Interactions between the national and foreign environments are complex because of national sovereignty issues and differing economic and social conditions.
3. Geographical separation, cultural and national differences, and variations in business practices tend to make control and communication between HQ and affiliate very difficult.
4. MNEs face extreme competition because of differences in industry structures.
5. MNEs are restricted in their selection of competitive strategies by various regional blocks and economic integrations (e.g. NAFTA, EU, MERCOSUR).

Iscor's expansion programme can be seen as a strategy to obtain specific advantages so that it can give the company a competitive edge, in other words, a proactive reason for international expansion. With Iscor currently ranked no. 29 in the world – measured on the basis of metric tonnes of crude steel output – and the growing demand for minerals and metals worldwide, the company decided to embark on an international expansion programme, and the following proactive reasons can be given for its international business ventures:

- **Economies of scale**: When the volume of production increases, the long-range average cost of a unit produced will decline. Iscor's economies of scale result from both technological and non-technological sources (higher levels of mechanisation, automation, long-term contractual agreements and specialisation). Iscor 'controls' its competitors by means of its economies of scale and simultaneous creation of entry barriers. This also puts it in a position to lower prices and offer a unique range of value-added steel grades, to become even more competitive in the international market-place.
- **Taxes:** Tax systems and tax rates differ from one location to another, thus presenting opportunities for companies to maximise their after-tax profits. Iscor also negotiates for tax incentives from the host country when opening up a new venture.
- **Labour cost**: High labour costs, such as

those which currently prevail in South Africa, can increase the overall price of the company's product or service. Iscor can find much cheaper labour in underdeveloped countries like Zaire.

- **Protection of home market**: By active involvement in a foreign country, a firm protects its own home ground, forcing competitors in that country to adopt a defensive strategy in their own market. This offensive strategy will result in competitors pulling back from their foreign activities. Iscor applies this strategy vigorously especially in the Sub-Saharan countries that are very close to its home market.
- **Power and prestige**: The international image can be seen in the following statement made by Mr Smith during an interview: 'I can confidently say that Iscor will have the pick of the best in the world when selecting co-developers. We will not experience the slightest difficulty with financing, nor with the acquisition of the needed expertise to launch big projects.'
- **New expanded markets**: There is great potential in foreign commodity markets and infrastructure (e.g. the iron ore harbour in China), as well as the demand for know-how and technologies from other steelmakers (e.g. Corex technology).
- **Social responsibility**: As stated by Mr Smith: 'Africa is the forgotten continent of the world. The only possible way we can really get off the ground and make the continent attractive to foreign investors and developers is to prove that we have confidence in our own future by coming up with imaginative projects and making them work.' Human resource development is recognised as strategically important if the company wishes to remain competitive internationally.

Iscor is confident that it has a sound foundation on which it can build a world-class global company. The elements of that foundation are a clear and finely focused vision, a robust balance sheet, a number of promising new projects, a strong innovative and entrepreneurial culture, and finally the will to win.

Generic strategies

Any company operating in the international environment has to contend with forces impacting on both the supply (or input) side and the demand (or output) side of its industry. South African companies operated in a protectionist environment up to 1994, when there was a change of government. International strategies were never really relevant, except for the sourcing and securing of raw materials not available locally, since the market was predominantly local, and export opportunities were subsidised by the Government Export Incentive Scheme (GEIS). Relatively sudden socio-political changes have caused an almost overnight removal of high entry barriers for foreign competitors in the local market. Simultaneously, removal of GEIS has put locally manufactured exports under tremendous pressure from overseas producers.

Selection of generic strategies

A company considering internationalisation has to address both the matter (i.e. what) and the method (i.e. how) within the boundaries of its opportunities/threats and strengths/weaknesses (SWOT) framework. Iscor's strategic options derive mainly from the generic value chain in which the company operates.

Strategies: mining

Current mining operations are located mainly in South Africa. An important and very interesting development on the mining side is the investment in a large-scale iron ore harbour in China. This represents a unique strategic thrust. China is currently (1999) the country with the largest aggregate (i.e in dollar terms) economic growth in the world, and infrastructure is, therefore, of the utmost importance to the country. At the same time, China is currently the world's largest steel producer, so that fixed investment in steel manufacturing would not have been a profitable exercise for Iscor. However, the direct investment in the iron ore harbour has huge potential spin-offs, since it could quite literally become the Rotterdam of Eastern Asia. Iron ore exports in 1996 to Western and Eastern Europe were R6,2 million and R1,8 million respectively, whereas exports to China and Japan were R3,4 million and R3,3 million respectively.

The iron ore harbour is also an opportunity to develop infrastructure to carry Iscor's ore to buyers in East Asia. Furthermore, China and the Pacific Rim countries generally show promise of becoming strong economic growth points in the future, so that an established presence in the region is a decided advantage.

Ticor Limited's (Australia) results were below expectation in 1997 due to production problems and low pigment prices, but improved results were expected in 1998.

Exploration is also being carried out in a number of Pacific Rim countries in association with Omax Resources Ltd, Rimfire Resources Ltd and Minerals International Ltd. Further exploration work at Moranbah in Queensland, Australia, was discontinued because of the depth of the reserves and oversupply in the coking coal market.

Strategies: steel

An example of the technology transfer strategy is the creation (by Iscor) of TransOrient Steel, a wholly-owned subsidiary in Taiwan, that sells specialised know-how to steelmakers in the Far East. The technical know-how for the Corex (iron-making) process, of which Iscor operates the only commercially functioning unit in the world, is being made available to a Korean steel-maker.

Internationalisation processes

The world is quickly changing from the industrial age to the information age, fostering urgency in actions within business organisations. One major aspect of change in the business environment is that of the global village. This requires organisations to undergo a process of internationalisation. This section focuses on aspects which characterise Iscor's internationalisation processes in this perspective.

Organisational structures and headquarters' influence over subsidiaries

Iscor consists of two major operating divisions, namely steel and mining. The company also has a separate group function consisting of four group departments, namely finance, business information, human resources and public relations, and legal and administrative services. The operating divisions each have their own business units, independent of those in the other divisions. The internationalisation of the company on any specific venture will, therefore, be part of one of the divisions, which will then be responsible to the executive chairman and the Iscor board of directors.

New trends in organisation structuring

Iscor is conducting investigations to implement user-friendly job evaluation (decision support) systems to adopt user-friendly methods for designing structures throughout the corporation and to ensure full participation on the part of line managers. This wave of change is likely to be incorporated into the foreign subsidiaries of the company. The company headquarters should not dictate to the subsidiaries what they must do, since local conditions may differ for different company operations.

Decentralisation process

The company's decentralised business units are characterised by local ownership and control over their markets. However, the parent company holds the 'purse' in terms of authorising capital expenditure of a certain financial magnitude, and this will probably be a characteristic of foreign subsidiaries during the early stages.

Headquarters' influence over subsidiaries

Although Iscor has made strides in creating decentralised business units, there is still some influence from the head office in local operations, which is also expected from investments abroad.

Organisational change

A major change in Iscor was its privatisation in 1989. This led to other major changes, including a shift toward strategic planning. The present executive chairman requires all operations to be bench-marked against the best practices in the world. He commissioned international consultants (McKinsey and Partners) to review the current operations of the company and establish their competitiveness against world-class performers.

London and Wueste state that the successful adoption of a change process is tied to career development and continuous learning (or organisation learning) which will put the company in a competitive position in its operations abroad. In the quest for the best practices in the world, key managers are sent to different countries to study and observe such practices. This will not only improve performance and productivity locally, but also in foreign operations. The executives who interact with their counterparts abroad will gradually develop a global mindset which is critical in foreign operations. Rhinesmith defines a mindset 'as a predisposition to see the world in a particular way that sets boundaries and provides explanations for why things are the way they are, while at the same time establishing guidance for ways in which we should behave'.

Financial control

As mentioned above, the executive chairman and the board require strong financial accountability from the company's subsidiaries, yet insist on authorising major capital expenditures in each business unit. This may lead to business opportunities being exploited suboptimally, because of the unavoidable time lag involved.

Downsizing

Iscor has been part of the world trend of corporate restructuring and downsizing in business organisations. The policy to downsize the corporate head office (and other parts of the company) will have a strong influence on foreign subsidiaries, which will be expected to have leaner organisational structures.

Corporate management attitude

The management philosophy of the executive chairman and the top executives is rooted in local ownership and individual worth. The head office has, therefore, only to give a broad framework of corporate strategic policies, while the business units formulate specific operating strategies according to their own local needs. This is somewhat contradicted by the centralised capital budgeting process, however.

The control over subsidiaries is based largely on the capital budget and financial performance. There is also a continuous flow of information between the business units and head office; the requirement for such information flow emphasises how valuable the executive chairman considers communication, which he strongly propagates. The administrative mechanisms used by the company to ensure control over its business units (or subsidiaries), in terms of Doz and Prahalad, are information systems, measurement systems, resource allocation procedures, strategic planning, and budgeting processes.

A major challenge facing the company, as it moves abroad, is managing cultural diversity. South Africa, where the company is based, is already an extremely diverse country in terms of different cultural values. The competency in managing local conditions may serve as leverage to manage international cultural issues. Cultural diversity should not be seen in a negative light, since it invariably brings substantial potential benefits, such as better decision-making, greater creativity and innovation, and more successful marketing, to different types of customers.

Generic enterprise types

Iscor is now involved in three different markets, namely commodities, technology transfer and the development of infrastructure, whereas the company was traditionally known only for its activities in the minerals mining business and the manufacturing of steel.

Iscor's medium-term future involvement as a global company is summarised in Table 2.2.

Iscor is well established as a company with a global focus, that is, competing worldwide, but only in a part of the commodities industry. By investing in copper and infrastructure in Africa, the iron ore harbour in China and the Trans-Orient Steel venture in Asia, Iscor is fast moving to an international focus. Iscor clearly chose China, the Pacific Rim and Sub-Saharan Africa to outperform global firms through cost advantage, differentiation and physical presence. Some of the advantages to Iscor are the additional resources, exploitation of its specific core competencies, taxes, economies of scale and new expanded markets.

Adler describes four phases of international corporate evolution or globalisation. Overall, Iscor is currently between phase 2 (international) and phase 3 (multinational), which can be seen in Table 2.1 (p. 51). Iscor's strategic plan clearly states that it is 'an integrated minerals and metals company which we visualise must be internationally competitive and top-rated in terms of financial performance, products, and service, adding real value for its shareholders'. According to Mr Smith, the company is the second-cheapest producer of steel in the world. The primary orientation is price, and the competitive strategy multinational; the world in terms of markets and competition is also extremely important (multinational). The products are completely standardised and the structure centralised.

The following phase 2 characteristics are discernible:

- shared technology (but not yet widely shared);
- exports are growing and there is high potential for growth;
- production locations are at the moment mainly domestic;
- the structure is functional with international divisions.

Table 2.2: Iscor's international exposure by generic enterprise type

Indicator	Commodities	Technology	Infrastructure
• Foreign sales: total sales (%)	25	100	20
• Foreign assets: total assets (%)	5	< 1	100
• Overseas subsidiaries (%)	20	7	13
• Intn'l experience (top management)	5	50	50
• Dispersion	50% local 50% overseas	100% Asia	Asia (Harbour) Africa (Zaire)

Conclusion

Iscor is clearly in the process of evolving into a multinational company. Steel is currently sold very profitably in Sub-Saharan Africa. Other steel clientele includes Japan, America and Britain, but these are not very profitable markets because of protectionism. A disadvantage in the international arena is that the South African government provides only a 5% tariff protection for local steel producers, while 10% is the internationally accepted rate. Another weakness is the high domestic corporate tax rate. While becoming a global player, Iscor will have to guard its own backyard with care, in order not to lose local customers to other international companies.

Mr Smith noted that Iscor's markets would be unlikely to recover significantly until 1999/2000. The production and marketing capabilities will be tested again, and financial management will have to contend with an ambitious capital expenditure programme.

? Questions

1 Do you think Iscor made the right decision to diversify into commodities, technology transfer and infrastructural development? (The company's core activity was in the minerals mining business and the manufacturing of steel.)
2 What would happen if the existing tariff protection for local steel producers were eliminated?
3 Write your own vision statement for Iscor.

Endnotes

1 Based on the essay 'Developing countries must insist on free and fair global trade'. www.fm.co.za, 10 March 1999.
2 Hill, C.W.L. 1998. *International business: competing in the global marketplace.* 2nd ed. Washington: Irwin/ McGraw-Hill, p. 5.
3 Dicken, P. 1992. *Global shift.* New York: Guilford Press.
4 Hill, ibid., p. 8.
5 Hill, ibid., p. 8.
6 Czinkota, R.C., Ronkainen, I.A., Moffet, M.H. & Moynihan, E.O. 1998. *Global business.* 2nd ed. New York: Harcourt Brace, p. 29.
7 Hill, ibid., p. 130.
8 Punnett, B.J. & Ricks, D.A. 1997. *International business.* 2nd ed. MA: Blackwell Business, p. 51.
9 Czinkota et al., ibid., p. 37.
10 Leontief, W. 1953. 'Domestic production and foreign trade: The American capital position re-examined'. *Proceedings of the American Philosophical Society,* 97, pp. 331–349.
11 Vernon, R. 1966. 'International investment and trade in the product cycle'. *Quarterly Journal of Economics,* pp. 190–207.
12 Porter, M.E. 1990. *The competitive advantage of nations.* New York: Free Press.
13 Mill, J.S. 1947. *Principles of political economy.* London: Standard Library, pp. 591–592.
14 Ingram, J.C. 1986. *International economics.* 2nd ed. New York: Wiley, p. 320.
15 Winters, L.A. 1985. *International economics.* 3rd ed. London: Allen & Unwin, p. 56.
16 Samuelson, P.A. 1980. *Economics.* 11th ed. Tokyo: McGraw-Hill Kogakusha, p. 651.
17 Winters, op. cit., p. 83.
18 See Unisa 'Advanced certificate programme in purchasing management', 1998. Pretoria: Centre for Business Management.
19 Sweeny, J. 1991. 'Business of the Southern Hemisphere', *The Economist,* 24 August, pp. 27–38.
20 COMESA website. www.comesa.int
21 'South Africa's participation in the Indian Ocean Rim Association for Regional Co-operation'. Report from the Indian Ocean Rim Business Forum, 30–31 March 1999. Issued by the Department of Foreign Affairs, March 1999.
22 Natrass, J. 1988. *The South African economy.* Cape Town: Oxford University Press, p. 271.
23 Data for the case was taken from:
ISCOR Annual Report, 1997; ISCOR Annual Report, 1996.
Gleasson, D. & van Huyssteen, A. 'Rumble in the jungle', *Financial Mail,* 21 June 1996, pp. 69–71.
Smith, H. 1996. Interviews with the Chief Executive Officer, ISCOR, June & July.
Adler, N.J. 1992. *International dimensions of organizational behaviour.* 2nd ed. Belmont, CA: PWS Kent, p. 4.
Pearce, J.A. & Robinson, R.B. 1995. *Strategic management: formulation, implementation and control.* (Alternate case edition.) Chicago, Ill: Irwin, p. 113.
Erwee, R. 1996. 'Strategies for internationalising South African companies', unpublished manuscript, University of Pretoria. January, pp. 1–21.
Stahl, M.J. 1995. *Management: total quality in a global environment.* Boston, MA: Blackwell.
London, L. and Wueste, R.A. 1992. *Human resource development in changing organizations.* London: Quorum.
Rhinesmith, S.H. 1992. *A manager's guide to globalization: six keys to success in a changing world.* New York: Irwin.
Doz, Y.L. & Prahalad, C.K. 'Headquarters influence and strategic control in MNCS', in Bartlett, C.A. & Ghoshal, S. (eds.)1992. *Transnational* , Chapter 5. Homewood, Ill: Irwin.
1991. 'The multicultural organization', *Academy of Management Executive,* Vol. 5, No. 2, pp. 34–47.

Appendix

South Africa/European Union negotiations

Trade, Development and Co-operation Agreement

A briefing document by the Department of Trade and Industry on the conclusion of the Agreement

25 March 1999

Briefing document on the conclusion of the RSA-EU negotiations for a Trade, Development and Co-operation Agreement

1 Background

This week marked the end of almost four years of negotiations with the European Union (EU) towards a Trade, Development and Co-operation Agreement. Minister Erwin and Commissioner Pinheiro finalised this historic agreement which has been endorsed by both the South African Cabinet and the European Council of Ministers. It means that the road has now been cleared for the signing and ratification of the Agreement which is of national and international importance. The expected implementation date is 1 January 2000, which will allow time for government structures as well as private sector operators to prepare for the procedural implications of a free trade area with our most important trading partner in the world.

1.1 The origins of the Agreement

The call for negotiations with South Africa was expressed as part of the desire on the part of the EU to support the country's new democracy and address the legacy of the past. The EU's mandate tempered South Africa's high expectations. South Africa, however, chose to engage and develop a strategic partnership with the EU, which is the country's major trade and investment partner.

As part of economic transformation, the government has adopted policies which seek to reposition and reintegrate the South African economy within a rapidly changing global economy. This necessitates the establishment of globally competitive economic enterprises. The move toward global competitiveness has to be accompanied by regional economic co-operation that advances a broad and integrated process of industrialisation in the economies of southern Africa.

A growing South African economy that facilitates intraregional economic trade and investment flows is a major opportunity for development in Africa – and more particularly southern Africa – in the medium term. Not only will it source a wider range of products from its neighbours, but it will also be able to invest in activities that will increase the region's exports. This will only be possible if South Africa is able to expand its production base by strengthening and enhancing its competitive advantage in the beneficiation of its natural resources. This, in turn, requires that there should be an increase in value-added production and a larger manufacturing sector.

The bold move toward a free trade Agreement with the EU is intended to contribute towards restructuring the economy. It is also aimed at consolidating the strategic links with the economies of the member states of the EU, securing preferential market access for South African products and providing certainty and added leverage for foreign investment in the South African economy.

2 Overall results

The Trade, Development and Co-operation Agreement with the EU covers a wide range of issues in a comprehensive field of co-operation. It includes, *inter alia:*

- political dialogue;
- provisions for a free trade area;
- trade-related issues;
- economic co-operation;
- financial assistance and development co-operation;
- social and cultural co-operation.

As part of establishing a comprehensive relationship with the EU, two other Agreements have been concluded, namely:

- the Science and Technology Agreement (signed in December 1996);
- partial membership of the Lomé Convention (agreed in April 1997).

At the request of the EU, South Africa agreed to negotiate a Wines and Spirits Agreement and a Fisheries Agreement. South Africa insisted, however, that such agreements should be mutually beneficial and that there should be no conditional linkage with the main Agreement. The main Agreement contains a so-called hook-clause providing for future negotiations for a co-operation agreement on fisheries, and there is also a side letter covering the political agreement on port and sherry.

3 Key features of the Agreement

3.1 Essential element and non-execution provisions

Respect for democratic principles, fundamental human rights, and the rule of law are established as key elements of the Agreement. Good governance is established as another important principle. Any violation of these principles by one party would lead to the other party taking appropriate measures, including withdrawing some concessions. South Africa insisted on the formulation of these provisions so that there is objectivity in the test for breach of the essential element of the Agreement without the risk of unilateral action nor the balance of economic or political interests becoming the determining factor. The agreed text has a better definition of good governance and circumstances under which the non-execution provision can be invoked.

3.2 Free Trade Area (FTA) provisions

3.2.1 General features

When South Africa presented its offer to the EU in June 1997, it called for free trade with asymmetrical coverage of all trade and sectors and special protocols to cover sensitive products. It also called for development and financial measures to support further regional integration and facilitate the adjustment process in Southern Africa. The outcome of the negotiations meets the WTO requirements of Article XXIV GATT 1994. The coverage of the FTA will be around 90% of current trade between the parties with the following elements:

- Community: full liberalisation of 95% of imports from South Africa at the end of the transitional period of 10 years;
- South Africa: full liberalisation of 86% of imports from EU at the end of the transitional period of 12 years;
- includes both traded and non-traded products;
- provides for the protection of South Africa's sectors (automobiles and components, textiles and clothing, red meat, sugar, winter grains, and dairy).
- includes the agricultural sector, alongside all other sectors with partial liberalisation, and provision for regular reviews on products on the reserve lists;
- commits the EU to provision of support for SACU for adjustment efforts resulting from the establishment of the FTA;
- contains several elements that assure a positive regional impact on the other countries of the South African Development Cooperation (SADC).

3.2.2 **Industrial sector**

Approximately 86% of South Africa's total exports to the EU consist of industrial products. While the EU's average tariff levels for industrial products are low, the removal of tariffs will nevertheless give South African exporters a relative advantage over some of their competitors in the EU market. The EU will eliminate its industrial tariffs either immediately or within three years after the entry into force of the Agreement. This includes most of the sensitive products of textiles and clothing (only about 20% of South Africa's textile exports to the EU will be phased out over a longer period, i.e. six years from the entry into force of the Agreement) At entry into force of the Agreement tariffs on auto-components will be reduced to 50% of the MFN rates[1] applied by the EU. Other products like ferrochromium, with tariff elimination starting in the fourth year, will continue to have a global duty-free quota. Only six lines of aluminium will remain on the reserve list. The products on the reserve list will nevertheless be subject to reviews.

As indicated, the transitional period for the phasing out of tariffs by South Africa is 12 years, to allow for adjustment by firms. Sensitive products, like automobiles and parts, will remain on the reserve list without any tariff elimination or reduction schedules at this point. This will be reviewed in the light of the outcome of the mid-term review of the Motor Industry Development Programme. With regard to other sensitive products, South Africa persuaded the EU to moderate its initial expectations. This will enable South Africa to have a slower phase-down. In the case of clothing and textiles, there is a commitment to reduce the tariffs applicable to imports from the EU. Depending on the segment of the market, by the end of the eighth year the tariffs will vary between 5% and 20%. Between the eighth year and the end of the transition period, EU products will enjoy a preference over the MFN rate of around 40%. The Agreement therefore takes into account the changes in these industries at a pace far beyond what was conceivable a few years ago.

3.2.3 **Agricultural sector**

The agricultural sector is traditionally the most protected sector in the EU and has generally been excluded by the EU in other free trade Agreements. In its mandate the EU's *a priori* excluded about 46% of agriculture from the FTA with South Africa.

- Agricultural safeguard clause

While the EU's Common Agricultural Policy (CAP) is still a matter of concern, the Agreement provides (with regard to agricultural policies) for consultation and compensatory adjustments for any changes which may affect the balance of concessions. The agricultural policies provision is supplemented by an agri-

1 The MFN rate is the rate applicable to all other contracting parties of the World Trade Organisation (WTO).

cultural safeguard clause which gives South Africa the right to challenge the EU should there be proof that increased imports of agricultural products are causing harm or threatening to cause harm to the domestic industry. The onus is on South Africa, and especially the agricultural industry, to put an effective monitoring system in place that will serve as an early warning signal in this regard.

- EU export subsidies

Although South Africa did not succeed in eliminating EU export subsidies completely, there are some important breakthroughs. Firstly, the EU has committed itself not to pay export refunds on cheese exported to South Africa under the tariff quota of 5 000 tons. Secondly, the EU is willing to eliminate export refunds on products South Africa might want to offer for front-loading during the implementation period. Refunds will be eliminated in full once tariff liberalisation starts. This is an important aspect of the Agreement, since most of the EU's agricultural products will not be competitive on the domestic market without refunds. South Africa will take up this challenge. Should the EU be unwilling or unable to eliminate export refunds, South Africa can simply retract its offer of front-loading.

- Tariff quotas

The introduction of tariff quotas is important in that it makes inroads into the EU reserve list. The tariff quotas for canned fruit (60 000 tons), fruit juices (5 000 tons) and cut flowers, especially proteas (900 tons), are of particular interest to the industry in South Africa. The quotas for wines and sparkling wines, as well as for cheese, are also significant.

- Reserve list

The EU list of exclusions has been reduced, i.e. from 46% to 38% (based on 1997 trade lists). If one takes tariff quotas into account, it has been reduced even further to 26%. This is an important development. In addition, it is now called a reserve list, which is subject to regular reviews with a view to a further opening-up of the market. South Africa will therefore be continuously pressing for a review of this list in the light of changing circumstances on EU and/or world markets.

3.3 Trade-related issues

While the South African law on the regulation of economic activities is consistent with international practices, the country took a view that provisions on trade-related issues in the bilateral Agreement with the EU should not go beyond the current multilateral conventions and disciplines agreed to in bodies like the WTO, WIPO, etc. This is particularly important, given South Africa's commitment to playing an active role in advancing the interests of the developing countries in the multilateral fora. A number of the trade-related issues put on the table by the EU are still subject to intense debates and examination in the multilateral fora. With regard to issues like government procurement and intellectual property rights, the Agreement provides for mechanisms for further dialogue with the EU. Generally speaking, the commitments that were made were regarded as necessary for the proper functioning of the free trade area. These include:

- Customs Unions (CUs) and FTAs

The Agreement provides for consultations to take into account the mutual interests in the event that the maintenance or establishment of CUs or FTAs affect each other's interests. For South Africa, this provision was regarded as essential for the protection of domestic interests against a change in the balance of rights which may arise from the future enlargement of the EU.

- Anti-dumping and countervailing measures

The Agreement provides for parties to consider alternatives (constructive remedies) before imposing definitive anti-dumping duties and countervailing duties. This creates an opportunity for the relevant firms to put options for undertaking on price, volume, and/or a combination of these, rather than to face prohibitive duties.

• Safeguards

There is a comprehensive provision covering regular, regional, and transitional safeguard measures. The regular safeguard provides for measures to be taken in the case of import surges which threaten or cause injury to domestic producers. This is supplemented by the non-reciprocal provision in terms of which South Africa will be able to take exceptional measures to protect infant industries or sectors facing serious difficulties caused by increased imports during the transitional period. There is also provision for measures to be taken to safeguard any of the other SACU[2] members against increased imports which threaten or cause serious deterioration in that member's economic situation. The comprehensive safeguard provision is important to ensure that South Africa and other SACU members can temporarily protect themselves or slow down the pace of liberalisation if the impact proves to be more than they can handle.

• Used goods

The exceptions clause provides for the protection of domestic producers against the importation of used goods.

• Competition policy

South Africa sought to ensure that the provisions do not go beyond those of the new competition policy and law. This provides for consultative mechanisms to attempt to accommodate the interests of each party with the application of domestic law. It does not regulate the provision of state aid, nor deal with services and government procurement as was proposed by the EU.

2 SACU (Southern Africa Customs Union) consists of Botswana, Lesotho, Namibia, South Africa, and Swaziland.

• Public aid

The agreed text recognises that it is in the interest of both parties to ensure that public aid is granted in a fair and transparent manner. It also takes into account the facilitating role that can be played by state support and involvement in the restructuring of the South African industry and the economy. It thus provides for consultation between the parties to find a satisfactory solution to situations where public aid distorts fair competition.

• Dispute settlement

To ensure that there are no unnecessary delays in the resolution of disputes, the Agreement sets out clear disciplines for the trade chapter. Other disputes on the general provisions of the Agreement or for those arising in areas such as Development Co-operation and Economic Co-operation, will be governed by a less tight procedure.

4 Economic co-operation

The Agreement provides for co-operation in a variety of fields, including industrial restructuring and modernisation, investment promotion and protection, trade development, development of SMMEs, information and communication technology, energy, mining and minerals, transport, tourism, services, and consumer protection.

5 Protocol on rules of origin

Rules of origin form the backbone of a preferential trade agreement like the one South Africa is about to sign with the EU. These rules prohibit the deflection of trade and thereby protect the integrity of the agreement. The protocol will therefore determine the administrative framework of the agreement between South Africa and the EU. It prescribes what would count as local content and has the same function as a person's passport. The rules determine the ability of economic operators in the contracting parties to reap the rewards of duty-free access to one another's markets. Important features of the protocol include:

- Cumulation

Cumulation of the rules of origin is an instrument[3] enabling parties to a free trade area to use material originating in certain other countries, i.e. without violating the rules of origin. The protocol provides for diagonal (or partial) cumulation between South Africa and the EU, as well as with materials originating in non-SACU African, Caribbean and Pacific (ACP) countries. As far as the SACU is concerned, it allows for full cumulation with materials originating in Botswana, Lesotho, Namibia, and Swaziland (BLNS).

As far as cumulation within the context of the Lomé Convention is concerned , i.e. trade in the direction from South Africa to all ACP countries to the EU – the EU has undertaken to remove the current ad hoc provision with regard to South Africa and to replace it with diagonal cumulation with South Africa. This means that ACP countries, including BLNS, will be able to cumulate with materials which have acquired originating status in South Africa.

- List rules

These are specific rules for specific products, based on the tariff nomenclature. This list, which is contained in Annexe II of the protocol, describes the working or processing to be carried out on non-originating materials in order that the final product can obtain originating status. South Africa's view was that some of these rules did not reflect the level of productive capacity in the country. These are 04.03 (cream, yoghurt); 09.02 9 (tea), 20.08 (peanut butter); 20.20.09 (fruit juices); 22.02 (beverages), and 25.25 (mica). This matter is still under consideration by the EU.

- General value tolerance rule

Article 5 allows a certain percentage of the value of the final product to be imported from other countries, notwithstanding the conditions set out in the list rule. The protocol makes provision for a general tolerance of 15%, with the exception of textiles (which will be covered by explanatory notes 5.1 and 6.1) fish, tobacco, and alcohol.

- Prohibition of drawback of, or exemption from, customs duties

The Commission's proposal contained in Article 14 of their draft protocol, specified that non-originating materials used in the manufacture of products destined for the EU or South African market shall not be subject to drawback of or exemption from customs duties. However, it did not preclude the application of the export refund system for agricultural products applicable in the EU.

This proposal was not acceptable to South Africa and the prohibition on drawback has therefore been deleted from the protocol.

- Definition of fishing vessels

As far as the definition of fishing vessels is concerned, a paragraph has been added at the end of Article 4.2 to reflect South Africa's position on the requirement for officers and masters, subject to the entry into force of tariff concessions on fishery products (which in reality will only be granted if South Africa is willing to grant the EU access to its fishing waters).

6 Sectoral agreements

6.1 Fisheries co-operation

The EU put South Africa under a lot of pressure for a Fisheries Agreement with provision for

3 There are basically two types of cumulation: a) partial or diagonal cumulation; and b) full cumulation. In terms of the former, imported material has to meet the rules of origin applicable to that specific intermediate product. In the case of the latter, the countries which are allowed to cumulate are treated as a single customer territory, which means that whatever value is added, in whatever part of the territory, will count towards meeting the rules.

access to the country's fishing resources. It thus made a linkage between the Fisheries Agreement and the market access concessions, as well as the overall Agreement.

From the outset South Africa explained its new fisheries policy and its efforts towards restructuring the industry and the conservation of fisheries. It emphasised that access to fishing resources would not be possible. An agreement regarding the future fisheries co-operation was reached in December 1998. This includes, *inter alia*:

- Both sides declare that they will make their best endeavours to negotiate and conclude a co-operation agreement no later than the year 2000.
- The EU wants to hold back the implementation of tariff concessions to South Africa on fisheries products. The most sensitive of these concessions are only envisaged in the light of the content and continuity of the future fisheries agreement.
- South Africa will abolish its tariffs on fisheries products in parallel with the elimination of duties of the corresponding tariff positions by the EU.

6.2 Wines and spirits

The political compromise on port and sherry which was reached in Davos on 29 January by Minister Erwin and Professor Pinheiro, contains the following main elements:

- Phase-out clause for the South African use of the names 'port' and 'sherry' in exports to third countries;
- Definition of South African domestic market to include all of the SACU;
- South Africa to continue the use of the names 'port' and 'sherry' on its domestic market throughout the transitional period of 12 years;
- Review the use of names within the transition to decide on the names to use after 12 years;
- The South African wine sector to enjoy a duty-free quota and financial assistance for restructuring the industry.

7 Conclusion

The Agreement with the EU will, among other things, establish for the next 12 to 15 years South Africa's trade relationship with its major trading partner and important trading bloc. The Agreement establishes as good concessions as each party can get at this point. There is room for improvement within the reviews as set out in the Agreement. The agreement reached between Minister Erwin and Commissioner Pinheiro is the basis for both parties to move forward after almost four years of protracted negotiations. It still has to be formally signed, after which it will be submitted for ratification by parliament. The venue for the signature of the Agreement is more than likely to be in South Africa, which would mark the historical agreement between South Africa and Europe.

25 March 1999

Compromise package on wines and spirits

1. South Africa reconfirms that the names 'port' and 'sherry' are not and will not be used for its exports to the EU.
2. South Africa will phase out the use of the 'port' and 'sherry' names on all export markets within five years, except in the case of non-SACU SADC countries, where an eight-year phase-out period would apply.
3. For the purpose of the Wines and Spirits Agreement, the South African domestic market is defined to cover SACU (South Africa, Botswana, Lesotho and Swaziland).
4. South African products may be marketed as 'port' and 'sherry' on the South African domestic market during a 12-year transitional period. Beyond that period the new denominations of these products which shall be used on the South African domestic market will be jointly agreed between South Africa and the EU.

5 From entry into force of the Agreement, the EU will provide a duty-free quota for wines covering the current level of trade of 32 million litres of South African exports to the EU, with allowance for the future growth of this quota.

6 As an additional effort toward the main objectives agreed for the development programme for South Africa to be funded by the EU, the EU will provide assistance of 15 million euro for the restructuring of the South African wines and spirits sector and for the marketing and distribution of the country's wines and spirits products. Such assistance will commence at entry into force of the Wines and Spirits Agreement.

7 A Wines and Spirits Agreement between South Africa and the EU will be concluded as soon as possible and no later than in September 1999, in order to ensure that the entry into force of the Wines and Spirits Agreement will take place before or in January 2000.

Berlin, 24 March 1999

SA Liberalisation Schedule

Summary – Industrial offer

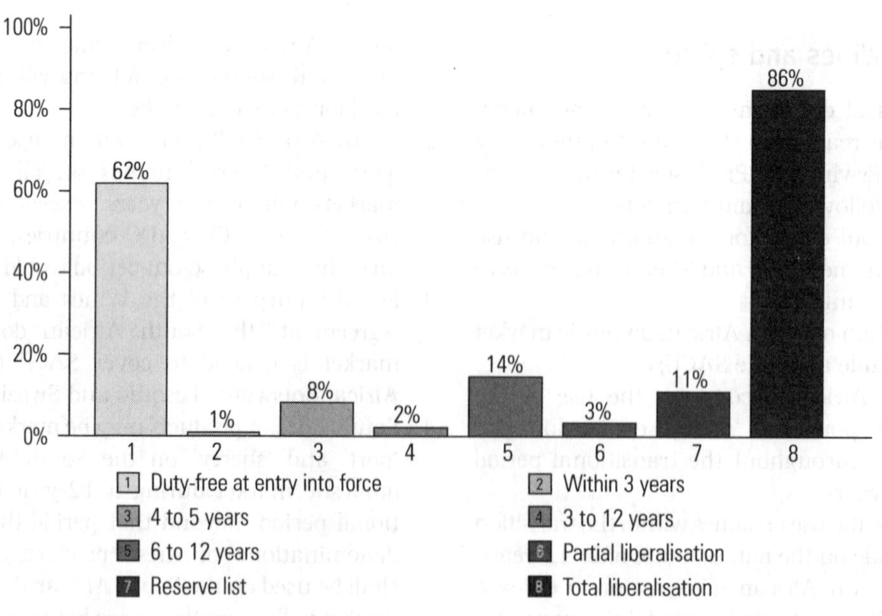

EU Liberalisation Schedule

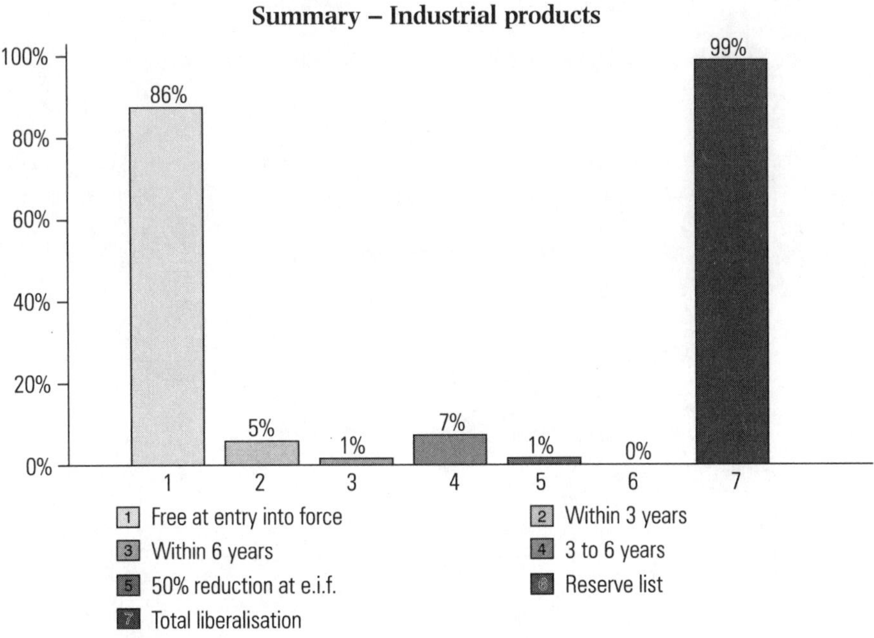

EU Liberalisation Schedule

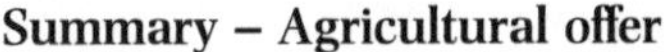

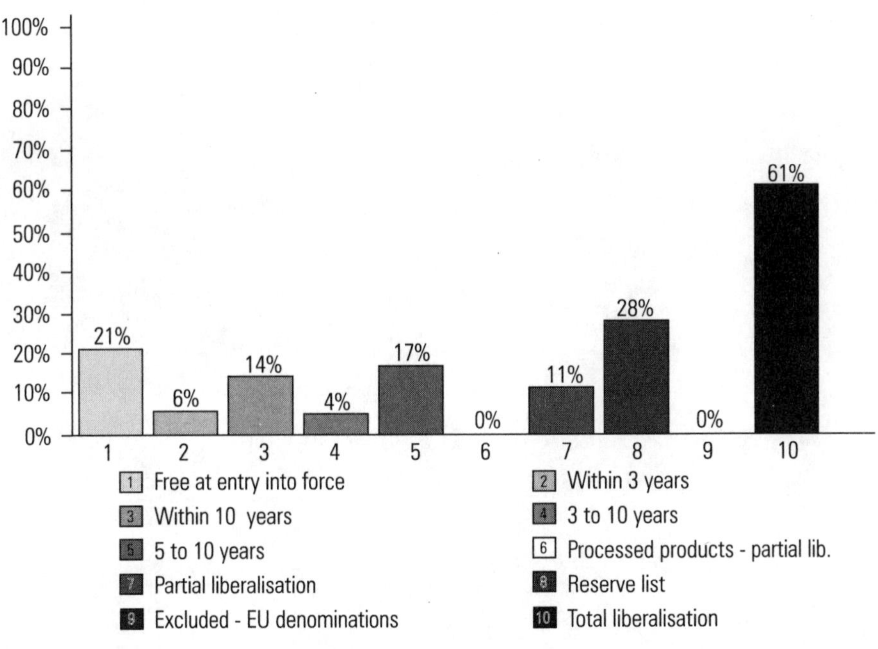

PART II

Global business environments

International cultural environments facing business

Key issues

- The nation as a definition of society
- The concept of culture
- Behavioural practices affecting business
- Importance of work
- Self-reliance
- Reconciliation of international differences
- Cultural needs in the internationalisation process
- Value systems

3.1 Introduction

The Parris-Rogers International (PRI) case[1] at the end of this chapter illustrates how behavioural differences give rise to different business practices in various parts of the world. International business is different to domestic business because countries are different. Understanding the cultures of groups of people is useful because business employs, sells to, buys from, is regulated by, and owned by people. An international company must consider these differences in order to predict and control its relationships and operations.

Further, it should realise that its accustomed way of doing business may not be the only or best way. When doing business abroad, a company first should determine whether a normal business practice in a foreign country differs from its home-country experience or from what its management ideally would like to see. If the practice differs, international management must then decide what, if any, adjustments are necessary to operate efficiently in the foreign country.

When individuals come into contact with groups whose cultures differ from their own, either abroad or within their own countries, they must decide if and how they can cope. We will discuss these differences in culture, economic systems, politics, and legal issues in this part of the book.

Some differences, such as those regarding acceptable attire, are obvious; others may be more difficult to perceive. For example, people in all cultures have culturally ingrained responses to given situations. They expect people from other cultures to respond the same ways as people in their own culture, and that people in similar stations or positions will assume similar duties and privileges. All of these expectations may be disproved in practice.

In the PRI case, the British salesmen budgeted their time and so regarded drinking coffee and chatting about non-business activities in a café as 'doing nothing', especially if there was 'work to be done'. The Arab businessmen, on the other hand, had no compulsion to finish at a given time, viewed time spent in a café as 'doing something', and considered 'small talk' a necessary prerequisite for evaluating whether they could interact satisfactorily with potential business partners. The Englishmen, because of their belief that 'you shouldn't mix business and pleasure', became nervous when friends of the Arab businessmen intruded. In contrast, the Arabs felt 'people are more important than business' and saw nothing private about business transactions.

Although the PRI case illustrates the folly of not adjusting, international companies have nevertheless sometimes been very successful in introducing new products, technologies and operating procedures to foreign countries. There have been times when this has not run counter to deep-seated attitudes in the host country, but at other times the host society has been willing to accept unwanted change as a trade-off for other advantages. In addition, in some cases the local society is willing to accept behaviour from foreigners that it would not accept from its own citizens. For example, Western female managers in Hong Kong have said that the local people regard them primarily as foreigners, not as women; thus, they are not subject to the same operating barriers that local females face as managers.[2] Members of the host society may even feel they are being stereotyped in an uncomplimentary way when foreigners adjust too much.[3]

3.2 The nation as a definition of a society

There is no universally satisfactory definition of a society, but in international business the concept of 'nation' provides a workable one, since the basic similarity between people is both a cause and an effect of national boundaries. The laws governing business operations apply primarily along national lines. Within the bounds of a nation, people share essential attributes perpetuated through rites and symbols of nationhood, flags, parades, rallies, a subjective common perception of and maintenance of their history, and through the preservation of national sites, documents, monuments and museums. These shared attributes do not mean that everyone in a country is alike. Nor do they suggest that each country is unique in all respects; in fact, nations may have various subcultures, ethnic groups, races, and classes. However, the nation is legitimised by being the mediator between the different interests.[4] Failure to serve adequately in this mediating role may cause dissolution of the nation, as occurred recently in the former Soviet Union and the former Yugoslavia, and almost happened in Canada through a Quebec separatist movement. In the mid-1990s there was ethnic unrest in the form of violence or strong separatist movements in about a third of the nations in the world; thus the boundaries of countries as we know them are far from secure.[5] Nevertheless, each country has certain characteristic physical, demographic and behavioural norms that constitute its national identity and may affect a company's methods of conducting business in that country.

In using the nation as a point of reference, it is important to remember that some countries have much greater internal variation than others. Geographical and economic barriers can restrict people's movements from one region to another, thus limiting their personal interactions. Decentralised laws and government programmes may increase regional separation, and linguistic, religious and ethnic differences usually preclude the fusion of the population into a homogeneous state. For example, for all the reasons just given, India is much more diverse than Denmark, and South Africa more so than Italy.

Of course, nationality is not the only basis on which to group people. Everyone belongs to various other groups; for example, those based on profession, age, religion, and place of residence. Many similarities can in some ways link groups from different countries more closely than groups within a country. For instance, regardless of the country, people in urban areas differ in certain attitudes from those in rural areas; and managers have different work-related attitudes to production workers.[6]

When comparing countries, therefore, it is necessary to examine relevant groups. There are thousands of possible relationships between human variables and business functions – too many to discuss exhaustively in one chapter.[7] However, keep in mind that different attitudes and values affect how any business function may be conducted, such as what and how products will be accepted, how they are best produced, and how the operation should be organised, financed, managed, and controlled. This chapter first concentrates on just a few of the variables that have been found to influence business practices substantially. It then highlights alternative approaches for determining and dealing with differences in foreign countries, as well as the changes that may occur in international companies as they come into contact with new human environments. More specifically, the cultural dimensions of international marketing are explored in Chapter 9 (Section 9.4.)

Ubuntu

In Africa, Ubuntu is the term used for group solidarity issues. 'In essence Ubuntu is a universal concept that can be applicable to all poor communities. The central belief here is that a man can just be a man through others. Its key values are group solidarity, conformity, compassion, respect, human dignity and collective unity.'

SOURCE: Mbigi, L. & Maree, J. 1995. *Ubuntu*. Randburg: Knowledge Resources.

3.3 The concept of culture

Culture consists of specific learned norms based on attitudes, values and beliefs, all of which exist in every society. Visitors remark on differences; experts write about them; and people managing affairs across countries find that they affect operating results.[8] Great controversy surrounds these differences because there is an acknowledged problem with measuring variances.[9] It is not easy to isolate culture from such factors as economic and political conditions and institutions. For example, an opinion survey may reflect a short-term response to temporary economic conditions, rather than basic values and beliefs that will have longer-term effects on managing business. Further, some national differences in specific work behaviour that have generally been attributed to culture may be due to other factors, such as climatic differences.[10] Despite these problems, considerable evidence indicates that some aspects of culture differ significantly across national borders and have a substantial impact on how business is normally conducted in different countries. Some evidence is derived by anthropologists or so-called country experts who rely on qualitative techniques, such as interviews and observations, to uncover people's ideas, attitudes and relationships to other people in the society. They then interpret processes and events and describe national character. Other evidence comes from researchers who compare the opinions of carefully paired samples of people in more than one country. For example, questionnaires may be used to determine attitudes toward specific business practices, such as an advertising message or shared decision-making in the workplace.[11]

3.3.1 Causes of cultural difference and change

Culture is transmitted by various patterns, such as from parent to child, from teacher to pupil, from social leader to follower, and from one peer to another. Studies among diverse societies indicate that the parent-to-child route is especially important in the transmission of religious and political affiliations.[12] Developmental psychologists believe that by age 10 most children have their basic value systems firmly in place, after which changes are difficult to make. These basic values include such concepts as evil versus good, dirty versus clean, ugly versus beautiful, unnatural versus natural, abnormal versus normal, paradoxical versus logical, and irrational versus rational.[13] The relative inflexibility of values helps explain the deeply-rooted opinions of an American female soldier and Saudi female doctor during the Persian Gulf War. The soldier said, 'I'm thankful I'm not a Saudi woman. I just don't know how they do it.' The doctor said, 'It is so strange. I am glad not to be an American woman. Women are not made for violence and guns.'[14]

However, because of multiple influences, individual and societal values and customs may evolve over time. Change may come about through choice or imposition.[15] Change by choice may take place as a by-product of social and economic change, or because of new contacts that present reasonable alternatives. For example, rural people had to change their previous customs when they chose to accept factory jobs in towns which required them to work regular hours and forego social activities with their families during working hours. When a person chooses to embrace a different religion, it becomes necessary to accept a new set of values and beliefs. Change by imposition, sometimes called cultural imperialism, occurred, for example, when colonial powers introduced their legal systems abroad by prohibiting established practices and defining them as being criminal.[16] The process of introducing some, but not all, elements of an outside culture is often referred to as creolisation, indigenisation or cultural diffusion.

Isolation is inclined to stabilise a culture, whereas contact tends to create cultural borrowing. In addition to national boundaries and geographical obstacles, language is a major factor that affects cultural stability. Although hundreds of languages are spoken around the world, a handful of languages predominate. Exhibit 3.1 shows the number of native speakers of the world's ten major languages.

Exhibit 3.1: Major languages of the world

Language	Number of native speakers (in millions)
Mandarin	836
Hindi	333
Spanish	332
English	322
Arabic	186
Portuguese	170
Russian	170
Japanese	125
German	98
French	72

SOURCE: *The world almanac and book of facts*. 1995. Mahwah, New Jersey: Funk & Wagnalls, p. 598.

When people from different areas speak the same language, culture is transmitted from one area to another much more easily. Thus there is more cultural similarity in English-speaking countries or in Spanish-speaking countries than there is between them. This is due partially to heritage and partially to the ease of communicating. Note also that there are hundreds of languages that are spoken in limited areas. When people speak only one of these languages, they tend to adhere to their own culture because meaningful contact with others is difficult.

For example, in Guatemala, the official language is Spanish; however, there are 22 ethnic groups, three main ethnic languages and derivations of those three. These groups have cultures that are much the same as those of their ancestors hundreds of years ago. The Guatemalan Nobel Peace Prize winner, Rigoberta Mench, is from the Quich group. She recounted that parents in that group do not permit their children to go to school, because all public schools use Spanish; if the children have to learn Spanish, their parents consider that they will lose their values and customs. She broke out of this linguistic isolation when she learned Spanish as an adult in order to fight government policies.[17] Her standpoint has been to promote the multicultural diversity within Guatemala rather than have ethnic groups either embrace a different culture or form separate countries.[18] In South Africa, 11 official languages are recognised, although English is spoken by almost everyone.

Religion is a strong shaper of values. Exhibit 3.2 shows the number of followers of the world's major religions. Within the major religions Buddhism, Christianity, Hinduism, Islam, and Judaism, there are many factions whose specific beliefs may affect business. For example, some Christian groups forego alcohol, but others do not. Differences among nations that practise the same religion can also affect business. For example, Friday is normally not a workday in predominantly Muslim countries because it is a day of worship; however, Tunisia adheres to the Christian work calendar in order to be more productive in business dealings with Europe.[19] When a religion is dominant in an area, it is apt to have a great influence on laws and government policies. It is also apt to limit acceptance of products or business practices that are considered unorthodox (refer to the Bahraini prohibition of pork in the PRI case). Consequently, foreign companies may have to alter their usual business practices. For example, because of criticism from fervent Hindus, McDonald's agreed not to serve beef in its restaurants in India.[20] In countries in which rival religions vie for political control, the resulting strife can cause so much unrest that business is disrupted. In recent years, violence among religious groups has erupted in India, Lebanon, Northern Ireland and the former Yugoslavia. The following discussion provides a framework for understanding how cultural differences affect business.

Exhibit 3.2: Major religions of the world

Religion	Number of followers (in millions)
Christian	1 870
Muslim	1 014
Hindu	751
Buddhist	334
Chinese folk	141
Local	111
Sikh	20
Judaic	18
Confucian	6

SOURCE: *The world almanac and book of facts*. 1995. Mahwah, New Jersey: Funk & Wagnalls, p. 31.

3.4 Behavioural practices affecting business

3.4.1 Group affiliations

The populations of all countries are commonly subdivided into groups, and individuals may belong to more than one group. Affiliations determined by birth, known as ascribed group memberships, include those based on gender, family, age, and caste, and ethnic, racial or national origin. Affiliations not determined by birth are called acquired group memberships, and include those based on religion, political affiliation, and professional and other associations. A person's affiliations often reflect his or her class or status in a country's social stratification system. Every society uses group membership for social stratification, such as by valuing members of managerial groups more highly than members of production groups. Social stratification also affects such business functions as marketing. For example, companies choose to use people in their advertisements who are from groups admired by their target audience.

3.4.2 Role of competence

In some societies, such as that of the United States, a person's acceptability for jobs and promotions is based primarily on competence. Thus the workplace is characterised more by competition than by co-operation. This does not mean, of course, that USA society does not discriminate against people on the basis of group affiliation. However, the belief that competence should be the deciding factor is valued so highly in the United States that legislative and judicial actions have aimed at preventing discrimination on the basis of sex, race, age, and religion. This value is far from universal. In many cultures, competence is of secondary importance, and the belief that it is right to place some other criterion before competence is just as strong in those cultures as the belief in competence is in the United States. Whatever factor is given primary importance, whether seniority, as in Japan (where the workplace is characterised more by co-operation than by competition), or some other quality, it will influence a person's eligibility for certain positions and compensation to a large extent.[21]

The more egalitarian, or open, a society is, the less difference ascribed group membership makes with regard to access to rewards; however, in less open societies, legal proscriptions sometimes enforce distinctions on the basis of ascribed group memberships. In other cases, group memberships prevent large numbers of people from getting the training that would provide them with equal qualifications. For example, in countries with poor public education systems, elite groups send their children to private schools, but the other children receive inferior schooling.

Even when individuals qualify for certain positions and there are no legal barriers to hiring them, social obstacles may make companies wary of employing them. Other workers, customers, local stockholders, or government officials may oppose certain groups, making it even more difficult for their members to succeed.

3.4.3 Importance of different group memberships

Although there are countless ways of defining group memberships, three of the most significant are in terms of gender, age and family. An international comparison reveals the wide differences in attitudes concerning these memberships and how important they are to business considerations.

(a) Gender-based groups

There are strong country-specific differences in attitudes toward males and females. The Chinese and Indians show an extreme degree of preference for males. Because of government and economic restrictions on family size and the desire to have a son to carry on the family name, the practices of aborting female foetuses and killing female babies are widespread despite government opposition to such practices.[22] In Afghanistan, the 1996 takeover by religious fundamentalists led to prohibitions against women attending school and working. They were also required to be shrouded from head to toe.[23]

In the PRI case the female editor could not get permission to enter Saudi Arabia, a country that exhibits an extreme degree of behavioural rigidity related to gender. Schools are separate, as is most social life, such as wedding parties and zoo outings. Women are legally prohibited from driving cars and socially restricted from riding in a taxi without a male relative. Only about 10% of women work outside the home, and those who do, remain separate from men. Most jobs for women are in professions that entail little or no contact with males, such as teaching or providing medical treatment to other women. When women do work in integrated organisations, the Saudis place partitions between them and male employees.

> **Perrier withdraws 'sexist' billboards**
>
> Paris – The French group Perrier-Vittel has decided to drop an advertising campaign in Belgium showing

doll-like women wearing only Perrier bottle-caps covering their nipples, a company spokesman said this week.

'The management of the Perrier-Vittel decided last Friday to halt its billboard campaign after realising that this advertising campaign, which was intended to be amusing, could upset some people,' the spokesman said.

The billboard ads, which began appearing this week, feature three nude women, their nipples covered with Perrier bottle-caps. The ad reads: 'Wonderbulles' or 'wonderbubbles.' The decision came after the European Women's Lobby threatened to boycott Perrier mineral water unless the company dropped its 'offensive ad campaign against women'.

SOURCE: *The Star*, 27 July 1996, p. 20

Even in countries where women constitute a large portion of the working population, there are vast differences in the types of jobs regarded as 'male' or 'female'. For example, in the United States, more than 40% of administrative and managerial positions are filled by women; in Japan, that figure is less than 10%.[24]

Culturally mandated male and female behaviours may carry over to other aspects of the work situation. For example, Molex, an American manufacturing company in Japan, invited its Japanese workers and their spouses to a company dinner one evening. Neither wives nor female employees appeared. To comply with Japanese standards, the company now has a 'family day', which the women feel comfortable attending.[25]

(b) Age-based groups

Attitudes toward age involve some curious variations. Many cultures assume that age and wisdom go hand in hand. These cultures usually have a seniority-based system of advancement. In the United States, retirement at age 60 or 65 was mandatory in most companies until the 1980s, and relative youthfulness has been a professional advantage. However, this esteem for youthfulness has not carried over into the political realm, where representatives must be at least 25, senators 30, and the president 35 – none of which posts carries a mandatory retirement age.

Barriers to employment based on age or gender are changing substantially in many parts of the world. Thus statistical and attitudinal studies that are even a few years old may be unreliable. One change has involved the growing numbers of women and men in the United States employed in occupations previously dominated by the other gender. For example, recently the proportion of male secretaries, telephone operators and nurses has risen substantially, as has the proportion of female architects, bartenders and bus drivers. Further, the proportion of the workforce made up by women has been increasing throughout most of the world; however, the increase is largely in part-time employment, where women dominate.[26]

(c) Family-based groups

In some societies, the family constitutes the most important group membership. An individual's acceptance in society is based largely on the family's social status or respectability rather than on the individual's achievement. Because family ties are so strong, there may also be a compulsion to co-operate closely within the family unit while distrusting links involving others. In societies where there is low trust outside the family, such as in China and southern Italy, family-run companies are more successful than large business organisations, where the people are from many different families. The difficulty in sustaining large-scale companies retards economic development in these countries.[27]

3.5 Importance of work

People work for a number of reasons. Many, especially in industrialised societies, could satisfy their basic needs for food, clothing and shelter by working fewer hours than they do. What motivates them to work more? The reasons for working and the relative importance of work among human activities may be explained largely by the interrelationship between the cultural and economic environments of the particular country. The differences in motivation help to explain management styles, product demand and levels of economic development.

3.5.1 Protestant ethic

Max Weber, a German sociologist, observed near the beginning of the 20th century that the predominantly Protestant countries were the most economically developed. Weber attributed this fact to the attitude toward work held by most of those countries, an attitude he labelled *the Protestant ethic.* According to Weber, the Protestant ethic was an outgrowth of the Reformation, when work was viewed as a means of salvation. Adhering to this belief, people preferred to transform productivity gains into additional output rather than into additional leisure.[28]

Although Weber's conclusions on the relationship between work and Protestantism were simplistic, there is evidence that some societies have more leisure than others. For example, on average, the Japanese take less leisure time than people in any other industrialised country. But in a survey of over 1 200 companies in more than 60 countries covering about 26 000 employees, the Japanese were the least satisfied with both their jobs and employers. (The Swiss were the most satisfied.) Thus it is not clear why the Japanese take so little time for leisure. In the United States, another country where incomes probably allow for considerably more leisure time than most people use, there is still much disdain, on the one hand, for the millionaire socialite who contributes nothing to society and, on the other hand, for the person who lives on welfare. People who are forced to give up work, such as retirees, complain strongly of their inability to do anything 'useful'. This view contrasts with those that predominate in some other societies. In much of Europe, the highest place in the social structure is held by th aristocracy, who have historically been asso ciated with leisure. Therefore, upward mobilit is associated with more leisure activities, bu only those that are broadening, such as takin trips, reading or sports endeavours, and no household-related activities, such as gardenin and taking care of children.[29] In rural India living a simple life with minimal materia achievements is still considered a desirable en in itself.

Today, personal economic achievement i considered commendable not only in industria lised countries but also in most rapidly devel oping ones. Some observers note that man economies, in contrast, are characterised b limited economic needs that are an outgrowt of the culture. If incomes start to rise, worker in these economies tend to reduce their effort since they are paid by the hour and ca therefore work fewer hours for more or les the same income.

This cultural trait has been noted as a essential difference that underpins national sel identity in many lower-income countries Rather than reject the labels of 'traditiona for themselves and 'progressive' for the higher income nations, their leaders have stressed th need for a superior culture – one that combine material comforts with spirituality.[30] Othe observers, however, have argued that limite economic needs may be a very short-live phenomenon because expectations rise slowl as a result of past economic achievement. Mos of us believe we would be happy with just 'a little bit more', until we have that 'little bi more', which then turns out to be not quit enough.

3.5.2 Belief in success and reward

One factor that influences a person's attitud toward working is the perceived likelihood o success and reward. The concepts of succes and reward are closely related. People generall have little enthusiasm for efforts that seem to easy or too difficult, that is, where the prob ability of either success or failure seems almost certain. For instance, few of us would be eager to run a race on foot against either a snail or a racehorse, because the outcome in either case is too certain. We are most enthusiastic when there is greater uncertainty, such as when racing against someone else of roughly equal ability. The reward for successfully completing an effort, such as winning a race, may be great or small as well. People will usually work harder at any task when the reward for success is high compared with the reward for failure.

The same tasks performed in different countries will have different probabilities of success and different rewards associated with success and failure. In cultures where the probability of failure is almost certain and the perceived rewards of success are low, there is a tendency to view work as necessary but ungratifying. This attitude may prevail in harsh climates, in very poor areas or in subcultures that are the objects of discrimination. At the other extreme, in areas such as Scandinavia, where the tax structures and public policies redistribute income from higher earners to low earners, there also is less enthusiasm for work. In this case, the probability of success is high and rewards also tend to be high, but the rewards are the same, regardless of how hard one works. The greatest enthusiasm for work exists when high uncertainty of success is combined with the likelihood of a very positive reward for success and little or no reward for failure.[31]

3.5.3 Work as a habit

Another factor in the trade-off between work and leisure is that the pursuit of leisure activities may itself have to be learned. After a long period of sustained work, a person may have problems deciding what to do with free time. This insight helps to explain the continued drive for greater achievement seen in some societies in which most people already have considerable material comforts. One study that attempted to determine why some areas of Latin America developed a higher economic level and greater desire for material achievement than others, attributed differences to the fact that some Spanish settlers did the work themselves rather than use slave labour. In such areas as Antioquia in Colombia, the Spanish settlers who laboured themselves developed a work ethic and became the industrial leaders of the country.[32] Clearly, when comparing the importance of work between one country and another, the effects of habit cannot be overlooked. An international company may thus find it easier in some societies than in others to motivate its workforce with shorter hours or longer vacation periods.

3.5.4 High-need achievement

The high-need achiever is a person who will work very hard to achieve material or career success, sometimes to the detriment of social relationships or spiritual achievements.[33] Three attributes distinguish high-need achievers:

1 They like situations that involve personal responsibility for finding solutions to problems.
2 They set moderate achievement goals and take calculated risks.
3 They want concrete feedback on performance.

The average manager's interest in material or career success varies substantially among countries. For example, one study compared the attitudes of employees from 50 countries on what was called a masculinity index. Employees with a high masculinity score were those who had (among other attributes) more sympathy for the successful achiever than for the unfortunate, preferred to be the best rather than like the others, had more of a money-and-things orientation than a people orientation, believed that it is better 'to live to work' than 'to work to live', and preferred performance and growth to quality of life and the environment. The masculinity index also included attitudes toward gender roles, with higher scores going for beliefs that roles should be differentiated by gender and that men should dominate. The countries with the highest masculinity scores were Japan, Austria, Venezuela, and Switzerland. Those with the lowest scores were Sweden, Norway, the Netherlands, and Denmark.[34] These attitudinal differences help explain situations in which the local manager reacts in ways that the international management may neither expect nor wish. For instance, a purchasing manager with a high need for smooth social relationships may be much more concerned with developing an amiable and continuing relationship with suppliers than with reducing costs and speeding-up delivery. Or local managers in some countries may place such organisational goals as employee and social welfare before the foreign company's priorities for growth and efficiency.

3.5.5 Needs hierarchy

Maslow's hierarchy of needs is a well-known motivation theory, which is shown schematically in Exhibit 3.3. According to this theory, people try to fulfil lower-order needs sufficiently before moving on to higher ones.[35] People will work to satisfy a need, but once it is fulfilled, it is no longer a motivator. This fulfilment is not an all-or-nothing situation. However, because lower-order needs are more important than higher-order ones, they must be nearly fulfilled before any higher-order need becomes an effective motivator. For instance, the most basic needs are physiological, including the needs for food, water and sex. Physiological needs may have to be nearly satisfied (say 85%), before a security need becomes a powerful motivator. The security need, centring around a safe physical and emotional environment, may have to be nearly satisfied before triggering the influence of the need for affiliation or social belongingness (acceptance by peers and friends). After the affiliation need is sufficiently satisfied, a person may be motivated by an esteem need, the need to bolster one's self-image through recognition, attention and appreciation for one's contributions. The highest-order need is that for self-actualisation which refers to self-fulfilment, or becoming all that it is possible to become. The relative fulfilment requirements are shown by the horizontal bars in Exhibit 3.3. For example, people represented by the lower hierarchy require more affiliation needs (3) to be met before a self-esteem need (4) will be triggered as

Exhibit 3.3: Maslow's hierarchy of needs and need-hierarchy comparison

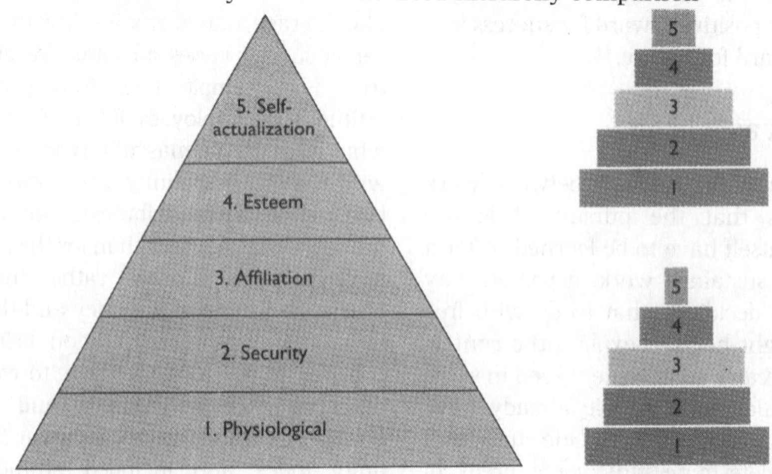

a motivator, compared with people represented by the upper hierarchy.

The hierarchy of needs theory is helpful for differentiating the reward preferences of employees in different countries. In very poor countries, most workers may be so deprived that a company can motivate them by simply providing enough food and shelter. Elsewhere, other needs have to be addressed to motivate workers. Researchers have noted that people from different countries attach different degrees of importance to various needs and even rank some of the higher-order needs differently. For example, studies have compared employees with regard to individualism versus collectivism. Countries with the highest individualism scores are the United States, Australia, the United Kingdom, Canada, and the Netherlands. Attributes of high individualism are low dependence on the organisation and a high desire for personal time, freedom and challenge. Countries with the highest collectivism scores (as opposed to individualism) are Guatemala, Ecuador, Panama, Venezuela, and Colombia. Attributes of high collectivism are high dependence on the organisation and a high desire for training, physical conditions and benefits.[36] In those countries with high individualism scores, one should expect that self-actualisation will be a workable motivator because employees want challenges; however, in countries with high collectivism scores, one may expect that the provision of a safe physical and emotional environment (security need) will be a workable motivator because employees depend more on the organisation.

3.5.6 Importance of occupation

In every society, certain occupations are perceived to bring greater economic, social or prestige rewards than others. This perception determines to a great extent the numbers and qualifications of people who will seek employment in a given occupation. Although overall patterns are universal (for example, professionals are ranked ahead of street cleaners), there are some national differences. For instance, university professors are more influential as opinion leaders in Korea and Japan than in the United States and the United Kingdom.[37]

The importance of business as a profession is also predictive of how difficult it may be for an international company to hire qualified managers. If jobs in business are not held in high esteem, a company may have to spend more to attract and train local managers, or it may have to rely more on managers transferred from abroad.

Another international difference involves the desire to work for an organisation rather than to be one's own boss. For example, the Belgians and the French, more than most other nationalities, prefer, if possible, to go into business for themselves. Thus Belgium and France have more retail establishments per capita than most other countries. One reason for this is that owning a small or medium-sized enterprise, rather than earning more income, is a means for Belgian and French people to get out of the working class and move up socially. Further, psychological studies show that Belgian and French workers place a greater importance on personal independence from the organisations employing them than workers in many other countries.[38]

Jobs with low prestige usually go to people whose skills are in low demand. In the United States, for example, such occupations as babysitting, delivering newspapers and carrying groceries, traditionally have been largely filled by teenagers, who leave these jobs as they age and gain additional training. In most less-developed countries, these are not transient occupations; instead, they are filled by adults who have very little opportunity to move on to more rewarding positions. (In South Africa, there is rising concern that many low-paying menial jobs are becoming more permanent, thus perpetuating income disparities.)

3.6 Self-reliance

3.6.1 Superior-subordinate relationships

In some countries, an autocratic style of management is preferred; in others, a consultative style prevails. Studies on what is known as power distance show that in Austria, Israel, New Zealand, and the Scandinavian countries, the consultative style is strongly preferred, but in Malaysia, Mexico, Panama, Guatemala, and Venezuela, the autocratic style is favoured. Interestingly, those preferring an autocratic style are also willing to accept decision-making by a majority of subordinates. What they don't accept is the interaction between superiors and subordinates in decision-making. Clearly, it may be easier for organisations to initiate certain types of worker-participation methods in some countries than in others.

3.6.2 Uncertainty avoidance

Studies on what is known as uncertainty avoidance show that in Greece, Portugal, Guatemala, Uruguay, El Salvador, and Belgium, employees prefer that rules should be set out and that they should not be broken even if breaking them is in the company's best interest. Further, these employees plan to work for the company for a long time. At the opposite end of the spectrum are Singapore, Jamaica, Denmark, Sweden, Hong Kong, the United Kingdom, and Ireland.[39] When uncertainty avoidance is high, superiors may need to be more precise and assured in the directions they give to subordinates.

3.6.3 Trust

Surveys that measure trust among countries by having respondents evaluate such statements as 'Most people can be trusted' and 'You can't be too careful in dealing with people', indicate substantial national differences. For example, 61,2% of Norwegians think that most people are trustworthy, but only 6,7% of Brazilians feel that way. Where trust is high, there tends to be a lower cost of doing business because managers do not have to spend time trying to write contracts that foresee every possible contingency and then monitoring every person's actions for compliance. Instead, they can spend their efforts on investing and innovating.[40]

3.6.4 Degree of fatalism

If people believe strongly in self-determination, they may be willing to work hard to achieve goals and take responsibility for performance. A belief in fatalism, on the other hand, may prevent people from accepting a basic cause-effect relationship. In this regard, religious differences play a part: conservative or fundamentalist Christian, Buddhist, Hindu, and Muslim societies tend to view occurrences as 'the will of God'. For example, Muslim mosques in the United States now generally rely on computer-generated programs to decide ahead of time when the new moon will be in the right place for Ramadan to begin; however, in conservative countries such as Saudi Arabia, the view is: 'How can you say six months before that it [the moon] will appear that day? You're not the one that controls the universe.'[41]

In a fatalistic atmosphere, people are less inclined to plan for contingencies; for example, they may be reluctant to buy insurance. Studies have shown national differences in degree of fatalism even among managers in economically developed societies.[42]

3.6.5 Individual versus group

Japan has a much more collectivist culture than the United States, one that values submergence of individual concerns to those of a group. For the Japanese, the dominant group loyalty is to the work group.[43] For example, an American scientist was invited to work in a Japanese laboratory, but he was treated as an outsider until he realised he had to demonstrate his willingness to subordinate his personal interests to those of the group. He did so by mopping the lab floor for several weeks, after which he was invited to join the experiment.[44]

Although China and Mexico are also characterised as collectivist cultures, they differ from Japan in that the collectivism is based on kinship that does not carry over to the workplace.[45] Further, the concept of family in China and Mexico includes not only a nuclear family (a husband, wife and minor children), but also a vertically extended family (several generations) and/or a horizontally-extended one (aunts, uncles and cousins). This difference affects business in several ways. First, material rewards from an individual's work may be less motivating because these rewards are divided among more people. Second, geographical mobility is reduced because relocation means other members of a family also have to find new jobs. Even where extended families do not live together, mobility may be reduced because people prefer to remain near relatives. Third, purchasing decisions may be more complicated because of the interrelated roles of family members. Fourth, security and social needs may be met more extensively at home than in the workplace.

3.6.6 Communication

Linguists have found that all societies have complex languages that reflect the environment in which their people live. Because of varying environments, translating one language directly into another can be difficult. For example, people living in the temperate zone of the Northern Hemisphere customarily use the word 'summer' to refer to the months of June, July and August. People in tropical zones may use that term to denote the dry season, which occurs at different times in different countries. Some concepts simply do not translate. In Spanish, for instance, there is no word to refer to everyone who works in a business organisation. Instead, there is one word, *empleados*, that refers to white-collar workers, and another, *obreros*, that refers to labourers. This distinction reflects the substantial class difference between the groups. Further, common language usage is constantly evolving. Microsoft purchased a thesaurus code for its Spanish version of Word 6.0, but many synonyms turned out to be too derogatory to be currently acceptable. The company corrected the software after newspapers and radio reports denounced the program.[46]

English, French and Spanish have such widespread acceptance (they are spoken prevalently in 44, 27 and 20 countries, respectively) that native speakers of these languages are generally not very motivated to learn others. Commerce and other cross-border transactions can be conducted easily with other nations that share the same language. When a second language is studied, it is usually chosen because of its usefulness in dealing with other countries. English and French traditionally have been chosen because of commercial links developed during colonial periods. But English is gaining in relative importance as countries such as Vietnam are switching to English studies. Further, more young people in Europe are learning English than in the past.[47] In countries that do not share a common language with other countries (such as Finland and Greece), there is a much greater need for citizens to study other languages in order to function internationally.

English, especially American English, words are being added to languages worldwide, partly because of USA technology that develops new products and services for which new words must be coined. When a new product or service enters another language area, it may take on an Anglicised name. For example, Russians call tight denim pants *dzhinsi* (pronounced 'jeansy'); the French call a self-service restaurant *le self*; and Lithuanians go to the theatre to see moving *pikceris*.[48]

An estimated 20 000 English words have entered the Japanese language. However, some countries, such as Finland, have largely developed their own new words rather than use Anglicised versions, although translating one language into another does not always work as intended.

Language problems

The following are examples of signs in English observed in hotels around the world:

France: 'Please leave your values at the desk.'

Mexico (to assure guests about the safety of drinking water): 'The manager has personally passed all the water served here.'

Japan: 'You are invited to take advantage of the chambermaid.'

Norway: 'Ladies are requested not to have children in the bar.'

Switzerland: 'Because of the impropriety of entertaining guests of the opposite sex in the bedroom, it is suggested that the lobby be used for this purpose.'

Greece (at check-in line): 'We will execute customers in strict rotation.'

Even within the same language there are often differences in usage or meaning. 'Corn', 'maize' and 'graduate studies' in the United Kingdom correspond to 'wheat', 'corn' and 'undergraduate studies', respectively, in the United States. These are among the approximately 4 000 words used differently in these two countries. Although the wrong choice of words is usually just a brief source of embarrassment, a poor translation may have tragic consequences. For example, inaccurate translations have been blamed for structural collapses and airplane crashes.[49] In contracts, correspondence, negotiations, advertisements, and conversations, words must be chosen carefully.

3.6.7 Silent language

Of course, formal language is not our only means of communicating. We all exchange messages by a host of non-verbal cues that form a silent language.[50] Colours, for example, conjure up meanings that are based on cultural experience. In most Western countries, black is associated with death; white has the same connotation in parts of Asia and purple in Latin America. For products to be successful, their colours and their advertisements must match the consumers' frame of reference.

Another aspect of silent language is the distance between people during conversations. People's sense of appropriate distance is learned and differs among societies. In the United States, for example, the customary distance for a business discussion is five to eight feet; for personal business, it is 18 inches to three feet.[51] When the distance is closer or further than is customary, people tend to feel very uneasy. For example, a USA manager conducting business discussions in Latin America may keep on moving backward to avoid the closer conversational distance to which the Latin American official is accustomed. Consequently, at the end of the discussion, each party may inexplicably distrust the other.

Perception of time, which influences punctuality, is another unspoken cue that may differ across cultures and create confusion. In the United States, participants usually arrive early for a business appointment. For a dinner at someone's home, guests arrive on time or a few minutes late, and for a cocktail party, they may arrive a bit later. In another country, the concept of punctuality may be radically different. For example, an American businessperson in Latin America may consider it discourteous if a Latin-American manager does not keep to the appointed time. Latin Americans may find it equally discourteous if an American businessperson arrives for dinner at the exact time given in the invitation.

Cues concerning a person's relative position may be particularly difficult to perceive. An American businessperson who tends to place a greater reliance on objects as prestige cues, may underestimate the importance of a foreign counterpart who does not have a large private office with a wooden desk and carpeting. A foreigner may react similarly if counterparts from the United States open their own doors and mix their own drinks.

Body language or kinesics (the way in which people walk, touch and move their bodies) also differs among countries. Few gestures are universal in meaning. For example, the 'yes' of a Greek, Turk or Bulgarian is indicated by a sideways movement of the head that resembles the negative shake of the head used in the United States and elsewhere in Europe. In some cases, one gesture may have several meanings: the joining of the index finger and thumb to form an O means 'okay' in the United States, 'money' in Japan, and 'I will kill you' in Tunisia.[52]

3.6.8 Perception and processing

We perceive cues selectively. We may identify what things are by means of any of our senses (sight, smell, touch, sound or taste) and in various ways within each sense. For example, through vision we can sense colour, depth and shape. The cues people use to perceive things differ among societies. The reason for this is partly physiological; for instance, genetic differences in eye pigmentation enable some groups to differentiate colours more finely than others. It also is partly cultural; for example, a relative richness of vocabulary can allow people to notice and express very subtle differences in colour.[53] Differences in vocabulary reflect cultural differences. Arabic, for example, has more than 6 000 different words for camels, their body parts and the equipment associated with them.[54]

Perceptions about breasts

Westerners require the covering of a woman's breasts in public. This is also applicable to Asian and Muslim tradition, where the breasts are considered private. However, it is different in African culture. The erect breasts of a young girl or woman indicate that she is a virgin or is unmarried. Married women generally only expose their breasts when feeding their babies. This act is performed with some amount of pride. When a baby begins crying out of hunger, people in the vicinity call on the mother to give the infant a breast: meaning to feed it.

SOURCE: Dadoo, Y., Ghyoot, V., Lephoko, D. & Lubbe, G. 1997. *Multicultural sensitivity for managers*. South Africa: Tsebanang, p. 168.

Regardless of societal differences, once people perceive cues, they process them. Information-processing is universal in that all societies categorise, plan and quantify. In terms of categorisation, people bring objects together according to their major shared function. A piece of furniture to sit on is called a chair in English, whether it is large or small, wooden or plastic, upholstered or not. The languages of all societies express the future and conditional situations; thus all societies plan. All societies have numbering systems as well. But the specific ways in which societies go about grouping things, dealing with the future and counting, differ substantially.[55] For example, in the United States telephone directories, the entries are arranged by surnames (last names or family names); in Iceland, they are organised by first (given) names. Icelandic last names are derived from the father's first name: thus Jon, the son of Thor, becomes Jon Thorsson, and his sister's last name is Thorsdottir (daughter of Thor).[56]

3.6.9 Obtaining and evaluating information

In spite of vast differences within countries, some countries, such as those in northern Europe, are categorised as being low-context cultures, that is, most people only consider information that they receive firsthand as relevant and bearing very directly on the decision they need to make. They also spend little time on 'small talk' in business situations. However, other countries, such as in southern

Europe, are high-context cultures, that is, most people consider that peripheral and hearsay information is necessary for decision-making because it is relevant to the context of the situation. Northern Europeans are also called monochronic, which means that most of them prefer to deal with situations sequentially (especially those involving other people), such as finishing with one customer before dealing with another. On the other hand, polychronic southern Europeans are more comfortable in dealing with all the situations facing them simultaneously. They feel uncomfortable if they do not deal immediately with all customers who need to be served.[57]

There are also national norms that govern the degree to which people will try to determine principles before they try to resolve small issues, or vice versa. In other words, they will tend toward either idealism or pragmatism. From a business standpoint, the differences manifest themselves in a number of ways. The idealist sees the pragmatist as being too interested in trivial details, whereas the pragmatist considers the idealist to be too theoretical. In a society of pragmatists, labour tends to focus on very specific issues, such as a pay increase of a dollar per hour. In a society of idealists, labour tends to make less precise demands and to depend instead on mass action, such as general strikes or support of a particular political party, to publicise its principles.[58]

3.7 Reconciliation of international differences

3.7.1 Cultural awareness

Where cultural differences exist, businesspeople must decide whether and to what extent they should adapt home-country practices to the foreign environment. But before making that decision, managers must be aware of what those differences are. As discussed earlier in this chapter, there is much disagreement about such differences. Building cultural awareness is not an easy task, and there is no foolproof method for doing so.

In any situation, some people are prone to say the right thing at the right time and others to offend unintentionally. Most people are more aware of differences in things they have learned consciously, such as table manners, than differences in things they have learned subconsciously, such as methods of problem-solving. Nevertheless, there is general agreement that awareness and sensitivity can be improved and that training with regard to other cultures will enhance the likelihood of success in operating within those cultures. This chapter has presented a framework of some of the human cultural factors that require special business adjustments on a country-to-country basis. By paying special attention to these factors, businesspeople can start building cultural awareness.

Reading about and discussing other countries and researching how people regard a specific culture can be very instructive. The opinions presented must be weighed up carefully. Very often they represent unwarranted stereotypes, an accurate assessment of only a subsegment of the particular country, or a situation that has since undergone change. By getting varied viewpoints, businesspeople are better able to judge assessments of different cultures. In a given society, managers can also observe the behaviour of those people who are well accepted, or those with whom they would like to be associated, in order to become aware of and learn to emulate acceptable behaviour. Samsung, Korea's largest company, is experimenting with a cultural awareness programme that involves sending 400 junior employees abroad for a year. In the United States, for example, they do not work; instead, they idle at malls, watch people and try to develop international tastes. The company is convinced that this programme will pay off in more astute judgements about what customers want.[59]

There are so many behavioural rules that businesspeople cannot expect to memorise all of them for every country in which business relations might be attempted. There are wide variations even in form of address; for example, it may be difficult to know whether to use a given name or surname, which of several surnames to use, and whether a wife takes her husband's name.[60] Fortunately, there are up-to-date guidebooks that have been compiled for particular geographical areas, based on the experiences of many successful international managers.[61] A manager may also consult with knowledgeable people at home and abroad, in government offices or in the private sector.

A person who moves to a foreign country or returns home after an extended stay abroad, frequently experiences culture shock. 'This is a generalised trauma one experiences in a new and different culture because of having to learn and cope with a vast array of new cultural cues and expectations, while discovering that your old ones probably do not fit or work.' [62]

People working in a very different culture may pass through certain stages. First, like tourists, they are charmed by 'quaint' differences. Later, they may feel frustrated, depressed and confused during the culture shock phase and their usefulness in a foreign assignment may be greatly impaired. Fortunately for most people, culture shock begins to wear off after a month or two as optimism and satisfaction improve.[63] Interestingly, some people also experience culture shock when they return to their home countries, a situation known as reverse culture shock, because they have become accustomed to what they encountered abroad.

3.7.2 Grouping countries

Some countries are relatively similar to one another, usually because they share many attributes that help mould their cultures, such as language, religion, geographical location, ethnicity, and level of economic development. In Exhibit 3.4 (p. 88), countries are grouped according to attitudes and values based on data obtained from a large number of cross-cultural studies. A company should expect fewer differences when moving within a cluster (a Peruvian company doing business in Colombia, for example) than when moving from one cluster to another (a Peruvian company doing business in Thailand).[64]

Such relationships must be used with caution, however. They deal only with overall similarities and differences between countries, and managers may easily be misled when considering specific business practices to use abroad. In fact, there is some tendency to expect that seemingly similar countries are more alike than they really are; thus a company may be lulled into a complacency that overlooks subtleties that are important for performance. For example, in the PRI case, the company expected the 12 Middle Eastern Arab countries to be more similar than they turned out to be, and the PRI experience only touches the 'tip of the iceberg' as far as national differences are concerned.[65]

3.8 Cultural needs in the internationalisation process

Not all companies need to have the same degree of cultural awareness. Nor must a particular company have a consistent degree of awareness during the course of its operations. As was discussed in Chapter 1, companies usually increase foreign operations over time. They may expand their knowledge of cultural factors in tandem with their expansion of foreign operations. In other words, they may increase their cultural knowledge as they move from limited to multiple foreign functions, from one to many foreign locations, from similar to dissimilar foreign environments, and from external to internal handling of their international operations. Thus, for example, a small company that is new to international business may have to gain only a minimal level of cultural awareness, but a highly involved company needs a high level.

When foreign functions are limited in a purely market-seeking operation, such as

Exhibit 3.4: A synthesis of country clusters

Anglo	Latin America	Nordic	Germanic	Latin European
Australia	Argentina	Denmark	Austria	Belgium
Canada	Chile	Finland	Germany	France
Ireland	Colombia	Norway	Switzerland	Italy
New Zealand	Mexico	Sweden		Portugal
South Africa	Peru			Spain
United Kingdom	Venezuela			
United States				
Near Eastern	**Arab**	**Far Eastern**	**Independent**	
Greece	Abu-Dhabi	Hong Kong	Brazil	
Iran	Bahrain	Indonesia	Israel	
Turkey	Kuwait	Malaysia	India	
	Oman	Philippines	Japan	
	Saudi Arabia	Singapore		
	United Arab Emirates	Taiwan		
		Thailand		
		Vietnam		

SOURCE: Ronen, S. & Shenkar, O. 1985. 'Clustering countries on attitudinal dimensions: a review and synthesis.' *Academy of Management Review,* Vol. 10, No. 3, p. 449.

exporting from the home country, a company must be aware of cultural factors that may influence the marketing programme. Consider advertising, which may be affected by the real and ideal physical norms of the target market, the roles of group membership in terms of status and buying decisions, and the perception of different words and images. A company undertaking a purely resource-seeking foreign activity can ignore the effects of cultural variables on advertising but must consider factors that may influence supply, such as methods of managing a foreign workforce. For multifunctional activities, such as producing and selling a product in a foreign country, a company must be concerned with a wider array of cultural relationships.

The more countries in which a company is doing business, the more cultural nuances it must consider. Think of the adjustments a manager from corporate headquarters who visits the company's foreign distributors would have to make. The more countries visited, the more cultural differences would be encountered on the trip and the more pre-departure training time would be needed.

There is a relationship in the similarity between countries and the relative need for cultural awareness. For example, an American firm starting a new business in Australia will find cultural differences that may be important enough to create operating problems; however, the number and intensity of these differences are apt to be less than if it were starting a new business in Japan.

A company may handle foreign operations on its own or contract with another company to handle them. The risk of making operating mistakes because of misunderstanding may be effectively reduced if foreign operations are turned over to another company at home or abroad that has had experience of the foreign country. In such a case, some cultural awareness is necessary because of nuances that may influence the relationship between the two companies, such as the means of negotiating an agreement or setting objectives for the operation. As a company takes on activities that had previously been contracted to another company, it will need to know much more about the cultures where it is doing business.

3.8.1 Polycentrism

In organisations characterised by polycentrism, control is decentralised so that 'our manager in Zimbabwe' is free to conduct business in what he thinks is 'the Zimbabwean way'. When the concept is taken to extremes, a polycentric individual or organisation is 'overwhelmed by the differences, real and imaginary, great and small, between its many operating environments'.[66] Since most discussions of international business focus on factors of uniqueness encountered abroad and the attendant problems that companies have experienced, it is understandable that many managers develop a polycentric view. Polycentrism may, however, be an overly cautious response. In reality, the extent to which companies adjust when operating abroad, is uncertain and it has not been established whether their practices abroad are any more prone to failure than those at home.

A company that is too polycentric may shy away from certain countries or may avoid transferring home-country practices or resources that may, in fact, work well abroad. For example, American Express assembled its worldwide personnel managers for an exchange of views. The complaints from the overseas managers centred on certain corporate directives that they claimed did not fit 'their' countries. The impression was created that foreign operations were so unique that each overseas office should develop its own procedures. Further talks, however, revealed that the complaints really focused on only one particular personnel evaluation form. If the company had delegated procedural control, as these overseas managers were suggesting, it would have risked not introducing abroad some of its other standard forms and procedures that would work reasonably well. Furthermore, it would have risked duplicating efforts, which might have been more costly than trying to administer the ill-suited form. The additional discussions also generated for the first time comments from personnel managers in offices in the USA who had received the same corporate instructions. They indicated that they had had just as many problems with the form as their foreign counterparts. Thus the problem, originally attributed to environmental differences, was seen to be universal.

To compete effectively with local companies, an international company must usually perform some functions in a distinct way. Polycentrism, however, may lead to such extensive delegation or such extensive imitation of proven host-country practices that innovative superiority is lost. Furthermore, control may be diminished if managers in each country foster local rather than worldwide objectives.

3.8.2 Ethnocentrism

Ethnocentrism is the belief that one's own group is superior to others. The term is used in international business to describe a company or individual so imbued with the belief that what worked at home should work abroad, that environmental differences are ignored. Ethnocentrism can be categorised into three types:

1 Important factors are overlooked because management has become so accustomed to certain cause-effect relationships in the home country that differences abroad are ignored. To combat this type of ethnocentrism, managers can refer to checklists of human variables in order to assure themselves that all the major factors are at least considered.

2 Management recognises both the environmental differences and the problems associated with change, but is focused on achieving home-country rather than foreign or worldwide objectives. The result may be diminished long-term competitive viability because the company does not perform as well as its competitors, and opposition to its practices may develop in another country.
3 Management recognises differences but assumes that the introduction of change is both necessary and easily achieved. (The problems accompanying this type of ethnocentrism are discussed in the next subsection, 'Geocentrism'.)

3.8.3 Geocentrism

Between the extremes of polycentrism and ethnocentrism are hybrid business practices that are neither exactly like the international company's home operations nor exactly like those of the typical host-country company. When the host-country environment is substantially different, the international company must decide whether to persuade people in that country to accept something new (in which case, the company would be acting as an agent of change) or to make changes in the company itself. Geocentrism refers to operations based on an informed knowledge of both home and host country needs, capabilities and constraints.

3.9 Value systems

It is much easier to adapt to things that do not challenge our value systems than to things that do. We can usually be flexible about whether we eat the salad before or after the main course, but we would probably think twice before exposing more of our bodies in public or paying bribes to government officials – actions that would require some moral adjustment if we do not do so in our own country. For example, Eritreans eat only 175 g of fish per capita per year (compared with 20 kg in the United States and 70 kg in Japan), despite having a long coastline rich in seafood and a recent experience with famine. The Eritrean government and the United Nations World Food Programme have faced formidable opposition in trying to persuade Eritrean adults to eat more seafood because their value systems are too set. Many have religious taboos about eating sea creatures that look like insects (such as shrimp and crayfish), and fish without scales, and most of them grew up believing that seafood tasted putrid. But there is little opposition from schoolchildren who are being fed seafood that adults find unpalatable. Their value systems and habits are not yet set, so they can be easily influenced.[67] The important lesson here is that the more a change disrupts basic values, the more the people affected will resist it. When changes do not interfere with deep-seated customs, accommodation is much more likely.

3.9.1 Cost benefit of change

Some adjustments to foreign cultures are costly to undertake; others are inexpensive. Some result in greatly improved performance, such as higher productivity or sales; others may improve performance only marginally. A company must consider the expected cost-benefit relationship of any adjustments it makes abroad. For example, Cummins Engines shuts down its plant in Mexico every 12 December so that workers may honour the Virgin of Guadalupe. It holds a celebration in the company cafeteria for employees and their families, as well as a priest who offers prayers to the Virgin at an altar.[68] The cost is small in relation to the resultant employee commitment to the company.

3.9.2 Resistance to too much change

When Germany's Gruner 1 Jahr bought the US magazine *McCalls*, it quickly began to revamp the format. Gruner 1 Jahr changed the editor, eliminated long stories and advice columns, increased coverage on celebrities, made the layouts more dense, initiated the use of sidebars and boxes in articles, and refused discounts for big advertisers. But there was an increase in employee turnover because of low morale, and revenues fell because advertisers considered the new format too different.[69] Acceptance by employees and advertisers might have been easier to obtain if Gruner 1 Jahr had made fewer demands at the same time and had phased in other policies more gradually.

3.9.3 Participation

One way to avoid undue problems that could result from change is to invite the prior participation of stakeholders, such as employees, who might otherwise feel they have no say in their own destinies. By discussing a proposed change with stakeholders in advance, the company may ascertain how strong the resistance to the change is, stimulate in the stakeholders a recognition of the need for improvement, and allay the fears of adverse consequences which may result. Managers sometimes think that delegation and participation are unique to highly developed countries, in which people have educational backgrounds that enable them to make substantial contributions. Experience with economic development and population control programmes, however, indicates that participation may be extremely important even in countries with a preference for authoritarian leadership. However, participation is limited to the extent that proposed actions do not violate conditions in the prevailing value system, nor are participants so fatalistic that they believe they can have no control over the results of actions taken.

3.9.4 Reward-sharing

Sometimes a proposed change may have no foreseeable benefit for the people whose support is needed to ensure its success. For example, production workers have little incentive to shift to new work practices unless they see some benefits for themselves. One solution may be for a company to develop a bonus system for productivity and quality.

3.9.5 Opinion-leaders

By discovering the local channels of influence, an international company may locate opinion-leaders who can help speed up the acceptance of change. Opinion-leaders may emerge in unexpected places. For example, in rural Ghana, government health workers frequently ask permission from and seek the help of village shamans before inoculating people or spraying huts to fight malaria. Doing this achieves the desired result without destroying important social structures. Characteristics of opinion-leaders may vary from one country to the next – opinion-leaders are generally the more mature people in India and Korea, while this is not the case in Australia.[70]

3.9.6 Timing

Many good ideas are never applied effectively because they are ill-timed. Change brings uncertainty and insecurity. For example, a labour-saving production method will create resistance because people are afraid of losing their jobs, regardless of what management says. However, there will be less resistance if the labour-saving method is introduced when there is a labour shortage rather than a surplus. Attitudes and needs may change slowly or rapidly, so keeping abreast of these changes helps in determining timing.

3.9.7 Value judgement and ethics

The way in which companies and business-people should react to cultural practices that run counter to their own values is in itself a value judgment. On the one hand, relativism affirms that ethical truths are relative to the groups holding them; thus intervention would be unethical. On the other hand, normativism holds that there are universal standards of behaviour that should be upheld; in such a case non-intervention would be unethical. Respect for other cultures is a Western cultural phenomenon that goes back at least as far as St Ambrose's fourth-century advice: 'When in Rome, do as the Romans do.'

Neither international companies nor their employees are expected to always adhere to the norms of a host society. This would seem to solve ethical questions; however, exposure to certain practices may be traumatic to foreigners. Many practices that are considered 'wrong' in home country cultures, for example, are either customary or only recently abolished and liable to be reinstated elsewhere, such as slavery, polygamy, concubinage, child marriage, and the burning of widows.[71] Some companies have avoided operating in locales in which such practices occur; others have pressured a host country to change the 'wrong' behaviours. An illustration of this was where complaints from international business leaders induced Papua New Guinea, which depends on foreign investment, to abandon policies of payback killings.[72]

Although the preceding examples are extreme and seldom, if ever, encountered by international managers, many other behavioural differences may violate a manager's own ethical code to a lesser degree. It is easier to adjust in these cases, although dilemmas still exist. For example, using gifts and flattery to gain business advantages may seem unethical to some people. But in many countries, particularly in Asia, failure to bring a small gift may not only be considered a breach of etiquette, but also be interpreted as indicating a lack of interest in doing business. Most Westerners are conditioned to express gratitude verbally, whereas most Asians, particularly the Chinese, are conditioned to express appreciation tangibly, such as with gifts.[73] Giving gifts to government officials may be particularly perplexing to Westerners, but in many places such gifts or payments are customary to obtain government services or contracts. Although this practice may be condemned officially, it is so well embedded in local custom and precedent that it is, to all intents and purposes, the prescribed enforcement of common law. In Mexico, for example, companies commonly give tips once a month to the mail carrier; otherwise their mail simply gets lost.[74] The going rate of payment is quite easily ascertained and is usually in accordance with the ability to pay. The practice of making payments to government officials is, in effect, a fairly efficient means of taxation in countries that pay civil servants low wages and do not have the means for collecting income taxes. Still, these payments are considered bribes by many multinational enterprises, and the practice is frequently viewed by home-country constituents as so unethical that home-country laws against it are enforced in foreign operations.

In situations such as making payments to government officials, companies may incur operational inefficiencies or loss of business if they do not comply with local custom. This raises the question of whether operational performance should be considered along with potential violation of ethical standards. For example, many people feel it is more acceptable to give payments to government officials when a large, rather than a small, amount of business is at stake and when small, rather than large, payments are expected.

3.9.8 Learning abroad

The discussion so far has centred on the interaction between an international company and the host society. This interaction is a two-way street. The company not only affects the relationship but is affected by it. It may change things abroad or alter its activities to fit the foreign environment; it also may learn things that will be useful in its home country or in other operations. This last point is the essence for undertaking transnational practices in which the company seeks to capitalise on diverse capabilities among the countries in which it operates. In fact, the management in a given foreign country may serve effectively as the worldwide headquarters for a specific product or function.

The national practices most likely to be scrutinised for possible use in other countries are those found in the countries with the best economies.[75] For example, in the 19th century, when Britain was the world economic leader, interest focused on the British cultural character. At the turn of the century, such attention was diverted to Germany and the United States. More recently, it has shifted toward Japan and the newly industrialised countries of Asia. Whether a company is importing or exporting business practices, managers must consider the same factors when questioning whether and how change can be introduced.

3.9.9 Countervailing forces

Contact across cultures is becoming more widespread than ever. This should lead to a levelling off of cultures, which, on the surface, seems to be occurring. People around the world wear similar clothes and listen to the same recording artists. Competitors from all over the world often buy the same production equipment, the use of which imposes more uniform operating methods on workers. This globalisation of culture is illustrated by the fact that Japanese tourists may hear a Philippine group sing an American song in a hotel in Thailand.[76]

However, below the surface people continue to hold fast to their national differences.[77] In other words, although some tangibles have become more universal, the ways in which people co-operate, attempt to solve problems and are motivated, have tended to remain the same. Religious differences are as strong as ever, and language differences continue to bolster separate ethnic identities. These differences fragment the globe into regions and stymie global standardisation of products and operating methods.

One factor that inhibits the levelling of cultures is nationalism. Without perceived cultural differences, people would not see themselves as being apart from other nationalities; thus cultural identities are used to mobilise national identity and separateness. This is done by regulating and encouraging the so-called national culture. Language is regulated in many ways, such as by designating an official language, preventing bilingual education, or requiring 'Made in____' labels printed in the language of the importing country. A religion may be designated as a country's official one or made a prerequisite for holding certain government posts or for voting.

Those things that are part of the essential national heritage are perpetuated by marketing them to visitors at home and abroad, such as where the image of Britain is used in promotions to foreign tourists. Parts of the national heritage may also be off-limits to foreign ownership. For example, the French government has prevented foreign acquisition of vineyards in France for reasons based on heritage. Canada prevents foreign ownership in culturally sensitive industries. And, although the game of baseball has spread in popularity from the United States to Japan, when a Japanese group bought the Seattle Mariners team, there was an uproar in the United States, not on economic or national security grounds, but on the basis of heritage. Maintaining a national identity may extend beyond heritage. Most countries have a national airline that is government-subsidised so that there is a national identity associated with the flag painted on the aircraft.

As long as nations seek to perpetuate themselves through the promotion of separate cultural or national identities, companies will be limited in their global competitive moves. International companies are likely to continue to face diverse cultural trends in different parts of the world and for different parts of their operations. In some areas, diversity will decrease as small cultural groups are absorbed into more dominant national ones. In recent years, for example, such absorption has led to the extinction of many regional languages, which is sometimes expedited by government assimilation programmes and bans on religious groups or the use of anything except the official language.[78] At the same time, there is evidence of more powerful subcultures within countries because of the influx of people from other countries, the global rise in religious fundamentalism, and the growing belief of ethnic groups that they should be independent.

All of these factors might cause future problems in defining culture along national lines. Subcultures may transcend borders, and the distinct subcultures within a country may have less in common with each other than they do with subcultures in other countries. Examples of transnational subcultures are the Inuits in Arctic lands and the Kurds of the Middle East. At the same time, cultural similarity will continue to be used to mobilise a sense of national identity: such as religious separatism in Iran or the independence movements among the Québeçois in Canada and the Tamils in Sri Lanka. Such activities may retard or even prevent the homogenisation of cultures.[79]

An interesting potential scenario is that cultural competition, the promotion of ideas, attitudes, norms, and values among nations, will become more important.[80] Now that the Cold War has ended, cultural competition may become a more important means of bringing about economic growth as nations try to harness their distinctive human resource capabilities as a means of outperforming other countries.

3.10 Summary

International companies must evaluate their business practices to ensure that national norms in behavioural characteristics are taken into account. There may be very distinct societies in a certain country. People may also have more in common with similar groups in foreign countries than with different groups in their own country.

Culture includes norms of behaviour based on learned attitudes, values and beliefs. Businesspeople agree that there are cross-country differences in these but disagree as to what the differences are. Cultural change may take place as a result of choice or imposition; however, isolation from other groups tends to stabilise cultures.

Group affiliations based on gender, family, age, caste, religion, political preference, professional associations, and ethnic, racial or national origin often affect a person's degree of access to economic resources, prestige, social relations, and power. An individual's affiliations may determine his or her qualifications and availability for given jobs.

Some people work far more than is necessary to satisfy their basic needs for food, clothing, and shelter. The relative importance of work is determined largely by the interrelationship of the cultural and economic environments. People are motivated to work for various reasons, which include the Protestant ethic, the belief that work will bring success and reward, habit, the need for achievement and the fulfilment of higher-order needs.

Different occupations bring varied economic, social and prestige rewards in different countries. People gravitate towards jobs in which they perceive they will receive high rewards. The many differences among societies result in varied attitudes towards working for business organisations. National groups differ as to whether they prefer an autocratic or a consultative working relationship, in the degree to which individuals trust others, in attitudes towards self-determination and fate, and in the importance placed on group memberships, especially family-based ones.

People communicate through both formal language and silent language based on culturally-determined cues. Information-processing is greatly affected by cultural background. Failure to perceive subtle distinctions can result in misunderstandings in international dealings.

Companies can encourage awareness of other cultures. The amount of effort needed to do this depends on the similarity between countries and the type of business operation undertaken. People working in a foreign environment should be sensitive to the dangers of either excessive polycentrism or excessive ethnocentrism. They should try to become geocentric instead.

In deciding whether to try to bring change to home or host country operations or to develop new practices to fit conditions, an international company should consider several factors, including how important the change is to each party, the cost and benefit to the company of each alternative, the possibility of participation in decision-making, the need to share the rewards of change, the use of opinion-leaders, and the timing of change.

Case Study

Parris-Rogers International (PRI)

In June 1996, a car bomb in Saudi Arabia killed 19 American servicemen. The victims were among the approximately 9 000 American troops remaining in Saudi Arabia, Kuwait, Bahrain and the United Arab Emirates since the end of the 1991 Persian Gulf War to liberate Kuwait from Iraq. Although no group claimed responsibility for the blast, most analysts reasoned that cultural conflict was an underlying cause. Traditionalists wanted to rid the area of Western influences, such as music, entertainment and dress, which they considered immoral. At the same time, a Western-educated middle class was questioning many c the traditional rules. The cultural conflict an accommodation are illustrated by the rule imposed by the USA army on female troop during the war. They were not permitted to jog drive or show their legs outside the militar base. In deference to USA sensitivities, Saud Arabia suspended beheadings in centra squares during the Gulf crisis.

A few years earlier, Parris-Rogers Interna tional (PRI), a British publishing house, had sol its floundering Bahraini operation. This branc had been set up to edit the first telephone an business directories for five Arab states on o near the Arabian peninsula, plus the sever autonomous divisions making up the Unite Arab Emirates (the region is shown in Exhibi 3.5). Although the USA Army had protoco officers to advise it on accepted behaviour, PR

Exhibit 3.5: The scope of PRI's business contract

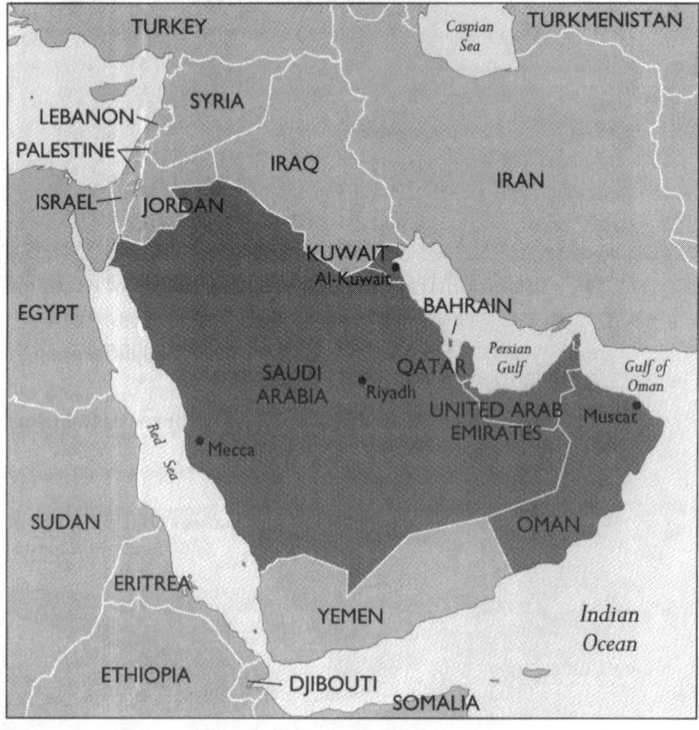

had no such guidance. Further, although the Saudis were willing to make some compromises to assure the defence of their country, PRI's directories were less important to the 12 Arab states. The ensuing lack of understanding between the Arab states and PRI, and PRI's failure to adapt to a different culture, contributed directly to the company's failure.

Most Middle-Eastern oil-producing countries have an acute shortage of local personnel, and have had to hire many foreign workers. The latter now make up a large portion of the population in those countries. In the United Arab Emirates in 1995, for example, 70% of the population was foreign, mainly from India and Pakistan. In Saudi Arabia, about 40% was foreign. Thus when PRI could not find sufficient qualified people locally, it filled four key positions through advertisements in London newspapers. Angela Clarke, an Englishwoman, was hired as editor and researcher, and three young Englishmen were hired as salesmen. The four new employees left immediately for Bahrain. Not one of them had visited the Middle East before; and they all expected to carry on business as usual. The salesmen, hired on a commission basis, expected that by moving aggressively they could make the same number of calls as they normally did in the United Kingdom. They were used to working about eight hours a day, to having the undivided attention of potential clients, and restricting most conversation to the specifics of the business transaction.

Instead, the salesmen found an entirely different situation. There was less time to sell, first, because the Muslims were required to pray five times a day and, second, because the workday was reduced even further during the sacred ninth month of the Muslim year, Ramadan, when there is fasting from sunrise to sunset. The Muslim year is based on a lunar rather than a solar calendar; thus Ramadan may begin in different solar months, such as in January for 1997, or December 1997 for 1998. Moreover, since the start of Ramadan is based on the sighting of a new moon, longitudinal, latitudinal and weather conditions usually cause it to vary by a day or two between countries and it cannot be determined in advance. The salesmen also felt that the Arabs considered appointments to be of little importance, and they seldom began at the scheduled time. When the salesmen finally managed to see Arab businessmen, they were often expected to go to a café where the Arabs would engage in what seemed to them to be idle chitchat. Whether in a café or in the office, drinking coffee or tea seemed to take precedence over business matters. The Arabs also frequently diverted their attention to friends who joined them at the café or in the office.

Angela Clarke, too, encountered considerable resistance as she sought to do her job. And, since she was paid a salary instead of a commission, PRI had to bear all of the expense resulting from her work being thwarted in unexpected ways. PRI had based its budgets for preparing the directories on its English experience. In Bahrain, however, preparing such books turned out to be more time-consuming and costly. For example, in the traditional Middle-Eastern city, there are no street names or building numbers. Thus, before getting to the expected directory work, Clarke had to take a census of Bahraini establishments, identifying the location of each with such prepositions as 'below', 'above' or 'in front of' some meaningful landmark.

Clarke encountered other problems because she was a single woman. She was in charge of the research in all 12 states and had planned to hire freelance assistants in most of them. But her advertisements for such assistants were answered by personal harassment and obscene telephone calls. In addition, Saudi authorities denied her entry to Saudi Arabia, while her visa for Oman took six weeks to process each time she went there. These experiences were particularly frustrating for her, because both Saudi Arabia and Oman sometimes eased the entry of a single woman when her business was of high local priority, and/or when she would be serving as a housemaid or nanny where her only contact would be with women and children. In the states she could enter, Clarke was sometimes required to stay only in hotels that government officials had approved for foreign women, and even there, she was prohibited from eating in the dining-room unless accompanied by the hotel manager.

PRI's salesmen never adjusted to working in the new environment. Instead of pushing PRI to review its commission scheme, they tried to change the way the Arab businessmen dealt with them. For example, after a few months they refused to join their potential clients for refreshments and began showing their irritation at 'irrelevant' conversations, delays and interruptions from outsiders. The Arab businessmen responded negatively. In fact, PRI received so many complaints from them that the salesmen had to be replaced. By then, however, irrevocable damage had been done to PRI's sales.

Clarke fared better, thanks to her compromises with Arab customs. She began wearing a wedding ring and registering at hotels as a married woman. When travelling, she ate meals in her room, conducted meetings in conference rooms, and had all incoming calls screened by the hotel operators. To avoid arrest by decency patrols, she wore long-sleeved blouses and below-the-knee skirts in plain blue or beige. Still, in spite of her compromises, the fact that she was unable to enter Saudi Arabia made it necessary for PRI to send a salesman, who was not trained to do the research, in her place.

The rapidly growing number of foreigners in the Middle East has created adjustment problems for both the foreigners and the local societies. In many cases, foreigners are expected to conform; in others, they are allowed to pursue their own customs in isolation from the local populace. For example, according to traditional Islamic standards, most Western television programming is immoral. However, in some places, foreigners are permitted to acquire descramblers to view Western programmes; local people may not. At the same time, although satellite dishes are technically illegal in Saudi Arabia, these 'devils' dishes' – a term used by hard-line Islamic fundamentalists – are seen on rooftops everywhere. Nevertheless, the BBC axed its Arabic Television Service in 1996 because of disagreements over programme content. This led a BBC executive to remark, 'Looking at the partners involved, the Saudis and the BBC, who would have thought two such different cultures could comfortably coexist?'

The Saudi government has also had second thoughts about some of its culture's double standards. A case in point is that at one time male and female hotel guests were allowed to swim in the same pools in Saudi Arabia, but this permission was later rescinded because Saudis also frequent the hotels. It was feared that they might be corrupted by viewing 'decadent' behaviour. Also, when Angela Clarke and the salesmen first arrived in Bahrain, there were prohibitions on the sale of pork products, including imported canned foods. This prohibition was later modified, but grocers had to stock pork products in separate rooms in which only non-Muslims could work or shop.

These dual and changing standards for both foreigners and local citizens hamper the efforts of foreigners to adapt. The situation has become even more complicated because the Middle East is going through a period of substantial, but uneven, economic and social transformation. As contact increases between Arabs and Westerners, cultural borrowing and meshing of certain aspects of traditional and modern behaviour will increase. These changes are apt to come slowly, perhaps more so than many people think.

Questions

1 'The Arab businessmen viewed time spent in a café as doing something, and considered "small talk" a necessary prerequisite for evaluating whether they could interact

satisfactorily with potential business partners.' Discuss this section and give your own perceptions about the Englishmen's attitude towards the Arab's way of doing business in Saudi Arabia.

2 Do you think Angela Clarke might have been even less effective for PRI if she had worn the traditional Arab woman's dress with veil? Give motivations for your answer.

3 Would you have called Angela back from Saudi Arabia?

4 After a company successfully identifies the differences in the foreign country in which it intends to do business, must it alter its customary or preferred practices in order to be successful there?

5 What would you have done differently if you were employed by PRI in Saudi Arabia?

Endnotes

1 Most data were taken from an interview with Angela Clarke, a protagonist in the case.
Additional background information taken from:
Harfoush, S.1980. 'Non-traditional training for women in the Arab world', *Bridge*, Winter, pp. 6–7.
'British premier visits Saudi Arabia', *New York Times*, 20 April, 1981, p. A2.
Karen Elliott House. 1981. 'Modern Arabia', *Wall Street Journal*, 4 June, p. 1.
Brooks, Geraldine. 1990, 'Mixed blessing', *Wall Street Journal*, 11 September, p. A1.
Horwitz, T. 1991. 'Thought police', *Wall Street Journal*, 2 May, p. A1.
Horwitz, T. 1993. 'Arabian backlash', *Wall Street Journal*, 13 January, p. A1.
Allen, T. 1995. 'Imported labour may not be cheap for Gulf states', *Financial Times*, 13 October, p. 5.
Morehouse, M. 1996. 'Western influence brings wealth, strain, to Saudi society,' *The Atlanta Journal*, 26 June, p. 10A.
Mackey, S. 1996. 'Perspectives on the Saudi bombing', *Los Angeles Times*, 28 June, p. B9.
Lippman, T.W. 1996. 'Mission to bolster Saudi security also provokes rulers' enemies', *Washington Post*, 27 June, p. A24.
Allen, R. 1996. 'Oil price alert on Saudi state finances', *Financial Times*, 26 June, p. 4.
'The shockwaves that unsettle', *Financial Times*, 26 July, 1996, p. 16.
Horsman, M. & Waller, E. 1996. 'The BBC's Arabian plight', *The Independent*, 16 April, p. 18.
Pearl, D. 1997. 'Moon over Mecca: It's tough to pinpoint start of holy month', *Wall Street Journal*, 7 January, p. A1+.

2 Westwood, R.I. & Leung, S.M. 1994. 'The female expatriate manager experience', *International Studies of Management and Organization*, Vol. 24, No. 3, pp. 64–85.

3 Francis, J.N.P. 1991. 'When in Rome? The effects of cultural adaptation on intercultural business negotiations', *Journal of International Business Studies*, Vol. 22, No. 3, pp. 421–422.

4 Foster, R.J. 1991. 'Making national cultures in the national Ecumene', *Annual Review of Anthropology*, Vol. 20, pp. 235–260, discusses the concept and ingredients of a national culture.

5 Binder, D. & Crossette, B. 1993. 'As ethnic wars multiply, US strives for a policy', *New York Times*, 7 February, p. A1+.

6 Segall, M.H. 1979. *Cross-cultural psychology: Human behaviour in global perspective.* Monterey, Calif.: Brooks/Cole, p.143.

7 Farmer, R.N. & Richman, B.M. 1970. *Comparative Management and Economic Progress.* Rev. ed. Bloomington, Ind.: Cedarwood, pp. 20–21.

8 Jamieson, I. 1980. *Capitalism and culture: A comparative analysis of British and American manufacturing organizations.* Farnborough, England: Gower Press, Chapter 1.

9 Adler, N.J. & de Villafranca, J. 1982–1983. 'Epistemological foundations of a symposium process: A framework for understanding culturally diverse organizations', *International Studies of Management and Organization*, pp. 7–22.

10 Van de Vliert, E. & Van Ypern, N.W. 1996. 'Why cross national differences in role overload? Don't overlook ambient temperature!' *Academy of Management Journal* Vol. 39, No. 4, pp. 986–1004.

11 Giovannini, M.J. & Rosansky, L.M.H. 1990. 'Anthropology and Management Consulting: Forging a New Alliance.' N.P.: *National Association for the Practice of Anthropology*, Bulletin 9, pp. 19–27. For discussion on grouping techniques into four categories, see Earley, P. C. 1995. 'International and intercultural management research: What's next?' *Academy of Management Journal*, Vol. 38, No. 2, pp. 327–340.

12 Cavalli-Sforza, L.L., Feldman, M.W., Chen, K.H. & Dornbusch, S.M. 1982. 'Theory and observation in cultural transmission', *Science*, Vol. 218, pp. 19–27.

13 Hofstede, G. 1991. *Cultures and organizations.* London McGraw-Hill, p. 8.

14 Le Moyne, J. 1990. 'Army women and the Saudis shock one another', *New York Times*, 25 September, p. A1.

15 Durham, W.H. 1992. 'Applications of evolutionary culture theory', *Annual Review of Anthropology*, Vol. 21, pp. 331–355.

16 Merry, S.J. 1992. 'Anthropology, law, and transnational processes', *Annual Review of Anthropology*, Vol. 21, p. 364.

17 Mench,R.1984. *An Indian woman in Guatemala.* London: Verso.

18. Mench, R. 1994–1995. 'Asserting our dignity'. *Harvard International Review*, Winter 1994–95, pp. 42–44.

19 Terpstra,V. & David, K. 1991. *The cultural environment of international business.* 3rd ed. Cincinnati: South-Western, p. 93.

20 *Business Week*, 1993. 'Big Mac vs. Sacred Cows', 1 March, p. 58.

21 Triandis, H.C. 1983–1983. 'Dimensions of cultural variation as parameters of organizational theories', *International Studies of Management and Organization*, Winter 1982–1983, pp. 143–144.

22 *Wall Street Journal*, 'China's gender imbalance', 7 June, 1990, p. A12.

23 Crossette, B. 1996. 'Afghans draw U.N. warning over sex bias', *New York Times*, 8 October, p. A1.

4 *Wall Street Journal*, 'Comparing women around the world', 26 July, 1995, p. B1.

5 Dreyfack, K.1987. 'You don't have to be a giant to score big overseas', *Business Week*, 13 April 1987, p. 63.

6 Lin, L.L.1996. *More and better jobs for women: an action guide.* Geneva: International Labour Organization.

7 Fukuyama, F. 1995. *Trust: the social virtues and the creation of prosperity.* New York: The Free Press.

8 Weber, M. 1969. 'The Protestant ethic and the spirit of capitalism', and Fullerton, K. 'Calvinism and capitalism', both in Webber, R.A. ed. *Culture and Management.* Homewood, Ill.: Richard D. Irwin, pp. 91–112

9 Boddewyn, J.J. 1992. 'Fitting socially in fortress Europe: Understanding, reaching, and impressing Europeans', *Business Horizons*, November-December, pp. 35–43.

0 Inden, R. 1986. 'Tradition against itself', *American Ethnologist*, Vol. 13, No. 4, pp. 762–775.
Chatterjee, P. 1986. *Nationalist thoughts and the colonial world: a derivative discourse.* London: Zed Books.

1 Triandis, op. cit., pp. 159–160.

2 Hagen, E.E. 1962. *The theory of social change: how economic growth begins.* Homewood, Ill.: D. Irwin, p. 378.

33 McClelland, D.C. 1961. *The achieving society.* Princeton, N.J.: Van Nostrand.
McClelland, D.C. 1962. 'Business drives and national achievement', *Harvard Business Review*, July-August , pp. 92–12.
Maehr, M.L. & Nicholls, J.G.1980. 'Culture and achievement motivations: a second look', in Warren, N.(ed.) *Studies in Cross-Cultural Psychology*, Vol. 2, Chapter 6. London: Academic Press.

34 Hofstede, G. 1983. 'National cultures in four dimensions', *International Studies of Management and Organization*, Spring-Summer, pp. 46–74.

35 Maslow, A. 1954. *Motivation and personality.* New York: Harper.

36 Hofstede, op. cit., pp. 46–74; and for an earlier comparison among countries, see Haire, M., Ghiselli, E. & Porter L. 1966. *Managerial thinking.* New York: Wiley, pp. 90–103.

37 Jordan, M. 1994. 'Respect is dwindling in the hallowed halls', *Washington Post*, 20 June, p. A3, citing data collected by the Carnegie Foundation for the Advancement of Teaching in a survey of 20 000 professors in 13 nations and Hong Kong.

38 Hofstede, op. cit., pp. 54-55; Boddewyn, op. cit., p. 36.

39 Hofstede, loc. cit.

40 Knack, S.1996. 'Low trust, slow growth,' *Financial Times*, 26 June, p. 12;
Fukuyama, F.1995. *The social virtues and the creation of prosperity.* London: Hamish Hamilton,.

41 Pearl, loc. cit.

42 Cummings, L.L., Harnett, D.L. & Stevens, D.J. 1971.'Risk, fate, conciliation and trust: An international study of attitudinal differences among executives', *Academy of Management Journal*, September, p. 294, found differences among the United States, Greece, Spain, Central Europe, and Scandinavia.

43 Kanter, R.M. 1991. 'Transcending business boundaries: 12 000 world managers view change', *Harvard Business Review*, May-June, pp. 151–164.

44 Reece, J.B. 1992. 'Book review of Patricia Gercik, *On the track with the Japanese* (Kodansha, 1992)', *Business Week*, 28 December, p. 20.

45 Lawrence, J.L. & Yeh, Reh-song. 1994. 'The influence of Mexican culture on the use of Japanese manufacturing techniques in Mexico', *Management International Review*, Vol. 34, No.1, pp. 49–66.
Earley, P.C.1993. 'East meets West meets Mideast: Further explorations of collectivistic and individualistic work groups', *Academy of Management Journal*, Vol. 36, No. 2, pp. 319–346.

46 Clark, D. 1996. 'Hey Amigo, can you translate the word "gaffe"?' *Wall Street Journal*, 8 July, p. B6.

47 Newman, B. 1995. 'Global chatter: The world speaks English, but often none too well', *Asia Wall Street Journal*, 23 March, p. 1+.

48 Ducat, V. 1986. 'American spoken here and everywhere', *Travel & Leisure*, Vol. 16, No. 10, October, pp. 168–169.
Bryson, B. 1990. *The mother tongue: English and how it got that way.* New York: Morrow.

49 Newman, op. cit.
Nicholson, M.1996. 'Language error was cause of Indian air disaster', *Financial Times*, 14 November, p. 1.

50 This term was first used by Hall, E.T. 1960. 'The silent language in overseas business', *Harvard Business Review*, May–June 1960, and included five variables (time, space, things, friendships, and agreements).

51 Ibid.

52 Ferrieux, E. 1989. 'Hidden Messages', *World Press Review*, July, p. 39.

53 For a survey of major research contributions, see Triandis H.C. 1980. 'Reflections on trends in cross-cultural research', *Journal of Cross-Cultural Psychology*, March, pp. 46–48.

54 Whorf, B.L. 1956. *Language, thought and reality.* New York: Wiley, p. 13.

55 Segall, op. cit., pp. 96–99.

56 Horwitz, T. 1990. 'Iceland pushes back English invasion in war of the words', *Wall Street Journal*, 25 July, p. A8.

57 For an examination of subtle differences within northern Europe, see Djursaa, M. 1994. 'North Europe business culture: Britain vs. Denmark and Germany', *European Management Journal*, Vol. 12, No.2, June, pp. 138–146.

58 Glenn, E. 1981. *Man and mankind: conflict and communication between cultures.* Norwood, N.J.: Ablex.

59 *Wall Street Journal.* 1992. 'Sensitivity kick', 30 December, p. A1.
60 Gosling, P. 1985. 'Culture and commerce: What's in a name?' *Southeast Asia Business,* No. 6, Summer, pp. 30-38.
Acuff, F.L. 1995. 'Just call me Mr Ishmael', *Export Today,* July, p. 14.
61 A list of books appears in Glover, K. 1990. 'Do's & taboos', *Business America,* 13 August, 1990, p. 5. See also Axtell, R. 1992. *Do's and taboos around the world.* New York: John Wiley.
62 Harris, P.R. & Moran, R.T. 1979. *Managing cultural differences.* Houston: Gulf, p. 88, quoting Kalervo Oberg.
63 Furnham, A. & Bochner, S. 1986. *Culture shock.* London: Methuen, p. 234.
64 Kedia, B.L. & Bhagat, R.S. 1988. 'Cultural constraints on transfer of technology across nations: Implications for research in international and comparative management', *Academy of Management Review,* Vol. 13, No. 4, October, pp. 559–571.
65 Miller, J.1996. *God has ninety-nine names.* New York: Simon & Schuster.
Lewis, B.1996. *The Middle East: 2000 Years of history from the rise of Christianity to the present day.* London: Weidenfeld & Nicolson.
66 Thorelli, H.B. 1966. 'The multi-national corporation as a change agent', *The Southern Journal of Business,* July, p. 5.
67 Brooks, G. 1994. 'Eritrea's leaders angle for sea change in nation's diet to prove fish isn't foul', *Wall Street Journal,* 2 June, p. A10.
68 Miller, M. 1992. 'A clash of corporate cultures', *Los Angeles Times,* 15 August, p. A1.
69 Reilly, P.M. 1995. 'Pitfalls of exporting magazine formulas', *Wall Street Journal,* 24 July, p. B1+.
70 Marshall, R. & Gitosudarmo, I. 1995. 'Variation in th characteristics of opinion leaders across cultural borders', *Journal of International Consumer Marketing,* Vol. 8, No. 1, pp. 5–21.
71 Lewis, B. 1988. 'Western culture must go', *Wall Stre Journal,* 2 May, p. 18.
72 Merry, op. cit., pp. 366–367.
73 De Mente, B. 1989. *Chinese etiquette and ethics in business.* Lincolnwood, Ill.: NTC.
74 Stockton, W. 1986. 'Bribes are called a way of life in Mexico', *New York Times,* 25 October, p. 3.
75 Lammi, P. 1992. 'My vision of business in Europe', in Mahoney, J. and Vallance, E. (eds).*Business ethics in new Europe.* Dordrecht, The Netherlands: Kluwer Academic, pp. 11–12.
76 The State (Columbia, SC). 1993. 'Golden arches raise eyebrows in Poland', 10 September, p. 5A.
77 Hope, K. 1996. 'Aristotle provides inspiration in figh for cultural crock of gold', *Financial Times,* 16 June, p. 22.
78 Jack, A. 1997. 'French Prepare to Repel English Advance', *Financial Times,* 7 January, p. 2.
79 Schafer, D.P. 1994. 'Cultures and economics', *Futures* Vol. 26, No. 8, pp. 830–845.
80 Kuyken, W., Orley, J., Hudelson, P. & Sartorius, N. 1994. 'Quality of life assessment across cultures', *International Journal of Mental Health,* Vol. 23, No. 2, pp. 5–27

4 The political and legal environments facing business

Key issues

- The political environment
- The political system and its functions
- The legal environment
- Evolution of legal and political strategies in the internationalisation process
- The future political situation
- Ethical dilemmas in global business

4.1 Introduction

Multinational enterprises (MNEs) must operate in countries that are characterised by different political, legal and economic frameworks, diverse levels of economic development and a variety of economic conditions. To each of an infinite number of situations, the MNE brings a frame of reference based on its domestic experience as well as its lessons from foreign settings. For the company to be successful, its management must carefully analyse the interaction between corporate policies and the political, legal and economic environments in order to maximise efficiency. Our case, Bata Shoes,[1] is such a company and we will discuss it in great detail at the end of this chapter.

This chapter discusses the political and legal systems that managers are likely to encounter and the factors they need to consider as they make strategic decisions about operations in different countries.

4.2 The political environment

Exhibit 1.2 (p. 5) identified the environments that influence managerial decisions. The political environments in a company's home country and the countries in which it does business are important external influences on management.

Countries have both market and non-market environments. The market environment involves the interactions between households (or individuals) and companies to allocate resources, free from government ownership or control. The non-market, or political, environment refers to public institutions (such as the government, government agencies, and government-owned businesses) and non-public institutions (such as environmental and other special interest groups that represent specific individuals or groups).[2] Managers must establish corporate strategies for both the market and non-market environments, both individually and combined.

4.3 The political system and its functions

The political system is designed to integrate the parts of a society into a viable, functioning unit. A country's political system has an enormous impact on how business is conducted domestically and/or internationally. It influences and is influenced by various factors. In Hong Kong, for example, political change was influenced by China because it took control of Hong Kong in 1997; by Britain because it had ruled Hong Kong and tried to institute more democracy before the takeover by China; and by the United States because of the strong trading relationship it had with Hong Kong, as well as the ongoing debate with China over human rights issues. The political system is also influenced by a variety of internal factors, such as the nature of the population, the size and influence of corporations and government bureaucracies, and the strength of the politicians. For example, important factors influencing the political process in Hong Kong are the general population, the large companies that are investing and doing business there, and emerging politicians.

Exhibit 4.1 illustrates the interaction between the process functions, inputs and outputs in any political environment. The process functions in the figure are interest articulation and aggregation, formulation of policy alternatives and implementation and adjudication of policies. Politicians, individuals, businesses, and interest groups provide inputs through the process of interest articulation, that is, making their desires known. These inputs are then aggregated through a process called interest aggregation so that policy alternatives can be formulated that stand a chance of making it through the political process. The alternatives are debated and policies are made, usually by political structures such as political parties, government bureaucracies, state and federal legislatures, and courts. Next the policies are implemented, and any controversial features are adjudicated through the court process to determine if they are legal.[3]

These process functions occur regardless of whether a country is democratic. This is true,

Exhibit 4.1: The political system and its functions

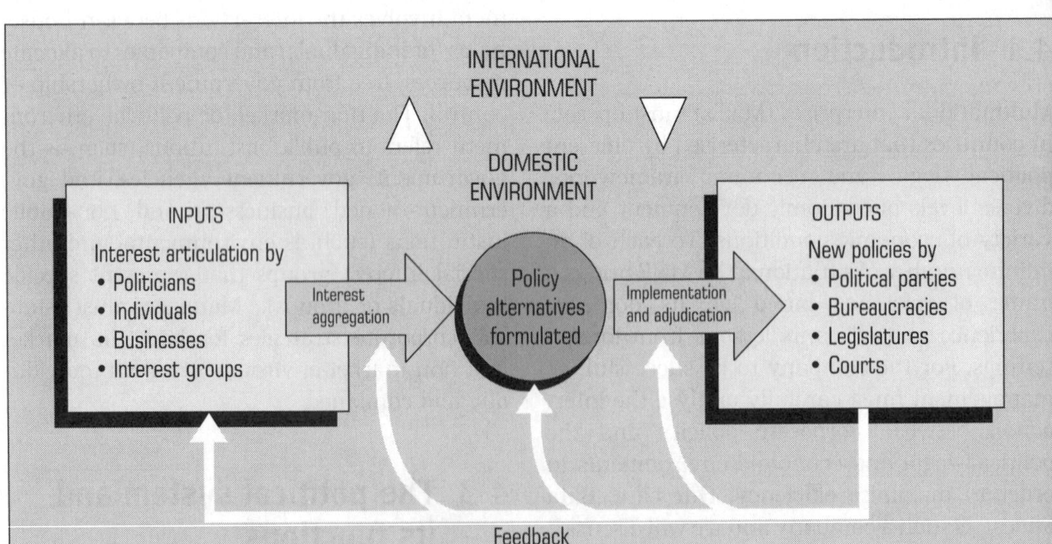

SOURCE: From *Comparative Politics Today: A World View,* 3rd Ed., by Gabriel A. Almond and G. Bingham Powell, Jr. Copyright © 1984 Gabriel A. Almond and G. Bingham Powell, Jr. Reprinted by permission Addison-Wesley Educational Publishers

for example, of the United Kingdom and Hong Kong, which differ in this regard only in degree. There is much wider interest articulation in the United Kingdom than in Hong Kong (although this is changing), and the steps of interest aggregation, policy-making, implementation, and adjudication involve more checks and balances in the UK than in Hong Kong.

4.3.1 Basic political ideologies

A political ideology is the systematic and integrated body of constructs (complex ideas), theories and aims that constitute a socio-political programme. Most modern societies are pluralistic from a political point of view; that is, different ideologies coexist within the society because there is no official ideology accepted by everyone. Pluralism is an outgrowth of the fact that groups within countries often differ significantly from each other in language (for example, the former Yugoslavia, with its many different languages and alphabets), ethnic background (for example, South Africa), or religion (for example, Northern Ireland). As noted in Chapter 3, these and other cultural dimensions strongly influence the political system.

The ultimate test of any political system is its ability to hold a society together despite pressures from different ideologies which tend to split it apart. The more widely different and strongly held the articulated ideas are, the more difficult it is to aggregate them and formulate policies that everyone can accept. Ideologies broke many countries apart in the 1990s, including the former Yugoslavia, the former Czechoslovakia, and the former Soviet Union.

However, ideologies, language, religion, and ethnic background also play an important role in bringing countries together. In one example involving violence, Serbs in the former Yugoslavia initiated conflict in that region and brought together Serbs from different regions of Yugoslavia in an attempt to form a new country, a 'Greater Serbia.' Also, one reason China why wants Hong Kong back is because of ethnic Chinese ties.

With the advent of communist rule after the Second World War, countries were often formed from different ethnic groups held together by totalitarian rule rather than by any particular logic. Yugoslavia, for example, comprised peoples that were ethnically and religiously very different from each other (Roman Catholic Croats, Greek Orthodox Serbs, and Muslim Bosnians). Further, the Croats and Serbs were on opposite sides during the Second World War, and Croats were accused of murdering thousands of Serbs. (Some have termed the bloodshed by Serbs in recent years 'a thousand years of payback' for earlier Croat atrocities.) The recent break-up of the Communist Bloc resulted in the disintegration of countries because of the loss of totalitarian control and ethnic and other differences. Understanding historical roots is essential to understanding the political environment.

(a) A political spectrum

Political ideologies are many and varied, so it is difficult to fit them neatly into a continuum that represents degrees of citizen participation in decision-making. Exhibit 4.2 (p. 106) presents a general scheme of the various forms of government. The two extremes are, in a theoretical sense, democracy and totalitarianism. From these two, various degrees of participation have evolved. Change continues to occur rapidly around the world, and many authoritarian regimes are being replaced by different types of democracies, as can be seen in East Germany's becoming a part of the new Germany, in former Eastern Bloc countries like Poland and the Czech Republic, and in former republics of the Soviet Union. Brazil, which had been ruled by the military since 1964, finally elected a president in 1984, although he died before taking office. Thus the first person to be elected president and to take office was President Collor in 1989.

(b) Democracy

The ideology of pure democracy derives from the ancient Greeks, who believed that citizens

Exhibit 4.2: The political spectrum

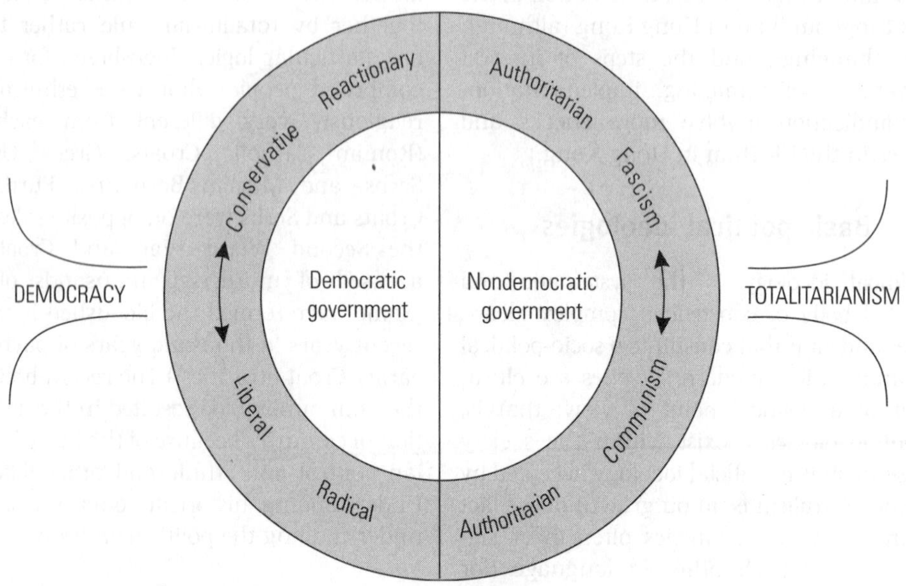

Although democratic and totalitarian governments are extremes, there are variations to each approach. For example, democratic governments range from radical on one side (advocates of political reform) to reactionary (advocates of a return to past conditions). The majority of democratic governments, however, lie somewhere in between.

should be directly involved in the decision-making process. According to the ideal, all citizens should be equal politically and legally, enjoy widespread freedoms and actively participate in the political process. In reality, the complexity of society increases as the population increases, and so full participation becomes impossible. Consequently, most modern democratic countries actually practise various forms of representative democracy, in which citizens elect representatives to make decisions rather than vote on every specific issue.

Contemporary democratic political systems share the following features:

1 freedom of opinion, expression and the press, and freedom to organise;
2 elections in which voters decide who is to represent them;
3 limited terms for elected officials;
4 an independent and fair court system with high regard for individual rights and property;
5 a relatively non-political bureaucracy and defence infrastructure;
6 a relative accessibility to the decision-making process. [4]

A key element of democracy is freedom in the areas of political rights and civil liberties. Each year, a list of countries ranked according to the degree to which these freedoms exist, is published by Freedom House – a non-profit organisation in New York that was established in 1941 and monitors political rights and civil liberties around the world.

The major indicators for political rights are:

- the degree to which fair and competitive elections occur;
- the ability of voters to endow their elected representatives with real power;
- the ability of people to organise into political parties or other competitive political groupings of their choice;
- the existence of safeguards for the rights of minorities.

The major indicators for civil liberties are:

- the existence of freedom of the press;
- equality under the law for all individuals;
- the extent of personal social freedoms;
- the degree of freedom from extreme government indifference or corruption.

Exhibit 4.3 illustrates how countries high in both political rights and civil liberties are classified as 'free', countries quite low in both political rights and civil liberties are classified as 'not free' and countries in between are classified as 'partly free'. See the Appendix to this chapter on p. 127 for the list of countries according to a survey by Freedom House.

The survey identifies the number of countries in each category as well as the percentage of the world's population in each category. In 1994, there were 114 countries that could be classified as democracies, double the number that were called democracies in the early 1970s. What some call the 'third wave' of democratisation started in the early 1970s and is still under way.[5] However, these democratic countries are considered a mixture of 'free' and 'partly free'. In fact, 37 of the democratic countries were considered 'partly free' in 1995.[6] The following identifies the percentage of the total population living in 'free', 'partly free', and 'not free' conditions in 1981, 1990, and 1995.[7]

	1981	1990	1995
Free	35,9%	21,6%	42,5%
Partly free	38,9%	21,6%	39,3%
Not free	20,0%	40,0%	40,0%

Exhibit 4.3: Comparative measures of freedom

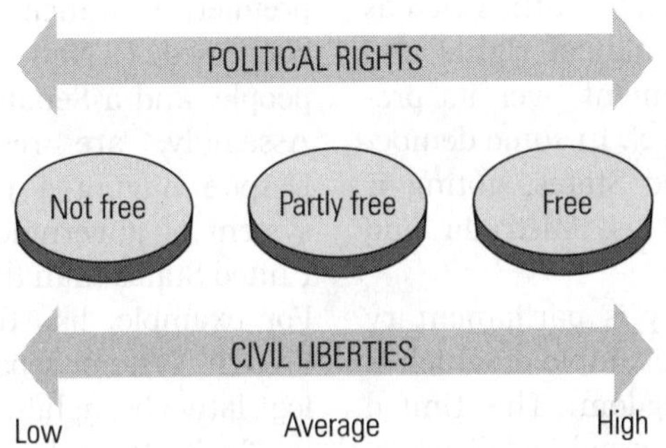

Countries classified as 'free' in a political sense have a high degree of political rights and civil liberties. Those classified as 'partly free' tend to be average to just below average in political rights and civil liberties. Those classified as 'not free' tend to be quite low in both political rights and civil liberties. Examples of countries in each classification: Free – Australia, Bahamas, Belgium, Canada, Chile, Czech Republic, Estonia, Japan, South Africa, South Korea; Partly Free – Brazil, Burkino Faso, Cambodia, Malaysia, Mexico; Not Free – Algeria, China, Egypt, Ethiopia, Iraq, Kenya, North Korea, Nigeria, Saudi Arabia

SOURCE: Original art based on Freedom House survey. Adrian Karatnycky, *Freedom in the World* (New York: Freedom House, 1995).

The problem is that many of the democracies that have emerged since the early 1970s are fragile and are confronted by challenges to stability and cohesiveness. These stem from internal division, corruption, militaries, and oligarchies (ruling power in the hands of a few), and destabilisation from abroad. Although there is a certain euphoria in the number of democracies that have surfaced, there is still concern over whether or not all of them will continue along the path to freedom in political rights and civil liberties.

Although pure democracy does not exist in modern countries, there are various forms of representative government in which citizens vote for individuals to represent them and make collective decisions. Voting eligibility may be based on gender, religious affiliation, the attainment of a certain minimum age, or racial classifications. In South Africa, for example, the policy of apartheid resulted in only 12,6% of the population being eligible to vote. In April 1994, after the fall of apartheid and the rise of new labour parties, a coalition government was elected with whites and blacks ruling together. The interim constitution guaranteed 'equality between men and women and people of all races, thus opening up the vote to all'.[8] It is interesting to note that Freedom House now classifies South Africa as 'free' and improving its political rights and civil liberties, an improvement over its previous position as 'partly free'. In some democracies, such as the United States, voting is optional; in others, such as Australia and Belgium, it is mandatory.

One form of democracy is parliamentary government, an excellent example of which is found in the United Kingdom. The United Kingdom is divided into geographical districts, and a representative is elected to represent each district in the House of Commons. General elections must be held at least every five years. After a general election, the monarch asks the leader of the party that has the majority of seats in the House of Commons, to form a government. The party with the second-largest number of seats becomes the opposition. Other parties can align with either the majority party or the opposition party. The members of each party select the person who leads that party. The leader of the majority party becomes the prime minister and selects a cabinet.

Although the people vote for their representatives in the House of Commons, also known as the members of parliament (MPs), the MPs select their own leader, who becomes the prime minister. In November 1990, the Conservative Party in the UK, with Margaret Thatcher as prime minister, was undergoing turmoil, so the Conservative MPs held an election to select their leader, and Thatcher did not have enough votes to continue. On the second ballot, John Major was elected as prime minister. In April 1992, a general election was held, and the Conservatives won a majority of the seats in Parliament, so Major carried on as prime minister. He was not directly elected by the people to be prime minister, but he did have to win re-election as an MP in his own district.[9]

The French form of parliamentary government involves the direct election of a president who is in power for seven years and selects a premier and, upon the recommendation of the premier, a Council of Ministers. A parliament composed of a National Assembly elected by the people, and a Senate selected by the National Assembly, are responsible for legislation. Despite having a parliament, France has a system of government more like that of the United States than that of the United Kingdom. For example, like the American system, the French system separates the executive and legislative branches.

To illustrate the French process, the French elections for President were held on 23 April and 7 May, 1995. Because there were so many candidates, a president was not elected on the first ballot. Lionel Jospin won 23% of the vote, Jacques Chirac won 21% and the rest of the votes were split among several other candidates. On the second ballot, however, only

Jospin and Chirac were on the ballot, being the two highest vote-getters on the first ballot. Chirac won the presidency with 53% of the vote.[10]

In most democratic countries, multiple political parties may participate in the election process. Many democracies have only a few dominant parties, so usually it is not difficult for them to form a government. The exceptions to this are Italy and Israel, in which there are so many political parties that the government in power is usually a minority government formed from a coalition of several minority parties. In these countries, whenever a vote of no confidence is taken, a new coalition must be formed before a new government can be formed. In 1996, the Israelis changed their election procedures and went to a direct vote for prime minister for the first time, rather than automatically have the head of the party that can make a coalition work as the prime minister. In a run-off election, Benjamin Netanyahu was elected prime minister over Shimon Peres by the slimmest of margins, but he still won a majority of the votes. This allowed him to rule without having to form tricky coalitions with smaller, but even more radical, parties.[11]

The United States is an example of a country that elects its president by a plurality vote of the electoral college instead of a majority vote. In 1984, Ronald Reagan was elected president with 59,2% of the popular vote; in 1988 George Bush was elected with 53,9% of the vote but, in 1992, Bill Clinton was elected with only 43% of the vote. In that election, Ross Perot won 18,9% of the vote as an Independent, making it virtually impossible for either Clinton or Bush to win a majority of votes. If the system was the same as that in France, a run-off election between Clinton and Bush would have had to be held within a few weeks of the first ballot.

In some democracies, a single dominant party controls political power, such as in Mexico. Mexico has been ruled by one political party, the Institutional Revolutionary Party (PRI), since it acquired its independence from Spain. Its members are Mexico's elite, who are the most educated and the most experienced in government. The PRI does not have a particularly ideological thrust; it is mainly interested in keeping the country together. In 1994, however, the PRI faced severe difficulties because the hand-picked president was assassinated during campaigns, and another leader of the PRI was also assassinated. In the murder conspiracy, the brother of the sitting president was implicated, throwing the PRI into even more turmoil. And even though Mexico is considered to be a democracy, it is ranked only as 'partly free' due to the relative power of the PRI and concern about the lack of political freedom, as well as, to a lesser extent, the abuse of civil liberties. Ernesto Sedillo of the PRI was elected president in 1995, and he has moved ahead with electoral reforms to try to eliminate some of the abuses of the past, especially at state and local levels. However, he has to deal with decades of graft and corruption, so change will not come easily.

Hong Kong is an interesting example of a quasi-democracy. Prior to the takeover by China, Freedom House classified Hong Kong as a partly free, related territory rather than as a free country. The British Parliament had served as the democratic check against any governor who was selected by the Queen. However, the Chinese residents of Hong Kong had little real democratic power because, although freedom of expression was guaranteed, freedom to select the government did not exist. Hong Kong's status should slip in future Freedom House surveys, because the Chinese government has made it very clear that freedom of expression in Hong Kong will be curtailed after 1 July 1997, and democratic institutions put into place by former Governor Patton will not be allowed to continue.

Democracies differ not only in the amount of citizen participation in decision-making, but also in the degree of centralised control. Canada, for example, gives significant political power to the provinces at the expense of its federal government. Thus a major difficulty in negotiating the Canada-USA Free Trade Agreement (FTA) was that many provinces had their own trade barriers that had to be considered. The provincial power and concern about lack of safeguards for French-speaking Canadians were two factors leading to the 1995 vote in Canada on whether or not to allow citizens of the province of Quebec to leave Canada and form their own country. Although the unity side won the election by 50,6% to 49,9% (only 53 498 votes), it was clear that Canadians are deeply concerned about the nature of their federal system and the role of the French-speaking province of Quebec.[12]

Democracy is being radically affected by technology through the Internet. The essence of politics is communication, and the Internet has made communicating much easier and cheaper. Government documents that used to be available only on hard copy or CD-ROM, are now available on the Internet. Lobbying groups can easily set up distribution lists for sending out information quickly and cheaply. Elected representatives can now communicate faster and more cheaply with their constituents. President Clinton averaged 1 000-2 000 e-mail messages daily in 1995, making him the world's most e-mailed person. He relies on e-mail and other messages from external constituents as part of the interest articulation and interest aggregation process, whereas his predecessor, President Bush, only received on average 800 messages daily.[13] The information flow to the President is increasing at a rapid rate, and electronic mail is an important component of that flow. Not only are companies using the Internet to get their message across to potential investors and customers, but politicians and lobbyists are doing so as well. The Internet will not replace elected representatives, because democracy still needs specialists who can interpret and compromise, but the Internet makes it easier to find the information on which to base an informed decision, and it allows the American Congress to keep more in touch with constituents.

(c) Totalitarianism

Democracy is at one end of the politic spectrum, and totalitarianism is at the othe As noted in Exhibit 4.2 (p. 106), totalitarianis takes several forms, including authoritaria ism, communism, and fascism. Mussoli defined the fascist side of authoritarianism a follows: 'The Fascist conception of the state i all-embracing; outside of it no human c spiritual value may exist, much less have an value. Thus understood, Fascism is totalitaria and the Fascist State, as a synthesis and a un which includes all values, interprets, develop and lends additional power to the whole life of people'.[14] In a totalitarian state, a single part individual, or group of individuals monopolise political power and neither recognises n permits opposition. Only a few individua participate in decision-making. One famou construct of totalitarianism contains the fo lowing six interdependent components or syn dromes: 'an ideology, a single party typically le by one man, a terroristic police, a communica tion monopoly, a weapons monopoly, and centrally directed economy',[15] In Exhibit 4.3(107), totalitarian regimes are in the 'partly fre and 'not free' categories.

Totalitarian governments typically take on of two forms: theocratic or secular. In the cratic totalitarianism, religious leaders are als the political leaders. This form is best exempl fied in Middle-Eastern Islamic countries such a Iran. In secular totalitarianism, the gover ment often imposes order through milita power and is based on worldly rather tha religious concepts. Examples of this form ar found in Cambodia and Iraq.

Looking at totalitarianism slightly diffe ently, Exhibit 4.2 (p. 106) defines totalitaria ism as being authoritarian, fascist, or comm nist. Examples of fascist totalitarianism in th past include Germany, Hungary, Romani Portugal, and Spain. Examples of communis include China, Cuba, Vietnam, and the forme Soviet Union. Examples of authoritarian total tarianism include Chile under Pinochet, an South Africa prior to the end of apartheid an the initiation of Black rule. Authoritarianism differs from communism, fascism, or Islamic fundamentalism in that the former simply wants to rule people, whereas the latter want to control people's minds and souls, to convert them to their own faith.[16]

Communism is a form of secular totalitarianism. Under communism, the political and economic systems are virtually inseparable. According to Karl Marx, the 19th-century German philosopher and political economist who founded world communism, economic forces determine the course taken by a society. He predicted that the capitalist societies would eventually be overcome by two types of revolution – political and social. The political revolution would precede and ignite the social revolution, which would be a long-term transformation based largely on eliminating economic inequities. This social revolution would be guided by what Marx called a dictatorship of the proletariat, that is, the working class. In theory, the proletariat dictatorship would remain in power only long enough to smooth the transition to communism. The government would be responsible for organising society into groups in order to obtain as much input as possible for the decision-making process. Then, as the social revolution neared completion, the dictatorship would disappear and full communism would take its place.

Even casual observation reveals that real-world communism has differed markedly from theoretical communism. Marx's concept of democratic centralism gave way to totalitarian or autocratic centralism, with no general participation in decision-making, especially from those with opposing viewpoints. In recent years communism has been discredited in most parts of the world. The Eastern European countries and the former Soviet Union have moved away from communism to various degrees. And, as communism moves toward democracy, the link between economics and politics in communist countries has been weakened, making it possible for there to be 'free' communist countries such as Estonia, Latvia and Lithuania. China, North Korea, and Vietnam, however, are still communist countries with strong centralised authoritarian control over the political process.

Totalitarian regimes fit primarily in the 'not free' category in Exhibit 4.3 (p. 107). Freedom House notes that 90% of the 'not free' countries share one or more of the following characteristics:

1 they have a majority Muslim population and frequently confront the pressures of fundamentalist Islam;
2 they are multi-ethnic societies in which power is not held by a dominant ethnic group (one that represents more than two-thirds of the population);
3 they are neo-communist or post-communist transitional societies.[17]

In fact, it is not uncommon to find at least two of these characteristics present in 'not free' countries. For example, it is common for politicians in formerly totalitarian (including former communist) countries to appeal to ethnic, religious, and racial differences to gain votes. This is very divisive and runs the risk of reverting to totalitarianism. Rwanda and Somalia are other examples of 'not free' countries torn apart by ethnic strife.

Although some would argue that Islamic fundamentalism is a growing force for totalitarianism, there is no evidence that a single, unified, fundamentalist movement will ever take place. Some of the countries where Islamic fundamentalism is growing, such as Algeria and maybe Saudi Arabia, are 'not free' for other reasons. Islamic fundamentalism is trying to replace a more secular totalitarianism, but is not having a great deal of success on a broad scale. The Islamic movement has turned out to be several different movements, often sowing seeds of conflict within nations, as well as across them. As noted by one expert, 'In many cases, tensions between Islamists are greater than the conflict between them and the government they oppose'.[18]

4.3.2 The impact of the political system on management decisions

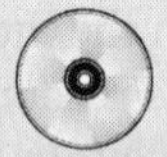

Compact disc

1 Mr Trevor Manuel gives a political perspective of FDI.

Every political system struggles with the balance between decentralised decision-making by individuals and centralised regulation and control of decisions by governments. Even democratic governments are faced with this dichotomy, but it is creating great conflict in the former totalitarian states of Eastern Europe and the former Soviet Union as their political systems evolve toward democracy and their economic systems move toward free-market economies.

Managers must deal with varying degrees of government intervention and, as was brought out in the Hong Kong case, varying degrees of political stability. To do so, they must understand the critical functions that a democratic government performs in the economy. For example:

1 It protects the liberty of its citizens;
2 It promotes the common welfare of its citizens;
3 It provides for public goods such as national defence and transportation and communications systems;
4 It handles market deficiencies such as entry barriers and insufficient consumer knowledge and power;
5 It deals with spillover effects and externalities.[19]

One type of public good whose development currently is under debate in many industrial countries is an information highway, a mechanism for the rapid, widespread transmittal of electronic data. Market deficiencies are barriers to the efficient and effective running of a market economy. They interfere with the supply of and demand for products, and with the ability of consumers to make rational choices. Examples of spillover effects are the many developments and applications that have commercial uses which the private sector can exploit. An example of a spillover effect is the American Air Force's Global Positioning System, which is composed of the linkage of personal computers with 24 satellites equally divided among six orbits. The satellites emit a radio signal that can be used to determine the location of the receiver within 20 to 300 metres of its exact position. The system is now available for civilian uses such as air-traffic control, wilderness search and rescue, car dashboard navigation systems, and truck-fleet management.[20] Externalities refer to by-products of the manufacturing process, such as pollution. Some governments largely ignore polluting externalities in the name of economic development, whereas others control pollution very carefully.

The political process also affects international business through laws that regulate business activity at both the domestic and international levels. Governments may deal with international transactions on a unilateral basis or through treaties and conventions. An MNE must be concerned with the laws in its home country that regulate cross-border transactions and must also understand legal requirements in each country in which it operates.

In addition to understanding government functions, managers must realise that government action is not always consistent. In the United States government, for example, significant conflict exists within government regarding how and to what extent international business activities should be regulated. There is no specific government agency which deals with international issues, so conflicting policies can be expected. For example, at least three different government agencies share responsibility for regulating non-agricultural exports: the State Department, the Department of Defence, and the Department of Commerce.

The State Department is responsible for the overall political relationships between the United States and other countries; Defence is responsible for national defence, and Commerce is responsible for facilitating commercial activities, including exports. These agencies also have three different viewpoints on how to regulate exports. For example, the Clinton Administration announced in 1993 that it intended to remove most of the restrictions on the sale of high-technology products, especially computers, that have possible uses for defence. Commerce and State had always favoured liberalising such restrictions, whereas Defence had always supported them.[21]

4.3.3 Formulating and implementing political strategies

Formulating political strategies is often more complicated than formulating competitive market-place strategies. Non-market issues attract different participants to market issues. In addition, important components of political strategies are implemented in public view – such exposure can constrain the actions of companies. Further, the logic of collective and political action is different from that of market action. Unlike market issues, which are resolved by voluntary agreements, political issues are resolved by institutions that have the power to compel action, regulate activities, and structure the conditions under which market participants operate.[22]

Political action is always a sensitive area. However, there are certain steps that a company must follow if it wants to establish an appropriate political strategy:

1 Identify the issue. What is the specific issue facing a firm: protectionism, environmental standards, worker rights?
2 Define the nature of the politics of the issue.
3 Assess the potential political action of other companies and of special interest groups. Who are the parties that are affected and able to generate political pressure? What are their strategies likely to be?
4 Identify important institutions and key individuals, legislatures, regulatory agencies, courts, and important personalities.
5 Formulate strategies. What are the key objectives, the major alternatives, and the likely effectiveness of alternative strategies?
6 Determine the impact of implementation. What will the public relations fallout be in the home and host countries if the action taken is unpopular?
7 Select the most appropriate strategy and implement it.[23]

Implementing a strategy involves marshalling whatever resources are necessary to accomplish the company's political objectives. In the United States, lobbyists are hired by a company, whether domestic or foreign, to educate and persuade decision-makers with regard to the merits of the company's position. However, there has been heavy criticism of the practice of hiring lobbyists who have recently departed from the government agency that is likely to take action against that company. On the other hand, lobbyists also perform an important role in communicating ideas to decision-makers. In a representative democracy, lobbyists represent constituencies and perform the important role of aggregating ideas and communicating them to decision-makers. Without the freedom of expression, democracy could not exist. Since the ethical dimensions of government/business relationships have gained prominence even in relatively totalitarian countries, companies have greater reason to examine their policy formulation and implementation strategies very carefully.

A company can also try to influence government action from the bottom up by using a grass-roots campaign, or by building coalitions of different groups that share the company's interests. For example, to fight trade protectionism in South Africa in the form of tariffs or quotas on imported motor cars, foreign car manufacturers might try to convince consumers that, as a result of such actions, they would be worse off because of higher prices or reduced availability.

Part of the problem with establishing a political strategy is that democracies deal with companies differently to totalitarian regimes. Democracies can generally be influenced through lobbying. However, companies sometimes abuse their power by engaging in bribery and other illicit activities. In a totalitarian regime, companies usually operate in a more stable environment. However, when such a regime is overthrown, the changes for business tend to be greater and more rapid than change typically is within a democracy. For example, when the Soviet Union broke up, companies that had entered into contracts with the former central government found that these contracts were not binding on the governments of the individual republics.

4.4 The legal environment

Closely related to the political system is the legal system, which is another dimension of the external environment that influences business. Managers must be aware of the legal systems in the countries in which they operate, the nature of the legal profession, both domestic and international, and the legal relationships that exist between countries. Both totalitarian and democratic countries have legal systems, but the independence of the law from political control may differ markedly from one to the other. In addition, some totalitarian systems, notably that of China, are not well equipped to deal with market economies in a legal sense, primarily because their legal system does not provide for issues that arise in such an economic environment.

4.4.1 Kinds of legal systems

Legal systems usually fall into one of three categories: common law, civil law and theocratic law. The United States and the United Kingdom are examples of countries with a common law system. Common law is based on tradition, precedent, and custom and usage, and the courts fulfil an important role in interpreting the law according to those characteristics. Because the United Kingdom originated common law in the modern setting, its former and current colonies, such as Hong Kong, also have common law systems.

The civil law system, also called a codified legal system, is based on a very detailed set of laws that are organised into a code which is the foundation for doing business. More than 70 countries, including Germany, France, and Japan, operate on a civil law basis.

The two legal systems differ primarily in that common law is based on the courts' interpretations of events, whereas civil law is based on how the law is applied to the facts. An example of an area in which the two systems differ in practice is contracts. In a common law country, contracts tend to be very detailed, with all contingencies spelled out. In a civil law country, contracts tend to be shorter and less specific, because many of the issues that a common law contract would cover are already included in the civil code. Civil law also tends to be less adversarial than common law, since judges rely on detailed legal codes rather than on precedent. This is one reason why British and American law firms encounter so much resistance when they enter civil law countries. They are used to the competitive, adversarial approach that the common law system engenders – an approach that tends to shake up the more orderly systems.

The third type of legal system is the theocratic law system, which is based on religious precepts. The best example of this system is the Islamic one, which is found in Muslim countries. Islamic law, known as Shair'a, is based on the following sources:

- the Koran, the sacred text;
- the Sunnah, or decisions and sayings of the Prophet Muhammad;
- the writings of Islamic scholars, who derive rules by analogy from the principles established in the Koran and the Sunnah;
- the consensus of the legal communities in Muslim countries.[24]

Since the 10th century AD, Islamic law has been frozen; in other words, it cannot be changed, modified or extended, even though conditions have changed significantly. Islamic law is a moral rather than a commercial law, and was intended to govern all aspects of life. Many Muslim countries have legal systems that are a unique blend of the Islamic law system and a common or civil law system derived from previous colonial ties.

An example of how Islamic law influences business can be found in banking. According to Islamic law, banks cannot charge or benefit from interest, which is viewed as usury, and investments in commodities such as alcohol or tobacco are forbidden.[25] There are approximately a hundred banks worldwide that offer Islamic banking, including the multinationals, Citibank and Barclays. The Malaysian government, in an attempt to bring more Muslim Malays into the economic system, announced in 1993 that all commercial banks should offer Islamic banking services. However, it is sometimes difficult to determine just what Islamic banking involves. There is no uniform Islamic-correct formula to structure leasing and other products which take into account issues such as inflation, the rising costs of imported equipment, and exchange rate fluctuations.[26] Malaysia, though, is considered to be at the forefront of Islamic banking, with more than 30 institutions offering Islamic banking services by late 1995.[27]

More conservative Muslim countries such as Saudi Arabia also interpreted the Shair'a to mean that equity investments were not permitted, presumably because of the fear that many companies were involved with non-Islamic practices, such as commerce, the sale of alcohol, and paying or receiving interest. Not all Islamic countries held the same view, however. Malaysia has a much more relaxed interpretation of the Shair'a, and the Islamic banking services mentioned above include investment banking as well. In 1994, however, the Islamic jurisprudence academy in Saudi Arabia issued a decree that permitted equity investment within certain parameters, such as in screened mutual funds involving companies that avoid non-Islamic activities, and the requirement that investors subtract from dividends any interest earned by the company from money on deposit. This interest is then donated to charities. As a result, a number of Islamic investment funds have been established, including funds initiated by Western banks.[28] Because of Islamic law's prohibitions against interest, those Muslims who save in these banks are paid a share of the profits made by the bank that uses the funds. The profit share is roughly the same as the current interest rate.[29]

Regardless of the legal system, the practice of law can be divided into criminal and civil. Although business practices can be found to violate criminal law, business issues are more commonly considered in the context of civil law. A study of civil law cases in the United States found that most of them involved small claims, divorces, and wills; only 14% involved contracts and 10% involved torts. Torts are wrongful acts; many tort cases are product-liability ones, in which an injured person tries to recover money for damages that are economic (such as medical expenses and lost wages), or non-economic (such as pain and suffering). The number of suits involving torts has increased dramatically in the United States for a variety of reasons. Almost unique characteristics of the American legal system are that

- lawyers take contingency fees (fees determined by a percentage of the final judgment if the case is won);
- groups can file class action lawsuits;
- pre-trial 'discovery' requires the submission of volumes of information by both sides;
- juries, rather than judges, decide cases and set damages.[30]

The cost of torts in the United States has reached 2,4% of the GNP, compared with between 0,4% and 0,8% of the GNP for most other industrialised countries.

Different legal systems provide various safeguards for consumers. For example, it appears that consumers have less access to and assistance from the legal community in Japan than in the United States. The United States has 312 lawyers per 100 000 of population, compared with only 101,6 lawyers per 100 000 in Japan. Also, the Japanese legal system differs from the USA in that legal prices are set by the Japanese Federation of Bar Associations, foreign lawyers are prohibited from advising on local law or hiring domestic lawyers to do so, and consumer information about legal services is limited by advertising restrictions. In addition, in Japan consumers are discouraged from filing civil suits because of the high cost of legal services and the long delays in the legal process. A survey of 194 big Japanese manufacturers found that only 24 had ever faced a product-liability suit at home and, of those, only seven had lost. Further, one motor car manufacturing company had been hit with 250 product-liability suits a year in the United States and only two in Japan.[31] Thus it appears that in Japan consumers have less legal protection and corporations have fewer legal problems than is the case in the United States.

4.4.2 The legal profession

Recently, discussion has increasingly focused on the growing number of lawyers and their impact on the world economy. MNEs have to use lawyers for a variety of services, such as negotiating contracts and protecting intellectual property. Lawyers and their firms practise law and service clients in different ways from one country to another.

Law firms that service international clients have changed over the years. Law firms are generally quite small. In the United Kingdom and the United States, for example, 60% of lawyers are in firms of five persons or fewer.[32] Although the business expansion in the 1960s and 1970s, especially in the area of mergers and acquisitions, led to the establishment of larger law firms, the 1980s slowdown in the world's economy resulted in a subsequent shrinking in firm size. There are still large firms servicing multinational clients, but many MNEs, concerned about upward-spiralling legal fees, have established their own in-house legal staffs and begun to rely on outside firms primarily for specialised work. However, smaller companies involved in international business still rely on outside legal counsel for help with a wide variety of issues, such as agent/distributor relationships and the protection of intellectual property.

Just as MNEs have invested abroad to take advantage of expanding business opportunities, law firms have expanded abroad to service their clients. Laws vary from country to country, and legal staffs need to understand local practices. There has definitely been an expansion of legal services across national boundaries, even though law firms have had to overcome significant barriers as they have expanded abroad. These barriers include restrictions on foreign firms hiring local lawyers, forming partnerships with local law firms, or even entering the country to practise law.

4.4.3 Legal issues in international business

National laws affect how critical elements of the management process are performed. They can relate to business within the country or business with other countries. Some national laws on local business activity influence both domestic and foreign companies, such as in the areas of health and safety standards, employment practices, antitrust prohibitions, contractual relationships, environmental practices, and patents and trademarks. There are also laws that govern cross-border activities, such as the investment of capital, the repatriation of earnings, and customs duties on imports. Business activity is governed by international laws as well, such as treaties governing the cross-border transfer of hazardous waste.

Several subsequent chapters discuss legal issues in international business, such as different laws for the regulation of trade and investments, taxes, intellectual-property pro-

:ection, regulation of financial flows and own-ership, reporting requirements, contractual relationships, extraterritoriality, international treaties, and dispute resolution.

4.5 Evolution of legal and political strategies in the internationalisation process

Companies deal with political and legal issues at different levels as they become more international. If a company selects exporting as the mode of entry, management is not as concerned with the political process, or with the variety of legal issues, as would be the case with a foreign direct investment. There are laws that relate to international trade, both at the export country level (such as with the export of defence-related products to an enemy), and the import country level (such as tariffs and quotas on imports), and also concern themselves with laws dealing with distributor relationships and the settlement of disputes. The political process can have a direct impact on the company, but home-country management is usually fairly removed from that process. Since it has not committed significant assets to the foreign country, it is not quite as affected by political decisions as it would be if it had established a foreign investment.

A major exception is companies that generate a significant percentage of their earnings from exports. In the past two decades, there has been a lot of pressure on the foreign motor car industry to reconsider its strategy to capture the market in the USA completely through exports. As a result, many exporters, such as Honda and Toyota, have invested significant assets in the United States as a way of mitigating the impact of tariffs and quotas on their market share, thus helping to preserve jobs in the USA.

As the company penetrates the foreign environment in increasingly more complex ways, such as through foreign direct investment, political and legal issues become more complex as well. For example, Japanese engaging in foreign direct investment in the United States may be questioned about their lobbying efforts, and they also have to worry about another set of laws, such as equal employment laws, gender discrimination, etc.

From a political point of view, foreign investors need to be concerned about the impact of their investment on the local environment and figure out how to work with local and national government officials and agencies. In more traditional societies, where democracy is not firmly entrenched, they have to be more aware of the importance of contacts and influence, and the possibility that they will be asked to behave in ways inconsistent with the way they behave in their own political and legal context, or in ways that might even be illegal.

Thus, as the degree of internationalisation increases, the nature, complexity, and breadth of the company's political and legal interactions also increase. Politics clearly affect corporate strategies through national policies and government influence on cross-border transactions. Because of differences in national laws, legal practices are multidomestic. It is, therefore, essential to acquire good legal counsel in the countries in which a company does business. Global legal firms provide legal assistance for MNEs doing business in different parts of the world, but their value is in having good lawyers in different countries, rather than a few lawyers who understand all laws in all countries.

Some legal issues, however, are cross-border in nature. A good example is the protection of intellectual property. Although each country has its own intellectual property laws, most countries are signatories to cross-national treaties and conventions that allow firms to acquire widespread protection for intellectual property. It is important to note that there are international agreements for such protection, such as the Paris Convention and the Trade-related Aspects of Intellectual Property Rights (TRIPs) Agreement of the World Trade Organisation. There are also regional agreements, such as those that are part of the European Union and the North American Free Trade Agreement. Thus companies can establish multidomestic strategies on protecting intellectual property, or they can use legal experts who are familiar with the appropriate cross-national treaties and conventions to establish global or regional strategies.

Differences in legal and political systems drive companies toward multidomestic or transnational rather than global strategies. Local differences require managers to make adjustments in virtually all areas of business, including marketing, finance, and human resources. Both political and legal dimensions are at the heart of sovereignty. Smaller countries are very concerned that they could be dominated politically by larger countries, and have tried to protect their interests against the larger countries with international trade agreements, such as the European Union and the North American Free Trade Agreement. This has been true, for example, of Denmark within the EU. In fact, Denmark nearly left the EU because it feared too many decisions affecting Danish individuals and companies would be made by EU bureaucrats.

Countries prefer to have their own laws enforced on their own soil. This is problematic for foreign companies, whose managers and workers might not understand local laws. Whether or not they have such an understanding, they usually have to use local courts to resolve local disputes. A country that tries to enforce its laws in another country through extraterritoriality threatens that other country's national sovereignty, and such action is usually met with significant resistance. As a counterbalance to sovereignty, treaties and conventions can modify or set aside national laws. The very purpose of treaties is to subjugate national law to the greater good of the group of countries that have signed a treaty. If no national laws were changed, treaties would not be needed. However, because treaties moderate sovereignty, they are difficult to implement.

4.6 The future political situation

What will happen to the political situation in the world? Will democracy continue to grow, or will authoritarianism creep back? Winston Churchill once said that democracy is the worst form of government, except for all the others. The next decade will test whether this hypothesis is true. The issue between democracy and totalitarianism is two-pronged. The first concern is whether the 40 or so countries that have become democratic in the past two decades will remain democratic or slip back into totalitarianism. The second is what path the next wave of 'not free' and 'partly free' countries will take as they develop economically.

Some argue that the movement toward democracy involves preconditions, such as economic development. Most non-oil-producing, high-income or upper-middle-income countries are democratic, whereas most of the remaining non-democracies are poor, non-Western, or both.[33] Others argue that democracy is the product of political leaders with the will and skill to see democratisation occur.[34] Some would argue that the move toward democracy in Russia occurred because of two men: Mikhail Gorbachev and Boris Yeltsin. When Gorbachev went as far as he could, Yeltsin was there to take the next steps. After Yeltsin, someone else will hopefully fill the void and take Russia to the next democratic plateau, although there is no guarantee that Russia will continue to democratise, or that Yeltsin's replacement, and those who support him or her, will continue to support the trend toward greater democracy. In reality, the movement toward democracy may require both preconditions and vision.

Democracy does not necessarily mean stability. In many elections in 1996, such as the one in Israel described earlier in the chapter and in India as well, established leaders were thrown out and new ones ushered in. The newer democracies are still unstable enough to possibly threaten war. A war between two democracies has not broken out in this century but this could happen as the new democracies try to find their way. In addition, some countries, such as Zambia, are backing away from experiments in liberal democracy and its freedoms.

There is an alternative to democracy that is being tested in Asia. With the exception of Japan, and to a lesser extent India, most Asian countries are not democracies, and their leaders do not appear to want democracy. Instead, they are attempting to forge a link between strong economic growth and totalitarian political systems. This is clearly the case with China, and to only a slightly lesser extent in Singapore. However, there are encouraging signs for those who favour increased democracy, such as the elections in Taiwan that nudged that island nation closer to democracy and farther away from the autocratic policies of the past and also from the encroachment of the People's Republic of China. The key at the present time is to consolidate the gains of democracy, and help the fledgling democracies of Eastern Europe, Africa, and Latin America strengthen their political rights and civil liberties. In some respects, the elimination of strong central controls with the advent of democracy has created problems in terms of ethnic, tribal, religious, and other constituencies, and the removal of individual moral constraints has resulted in crime, corruption, and an atmosphere of amorality.[35] The threat to democracy could come from the return to communism, from the electoral victory of antidemocratic forces (such as Islamic fundamentalism), or from the concentration of power in a leader. The latter seems to be the approach in many of the countries of East Asia. It will therefore be necessary to define democracy in different national contexts.

4.7 Ethical dilemmas in global business

Ethical dilemmas involve a balancing of means and ends. Means refer to the actions that are taken, which may be right or wrong; ends have to do with the results of the actions, which may also be right or wrong. Ethics teach that 'people have a responsibility to do what is right and to avoid doing what is wrong'.[36] Questions of right and wrong refer to intentions, which are a function of the various cultural issues that were discussed in Chapter 3. Some people argue that cultural relativism, or the belief that behaviour has meaning only in its specific cultural or ethical context, implies that there is no specific method for deciding whether behaviour is appropriate. However, the authors contend that individuals must seek justification for their behaviour, and justification is a function of cultural values (many of which are universal), legal principles, and economic practices.

Some people also argue that the legal justification for ethical behaviour is the only important one. According to this standard, a person or company can do anything that is not illegal. However, there are five reasons why the legal argument is insufficient:

1 The law is not appropriate for regulating all business activity because not everything that is unethical is illegal. This would be true of many dimensions of interpersonal behaviour, for example.
2 The law is slow to develop in emerging areas of concern. Laws take time to be legislated and tested in courts. Further, they cannot anticipate all future ethical dilemmas; basically, they are a reaction to issues that have already surfaced. Countries with civil law systems rely on specificity in the law, and there may not be enough laws actually passed that deal with ethical issues.
3 The law is often based on moral concepts that are not precisely defined and cannot be separated from legal concepts. Thus moral concepts must be considered along with legal ones.
4 The law is often in need of testing by the courts. This is especially true of case law, in which the courts establish a precedent.
5 The law is not very efficient. A reliance on legal rulings on every area of ethical

behaviour would not be in anyone's best interests.[37]

In spite of the pitfalls of using the law as the major basis for deciding ethical disputes, there also are good reasons for at least complying with it:

1 The law embodies many of a country's moral beliefs and is thus an adequate guide for proper conduct.
2 The law provides a clearly defined set of rules. Following those rules at least establishes a good precedent. Some are afraid to go beyond the law because of the potential legal liability that could result if they did.
3 The law contains enforceable rules that everyone must follow; each person is on an equal footing. Thus, everyone working for a company established in the United States must comply with the *Foreign Corrupt Practices Act*, which prohibits bribery of foreign government officials for business benefit. As long as everyone complies with the law, no one will have an edge due to bribery. Still, laws are subject to interpretation and often contain loopholes.
4 The law represents a consensus derived from significant experience and deliberation. It should reflect careful and wide-ranging discussions.[38]

The problem for companies that use a legal basis for ethical behaviour is that laws differ between countries. For example, a major area of contention between industrialised and developing countries during the GATT Uruguay Round was the protection of intellectual property, such as computer software. The industrial countries, which have strong laws concerning intellectual property rights, argued that developing countries need to strengthen such laws and their enforcement. American software manufacturers have noted that in some Asian countries it is possible to buy a heavily discounted pirated version of new software in one store and then go next door and purchase a photocopy of the documentation for the software. Using a legal basis for ethical behaviour would mean that such purchases are ethical because they occur in countries that either do not have laws on intellectual property rights or do not enforce such laws. Although the Agreement on Trade-Related Aspects of Intellectual Property Rights (TRIPs) of the World Trade Organisation, which came about as a result of the Uruguay Round of GATT, provides for better protection of intellectual property, it is up to the member countries to implement the provisions, but this is proceeding at a very slow rate in those countries that are the traditional violators of intellectual property.

One could argue that the moral values that cross cultures will be embodied in legal systems but, as in the software example, that is too simplistic. Not all moral values are common to every culture. In addition, strong home-country governments may try to extend their legal and ethical practices to the foreign subsidiaries of domestically headquartered companies – an action known as extraterritoriality. For example, a subsidiary of an American company operating in China might be forced to follow some American laws, even though China has no comparable laws and other companies operating there are not subject to the laws of the USA. In some cases, such as with health and safety standards, extraterritoriality should not cause problems. In other cases, such as with restrictions on trade with enemies of the United States, extraterritoriality may cause tension between the foreign subsidiary and the host-country government.

As noted, the law provides a clearly defined set of rules, which companies often follow strictly because of concerns about potential legal liability. However, a company may seek a loophole in order to accomplish some important objective. Evaluating potential liability and legality of actions varies between countries with civil law systems and those with common law systems. Civil law countries tend to have a large body of laws that specify the legality of various behaviours; common law countries tend to rely more on cases and precedents than on statutory regulations. A company must pay attention to laws to ensure the minimum level of compliance in each country in which it operates. When faced with conflicting laws, management must decide which applies. The forces of national sovereignty may encourage managers to follow the adage 'When in Rome, do as the Romans do'.

4.8 Summary

To be successful, managers must learn to deal with public institutions (such as the government, government agencies and government-owned businesses) and non-public institutions (such as environment and other special interest groups) in addition to market forces.

The political process involves inputs from various interest groups, articulation of issues that affect policy formulation, aggregation of those issues into key alternatives, development of policies, and implementation and adjudication of the policies.

Most complex societies are pluralistic; that is, they encompass a variety of ideologies.

The ultimate test of any political system is its ability to hold a society together despite pressures from different ideologies.

In democracies, there is wide participation in the decision-making process; in totalitarian regimes, only a relatively few may participate, although some are beginning to allow greater participation in the decision-making process. Totalitarian regimes can be either secular or theocratic.

Factors considered in measuring freedom include the degree to which fair and competitive elections occur, the extent to which individual and group freedoms are guaranteed, and the existence of freedom of the press.

Managers of MNEs must learn to cope with varying degrees of government intervention in economic decisions, depending on the countries in which a company is doing business.

As governments become more democratic, they influence their citizens and institutions by protecting liberty, promoting the common welfare of citizens, providing for public goods, handling market deficiencies, and dealing with spillover effects and externalities.

The political impact on international business activities is relatively complex because the domestic political process is subject to various influences and managers must deal with various political processes in different countries.

In formulating political strategies, managers must consider the possible political actions that could affect the company, the different constituencies that might influence those political actions, the political strategies that would be in the best interests of the company, and the costs of implementing those strategies.

Common law systems are based on tradition, precedent, and custom and usage. Civil law systems are based on a detailed set of laws organised into a code. Theocratic legal systems are based on religious precepts, as exemplified by Islamic law.

Many law firms have increased their size in order to better service corporate clients in domestic and international mergers and acquisitions.

There are national laws that govern local business activities of both domestic and foreign firms, national laws that govern cross-border activities, and international laws that govern cross-border activities.

The legal environment can influence international companies in various ways; for example, by regulating trade and investment and protecting intellectual property.

Although there is legal justification for some ethical behaviour, the law is not an adequate guide for all such behaviour. The legality of an action is one element that should be considered, but not the only one.

Case Study

Bata Shoes

In 1996 Bata Ltd was struggling to determine its future, both in defining its long-term strategy and in finding a top management team who would move the company into the 21st century. And in doing so, it was being deeply affected by the dramatic political changes taking place in Eastern Europe, South Africa and elsewhere.

As war swept across Europe in 1939, Tom Bata Sr was faced with a difficult situation. His father, who representated the ninth generation of a family of Czechoslovakian shoemakers, had built a worldwide shoe network in 28 countries, using machinery and the mass-production technology of the 1920s. On his father's death, Tom Bata Sr was left with the responsibility of expanding that empire during a period of great political uncertainty worldwide. Because of the Nazi invasion of Czechoslovakia and the uncertain future engendered by the resulting occupation, he sought to preserve his father's business by abandoning his Czechoslovakian operations and emigrating to Canada with a hundred of his managers and their families. His Czech operations were subsequently taken over by the communists after the Second World War.

Since that time, Bata's decision has been ratified through strong growth worldwide. The company is a family-owned business that is the world's largest manufacturer and retailer of footwear. Activities are carried out in over 60 countries on virtually every continent, employing more than 67 000 people worldwide. Bata operates 6 300 company-owned stores worldwide, and has over 100 000 independent retailers and franchisees. It owns over 70 manufacturing units worldwide, including shoe manufacturing plants, engineering plants producing moulds, quality control laboratories, hosiery factories and tanneries. Bata produces about 170 million pairs of shoes annually and sells about 270 million pairs worldwide (see Bata's web page for current information).

It would appear that Bata is a multidomestic company where local managers are free to adjust operating procedures to local environments, within certain parameters. As one outsider noted, 'Wherever you had a strong Czech, you had a strong company. Where you had a lousy Czech, you had a lousy company.' However, Bata's core philosophies and strategies are tightly controlled by Bata himself, who was 82 in 1996. In 1994, he hired the company's first non-family chief executive in an attempt to reinvigorate the paternalistic company, but disagreements over the future of the company forced the resignation of the CEO and two of the top members of his management team in October 1995. In announcing his resignation, the CEO stated that he had tried to balance the strong values of the company with the need for change. But he appeared to have overestimated his ability to operate independently of the family shareholders. As one executive stated, 'Tom Bata is a charismatic personality who exerts an awful lot of personal authority.'

The problem is that the shoe business is changing, and Bata is being affected like any other company. The key to the company's success has traditionally been a low-cost manufacturing base tied to an extensive distribution network. But Nike and Reebok turned the footwear industry into one that was market-driven, instead of manufacturing-driven. Several retail outlets began losing money, and Bata was forced to close down 20% of these in 1995 and 1996.

Although Bata has factories and operations of various forms in many countries, it does not own all of those facilities. Where possible, it owns 100% of them. The governments of some countries, however, require less-than-majority ownership. In some cases, Bata provides licensing, consulting and technical assistance to companies in which it has no equity interest.

The company's strategy for serving world markets is instructive. Some MNEs try to lower costs by achieving economies of scale in production, which means they produce as much as possible in an optimal-sized factory and then serve markets worldwide from that single production facility. Bata serves its different national markets by producing in a given market nearly everything it sells in that market. It does this partly because substantial sales volumes in the countries in which it produces enable it to achieve economies of scale very quickly. It may seem difficult to believe that Bata can always achieve economies of scale, especially since the company has production facilities in some small African nations. However, Bata's management believes that the company can achieve scale economies very easily because its shoe production is a labour-intensive operation. It also tries to buy all its raw materials locally, although this is not always possible, especially in some poorer countries.

Bata also prefers not to export production; when possible, it chooses local production to serve the local market rather than imports. However, sometimes Bata does become entangled with local governments when it imports some raw materials but does not export. In such cases, it must adjust to local laws and requirements for operation.

Bata avoids excessive reliance on exports, partly to reduce its risks. For example, if an importing country were to restrict trade, Bata could possibly lose market opportunity and market share. In addition, Tom Bata noted the benefit to a developing country of not exposing itself to possible protectionism:

> We know very well what kind of a social shock it is when a plant closes in Canada. Yet in Canada we have unemployment insurance and all kinds of welfare operations, and there are many alternative jobs that people can usually go to. In most of the developing countries, on the other hand, it's a question of life and death for these people. They have uprooted themselves from an agricultural society. They've come to a town to work in an industry. They've brought their relatives with them because by working in industry, their earnings are so much higher. Thus a large group of their relatives have become dependent on them and have changed their lifestyle and standard of living. For these people it is a terrible thing to lose a job. And so we are very sensitive to that particular problem.

Bata operates in many different types of economies. It has extensive operations in both industrialised democratic countries and developing countries. However, it was soundly criticised for operating in South Africa and thus tacitly supporting the white minority political regime. It has also been censured for operating in totalitarian regimes, such as that in Chile. In the latter case, Tom Bata countered by pointing out that the company had been operating in Chile for over 40 years, during which time various political regimes had been in power.

Although Bata's local operations have not been nationalised often, the company has had some fascinating experiences with such actions. For example, in Uganda, Bata's local operations were nationalised by Milton Obote, denationalised by Idi Amin, renationalised by Amin, and finally denationalised again by Amin. During that time, the factory continued to operate as if nothing had happened. As Tom Bata explained, 'Shoes had to be bought and wages paid. Life went on. In most cases, the governments concluded it really wasn't in their interest to run businesses, so they cancelled the nationalisation arrangements'.

Despite Bata's ability to operate in any type of political environment, Tom Bata prefers a democratic system. He feels that both democratic and totalitarian regimes are bureaucratic, but a democracy offers the potential to discuss and change procedures, whereas under totalitarianism it is sometimes wisest to remain silent.

Bata has a multifaceted impact on a country. Its product is a necessity, not a luxury. The company's basic strategy is to provide footwear at affordable prices for the largest possible segment of the population. The production of shoes is labour-intensive, so jobs are created, which increases consumers' purchasing power. Although top management may come from outside the country, local management is trained to assume responsibility as quickly as possible. Because the company tries to get most of its raw materials locally, sources of supplies are usually developed. Further, it likes to diversify its purchases, so it usually uses more than one supplier for a given product, which leads to competition and efficiency.

> South Africa presented unique challenges for Bata management. The size of the country's population is just under that of Nigeria, Egypt or Ethiopia. Thus South Africa had long been considered a good place in which to invest because of its large market size. Further, South Africa's per capita GNP was the largest in Africa. However, the country's main attraction was the incredibly high rate of return that companies could earn, which was largely the result of low labour costs and extensive mineral wealth. The large market allowed companies to achieve economies of scale in production while exploiting the low labour costs.

But the situation deteriorated rapidly in the early 1980s. A relatively stagnant economy, political strife resulting from apartheid, including the policy of not granting political freedom and civil liberties to blacks, prompted foreign companies and governments to put pressure on the government for political reforms. The Canadian attitude toward South Africa was very negative. Canada's government issued very conservative voluntary guidelines on new investments in that country. As a result, Bata sold its holdings there in 1986. It did not identify the buyer or the sales price, and denied that apartheid was the reason for pulling out. Company personnel stated, 'It really was a business decision that took into account all of the factors with respect to investment in South Africa at the present time.' Under the terms of the sale, the Bata company name and trademark could no longer be used in South Africa, and all ties with Canadian headquarters were broken. In addition, the new buyer apparently assured that the jobs of the workers, most of whom are black, would be preserved.

Bata also faced problems trying to get back into Slovakia. As noted earlier, the Bata operations had started in the former Czechoslovakia, and as Eastern Europe opened up, they immediately tried to recover lost investments in the Czech Republic and Slovakia. The problem was that the Czech and Slovak governments wanted compensation for the factories, but Tom Bata (known as Tomas Baoa in his homeland) felt the factories were still his. He eventually opened one factory in the Czech Republic and 48 retail outlets where the company sold 3 million pairs of shoes in the first year, capturing 11% of the Czech shoe market.

However, things were not so rosy in Slovakia. Bata said that the problem was that his 'company's former Slovak properties ended up in the hands of the Slovak government, which isn't interested in giving them up'. Instead, he is expected to rebuild his Slovak business using his own resources. He says that he is still waiting for the government to keep the promise it made when his 45 000-employee factory in Slovakia was nationalised. Compensation was promised by the communists but never paid.

The official position of the Czech government is that a new restitution law has been put into effect and that Bata has to raise his ownership claims with the new owner of the factory. If the two parties cannot agree to a joint solution to the problem, Bata is welcome to file a lawsuit against the new owner to be settled in Slovakian courts. Despite his success in the Czech Republic, Bata had not sold one pair of shoes in Slovakia by the beginning of 1996.

? Questions

1 Evaluate the different ways in which Bata has interacted with foreign political systems in its investments and operations abroad.

2 Do you think Bata made the correct decision to pull out of South Africa? How do you think the political events in South Africa in the past few years might change Bata's strategy for South Africa? How should Bata formulate a strategy for determining whether or not to re-enter South Africa?

3 What are the advantages and disadvantages to both Bata and the Republic of Slovakia of having Bata take over his former operations? Why do you think the Czech Republic allowed Bata to re-enter the market, but Slovakia had not, as at the end of 1995? Why do you think Bata is appealing for a political solution to his problems rather than going through the courts to get back his property? What type of political system do the Czech Republic and Slovakia have? How might that help explain Bata's problems?

4 Check the Internet for country pages, the CIA Factbook, or other sources of information on South Africa, the Czech Republic or Slovakia, that will help you understand more about the changing political and economic climates in those countries.

5 Why do you think Tom Bata has joined the list of entrepreneurs who cannot bear to loosen their grip on businesses they started? What is the risk to Bata Ltd if Tom Bata cannot find a way to retire?

Endnotes

1 The material for the case was taken from the following sources:
Walker, D. 1981. 'Shoemaker to the world'. *Executive*, January, pp. 63–69.
Vineberg, G. 1983. 'Bata favors free trade but tempers Asia stance'. *Footwear News*, Vol. 39, No. 24, 13 June, p. 2.
Breskin, I. & Vinesbert, G. 1983. 'Parent Bata looks after far flung footwear family'. *Footwear News*, Vol. 39, No. 23, 6 June, p. 1.
'After Sullivan', *The Economist*, 13 June, 1987, p. 71.
Collison, R. 1990. 'How Bata rules its world', *Canadian Business*, September, pp. 28–34.
Newman, P.C. 1990. 'The return of the native capitalist', *Macleans*, 12 March, p. 53.
Gutner, T. 1990. 'Bringing back Bata', *International Management*, November, pp. 41–43.
'Faded euphoria,' *Fortune*, 1 July, 1991.
'Pulled up by the bootlaces', *Financial Times*, 9 October, 1995, p. 23.
Anderson, J. 1995. 'Bata property still held by Slovak government', *The Prague Post*, 26 July, pp. 1+. Available: NEXIS Library: NEWS: CURNW.;
Simon, B. 1995. 'Bata executives quit in strategy row ...', *Financial Times*, 9 October, p. 25.
Simon, B. 1996. 'Footwear goes out of fashion', *Financial Times*, 6 June, p. 18.

2 Baron, D.P. 1993. *Business and its environment.* Englewood Cliffs, N.J.: Prentice-Hall, pp. 7–9.

3 Almond, G.A. & Powell,G.B. Jr general eds. 1984. *Comparative politics today: A world view.* Boston: Little, Brown. pp. 1-9.

4 Wesson, R. 1985. *Modern government democracy and authoritarianism.* 2nd ed. Englewood Cliffs, N.J.: Prentice-Hall, pp. 41–42.

5 Huntington, S. 1995. 'Democracy for the long haul', *The Strait Times*, 10 September, p. 1. Available: NEXIS Library: News: Curnws.

6 Karatnycky, A. 1995. *Freedom in the world.* New York: Freedom House, pp. 3–5.

7 Ibid., p. 4.

8 'South Africa: The joys of normality', *The Economist*, 20 May, 1995, Survey pp. 1–26.

9 *Europa World Year Book 1995*. London: Europa Publications Limited, pp. 3130–3131.

10 *Europa World Year Book 1996*. London: Europa Publications Limited, pp. 1222–1223.

11 'Netanyahu's day', *The Economist*, 1 June 1996, p. 39.

12 'That's that, until Quebec tries again', *The Economist*, 4 November, 1995, p. 45; 'Canada may be intact, but it is not united; Separatists vow: Until next time', News Services. Available: Nexis Library: NEWS:

13 'Democracy and technology', *The Economist*, 17 June, 1995, pp. 21–23.

14 Piekalkiewics, J. & Penn, A.W. 1995. *Politics of ideocracy* . Albany, New York: State University of New York Press, p. 4.

15 Friedrich, C.J & Brsesinski, S.K. 1964. *Totalitarian dictatorship and autocracy*. New York: Praeger Publishers, as quoted in Piekalkiewics and Penn, p. 9.

16 Piekalkiewics and Penn, op. cit., p. 17.

17 Karatnycky, op. cit., pp. 6–7.

18 Pearl, D. & Dockser, M. A. 1996. 'Political Islam's hope of unified movement has failed to solidify', *The Wall Street Journal*, 3 July, p. A1.

19 Marcus, A.A. 1993. *Business & society: Ethics, government, and the world economy.* Homewood, Ill.: Richard D. Irwin, p. 216.

20 Markoff, J. 1996. 'Finding profit in aiding the lost', *The New York Times*, 15 March, p. D1.

21 Pasztor, A. & Fialka, J.J. 1993. 'Export controls to be relaxed', *Wall Street Journal*, 20 September, p. 2.

22 Baron, op. cit., p. 162.

23 Baron, op. cit., pp. 177–179.

24 August, R. 1993. *International business law: Text, cases, and readings*. Englewood Cliffs, N.J.: Prentice-Hall, p. 51.

25 Sullivan, A. 1993. 'Westerners look at risks and rewards of Islamic banking', *International Herald Tribune*, 30 January, p. 1.

26 Allen, R. 1995. 'In search of an identity', *Financial Times*, 28 November, p. iii.

27 Cooke, K. 1995. 'Two systems exist side by side', *Financial Times*, 28 November, p. iv.

28 Taylor, R. 1996. 'Western funds scent rich rewards in Islam', *The Financial Times*, 13 February, p. 17.

29 'For God and GDP', *The Economist*, 7 August, 1993, pp. 34-35.

30 'Survey: The legal profession', *The Economist*, 18 July , 1992, p. 11.

31 Ibid., p. 14.

32 Ibid., p. 5.

33 Ibid.

34 Ibid.

35 Ibid.

36 Marcus, op. cit., pp. 49–52.

37 Boatright, J.R. 1993. *Ethics and the conduct of business*, Englewood Cliffs, N.J.: Prentice-Hall, pp. 13–16.

38 Ibid., pp. 16–18.

Appendix

Comparative measures of freedom

Country	Political rights	Civil liberties	Country	Political rights	Civil liberties
FREE					
Andorra	1	1	Hungary	1	2
Argentina	2	3	Iceland	1	1
Australia	1	1	Ireland	1	2
Austria	1	1	Liechtenstein	1	1
Bahamas	1	2	Lithuania	1	3
Barbados	1	1	Luxembourg	1	1
Begium	1	1	Malawi	2	3
Belize	1	1	Malta	1	1
Benin	2	3	Marshall Islands	1	1
Bolivia	2	3	Mauritius	1	2
Botswana	2	3	Micronesia	1	1
Bulgaria	2	2	Monaco	2	1
Canada	1	1	Mongolia	2	3
Cape Verde	1	2	Namibia	2	3
Chile	2	2	Naura	1	3
Costa Rica	1	2	Netherlands	1	1
Cyprus	1	1	New Zealand	1	1
Czech Republic	1	2	Norway	1	1
Denmark	1	1	Palau	1	2
Dominica	2	1	Panama	2	3
Ecuador	2	3	Poland	2	2
Estonia	3	2	Portugal	1	1
Finland	1	1	St Kitts & Nevis	2	2
France	1	2	St Lucia	1	2
Germany	1	2	St Vincent & The Grenadines	2	1
Greece	1	3	San Marino	1	1
Grenada	1	2	Sao Tome and Principe	1	2
Guyana	2	2	Slovakia	1	3

NOTE: 1 represents most free and 7 the least free category.

Country	Political rights	Civil liberties	Country	Political rights	Civil liberties
			FREE		
Slovenia	1	2	Kiribati	1	1
Solomon Islands	1	2	Korea, South	2	2
South Africa	2	3	Latvia	3	2
Spain	1	2	Trinidad & Tobago	1	2
Sweden	1	1	Tuvalu	1	1
Switzerland	1	1	United Kingdom	1	2
Israel	1	3	United States	1	1
Italy	1	2	Uruguay	2	2
Jamaica	2	3	Vanuatu	1	3
Japan	2	2	Western Samoa	2	2
			PARTLY FREE		
Albania	3	4	Jordan	4	4
Antigua & Barbados	4	3	Kuwait	5	5
Armenia	3	4	Kyrgyz Republic	2	3
Bangladesh	2	4	Lebanon	6	5
Belarus	4	4	Lesotho	4	4
Brazil	2	4	Macedonia	4	3
Burkina Faso	5	4	Madagascar	2	4
Cambodia	4	5	Malaysia	4	5
Central African Republic	3	4	Mali	2	4
Colombia	3	4	Mexico	4	4
Comoros	4	4	Moldova	4	4
Congo	4	4	Morocco	5	5
Croatia	4	4	Mozambique	3	5
Dominican Republic	4	3	Nepal	3	4
El Salvador	3	3	Nicaragua	4	5
Fiji	4	3	Niger	3	5
Gabon	5	4	Pakistan	3	5
Georgia	5	5	Papua New Guinea	2	4
Ghana	5	4	Paraguay	4	3
Guatemala	4	5	Peru	5	4
Guinea-Bissau	3	4	Philippines	3	4
Haiti	5	5	Romania	4	3
Honduras	3	3	Russia	3	4
India	4	4	Senegal	4	5

Country	Political rights	Civil liberties	Country	Political rights	Civil liberties
PARTLY FREE					
Seychelles	3	4	Turkey	5	5
Singapore	5	5	Uganda	5	5
Sri Lanka	4	5	Ukraine	4	4
Suriname	3	4	Venezuala	4	3
Taiwan (Rep of China)	3	4	Zambia	4	4
Thailand	3	5	Zimbabwe	5	5
Tonga	5	4			
NOT FREE					
Afghanistan	7	7	Korea, North	7	7
Algeria	7	7	Laos	7	6
Angola	7	7	Liberia	7	6
Azerbaijan	6	6	Libya	7	7
Bahrain	6	6	Maldives	6	6
Bhutan	7	7	Mauritania	7	7
Bosnia-Hercegovina	6	6	Nigeria	7	6
Brunei	7	6	Oman	6	6
Burma (Myanmar)	7	7	Qatar	7	6
Burundi	6	7	Rwanda	7	7
Cameroon	6	5	Saudi Arabia	7	7
Chad	6	5	Sierra Leone	7	6
China (PRC)	7	7	Somalia	7	7
Cuba	7	7	Sudan	7	7
Djibouti	6	6	Swaziland	6	5
Egypt	6	6	Syria	7	7
Equatorial Guinea	7	7	Tajikistan	7	7
Eritrea	6	5	Tanzania	6	6
Ethiopia	6	5	Togo	6	5
Gambia	7	6	Tunisia	6	5
Guinea	6	5	Turkmenistan	7	7
Indonesia	7	6	United Arab Emirates	6	5
Iran	6	7	Usbekistan	7	7
Iraq	7	7	Vietnam	7	7
Ivory Coast	6	5	Yemen	5	6
Kazakhstan	6	5	Yugoslavia (Serbia & Montenegro)	6	6
Kenya	6	6	Zaire	7	6

SOURCE: Karatnycky, A. *Freedom in the World.* New York: Freedom House, pp. 678–679.

5 The economic environment

Key issues

- Classifying economic systems
- Classifying countries
- Key macro-economic issues in international business
- Transformation to a market economy
- Keys to a successful transition to market economies
- Adapting to foreign economic environments in the internationalisation process
- Ethical dilemmas

5.1 Introduction

When a company is considering where to build factories and sell products, it must analyse the countries in which it contemplates doing business. Understanding the economic and political environments of these countries can help predict how trends and events in those environments might affect its future performance there. Pizza Hut[1] has been chosen as a case for this chapter because of its international operations in various countries.

In this chapter, we discuss the economic environments of the countries in which a company may want to operate, but not the specific decision about whether to invest in or do business with a certain country. This country analysis 'examines the economic strategy of the nation state. It takes the holistic approach to understanding how a country and, in particular, its government, has behaved, is behaving, and may behave'.[2] Country analysis requires, to a certain extent, understanding national goals, priorities, and policies. It also involves understanding economic performance as indicated by economic growth, inflation, and budget and trade deficits. We will discuss these in the next few chapters as we lay the economic foundation for an analysis of international business. This chapter focuses on the various types of world economies and how differences between them affect managerial decisions. In particular, we will first classify economic systems into market economies, planned economies, and mixed economies; second, we will discuss different ways of classifying countries according to per capita income and quality of life measures; third, we will discuss key macro-economic factors that influence one country's competitive advantage *vis-a-vis* other countries; and, finally, we will discuss the problems of transition or transformation from planned to market economies.

5.2 Classifying economic systems

Economic systems are usually classified as capitalist, socialist, or mixed. The term 'mixed' may be a little misleading in that all economies are really mixed. No country has a purely market or purely command economy, but each one tends to lean toward one direction or another. If it is considered to be a market economy with private ownership (Exhibit 5.1, block A), it is classified as such because the market and private ownership dominate the economy. There may be some government control of decision-making and government ownership of resources, but not in any significant way. However, as the economy moves to more balance between market and command, or between public and private ownership, it is considered mixed. France would be a mixed economy that is more weighted to public ownership than the United States, because the French government is much more actively involved in the ownership of large companies. It is also possible to classify economic systems according to two other criteria:

- type of property ownership, private or public;
- method of resource allocation and control; a market economy or a command economy (in which resources are allocated and controlled by the government).

These two criteria can be expanded to include mixed ownership and control. Exhibit 5.1 shows these classifications. Note that Hong Kong probably fits in block A, whereas China is best located in the upper left-hand corner of block I but may soon be in block E, B, or H. The United States probably lies in the upper part of block D. Ownership of the means of production ranges in theory from complete private ownership to complete public ownership, although, in reality, these extremes do not exist. Most countries lie somewhere in the mixed ownership range. For example, the United States is considered to be the prime example of a private enterprise system, yet the government does own some means of production and actively produces in such sectors of the economy as education, national parks, the postal service (which is in the quasi-public sector), and certain utilities. Similarly, the control of economic activity ranges in theory from market to command.

The next several sections examine more closely market, centrally planned, and mixed economies.

Exhibit 5.1: Interrelationships between control of economic activity and ownership of production factors

CONTROL	OWNERSHIP		
	Private	Mixed	Public
Market	A	B	C
Mixed	D	E	F
Command	G	H	I

Control/Ownership		Control/Ownership		Control/Ownership	
A	Market/private	D	Mixed/private	G	Command/private
B	Market	E	Mixed/mixed	H	Command/mixed
C	Market	F	Mixed/public	I	Command/public

5.2.1 Market economy

In a market economy, two societal units play important roles: the individual and the company. Individuals own resources and consumer products; companies use resources and produce products. The market mechanism involves an interaction of price, quantity, supply and demand for resources and products, as follows:

- Labour is supplied by the individual if the company offers an adequate wage.
- Products are consumed if the price is within a certain acceptable range.
- A company sets its wages on the basis of the quantity of labour available to do a job.
- Resources are allocated as a result of constant interplay between individuals and companies, between individuals, and between companies (for example, when the output of one company is the input of another).

The key factors that make the market economy work are consumer sovereignty, that is, the right of the consumer to decide what to buy, and freedom of the enterprise to operate in the market. As long as both the individual and the company are free to make economic decisions, the interplay of supply and demand should ensure proper allocation of resources.

More specifically, a market economy implies a degree of economic freedom, which can be measured in a variety of ways. Freedom House, which developed the comparative measure of freedom from a political rights and civil liberties point of view, has also developed a measure for economic freedom. Their feeling is that economic freedom has two dimensions. The first is the freedom from government restraints on wages, prices, trade flows, and business formation. The second is the establishment of rules that govern the economic game. In particular, Freedom House measures the extent to which 'government hinders or prevents its citizens from exercising their right to own property, earn a living, operate a business, invest their earnings, trade internationally, and participate equally in all aspects of the market economy'.[3] The key to the first dimension is the degree of state intrusion. The less the intrusion, the more likely the country is to have a free economy. The key to the second is the nature of the legal and institutional frameworks of a country in safeguarding the ability of all citizens, including women and minorities, 'to enter the professions, open businesses, own and transfer property, and participate in the economy'.[4]

5.2.2 Centrally planned economy

In a centrally planned economy, the government co-ordinates the activities of the different economic sectors. Goals are set for every enterprise in the country; the government determines how much is produced, by whom and for whom. In this type of economy, the government is assumed to be a better judge of how resources should be allocated than businesses or consumers. As a result of the recent political and economic changes in Eastern Europe and the former Soviet Union, however, few countries use strict central planning today. Most countries in this category have been moved into a new one called historically planned economies (HPEs), which comprises countries that previously used central planning as their primary economic system but may no longer do so.

5.2.3 Mixed economy

In reality, no economy is either purely market determined or completely centrally planned. Hong Kong and China represent opposite ends of the spectrum of mixed economies. In practice, however, what we call mixed economies generally have a higher degree of government intervention than is found in Hong Kong, and a greater degree of reliance on market forces than is found in China. The two ends of the spectrum, from the Freedom House point of view, are 'Free' and 'Not free'. Countries in the mixed categories would be 'Partly free' and

Mostly not free'. Examples of countries that are Partly free' are Hungary, Israel, and Taiwan; xamples of countries that are 'Mostly not free' re India, Mexico, Brazil, and Russia. Countries hat are 'Not free' would not necessarily be entral command economies, however. They night have a form of state capitalism where the narket is severely impaired, such as in Haiti, ndonesia, and Saudi Arabia. In some cases hey might be central command, such as in ietnam, China, Cuba, and North Korea. ountries that have historically classified themelves as central command, are rapidly moving oward the market, as we will discuss later in he chapter. Government intervention can be egarded in two ways: government ownership f the means of production and government nfluence in economic decision-making. Ownrship is easy to quantify statistically; influence, owever, is a matter of policy and custom and therefore more difficult to measure precisely.

Many high-income countries, such as Gernany and Sweden, have relatively low levels of overnment ownership but a strong tradition of ocial welfare supported by taxes and therefore igh total expenditures as a percentage of gross ational product (GNP). France has a similar ystem, although the government is more eavily involved in corporate ownership.

Japan offers an illustration of government ntervention in the form of influence. At the close of the Second World War, Japan, unlike other countries involved in the war, such as France and Italy, decided to leave ownership of the means of production in the private sector rather than nationalise key industries. Japanese policy-makers focused on setting targets and using fiscal incentives to direct the flow of investment. The Ministry of International Trade and Industry (MITI) was organised to guide industrial development through 'strategic planning and authority (both formal and informal) over investment and production priorities'.[5] MITI was more concerned with developing a vision for the economy than with setting up a blueprint for it.

Exhibit 5.2 summarises the number of countries, population, and gross domestic product (GDP) of countries according to economic freedom. Those in the 'Free' category would be considered market economies, those in the 'Partly free' and 'Mostly not free' categories would be considered mixed economies, and those in the 'Not free' category would be considered state capitalist and command economies. It is interesting to note that only 17% of the world's population lives in countries that are free economically, but they represent 81% of the world's GDP. In contrast, 36% of the world's population lives in countries that are 'Not free', and they represent only 5% of the world's GDP.

xhibit 5.2: Economic freedom

	Number of countries	Population (in millions)	Gross domestic product (trillions of U.S. $)
Free	27	942 (17%)	18.8 (81%)
Partly free	22	395 (7%)	1.1 (5%)
Mostly not free	13	1,645 (30%)	1.9 (8%)
Not free	20	1,974 (36%)	1.1 (5%)
Not surveyed	109	546 (10%)	.2 (1%)
Total world	191	5,502	23.1

URCE: Messick, R.E. 1996. The World Survey of Economic Freedom, *Freedom Review*, Vol. 27. No. 2, p. 10.

5.2.4 Political-economic synthesis

Except for central planning and communism, we have made no attempt to link an economic philosophy or system with a particular political philosophy or regime. A logical linkage is a democratic form of government with a market economy and private ownership of the means of production. The assumption is that voters, like consumers, are rational, understand their own self-interest, and prefer to make their own decisions. Japan, the United States, Switzerland, Germany, Canada, Colombia, Ecuador, and Argentina have this combination of political and economic systems.

Democratic socialists, however, have a different viewpoint. They believe that because economics and politics are so closely connected, voters should rely on their elected government to control the economic system; that is, the part of the economy not owned by the government should be regulated by the government. Democratic socialists reason that, in order to have an economy that is democratically controlled and provides the security necessary for liberty, resources and production factors must be owned or regulated by a welfare-oriented government. France, when controlled by the socialists, was a good example of democratic socialism. Radical democratic socialists support a mix of government-owned companies, co-operatives, small-scale private companies, and 'freelancers' (for example, journalists and artists).[6]

Clearly, numerous combinations of political and economic systems are possible. Generally, the more a country leans toward political totalitarianism, the greater is its reliance on government intervention in the economy. However, most democratic countries have experimented with different degrees of government intervention in the economy, and many totalitarian countries have not resorted to ownership of the factors of production as a method of control. The extremes tend to converge toward a mix of public and private interaction in matters of ownership and control. In the case of the industrialised countries, the emphasis seems to be on control rather than on ownership.

The Freedom House survey found that, with few exceptions, countries rated as economically 'Free' were 'Free' in terms of political rights and civil liberties. Similarly, those 'Not free' economically tended to be 'Not free' in terms of political rights and civil liberties. Seventy-nine per cent of the countries were classified correctly in economic and political terms.[7] An example of a country that did not match up was South Korea, which was considered to be 'Free' in political terms but 'Mostly not free' in economic terms because of the government's policy of encouraging the growth of the large chaebol (large Korean business groups that tend to be diversified into different businesses and are held together by ownership, management and family ties) at the expense of small firms. However, the political scandals of 1995 and 1996 are sure to break the influence of the chaebol and move South Korea closer to the 'Free' economic category.

5.3 Classifying countries

The classification of countries is always a difficult proposition because of the different methods of classification. A country's international competitiveness is a function of several factors, including factor conditions and demand conditions, which are relevant to this chapter. Factor conditions, also known as production factors, include essential inputs to the production process, such as human resources, physical resources, knowledge resources, capital resources, and infrastructure.[8] Demand conditions include three dimensions: the composition of home demand (or the nature of buyer needs), the size and pattern of growth of home demand, and the internationalisation of demand.[9] The composition of demand is known as the quality of demand, and the size is known as the quantity of demand.

In this chapter, we will look at several economic indicators that are helpful in understanding the economic performance of a country. One of the challenges is gaining access to good current data. At this point, it is impossible to identify all good sources of information on economic data, but the Internet is rapidly becoming one of the best places to obtain current data on a country. Looking for a specific country on the Internet, using one of the many search engines, will bring up country home pages by governments themselves, as well as individuals and organisations that are interested in the country. The authors use the Internet heavily in the endnotes to the chapters, and there are also good references included in our book's home page. In addition to the Internet, there are a number of good on-line databases, such as LEXIS/NEXIS, that can be used to search for information on companies, countries, and special topics. CD-ROMS are being used to store large amounts of data. Two examples are the World Bank socio-economic indicators and the National Trade Data Bank (NTDB) by the International Trade Administration of the USA Department of Commerce. The NTDB, which contains about 120 000 pages of information and is updated monthly, allows you to perform different types of searches, including searches by country. Be sure to check our home page for a more detailed description of these different databases and for some good Internet links that you can use to get updated information on countries.

Two important components of demand are population size and per capita income. Although it is hard to capture every concept in one measure, the two most widely used measures for categorising countries are per capita gross national product and per capita gross domestic product.

Gross national product (GNP) is the broadest measure of economic activity and is defined as 'the market value of final goods and services newly produced by domestic factors of production'.[10] Note that the production by domestic factors could take place at home or abroad. It comprises gross domestic product (see below) plus net factor income from abroad, which is the income residents receive from abroad for factor services (labour and capital), less similar payments made to non-residents who contribute to the domestic economy.[11]

Gross domestic product (GDP) measures the value of production that occurs within a country's borders without regard to whether the factors of production are domestic or foreign. For most countries, GNP and GDP are very similar, although GDP reflects economic activity within a country's borders more accurately. Per capita GNP is the approach used by the World Bank for operational and analytical purposes.

Every economy is classified into one of the following categories according to their per capita GNP:[12]

Low-income	\$725 or less in 1994
Middle-income	\$726-\$8,955
Lower-middle-income	\$726-\$2,895
Upper-middle-income	\$2,896-\$8,956
High-income	\$8,956 or more

This classification has changed in recent years because of rapid changes in political and economic systems. In the 1985 issue of the *World Development Report*, for example, the categories were: low-income economies, middle-income economies, upper middle-income economies, high-income oil exporters, industrial market economies, and East European non-market economies.

The low-income and middle-income countries are often known as developing countries, but the East European non-market economies are put into their proper per capita income classification rather than separated. In the past, we have referred to countries like Cuba, China, and Russia, as Second-World, socialist, or communist countries. Today, it is more common to refer to them as countries with economies in transition (CEIT), since most of them are moving in various degrees from central command to a market economy. **The high-income countries are less likely to be known as industrial market economies, because most of them generate less than half of their GNP from industry**. It is interesting to note that five of the high-income countries in terms of per capita GNP are referred to as developing countries by the United Nations: namely Israel, Hong Kong, Kuwait, Singapore, and United Arab Emirates.

In Exhibit 5.3 (p. 137), countries are classified into different economic categories according to per capita GNP. The world's wealth is located primarily in the high-income countries. The low- and middle-income countries where the vast majority of the world's population lives, do not have a proportional share of per capita income. It is interesting to note that the high-income countries are north of the equator (except for Australia and New Zealand). Thus, the so-called North-South dialogue consists of discussions on economic development between the rich northern hemisphere countries and the poorer southern hemisphere countries.

The relative importance of the high-income countries in the world economy is interesting since they represent only 21% of the number of economies and 15,2% of the population, but they generate 79,5% of the world's GNP. On the other hand, the low-income countries account for 30,6% of the number of economies in the world, 56,7% of the population, but only 4,9% of the GNP. The middle-income countries fit in between with 28,1% of the world's population and 15,6% of its GNP, while representing 48,3% of the total countries.[13]

5.3.1 Purchasing power

Per capita GNP is an important measure of wealth, but not the only one. In particular, the World Bank is quick to point out that per capita GNP does not measure welfare or success in development, nor does it measure factors such as the costs and benefits of development to the environment. An alternative measure of wealth is purchasing power parity (PPP) estimates of per capita GNP. The basic idea of PPP is to identify the number of units of a country's currency required to buy the same amount of goods and services in the domestic market as one dollar would buy in the United States.[14] Exhibit 5.4 (p. 139) compares the traditional per capita GNP of several countries with their PPP per capita GNP. It is interesting to note that some countries, such as China, have a higher PPP per capita GNP, whereas in others, such as Japan, it is lower. Although there are several countries with a traditional per capita GNP that is higher than that of the United States, only Luxembourg has a higher PPP per capita GNP than the United States. Thus, even though per capita GNP is the primary measure of wealth in a country, purchasing power GNP is an alternative way to measure wealth that is more indicative of the purchasing power of a country's currency.

5.3.2 Quality of life

Per capita income, as noted above, does not represent quality of life. The United Nations publishes an annual *Human Development Report* in which it ranks countries according to various measures of human happiness, such as life expectancy, educational standards, individual purchasing power, health, sanitation, treatment of women, and other important aspects of life. The top five countries in the 1996 survey are Canada, the United States, Japan, the Netherlands, and Norway. In that list of 174 countries, Russia ranks 57th, China 108th, and India 135th.[15] The 1996 survey also determines a capability poverty measure, which is an index that measures factors that could lead to poverty or result in conditions that can negatively affect the future of a country. The index includes measures such as the percentage of children under five who are underweight, the proportion of unattended births, the number of children in school, and the rate of female illiteracy.[16] The objective of this measure is to get countries to look at all factors that might affect their future and not focus strictly on income growth.

Another key issue in examining the wealth of a country is to note the widening gap between the rich and poor. The *Human Development Report* referred to above also notes that the gap between rich and poor is not only widening in the United States, but worldwide. An indication of this gap is where the national

Exhibit 5.3: World Bank categories for economies

High-income economies (42 countries with 1994 per capita GNP of $8,956 or more)	Upper-middle-income economies (36 countries with 1994 per capita GNP between $2,896 and $8,956)	Lower-middle-income economies (65 countries with 1994 per capita income between $726 and $2,895)	Low-income economies (65 countries with 1994 per capita income of $725 or less)
Andorra	American Samoa	Algeria	Afghanistan
Aruba	Antigua and Barbados	Angola	Albania
Australia	Argentina	Belarus	Armenia
Austria	Azerbaijan	Belize	Azerbaijan
Bahamas, the	Bahrain	Bolivia	Bangladesh
Belgium	Barbados	Botswana	Benin
Bermuda	Brazil	Bulgaria	Bhutan
Brunel	Chile	Colombia	Bosnia and Herzegovina
Canada	Czech Republic	Costa Rica	Burkina Faso
Cayman Islands	French Guiana	Croatia	Burundi
Channel Islands	Gabon	Cuba	Cambodia
Cyprus	Greece	Djibouti	Cameroon
Denmark	Guadeloupe	Dominica	Cape Verde
Faeroe Islands	Guam	Dominican Republic	Central African Republic
Finland	Hungary	Ecuador	Chad
France	Isle of Man	El Salvador	China
French Polynesia	Korea, Rep	Estonia	Comoros
Germany	Libya	Fiji	Congo
Greenland	Malaysia	Grenada	Côte d'Ivoire
Hong Kong	Malta	Guatemala	Egypt, Arab Rep.
Iceland	Martinique	Indonesia	Equatorial Guinea
Ireland	Mauritius	Iran, Islamic Rep.	Eritrea
Israel	Mayotte	Iraq	Ethiopia
Italy	Mexico	Jamaica	Gambia
Japan	New Caledonia	Jordan	Georgia
Kuwait	Oman	Kazakhstan	Ghana
Luxembourg	Puerto Rico	Kiribati	Guinea
Macao	Reunion	Korea, Dem. Rep.	Guinea-Bissau
Netherlands	Saudi Arabia	Latvia	Guyana
Netherlands Antilles	Seychelles	Lebanon	Haiti
New Zealand	Slovenia	Lithuania	Honduras
Norway	South Africa	Macedonia, FYR	India
Portugal	St. Kitts and Nevis	Maldives	Kenya
Quatar	St. Lucia	Marshall Islands	Kyrgyz Republic
Singapore	Trinidad and Tobago	Micronesia, Fed. Sts.	Laos PDR
Spain	Uruguay	Moldova	Lesotho
Sweden		Morocco	Liberia
Switzerland		Namibia	Madagascar
United Arab Emirates		Northern Mariana Is.	Malawi
United Kingdom		Panama	Mali
United States		Papua New Guinea	Mauritania
Virgin Islands		Paraguay	Mongolia

High-income economies (42 countries with 1994 per capita GNP of $8,956 or more)	Upper-middle-income economies (36 countries with 1994 per capita GNP between $2,896 and $8,956)	Lower-middle-income economies (65 countries with 1994 per capita income between $726 and $2,895)	Low-income economies (65 countries with 1994 per capita income of $725 or less)
		Peru	Mozambique
		Philippines	Myanmar
		Poland	Nepal
		Romania	Nicaragua
		Russian Federation	Niger
		Slovak Republic	Nigeria
		Solomon Islands	Pakistan Rwanda
		St. Vincent	Sao Tome and Principe
		Suriname	Senegal
		Swaziland	Sierra Leone
		Syrian Arab Republic	Somalia
		Thailand	Sri Lanka
		Tonga	Sudan
		Tunisia	Tajikistan
		Turkey	Tanzania
		Turkmenistan	Togo
		Ukraine	Uganda
		Uzbekistan	Vietnam
		Vanuatu	Yemen, Rep.
		Venezuela	Zaire
		West Bank and Gaza	Zambia
		Western Somoa	Zimbabwe
		Yugoslavia, Fed. Rep.	

SOURCE: World Bank, World Development Report 1996 (New York: Oxford University Press, 1996), p. viii; International Bank for Reconstruction and Development/World Bank. The World Bank Atlas 1996 (Washington, D.C.: The World Bank, 1995), pp. 18–19. The World Bank provides the data for both the World Bank Atlas and the World Development Report, and both sources are used for different discussions. The Atlas provides data for 209 countries, whereas the World Development Report provides data for 133 countries. The difference between the two is that the World Development Report tables do not include countries with populations of less than 1 million or those with incomplete data. Some of the categories in the Atlas contain countries for which data is estimated. In addition, data from the former USSR is preliminary. The classifications used in this table are from the World Development Report, but the countries listed in the table are from the more complete World Bank Atlas.

average per capital GNP is at least four times the average income of the poorest fifth of the country. The ratio of the top 20% of USA incomes to the poorest 20% is now 9 to 1, and the average income of the poorest fifth as a percentage of the average per capita income as a whole, is 24%. In contrast, the latter figure in Japan is 43.5% and the Netherlands 41%. Comparable numbers for the United Kingdom are 23%, basically the same as that of the United States, whereas it is only 10.5% in Brazil.[17] Some might argue, however, that equitable income distribution is not the most important issue. A more important factor is whether the bottom fifth of the population has a good overall standard of living, not whether it is the same as the top fifth. Equal distribution gets to the heart of a social welfare economic/political system, whereas a market system is concerned with overall economic gains in a

Exhibit 5.4: Per capita income measured two ways

Country	GNP per capita dollars 1994	PPP estimates of GNP per capita current international dollars 1994
Brazil	3,370	5,630
China	530	2,510
Czech Republic	2,710	7,910
France	23,470	19,820
Japan	34,630	21,350
Mali	250	520
Mexico	4,010	7,050
Russia	2,650	5,260
Thailand	2,210	6,870
U.S.	25,860	25,860

SOURCE: The World Bank, 1996. The World Bank Atlas, Washington, D.C.: pp. 18–19.

country and not whether the gains are evenly distributed.

In a far less analytical approach to quality of life, the Gallup Poll conducted an international survey of 18 countries to determine if people were satisfied with their lives, and in all but two of the countries surveyed (Mexico and Hungary), more people say they are satisfied than dissatisfied with their lives. The top five countries were Iceland, Canada, Germany, Thailand, the United States, and France. Although people tended to be more satisfied with their family situation and material possessions, they were least satisfied with their overall financial situation.[18] In explaining Iceland's top ranking, a Professor of Sociology at the University of Iceland feels that the secret of their success is their harsh environment: 'Our culture is colored by the harshness of nature. That's why Icelanders have a more tolerant attitude to the problems of life. They don't expect the same sort of stability often expected in other nations.'[19] Interestingly, the survey found that, although respondents felt that the world in which they live today is better than the one in which their parents grew up, the world in which the next generation of children will live will not be better than their own. Quality of life is an important way to compare countries, even though perceptions are relatively subjective.

5.3.3 Structure of production

A final way to classify countries is according to structure of production, which refers to the percentage of GDP generated by agriculture, industry, manufacturing (which is a subcategory of industry), and services. Exhibit 5.5 (p. 140) provides this information for the World Bank country categories and a few illustrative countries per category. It is interesting to note that the data for high-income countries was not available in the 1996 *Human Development Report* for 1994, but information was provided for a few representative countries. The key is to note that, as income rises, the percentage of GDP devoted to agriculture falls, while the percentage devoted to services rises. This is also true over time. In 1980, for example, 34% of the GDP of low-income countries went to agriculture, whereas it was only 28% in 1994. Industry went from 32% to 34%, and services from 32% to 36%.

Exhibit 5.5: Structure of the economy: distribution of gross domestic product (%)

	Agriculture	Industry	Manufacturing	Services
Low-income	28	34	25	36
China	21	47	37	32
Tanzania	57	17	8	26
Middle-income	10	36	20	52
Brazil	13	39	25	49
Indonesia	17	41	24	42
Russia	7	38	31	55
High-income	N/A	NA	NA	NA
Japan	2	40	27	58
United Kingdom	2	32	22	66

SOURCE: World Bank, 1996. The World Development Report 1996, New York: Oxford University Press, pp. 210–211.

5.4 Key macro-economic issues in international business

Developing countries share many problems and characteristics, although they vary from region to region and country to country. Some of the most frequently mentioned problems are inflation, heavy external debt, weak currencies, shortage of skilled workers, political and economic instability, over-reliance on the public sector for economic development, war and insurrection, mass poverty, rapid population growth, weak commodity prices, and environmental degradation. Some of these same problems plague the high-income countries, although they tend to focus on other issues as well. Europeans, for example, have been overly concerned about high unemployment, excessive regulation, competition from the developing countries of Asia, and the assimilation of the former centrally planned economies of Eastern Europe. Economic growth in Europe and North America has also been relatively weak in recent years.

In any event, we cannot discuss all aspects of the economic environment in this chapter, and some issues, such as currency, will be discussed in other chapters. However, we will focus on a few important macro-economic factors at this point, namely economic growth, inflation, and deficits and debt, both internal and external. After that, we will discuss some unique problems of countries in transition from planned to market economies.

5.4.1 Economic growth

An ideal situation would be if every country had political stability, a low inflation rate, and a high real growth rate. If this were the case, even if a company did not expand its share in each market, it would still be able to increase revenues at the same pace as the general growth in the economy. However, there are significant differences in growth rates worldwide.

In recent years, growth has been especially strong in East and South Asia, where it has been boosted by the region's tremendous market size – Asia's population is ten times that of North America and six times that of Europe. In contrast, the high-income countries have experienced relatively slower growth – a troublesome sign because, historically, they have tended to fuel growth in the rest of the orld. Further, although high-income coun-ies accounted for 80% of the world's GNP in 994, compared with only 8% for Asia (exclud-ıg Japan), the growth rates in Asia today are veraging about 8% annually, compared with ss than 2% in the high-income countries.

Projections of growth trends are dramatic. or example, the World Bank projects the rowth of the high-income countries as 2,7% r the period 1994-2003, whereas the devel-ping countries are expected to grow at nearly vice that rate, namely 4,8%. Within developing ountries, the greatest growth is expected to take ace in East and South Asia, namely 7,6% and ,3%, respectively. East Asia and Asia, excluding pan, comprise 53% of the world's population, ut only 7% of its GDP. Using projected growth ıtes and measuring national income according purchasing power parity, the high-income ountries might account for less than half of the orld output by the end of the decade, and less ıan 40% of the total by the year 2020, by hich time as many as 9 of the top 15 eco-omies in the world could be from developing ountries.[20] Thus, companies seeking greater les and earnings will increasingly look toward ıe faster-growing economies of Asia rather ıan the slower-growing economies elsewhere.

This disparity in growth rates creates a ıajor problem: high-income countries tend to ıvest in the fastest-growing economies, and ıch investment increases the disparity. For xample, of the total foreign investments in the eveloping world between 1986 and 1991, 5% went to six countries: Mexico, China, alaysia, Argentina, Brazil, and Thailand. The oorest of the poor, such as Pakistan and Mali, ceived very little.[21]

When economic and political crises hit exico in late 1994 and early 1995, the sulting instability rippled through Latin merica and even other emerging markets ıtside of Latin America, causing some com-ınies to pull back on their plans to expand in ıose markets. As economic growth began to ck up, and the markets became more attrac-ve again, their confidence also began to grow. However, during the period 1985-1994, 68 countries suffered a decline in per capita income, and most of these were developing countries. At the same time, 28 countries enjoyed average annual growth rates of 3% or more, representing 30,5% of the world's population and 38,7% of its GNP. Those countries as a group, represented primarily in East and South Asia, are important markets for MNEs and prime locations for investment. Their size and growth rates are significant location-specific advantages that cannot be ignored by companies that want to establish global strategic advantage.

5.4.2 **Inflation**

Inflation is a dimension of the economic environment that affects interest rates, exchange rates, the cost of living, and the general confidence in a country's political and economic system. For example, the constitutional charge of the Bundesbank, the central bank of Germany, is to control inflation. When East Germany began to assimilate with West Germany after the fall of the Berlin Wall in 1989, inflation rose to 2,7% in 1990 and reached a high of 4,1% in 1993. However, high inflation tends to force interest rates up for two reasons. The first is that interest rates must be higher than inflation so that they can reflect a real return on interest-bearing assets, otherwise no one would hold those assets. Second, monetary authorities use high interest rates to bring down inflation. Thus companies must watch the governments of high-inflation countries to determine what economic policies will be used to counteract inflation. If the government uses high interest rates to try to wipe out inflation, economic growth could slow down as well, making the market a less attractive place to do business.

The oil price shocks of the 1960s and 1970s brought with them an increase in inflation, especially in the developing countries. Although inflation continued on a downward trend in the early 1990s, it picked up again in 1993 and 1994, due largely to an increase in inflation in the developing countries. At the beginning of the 1990s, the countries in the IMF survey with inflation of more than 100% per year were Sierra Leone, Zambia, Poland, Yugoslavia, Argentina, Brazil, Nicaragua, Peru, and Uruguay. The high-inflation countries at the end of 1995 were Russia, Suriname, the Ukraine, and Zaire. The improvement was due to the overall drop in the inflation rate in the developing countries from 66% in 1994 to 27,6% in 1995. Russia and the Ukraine were not included in the 1990 IMF survey but were undoubtedly highly inflationary at that time as well. Brazil, a country that registered high inflation at 2 937,8% in 1990, improved to 84,4% for 1995, and was less than 30% on an annual basis for the first quarter of 1996. The government's resolve to control inflation seemed to be working.

Companies with dealings in high-inflation countries have difficulty planning for the future and running profitable operations. They must change prices almost daily in order to maintain sufficient cash flow to replace inventory and keep operating. Accurate inflation forecasting is also difficult, and so companies end up either underpricing or overpricing products. This practice results in a cash-flow shortage or a price that is too high for the company to maintain market share.

Inflation of the magnitude seen in Brazil in the early 1990s, and in Russia, also creates problems for companies that deal in imports and exports. If the exchange rate depreciates at the same pace as inflation rises, then the prices foreigners pay for exports from the inflationary country will not change. However, an exchange rate that depreciates more slowly than inflation rises causes prices to increase in importing countries. The local companies soon find they cannot compete in world markets. A depreciating currency also increases the cost of inputs, thereby further fuelling inflation. To keep its costs from being affected much by exchange-rate changes, the Moscow McDonald's developed a strategy of purchasing as many inputs as possible in Russia. However, inflation in Moscow is pushing up local costs and forcing McDonald's to raise prices as well.

Inflation causes political destabilisation. If the government tries to control inflation by controlling wages, the real income of the population declines and frustration sets in. If the government decides to do nothing, the economy may deteriorate to the point where real incomes fall anyway. Instituting tighter fiscal controls when the government is already in a fragile position, is very difficult. This is clearly the problem that faces both Brazil and Russia and strikes fear into the Chinese government. As mentioned earlier in this chapter China has been experiencing rapid economic growth that began in the early 1990s. However, this growth, if allowed to get out of hand could re-ignite inflation, thus devaluing the Chinese currency and forcing the government to slow down economic growth. Such instability concerns foreign investors, who hesitate to invest significant amounts of money in the country.[22]

5.4.3 Surpluses and deficits – international transactions

The transactions between the residents of one country and all other countries are captured in the balance of payments of that country. These transactions constitute either an export or an import. For each transaction, payment must either be received from a foreign resident (an export) or made to a foreign resident (an import). The major balance of active transactions (those for which payment must be received or made) included in the balance of payments is called the current account balance and it is comprised of the following transactions

- merchandise trade account;
- services account;
- income receipts and payments on assets accounts;
- unilateral transfers account.

The **merchandise trade account** measures the trade deficit or surplus. Its balance is derived by subtracting merchandise imports from merchandise exports. A negative result indicates a balance-of-trade deficit; a positive result, a balance-of-trade surplus. An export is considered positive because it results in a payment received from abroad and inflow of cash. Conversely, an import is considered negative because it results in a payment made to a seller abroad and outflow of cash. For example, in 1995, the United States had a deficit in the balance of merchandise trade (also known as goods) of $174 billion, of which $59,3 billion was the deficit with Japan. In 1995, the deficit with China was $33,8 billion, and in June 1996, the deficit with China exceeded that of Japan.[23] In 1996, the merchandise trade deficit with Japan narrowed to $47,7 billion, and the deficit with China widened to $39,5 billion.

The **services account** measures the following transactions: travel and transportation, tourism, and fees and royalties. For example, when a German tourist vacations in the United States, that person's total expenditures are considered to be a service export, that is, a cash inflow from Germany. When an American tourist vacations in Germany, that person's total expenditures are considered to be a service import, that is, a cash outflow to Germany.

Income receipts and payments on assets accounts measure foreign investment in the United States and USA investment abroad. For example, a dividend received by an American company from one of its subsidiaries in Brazil is considered to be an income receipt. A dividend sent, for example, by BMW of America to its parent company in Munich, is considered to be an income payment.

Unilateral transfers are payments made to a country for which no goods or services are received. For example, to help defray the cost of the Gulf War in 1991, many countries made payments to the United States. These payments were represented by a positive entry under unilateral transfers in the USA balance-of-payments accounts.

5.4.4 Impact of different balances on business

What difference does it make whether a country has a current account surplus or deficit? There probably is no direct effect; however, the events that comprise the balance-of-payments data influence exchange rates and government policy, which, in turn, influence corporate strategy. The size of the deficit can be measured in absolute terms or as a percentage of GDP. In 1994, for example, the current account deficit of the United States was $136,5 billion, whereas the current account surplus of Japan was $133,9 billion. These respective balances were by far the largest in the world. Closest to the United States was Mexico, with a deficit of $28,9 billion, and closest to Japan was Italy, with a surplus of $21,5 billion.[24] As a percentage of GDP, however, the United States did not look so bad, with a deficit of just 2,1%. There were 60 countries with deficits that were a larger percentage of GDP, including Mozambique, with the largest deficit of 71,4%.[25]

The policy implications of current account deficits are illustrated in several countries in South-east Asia, including Thailand and Malaysia, which were suffering current account deficits in 1996. Thailand's deficit was expected to reach 8% of GDP by the end of 1996, whereas that of Malaysia was expected to reach 10%.[26] Although the deficits were partly a result of slower export growth, the governments were focusing on policy issues to curtail imports. Malaysia's prime minister argued that 'if Malaysians could not restrain themselves from buying imports, then duties should be raised and, if that did not work, quotas and import permits should be imposed on certain non-essential goods. This would be better than to try and stifle growth by increasing interest rates.'[27]

Thus it appears that two ways to help solve a country's payments imbalance are to restrict imports or slow down economic growth through raising interest rates, so that demand for imports also slows down. In the first case, companies exporting to the country will suffer, as will foreign investors inside the country that rely on the import of essential materials and components. In addition, it might be more difficult to gain access to foreign exchange to remit dividends to the parent company. In the second case, the general slowdown of the economy would affect demand, thus making the country a less attractive place as a market or a location for investment.

5.4.5 External debt

One consequence of the rapid increase in oil costs during the 1970s was the equally rapid increase in many countries' external debt. This burgeoning debt resulted as developing countries sought help from foreign private or government institutions to finance oil imports and other products necessary for development. At the time, the two regions where the largest borrowing occurred were Latin America and Africa.

As noted in Exhibit 5.6, there are at least four different ways to measure external debt: the actual amount, external debt as a percentage of GNP, external debt as a percentage of exports of goods and services, and the debt-service ratio. External debt as a percentage of GNP helps keep the size of debt in perspective. As noted in the exhibit, it is quite high for Sub-Saharan Africa. For most countries in Africa, debt as a percentage of GNP exceeds 100%. The worst country is Nicaragua, however, with debt equal to 800% of GNP.[28]

External debt as a percentage of exports of goods and services relates the size of the debt to the capacity of the company to generate foreign exchange to pay off the debt. Sub-Saharan Africa, South Asia, and Latin America and the Caribbean are about the same, with debt of more than 200% of exports. In Nicaragua and Rwanda, debt is more than 2 000% of exports.[29]

The final measure is the debt-service ratio, which is the ratio of interest payments plus principal amortisation to exports. South Asia and Latin America and the Caribbean are the regions with the highest debt-service ratios, although all regions have countries with ratios in excess of 20%. An increasing share of many countries' export earnings goes to service their debt; thus, less is available for economic development. A total of 28 countries have to use at least one-quarter of their export earnings just to service their external debt, which is a real brake on local economic development.[30] If the debt is invested in capital development, it should help improve the location-specific advantage of the borrowing country. However, if the debt gets too big, it becomes a drag on the economy.

Exhibit 5.6: External debt indicators, 1994

Developing country regions	External debt as a percentage of GNP	Exports of goods and services	Debt-service ratio
Sub-Saharan Africa	78,7	265,7	14,0
East Asia and Pacific	30,9	93,3	12,0
South Asia	42,0	271,6	25,6
Europe and Central Asia	32,8	153,7	14,6
Middle East and North Africa	41,7	148,5	15,4
Latin America and Caribbean	37,2	258,6	27,5

SOURCE: *World Development Report.* 1996. Washington, DC: World Bank, p. 221

The interrelationship between deficits and debt is obvious, especially given the importance of linking exports to the ability to repay debt. As noted above, some countries in South Asia are suffering from current account deficits. Although Indonesia's deficit as a percentage of GDP was expected to be only 3,8% in 1996, compared with Thailand's 8% and Malaysia's 10%, there was still concern in Indonesia because of its external debt of nearly $100 billion. In 1994, Indonesia's external debt as a percentage of GNP was 57,4%, its external debt as a percentage of exports of goods and services was 211,3%, and its debt-service ratio was 32,4%.[31] As a result, Indonesian President Suharto warned that 'a surge in imports may have a far-reaching impact on growth and equitable distribution',[32] and encouraged people to buy local rather than imported products.

In response to the increasing uncertainty regarding repayment of loans to developing countries, many banks began setting aside large reserves in case those debtors defaulted. A bank establishes reserves by funnelling some of its earnings into a reserve account. This makes it possible to reduce earnings a little each year, especially during profitable years, rather than being surprised by a major default and having to reduce earnings all at once. However, the practice of setting aside large reserves is problematic because it weakens the bank's lending ability and financial strength.

The International Monetary Fund (IMF) has played a crucial role in helping debtor nations restructure their economies. In country after country, the IMF has recommended strong economic restrictions as a precondition to granting a loan. These restrictions have typically involved a combination of export expansion, import substitution and drastic reductions in public spending. In many developing countries, IMF restrictions have touched off heated debate and sorely tested the political stability of their governments.

In many cases, an IMF loan is a prerequisite for persuading international commercial banks to reschedule a country's debts. Usually, the IMF periodically monitors the targets it sets as a precondition to releasing funds. Private international banks often use these results to determine their lending policies with regard to the monitored country.

Managers of MNEs are concerned about high debt because of the difficulty of operating in an environment that is politically and economically unstable, since imports are often curtailed and hard currency is difficult to obtain. In addition, governments may institute a variety of macro-economic measures to control debt, including slowing down economic growth, which could have a negative impact on companies' sales opportunities.

5.4.6 **Deficits**

A constant problem for governments, in high-income as well as in developing countries, and in market as well as command economies, and also at federal, state, provincial, and local levels, is the balance between revenues and expenditures, with expenditures usually exceeding revenues. In 1994, for example, only two high-income countries, New Zealand and Singapore, had a central government surplus. A good measure of the size of the deficit is the ratio of the deficit to GDP or GNP. However, as noted by the World Bank, 'Because of differences in coverage of available data, the individual components of central government expenditure and revenue shown may not be strictly comparable across all economies. Inadequate statistical coverage of state, provincial, and local governments requires the use of central government data; this may seriously understate or distort the statistical portrayal of the allocation of resources for various purposes, especially in countries where lower levels of government have considerable autonomy and are responsible for many economic and social services.'[33]

However, the problem is still an important one to consider. The European Union identified several criteria that countries must meet as they move toward establishing a common currency. Two of the criteria refer to deficits and debt. National budget deficits must be less than 3% of GDP, and the public debt ratio (total debt to GDP) must not exceed 60%.[34] The World Bank measures a country's surplus/deficit as current revenue of the central government less current expenditure. Specifically excluded are grants and the capital account.[35] Seven of the 25 countries listed by the World Bank as high-income countries had deficits greater than 3% of GNP, and included seven members of the European Union. Although there is serious political debate in the United States over the size of the budget deficit, it was only 2,2% of GNP in 1994. However, it was only 0,4% in 1980. The problem is that the size of the deficit is significant, even though it is a relatively small percentage of GNP.[36]

It is clear that countries have been moving towards reducing their deficits and have been successful in doing so. This has been due in large part to the reaction of financial markets to government fiscal policies and the recognition by governments that they need to bring their deficits under control. In the early years of the Clinton presidency, budget battles with Congress and the inability to reach a consensus to establish a balanced budget put significant downward pressure on the dollar. However, in the fiscal year 1995, the average budget deficit of high-income countries in the Organisation for Economic Co-operation and Development was expected to be only 3,4% of GDP. The United States was expected to have 'the smallest budget deficit, the lowest level of government expenditure and the lowest tax burden, relative to economic size'.[37]

Government internal deficits typically occur for one of several reasons:

- the tax system is so poor that the government cannot collect all the revenues it wants to;
- government programmes, such as defence and welfare, are too big for the revenue side to adequately cover, and
- the government gets involved in the ownership of assets.

In addition, there is the constant battle between liberals and conservatives, as illustrated in the United States, over whether cutting taxes will lead to greater personal freedom but higher budget deficits, or result in the stimulation of growth and the collection of higher revenues, but at lower personal rates. Thus all governments, including those in transition from command to market, struggle with several issues, such as rightsizing government, setting spending priorities, working toward better expenditure control and budget management, improving tax policy and administration to close the revenue gap, and the degree to which services should be decentralised.[38]

5.4.7 Privatisation

As countries move to control expenditures and reduce their budget deficits, a major target is state-owned companies. The movement of ownership from the public to the private sector is known as privatisation, and it involves all types of countries. There are many benefits to privatisation, which include:

- improving enterprise efficiency and performance;
- developing a competitive industry that services consumers well;
- assessing the capital, know-how, and markets that permit growth;
- achieving effective corporate governance;
- broadening and deepening capital markets, and
- securing the best price possible for the sale.[39]

However, privatisation is not easy. It is a political as well as an economic process, and political objectives do not always result in the best economic results. In addition to political objectives, there are political impediments, such as the obstructive attitudes of existing managers and employees of state-owned enterprises.[40]

The term 'privatisation' began with the sale of British Telecom in 1984, and most of the significant earlier privatisation efforts took lace in Britain. The process gradually spread ɔ other high-income countries and eventually ɔ the developing countries. After the fall of the erlin Wall in 1989, the privatisation effort noved to the countries of Eastern Europe and he former Soviet Union, which will be discussed more in the final sections of the chapter. 'he privatisation efforts in the non-communist vorld took place primarily through cash sales. s noted by the International Finance Corporaon, 'a database of larger [cash] sales records 2 55 transactions in 95 countries between 988 and 1993, yielding US$271 billion in evenues. Industrialised countries accounted or US$175 billion of this, and 15% of the umber of transactions, so over the period eveloping countries accounted for 85% of ales and 35% of all revenue generated'.[41]

In the developing countries, the privatisation novement began in Latin America and the 'aribbean, where 57% of the value of total eveloping-country privatisations was taking lace, followed by Europe and Central Asia vith 18.7%, and only minimal privatisations ı Sub-Saharan Africa, the Middle East, and Jorth Africa.[42]

The key to successful privatisation is the vailability of capital. Although privatisation is lofty goal preached by governments worldvide, Europeans alone will have to come up vith more than $150 billion before the end of he decade to pay for numerous efforts ranging om vehicle manufacturers to banks to oil and elecommunications companies.[43] This implies olid capital markets and both domestic and oreign investors willing to purchase the stateowned companies.

France provides an example of the privatisaion experience. Most efforts at privatisation in 'rance have involved selling minority interests n state-owned enterprises, with little initial nvolvement by foreign investors. When the 'onservatives came into power in 1993, they owed to privatise all banks, insurance companies, and competitive enterprises such as Renault, Elf Aquitaine, and Pechiney. To help und the country's privatisation effort, the Conservatives have sought to attract significant foreign capital by encouraging increased foreign involvement and allowing foreigners to hold a larger percentage of French companies.[44]

The problems that France has faced are no different to those of other European countries that are privatising state-owned assets. Some of the factors that seem to have an impact on the success of privatisation are:

1 the relative health and stability of the local stock market as well as those in surrounding countries;
2 the number of offers in the market, both at home and abroad;
3 tight monetary policy, which can prolong a recession and depress corporate profits, making it more difficult for local companies to generate the cash necessary to get involved in the privatisation efforts, and
4 the perceived openness of the bidding process. Many French, for example, feel that the government has a tendency to sell major stakes in privatised companies to hard cores of friendly buyers in France, which helps to insulate the companies against unfriendly takeovers.[45]

In 1996, the French government embarked on a new plan to move protected state-owned defence and industrial companies out of the government support mechanism by permitting consolidation among competitors inside France and then allowing the surviving companies to establish strategic alliances with similar companies in Europe. Given the deep roots of state support for national industry in France, the policy shift is not insignificant. The French government's budget deficit reduction plan has forced it to follow the policy of moving away from state-owned enterprises.[46] However, the privatisation efforts have not been as extensive as advertised. The same is true of developing countries such as Venezuela, Argentina, and Mexico. Even though the governments have announced major privatisation efforts, the actual experience has not been as advertised.

In most of the countries, the problem with privatisation lies in selling the inefficient, unproductive enterprises, not those that have a chance to survive. Where permitted, the privatisation process enables foreign companies to pick up assets and gain access to markets through acquisition. In addition, international managers accustomed to dealing with state-owned enterprises, are finding a new breed of managers in the newly privatised enterprises with which they do business.

5.5 Transformation to a market economy

The demolition of the Berlin Wall and the overthrow of Eastern European communist dictatorships in 1989 renewed Western interest in doing business in countries that had previously been considered off-limits. These countries were those that had had non-market economies (NMEs), centrally planned economies (CPEs), or had been commonly called the Second World or the Eastern Bloc. (The latter term was political rather than geographical. East-West trade referred to business between communist and non-communist countries rather than to trade between the eastern and western hemispheres.)

Most of the CPEs are in the process of transition to a market economy, hence the designation CEIT, as defined earlier in the chapter. In a report by the United Nations on demographic changes in CEITs, the discussion was generally grouped around the European successor states of the former USSR (Estonia, Latvia, Lithuania, Belarus, Republic of Moldovia, Russian Federation, and the Ukraine), the Asian successor states of the former USSR (Armenia, Azerbaijan, Georgia, Kazakhstan, Kyrgyzstan, Tajikistan, Turkmenistan, and Uzbekistan), and other European countries (Bulgaria, Czech Republic, Hungary, Poland, Romania, Slovakia, Albania, Bosnia and Herzegovina, Croatia, Slovenia, Macedonia, and Yugoslavia). In addition, there are CPEs in other parts of the world that are going through transition, including Cuba, Vietnam, China and North Korea.[47] The transition is also taking place at radically different rates. One could argue that Cuba and North Korea are not making any transition at all at this point. Even though significant demographic economic transitions are taking place in these countries, there is no common pattern. In addition, data is not reliable for all countries.

One could also argue that all countries are going through transitions of different types. For example, the statist economies of Latin America are also moving more toward democracy on a political scale and are privatising state-owned companies in order to downsize government and introduce market reforms. However, the CEITs are going through a much more significant transition from one economic system to a radically different one. Thus we will focus on the problems of these particular countries rather than all countries in transition.

The process of transformation to a market economy differs from country to country; no single formula can be applied to all. In addition, the various CEITs differ greatly in their commitment to and progress toward transformation of their centrally planned economies into market economies. At one end of the spectrum is the former German Democratic Republic (East Germany), which has been reunited with and absorbed into the German Federal Republic (West Germany), although with great difficulty. At the other end of the spectrum is Cuba, which has committed to neither reforms nor market transformation. It is unlikely that Cuba will embark on transformation any time soon. Fidel Castro, Cuba's leader, said in 1989, in reference to the political liberalisation and other changes within Eastern Europe, 'We are witnessing sad things in other socialist countries, very sad things. We are astonished at the phenomena that we see.'[48]

In the middle of the spectrum of economic transformation are the other CEITs. Hungary and the Czech Republic are in the process of transformation, but Bulgaria and Romania still naintain that a combination of central planning and market economy is possible.[49] Poland s committed but has not had time to complete he change. China, like Bulgaria and Romania, s committed to a combination of central lanning and market economy; thus it has mbarked on some reforms but still adheres to ommunistic and central planning principles.

Why do these changes bring renewed Vestern interest in doing business with EITs? The answer is partly political, partly conomic. Most CEITs experienced slow eco-omic growth during the 1970s and 1980s; onsequently, the outlook for expanded com-iercial activities seemed bleak. However, along rith reforms and transformation has come a iawing of Cold War tensions. There is also the ope that governments of these countries will liminate their trade barriers, thereby encoura-ing rejuvenated economic growth and icreased business opportunities.

Much of the recent optimism has centred round business possibilities in Eastern Europe nd China. Interest in the former is due to its vel of economic development, and the latter as been the focus of attention because of its uge population and rapid economic growth. hese conditions help explain why McDonald's as entered Hungary, Russia and China, but ot Mongolia.

China is a special case. Although its per apita income is only about one-quarter of that f Eastern European countries, its recent eco-omic growth rate is much higher, rivalling iose of its East Asian neighbours. As noted arlier in the chapter, even the World Bank oncedes that its low per capita income figures iay not accurately describe the dynamic hinese economy. Because of China's large conomy and understated per capita income, iere is greater market potential in that ountry than might seem apparent.

.5.1 Political and economic volatility

Vestern business with CEITs has been com-ared to a light switch: it turns on and then turns off.[50] The McDonald's case illustrates how business volatility is created by changing political attitudes. McDonald's negotiations with the Soviets began in 1976 and continued without significant progress until the Soviets enacted joint venture legislation in 1987. From that point, negotiations concluded swiftly and start-up followed soon afterward.

Sometimes volatility has resulted from unpopular actions by CEITs (such as the Soviet invasion of Afghanistan). In some cases, it may result from the ascendancy either of new political decision-makers in the East or leaders in the West who hold differing philosophies about business interactions with dictatorships and/or countries with central planning (for example, American trade sanctions against Cuba). Although relations between most CEITs and the Western industrialised countries have been more congenial since 1989, the risk of future sanctions by the West still exists.

Most companies prefer to invest their capital and human resources in endeavours that can be expected to continue for a long time. For this reason, persistent uncertainty about political relations with certain CEITs causes some companies to hesitate to commit resources to business development in those countries. On the one hand, Western businesses have witnessed increased political interactions, while, on the other, they also realise that past experience shows how rapidly business can change because of politics and how it can continue to fluctuate over time.

It is also important to realise that a country's attaining a market economy does not guarantee its economic success; in fact, most of the world's developing countries currently qualify as market economies. The CEITs vary widely in terms of factors that may affect their growth, with or without a high degree of transformation. These factors include the following:

- educational level of the population;
- quantity and distribution of natural resources;
- degree of national cohesiveness;

- access to investment capital;
- extent of existing industrial structure;
- entrepreneurial experience among the population;
- development of infrastructure.

Companies contemplating commercial activities in CEITs should examine development potential as well as prospects for economic transformation. The key to successful transformation to a market economy is achieving certain changes in the general economic environment, including monetary stabilisation, currency convertibility, and price and trade liberalisation.[51] Once a private sector appears, these economic changes are the ones that will keep the transformation process working.

5.5.2 The process of transformation

The World Bank, in its *World Development Report 1996*, entitled 'From Plan to Market', described the legacy of planning and its problems. Although there were early gains in economic growth and industrialisation, in the equal distribution of income and in the welfare of people, the planning process was very unstable and inefficient, leading to a poor utilisation of resources and a worsening of social indicators. 'In response, most of these economies have rejected all or much of central planning and have embarked on a passage, a transition toward decentralised market mechanisms underpinned by widespread private ownership.'[52] However, the report also noted that the transition is not the same in all countries because of 'different histories, cultures, and resource endowments'.[53]

5.5.3 Russia's transformation

For Russia, transformation to a market economy has been difficult because the government has been trying to change the country's economy and its political system simultaneously, while still coming to grips with the end of an empire whose various parts were politically and economically interdependen The resulting political turmoil is exacerbate by the battle between conservatives, who ar afraid of moving too fast, and reformers, wh want to install capitalism quickly throug privatisation and price decontrol.

The Soviet economy was cumbersom inefficient and corrupt, but somehow it seeme to function. However, the breakup of th central Soviet government, and the loss of th relationship Russia had with the other 1 Soviet republics and the former Eastern Blc countries, resulted in the implosion of th economy. For example, in 1992, Russia's GD fell by about 23% and unemployment rose fro 5 000 in January to 905 000 in Novembe Also in 1992, prices were decontrolled. Prior t that, they were controlled by the governmen and goods were distributed by means of co sumers waiting in long queues, because shortages. Price decontrol resulted in mor products being brought to market, but at th cost of significantly higher prices and inflatio that soared to over 1 000% annually. Ful two-thirds of the Russian people live below th poverty line. From the period from 1990–199 the average annual growth in GDP wa 210,6%, the average annual growth in pe capita GNP from 1985–1994 was 24,1%, an the average annual inflation from 1984–199 was 124,3%.[54] The Russian ruble, valued a 120 per US dollar in early 1992, had fallen t 5 683 rubles per dollar by the end of Februar 1997.

However, as noted earlier in the chapte Russia is starting to make real progress in th transformation process. Although data comin from Russia looks a little bleak, it is als inaccurate. Over 95% of Russia's shops ar privately owned, and retailing now accoun for half of that country's GDP. However, abou 25% of the Russian economy is unrecorded, s economic activity is not as bad as it might seen To continue the transformation process, Russi needs to stabilise the economy, enforce prop erty rights and reform local government. Infla tion is out of control, largely because of th huge government deficit, half of which is the result of subsidising inefficient enterprises.[55]

5.5.4 Eastern Europe's transformation

In the three years following the overthrow of communism in 1989 and 1990, economic growth in Eastern Europe ground to a halt. From 1990 to 1992, GNP fell by 40% in Czechoslovakia, 32% in Hungary and 32% in Poland. However, by 1992, the worst appeared to be over. Poland exhibited solid real growth in 1993 and 1994. Hungary showed a drop in real GNP in 1993, but it had real growth of 2,9% in 1994. The Czech Republic showed real growth in GDP of 2,6% in 1994 and 4,8% in 1995. Thus the big three in Eastern Europe, namely Poland, Hungary, and the Czech Republic, appear to be well on the way to positive growth.[56]

The process of transforming CEITs to market economies attempts to solve two types of problems that are universal in Eastern Europe: macro-economic problems that involve shortages and inflation, and micro-economic problems that involve investments in the wrong industries. As price controls ended and markets opened up all over Eastern Europe, shortages began to disappear fairly quickly. However, central planning had resulted in highly inefficient industries and the transformation of state-owned enterprises resulted in a sharp drop in production, much of which was unwanted and unnecessary anyway. Today, the output of the private sector is growing much more rapidly than that of the remaining public sector.[57]

As Eastern European countries transform, they are finding their budget deficits rising, not because of higher government expenditures, but because of weak revenue collections. Failing enterprises are not paying taxes, resulting in continuing revenue shortfalls.

5.5.5 China's transformation

In 1978, China's government launched reforms designed to transform the Chinese economy on the basis of a new vision – a turning away from central planning, government ownership and import substitution, and a movement toward greater decentralisation and opening up of the Chinese economy. Since then, the Chinese economy has grown to four times its size in 1978; by 2002, it is estimated to be eight times as large as in 1978.[58]

The Chinese approach to transformation differs significantly from the approaches followed in Russia and Eastern Europe. Chinese leadership is not at all interested in democratic reform and continues to hold tight to totalitarian political control, while trying to pacify citizens with economic growth. Recently, most of such growth has been along the coast and near the special economic zones, but current reforms are rapidly moving economic changes into the much poorer interior. Privatisation is not an issue, but economic activity has been decentralised swiftly. Centralised state-owned enterprises now control only half of the GNP, and their share is rapidly dwindling as economic power is pushed down to the regional and local levels, resulting in what looks like a loose federation of regional economies.[59]

One major advantage China enjoys is a high rate of investment by Chinese overseas. 'Today, at least 75% of the mainland's roughly 28 000 enterprises with significant foreign equity are financed by ethnic Chinese who live outside China. Hong Kong and Taiwan account for two-thirds (Hong Kong is the largest source of foreign investment in China).'[60] In contrast to Russia and Eastern Europe, significant foreign investment is moving into China.[61]

5.6 Keys to a successful transition to market economies

There are several keys to a successful transition to the market economy, including the following:

1 It is important for countries to establish firm and persistent application of good policies, but the way this is done is partially

determined by the history, geography, and culture of the country. As noted above, not every country can succeed in the same way.

2 'Extensive liberalisation and determined stabilisation are needed for improved productivity and growth, and sustaining these policies requires rapid structural change as well as institutional reform.' This statement implies the liberalisation of prices and trade regimes, hard budgets, and the entry of new businesses. A hard budget is one set by market conditions without government subsidies. In a soft situation, the government subsidises the revenues of the enterprise so that expenses will always be covered. Thus the enterprise cannot go bankrupt.
3 Privatisation is important, and so is the way it is done, as we will discuss below. Incentives must flow from defined property rights for a market economy to work.
4 Legal systems, financial systems, and governments must be put into place for reforms to succeed. In addition, attention must be paid to the development of human capital to cope with a market economy.[62]

Special mention must be made of five issues: the economic shocks that accompany rapid economic reform, the establishment of hard budgets, environmental damage, the development of human capital, and the privatisation of state-owned enterprises.

5.6.1 Economic shocks

As part of bringing about a market transformation, some negative economic consequences are inevitable, at least in the short term. The basic problem is that the costs are up front, but the benefits come much later. For example, increasing efficiency, through allowing foreign competition, brings with it unemployment. But CEITs are not accustomed to unemployment and do not have the safety nets of fall-back compensation, retraining facilities and job-relocation assistance that have been developed over a long period in industrialised countries. In addition, price decontrol brings rapid inflation because the old prices were below the true market values. When Poland deregulated most of its prices, a standard joke among its citizens was, 'We used to have long lines and empty shelves. Now we have no lines, full shelves, but no money to buy what's on the shelves.'

Economic shocks are politically dangerous. Workers and consumers have high expectations for economic transformation – perhaps too high. To the extent that they are adversely affected by unemployment and higher prices (a lowering of real income), even in the short term, they may lose confidence in the elected political leadership and in the transformation process itself, thus slowing down or preventing change.

5.6.2 Soft budgets

A soft budget is a financial condition in which an enterprise spends more than it earns and the difference is met by some other institution, typically the government or a government-controlled financial institution. The CEITs all have legacies of soft budgets from the period when it was unthinkable that an enterprise would not survive. Even within an environment of transformation, pressures remain to continue soft-budget practices. Cushioned by a soft budget, management has an incentive to make deals with authorities, instead of effecting efficiencies in the company that could help it survive.

5.6.3 Environmental damage

Environmental damage is another major concern for CEITs. Since harm to human health is the most important consequence of such damage, the two most important problems are air and water pollution. The former results from suspended metal dusts and particulate materials. The latter is exacerbated by careless disposal of toxic or nuclear waste that threatens the quality of surface and groundwater in some areas.[63] The major causes of environmental pollution are heavy coal use, old technology, especially in the metallurgy industry, and low energy prices, which serve as a disincentive to save energy and raw materials.

Some argue that air pollution in the main towns and cities of Eastern Europe is no worse than in Western European cities, such as Athens, Madrid, and Milan, that have similar income levels and industrial structures. These analysts claim that environmental problems in Eastern Europe today are at the level they were in Western Europe and North America 20 to 30 years ago. In reality, water pollution and environmental damage from inadequate nuclear waste management are far more serious in Eastern Europe today than they were in industrialised countries 30 years ago. The cost of environmental cleanup will be significant and will reduce the amount of investment capital available to transform CEITs to market economies. China is also facing an environmental crisis as it modernises its economy. Major concerns are the pollution of air, water, and farmland. Even the World Bank has warned China of the consequences of the lack of enforcement of environmental controls on all sources of pollution.

5.6.4 Human capital

Many government-owned enterprises are plagued by mammoth bureaucracies that are difficult to replace. As a government eliminates central planning without also substituting knowledgeable owners to whom enterprise managers can report, there is little control over these managers' actions. Another problem, more acute in countries in which people have no memory of market operations, is that most managers have no experience in operating without a central plan that tells them what to produce and to whom to sell. They may also lack experience in controlling subordinates by hiring and firing them, or finding means of compensation as a way of motivating them. Very few of these managers understand how to read or compile financial statements, respond to market signals (such as changes in demand), or market products when there is competition and no pent-up demand, especially in Western export markets. They may also lack a strong work ethic because of their experiences with low pay and high job security. Further, egalitarian attitudes, especially in Russia and China, result in successful entrepreneurs sometimes being seen as speculators – a contemptuous label.[64]

5.6.5 Privatisation in CEITs

A characteristic of CEITs is the existence of large companies before the transition to a market economy. An important dimension to the transition process, and one where foreign investors can play a role, is the privatisation of large, state-owned companies. There are basically five objectives of privatisation: better corporate governance, speed and feasibility, better access to capital and skills, more government revenues, and greater fairness.[65]

There are three major methods used to privatise: sale to outside owners, management-employee buyout, and equal-access voucher privatisation.[66] Sale to outside owners, the method most widely used initially, leads to better corporate governance, better access to capital and skills, and more government revenue, but not to speed or flexibility and greater fairness. This is the process used most widely in Estonia and Hungary.

Management-employee buyout is the most-used approach in Russia, Croatia, Poland, Romania, and Slovenia. This approach is relatively fast and easy to implement, but it results in employees in good companies getting vouchers with value, and those in bad companies getting vouchers worth little. In addition, the government does not raise as much revenue as would be the case in an outright sale. In Russia, privatisation favours keeping insiders in control of enterprises. Each Russian citizen receives a voucher that can be used to purchase stock in former state-owned enterprises or investment funds that, in turn, invest in companies. Although the system appears to be a voucher system, insiders could buy up to

51% of their enterprise at 1,7 times book value, not adjusted for inflation. In addition, investment funds could not own more than 10% of the shares in any one company. Further, because workers usually ended up with more power, there is more incentive to put earning into wages and bonuses than into dividends, a practice that discourages investment.[67] Eventually, insiders bought about two-thirds of the shares of 15 000 privatised firms. Outsiders obtained about 20% to 30% of the shares, investment funds and individual investors picked up 10% to 15%, and the rest went to the government.[68]

Equal-access voucher privatisation is the most widely used approach, and is especially popular in the Czech Republic, Lithuania, Mongolia, and more recently, the Ukraine and Poland. Assets are spread equally among voucher-holders, and the system is quick and easy to implement, but it does not raise much revenue nor does it improve corporate governance. With the voucher system, vouchers are given to the general public and they are exchanged for shares in privatising companies.

In the Czech Republic, for example, the government sold booklets of vouchers for a nominal fee, which was then used to buy shares in huge public auctions of enterprises. In two waves of privatisation, the Czech government has transferred about 50% of the state-owned assets into private hands. However, more than two-thirds of the voucher-holders invested their vouchers in investment funds rather than directly in the enterprises. Many of these investment funds were controlled by banks, resulting in a concentration of ownership.[69]

5.7 Adapting to foreign economic environments in the internationalisation process

A company based in the United States is accustomed to and has devised ways to survive in the American economic system. However, when such a company wants to do business in another country for the first time, it needs to find answers to questions such as the following:

1 Under what type of economic system does the country operate?
2 Is the company's industry in the public or private sector of that country?
3 If it is in the public sector, does the government also allow private competition in that sector?
4 If the company's industry is in the private sector, is it moving toward public ownership?
5 Does the government view foreign capital as being in competition with or in partnership with public or local private enterprises?
6 In what ways does the government control the nature and extent of private enterprise?
7 How much of a contribution is the private sector expected to make in helping the government formulate overall economic objectives?

These questions appear simple; however, because of the dynamic nature of political and economic events, the answers are complex. Many foreign companies are still investing in Hong Kong even though it reverted to China on 1 July 1997, and there is some uncertainty as to how China will affect the business environment of Hong Kong in the future. Hong Kong companies, such as Swire, are investing outside of that country because of the same uncertainty. Companies attempting to invest in Eastern Europe and the former Soviet Union are experiencing enormous difficulties because the economic environment in those countries is very different to any other in the world, and the changes taking place there are rapid and unpredictable.

Companies intending to do business in foreign markets must be aware of how their own experiences have helped shape their managerial philosophies and practices. In addition, they must determine how the new environment differs from their more familiar domestic one, and decide how managerial philosophy and practice must be changed to adapt to the new conditions.

A major issue of social responsibility implied in this chapter concerns the obligations of high-income countries to assist those which are still developing. Some of the areas in which the high-income countries might be considered to have an ethical obligation to provide support are access to markets for developing countries' exports, foreign aid, and repayment of loans.

First, developing countries must have access to markets in high-income countries in order to sell products. Many developing countries have domestic markets of limited size, and their trade with each other is not significant. For example, Latin-American countries on average export only about 10% of their products to other Latin-American countries but almost 20% of these to the United States. However, during the recent period of relatively high unemployment in industrial countries, protectionism has threatened to cut off developing countries' access to industrial markets. If high-income countries discriminate against exports from developing countries, they are hurting those countries' prospects for further development.

As for foreign aid, there has been increasing pressure in the United States to cut down the amount of such aid in order to put the funds to use in improving the domestic economy. However, the United States and other high-income countries benefit from trade with developing countries, not only through gaining access to their markets, but also through utilising their resources. Some high-income countries view foreign aid as a means of putting resources back into developing countries. For example, the Scandinavian countries contribute a larger percentage of their GDPs to foreign aid than the United States and Japan. And other high-income European countries, such as Germany and the Netherlands, provide funding to their developing neighbours, Spain and Portugal, to help them improve their infrastructure. In contrast, when the United States and Mexico were debating NAFTA in 1993, much of the opposition to the agreement came from people who wondered how it was going to be funded, rather than how the United States could provide more resources to Mexico to help develop the economy.

A third ethical issue concerns the repayment of loans. Because of the overwhelming size of the external debt of many developing countries, one possible solution is writing off some or all of such debt. Another possibility is to restructure it so that repayment is less burdensome to a developing country's economic growth. Writing off debts might be more appropriate for loans made by governments of high-income countries than for those made by private-sector banks. But, in any case, some feel the high-income countries need to make an effort to be part of the solution to the debt crisis rather than just part of the problem.

5.8 Ethical dilemmas

Small companies that do business with developing countries and CEITs potentially face the problems of inadequate financial resources, managerial expertise, and/or the patience required to succeed. The resource commitment is significant, as illustrated by the McDonald's case. However, many small companies successfully trade with or invest in developing countries by exploiting a product niche. For example, before McDonald's opened its first restaurant in Moscow, an American entrepreneur with limited financial resources operated a Nathan's Famous Hot Dogs mobile unit in that city. From one pushcart, he served about 1 000 customers a day, and the venture was very profitable. To ensure that he could always obtain needed supplies, he bought meat each day from the Central Market, where farmers sell from their private production at a significant premium over the prices offered by the state stores.[70]

Another major issue is national sovereignty. As CEITs go through the transition to market economies, they are getting a lot of advice from Western countries that are providing financial aid, as well as from international organisations such as the IMF. Although the CEITs need the aid and the advice, they are trying to develop strategies that fit their unique situations and so they do not always follow all the advice offered. This is especially a problem when their actions are contrary to the advice offered by aid-granting countries and organisations.

5.9 **Summary**

The economic system determines who owns and controls resources. In a market economy, individuals allocate and control resources; in a centrally planned economy, the government allocates and controls resources.

Consumer sovereignty was defined as the freedom of consumers to influence production, while economic freedom was defined as freedom from government constraints, and legal and institutional frameworks to safeguard freedoms. 'Free' countries tend to be high-income market economies, and 'Not-free' countries tend to be state capitalist and command economies.

Countries were classified according to three income levels: high, middle, and low. The middle- and low-income countries are often called developing countries, while developed or high-income countries represent 21% of the countries and 15,2% of the population, but 79,5% of the GNP.

As countries become more prosperous and their economies shift from low-income to high-income categories, the percentage of GDP derived from agriculture decreases and that derived from industry and services increases.

High-income and developing countries are trying to privatise government-owned enterprises in order to help eliminate their budget deficits. This has resulted in the reduction of inflation and, therefore, the number of countries considered to be highly inflationary has also been reduced.

Political and economic changes within the former communist countries have led to optimism in the West about doing business in those countries because there may be fewer political barriers and economic growth will enhance market potential. Another feature of the 20th century is that political relationships between Western countries and CEITs have varied significantly, resulting in business relationships that also have fluctuated substantially. This has been especially true of trade between the United States and the former Soviet Union.

Russia's transformation has been complicated by its transition to democracy, the breakup of the Soviet empire, and the political problems of balancing conservative efforts to retain central control over the economy and reformist efforts to move quickly to a market economy. Eastern European countries have approached transformation of their economies differently, and their private sectors are creating significantly more economic growth than their public sectors. China's transformation has involved large infusions of capital from overseas Chinese and decentralisation of economic decision-making.

Case Study

Pizza Hut in Brazil

In 1994, Pizza Hut celebrated the opening of its 10 000th restaurant worldwide by featuring the former Brazilian soccer star, Pélé, kicking an autographed soccer ball through a ceremonial ribbon to open a store in Sâo Paulo, Brazil. This event was viewed by people in 12 countries in Europe and the United States via an international satellite broadcast. Because of to changing economic conditions in Brazil, however, Pizza Hut was re-examining its strategy in 1996 to determine what changes it needed to make to be competitive in Brazil and to add value to the bottom line of its parent company, PepsiCo. Although PepsiCo announced in 1995 that it planned to invest an additional $2,1 billion in Brazil, through to the year 2000, for the construction of soft-drink factories and new Pizza Hut restaurants, that investment could be in jeopardy if the Brazilian economy soured.

PepsiCo, one of the largest consumer products companies in the world, was organised into three major business units in 1996; beverages, snack foods and restaurants. Exhibit 5.7 identifies PepsiCo's sales and profits by division in 1995. The snack foods division, Frito-Lay, is organised around key brands, such as Fritos, Lay's potato chips, Cheetos, Doritos, and Tostitos. The restaurant division is divided into Pizza Hut, KFC, and Taco Bell. As noted in Exhibit 5.7, the restaurant division is not very profitable, which resulted in the announcement in late 1996 that it would be sold off from PepsiCo.

As noted in Exhibit 5.8 (p. 158), 71,3% of PepsiCo's revenues are from domestic operations, although beverages and snack foods, are much more international than the restaurant division. PepsiCo's largest market internationally is Europe, with 9,1% of net sales being generated there. Their next two largest markets are Mexico and Canada, which are also involved with the United States in the North American Free Trade Agreement (NAFTA), which was discussed in Chapter 2.

Pizza Hut has more restaurant units worldwide than Taco Bell or KFC. It operates through company-owned stores, joint ventures with

Exhibit 5.7: PepsiCo's net sales and profits by divisions, 1995

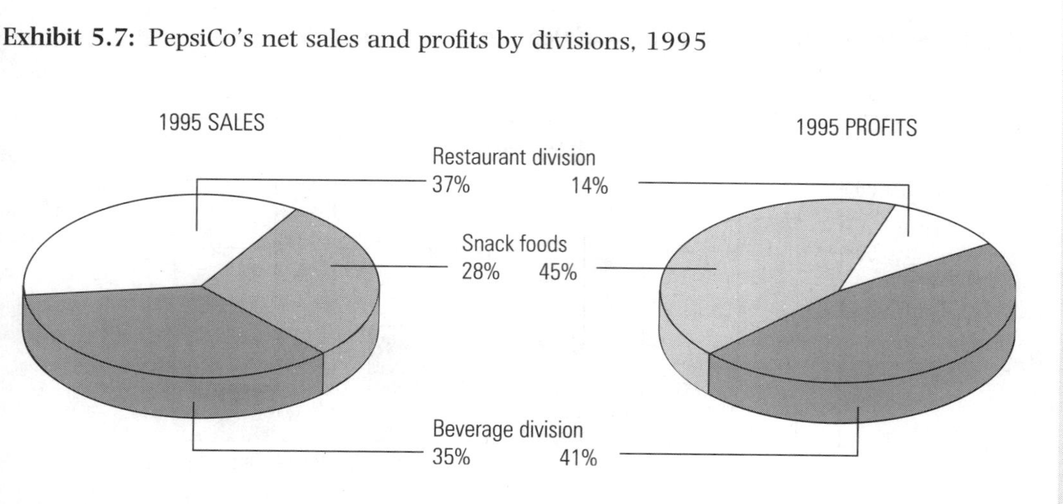

other partners where Pizza Hut has an equity interest in the stores, and franchises. In the case of franchises, Pizza Hut does not own an equity interest in the local stores, but it allows a local investor to own the store and pay a royalty and other fees to Pizza Hut. Operating results for the restaurant division in general, and Pizza Hut in particular, have been disappointing in recent years. As noted in the 1994 annual report, 'There were two reasons for the decline (in Pizza Hut's volume). First, we were less successful than usual at introducing the kind of big new products that really excite consumers and attract lots of them to our restaurants. Second, with beef prices unusually low, the hamburger chains were able to keep their prices down. That led to pretty fierce competition across most of the quick service restaurant industry.'

What role will Brazil play in the growth of Pizza Hut worldwide? The three largest markets for Pizza Hut internationally are (1) the United Kingdom, (2) Canada, and (3) Australia. However, Pizza Hut's ten-year plan would put Brazil as the second- or third-largest market in the world. Brazil offers a number of location-specific advantages. The first is its massive size. In 1993, Brazil was the fifth-largest country in the world in population, with 156 million people, the 12th-largest country in the world in GNP, but only ranked 103rd in per capita income. It was also the seventh-largest country in the world in land mass. Brazil is very urbanised, with Sâo Paulo the second-largest city in the world after Cairo, and Rio de Janeiro the 16th-largest city in the world. It is ranked 42nd in the world in urbanisation, but only 175th in population density, even lower than the United States.

From a political standpoint, Brazil's democracy was replaced by a military dictatorship in 1964, and it stayed a totalitarian state until 1984. In 1984, a new president was elected, but he died before he could take office in 1985. His vice-president, José Sarney, served as president until 1990. When Fernando Collor de Mello took office in 1990, he was thus the first democratically elected president since 1960. In 1994, Fernando Henrique Cardoso, previously the finance minister, was elected president and took office in 1995. Thus Brazil's nascent democracy seems to be taking hold. When Cardoso took office, the Brazilian constitution did not permit the president to succeed himself, but, by early 1997, he was working hard to

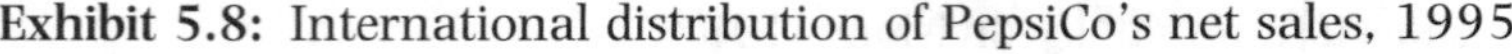

Exhibit 5.8: International distribution of PepsiCo's net sales, 1995

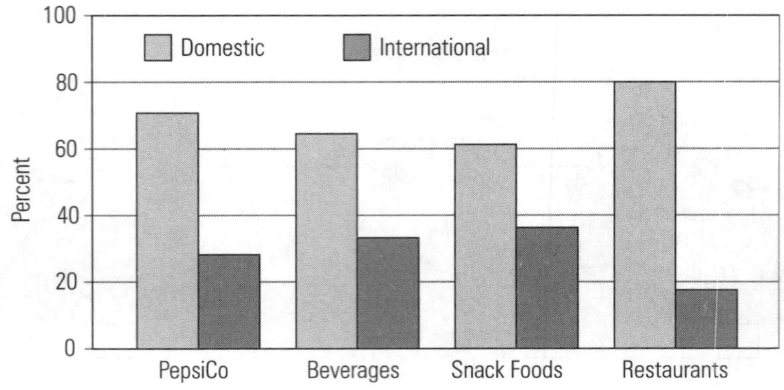

amend the constitution to allow him to run for a second five-year term, so that his economic reforms could be put into place.

From an economic standpoint, Brazil is a land of tremendous opportunity. Historically, Brazil's governments followed an economic policy based on import substitution and the transition from agriculture to industry. Protective tariffs and import quotas were essential to stimulate domestic industry. State-owned enterprises were established in steel, oil, infrastructure, and other industries, and they received subsidised, long-term credit to expand.

When the military took over in 1964, power was centralised from the states and from congress to the executive branch of government. As the economy began to heat up during the late 1960s and early 1970s, inflation also began to rise, averaging about 20% per annum. The government tried traditional means of slowing it down, such as raising interest rates, but the large concentration of industrial power resulted in price inflexibility, the indexing of prices above costs, and the passing on of higher interest rates as an additional cost. Because of protection, foreign trade remained a small percentage of GDP.

The first oil shock in 1973 created problems for Brazil, because, in spite of its wealth of natural resources, the country relies on imported oil. Economic growth expanded the demand for oil, and the rise in prices worsened its trade balance. However, import controls gave the government some breathing space. In spite of this, it was forced to borrow money from abroad, and about 50% of the foreign debt was tied to state-owned enterprises. Inflation during the later 1970s increased to an annual rate of about 40%, and the private sector began to show significant resentment to the favouritism shown to the state-owned enterprises. The second oil shock in 1979 was accompanied by rising interest rates on foreign debt, and the country went into more severe shock. The economy actually fell 2% in 1981, and Brazil was hit by recession, devaluation of the currency, rising real interest rates, real wage reductions, and a widening federal deficit.

The newly elected governments of 1985 and 1990 focused on foreign debt, inflation, and exchange rate policies. Real per capita incomes actually fell 6% during the 1980s, and cumulative inflation during the 1980s reached 39 043,76%. Before he resigned from office because of a corruption scandal, President Collor had begun to tackle Brazil's serious economic problems, but he ran out of time. However, Cardoso instituted a new economic plan, while he was finance minister, that slowed down Brazil's inflation and stabilised the exchange rate. Prices that had been rising by 30% to 50% per month suddenly slowed to rises of single-digit figures, and Cardoso's popularity soared, allowing him to win the election with 54% of the vote. However, Brazil continues to face serious economic and social problems. The state is still a dominant force in the economy, and privatisation has been difficult. The vast gap between the rich and poor has widened in recent years, and there are problems with decent housing, clean water, and good sewage systems. However, trade restrictions have fallen away and Brazil is attracting a lot of foreign investment, both direct and portfolio.

Pizza Hut first entered Brazil through a franchisee in 1988 during a period of high inflation and economic instability. At that time, Pizza Hut did not have a specific strategy for Brazil but, in 1989, opened a mall unit in Sâo Paulo, and in 1991, set up an office in Brazil dedicated to establishing a plan for the country. In addition to Pizza Hut, KFC is also operating in Brazil. However, the two restaurants have different strategies. KFC is expanding through unit-by-unit franchising, whereas Pizza Hut does so through corporate franchises. In a unit-by-unit franchise, an individual restaurant is franchised to a particular franchisee. In a corporate franchise, the corporate franchisee is given a whole territory, generally the same as a state boundary, with the exception of Sâo Paulo, and is not allowed to subfranchise (sell a franchise to someone else). Because of its size, São Paulo is divided up into five different franchises.

The initial idea of using strong corporate franchises made sense to Pizza Hut, because they wanted franchisees with strong financial backing and experience in operating in an inflationary environment. However, the franchisees wield a great deal of power, which could affect Pizza Hut's implementation of a Brazilian strategy. Pizza Hut establishes targets for all franchisees in terms of how they must let the business grow in order to maintain the franchise. One of Pizza Hut's original franchisees in São Paulo, United Food Companies (UFC), also became a supplier of cheese products to the franchisees, allowing UFC to move down the value chain and the other franchisees to get access to cheese. Now Pizza Hut has diversified to other suppliers, and is importing cheese from abroad.

By 1993, UFC had established 35 stores in São Paulo, generating sales per store unit that were between 33% and 50% greater than at its counterparts in the USA. However, Brazil was also the only region in the world serviced solely by franchises. Pizza Hut had no equity interest in any of its stores. Management decided that it needed to own some stores in order to develop operating knowledge and expertise that it could share with its franchisees. The franchise value increases when the franchisor can make a valuable contribution to the franchisees, and Pizza Hut felt that it was lacking an important piece of operating knowledge. It was fairly easy to track the revenues and taxes of its franchisees, but it did not have a good understanding of the cost structure of the business. Therefore, Pizza Hut decided to buy UFC's 35 units in December 1993. Management soon found out that the restaurants were not very cost-efficient, but they could get away with their inefficiencies because of the high prices they were charging. However, the environment was beginning to change.

A major aspect of the economic environment affecting Pizza Hut's profitability in Brazil was inflation. Between 1964 and 1993 when Pizza Hut bought its first 35 units, the annual increase in the consumer price index (CPI) in Brazil had been less than 20% only twice – in 1972 and 1973. In the 1990s, inflation was out of control, with a 2 938% increase in 1990, 441% in 1991, 1009% in 1992 and 2148% in 1993. In early 1994, the CPI was rising at the rate of 1% per day. Then in June 1994, the government instituted the Plan Real, and inflation began to slow down. The new currency, the Real, was pegged to the US dollar, meaning that the government established an exchange rate between the Real and the dollar and would not allow this rate to change as it had done in the past. In addition, inflation dropped from an annual rate of 4 060% in the third quarter of 1994 to 33,4% by September 1995.

In the first six months of operations, several problems arose. The first was management culture. Store managers had been operating relatively independently without any outside control, and now they had to adopt Pizza Hut's control process – not an easy thing to do. They rebelled against the outside control and did not appreciate having to manage differently and be held accountable for their actions. Second, staff at the stores were more numerous than Pizza Hut management realised. It was easy for the original franchisee to hide costs and the number of employees during the initial negotiations, and when Pizza Hut found this out, it was too late to go back to the original owners and complain.

The third major problem was inflation, which affected business in many different ways. When the new currency came in and inflation slowed down, the stores took a big payroll hit. Although store managers had a fixed salary, they also received a bonus based on sales. Previously, the bonus had been delayed by 45 days, and price increases allowed stores to cover the bonuses with cheaper money. Inflated sales were immediately invested so that the store could generate interest income. However, the inflationary benefit disappeared, effectively increasing bonuses by the lost inflation as much as 45% in that period. The same problem affected purchases and mall leases. In the case of purchases, Pizza Hut used to collect sales immediately, since the stores operate on a cash-and-carry basis, and delay the payment of supplies, which allowed them to pay for supplies with inflated sales revenues. However, this benefit disappeared once inflation slowed down. Mall leases are based on 6% of sales and are typically delayed 30 to 45 days, thus allowing stores to use inflated revenues to pay for the leases. However, the drop in inflation meant that mall lease payments basically went up 30% to 45%.

In addition, the slowdown in inflation has made consumers more knowledgeable. When inflation was running wild, no one really knew how to compare prices. Prices were changing daily, and salaries were going up as well, so there was no reliable point of reference. Now, however, consumers, as well as franchisees, are beginning to compare prices and make more informed decisions. At approximately $19 to $20 for a medium pizza, many consumers are wondering if Pizza Hut is worth the price, given the alternatives. For example, Mr Pizza, the largest Brazilian-brand fast-food operation, was thrilled to have Pizza Hut as a competitor, because it no longer had the most expensive pizza in the market but fell into the medium-price range.

At the same time that Pizza Hut is attempting to control costs in Brazil, PepsiCo is trying to improve the profitability of its restaurant division worldwide. In November 1994, PepsiCo established PRI (PepsiCo Restaurants International) with Roger Enrico, former head of the successful Frito-Lay products division, as the head of PRI. The objective of the new PRI is to consolidate the international aspects of the restaurants in order to cut costs and improve profitability. Prior to that time, each restaurant group – Pizza Hut, KFC and Taco Bell – had its own staffs, including human resources and finance. The same was true of each country. In Brazil, for example, Pizza Hut and KFC were relatively independent with their own local staffs. Thus PRI, which is headquartered in Dallas, is responsible for all restaurants outside the United States and Canada. There will still be three North American restaurant divisions with the remainder consolidated in PRI. In 1995, Enrico's responsibilities were expanded when he was made responsible for the entire restaurant division in North America and worldwide so that he could help establish a co-ordinated restaurant strategy.

Beginning in 1995, Pizza Hut Brazil was faced with having to adapt to the new organisational structure as well as the new Brazilian operating environment. Because of the stabilisation of prices and the exchange rate between the US dollar and the Brazilian Real, sales in Pizza Hut's Sâo Paulo units dropped by nearly one-half from December 1994 to December 1995, even though the number of units increased. As people perceived the relatively high prices of Pizza Hut pizzas, store traffic fell. Although Pizza Hut's target increase in volume annually in Brazil was 19%, it was only growing by 6%. In order to stimulate sales, Pizza Hut attempted two different strategies. PRI told the franchisees to reduce prices by 25% in order to be more price-competitive. McDonald's, the leading fast-food chain in Brazil, increased prices by 40% in January 1992 in order to catch up to inflation, but later reduced them by 20% and advertised the drop as a vote of confidence in Brazil. The campaign was widely successful and helped McDonald's to continue to grow. Many Pizza Hut units, on the other hand, dropped prices in the last week of October and first week of December 1995, and used the samba (a Brazilian dance of African origin) to announce the decision. However, this campaign was seen as a failure. The press covered it as a desperation move to keep pace with McDonald's, and many felt that in adopting the samba, Pizza Hut had followed a strategy very inconsistent with the American brand image that it had worked so hard to cultivate. In addition, one franchisee in Rio maintained that Pizza Hut would be better off putting more money into marketing than dropping prices. Using this strategy, he was able to increase his volume, whereas those that dropped prices found that volume initially went up but then dropped back to the previous level.

By the end of 1996, Pizza Hut was continuing to struggle worldwide, and PepsiCo announced that it was selling its restaurant division sometime in 1997. Would Pizza Hut continue its expansion in Brazil under new management, and would it be successful?

? Questions

1 What are the location-specific advantages that Brazil has to offer? How do these advantages differ from those offered by other markets in Latin America?

2 Should Pizza Hut put more of its efforts in expanding in Brazil or somewhere in South-East Asia? Why?

3 What dimensions of the local political and economic environment have an impact on Pizza Hut's success in Brazil in volume, revenues, and profitability? How could a change in those dimensions affect Pizza Hut's future success?

4 Why did Pizza Hut decide to purchase some stores in Brazil instead of continuing to expand through issuing franchises? What are the strengths and weaknesses of this strategy?

Endnotes

1 PepsiCo 1994 and 1995 Annual Reports; 'Pepsi-Cola wins second stadium account', *Nation's Restaurant News*, 28 August, 1995, p. 46 .
Penteado, J.R.W.1993. 'Fast food franchises fight for Brazilian aficionados', *Brandweek*, 7 June, pp. 20-24.
'Pélé kicks open 10 000th Pizza Hut outlet', *Public Relations Journal*, May 1995, p. 16.
'Pizza Hut cooks in Brazil', *Advertising Age*, 4 April, 1994, p. 45.
Simmerman, M. 1995. 'The new Pepsi challenge: Annual profit growth of 15%', *Buffalo News*, 24 September, p. 18B.
Whalen, J. 1995. 'PepsiCo restaurants cook with Enrico', *Advertising Age*, 5 June, p. 4. *International Financial Statistics Yearbook*, 1993.
Interviews with Pizza Hut employees in Brazil.
2 Scott, B.R. 1984. 'Country analysis', *Harvard Business School*, March, pp. 82–105.
3 Messick, R E. 1996 . 'The world survey of economic freedom', *Freedom Review*, March-April, pp. 7–8.
4 Ibid., p. 8.
5 *World Development Report 1984*.Washington, DC: World Bank, p. 67.
6 Freeman, J R. 1989. *Democracy and markets: The politics of mixed economies.* Ithaca, NY: Cornell University Press, p. 7.
7 Messick, op. cit., p. 14.
8 Porter, M.E. 1980. *The competitive advantage of nations.* New York: The Free Press, pp. 74–75.
9 Ibid., p. 86.
10 Abel, A.B. & Bernanke, B. S. 1992. *Macro-economics.* Reading, MA: Addison-Wesley, p. 30.
11 The World Bank. 1996. *World Development Report.* New York: Oxford University Press, p. 224.
12 Data are from *The World Bank Atlas* 1996, p. 20.
13 Ibid.
14 *World Development Report 1996*, pp. 224–225.
15 Crossette, B. 1996. AUN survey finds world rich-poor gap widening', *New York Times*, 15 July, (international edition), p. A3. Quotes information contained in the Human Development Report published by the United Nations.
16 Ibid.
17 Ibid.
18 Moore, D.W. & Newport, F. 1995. 'People throughout the world largely satisfied with personal lives', *The Gallup Poll Monthly*, June 1995, p. 2.
19 Morais, R.C. 1995. 'Saga of fire and ice', *Forbes*, 23 October, p. 162.
20 'The global economy: A survey', *The Economist*, 1 October, 1994, p. 4.
21 Carrington, T. 1993. 'Economic disparities vex developing world', *Wall Street Journal*, 27 September, p. A1.
22 Barnathan, J. & Curry, L. 1993. 'Inflation has China running scared', *Business Week*, 14 June, pp. 48–49.
23 *Business America*, March 1996, pp.11–13;.
Greenberger, R.S. 1996. 'June trade gap narrowed, but deficit with China overtakes Japan's as largest', *Wall Street Journal*, 21 August, p. A3 (Western Edition).
Greenberger, R.S. 1997. 'U.S. trade gap hit eight-year high in 1996, widened by rise in imports', *Wall Street Journal*, 20 February, p. A2 (Western Edition).
24 *World Development Report 1996*, p. 219.
25 Ibid., pp. 190–191.
26 'States of denial', *The Economist*, 10 August, 1996, p. 57.
27 Ibid.
28 *World Development Report 1996*, pp. 220–221.
29 Ibid.
30 Ibid.
31 Ibid., p. 220.
32 'States of denial', p. 57.
33 *World Development Report 1996*, p. 233.
34 'How to get good marks, or ECUs', *The Economist*, 14 December, 1991, p. 52.
35 *World Development Report 1996*, pp. 225–226.
36 Ibid., p. 191.
37 Strassheim, D. 1996. 'Economic Viewpoints', *Business Insights* (Merrill Lynch, January), pp. 1–2.
38 *World Development Report 1996*, pp. 113–120.
39 International Finance Corporation. 1995. *Privatisation Principles and Practice.* Washington, DC: IFC, p. 1.
40 Ibid.
41 Ibid., p. 9.
42 Ibid.
43 'The perils of privatisation', *Business Week*, 16 May, 1994, p. 48.
44 Casassus, B. 1993. 'How French privatisation could go into fast-forward', *Global Finance*, March, p. 59.
45 Toy, S. & Glasgal, W. 1994. 'France: Investors may be sated', *Business Week*, 16 May, p. 48.
46 Lavin, D. 1996. 'Paris retreats from protected industries', *Wall Street Journal*, 24 July, 1996, p. A15.
47 United Nations Population Division, Department for Economic and Social Information and Policy Analysis. The Demography of Countries with Economies in Transition [on line]. Available: gopher://gopher.undp.org:70/00/ungophers/popin/wdtrends/transit.
48 'Castro laments sad events in other communist nations', *New York Times*, 9 November, 1989, p. A6.
Howard, W. F. 1990. 'Dreary Havana flirts with capitalism', *New York Times*, 6 December, p. A4.
49 Marer, P. 1990. 'Roadblocks to economic transformation in Central and Eastern Europe and some lessons of market economies', in Clark, Dick, ed. *United States-Soviet and East European relations: Building a*

. Queenstown, Md.: Aspen Institute,

by R. D. Schmidt, vice chairman of
AUS-USSR trade: An American
ssman's viewpoint', *Columbia Journal of World Business*, Vol. 18, No. 4, Winter 1983, p. 36.

51 Frydman, R. & Rapacsynski, A. 1993. 'Privatisation in Eastern Europe: Is the state withering away?' *Finance & Development*, June, p. 10.
52 *World Development Report 1996*, pp. 1–3.
53 Ibid.
54 Ibid., pp. 189, 191, and 209.
55 'Putting Russia right', in 'Russia's emerging market: A survey', *The Economist*, 8 April, 1995, pp. 16–21.
56 'East Europe survey: More than half-way there', *The Economist*, 13 March 1993, p. 9.
57 Ibid.
58 'China survey: The titan stirs', *The Economist*, 28 November, 1992, pp. 3–4.
59 Barnathan, J. & Curry, L. 1993. 'Inflation has China running scared', *Business Week*, 14 June, pp. 55–57.
60 Brick, A. in Melloan, George. 1993. 'China's miracle workers mostly live elsewhere', *Wall Street Journal*, 8 March, p. A11.
61 'The overseas Chinese: 'A driving force', *The Economist*, 18 July, 1992, p. 21.
62 *World Development Report 1996*, p. 5.
63 Hughes, G. 1992. 'Cleaning up Eastern Europe', *Finance & Development*, September, pp. 17–18.
64 Sachs, J. 1991. 'Poland and Eastern Europe: What is to be done?' in Andris Kšves and Paul Marer, eds. *Foreign economic liberalisation: Transformations in socialist and market economies*. Boulder, Co.: Westview, pp. 238–239.
Kraljic, P. 1990. 'The economic gap separating East and West', *McKinsey Quarterly*, Spring, pp. 62–74.
'Now for the acid test', *Euromoney*, November 1990, pp. 40–47.
65 *World Development Report 1996*, p. 52.
66 Ibid.
67 Frydman and Rapacsyruski, op. cit., p. 12.
68 *World Development Report 1996*, p. 55.
69 Ibid., p. 56.
70 Poe, R. 1990. 'Guerrilla entrepreneurs', *Success*, September, pp. 34–36.

6 The global monetary system and foreign exchange market

Key issues

- The International Monetary System
- The foreign exchange market
- Foreign exchange markets and rates
- Exchange rate determination
- Exchange rate forecasting
- International capital markets

The brief outline of the International Monetary System sets the scene for a closer look at the scope, nature, and functions of the foreign exchange market and international capital market. Given this global financial environment, the approach in this chapter provides a frame of reference for international financial management and decision-making, which are discussed in Chapter 10.

6.1 Introduction

Money became increasingly important as the generally accepted medium of exchange when barter was no longer used. The growth of international trade and investments in recent decades promoted the development of international and global financial markets, systems and institutions in support of the ever-increasing international financial activities worldwide.

The international economy was discussed in Chapter 5. This chapter deals with the global financial market as the frame of reference and basis for all international financial activities. More specifically, it discusses the following important aspects of the global financial market:

- the International Monetary System, including the European Monetary System and the Economic and Monetary Union;
- the foreign exchange market;
- the international capital market.

6.2 The International Monetary System[1]

The International Monetary System (IMS) is an important part of the broader international financial system and represents a set of rules and regulations aimed at facilitating international trade without jeopardising either individual national economies or the entire world economy. The IMS accordingly provides the institutional framework within which the foreign exchange market functions and the rationale for government intervention.

This section looks at the historical development and current status of the IMS as a frame of reference for international monetary activities and the functioning of the foreign exchange market. The foreign exchange market and its implications for international financial management are addressed in Section 6.3.

6.2.1 Development of the International Monetary System

In order to know how the foreign exchange market functions within the institutional framework of the IMS and how it serves as a frame of reference for international financial decision-making, it is necessary to trace the origin and evolution of the IMS. The historical development of the IMS, the European Monetary System (EMS), the Economic and Monetary Union (EMU), and the foreign exchange market will now receive attention.

6.2.2 The gold standard, 1876–1944

From very early times, gold was used as a universal medium of exchange. At its inception in Europe during the 1870s, the gold standard constituted the first formal international monetary system. According to the rules governing the **gold standard**, the countries concerned had to determine rates at which their paper or coin currency could be converted to a specific weight of gold.

The overall confidence in this system was undermined by distortions in the international financial markets, particularly from the First World War in 1914 until 1944, as the Second World War was drawing to a close. These distortions resulted primarily from the inadequate monetary policies of many countries, competitive currency devaluations, and deliberate speculative actions in the international financial markets. For these reasons, in particular, as well as the need for greater stability, the gold standard was gradually phased out during the 1930s, and from 1934 to the end of the Second World War, exchange rates were basically determined by the value of each country's currency in terms of gold.

6.2.3 The Bretton Woods Agreement 1944–1973

The adoption of the **Bretton Woods Agreemen** of fixed exchange rates in 1944 ushered in th next important phase in the development of th IMS. This agreement provided for a US dollar based international monetary system and th establishment of two important institutions, th **International Monetary Fund (IMF)** and th **World Bank (WB)**, each with its own specifi role, mandate, and functions.

With this new fixed exchange rate, all othe currencies were **pegged** to the US dollar, an countries had to obtain the prior approval (the IMF before embarking on any significar exchange rate devaluation. The onus wa therefore, on the IMF to maintain monetar discipline in and provide stability to the inter national financial markets and the IMS afte 1944.

The **fixed exchange rate system** came unde pressure during the 1960s as world trad expanded, and finally collapsed around 197 mainly because of the divergent monetar policies adopted by various countries, th different inflation rates between countrie and, more importantly, an increasing inflatio rate and continuous balance-of-payments de icits in the United States during the late 196(and early 1970s.

6.2.4 The floating exchange rate system, 1973–present

The demise of the fixed exchange rate regime le to the introduction of the **floating exchange rat system** in 1973, which was formalised durin 1976 in terms of the **Jamaica Agreement**.

However, the floating exchange rate syster made exchange rate fluctuations inherentl more unpredictable than before. This phase i the evolution of the IMS understandably gav rise to greater uncertainty in the foreig exchange market, which was intensified b the 'oil crisis' of 1973, and the subsequer volatility in commodity prices. Companies an individuals involved in international business and finance had to contend with a rapidly changing international monetary scene and a highly unpredictable and volatile foreign exchange market.

During the period from 1980 to 1985, the value of the trade-weighted US dollar increased dramatically against other major currencies with devastating consequences for the competitiveness of United States exports. This situation prompted the ministers of finance of the so-called Group of Five or G5 countries (France, Germany, Great Britain, Japan, and the United States) into action in 1985. Their deliberations resulted in the **Plaza Accord**, which provided for most major currencies to appreciate against the dollar, and a pledge by the finance ministers of the Group of Five countries to intervene in the foreign exchange market whenever necessary. The decline in the value of the dollar started in 1985, and continued until 1987, when the Group of Five countries met again in Paris in a renewed attempt to achieve some stability in the international financial markets. Agreement was reached in terms of the **Louvre Accord**, which allowed governments to intervene in the international financial markets by selling or buying currency, as circumstances required.

By early 1988, the value of the dollar had levelled off against other currencies and remained fairly stable against most major currencies well into the 1990s, the exception over the long term being the effect of the continued strength of the Japanese yen and the German mark relative to the dollar.

While overcoming some of the inherent shortcomings of fixed exchange rate systems, the floating exchange rate regime has undoubtedly contributed to the increasing complexity, uncertainty and sophistication of the international financial market during the last two decades. This situation is furthermore underlined by the ongoing debate regarding the relative merits of fixed as against floating exchange rate systems. As a result of the Plaza and Louvre Accord interventions, the floating exchange rate regime is also referred to as a **managed float system** or a **dirty float system** of exchange rates.

Although many different currency arrangements exist today, and despite the fact that the most widely-traded currencies (the US dollar, the Japanese yen, the German mark, the British pound and, more recently, the euro) float against one another, it is important for a firm's financial management to understand the specific currency arrangements that apply to the markets in which it operates.

The IMF currently classifies existing currency arrangements in the following seven categories:

- pegged to another currency;
- pegged to a basket;
- flexible against a single currency;
- joint float;
- adjusted according to indicators;
- managed float;
- independently floating.

According to the IMF, South Africa is one of more than 40 countries that allow full flexibility in terms of an 'independent float', where central banks allow exchange rates to be determined by market forces alone, although some central banks intervene in the market from time to time, especially to counter speculative pressures.[2]

6.2.5 Development of the European Monetary System and the Economic and Monetary Union

An important development within the international monetary system was the establishment of the **European Monetary System (EMS)** in 1979. The EMS was founded with the following three objectives in mind:

- to create a zone of monetary stability in Europe (by reducing exchange rate volatility and through the converging of interest rates);
- to control inflation through the imposition of monetary discipline;

- to co-ordinate exchange rate policies versus non-European currencies like the US dollar and the Japanese yen.

Subsequently, a fourth objective was added: the introduction of a common currency for the EMS by 1 January 1999. **European Union (EU)** member states formally committed themselves to this last objective by way of the **Maastricht Treaty** in December 1991. As early as 1990 speculative exchange rate developments had begun to put the EMS under pressure.

The European Union relied on the **European Currency Unit (ECU)** and the **exchange rate mechanism (ERM)** to achieve the four objectives outlined above. The ECU was introduced as a basket of EU currencies to serve as the unit of account for the EMS. The value of the ECU comprised defined percentages of the currencies of EU member states, where the weighted share of each country's currency in the ECU depended on that country's relative economic weight within the EU. According to the ERM, at one level each national currency would be assigned a central rate in relation to the ECU, and this rate could only be changed on the basis of a commonly agreed realignment. At another level, a series of bilateral rates between the currencies of individual countries would apply, resulting in a network of exchange rate interactions within the EU, known as the **parity grid**.

Prior to 1992, EU countries were compelled to intervene in the foreign exchange market when exchange rates deviated more than 2,25 % from the prescribed bilateral rate with another currency. Because the ERM was, by implication, based on the principles underlying a fixed exchange rate system involving both weaker and stronger currencies, it was, in effect, not immune to the inherent dangers of speculative pressures. As could be expected, when speculative pressures occurred in September 1992, the value of the British pound and the Italian lira fell dramatically against the German mark, despite government intervention. This resulted in the withdrawal of Britain and Italy from the ERM. The vulnerability of fixed exchange rate systems to speculative pressures was once again reaffirmed.

These events triggered two important changes in the EMS in August 1993. Firstly, the prevailing exchange rate fluctuation band of 2,25% was widened to a more accommodating band of 5% with the objective of reducing the scope for speculation. Secondly, countries with stronger currencies were no longer compelled to intervene in the foreign exchange market, a measure that largely condoned what had already been experienced in the crisis of September 1992. Although these modifications brought some stability to the EMS, by July 1997 Britain and Italy had not yet rejoined the ERM. This resulted in a loss of credibility at a time of concerted efforts to strive for a European monetary union and a single EU currency, the euro, to be introduced on 1 January 1999 as legal tender for 11 of the European Union's 15 nations in the year 2002 (the 11 nations involved are Austria, Belgium, Finland, France, Germany, Ireland, Italy, Luxembourg, the Netherlands, Portugal, and Spain). At the time of writing, these countries will participate in the Economic and Monetary Union (EMU).

According to Charlton, the **Economic and Monetary Union (EMU)**, as conceived by the Maastricht Treaty, is a monetary union, an economic union to a limited extent, but not a political union. It is a monetary union because national monetary competencies are pooled within a **European Central Bank (ECB)** which defines and implements a single monetary policy, in a single currency – **the euro** – for the whole of the EMU area.[3]

The composition and current status of the EMU area are presented in Exhibit 6.1 (p. 169).

The transition to a single currency involved three phases, for which definite dates had been set. Phase A involved the launch of the third stage of the EMU, which was the formal creation of the ECB, following an announcement of the participating member states in May 1998. During 1998 all arrangements for the single monetary and exchange rate policy were

Exhibit 6.1: The Economic and Monetary Union area

Eleven countries of the European Union will participate in EMU from 1 January 1999:	Four countries are in the EU but will not participate in the first wave (they are usually described as 'pre-ins'):
Austria Belgium Finland France Germany Ireland Italy Luxembourg Netherlands Portugal Spain	Denmark Greece Sweden United Kingdom
With effect from 1 January 1999 the official national currency of the participating 11 countries is the euro. The rate of exchange between the euro and the old national currency will be irrevocably locked, each rate expressed to six significant figures, e.g., 1 euro = 6,54321 French francs.	

SOURCE: Charlton, C. 1999. *Euro – Impact and Reality.* London: Financial Times Pitman Publishing, p. 14.

finalised, and the production of euro banknotes commenced.

Phase B signalled the effective start of the EMU. On 1 January 1999 the ECB took over the monetary policy from the member states and the rates of conversion between the euro and the participating national currencies were irrevocably fixed, so that the euro became a currency in its own right. As explained by Charlton,

> The currencies of the participating Member States are replaced by the euro which is denominated both in its own unit (1 euro) and sub-units (100 cents) and in national currency units (NCUs), i.e. the former national currencies of the participating Member States.[4]

Phase B ends on 31 December 2001, and there will be no physical euro notes and coins during this phase, since they will not be introduced until 1 January 2002.

Phase C involves the definitive changeover to the euro on 1 January 2002. Amounts which, on 31 December 2001, are still in national currency units of participating member states will be taken to be expressed in euro units, converted at the official rates. From 1 January 2002, new euro banknotes and coins will be in circulation to substitute for old national currency units. According to Charlton, this operation will end by 1 July 2002 at the latest, after which date euro banknotes and coins will replace marks, francs, schillings, lira, markka, pesetas, gulden, escudos, punts, and perhaps drachmas, as the only legal tender in participating member states. As mentioned earlier, Britain's pound sterling is expected to remain a holdout, at least for the foreseeable future.

The impact of the euro

Since the early 1960s economists have speculated about the possibility and potential benefits of a single currency for Europe. It was argued that cross-border sharing of a single currency would lead to more transparent prices, lower transaction costs, relatively greater certainty for investors, and enhanced competition. Uncertainty regarding the effects on issues such as the free flow and mobility of labour, flexibility of wages and prices, and appropriate mechanisms for transferring fiscal resources to affected countries, however, raised a number of questions, especially where the countries concerned – in this case the EU member states – do not have similar economic structures, and have economic cycles which are far from being in harmony with one another.[5]

It has been suggested that volatility in interest rates, especially with regard to those of the 'stronger' and 'weaker' member countries of the EMU, will depend largely on monetary policy instruments in the ECB, and the frequency of possible market inventions.

With regard to exchange rates, the elimination of foreign exchange risk between member countries, as a result of the single currency system, can reduce costs and enhance competition, but, above all, promote, stimulate, and increase cross-border trade between member countries. It has been suggested that the businesses affected immediately on the introduction of the euro, other than the financial sector, include:

- exporters and importers to and from the euro zone having to or likely to come under pressure to quote/deal with the euro as currency;
- multinational enterprises operating in the euro zone having to deal with the euro as currency;
- firms in supply chains that include organisations that are or will be using the euro.

The introduction of the euro has given rise to a number of accounting and taxation issues, especially with regard to accounting for foreign subsidiaries, translation of financial statement data in multinational enterprises, and exchange rates for translation of historical data, apart from the general regulatory requirements with which multinational enterprises are normally concerned. It is clear that the coming of the euro has not only created opportunities for business and development, but will also demand greater efficiency for global competitiveness.[6]

From a South African perspective, Europe, including the United Kingdom (UK), will remain an important trading partner. It is, therefore, important that financial institutions and the financial managers of South African firms that are internationally involved, know how the European Union, the EMU and the ERM function, and are also aware of the challenges, opportunities and constraints that the EU environment holds. More specifically, the financial managers of South African firms should have a thorough knowledge of the following:

- the functioning of the EMS, the ERM, and the EMU, as well as how and why they have developed up to this stage;
- the financial implications of import and export activities involving EU member states, including the assessment and management of foreign exchange risks in this regard;
- the implications of tariffs for both exports and imports in terms of the **General Agreement on Tariffs and Trade** (**GATT**) where it still may apply, the **World Trade Organisation** (**WTO**), and the bilateral agreement between South Africa and the EU in this regard.[7]

The development and functioning of the EU, as well as the bilateral trade agreement between South Africa and the EU, were discussed in Section 2.5. An understanding of these developments and the current status of the International Monetary System, the European Monetary System, and the Economic and Monetary Union should provide valuable insights into the potential opportunities, benefits, and risks in the context of international financial management.

The foreign exchange market and its implications for international business are dealt with in the following section.

6.3 The foreign exchange market[8]

All countries in the world, to a greater or lesser extent, are part of the international trade and global business environments. With the exception of developments such as the Economic and Monetary Union in the EU, every country has its own currency. The most unique characteristic that distinguishes international finance from purely domestic finance is the concept of **foreign exchange**. Financial and capital flows resulting from international trade and investments are subject to exchange rates and are facilitated by the foreign exchange market. This discussion provides a brief overview of the structure and functions of the foreign exchange market.[9]

6.3.1 The functioning of the foreign exchange market

The **foreign exchange market** is a world-wide financial market that provides the physical and institutional structure for foreign exchange transactions. This market is not an organised exchange like many stock markets or futures markets, has no fixed location, and market participants are located mostly in major commercial banks around the world.

In some countries trading is also conducted by means of open bidding on the official floor of stock exchanges. Authorised foreign exchange traders and dealers are connected by means of advanced telecommunication and electronic networks. Dealing in foreign exchange markets can also take place through **currency brokers**, who handle roughly half the transaction volume in these markets. Because of the international time difference between countries, this world-wide market operates 24 hours a day. The **Bank for International Settlements (BIS)** was established after the Second World War for the netting of payments among **European Payment Union** members, which greatly reduced the volume of gross international payments. Recently the BIS has been acting as a club for central bankers and regulators, and gathers data on exchange markets, euromarkets and new financial instruments. The designation of and symbols for selected international currencies appear in Exhibit 6.2 (p. 172).

Specific **functions of the foreign exchange market** in an international context involve the following:

- transfer of purchasing power;
- provision of credit;
- minimising foreign exchange risk related to exchange rate movements.

These functions are well documented in the literature and will not be discussed further here.[10]

6.3.2 The foreign exchange market – structure and participants

The foreign exchange market comprises the following two levels:

- the **wholesale market** or **interbank** which constituted an informal network of about 500 banks and brokerages in the late 1990s, dealing among each other and with large companies; and
- the **retail** or **client market**, which caters primarily for the foreign exchange needs of individuals.

The foreign exchange market consists of two further segments, the **spot exchange market** and the **forward exchange market**. In the spot exchange market, transactions are executed immediately with settlement (payment and delivery of currency) within two business days.

In the forward exchange market, payment and delivery of foreign currency takes place at a specified future date. These two important types of transactions are discussed more fully in Section 6.4.1.

The following five broad categories of **participants** are involved at the interbank and client levels, and in the spot and forward foreign exchange markets:

Exhibit 6.2: Selected international currency symbols

COUNTRY	CURRENCY	SYMBOL
Australia	Dollar	A$
Austria	Schilling	Sch
Belgium	Franc	BF
Canada	Dollar	Can$
Denmark	Krone	DKr
European Union*	Euro	€
Finland	Markka	FM
France	Franc	FF
Germany	Deutsche Mark	DM
Greece	Drachma	Dr
India	Rupee	Rs
Iran	Rial	Rl
Italy	Lira	Lit
Japan	Yen	¥
Kuwait	Dinar	KD
Mexico	Peso	Ps
Netherlands	Guilder	FL
Norway	Krone	NKr
Saudi Arabia	Riyal	SR
Singapore	Dollar	S$
South Africa	Rand	R
Spain	Peseta	Pts
Sweden	Kronar	SKr
Switzerland	Franc	SF
United Kingdom	Pound	£
United States	Dollar	$

* Economic and Monetary Union (EMU)

- bank and non-bank foreign exchange dealers;
- individuals and firms conducting international commercial and investment transactions;
- speculators and arbitrageurs;
- central banks and treasuries;
- foreign exchange brokers.

International monetary activities and transactions, which are indispensable to international trade and investment, are greatly facilitated and enhanced by a dynamic and efficient foreign exchange market.

6.4 Foreign exchange markets and rates

International trade, as well as international money and capital movements form the basis of an ongoing need for foreign exchange transactions and related activities. The foreign exchange market provides a global mechanism that facilitates the exchange of one country's money for that of another.

In this section, and also in Sections 6.5 and 6.6, the following features and characteristics of foreign exchange markets and rates are discussed:

- terminology and conventions related to foreign exchange markets and rates;
- foreign exchange transactions and activities;
- the determination of exchange rates;
- exchange rate forecasting.

The concepts, frameworks and methodologies presented here provide the necessary insights and serve as basic frame of reference for effective international financial management and decision-making.

6.4.1 Concepts in foreign exchange[11]

Some important concepts related to the foreign exchange market, foreign exchange market activities, and foreign exchange dealings are now defined, and the meaning and application of currency swaps, cross-rates, and arbitrage are explored below. This discussion provides the background for foreign exchange risk management which is discussed in Chapter 10.

Foreign exchange is the money or currency of a foreign country, usually in the form of claims, drafts or bank deposits, denominated in one or more foreign currencies. The **exchange rate** is the rate at which the currency of one country is exchanged into that of another. A **foreign exchange transaction** is an agreement between a buyer and seller that a fixed amount of one currency be delivered for some other currency at a specified rate and time. One currency can be converted to another by means of a **spot transaction** or a **forward operation.**

Banks, the most important foreign exchange dealers, form a vital link between foreign exchange supply and demand. Foreign exchange banking activities, involving advanced, sophisticated communications technology, largely ensure that information on foreign exchange transactions is readily available, resulting in relatively uniform price ranges for any particular currency throughout the major financial centres in the world. The sheer magnitude of the foreign exchange market becomes evident when it is realised that more than $1 trillion is **traded daily** in the foreign exchange markets worldwide, with **annual trading** in excess of $250-300 trillion. According to the June 1999 Quarterly Bulletin of the South African Reserve Bank, the **average net daily turnover** in the South African foreign exchange market amounted to $9,4 billion for the first quarter of 1999.

Foreign exchange rate quotations appear daily in all major international newspapers such as the *Financial Times* and the *Wall Street Journal*, in most local newspapers and financial journals, as well as on the Internet, for example, as provided by banks (see Exhibit 6.3 on p. 174).

Exchange rate quotations can be direct or indirect. A **direct quote** gives the home currency price of one unit of the foreign currency. If the South African rand is the home currency, and the United States dollar the foreign currency, the exchange rate between the rand and the dollar in a direct quote would be:

R6,1625/$ (6,1625 rand per dollar)

This method of exchange rate quotation is refered to as **American terms** and is normally used in the wholesale foreign exchange market or interbank for quotations of the British pound, Australian dollar, New Zealand dollar, the Irish punt, and the euro, as well as quoting the rates for most foreign currencies and futures. For historical reasons, the British pound is quoted as the foreign currency price of one pound.

Exhibit 6.3: South African spot and forward markets

	SPOT	1M	3M	6M	12M
R/$	6,1625	6,2055	6,2765	6,3665	6,5375
R/€	6,6370	6,6987	6,8069	6,9516	7,2318
¥/R	18,5931	18,3807	18,0067	17,4925	16,5568
R/£	10,00	10,07	10,19	10,35	10,63
DM/R	0,2948	0,2922	0,2876	0,2816	0,2708
FF/R	0,9889	0,9801	0,9646	0,9446	0,9081
SF/R	0,2412	0,2386	0,2343	0,2286	0,2182

NOTE: Spot = spot exchange rate
M = month (30 days)
For the various symbols such as R and $ refer to Exhibit 6.2

SOURCE: ABSA Bank Treasury, Thursday 05 August 1999 (http://www.absa.co.za/treasury)

An **indirect quote** gives the number of units of foreign currency needed to buy one unit of home currency. Again taking the South African rand as the home currency and the US dollar as the foreign currency, the exchange rate between the rand and the dollar in an indirect quote would be:

$0,1623/R (0,1623 dollars per rand)

This method of indirect exchange rate quotation is also referred to as **European terms**, expressing the exchange rate as the foreign currency price of one unit of home currency, in our case the dollar price of one rand. Worldwide, most of the interbank quotations are stated in European terms. On 5 August 1999, the exchange rates between the South African rand and the US dollar appeared as follows (see Exhibit 6.3):

R1=Foreign unit ($)	One foreign unit ($)=R
0,1623	6,1625

(Note that the direct quote is the reciprocal of the indirect quote, and vice versa.)

The rate on the left shows the indirect quote, the amount of foreign currency (US$) per rand. The rate on the right indicates the number of rand needed to buy one unit of foreign currency (US$) as a direct quote.

Up to now, we have regarded exchange rate quotations as being one single quotation. In actual interbank requests, however, dealers would give quotations as a **'bid'** or **'buy'**, and an **'ask'**, **'offer'** or **'sell'**. The bid is the price at which the bank will buy foreign exchange from another bank, and the ask or offer is the price at which the bank will sell foreign exchange. Banks bid or buy foreign exchange at lower rates, and ask or sell at higher rates. The difference between the selling and buying rates is called the **spread**, and basically represents the dealer's profit margin.

On 5 August 1999, the single direct quote for the rand and the US dollar from a South African perspective was $1 = R6,1625, and a typical spread in this case could be as follows:

	Bid/buy	Ask/Offer/Sell
Spot exchange rate (direct quote)	6,1620	6,1630

A **single rate** is the average of a buying and a selling rate and is referred to as a **mid-rate**, which in our case is $1 = R6,1625.

At any given point in time, the spread will vary according to the individual dealer, the currency being traded, and the trading bank's overall view of conditions in the foreign exchange market. The spread will most likely increase in the case of thinly traded currencies, or when the risks associated with the trading are perceived to be increasing.

Spot transactions, **forward transactions**, and **currency swaps** constitute vital mechanisms in international finance in general, and in foreign exchange market operations in particular. These mechanisms are indispensable for international financial management and decision-making.

A **spot transaction** in the foreign exchange market involves the purchase of foreign exchange with settlement (delivery and payment) to be completed within two business days following the date of transaction.

The **spot foreign exchange rate** or, more generally, the **spot rate**, is the price at which one currency trades for another in a spot transaction. Spot rates for the South African rand against various other currencies appear in Exhibit 6.3 (p. 174). For example, the price of one rand in US dollars on 5 August 1999 could have been quoted as $0,1623 = (R1 ÷ 6,1625) in an indirect quote.

A **forward exchange rate** or **forward rate** is the price agreed on today for the purchase or sale of foreign exchange at a future date. Such a transaction is called an **outright forward transaction** or, more generally, a **forward transaction**, and requires delivery of foreign exchange on a designated future date, either on an **outright** basis, or by means of a **futures contract**.

Forward exchange rates are normally quoted for **maturities** or future **value dates** of one, three, six, and twelve months, as indicated in Exhibit 6.3. **Forward contracts** should be settled by the second business day after expiry of the contractual time period. For example, a three-month contract entered into on 2 June will be for a value date of 4 September, or the next business day, if 4 September happens to fall during a weekend or on a public holiday.

As far as terminology is concerned, **'buying forward'** or **'selling forward'** can be used to describe the same transaction. For example, a forward transaction to deliver German marks for South African rand in three months could be said to involve 'buying rand forward for marks' or 'selling marks forward for rand'.

Forward quotations for exchange rates are either at a **premium** or a **discount** from the spot rate. We recall the following data in Exhibit 6.3 regarding the rand-dollar spot and forward exchange rates:

Direct rate (quote)

		Rand
US$	spot rate	6,1625
1	month forward rate	6,2055
3	months forward rate	6,2765
6	months forward rate	6,3665
12	months forward rate	6,5375

Much of the international trade today is contracted in advance of delivery and payment. Suppose a South African importer places a $30 000 order with a computer company in the United States for the delivery of goods to the South African firm, and payment to the American supplier in 3 months, assuming that the above exchange rate quotations apply.

At the current spot rate of 6,1625 (on 5 August 1999) the order amounts to R184 875. What options are open to the importer in this case? One option would be to wait three months and then buy the $30 000 required. However, the exchange rate could change to the South African importer's disadvantage over the next 3 months, since there is no guarantee that the spot exchange rate will remain unchanged. Should no immediate payment take place in the above example, the importer could enter into a 3-months forward contract to take delivery of US dollars at a direct forward rate of 6,2765 at that time to settle the account. Since the US dollar is more expensive in the forward market (R6,2765 compared to the spot rate of R6,1625), the US dollar is selling at a **premium** relative to the rand. On the same basis it is argued that the rand is selling at a **discount** relative to the US dollar.

From a US dollar perspective, the premium is calculated as follows:

$$\frac{F_3 - S_0}{S_0} = \frac{6{,}2765 - 6{,}1625}{6{,}1625}$$
$$= 0{,}0185$$
$$= 1{,}85\%$$

where S_0 = spot exchange rate
F_3 = 3-months forward exchange rate.

In this case, the rand is selling at a discount relative to the US dollar from the perspective of the South African importer. It would therefore take more rand to buy a given quantity of dollars. The importer has to pay R188 295 in 3 months' time. The difference between R188 295 and R184 875 is R3 420, or 1,85%, on the basis of the spot rate. If the direct forward exchange rate of a currency is less than the current spot rate, the currency is said to be selling at a discount relative to the other currency.

The advantage of the forward market is that it allows companies and individuals alike to contractually agree today on a future exchange rate that is fixed, thereby eliminating any risk from unfavourable exchange rate movements.

For financial decision-making purposes it is important to note the following from our example:

- If the future (3-months) spot rate (which is unknown at the moment) should be higher than R6,2765, the importing company would experience a loss greater than the difference of R3 420 (discount of 1,85%) **in the absence of a forward contract.** If the future (3-months) spot rate (unknown at the moment) should be lower than the current spot rate of R6,1625, then the importer's profit would be larger than expected **in the absence of a forward contract**.
- Forward cover is not free – in the above example, the cost of forward cover would be 7,42% of the spot rate annualised (the cost of forward cover for a number of foreign currencies as on 5 August 1999 appears in Exhibit 6.4 on p. 177).

Remember that, with few exceptions, exchange rates are generally quoted as the amount of foreign currency per one US dollar, where reference is made to rising or declining exchange rates.

6.4.2 Currency swaps

A **currency swap** could be regarded as a sophisticated type of forward exchange. It is a trade involving two currencies by means of the simultaneous purchase and sale of a given amount of foreign exchange for two different value dates. Swaps are extremely useful in international finance because:

- they allow moving out of one currency into another for a specified time period without incurring foreign exchange risk;
- they allow companies to obtain long-term foreign currency financing at lower costs than would have been possible with direct borrowing.

A common type of currency swap is referred to as **spot against forward**. To explain how a currency swap works, consider a South African manufacturer of domestic heaters, who has to import sophisticated heater elements from a company in the United Kingdom. A significant proportion of the total production output of heaters is also sold in the United Kingdom. The South African manufacturer, in effect, buys from and sells to firms in the United Kingdom. Further assume that the South African firm has to obtain £40 000 today to pay the UK firm for a consignment of heater elements. Since the South African firm at this stage also knows that, in 180 days, it will be paid £40 000 for a batch of heaters by a UK importer, it would need to convert these pounds into rand at that stage.

From Exhibit 6.3 (p. 174), we note that the spot exchange rate for the British pound in terms of the South African rand is £1 = R10,000, and

Exhibit 6.4: Cost of forward cover (% of spot annualised)

	1M	3M	6M	12M
R/$	8,22	7,42	6,60	6,09
R/EURO	10,94	10,27	9,45	8,96
R/¥	13,27	12,48	11,64	10,80
£/R	8,29	7,60	6,89	6,26
R/SF	12,28	11,38	10,28	9,40

NOTE: M = month (30 days)

SOURCE: ABSA Bank Treasury, Thursday 5 August 1999 (http://www.absa.co.za.treasury).

that the 180-day forward exchange rate is £1 = R10,3500. Through its bank the South African firm sells R400 000 to the bank at the spot exchange rate in return for £40 000, and can pay the UK manufacturer. At the same time, the South African manufacturer enters into a 180-day forward exchange contract with its bank for converting £40 000 into rand. Therefore, in 180 days the said manufacturer will receive R414 000 (£40 000 x 10,35).

Since the £ is trading at **a premium** in terms of the rand on the 180-day forward market, the South African manufacturer ends up with more rand than it had started with (remember that the opposite could also occur).

According to Hill, the swap deal is just like a conventional forward deal in one important respect.[12] It enables the South African manufacturer to insure itself against foreign exchange risk, and by engaging in a swap the firm **knows today** that the £40 000 payment it will receive in 180 days will yield R414 000.

As mentioned before, swaps are an efficient way to meet a firm's need for foreign currencies because swaps combine two separate transactions into one. Firms can accordingly avoid foreign exchange risk by matching the liability created by borrowing foreign currencies with the asset created by lending domestic currency, both to be repaid at the **known** future exchange rate. This technique is known as **hedging** foreign exchange risk.

6.4.3 Cross-rates and arbitrage

A **cross-rate** is the exchange rate between two currencies, calculated on the basis of their common relationship with a third currency. More specifically, it is the exchange rate between two currencies (usually non-US and often infrequently traded currencies), when both are quoted in some third currency, usually the US dollar. However, cross-rates can be calculated for any two currencies, based on the above approach. Where the exchange rate between two currencies is not available, individuals and companies often have to rely on a cross-rate, as illustrated in the following example.

Assume that a US dollar quotation for the Swiss franc is not available, but that the British pound is quoted in New York, and the Swiss franc is quoted in London:

British pound quote in the United States: \$1,763/£
Swiss franc quote in London: SF2,681/£

The cross-rate in this case is:

$$\frac{\text{Swiss francs per £}}{\text{US dollars per £}} = \frac{\text{SF}2{,}681/\text{£}}{\$1{,}763/\text{£}} = \text{SF}1{,}52/\$$$

A situation as reflected in this example would rarely occur since the Swiss franc/US dollar exchange rate would normally be available.

Of greater importance, however, is the role of cross-rates in respect of **arbitrage activities** in the foreign exchange market.

Worldwide, exchange rates tend to converge to the same value since information is readily available. Where this is not the case, there will be profit opportunities from simultaneously buying a currency in one market and selling it in another. This arbitrage activity of buying a currency where it is too low would raise the exchange rate of the currency in that market (owing to the effect of increased demand), and selling the currency where it is too high would again tend to lower the exchange rate in that market (owing to the effect of increased supply). **Arbitrage** would continue until the difference in these exchange rates becomes so small that it would no longer justify the costs of buying and selling, thereby effectively eliminating the profit opportunity.

Arbitrage often involves more than two currencies. Since banks generally quote exchange rates in terms of the US dollar, the exchange rates between the US dollar and foreign currencies are readily available. For example, if the dollar price of the British pound ($/£) as well as the dollar price of the German mark ($/DM) are known, the pound price of the mark (£/DM) can be readily determined.

Consider an arbitrage involving the above three currencies in the following hypothetical examples (for the sake of simplicity ignore the bid-ask spread and assume that we can buy or sell at the same price). Suppose in London, $/£ = $2,2 and in New York $/DM = $0,70.

The cross-rate between the pound and the mark is calculated as follows:

$$\text{£/DM} = \frac{\$/\text{DM}}{\$/\text{£}} = \frac{0{,}70}{2{,}20}$$
$$= 0{,}318$$

If any one of the three exchange rates is out of line with the remaining two, an arbitrage opportunity exists. For example, assume that the £/DM is 2,20 in Frankfurt, the $/DM = 0,70 in New York, but in London the $/£ = 2,10. As soon as the discrepancy in the $/£ exchange rate is observed, a trader could buy £1 million in London for $2,1 million ($/£ = 2,10). The pounds are now used to buy marks at £/DM = 0,318, resulting in £1 million = DM 3 144 654. This last amount of DM 3 144 654 can now be used to buy US dollars in New York at $/DM = 0,70. This would give DM 3 144 654 = $2 201 258. The initial $2,1 million dollars would now return a profit of $161 258 ($2 201 258 – $2 100 000) as a result of **triangular arbitrage.** Bear in mind that, in a real-world situation, transaction costs would decrease this profit.

In this example of triangular arbitrage:

- the initial $ price of the £ in London was too low;
- arbitrageurs selling $ for £ in London will make the £ relatively more expensive (increase in demand for £), which at the same time will tend to make the $ in London slightly less expensive, through increasing the supply in London;
- the net effect of this arbitrage will be **raising the price** of the £ from the level of $2,10 towards the (equilibrium) level of $2,20, while the influence in other markets will tend to **raise the £ price of marks**, and **lower the $ price of marks**, converging towards a **new equilibrium for the $ price of pounds** somewhere between $2,10 and $2,20.

As explained earlier, on the basis of demand and supply, arbitrage will tend to eliminate any existing discrepancies in exchange rates and ensure that they quickly return to internationally comparable levels.

In the explanation of cross-rates and arbitrage, an exchange rate discrepancy between the £ and $ was merely assumed. The same logic would obviously apply if the discrepancies had been between the $ and DM, or £ and DM.

The concepts related to foreign exchange markets and rates, the mechanisms involved in foreign exchange markets, spot and forward exchange transactions, and currency swaps, as well as cross-rates and arbitrage, are indispensable for effective financial management in an international context.

6.5 Exchange rate determination[13]

As we have seen, international trade and investments are facilitated by the foreign exchange market, where one currency can be transformed into another. The process of deciding how one currency will be converted into another is known as **exchange rate determination**. This section briefly explores how exchange rates are determined in the context of the international financial and foreign exchange markets as outlined in Sections 6.2 and 6.3.

6.5.1 Exchange rate determinants

It is generally accepted that exchange rates are determined by the demand and supply of one currency relative to the demand and supply of another. While differences in relative demand and supply explain how exchange rates are determined, this explanation does not tell us what factors inherently affect the demand and supply of a currency, when demand will exceed supply (and vice versa), or under what conditions a currency will be in relatively higher demand than otherwise.

Basically, the main motivators for the **demand** of a foreign currency are people's desire for foreign goods and services, foreign investments, international financial instruments, and to capitalise on speculative opportunities. Similarly, people's desire to sell their products and services creates a **supply** of foreign currency.[14]

Notwithstanding the complexity of exchange rate determination and a lack of consensus regarding the determinants of exchange rates, there is general agreement that the following three factors appear to have a significant influence on future exchange rate movements in a currency. These are the country's inflation rate, its interest rate, and its market psychology. To this end, we will look at the role of purchasing power parity, interest rate parity, and of market effects and investor behaviour respectively.

6.5.2 Exchange rates and price levels

The relationship between price levels and exchange rate movements is largely explained by the theory of purchasing power parity, based on the economic proposition of the law of one price.

(a) The law of one price

According to the **law of one price**, identical products sold in different countries must sell at the same price when the price is expressed in the same currency, assuming the existence of competitive markets free from barriers of trade and transportation costs.

(b) Purchasing power parity

The accepted economic theory of **purchasing power parity (PPP)** states that the exchange rate between any two currencies adjusts to reflect differences in price levels in the two countries. In simple terms it states that the price of a basket of goods should be the same in each country, and predicts that the exchange rate will change if relative prices change. Differences in national inflation rates are therefore the major cause of changes in the relative prices of goods and services in a country. These price changes, in turn, are the major cause of changes or adjustments in exchange rates, where a country's inflation rate is believed to be a function of the growth in its money supply. In the final instance, the exchange rate adjusts to keep the purchasing power constant between currencies.

A distinction is made between **absolute purchasing power parity** and **relative purchasing power parity**. Absolute PPP means that a commodity or service costs the same, regardless of where it is sold or what currency is used. Relative PPP does not serve as an indicator of the absolute level of exchange rates, but rather of the change in exchange rates over time.[15]

According to relative PPP, a change in the exchange rate is determined by the differences in the inflation rates between the two countries, and the expected exchange rate $E[S_t]$ at some future date (t) is calculated as follows:

$$E[S_t] = S_o \times [1 + (h_{FC} - h_{HC})]^t$$

where
$E(S_t)$ = expected exchange rate in (t) periods
S_o = spot exchange rate at time t_o
h_{HC} = inflation rate in the home country
h_{FC} = inflation rate in the foreign country

Relative PPP tells us that the exchange rate between South Africa and some foreign country will rise (when quoting the rand per unit of foreign currency) if the South African inflation rate is higher than that of the foreign country. What really happens is that the rand depreciates in value, and therefore weakens relative to the foreign currency, so that it takes more rand to buy a unit of foreign currency.

For example, if the South African exchange rate is currently R3.3921 per German mark (spot exchange rate on 5 August 1999), what will the exchange rate be two years from now if the average annual inflation rates in South Africa and Germany are expected to be 7% and 2% respectively over the next few years?

$$\begin{aligned} E(S_2) &= S_o \times [1 + (h_{SA} - h_G)]^2 \\ &= 3{,}3921 \times [1 + (0{,}07 - 0{,}02)]^2 \\ &= 3{,}3921 \times (1 + 0{,}05)^2 \\ &= 3{,}3921 \times (1{,}05)^2 \\ &= 3{,}74 \text{ rand per mark} \end{aligned}$$

Similarly, the expected exchange rate four years from now would be

$$\begin{aligned} E(S_4) &= 3{,}3921 \times (1{,}05)^4 \\ &= 4{,}12 \text{ rand per mark} \end{aligned}$$

Note: While the German mark has been used in this illustration, bear in mind that on 1 January 2002 all national currency units of member states of the Economic and Monetary Union will be converted to the euro as currency, as indicated in Section 6.2.5.

Most economists agree that the PPP theory explains long-term trends in exchange rate movements reasonably well, but that it is not suitable for predicting short-term changes.

6.5.3 Exchange rates, interest rates and inflation rates

(a) The Fisher effect

While PPP theory essentially explains why exchange rates adjust to keep the purchasing power among different currencies constant, the relationship between spot exchange rates, forward exchange rates and interest rates needs to be investigated for a more complete understanding of how the exchange rate is determined.

Irving Fisher first formulated the **Fisher effect**, a parity relation which holds that nominal interest rates (*i*) in a given country are equal to a real interest rate (r) plus the expected rate of inflation (h). This relationship supports economic theory in that interest rates reflect expectations about likely future inflation rates. The Fisher equation is as follows:

$$i = r + h$$

Investors, however, require positive real returns on their investments. When inflation is expected to be high, interest rates will also tend to be high to compensate investors for a drop in the value of their money. In a world without government intervention and in which the free transfer of capital is allowed, real interest rates should, theoretically, be the same in every country. From the Fisher effect it follows that an increase in expected inflation will tend to increase the nominal interest rate.

If, on the basis of the PPP, we already know, at least in theory, that there is a link between inflation rates and exchange rates, and since interest rates reflect expectations about future inflation, there should logically also be a link between interest rates and exchange rates. We now explore the relationship between exchange rates, interest rates, and inflation rates. A number of important concepts and relationships are illustrated in Exhibits 6.5 to 6.9. The prime overdraft (o/d) rate, the bankers' acceptance (BA) rate, and the rate on R150 government stocks as from 1996 appear in Exhibit 6.5.

(b) The International Fisher effect

This important relationship between exchange rates, interest rates, and inflation rates is embodied in the **International Fisher effect (IFE)**, which states that, for any two countries,

Exhibit 6.5: Interest rates – South Africa

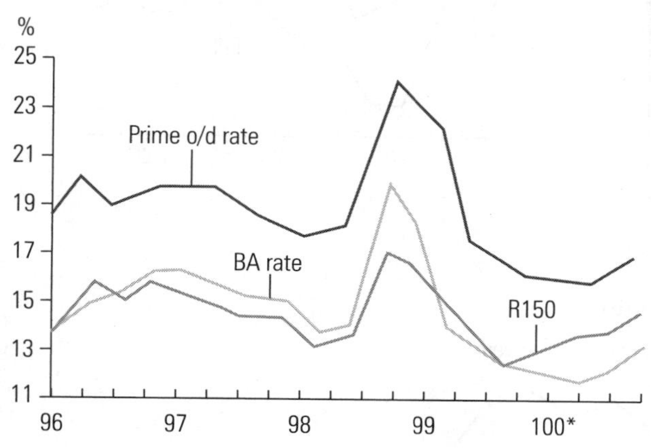

* Year 2000.

SOURCE: ABSA Bank, Quarterly South African Economic Monitor, Second Quarter 1999, p. 14.

Exhibit 6.6: Real prime interest rates – selected countries

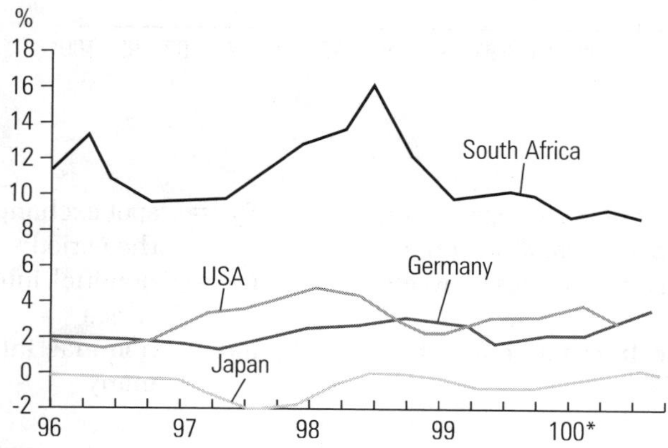

Year 2000.

OURCE: ABSA Bank, op. cit., p. 14.

Exhibit 6.7: Consumer Price Index (CPI) and Producer Price Index (PPI) inflation rates

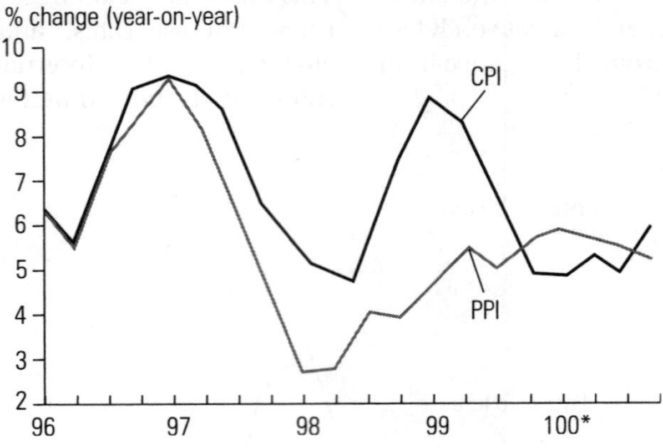

* Year 2000.

SOURCE: ABSA Bank, op. cit., p. 14.

Exhibit 6.8: Inflation rates

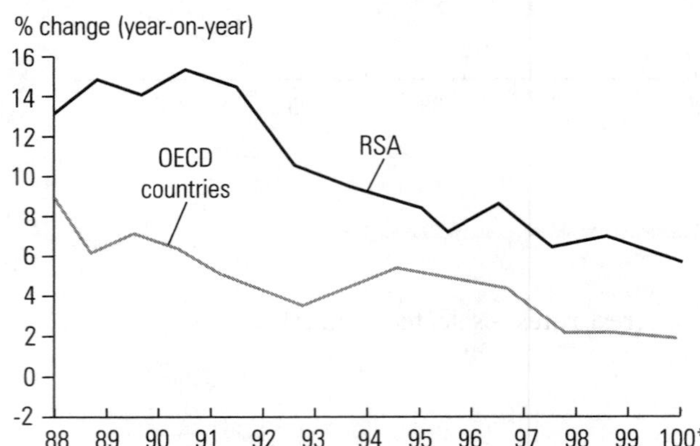

* Year 2000.

SOURCE: ABSA Bank, op. cit., p. 14.

the spot exchange rate should change in an equal amount, but in the opposite direction, to the difference in nominal interest rates between the two countries.

The equation for the International Fisher effect states that:

$$\frac{S_1 - S_2}{S_2} \times 100 = i_R - i_{DM}$$

where S_1 = spot exchange rate at the beginning of the period

S_2 = spot exchange rate at the end of the period

i = nominal interest rate in South Africa

i_{DM} = nominal interest rate in Germany

If, for instance, the expected South African interest rate of 7% is higher than the German interest rate of 2%, reflecting relatively higher expected inflation rates for South Africa com

Exhibit 6.9: Exchange rates – South Africa

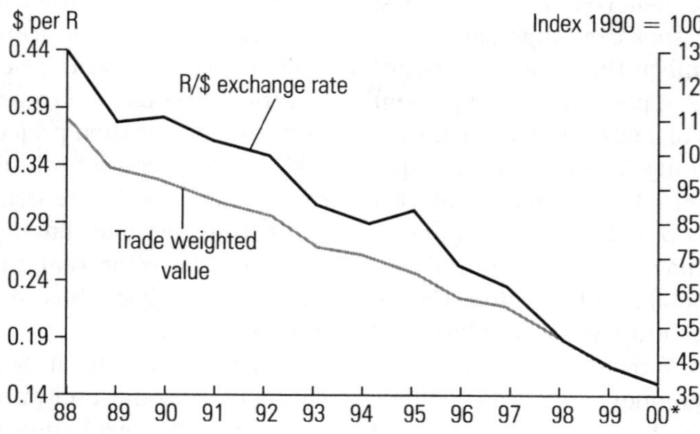

* Year 2000.

SOURCE: ABSA Bank, op. cit., p. 14.

pared to those for Germany, the value of the rand should decrease by 5% (7 – 2) against the mark over the period concerned.

According to the underlying theory of the IFE, it is clear that the difference in returns (nominal interest rates) between two countries (foreign country and home country) is equal to the difference in their inflation rates, confirming the IFE theory that real interest rates are equal across countries. In theory these relationships should hold for any two countries.

As with the PPP approach, evidence suggests that interest rate differentials do have some value in predicting future currency movements, and therefore predicting exchange rates **in the long term**. Both the PPP and the IFE, however, are poor predictors of short-term changes in spot exchange rates.

6.5.4 Market effects and investor behaviour

Hill points out that various **psychological factors**, as opposed to purely **macro-economic fundamentals**, have become increasingly important in determining the expectations of traders in the foreign exchange market.[16] For instance, the **bandwagon effect**, where the 'herd instinct' leads to certain types of mass trading behaviour and actions, does seem to have a significant influence on **short-term** exchange rate movements. The inherent problem, however, is that the occurrence, frequency and potential effects of these events are extremely difficult to predict.

6.6 Exchange rate forecasting

6.6.1 Market efficiency and exchange rate forecasting

In an environment primarily characterised by floating exchange rates, it is extremely difficult to forecast spot exchange rates. This difficulty is mainly due to unpredictable exchange rate volatility as well as the unexpected influence of numerous factors of a fundamental, technical, and behavioural nature. However, the greater the accuracy with which spot exchange rates can be forecast, the less should be the effect of foreign exchange risk.[17]

Regarding the formality and desirability of predicting or forecasting exchange rates, two distinct schools of thought have developed over time: the efficient market school and the inefficient market school. These concepts are now briefly discussed.

In the **efficient market school**, forward exchange rates are believed to be the best predictors of future spot exchange rates. It is important to remember that quoted forward exchange rates at any point in time represent the combined views of a vast number of market participants concerning a possible future spot exchange rate. The belief of the efficient market school of thought is based on the assumption that the exchange market is efficient, and that prices reflect all available information. Consequently, any further attempts at analysis will not result in superior forecasts and will only be a waste of time and money. Forward exchange rates should therefore be regarded as unbiased predictors of future spot exchange rates, and any inaccuracies that might occur would be of a random nature.

There has, however, been increasing evidence that forward exchange rates are not unbiased predictors of future spot exchange rates, and that forecasts could be improved by the effective use of publicly available information.

The **inefficient market school** accordingly believes that foreign exchange markets are inefficient to varying degrees and that so-called **market imperfections** do exist. Analysts can, therefore, improve on the foreign exchange market's predictions and it is argued that forward exchange rates are not the best predictors of future spot exchange rates. Investing in professional or other forecasting services would therefore seem to be worthwhile.

6.6.2 Approaches to exchange rate forecasting

Supporters of the inefficient market school basically follow two approaches to exchange rate forecasting: fundamental analysis and technical analysis.

Fundamental analysis is based largely on economic theory and includes variables such as fundamentally determined forward exchange rates, recognised lead indicators, relative money supply data, growth rates, interest rates, inflation rates and, more indirectly, balance of payments information.

Technical analysis primarily makes use of relevant volume and price data to identify historical trends and repetitive cyclical patterns, which are then projected into the future, taking into account various market and other relevant factors. There is fairly general agreement that, despite having no fundamental economic basis or real theoretical rationale, technical analysis has nevertheless become more popular.

Recent research in South Africa on the effects of seasonal and public holidays on the rand/US dollar exchange rate for the period 1984 to 1995 has provided new insights into the seasonal behaviour of this exchange rate, as illustrated by the following results.[18] These are presented for the period 1984-1989 (period 1), 1990-1995 (period 2), and 1984-1995 (total period):

- The most volatile times in the South African currency market occur on Mondays, in August/September, at the turn of the month, and during the first trading week of the month.
- The foreign exchange market is usually the least volatile on Thursdays, in December, and during the turn-of-the-year days, as well as on a trading day immediately prior to a public holiday.

In the context of the ongoing debate regarding the efficient market as opposed to the inefficient market approaches to exchange rate forecasting, the authors state the following:

> Persistent appreciation of the rand during January non-turn-of-the-month days and on a trading day prior to public holidays shows some inefficiencies in the South African foreign exchange market. An active forex trader may capitalise on the detected seasonalities by adhering to a simple trading strategy: buy US dollars/sell South African rand in January and immediately before public holidays,

> while holding back or taking the opposite position in these currencies during other periods. Even if transaction costs tend to neutralise the expected benefits of such a trading rule, some additional income can be derived by delaying the planned purchases/sales of currencies until seasonably favourable periods ... the seasonal effects observed in the variance of the daily exchange rate changes will have important consequences for the pricing of foreign exchange options, (and) the specification of risk/return relationships.[19]

Operators in foreign exchange markets generally rely on quoted forward exchange rates as being reliable and unbiased predictors of future spot exchange rates. Knowledge of accurate future spot rates would greatly facilitate the management of foreign exchange exposure. Based on existing evidence, it would appear that foreign exchange markets are not totally efficient and do present opportunities for superior forecasts of future exchange rates, which would inevitably provide support for the inefficient market school. The debate continues with regard to the relative merits of fundamental and technical analysis.

6.7 International capital markets

In any domestic setting, business firms are in continuous interaction with financial markets and financial institutions. **Financial markets** bring together those with surplus funds who wish to invest money and those who are in need of and wish to borrow money. In this regard, **financial institutions** act as **intermediaries** and facilitate the flow of funds in the process of satisfying the financial needs of investors and borrowers alike.

Financial markets are traditionally distinguished into **money markets**, which relate to short-term activities, and **capital markets** that are concerned with long-term financial market activities. Capital markets are primarily involved in **equity** and **debt** financing activities in the business sector, where equity and debt are characterised by their own specific risk and return characteristics.

The line demarcating money and capital markets is traditionally based on the term to maturity of the securities traded in the two markets, and is arbitrarily fixed at one year. Money and capital markets include the primary or new issues market and the secondary market. Accordingly, the capital market is defined as the market for the issue and trading of long-term securities involving equity and debt, while the money market deals with the issue and trading of short-term securities.

The arbitrary distinction of one year should not be seen as a definitive basis for the classification of money and capital market activities. Whether some activities, such as repurchase agreements and interest rate swaps, are regarded as capital or money market transactions, depends on the term of the agreement in a particular case.

The primary function of financial institutions in South Africa is financial intermediation, although some of them are in the business of making markets in financial instruments. With regard to their essential role of intermediation, there appears to be little distinction between banks, finance houses, insurance companies, and other types of financial institutions.

In the next section we will take a brief look at the scope, structure and functions of international capital markets from an international and multinational perspective.

6.7.1 Scope, structure and functions of International capital markets

Firms that become internationally involved are exposed to a vastly different financial environment to those that only operate domestically. For example, even in the first phase of internationalisation, where firms are primarily involved in import and export activities, **international capital markets** facilitate import and export financing, and involve more as well as different types of risk compared to purely domestic operations. As a consequence, and apart from political and other non-financial risks, an intricate knowledge of the international monetary system, the foreign exchange market, and international capital markets is imperative if the international business firm is to succeed.

In subsequent phases of internationalisation, multinational enterprises (MNEs) face an even more daunting situation, especially with regard to subsidiaries which are generally located in a number of different foreign countries. The scope of international capital markets as a frame of reference for international financial management is reflected by some of the demands in this regard on international financial management. These would include the following:

- international financing, investment and dividend decisions, including decisions regarding the repatriation of capital and dividends;
- identification of appropriate financing sources, located in different countries, that could lower the firm's cost of capital;
- overcoming host country limitations on financing in general, and host country debt financing in particular;
- effectively dealing with host country tax laws, accounting practices, rules, and regulations;
- global money management, based on efficiency and tax considerations;
- effective management of foreign exchange risk.

As far as the structure of international financial markets is concerned, London and New York have established themselves as the main international financial centres, with Tokyo running a close third place. They are followed by Amsterdam, Paris, Zurich, and Frankfurt. According to Hill, Hong Kong has the potential for significant growth in view of current and expected future developments in China.[20]

In their overall functioning, international capital markets have distinct advantages for **investors** and **borrowers** alike. For investors, there is a much wider range of investment opportunities when compared to domestic capital markets. International capital markets allow investors to diversify their investment portfolios internationally, thereby minimising their portfolio risk to below the levels obtaining in domestic markets.

Where borrowers are concerned – and here MNEs figure prominently – the added advantages of access to international capital markets bring greater scope, better financing opportunities, greater liquidity, and the potential for lowering cost of capital. Because of these advantages, and supported by significant advances in information technology, as well as an increasing trend towards deregulation, international capital markets have grown significantly over the past two decades.

6.7.2 The eurocurrency market[21]

The **eurocurrency market** has grown dramatically since the early 1980s. A **eurocurrency** is any domestic currency banked or on deposit in another country. The value of a specific eurocurrency is identical to that of the same currency at home, a eurodollar being a US dollar-denominated interest-bearing deposit in a bank outside the United States. A eurocurrency can be created anywhere in the world, since the 'euro'-prefix only indicates the European origin of this special market. 'Eurocurrencies' in this regard should not be confused with the 'euro' as the single currency of the European Union and the Economic and Monetary Union, as discussed in Section 6.2.5. Other important eurocurrencies when banked outside their country of origin are euromarks, eurofrancs, eurorands and eurosterling (British pounds banked outside the UK). However, eurodollars account for well over two-thirds of all eurocurrencies. The **London Interbank Offer Rate (LIBOR)** is the rate most international

Exhibit 6.10: London Interbank Offer Rates

	1M	3M	6M	12M
USD	5.21	5.37	5.77	5.97
GBP	5.27	5.30	5.60	5.89
EUR	2.63	2.70	3.04	3.23

SOURCE: ABSA Markets and Trading, http://www.absa.co.za/treasury/treasure_daily/DAILYN.htm, 5 August 1999.

banks charge one another for loans of eurodollars overnight in the London market, and interest rates are frequently quoted as a certain spread over the LIBOR. This rate for the US dollar, the British pound, and the euro, is illustrated in Exhibit 6.10.

Eurocurrency markets serve the following two important purposes:

- eurocurrency deposits are an efficient and convenient money market device for holding excess corporate liquidity; and
- the eurocurrency market is a major source of short-term bank loans to finance corporate working capital needs, including import and export financing requirements, as well as financing for other off-shore ventures.

One of the most important advantages of the eurocurrency market is that it is largely free from government regulation and interference, and is therefore beneficial for both investors and borrowers. One of the reasons for this is that the spread between the eurocurrency deposit and lending rates is less than the spread between the domestic deposit and lending rates.

It would seem, however, that the eurocurrency market has two major drawbacks or limitations:

- In an unregulated system such as the eurocurrency market, the probability of a bank causing depositors to lose their money is greater than in a regulated system.
- Because international loans do not offer complete assurance against risk, companies are still exposed to foreign exchange risk, despite the advantage of being able to use the foreign exchange market.

6.7.3 The international bond market

Bonds constitute an important means of corporate financing, where **fixed-rate bonds** are most commonly found. There are, however, two types of international bonds: foreign bonds and eurobonds.

Foreign bonds are normally sold outside the country of the borrower, but are denominated in the currency of the country of issue. **Eurobonds** are normally underwritten by international banking syndicates or consortia. The placement of the bonds is in countries other than the country in whose currency the bond is denominated. Eurobonds are by far the most popular type of bond in the international capital market.

It is evident that the rapid growth of the eurobond market in recent years can be ascribed to the following:

- the absence of regulatory interference;
- the situation of less stringent disclosure requirements when compared to most domestic bond markets;
- a relatively favourable tax status, where the majority of industrialised countries have abolished the custom of withholding tax on interest payments to foreigners.

6.7.4 The international equity market

Since there is no international **equity market** in the true sense of a specific location, this development reflects the trend whereby investors increasingly take ownership in companies in foreign countries where regulatory and other systems allow such a practice. In a gradual evolution, this practice has expanded in recent years to a situation where companies list their shares on stock exchanges in foreign countries. This, in turn, is seen as a preliminary step to the actual issuing of a company's shares on a foreign stock market, which undoubtedly increases its access to other financing sources, and also has the potential of lowering its cost of capital.

These trends seem to underline the importance and continuous development of international capital markets for international business.

It is clear that developments in international capital markets, including the eurocurrency market, have created numerous opportunities for multinational financial management in particular, notwithstanding the concomitant risks related to these developments. The major advantages of international capital markets are that they have broadened the access to financing and investment opportunities for multinational companies, with the added benefits of risk diversification and cost-effectiveness.

6.8 Summary

In this chapter we looked at the international financial market and its important constituent parts from a financial management perspective. The development of the International Monetary System, the European Monetary System, and the Economic and Monetary Union was traced to their current status in the international financial market.

It is evident that the management of firms involved in international operations necessitates an intricate knowledge of the way in which the IMS, the EMS, and the EMU function, especially with regard to the various exchange rate systems and practices in those markets in which they are active. The increased uncertainty, complexity and sophistication of financial markets have accordingly made international financial management much more demanding and challenging.

This was followed by a discussion of the nature, scope, functions, and activities of the foreign exchange market as a vital mechanism in international money, capital, and investment flows. More specifically, various concepts related to foreign exchange and foreign exchange activities were presented and the importance of spot and forward exchange rates and transactions, as well as currency swaps, cross-rates, and arbitrage were explained from a financial management perspective.

In conclusion, there was an overview of the international capital market, including the all-important euromarket. While the international capital market has some inherent disadvantages, its advantages are becoming increasingly important for international financing and investment decisions. The most important of these are opportunities for greater access to financing, risk reduction through diversification, and lowering of the overall cost of capital.

To sum up, the internatonal financial market is the cornerstone of all international financial activities and presents challenging opportunities, as well as unique risks, to everyone involved in international business and finance.

Case Study

The Zimbabwean foreign exchange market

As long as currencies remain the medium of exchange for international business transactions, market fluctuations in relative currency values will be of importance to exporters and importers, manufacturers, investors, bankers, speculators, and policy-makers alike. The Zimbabwean foreign exchange market is no exception to the rule. In effect, the status of Zimbabwe as a developing economy adds to the complexities inherent in foreign exchange markets.

In the discussion that follows, the macro-economic situation in Zimbabwe will be explored, as well as the applicability of the above theories and concepts of foreign exchange to the Zimbabwean foreign exchange market.

Zimbabwe: a macro-economic overview

The Zimbabwean economy has been particularly hard-hit by the world-wide economic and currency crises experienced in emerging markets from 1997 to 1999, and its experience during 1998, in particular, has been one of the most traumatic in the southern African region.

The Zimbabwean Stock Exchange and exchange rates have suffered the steepest decline in the region (ahead of South Africa and Malawi), and the inflation rate in 1998 was one of the highest in the region, after Angola and the Democratic Republic of the Congo. A combination of macro-economic and governance issues have, together, adversely affected the external accounts and resulted in a severe erosion of market sentiment. Although the worst effects were felt in the financial sector of the economy and the balance of payments, the crisis inevitably worked its way through to the real economy, with the GDP growth rate falling steadily from 7,3% in 1996 and 3,2% in 1997 to a projected 0,8% in 1998.

Zimbabwe's balance of payments had increasingly come under fire in recent years. Pressure intensified in the period beginning September 1997, and culminated in a sharp depreciation of the Zimbabwean dollar on 14 November 1997.

The situation had been aggravated by the fact that proceeds from tobacco, the country's major export-earning product, were lower than expected. Compounding the already critical situation was the fall in mineral prices on international markets, especially those of gold, ferrochrome, copper, asbestos, and nickel. These adverse developments took their toll on official foreign exchange reserves.

Imports which were expected to grow by only 5% from the 1996 level, had increased almost 17% by mid-1997. In the absence of significant capital inflows, stability of the foreign exchange market at that stage could only be maintained by either running down official foreign exchange reserves to meet import demand, or by raising the price of foreign exchange reserves to meet import demand, or a combination of both. Raising the price of foreign exchange would inevitably mean a sharp depreciation of the Zimbabwean dollar against major trading partner country currencies.

The Reserve Bank managed to stabilise the exchange rate between August and December 1997 at the expense of foreign exchange reserves. Official foreign exchange reserves declined further as the Reserve Bank continued to intervene in the foreign exchange market to ensure sufficient liquidity. Pressures intensified from September 1997 onward, initially reflecting the market's concern over the level of gross official foreign exchange reserves, but increasingly as a strong speculative element on the part of both banks and holders of foreign currency accounts began to surface. Negative perceptions of macro-economic fundamentals by the market, especially after the government's decision to compensate war veterans, which entailed large expenditure outlays, also brought more pressure to bear on the foreign exchange market, and speculation intensified.

To ease the pressure on the official foreign exchange reserves, the Reserve Bank took the following corrective measures with the objective of increasing the level of usable foreign exchange reserves:

- It increased the re-discount rate.
- It closed all corporate foreign currency accounts and off-loaded them on to the foreign exchange market.
- It regarded the Foreign Exchange Bureau, that had previously operated outside the interbank foreign exchange market, as part of the interbank foreign exchange market from November 1997 onwards.
- It introduced new controls as from 17 November 1997, which meant that banks could hold net foreign exchange balances of up to US$50 000, or 20% of their capital base, whichever is lower, where previously they were allowed to hold net foreign exchange balances of up to 20% of their capital base for transaction purposes.

These measures were meant to be short-term solutions. However, they subsequently limited the ability of the foreign exchange market to adjust its flexibility. Sustainable stability in the foreign exchange market required addressing the macro-economic fundamentals which, it was hoped, would, in turn, improve market perceptions about the macro-economic situation, which could hopefully guarantee the necessary balance of payments support from the World Bank and the donor community.

Inflation had been on a sharp upward trend, driven by a number of cost-push factors, the most notable of which stemmed from the exchange rate decline. Rising real wages, as well as food and energy price pressures, were additional cost-push forces. Headline inflation was expected to rise to a peak of just over 35% in November 1998 (up from 20% at the end of 1997). Interest rates also increased sharply during 1998, with the rediscount rate having risen from 25,5% to 35% during 1998.

It would appear that the Zimbabwean economy had been characterised by high inflation rates, high interest rates, and falling exchange rates. Investor confidence declined to its lowest ebb by the end of 1998, especially in the light of the contentious land issue and other political decisions which were taken by government, such as intervention in the war in which the Democratic Republic of the Congo was involved.

The foreign exchange market in Zimbabwe

Prior to 1994, Zimbabwe had a fixed exchange rate system, with the exchange rate value pegged by the country's Central Bank. In order to maintain the fixed exchange rate, the government needed large reserves of foreign currencies for the Central Bank in order to buy the local currency during those periods when its value was likely to fall.

Since January 1994, Zimbabwe had operated a unified exchange rate, determined by the demand and supply of foreign exchange in the interbank market. However, there have been substantial reversals in this liberalised system in the wake of the exchange rate crisis. In particular, the termination of foreign currency accounts held by resident companies within the domestic banking system had a severely negative impact on domestic and foreign investor confidence.

The Zimbabwean market is a thin market in terms of volume. The number of players has been limited, a violation of one of the basic assumptions of perfect markets, namely that there should be a large number of players, none of which is big enough to control the market, for markets to be efficient. In Zimbabwe, one big player, a merchant bank, could actually dictate the pace and sentiment of the market.

The market has also been imperfect because information dissemination was not very efficient. The efficient market hypothesis assumes that new information comes to the market in a random, independent fashion. In Zimbabwe, however, it was shown that market participants with inside information had reaped profits on the foreign exchange market at the expense of those who did not have access to such information.

The market was also illiquid in terms of availability of foreign exchange reserves. As at the end of October 1998, it was reported that the Central Bank's foreign reserves could only cover one month's import requirements.

Although on paper Zimbabwe was supposedly operating on a managed exchange rate system, the Central Bank's intervention policy was, at times, not clear. For example, in October 1998, when the Zimbabwean dollar depreciated by 10% against the US dollar, the Central Bank did not intervene, and no public announcement in this regard was made. As a result of the above factors, Zimbabwe had an imperfect foreign exchange market, which was not consistent with the efficient market hypothesis.

Inflation rates and foreign exchange markets

Based on the PPP, which predicts that the exchange rate changes to compensate for differences in inflation between two countries, it is important to note that Zimbabwe's inflation rate was considerably higher – five to ten times higher – than that of all its important trading partners (USA, South Africa, Germany) and was showing little prospect of decreasing in the near future. The fall in the value of the Zimbabwean dollar had for the 13 months previous to the end of 1998, matched the domestic inflation rate, and this seemed consistent with the PPP theory. On the basis of projected inflation differentials between Zimbabwe and its major trading partners, the nominal trade weighted exchange rate should have been allowed to adjust (if it had been managed flexibly) by about 24% in nominal terms over the next 12-month period.

There was considerable doubt about whether the authorities were capable of implementing a credible and sustainable anti-inflation policy. It appeared that monetary expansion would remain a potent source of inflationary pressure in the economy throughout 1999, ruling out any chance of a return to single-digit inflation in the year 2000. With the widening gap between domestic and trading partner inflation, further depreciation appeared both likely and necessary if international competiveness was to be restored. Exhibit 6.11 (p. 192) shows the relationship between exchange rates and inflation in Zimbabwe for the period 1990 to 1998.

Based on 1998 inflation projections, interest rates in Zimbabwe seemed likely to rise further during the next 12 months. The rediscount rate at the end of 1998 was 35% compared to the repo rate of 15-20% in South Africa. Excessive pressure on the Zimbabwean dollar exchange rate and its decline to levels that were too far removed from realistic values, prompted the Reserve Bank to raise interest rates in an effort to halt its decline.

The Reserve Bank's rediscount rate was increased from 31,5% to 35% on 3 August 1998. Unfortunately, this did not arrest the fall in the value of the dollar for long. A sustained decline in business sector confidence in South Africa led to a decline in the rand exchange rate that had a further impact on the stability of the Zimbabwean dollar.

The above event seems to imply that inflation and interest rate differentials alone are not the major determinants of foreign exchange rate movements. Other factors which are explored in more detail below, also come into play.

Speculation

The actions of speculators can play havoc with a currency, as experienced in Zimbabwe during the second quarter of 1998. The Zimbabwean dollar was fairly stable against most major currencies, but this situation was disrupted by major movements in the rand/US dollar rela-

Exhibit 6.11: Money, prices and the exchange rate

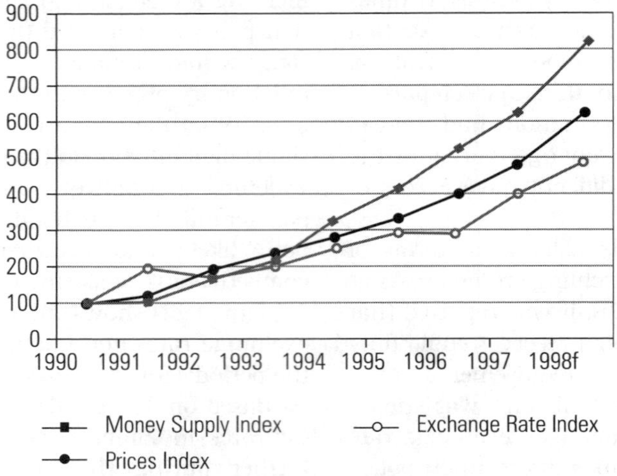

SOURCE: Standard Chartered Bank Zimbabwe Ltd: May 1998 (*Business Trends Zimbabwe*)

tionship, resulting in an import pressure build-up. Speculative attacks on the Zimbabwean dollar resulted in a strained balance of payments position and a precarious foreign exchange reserve position. These factors resulted in a further devaluation of the local currency.

Political decisions

The land redistribution policy in Zimbabwe seriously affected investor confidence in that country, and consequently, the exchange rate. The situation was not helped by the government's decision to intervene in the war in the Democratic Republic of the Congo. This intervention did not find favour with foreign investors, the impact resulting in a further weakening of the Zimbabwean dollar. The International Monetary Fund had promised to inject some foreign currency into the country to boost the Central Bank's foreign currency reserves. However, this 'help' was postponed until such time that the government clarified its policy on land distribution and its intervention in the DRC, among other issues.

Money supply and exchange rates

According to the money supply approach, an economy with a high relative money supply growth will experience a weakening exchange rate. Accordingly, both high nominal interest rates and weakening currencies flow from high relative money supply growth.

In Zimbabwe, money supply data through October 1998 indicated that there had been a resurgence of broad money growth. In the third quarter of 1997, M3 expanded by 114% on an annualised basis, after averaging a mere 14% (annualised) in the previous fourth quarter. On a year-on-year basis, the rate of broad money growth rose to 34,9% in December 1997, from an average of 22,1% in the previous 12-month period. Thus, while the money supply had been growing, there was a simultaneous deterioration in the exchange rate.

This was in line with the hypothesis of the money supply approach as defined above, which suggested that the exchange rate and monetary policy should be addressed concurrently, in order to achieve the country's stabilisation and inflation-reduction objectives. While Exhibit 6.11 (p. 192) shows the relationship between money supply index, price index, and exchange rate index in Zimbabwe for 1990 to 1998, Exhibit 6.12 shows the growth in money supply for the period 1994 to 1998.

Exchange rates and tobacco prices

Weak tobacco prices at the beginning of the season in April 1998 and uncertainty surrounding IMF support in the matter of balance of payments, contributed to an unstable Zimbabwean dollar against major currencies as from May 1998. The weak tobacco prices had resulted in doubt as to whether the foreign exchange markets could sustain the usual stability that prevailed during the tobacco season.

The pressure on the local currency had increased further as a result of relatively low commodity prices (e.g. gold) on the international market. Furthermore, the anticipated balance of payments facility had not been forthcoming from the IMF.

It was argued that stability in the foreign exchange market would depend (among other factors) on the ability of the government to reduce both inflation and government domestic debt to allow the Central Bank to tighten domestic credit and build up foreign reserves.

Import cover and exchange rates

One statistic which is not always available from the Central Bank but is critical in determining the future direction of exchange rates, is the level of import cover.

One of the major factors behind the 40% crash of the Zimbabwean dollar on 14 November 1997 was market concern about the level of official external reserves held by the Zimbabwean Reserve Bank. Mirroring the deterioration in the current account, external reserves fell sharply in 1997, dropping from a peak level of US$930 million in August 1996 (equal to five months' imports) to US$482 million by the end of the first quarter of 1997. By the end of 1997, official reserves (including gold holdings) had declined to around US$200 million as the Reserve Bank ran down reserves to finance imports on the back of a significant fall in export receipts. The low level of reserves could

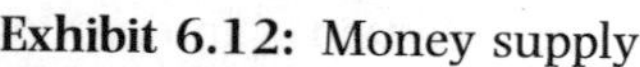

Exhibit 6.12: Money supply

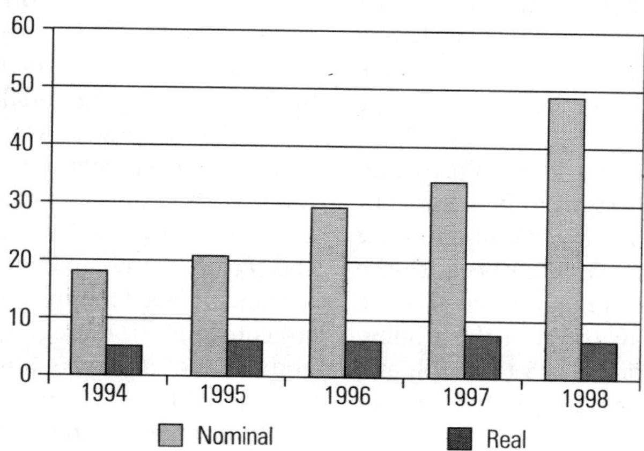

SOURCE: Standard Chartered Bank Zimbabwe Ltd: May 1998 (*Business Trends Zimbabwe*)

be explained by the fact that the 1997 current account deficit of over US$500 million had been financed largely by running down external reserves (and also the fact that there was very little capital inflow into the country during 1997).

The implications of the above were that exchange rate movements were also affected by the balance of payments position and external reserves held by the Central Bank.

Concluding remarks

It appears that the Zimbabwean foreign exchange market could still be regarded as an emerging market, and one with few significant players. Because it could be dominated by one big player, as well as the intervention policy of the Central Bank and government controls, the Zimbabwean foreign exchange market could be regarded as an imperfect one. The President of Zimbabwe is on record as saying that only five banks in Zimbabwe controlled the foreign exchange market.

A few banks can control the pace of the foreign exchange market because exporters deposit their foreign currency earnings with the established banks. The exporters will then sell the foreign currency on the local market when rates are favourable. Thus the foreign receipts will be in the hands of a few banks which can then influence the exchange rates on the market, depending on the timing of their transactions

The theory of Purchasing Power Parity and interest rate differentials seem to be consistent with what is happening in the Zimbabwean foreign exchange market, mainly because the country's interest and inflation rates were significantly higher than those of the trading partners during the period 1995 to 1998, and the currency depreciated to compensate for these differentials.

However, there were other factors such as speculation, political decisions, balance of payments positions, money supply, and external reserves, which affected the foreign exchange market. The foreign exchange market was – and still is – dependent on international tobacco sales, the major foreign exchange earner in Zimbabwe.

Because of the volatility in the Zimbabwean foreign exchange market, forecasting exchange rate movements is a daunting, if not an impossible, task. Since financial institutions are aware of this, they load a prohibitive premium on forward contracts, which further adds to the problems of commerce and industry in the Zimbabwean economy.

The way forward

The Zimbabwean dollar halved in value during the first four years after independence in 1980, halved again during the next seven years, and again during the next two years. It halved yet again during the next four-year period and then, during 1997/1998, halved again in less than one year. Valued at about three US cents, compared to 140 US cents in 1980, the Zimbabwean dollar bears all the battle scars of front-line soldiers in an unequal contest. The trend in the exchange rate of the Zimbabwean dollar against the US dollar for the period 1992/93 to 1997/98 is illustrated in Exhibit 6.13 (p. 195).

Notwithstanding certain international events beyond the control of an individual country, such as the economic and currency crises of 1997/98 which had a significant impact on emerging and developing economies in particular, other issues or forces are the result of government decisions at the policy level in the countries concerned. Also, countries venturing into international markets, and specifically the companies in various industrial sectors involved in international business, have to compete in increasingly demanding and competitive markets, but at the same time operate within an economic and policy framework unique to the specific country. They should therefore be given the necessary support to be effective in the international marketplace. In the case of Zimbabwe, it seems that

Exhibit 6.13: Z$:US$ average exchange rates 1992/93 – 1997/98

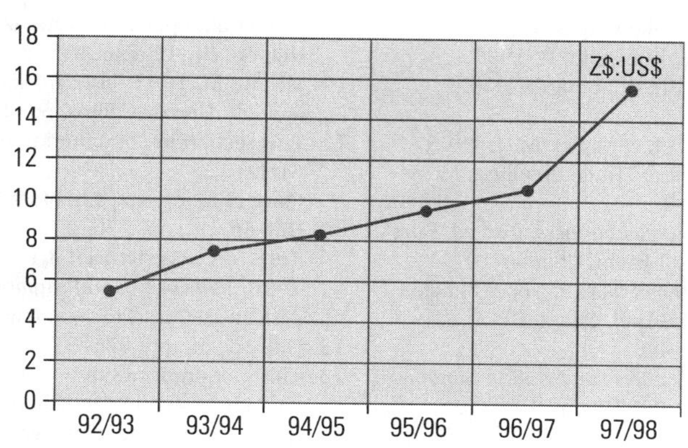

there is much to be done to attain economic stability and an optimal position in international business and in the international financial market.

Questions

The following questions are based on the case-study information as well as on Chapters 5 and 6:

1 What external international events and environmental forces during the late 1990s contributed to Zimbabwe's declining economic situation?
2 Which major internal factors during the late 1980s and the 1990s negatively influenced Zimbabwe's economic situation and specifically its export position?
3 Based on economic, money supply, and exchange rate theories, what would you recommend as appropriate government actions or initiatives to get the Zimbabwean economy (*inter alia*, characterised by high inflation resulting in high interest rates and a declining exchange rate), and especially its export industry, back on track?
4 Could the role of the established banking sector and the Central Bank be improved to support your recommendations in 3 above? Explain.
5 Can commerce, industry, mining, and agriculture contribute to an improvement in Zimbabwe's overall economic position? If so, in what way?

(Access the Internet for current information on the above-mentioned issues with regard to Zimbabwe's economy.)

Sources

This case study is based on a Research Working Paper entitled 'Foreign exchange rate movements: Zimbabwe foreign exchange market' submitted by T. Mbabvu in part fulfilment of the requirements for the Master's Degree in Business Leadership of the University of South Africa, Pretoria, November 1998. Adapted and reprinted with the permission of the Graduate School of Business Leadership, Unisa;

Sikhakhane, Jabulani. 1999. 'Beyond the Limpopo banks', *Financial Mail*, 11 June, pp. 52-53; and

Deketeke, Pikirayi. 1999. 'Amid the turmoil: A president's optimism', *Business in Africa*, Vol.7, No.4, July/August, pp.48-49.

Endnotes

1 This section draws on the following works:
Clark, E., Levaisseur, M. & Rousseau, P. 1993. *International finance*. London: Chapman & Hall, Chapter 4.
Eiteman, D.K., Stonehill, A.I. & Moffet, M.H. 1995. *Multinational business finance*. 7th ed. Reading, Mass: Addison-Wesley, Chapter 2.
Hill, C.W.L. 1997. *International business*. 2nd ed. Burr Ridge, Illinois: McGraw-Hill Irwin, Chapter 10.
Baker, J.C. 1998. *International finance*. Upper Saddle River, New Jersey: Prentice Hall, Chapter 2.

2 Eiteman, et al., op. cit., p. 40.

3 Charlton, C. 1999. *Euro – impact and reality*. London: Financial Times Pitman Publishing, p. 14.

4 Charlton, op. cit., p. 15.

5 Hill, op. cit., pp. 227–236.
Sercu, P. & Uppal, R. 1995. *International financial markets and the firm*. London: Chapman & Hall, pp. 14–24;
Charlton, op. cit., p. 15–17

6 Odendaal, J.A. & Prinsloo, F. 1999. *'The impact of the introduction of the euro as single currency on international and local companies'*, Unpublished Research Report, University of Pretoria, pp. 6–10.

7 Odendaal & Prinsloo, op. cit., p. 9–11.

8 Eng, M.V., Lees, F.A. & Mauer, L.J. 1995. *Global finance*. New York: Harper Collins, Chapter 4.
Eiteman, et al., op. cit., Chapter 4.

9 Eng, et al., op. cit., Chapter 4.
Hill, op. cit., Chapter 9.

10 Melvin, M. 1995. *International money and finance*. London: Harper Collins, pp. 2–3.

11 This section in combination draws on the following works:
Clark et al. op. cit., Chapters 6 and 19;
Hill, op. cit., pp. 270–276;
Ross, S.A., Westerfield, R.W., Jordan, B.D. & Firer, C. 1996. *Fundamentals of corporate finance*. First South African edition. Chicago: Irwin, Chapter 21.

12 Hill, op. cit., pp. 275–276.

13 This section draws on:
Eiteman et al., op. cit., Chapter 5.
Ross et al., op. cit., Chapter 21.

14 Kefalas, A.G. 1990. *Global business strategy*. Cincinnatti, Ohio: South Western, pp. 177–179.

15 Melvin, op. cit., pp. 92–93.

16 Hill, op. cit., p. 285.

17 Eng, et al., op. cit., p. 110.

18 Greshner, D.N. & Smit, E.v.d.M. 1997. 'Seasonal and public holiday effects in the commercial rand/dollar exchange rate during the period 1984 – 1995'. *South African Journal of Business Management*, Vol. 28, No. 1. March, pp. 6–14.

19 Greshner & Smit, op. cit., pp. 13–14.

20 Hill, op. cit., p. 329.

21 Eiteman, et al., op. cit., pp. 46–52.

PART III

Global business leadership and strategies

7 International management and leadership: developing a global mindset

Key issues

- International management and leadership
- The need for a global mindset
- Developing global competencies
- Focus on training efforts
- Socialising the new breed of global managers in multinational corporations

7.1 **Introduction**

The development, growth, and dynamics of international business, the increasing importance of international trade and investment, and the continuing trend towards economic integration were the topics of Part I. The discussion in Part II focused on the global business environments facing international business enterprises. These comprised the dynamic and continuously changing, often volatile, economic, political, legal, and cultural environments. Given the increasing importance of financial issues worldwide, the global monetary system was explored as an important dimension and extension of the international economic environment.

A thorough knowledge of the characteristics, scope, and dynamics of international business as defined in Chapter 1, as well as of the environments of international business, is required for effective international management and global leadership. More specifically, international business and its environments provide the framework of opportunities, challenges, threats, risks, and constraints within which organisational strategies are conceived and executed – the essence of international management and leadership. The four basic strategies that firms use to enter and compete in the international environment are discussed in Section 8.1.

This chapter initially sets out to explain and clarify a number of relevant concepts and terms in the context of international management and leadership. This is followed by a brief exploration of the environment of international management and leadership, the role of international management, and the requisite skills and attributes to fulfil these roles. A discussion of the increasing importance of cross-cultural leadership completes the first part of this chapter.

Notwithstanding the increasing demands on international management and leadership, recent evidence unequivocally supports the notion that, to ensure continued success, international companies and business leaders must cultivate a global mindset.[1] Accordingly, this chapter is concluded by identifying the need for a global mindset, arguing why mindset matters, indicating how global mindsets are developed, and how the new breed of global managers are to be socialised for the successful management of multinational companies in the 21st century.

7.2 International management and leadership

In an intensely competitive international business environment, many factors are increasingly impacting on international business involvement, an issue that has already been referred to in Chapters 1 and 2. As a result, the importance of effective **international management and leadership** has increased dramatically, especially with regard to the increased levels of complexity, ambiguity, and anxiety as the business organisation moves from being a 'local player' to being a 'local-player-cum-exporter', then a 'multinational' and finally a 'transnational' or 'global player'.[2]

It is clear that the international manager and leader have to master new concepts and theories, cultivate new insights, command new skills, and above all, develop a **global mindset** conducive to global thinking and strategising beyond those which have been successful in the past.[3]

In this section, a number of relevant concepts are first defined, after which the environment and role of the international manager and leader, their attributes and the skills they require, are examined. Lastly, the requirements for success in cross-cultural leadership are briefly explored. The important issue of global mindsets is dealt with in Sections 7.3 to 7.6 of this chapter.

7.2.1 Basic concepts

In Parts I and II we considered the development and the environments of international business respectively. Part III deals primarily with the management, leadership, strategies, and functional activities of international business enterprises. With this in mind, it is necessary to define and clarify some concepts and terms in the context of Part III, starting with the concepts of international management and leadership, exploring the distinction between management and leadership, and in conclusion, defining a number of strategic and institutional concepts. Given the divergent and interdisciplinary character of international business, clarification of concepts should facilitate discussion and enhance the understanding of this exciting subject area.

(a) International management

In emphasising the difference between domestic and international management, Dessler defines **international management** as

> the performance of the management functions of planning, organising, leading, and controlling across national borders.[4]

The broader definition of Phatak, however, is preferred. He defines international management as

> a process of accomplishing the global objectives of a firm by effectively co-ordinating the procurement, allocation, and utilisation of the human, financial, intellectual, and physical resources of the firm within and across national boundaries, and effectively charting the path toward the desired organisational goals by navigating the firm through a global environment that is not only dynamic but often very hostile to the firm's very survival.[5]

The value of this definition is that, apart from articulating the demands on international management, it also provides for the important interface between the enterprise and its external environment.

(b) International management and leadership

In the relevant management and international business literature the concepts of **management** and **leadership** are distinguished, but are, in effect, inseparable in practice.

In the first definition of management above, 'leading' is mentioned as one of the four basic functions of management. Accordingly, managers get the job done by working through people, making leadership the key ingredient among many in the management task.[6]

Because managers are required to work with their people – constituting the 'behavioural side of management' – leading applies to almost anything, besides planning, organising, and controlling. It will become clear as we go on that the internationalisation and globalisation of business decidedly impact on the behavioural side of leading the firm.

Despite the fact that the concepts of management and leadership seem to be converging gradually, as is evidenced by the appearance of terms such as 'global manager' in the more recent literature,[7] there is still a definite distinction between management and leadership. Nancy Adler contends that

> Leaders create vision, the meaning within which others work and live. Managers, by contrast, act completely within a vision.... Leadership and vision remain fundamental to the understanding of a people and their institutions.[8]

She accordingly defines the concept of **leadership** as follows:

> Leadership involves the ability to inspire and influence the thinking, attitudes and behaviour of people.[9]

Warren Bennis also acknowledges this distinction by stating that

> too many of today's organisations are overmanaged and underled.[10]

(c) Enterprise, firm, company, and corporation

Unless evident from the context, or specified otherwise, the terms **enterprise**, **firm**, **company**, and **corporation** will be used interchangeably. In Section 1.8 the **multinational enterprise (MNE)** was described as a specific type of institution (also generally referred to as multinational corporation/company – MNC – especially in the American literature, and used synonymously with MNE). The term **organisation** is often used in a generic sense to denote 'enterprise'.

(d) Affiliates and subsidiaries

Notwithstanding the possibility of subtle or legal differences which may exist, the terms **affiliates** and **subsidiaries** will be used interchangeably.

(e) International, multidomestic, global, and transnational

The terms **international**, **multidomestic**, **global**, and **transnational** could refer or apply to firms, industries (and, by implication, products and services), and strategies. The context in which they are used will appropriately reflect the intended meaning of each of these terms.

In reference to firms, **multidomestic firms** follow a multidomestic strategy that focuses on local responsiveness in foreign markets. **Firms with an international strategy** strive towards creating value by transferring core competencies from home to foreign business units, and towards a balance between globalisation and local responsiveness. **Global firms** (also referred to as globally integrated firms) follow global strategies that emphasise the realisation of location and experience curve economies in the production and marketing of largely low-cost, standardised products. **Transnational firms** focus relentlessly on the simultaneous attainment of location and experience curve economies, as well as local responsiveness, through global networks and the multidirectional transfer of core competencies.[11] Where the above terms specifically refer to strategies, these are explored further in Chapter 8.

(f) International, global and worldwide

The term **international** will refer to any activity or object connected with doing business outside the home country. The term **worldwide** will be used as a neutral designation, and **global** will mean encompassing extensive networking linkages internationally. Alternatively, **global** will also refer to types of worldwide strategy.[12]

7.2.2 The environment of international management

(a) Environments and management

While the international business environment comprises the total world environment in its broadest sense, the relevant international environment for a multinational enterprise would be the sum total of the environments of each of the nation-states or countries with which the company trades or may have foreign affiliates. Global issues and forces such as ongoing shifts in international financial markets, increasing economic integration, global trends in trade liberalisation and deregulation, far-reaching technological advances, and the increasing importance of emerging economies and markets, can affect the environments of countries concerned in various ways – confirming Miller's views of an exponential increase in the level of complexity as businesses become more international in scale and in scope.[13] In the discussion of the environments in Part II, some implications and influences of environmental factors were discussed. According to Coade, the following six key areas have a direct impact on a company's understanding of the international business environment:

- success and failure in understanding the business environment;
- the changing nature of the international business environment;
- the competitive factors influencing the business environment;
- the need for general environmental scanning;
- systemising the search for international business opportunities;
- the key factors driving the competitive environment.[14]

Effective international management requires systematically addressing these key issues and gathering relevant information to facilitate market and competitor analysis as a basis for strategic planning and strategy formulation – an approach which will most likely decrease risk and uncertainty, enhance performance, and achieve a competitive advantage in the global market-place. (International market assessment is discussed in Chapter 9.)

The relevant environments and their implications for international business were discussed in Chapters 3 to 6. In addition to these challenges we briefly consider the aspect of risk in the international environment and how it should be managed internationally.

(b) Risk in the international environment

Risk can adversely affect carefully planned outcomes and expectations in international business.

Mead[15] identifies two types of risk, **internal risk** and **environmental risk**, which he defines as follows:

> Internal risk is defined as the threat that internal events will adversely affect the company's ability to implement its strategy and achieve its goals. .... In a multinational company this risk is heightened to the extent that the subsidiary is more autonomous – free of headquarters management distant from headquarters – geographically and culturally less involved in headquarters operations.
>
> Environmental risk is defined as the threat that events in the environment will adversely affect the company's ability to implement its strategy and achieve its goals.

As far as internal risks are concerned, firms try to protect themselves against risks, such as fraud and incompetence, by implementing effective risk-management systems and encouraging a positive organisational culture. Environmental risks are extremely difficult – if not impossible – to forecast or predict and usually occur unexpectedly. Environmental risks mentioned by Mead include unexpected government-imposed

- discriminatory taxation;
- import and export controls;
- bad payments;
- interference with operations;
- legal disputes (e.g. trade issues);
- industrial disputes (e.g. labour relations);
- unfair competition from the local public sector.[16]

In addition to the abovementioned examples, environmental risks also include:

- political events such as government takeovers, the nationalisation of industries, the expropriation of property and assets, and piracy of intellectual property rights;
- public sector corruption;
- regional hostilities, military interventions and wars.[17]

Because events such as these almost always occur without prior warning, they can result in crises that could devastate the firm. Risk is one of the elements in the international firm's environmental frame of reference, which means that the international manager should strive to be aware of potential crises, and also devise ways in which to anticipate such events and minimise their effects on the business. As a first step, international managers need to have effective and appropriate competitive intelligence and environmental scanning systems in place to provide timely information for proactive action. In this regard, country risk profiles and ratings that regularly appear in the *Euro-money Magazine*,[18] or are published by the *Business Environmental Risk Index* (BERI),[19] provide valuable information for the initial screening of countries as potential destinations for foreign investment and international business.

A recent risk-assessment survey of 45 emerging economies highlights some of the risks and problems in developing countries with which multinational companies have to contend.

South Africa 14th on list of riskiest places to do business

According to a survey in early 1999 of multinational companies in 45 countries by the Merchant International Group, a London-based risk-assessment firm, South Africa was found to be 14th on the list of riskiest countries with whom to do business, and was also 'way above average on the danger scale in terms of corruption in business dealings'. Other factors evaluated in the survey included organised crime, counterfeiting, extreme political groups, unfair competition, and cultural and ethical differences.

In this survey based on cumulative ratings and applied to 45 emerging nations, Singapore was rated least corrupt (19%), and Pakistan the most (91%). Indonesia (84%), Russia (83%), Colombia (81%), and South Africa (68%) exhibited most of the negative factors mentioned above. However, after China, South Africa was pin-pointed as an outstanding potential emerging market, but Merchant International stated that '... in general, multinationals are fed up with business practices in emerging countries ... losses of UK multinationals alone due to inability to cope with bad business practices, corruption, and crime in emerging markets, total £15 billion a year – about 10% of expected returns on foreign investments'.

SOURCE: Behrman, Neil. *Business Day*, http:\w.w.w.bday.co.za/99/03/15/news/news4.htm

Fatehi recommends that, besides insuring against certain risks, ways to protect the firm against some uninsurable risks include:

- investing in countries through direct foreign investment and joint ventures;
- investing in industries which have been earmarked for encouragement by host governments;
- using local financing sources.[20]

The effective management of risk, both internal and external, in the international environment, however difficult it may be, constitutes an important element of the all-embracing task of the international manager.

7.2.3 Managing in the 21st century

What will managing in the 21st century involve and what will be required to make it successful? As far back as 1987, Ian Mitroff sounded the following warning:

> For all practical purposes, all business today is global. Those individual businesses, firms, industries, and whole societies that clearly understand the new rules of doing business in a world economy, will prosper; those that do not, will perish.[21]

The complexities that international managers and leaders face as a result of environments that vary across countries, and also change over time, provide the background against which the future role of the international manager is briefly explored.

As we have seen so far, international managers need to cope with and manage a host of current and emerging global issues, the most important of which include deregulation, privatisation, technological and biotechnological progress, changing political systems, changing demographics, increasing economic integration, and formulation of trading blocks, all of which contribute in some way to the process of globalisation.

More specifically, Coade[22] outlines the direction in which international business in general is developing and identifies a number of inescapable competing factors for the future. These factors are grouped into four categories, as depicted in Exhibit 7.1.

These groups of competing factors include aspects of the business environment and the initiatives of companies that will not only impact on the task of the international manager, but also on the success of international

Exhibit 7.1: Groups of competing factors

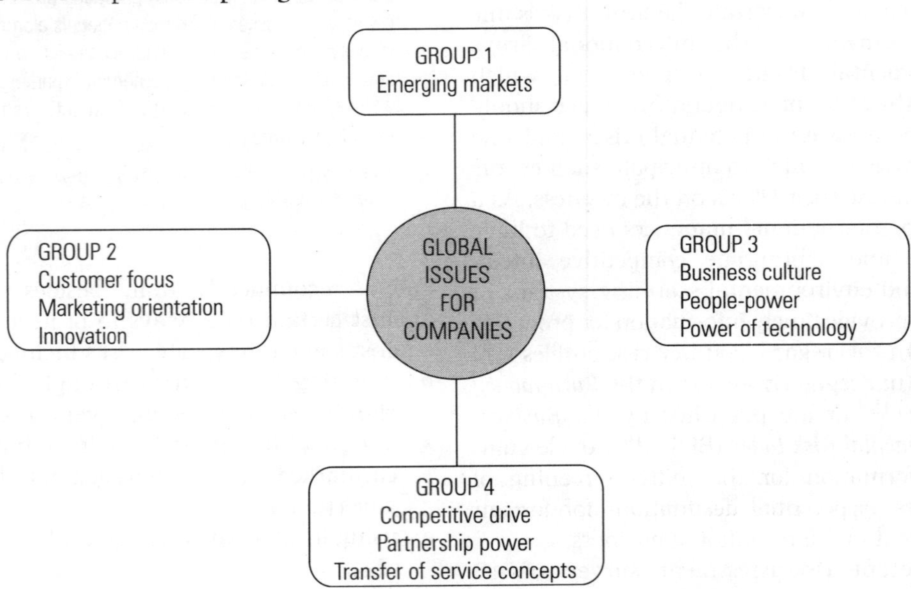

SOURCE: Coade, N. 1997. *Managing international business*, London, International Thomson Business Press, p. 88.

companies in their search for competitive advantage and sustainable growth.

The first group of factors includes the market opportunities and investment strategies of international companies, and emphasises the fact that the future growth in international business will be largely in developing economies and emerging markets. It is predicted that the top 10 emerging markets will double their 1991 share of global GDP by 2010, and that foreign direct investment (FDI) into and exports from emerging economies in the next decade will significantly alter the international competitive landscape. Garten has identified ten major emerging markets which he believes are on track to grow two to three times as fast as the United States and the other industrial countries, and which present enormous economic opportunities. These ten prominent emerging markets are Argentina, Brazil, China, India, Indonesia, Mexico, Poland, South Africa, South Korea, and Turkey.[23]

The second group of factors involves an increased emphasis on the customer, and more specifically includes service excellence, quality, customer care, and user-friendly technology-customer interfaces like electronic home shopping and e-commerce. Creative marketing strategy and innovation as means of pursuing competitive advantage will be the driving forces for international firms.

The third group of factors emphasises the need for visionary leadership, the importance of the extent and success of an appropriate, enhancing business culture, and the ability of companies to adapt their business cultures to a changing business environment. Excellence in leadership, effective management, and human resource strategies that allow 'people-power' to become an integral part of international business strategy will contribute to ultimate success. Most of these factors will crop up again in our discussion of the need for and the development of global mindsets in the new emerging international business scene, and will be explored further in Sections 7.3 to 7.6.

The fourth group of factors emphasises strategic business reviews and organisational transformation. The growing importance of partnership power and intracompany co-operation in every aspect of the supply chain, and an innovative approach to the development of global strategies to introduce, develop and transfer business and service concepts, will give international firms a competitive edge.

In his assessment of the situation regarding progress in the globalisation of South African companies, Miller[24] states that successful managers should:

- possess appropriate knowledge and have the requisite experience to deal with high levels of complexity and ambiguity;
- possess the conceptual scope required to deal with the macro-issues of global management beyond what is required for dealing with the micro-issues required to operate local businesses;
- have realistic time frames for global strategy implementation;
- effectively overcome cultural barriers and develop an appreciation of cultural issues – South African managers have a tendency to treat other cultures as being much the same as their own, with only slight differences;
- develop and implement effective human and organisational networks, with sufficient time and resources allowed for these developments on a global scale;
- be able to identify global needs and products in the context of a market-driven, comprehensive, and integrated globalisation process;
- build globally distributed teams (GDT), whose members will frequently communicate by means of electronic and teleconferencing technologies, have infrequent personal contact, and be able to provide strategic information based on global thinking and learning.

As we will see below, these requirements already bear a marked resemblance to the competencies necessary for the development of a global mindset. Miller believes that, despite the enormous challenges of the transition to globalisation, the indications are that South African firms have already built up a core of high-potential global managers and that these companies probably have a head start in the race to become more competitive.[25] Notwithstanding Miller's pronouncement regarding this core of high-potential global managers, the reality of South Africa's poor ranking in respect of internationalisation in the *World Competitiveness Yearbook* is far from reassuring (see Section 1.1).

Given the broader global issues which were initially mentioned, Coade's competing factors that will impact on international business and management, and Miller's views on the managerial attributes required by South African managers, we can now attempt to identify some executive traits required for the future. A comparison of contemporary executive traits with those of the future, underlines the crucial importance of the new directions in which international management is developing. This comparison of current and future traits is summarised in Exhibit 7.2. The future traits, in particular, provide an overarching frame of reference for the traits and requirements for a global mindset, and should be integrated with those discussed in Sections 7.3 to 7.6.

According to Beamish, substantive issues that managers in diversified multinational corporations increasingly face include:

- integrating large international acquisitions;
- understanding the meaning of performance and accountability in a globally integrated system of product and service flows;
- building and managing a world-wide logistics capability;
- developing country-specific strategies that take into account the political as well as the economic imperatives;
- forming and benefiting from collaborative arrangements around the world;
- balancing the pressures for global integration and local demand.[26]

It is evident that global managers who want to succeed in the competitive business environment of the 21st century will need the ability to:

- develop and use global strategic skills;
- manage change and transition;

Exhibit 7.2: Executive traits now and in the future

Now	The Future
All knowing	Leader as learner
Domestic vision	Global vision
Predicts future from past	Intuits the future
Caring for individuals	Caring for institutions and individuals
Owns the vision	Facilitates vision of others
Uses power	Uses power and facilitation
Dictates goals and methods	Specifies processes
Alone at the top	Part of an executive team
Values order	Accepts paradox of order amidst chaos
Monolingual	Multicultural
Inspires the trust of boards, shareholders	Inspires the trust of owners, customers, and employees

SOURCE: Galagan, P.A. 1990, Executive Development in a Changing World, *Training and Development Journal,* June, pp. 23–41.

- manage cultural diversity;
- design and function in flexible organisation structures;
- work with others and in teams;
- communicate;
- learn and transfer knowledge in an organisation.[27]

These abilities and attributes are covered in greater detail in the context of global mindsets which are considered below in Sections 7.3 to 7.6.

7.2.4 Towards cross-cultural leadership

Increasingly, leaders will have to manage and lead people effectively by focusing on the identification and development of the skills that international managers need to succeed as leaders. Even more important, leaders will have to adapt their leadership styles to effectively address the needs inherent in different cultural situations. Chapter 3 was devoted to a discussion of cultural environments. In this section we look at the need to adapt international business activities effectively to different cultures as one of the major challenges of international management and leadership. This requires an intimate understanding of cultural diversity, perceptions, attitudes, stereotypes, and values related to those countries with which business is done.[28]

In Chapter 3, **culture** was broadly referred to as

> acquired knowledge that people use to interpret experience and generate social behaviour.[29]

Understanding culture is important because it affects how people think and behave, how managers and employees make decisions, and how they interpret their roles. All of this could have far-reaching effects on business performance due to misinterpretation and misunderstanding because of culture. As a point of departure, therefore, it is important for leaders to understand that:

- a culture is particular to one specific group and not to others,
- culture influences the behaviour of group members in uniform and predictable ways;
- culture is learned, not innate; it is passed down from one generation to the next;
- culture includes systems of values.

As far as groups in particular are concerned, leaders should know that:

- different social groups have different cultures;
- different social groups may respond to similar situations in different ways.[30]

Essentially, international leadership requires an open mind as well as an understanding and appreciation of the various international cultures and their differences as prerequisites for the attainment of a global mindset.

As far as leadership as such is concerned, research has shown that:

- the meaning of leadership may vary across cultures;
- the values that leaders have may vary across cultures;
- the behaviour, power sources, and influence tactics of leaders may have to be modified to be effective in specific international cultural environments;
- more effective leaders can be developed, given the future challenges of international business.[31]

We will now explore some of these important aspects related to leadership in a cross-cultural context.

(a) Differences in the meaning of leadership across cultures

It would appear that the culture in which leaders grow up strongly influences their attitudes and behaviours.[32] As a result, the actual **meaning of leadership** can vary across countries because every person is firmly embedded in his or her own specific culture of origin. It is noteworthy that:

- Americans tend to perceive leadership as an influence process, which affects the attitudes and behaviour of employees to attaining objectives;
- in Germany, leadership emphasis is on problem-solving and task allocation;
- American, Dutch, and Swedish leaders generally see their leadership role as motivating subordinates to solve their own problems, rather than initially supplying them with solutions;
- German, French, Italian, Indonesian, and Japanese managers generally have precise answers ready for subordinates because they regard it as the leader's responsibility to project an image of expertise that provides for an organisational culture of comfort and stability;
- the Chinese generally have a paternalistic view of leadership – instead of formal policies and procedures, Chinese leadership in business generally relies on networks and personal relationships where wisdom is defined in terms of the leader's judgement.[33]

If the meaning of leadership can vary across cultures and countries, of what value is this knowledge to international management and leaders? Apart from hopefully being able to avoid blatant mistakes due to ignorance with regard to cultural issues, the ability to predict how management and employees in different countries might behave can help international leaders to:

- select and appoint appropriate managers and employees in foreign operations;
- develop appropriate management education and training programmes;
- decide on appropriate approaches for strategy formulation and implementation.

We now briefly address the question of whether the values of leaders as such could vary across cultures.

(b) The extent to which the values of leaders may vary across cultures

International managers need to understand that the values which leaders need for being successful in meeting expectations, vary from one country to another. Research has confirmed the existence of the following cultural distinctions that can affect the values associated with leadership:

- traditionalism and modernism;
- particularism and universalism;
- outer-directed versus inner-directed world values.[34]

Traditionalism and modernism: In traditional cultures which are strongly based on history, family, and class, autocratic leadership may elicit a positive response, since the leader is normally an older and respected head of a specific grouping.

Modernism, on the other hand, is characterised by cultures in which reason and advancement on merit are the accepted norm. In modernism, therefore, the tendency is more towards sharing the decision-making authority. Traditionalism is generally more predominant in developing countries where collective values also predominate and a more structured work environment is preferred. Modernism, which is more prevalent in developed countries, is more future and goal-oriented, and also conforms to the idea of reward for performance based on merit.

This knowledge is of crucial importance to international leaders for the management, deployment, motivation, and reward of people in foreign subsidiaries of the company.

Particularism and universalism: This characteristic is indicative of whether leaders have particular or universal values, especially with regard to the application of rules. Universalism is where one set of rules applies to everyone, while with particularism the rules have to be modified, depending on the specific situation and cultural setting. It could be concluded, within reason, that a particularist culture emphasises good relationships (family, friends employees), while universalism stresses performance. It should be evident that apart from the cultural implications, these two approaches can result in different degrees of productivity which, in turn, could affect the competitiveness and profitability of the subsidiaries of a multinational company. This once again underlines the value of this knowledge for the astute international leader.

Outer-directed and inner-directed world views: It has also been shown that leaders may differ across cultures with regard to their world views.

Outer-directed managers and leaders tend to align their behaviour to their situation in life. This view inherently embraces tribalistic, conformist, and sociocentric values. Inner-directed managers are more intent on changing their environment and pursuing their own goals and objectives. This view inherently embraces egocentric, manipulative, and existential values.

Depending on the view that generally prevails with regard to the culture in the country with which business is done or operations established, the international leader who is knowledgeable about the three cultural distinctions is in a relatively favourable position to make informed decisions regarding matters such as:

- development and implementation of strategies and policies;
- selection, appointment, training, development, and rewarding of people;
- business-government relations.

Finally, it should be clear that the international leader's knowledge of the above cultural distinctions enables him or her to assess cross-cultural situations and decide on the most appropriate action in each specific situation.

(c) Attributes and skills in cross-cultural leadership

The relationship between culture and leadership attributes appears to be complex, as is evident from the following statement:

'Culture may affect assumptions about the characteristics of successful leaders ... However, there is also evidence that attitudes about what makes for effective leadership have been changing.'[35]

Research seems to confirm that there are differences with regard to the necessary attributes for leaders in different international settings, and that these differences can, to a certain extent, be explained by differences in culture.

In research by Yeung and Ready,[36] senior managers in MNCs in eight different countries were asked to give their views concerning the importance of 13 leadership characteristics or attributes to each of them. The rankings for the top five leadership characteristics by the senior managers appear in Exhibit 7.3 (p. 210).

The data in Exhibit 7.3 is summarised further in Exhibit 7.4 (p. 211) to emphasise the relative importance of the ranked characteristics in relation to the countries and cultures of the managers in the survey.

At this point, the following important conclusions with regard to international leadership characteristics and attributes may be drawn from the preceding research findings:

- One characteristic, 'the ability to articulate a tangible vision', was ranked first by four of the eight senior managers, which confirms the importance of this leadership characteristic in the countries concerned;
- Not one of the eight countries had identical rankings of the top five characteristics in each case;
- The way in which the top five characteristics were ranked for each country evidently reflects some important aspects regarding differences in culture;
- Interestingly, the characteristic, 'possesses a global mindset', was only ranked by two of the eight countries, namely Japan and South Korea – and then only as fourth most important in both cases – despite the fact that the issue of 'acquiring a global mindset' appears to have become of crucial importance in recent times, as discussed in Sections 7.3 to 7.6 of this chapter.

Exhibit 7.3: Rankings for the top five leadership characteristics selected by senior managers in different countries

Leadership characteristic	Australia	France	Germany	Italy	Japan	South Korea	U.K.	U.S.
Can create strategic change	–	5	2	–	5	1	–	3
Can create cultural change	3 & 4	2	–	1	–	–	4	5
Is flexible and adaptable	–	–	–	2	–	–	–	–
Possesses a 'global mindset'	–	–	–	–	4	4	–	–
Can articulate a tangible vision	1	1	1	–	2	2	1	2
Can communicate effectively day-to-day	–	3	3	4 & 5	–	–	–	–
Can manage internal and external networks	–	4	–	–	–	–	–	–
Can think about the total business	–	–	–	–	3	5	–	–
Has integrity and trust	–	–	–	–	–	3	–	–
Has a customer orientation	5	–	5	4 & 5	–	–	3	4
Can manage quality improvement	–	–	–	–	–	–	5	–
Can empower others	3 & 4	–	4	–	1	–	–	–
Manages strategy to action/gets results	2	–	–	3	–	–	2	1

SOURCE: A.K. Yeung and D.A. Ready, 'Developing Leadership Capabilities of Global Corporations: A Comparative Study in Eight Nations,' *Human Resource Management, 34 (1995): 529-547.*

Apart from the fact that culture affects the views of managers and leaders with regard to the relative importance of leadership attributes and skills as we have seen above, research has also shown that managers in different countries – and by implication, different cultures – have different perceptions of the managerial goals of business. More specifically, managers in three countries, namely the United States, Japan, and South Korea, had to rank nine alternatives from 0 (low in importance) to 3 (high in importance). The results of the survey with the ranking of items for each country appear in Exhibit 7.5 (p. 211).

The survey provides interesting findings firstly that 'Return on Investment' is ranked first by managers in America, and, although this item also appears to be of importance to Japanese and Korean managers (rankings of 2

Exhibit 7.4: Frequency of ranking and importance of the top five leadership characteristics

Leadership characteristic ranked by country (in descending order of frequency)	Frequency of top-ranking characteristic	Countries
• Can articulate a tangible vision	4	Australia, France, Germany, UK
• Can create strategic change	1	South Korea
• Can create cultural change	1	Italy
• Can empower others	1	Japan
• Manages strategy to action/get results	1	US

SOURCE: Summary from Yeung & Ready, op.cit., pp. 529–547.

Exhibit 7.5: Rating of goals in three countries

Items	USA	Japan	Korea
Return on investment	2.43 (1)	1.24 (2)	1.23 (3)
Stockholders' gains	1.14 (2)	0.02 (9)	0.14 (8)
Market share	0.73 (3)	1.43 (1)	1.55 (1)
Product portfolio	0.50 (4)	0.68 (5)	0.19 (6)
Operational efficiency	0.46 (5)	0.71 (4)	0.47 (5)
Financial structure	0.38 (6)	0.59 (6)	0.82 (4)
Product innovation	0.21 (7)	1.06 (3)	1.24 (2)
Corporate image	0.05 (8)	0.20 (7)	0.12 (9)
Working conditions	0.04 (9)	0.09 (8)	0.15 (7)

SOURCE: Chow, I, Holbert, N. Kelley, L & Yu, L. 1997. *Business Strategy – An Asia-Pacific Focus*, New York, Prentice Hall, p. 6.

and 3 respectively), they ranked market share first, with product innovation also being given a high ranking.

Commenting on these findings, Chow et al.[37] argue that the culture of Asian business and leadership focuses on the longer-term goals of market share and product innovation, compared to the shorter-term emphasis on predominantly financial criteria on the part of managers in the USA. It can therefore be accepted that, within limits, these managerial and leadership perceptions will influence managerial and leadership behaviour and expectaions differently across cultures.

There are, however, indications that attitudes towards leadership are converging worldwide, partly as a result of increased globalisation and industrialisation, and also because emergent and developing economies are acquiring a more developed character.

Despite these global developments, substantial evidence seems to support the view that culture continues to be important for leadership success across cultures, as we have briefly outlined in this section.

Having considered some attributes that seem to be associated with effective international leadership, we now briefly turn to the cross-cultural skills of the global manager and international leader.

Mead[38] contends that the cross-cultural skills which are required in international leadership settings and are directly related to management systems, include:

- communicating with members of the cultures;
- managing in structures;
- motivating and rewarding;
- resolving disputes;
- negotiating.

He then summarises the following performance goals required by international managers and leaders:

- understanding the nature of culture, and how it influences behaviour in the workplace;
- learning about specific cultures – the other, and one's own;
- recognising differences between cultures;
- recognising which cultural factors influence the expression of business structures, systems and priorities, and how they do so;
- implementing the structures and other aspects of the other culture;
- recognising how far structures and other factors of one's culture can be implemented within the other culture, and vice versa.

It is also evident that these performance goals are aligned to the requirements for leaders in the process of acquiring a global mindset.[39]

Commenting on leadership of the future, Warren Bennis maintains that leaders, whether male or female, need to have:

- a strongly defined sense of purpose – a sense of vision;
- the capacity to articulate a vision clearly.[40]

Kotter emphasises another important dimension of leadership when he states that it is only through leadership that you can timeously develop and nurture a culture that is adaptive to change.[41]

The views of both Bennis and Kotter support the notion that a strong sense of vision, the ability to cope with change, effective cross-cultural management, communication, and interpersonal skills will undoubtedly contribute to successful international leadership.

(d) Leadership behaviour and styles in the international context

Despite extensive research into various dimensions of leadership, it appears that two basic types of leadership behaviour, namely task-oriented and relationship-oriented behaviour, are useful in explaining organisational leadership behaviour. Whereas task-oriented behaviour involves clear performance specifications and specific procedures, relationship-oriented behaviour is more inclined towards personal concern and empathy toward employees' needs.[42]

Rather than looking at this dichotomy of leadership behaviour as two extremes, the most effective type of behaviour in any specific cultural situation could be seen to lie on a continuum somewhere between the two.

From an international leadership perspective, the preferred type of leadership behaviour would depend on the specific circumstances and the cultural situation concerned, which means that leaders may need to use different combinations of task- and relationship-oriented behaviours at any one time to be effective. However, Ayman and Chemers warn that

> research findings on leadership issues that have been obtained without provision to accommodate cultural differences should be treated with caution.[43]

It is imperative that international managers and leaders constantly keep in mind that culture affects how employees basically perceive the meaning of leadership, the values of leadership, and leadership style and behaviour. The following example by McFarlane and Sweeny illustrates how employees interpret leadership behaviour.

In one study, Japanese managers had less impact on American than Japanese subordinates, and generally had less influence than American supervisors. However, American subordinates performed **better** when a Japanese supervisor was friendly and supportive, but they performed **worse** when an American supervisor did basically the same thing. This suggests that the supervisor's nationality affects the interpretative framework used by subordinates. Friendliness by an American supervisor may imply weakness that can be taken advantage of, while the same behaviour from a Japanese supervisor may imply a focus on getting things done.[44]

Some recent developments that have in a way revolutionised the understanding of leadership include the emergence and recognition of charismatic leadership, transactional leadership and transformational leadership.

- A **charismatic leader** is a person who is dominant, self-confident, convinced of the moral righteousness of his or her beliefs, and able to arouse a sense of excitement and adventure in subordinates.
- A **transactional leader** manages through business transactions in which leaders use their legitimate, reward, and coercive powers to give commands and exchange rewards for services rendered.
- A **transformational leader** is one who transforms a vision into reality and motivates people to transcend their personal interests for the good of the group.

In South Africa, black empowerment in business and management has been a priority in recent years. One option for management development in the African context that has gained popularity, embraces the concept of **ubuntu.**[45] (This is also referred to in Section 3.3.) A model which has been proposed with regard to this approach is illustrated in Exhibit 7.6.

Ubuntu basically views the enterprise as a community of relationships which reflects the group solidarity prevalent in many African cultures.[46] This approach furthermore emphasises sharing, supportiveness, co-operation and participative decision-making, based on collective values.[47]

It is evident that an understanding of concepts such as these is of great importance also to those international enterprises involved in trade with or investment in South Africa.[48]

Because of its strong relationship with charismatic leadership and its positive attributes, transformational leadership appears to

Exhibit 7.6: A model for management development in South Africa

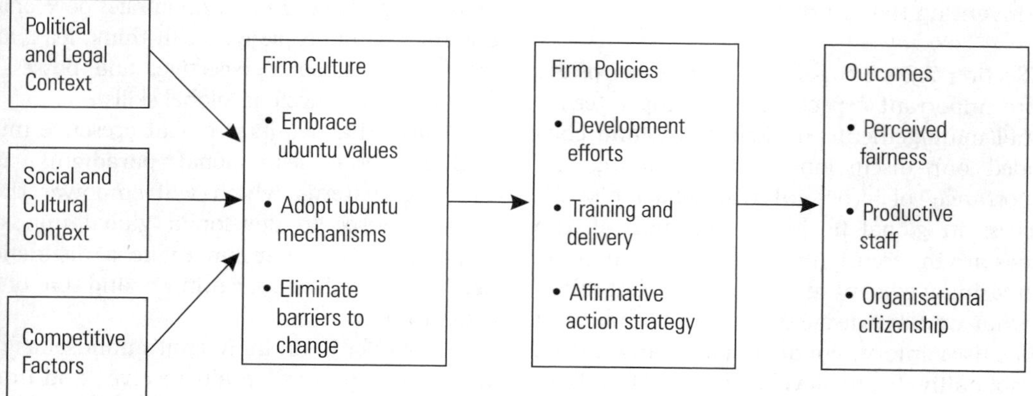

SOURCE: McFarlane, D.B. & Sweeney, P.D. 1998, *International Management*. Cincinnati, Ohio: South Western College Publishing, p. 237.

be superior to the relatively dispassionate transactional leadership style.[49] From what we have discussed with regard to cross-cultural leadership thus far, it is evident that transformational leadership could have a positive impact on follower satisfaction in international organisations.

We conclude the discussion in this section on international management and leadership and the importance of cross-cultural leaders by bringing together the loose ends in Rowan Gibson's exemplary views in this regard. His views are worth quoting at some length, since they touch on the very aspects which are seen to ensure excellence in leadership.

> So how will the twenty-first century organisation develop a sense of foresight about where it needs to be heading? How will it create a meaningful vision and purpose; a goal that is uniquely its own, and that will give it a sustainable competitive advantage; something that it can stand for in a crowded and confusing world? The answer, in a word, is leadership. Not traditional leadership, but twenty-first century leadership ... new kinds of leaders. They will decentralise power and democratise strategy by involving a rich mixture of different people from inside and outside the organisation in the process of inventing the future.[50]

In Section 7.2 we highlighted a number of the more important aspects surrounding international management and leadership, and concluded our discussion by accentuating the importance of cross-cultural leadership for success in global business. Although all the issues are inherently important, it has become increasingly evident in recent times that much of what we have discussed so far will not be of much use if international managers and leaders do not cultivate and develop a 'global mindset'. This important topic is addressed in the remainder of this chapter.

7.3 The need for a global mindset

7.3.1 Overview and definition of a global mindset

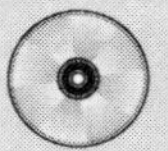

Compact disc

1 Mr Jan de Bruyn of the Industrial Development Corporation (IDC) explains the role of the IDC in the regional development of the SADC.

For most South African organisations, an those of southern Africa, to make up leewa in the global arena there would have to be strong input, particularly in the developmen and training of people who already hav developed or could develop a global perspectiv and obtain global skills. On the other hanc multinational enterprises which have neve invested in South Africa, or withdrew durin the years of sanctions, will now have to enter re-enter into a new dispensation.[51]

It is particularly on the African continen where South African organisations as well a multinational corporations (MNC) with interest in South Africa, should play a major role. Pucik[5 states that successful development and manage ment of a global organisation implies developin and managing people who can think, lead, an act from a global perspective, and possess 'global mind' as well as 'global skills'.

A firm that wants a global presence mus facilitate processes, global paradigms an thinking patterns which will empower thei working force to develop a global mindset Gupta and Govindarajan make a distinctio between an individual's mindset and that of a organisation. [53]

They refer to an individual's mindset as th way that a person's brain receives and inter prets information, while the organisation' mindset is defined as the aggregated mindse of a collective of individuals adjusted for the distribution of power and mutual influence among the people making up this collective of individuals. Thus it would be wrong to assume that the personal mindset of the executive manager or the mindsets of the people on the board of a company represent the organisation's mindset.

When we try to define a global mindset of an organisation it is clear that it is not as simple as the above definitions because the 'collective of individuals' operates in a global village which is not just a large market-place but also a source of perceptions, ideas, strategies, technologies, nationalities, values, cultures, and choices.

A global mindset of an organisation, therefore, is the ability of a company to:

- be open to new experiences and to change over time;
- be willing to learn new skills and competencies in order to exploit a global presence;
- operate on the premise that cultures can be different without being better or worse than one another;
- dedicate itself to becoming well informed about different value systems, norms of behaviour and assumptions regarding reality;
- accept diversity and heterogeneity as natural and as a source of opportunities and strengths rather than a necessary evil. [54]

Does your organisation have a global mindset?

- Is your company a leader rather than a laggard in discovering and pursuing emerging market opportunities in the world?
- Do you consider every customer, regardless of country, to be as important as a customer in your own domestic market?
- Do you draw your employees from the worldwide talent pool?
- Do employees of every nationality have the same opportunity to move up the career ladder to the top?
- In scanning the horizon for potential competitors, do you examine all economic regions of the world?
- In selecting a location for any activity, do you seek to optimise the choice on a global basis?
- Do you view the global arena as not just a 'playground'(that is, a market to exploit) but also a 'school' (that is, a source of ideas and technology)?
- Do you perceive your company as having a universal identity and many homes rather than a national identity?

SOURCE: Gupta, A.K. & Govindaranjan, V. 1999. 'Success is all in the mindset'. *Mastering global business series,* No. 5, *Business Day*, June, p. 3.

7.3.2 Traditional and global mindsets

Rhinesmith[55] draws the following comparisons between traditional and global mindsets of organisations:

Traditional mindsets	Global mindsets
Specialisation	Drive for broader picture
Prioritisation	Balance of contradictions
Manage job	Engage in processes
Control results	Flow with change
Manage self	Value diversity
Learn domestically	Learn globally

The big differences between the traditional or domestic global mindsets of organisations stem from new, diverse, and constantly changing global environments as discussed in Chapters 2 to 6. The impact of these new environments means that thinking styles based on habits, customs, stereotypes, current situations, or preoccupation with the immediate outcome, are inadequate to develop effective strategies and scenarios. Personnel must be able to assess relevant information based on a broad awareness of these bigger environments, diversity and interlinking processes in order to create opportunities for possible innovation.

Although a great deal can be done to develop and train global managers, certain personal qualities will always be found in such managers. This brings us to the next topic in the search for a global mindset, namely the 'link' between global mindsets and personal characteristics.

7.3.3 Global mindsets and personal characteristics

The above-mentioned global mindsets and the personal characteristics are interlinked, as shown in the explanation below. It should be borne in mind that these characteristics are only the most noted of the total spectrum of possible characteristics that might play a role in developing a global mindset. [56]

Global mindsets	Personal characteristic
Drive for broader picture	Knowledgeable
Balance contradictions	Analytical
Engage in processes	Strategic
Flow with change	Flexible
Value diversity	Sensitive
Learn globally	Open

A short discussion of these personal characteristics follows.

Knowledgeable

Technical, business and industrial knowledge, on a broad basis as well as in depth, is the most fundamental quality for the successful management of any competitive process.

Analytical

This characteristic is necessary to deal with the complexity of a global organisation: the ability to understand different levels of vision, mission, and strategy, as well as the ability to balance contradictory forces and handle complicated issues.

Strategic

This allows the managers to meet the needs of the organisation, focus on the important issues, and constantly adjust to global and local demands through co-ordination and allocation of the organisation's resources.

Flexible

The speed and constancy of change in global organisations, as well as their complexity, leads to uncertainty. Uncertainty requires new levels of judgment which enable the manager to see change as an opportunity, creating a process by which such a manager will be able to make intuitive decisions with inadequate information based on experience rather than empirical data. This necessitates a mix of self-confidence and humility – confidence in experience, but humility in the knowledge that there is seldom one right answer.

Sensitivity

To operate cross-culturally is a continuous learning experience which requires not only sensitivity to others, but also a fairly well-developed ego and self-concept. The goal is a well-developed philosophy and approach to life, which is inclusive, rather than exclusive, of others.

Open

Openness and reflection lead to continuous improvement since they provide the necessary perspective for dealing with future challenges. They indicate an urge for continuous learning and development.

In the McDonald's case study at the end of this chapter we discuss the problem of insufficient sugar, flour, mustard, iceberg lettuce, pickling cucumbers, Russet Burbank potatoes, milk, cheddar cheese, and beef for their Moscow restaurants. We point out the innovative and creative ways in which management dealt with these shortages by judging this as an opportunity and therefore creating problem-solving processes by which to achieve the necessary results. They did not panic and throw their hands in the air, but decided to 'see the bigger picture'.

Adler and Bartholomew[57] explain that leading corporations are losing control since their strategic thinking has far outdistanced the organisational capabilities and thus strategy is internationalising faster than individual managers and executives themselves.

The key to retaining control of global companies is the ability of top management to turn the perceptions, capabilities, and relationships of individual managers into the building blocks of the organisation. Top managers inside and outside the human resource function must be leaders in the recruitment, development, and assignment of the company's vital human talents.[58]

In this regard Bassiry[59] confirms that the above-mentioned realities create the necessity for the development of a different kind of corporate culture which will enable MNCs to become the vehicles for global economic integration. This, according to Bassiry, is not possible without the inclusion of the resources and populations of the less developed countries. Here he opts for a strategy guided by flexibility, rational consideration of long-term factors, and mutual self-interest, which require a substantial reorientation in the business culture of global firms and the training and attitudes of managerial personnel.

Global management is unique in the sense that, *inter alia*, it develops relationships between people who can facilitate communication and understanding and therefore reduce social distance between disparate cultures.[60] This would minimise risks and assure a continuing flow of high profits over a long period.

Therefore, the true test for global leaders lies in their ability to design structures, internal cultures, and human resource systems that can mobilise managers and employees to implement a successful global vision.[61]

7.4 Developing global competencies

Today's operating environment demands more than efficient central management and flexible local operations – it requires companies to link their diverse organisational perspectives and resources in a way that will allow them to combine their capabilities for achieving global co-ordination and national flexibility simultaneously.[62]

Rhinesmith[63] developed a model of six competencies which he uses to systematically describe the relationships between a global mindset and effective management behaviour. It builds up to what he calls 'a global manager's guide to action'. These six competencies refer to the ability to:

1 manage competitiveness by being knowledgeable and driving for the broader picture;
2 manage complexity by being analytical and balancing contradictions;
3 manage alignment by being strategic and engaging in processes;
4 manage change by being flexible and flowing with change;
5 manage teams by being sensitive and valuing diversity;
6 manage learning by being open and learning globally.

The global manager is ultimately the facilitator of personal and organisational development on a global scale. To achieve this, it is not only necessary to be attentive to and a developer of organisational cultures, values, and beliefs that reach well beyond one's own cultural, technical, and managerial backgrounds, but also a consummate reframer of the boundaries of the world in which one operates.

These boundaries include those of:

- space, time, scope, structure, geography, and function;
- functional, professional, and technical skills relevant to a past age;
- thinking and classification of rational versus intuitive, national versus foreign, 'we' versus 'they';
- cultural assumptions, values, and beliefs about the world, our relationships with others, and our understanding of ourselves.

The aims in developing these competencies are:

- to inculcate a common vision and shared values (cultural and spiritual training);
- to broaden management perspectives and capabilities by teaching people how to manage complexity instead of merely making room for it.[64]

This process of transformation is not an easy one and in the end, to be successful, global managers must find new paradigms for living and working in global organisations.

7.4.1 Competencies and characteristics

As outlined below, every competency is linked to a characteristic while a description of possible key practices is given in the following paragraphs in order to achieve the relevant competency.

Characteristic	Competency
Knowledgeable	Managing competitiveness
Analytical	Managing complexity
Strategic	Managing alignment
Flexibility	Managing change
Sensitivity	Managing teams
Openness	Managing learning

(a) Managing competitiveness[65]

Managing competitiveness means the ability to gather information on a global basis concerning the global sourcing of capital, technology, suppliers, facilities, market opportunities, and human resources, and the capacity to utilise the information to increase the competitive advantage and profitability of the organisation.

This demands curiosity and constant attentiveness to changes in social, economic, and political conditions. Managers must strike a balance between national responsiveness and exploitation of global economies of scale. This is the ability to think globally, but act locally. One aspect of managing this balance will include moving the decision-making authority as close to the customer as possible to ensure that local requirements are satisfied. Local managers will need to know and understand the global strategy and yet act within the context of their local environment.

Key practices would be:

- setting critical success factors for the organisation's competitiveness and using these as a framework to filter global information for key trends;
- establishing personal and organisational information systems that scan globally for trends, best practices, and resources that provide new opportunities for increased competitive advantages and profits;
- establishing information-processing systems that deliver the right level of information to the right people at the right time for the most effective and timely decision-making on a worldwide basis;
- tracking global merger and acquisition activity and foreign investment patterns of competitors and potential competitors;
- monitoring international trade, tariff, economic, social, and political changes that may affect local, regional, or international competitiveness.

(b) Managing complexity[66]

Managing complexity demands the ability to identify, analyse, and intuitively manage complex relationships on a global basis which affect personal and organisational effectiveness.

Global organisations are more complex than domestic firms and therefore require the ability to see – on a mental as well as on an interpersonal level – the validity of conflicting viewpoints while making decisions that are in the best interests of the organisation.

Key practices are:

- manage relationships which are simultaneously co-operative and competitive, such as strategic alliances, headquarters/subsidiary relations, and functional, geographic, and product matrices;
- identify contradictions and paradoxes in the work environment and determine how to manage them creatively instead of eliminating them;

- use intuitive as well as analytical skills to assess the feel for the information gathered and directing activities accordingly.

(c) Managing alignment[67]

This is the ability to appropriately centralise and decentralise decision-making for various businesses, functions, and tasks to provide the quickest, best, and most co-ordinated decisions and actions on a global basis, and to develop and dissolve temporary teams and mechanisms to deal with environmental change.

The best managers are already creating borderless organisations where the ability to learn, be responsive and efficient, develops within the firm's administrative heritage. In this sense, managers will need the ability to create an alignment of authority and responsibility between home office and field offices that moves decision-making as close as possible to the customer. To operate effectively in global organisations will take new skills and old skills honed to a new sharpness. Some of the abilities and characteristics needed by the global manager to function in flexible organisations will be:

- a high tolerance for ambiguity, new levels of creativity, and inventiveness in organisational design;
- the ability to identify diverse managerial behaviours for ongoing renewal of the organisation;
- the ability to learn, be responsive, and become more efficient;
- the ability to co-ordinate complicated financial, human resource, marketing, and manufacturing interdependencies;
- the ability to recognise different manufacturing, marketing, and organisational problems and priorities across different locations and accommodate these with new structures and processes.

The capacity to respond to rapid changes in the environment lies in the ability to manage the global corporate culture effectively. This means to occasionally break the rules, be committed to change, and be able to thrive on chaos.

Key practices are to:

- determine which decisions should be centralised for coherency and efficiency and which decisions should be decentralised for local responsiveness by business, function, and task;
- develop a global strategy and structure that is fixed, but a global corporate culture that is process-driven and flexible to changing world conditions through the use of global task forces, temporary decision committees, regional co-ordination groups, and global integrators.

(d) Managing change[68]

Managing change in an organisation means having the ability to manage continuous change and uncertainty on a personal and organisational level, ensuring that an adequate blend of flexibility and control are achieved, which enables the organisation to be responsive to changes in the environment in a timely fashion.

Managing change requires overcoming the sense of uncertainty that comes from knowing that some process may be out of control. Effective global managers will need the skills to manage the transition from independence/dependence to interdependence, from control to co-ordination and co-operation, and from symmetry to differentiation. Therefore, global managers will need to act more as equals and less as dominant decision-makers operating from a 'headquarters'. For this reason it is also important that managers in other countries are in agreement with the strategy.

Key practices are to:

- work with continuous global change, rather than stability, as the norm;
- create new opportunities out of change and chaos, rather than try to re-establish the old order;
- manage change as a cyclical process of taking charge and letting go, using right-brain as well as left-brain thinking skills.

(e) Managing teams[69]

Managing teams in an international context demands the ability to manage teams that represent diversity in functional skills, experience levels, and cultural background, with cultural sensitivity and self-awareness.

Global managers must be able to recognise that cultural differences operate both internally and externally. It is also important to understand the influence of the home office's own cultural filters when dealing with foreign affiliates, and to accept that the home office way of doing things will not be appropriate in all instances. In today's global environment, a firm's home culture must no longer dominate that of the entire organisation. Learning to manage global cultural diversity effectively can start with the recognition of cultural diversity at home, especially in South Africa.

It is essential to cultivate cross-cultural sensitivity in all managers, whether domestic or international, in order for them all to respond well to global customers, suppliers, and competitors. The ability to work effectively with other people and in teams will be critical to the successful implementation of a global strategy. Participation in global teams should occur early in the careers of managers in order to transform these developing people into globally effective managers (see Section 7.2.4).

Key practices are to:

- learn and use an understanding of the basic dimensions of cross-cultural behaviour and their impact on managerial style and organisational functioning;
- develop cultural self-awareness which allows one to contrast one's own culture with other cultures to allow flexible movement from one culture to another.

(f) Managing learning[70]

Managing learning is the ability to manage personal and organisational learning and improvement on a continuous basis through the exploration of new fields of knowledge and new cultural perspectives.

This requires a commitment to life-long learning as a central part of life. It requires an integrated approach to the world that leads to the capacity to flourish, while knowing that this capacity will never be enough to replace a sense of purpose, mission, and the willingness to trust the process and let go.

At the individual level one would expect broad interests, an openness to a variety of experiences, and a willingness to experiment and take risks, to all be ingredients of success. At the organisational level even more can be done. Managers should be encouraged to look for opportunities in one country that can be transferred elsewhere. These opportunities or experiments are the responsibility of national managers, while their transfer is the responsibility of management at headquarters.

Key practices are to:

- develop a capacity for systems thinking at every level of personal and organisational functioning, and search for contexts and broader influences on a global basis that may affect personal or organisational success;
- develop a working knowledge of international relations, international economics, and cross-cultural differences that will allow effective interaction with foreign suppliers, customers, and partners;
- develop a sense of meaning and purpose in personal and organisational life that transcends the immediate job or annual objective, and can be related to a higher or broader contribution to the human condition.

7.5 Focus on training efforts

Traditionally, international training centred around cross-cultural knowledge. Today, training goals must be linked directly to the strategic goals of the organisation and this cannot be done if such strategies are vague. [71]

Modern organisations have more complex organisational structures, and the more diverse the employee mix, the greater the need has become for effective management development programmes.[72] Multinational enterprises incorporate the importance of training at all categories of employees, including those from host-country and third-country nationals, in order to have high-calibre staff available where and when needed. [73]

Training programmes have to deliver new information about country environments and comparative management practices in other countries to meet organisational needs for a cadre of competent managers. This also implies 'unlearning' of inappropriate expectations and attributions with respect to the country of assignment.[74]

Globalisation requires managers who are able to manage decentralised, multicentred, flat-layered organisations through having complex interpersonal and cross-cultural skills.[75] It is particularly in this regard that training programmes, such as international management simulation games, prove to be helpful. Through case histories, setting of realistic rules guiding business decisions, as well as a computerised mathematical model which simulates a dynamic market complete with business cycles and other seasonal fluctuations, the international managers are taught fundamental aspects such as cross-cultural decision-making and understanding; teamwork and co-operation across cultures; consistency planning; human resource management, and labour relations differences across cultures, as well as dealing with male and female relationships across cultures.[76]

Other strategies to improve global productivity include organisational support in the form of improved job training, language training, pre- and post-assignment mentoring, and health and stress-reduction training. This support should also be extended to the spouse and other family members where applicable. [77]

A study done by Domsch and Lichtenberger[78] on pre-departure training and development for German expatriates in China and Brazil, showed that management, team and communication skills in intercultural situations, as well as successful business management in different cultural environments, are the most important educational requirements for international management. Training in behavioural skills should take precedence over cognitive skills.

7.5.1 Training for different types of global operations

The key consideration when planning for a training and development programme should be the type of international operation concerned. Dowling[79] described this trying and complex issue by means of the following four categories:

Limited relationships

These are depicted by MNEs with export offices, sales representatives, joint ventures, or distributor relationships. Training and management development is mostly limited to the firm's own managers.

Subsidiaries

These imply firms with foreign subsidiaries. Although an expatriate is sometimes used to set up the subsidiary, training and development should incorporate opportunities for host-country nationals to learn how the subsidiary operates and thereby develop the skills to fulfil their managerial role.

Regional business

Developmental assignments abroad for expatriates should be incorporated before such people can take up these more complex positions. Secondly, host- and third-country nationals also require developmental assignments and training in strategic leadership skills and financial analysis. The prediction is made that the future CEOs will most likely develop from this cadre.

Global business

Here management development programmes need to emphasise worldwide information-sharing on economic, social, political, technological, and market trends, and focus on building teamwork across related business lines, as well as across functional and country/regional lines.

7.6 Socialising the new breed of global managers in multinational corporations

In the past, an international assignment might have indicated a mid-career derailment, but today it is increasingly associated with the idea that the person is a high-potential employee being given a developmental assignment as a route to a top position. Fiat identified that human resource management should be a balance between strategic considerations (investment in junior staff resources and individual careers) and managerial considerations (care in the phases of expatriation and re-entry), with a precise and significant role also given to education and training.[80] Newcomers should be given realistic career previews as well as realistic job previews. This will help potential employees to make the decision to remove themselves from the applicant pool if the job offered is a poor fit. It can also inoculate newcomers against the inevitable disappointments new jobs can bring.[81]

Newcomers should be provided with technical training to build upon and enhance their international background in early assignments, but they should also be given the following learning opportunities and taught the necessary skills:

- how to communicate their competence effectively through the maze of political and socially different demands in organisations that have no boundaries;[82]
- how to learn about international finance, international marketing, and other international functional areas;[83]
- how to work with, or manage, a multicultural workforce;[84]
- how to incorporate a logical framework of career itineraries rather than just following opportunities;[85]
- how to build some type of meaningful, challenging,[86] and significantly rewarding[87] expatriate assignment into their career paths within the first three to five years;
- how to develop mentor relationships between expatriates and people in the corporate headquarters for the purposes of social support, information exchange, and general advice;[88]
- how to plan ahead for a specific assignment for the returning expatriate, and provide opportunities for the expatriate to use the knowledge and skills learned overseas.[89]

It is thus imperative that successful international managers should not be relegated to the 'slow track' because of their overseas assignments, but preferably be promoted into positions where their acquired knowledge and skills can be used to the best effect.

7.7 Summary

A number of relevant concepts and terms in the context of international management and leadership were explained and clarified in this chapter. This was followed by exploring the environment of international management and leadership, the role of international management, and the requisite skills and attributes to fulfil these roles.

The increasing importance of cross-cultural leadership, as well as leadership behaviour and styles in the international business environment, was discussed.

The notion that international companies and business leaders must cultivate a global mindset was analysed and the need for a global mindset emphasised. The importance of mindset was explained, while indicating how global mindsets are developed, and also how the new breed of global managers is to be developed for the successful management of multinational enterprises in the 21st century.

Case Study

McDonald's Corporation[90]

Some historians trace the origin of the hamburger to Russia. Supposedly, sailors took a dish made of raw ground beef and hot spices from Russia to the port of Hamburg, where the recipe was altered, popularised, and given its name. Hamburgers eventually showed up in England and then North America. If this historical account is accurate, then when McDonald's Corporation opened its first Moscow restaurant in 1990, the hamburger's round-trip journey was complete.

McDonald's entry into Russia capped a long and involved negotiation process. During the 1976 Olympic Games in Montreal, George A. Cohon, president of McDonald's Canadian subsidiary, made the first contact with Soviet officials. This began lengthy negotiations that culminated in the signing of a protocol agreement in 1987, shortly after the Soviets enacted legislation permitting joint ventures with Western companies. After that, the pace of negotiations quickened, until a formal agreement was signed in 1988. In the meantime, McDonald's had opened restaurants in Hungary and Yugoslavia, thus providing the company with valuable experience in operating in communist countries.

These moves were highly compatible with McDonald's growth strategy. By the mid-1980s, the company was expanding more rapidly outside the United States than inside, and company executives reasoned that, if they were to meet the company's rapid growth objectives, that trend must continue. It did. By the end of 1995, McDonald's had 18 380 restaurants in over 79 countries. Its foreign sales had reached 47% of total company sales, up from 37,2% in 1991 and 19% in 1981.

From 1990 to 1995, 56% of the new McDonald's restaurants were opened outside the United States. Of the 1 007 restaurants added in 1995, 42% were in the six largest foreign markets, namely Australia, Canada, England, France, Germany, and Japan, with Japan alone adding 313 of the new restaurants. This, compared with 57% in 1992 and 51% in 1994 of the new additions coming from the big six, demonstrates the importance of new emerging markets. McDonald's hopes to increase its expansion outside the United States by adding between 1 200 and 1 500 traditional restaurants and 350 to 500 satellite restaurants annually for the next few years. As noted in their 1995 Annual Report:

> At year-end 1995, 38% of system-wide restaurants were outside the USA, compared with 36 % in 1994 and 27% five years ago. Restaurants outside the USA comprised 53 % of traditional company-operated restaurants and 27% of traditional franchised restaurants. About 29% of the traditional restaurants outside the USA were company-operated, 47% were franchised and 24% were operated by affiliates. Approximately 69% of traditional company-operated restaurants were in England, Canada, Germany, Australia, Taiwan, and Brazil. About 6% of traditional franchised restaurants were in Canada, Germany, Australia, France, England, and the Netherlands. Restaurants operated by affiliates were principally located in Japan and other Asia/Pacific countries. Approximately 81% of satellite restaurants outside the USA were operated by franchisees and affiliates at year-end 1995. The vast majority were located in Japan, Canada, and Brazil (p. 21).

The McDonald's-Russian joint venture is between McDonald's Canadian subsidiary and the Moscow City Council. McDonald's has a 49% interest, the maximum allowed by Soviet law when the formal agreement was signed in 1988. (Since 1990, foreigners may own a 99%

interest in a joint venture.) The minority ownership has not proved to be a problem, however, because Russian law requires at least a three-quarters majority vote to approve important decisions. Therefore, the representatives of McDonald's and the City Council must agree on all major decisions. On the other hand, supply procurement was a major hurdle, as it has been for most foreign companies operating in Russia. The problem has several causes:

- the rigid bureaucratic system;
- supply shortages caused by distribution and production problems;
- available supplies not meeting McDonald's quality standards.

Even with the Moscow City Council as majority owner in the venture, not to mention having the backing of the Kremlin, the company repeatedly ran into negative responses, such as 'Sorry, you're not in my five-year plan', when it attempted to obtain such materials as sand or gravel to build the restaurant. The company had to negotiate to ensure it would be allocated, in the Soviet central plan, sufficient sugar and flour, which were in chronically short supply. Even for some products in sufficient supply, such as mustard, government regulations prevented Soviet manufacturers from deviating from standard recipes in order to comply with McDonald's needs. In other cases, strict allocation regulations dictated that Soviet plants sell all output to existing Soviet companies, thus leaving them no chance to produce products for McDonald's. Yet another problem was that some supplies were simply not produced or consumed in the Soviet Union, including iceberg lettuce, pickling cucumbers, and the Russet Burbank potatoes that are the secret behind McDonald's French fries.

To handle these problems, McDonald's scoured the country for supplies, contracting for such items as milk, cheddar cheese, and beef. To help ensure ample supplies of the quality products it needed, it undertook to educate Soviet farmers and cattle ranchers on how to grow and raise those products. In addition, it built a $40-million food-processing centre about 45 minutes from its first Moscow restaurant. And because distribution was as much a cause of shortages as production, McDonald's carried supplies on its own trucks. The company had to import some other needed supplies. (Today, 98% of supplies come from the Commonwealth of Independent States, which comprises most of the former republics of the Soviet Union.)

The company placed one small help-wanted advertisement and received about 27 000 Russian applicants for its 605 positions. It sent six Russian managers to its Hamburger University outside Chicago for six months' training and another 30 managers for several months' training in Canada or Europe. The company translated training and operations manuals and videotapes into Russian so that trainees could learn everything from how to wash windows and mop floors to how to assemble a Big Mac. In order to establish a Western image, McDonald's used its name and familiar golden arches in Moscow. However, in 1993 a law was passed in that city requiring all stores to have Russian names, or at least names transliterated into the Cyrillic alphabet. Just as PepsiCo chose Cyrillic letters to convey the sound of 'Pepsi' in Russian, McDonald's used the following Cyrillic letters that retain the sound of its name: **МАКДОНАЛДС**.

One problem McDonald's did not encounter was attracting customers. When the company opened its restaurant in Hungary, it quickly had to stop its advertising because of unexpectedly heavy consumer response. On the basis of this experience, McDonald's did no advertising prior to its Moscow opening. However, Russian television covered the upcoming event extensively. When the restaurant's doors opened for the first time in January 1990, it was almost impossible to accommodate the crowd, even though the 700 indoor seats made it the largest McDonald's anywhere in the world. (An additional 200 seats outside could not be used because of cold weather.) An estimated 30 000 people were served the first day, eclipsing the previous daily record of 9 100 set in Budapest. The crowds continued to arrive, even though the price of a Big Mac, French fries, and soft drink equalled a Russian worker's average pay for four hours of work. In contrast, lunch at a state-run or private sector café cost 15–25% as much as a meal at McDonald's.

However, McDonald's was not satisfied with only one restaurant in Moscow. In 1993, Moscow was the fourth-largest city in the world with nearly 9 million people, after Cairo, São Paulo, and Seoul, and just above Mexico City. It was obvious to McDonald's management that Moscow's 3 million commuters who were used to poor, slow service, would warm to McDonald's immediately. For example, the first Moscow McDonald's in Pushkin Square serves an average of 40 000 to 50 000 customers per day, whereas the restaurant which had formerly occupied the space, served only 200 customers per day. To illustrate the potential, the United States has a population of 240 million people and 8 500 McDonald's restaurants, whereas Russia had 149 million people and only 10 restaurants by the end of 1996 or early 1997. However, business was booming to such an extent in Moscow that McDonald's projected as many as 40 restaurants by 1998.

Since McDonald's joint venture partners are the Moscow City catering officials, it is relatively easy to get access to prime commercial property to open new sites. In most market economies, it would be considered a conflict of interest to have local government officials as partners in a commercial interest, but Russia's brand of capitalism involves significant state intervention.

The Pushkin Square McDonald's was so successful that they opened up a second restaurant on Ogareva Street on 1 June 1993; renovated two 18th-century Arbat Street buildings to house their third restaurant, which was opened 3 July 1993 and could seat up to 400 customers at one time; opened a fourth restaurant at Prospect Mira that can seat 300 customers at one time; and opened the Sokolniki restaurant next to Moscow's fire observation tower in 1995. When the Arbat Street McDonald's opened, 10 000 people lined up to get in, and 60 000 were served on the first day. Since then, the Arbat Street McDonald's has served 70 000 people per day, every day.

Although McDonald's is reinvesting its ruble profits in new stores, it has entered into a special barter arrangement with the Soviet government that allows it to earn some hard currency on its operations. It is hypothesised that McDonald's might be selling Soviet products like metals and other raw materials to help cover the cost of items like cups and restaurant equipment that it needs to import.

The employment record of McDonald's is impressive. Although it opened with 80 to 90 expatriates, it had replaced most with locals by the end of 1995. McDonald's employs 2 200 Russians at the five McDonald's restaurants and its food-processing and distribution centre, McComplex. A reporter from Pravda noted that 'people working in the service industry in the Soviet Union have a reputation for being lazy, slovenly, and a little like petty thieves. ... All around us, no matter where you look, there is ruin, irresponsibility, laziness, boorishness, lack of professionalism, and theft'. However, McDonald's is very satisfied with the performance of its employees, who have excellent pay and benefits. As noted by Cohen, 'There is no other restaurant in the world that could serve up the 55 000 people in a day. I could take the Soviet crew from the Pushkin Square restaurant, send them to any country, and be absolutely certain that they would do well anywhere'. The strong investment in training has paid off.

What is the future of McDonald's in places such as the former Soviet Union, Eastern Europe, and China? Since opening its first restaurants in China and Russia, the company has opened more in those countries. It also is studying the feasibility of opening restaurants in Ukraine, St Petersburg, and the Balkan states. The managing director of McDonald's Development Corporation said, 'We'll do one store, one country at a time, and plans will be made as we grow and develop.'

Several factors control McDonald's expansion abroad. Key among these are the size and growth rate of different economies. As noted above, most of the company's foreign restaurants are in high-income countries (those with per capita incomes of $8 956 or more in 1994). Although the main thrust of McDonald's expansion has been in the high-income countries, the developing countries have significant expansion potential. The following developing countries (those with per capita incomes of less than $8 956 in 1994) already have restaurants: Brazil, Hong Kong, Taiwan, Philippines, Singapore, Puerto Rico, and Mexico. Working with these countries involves challenges very different to those connected with doing business in high-income countries.

Questions

1 What are the location-specific advantages that Moscow/Russia has to offer for McDonald's? How would these advantages add to increase the 'global mindset' of the American management?

2 'The strategic objective of a globally competitive firm is the creation of continuously evolving and interdependent layers of organisational capabilities that reinforce and enhance each other across all core businesses, functions, and markets.' Do you think McDonald's has achieved this objective by opening in Russia?

3 What dimensions of the local political and economic environment have an impact on McDonald's success in Moscow/Russia in volume, revenues, and profitability? How could a change in those dimensions affect McDonald's future success?

4 How successful would you say McDonald's Russian (country) manager is in being:
   (a) sensitive to the local culture in order to interpret local opportunities and threats;
   (b) a builder of local resources and capabilities to stimulate entrepreneurship and innovation;
   (c) a contributor to and active participant in the firm's global strategy?

Endnotes

1 Gupta, A.K. & Govindaranjan, V. 1999. 'Success is all in the mindset'. Mastering global business series no. 5. *Business Day*, June, p. 2.
2 Miller, P. 1997. 'SA managers struggle with the transition from local operations to globalised business', *Perspectives*, Graduate School of Business, University of Cape Town, Winter, p. 12.
3 Beamish, P.W., Morrison, A. & Rosenzweig, P.M. 1997. *International management*, 3rd ed, Burr Ridge, Illinois: Irwin, p. 182.
4 Dessler, G. 1998. *Management*, Upper Saddle River, New Jersey: Prentice Hall, p. 44.
5 Phatak, A.V. 1997. *International management*. Cincinnati, Ohio: South-Western College Publishing, p. 3.
6 Dessler, op. cit., p. 11.
7 Beamish et al, op. cit., p. 181.
8 Adler, N., 1997. *International dimensions of organizational behaviour*. 3rd ed. Cincinnati, Ohio: South Western College Publishing, p. 152.
9 Adler, op. cit., p. 154.
10 Bennis, W. 1998. 'Becoming a leader of leaders', in Gibson, R. (ed). *Rethinking the future*. London: Nicholas Brealey Publishing, p. 154.
11 Hill, C.W.L. 1998. *International business*. 2nd ed. Burr Ridge, Illinois: McGraw-Hill Irwin, pp. 396–400.
12 Yip, G.S. 1995. *Total global strategy*. Business School Edition. Englewood Cliffs, New Jersey: Prentice Hall, p. 8.
13 Miller, op. cit. p., 12.
14 Coade, N. 1997. *Managing international business*, London: International Thomson Business Press, p. 1.
15 Mead, R. 1998. *International management*. 2nd ed. Oxford: Blackwell Business Publishers, pp. 109–110 and 350.
16 Mead, op. cit., p. 350.
17 McFarlane, D.B., & Sweeney, P.D. 1998. *International management*. Cincinnati, Ohio: South Western College Publishing, p. 23.
18 Hill, op. cit., pp. 568–571.
19 Kefalas, A.G. 1990. *Global business strategy*. Cincinnati, Ohio: South Western Publishing, p. 477.
20 Fatehi, K. 1996. *International management*. Englewood Cliffs, New Jersey: Prentice Hall, pp. 495–96.
21 Mitroff, I. 1987. *Business not as usual*. San Francisco: Josey-Bass, in Adler, op. cit., p. 151.
22 Coade, op. cit., pp. 87–88.
23 Grose, T.K. 1997. 'Ten risky businesses', *Time*, 7 July, p. 60.
24 Miller, op. cit., pp. 12–13.
'The huge cost of not managing change', *Boardroom*, No. 2, 1999, p. 13.
25 Miller, op. cit., pp. 12–13.
26 Beamish et al., op. cit., p. 182.
27 Beamish et al., op. cit., p. 184;
McFarlane & Sweeney, op. cit., p. 30.
28 Hodgetts, R.M. & Luthans, F. 1997. *International management*. 3rd ed. New York: McGraw-Hill, p. 95.
29 Hodgetts & Luthans, op. cit., p. 96.
30 Mead, op. cit., pp. 3–5.
Hodgetts & Luthans, op. cit., p. 96.
31 McFarlane & Sweeney, op. cit., p. 133.
32 Adler, op. cit., p. 154.
33 Laurent, A. 1983. 'The cultural diversity of Western conceptions of management', *International Studies of Management and Organizations*, No. 13 (Spring-Summer), pp. 75–96.
34 McFarlane & Sweeney, op. cit., p. 138.
35 Ayman, R., Kreicker, N.A. & Masztal, J.J. 1994. 'Defining global leadership in business environments', *Consulting Psychology Journal*, No. 46, pp. 64–73.
36 Yeung, A.K. & Ready, D.A. 1995. 'Developing leadership capabilities of global corporations: A comparative study in eight nations', *Human Resource Management*, Vol. 34, pp. 529–547.
37 Chow, I., Holbert, N., Kelley, L. & Yu, L. 1997. *Business strategy – An Asia-Pacific focus*. New York: Prentice Hall, pp. 6–7.
38 Mead, op. cit., p. 17.
39 Gupta & Govindaranjan, op. cit., pp. 2–4. (See also Section 7.3.1.)
40 Bennis, W. 'Becoming a leader of leaders', in Gibson, op. cit., p. 154.
41 Kotter, J. 'Cultures and coalitions' in Gibson, op. cit., p. 166.
42 McFarlane & Sweeney, op. cit., p. 146.
43 Ayman, R. & Chemers, M.N.M. 1983. 'Relationship of supervisory behaviour ratings to work group effectiveness and subordinate satisfaction among Iranian managers', *Journal of Applied Psychology*, Vol. 68, pp. 338–341.
44 McFarlane & Sweeney, op. cit., p. 148.
45 McFarlane & Sweeney, op. cit., p. 236
46 Nieman, G.H. 1997. 'The need to reconsider management styles in Africa'. Paper presented at the Conference of the Academy of International Business, Leeds, UK, 4–5 April.
47 Dreyer, W.W. & Neuland, E.W. 1996. 'Afrocentricity in South African management'. Proceedings of the Conference of the Southern Africa Institute for Management Scientists, Grahamstown, 1–3 July.
48 McFarlane & Sweeney, op.cit., p. 236.
49 Bateman, E. & Snell, A. 1999. *Management*. 4th ed. New York: McGraw-Hill, pp. 422–424.
50 Gibson, op. cit., pp. 10–11.
51 Van Schalkwyk, E. 1997. 'Developing a global mindset'. Unpublished research paper. University of Pretoria, p. 2.

52 Pucik, V. 'Globalization of human resource management', in Pucik, V., Tichy, N. M. & Barnett, C.K. 1992. 'Globalizing management: Creating and leading the competitive organization'. New York: John Wiley & Sons. p. 3.
53 Gupta, A.K & Govindaranjan, V., op. cit.
54 Ibid., p. 3.
55 Rhinesmith S.H. 1993. *A manager's guide to globalization: Six keys to success in a changing world*, 2nd ed. New York: lrwin, p. 28–29.
56 Ibid., p. 30.
57 Adler, N.J. & Bartholomew, S. 1992. 'Managing globally competent people', *Academy of Management Executives*, 6(3), p. 52–65.
58 Ibid., p. 52.
59 Bassiry, G.R. 1991. 'Multinational corporations in less developed countries: An alternative strategy', *Human Systems Management* ,10(1), p. 61–69.
60 Black, J.S., Gregersen H.B. & Mendenhall, M.E. 1992. *Global assignments: Successfully expatriating and repatriating international managers*. San Francisco: Jossey-Bass lnc Publishers, p. 7.
61 Tichy N.M., Brimm, M. & Charan, R. 'Leadership development as a lever for global transformation', in Pucik V., Tichy, N.M. & Barnett, C.K. 1992. *Globalizing management: Creating and leading the competitive organization*. New York: John Wiley & Sons, p. 43.
62 Bartlett, C.A. & Ghoshal, S. 1992. 'Matrix management: Not a structure, a frame of mind', in Pucik, V. Tichy, N.M. & Barnett, C.K. *Globalizing management: Creating and leading the competitive organization*. New York: John Wiley & Sons, p. 115.
63. Rhinesmith, op. cit., p. 36.
64. Bartlett, C.A. & Ghoshal, S. 1988. 'Organizing for worldwide effectiveness: The transnational solution'. *California Management Review*, 31(l), p.54–55.
65 Rhinesmith, op. cit., p. 64–67.
66. Ibid., p. 98–100.
67 Ibid., p. 127–129.
68 Ibid., p. 149–150.
69 Ibid., p. 189–192.
70 Ibid., p. 223–224.
71 Dowling, J.P., Schuler, R.S. & Welch, D.E. 1994. *International dimensions of human resource management*. California: Wadsworth Publishing, p. 32.
72 Bailey & Shenkar, op. cit., p. 17.
73 Dowling et al., p. 121.
74 Dunbar, R.L.M. & Bird, A. 1992. 'Preparing managers for foreign assignment: The expatriate profile program', *Journal of Management Development*. 11(7), p. 63.
75 Bailey & Shenkar, op. cit., p. 17.
76 Keys, J.B., Wells, R. & Edge, A. 1993. 'International management games: Laboratories for performance-based intercultural learning', *Leadership & Organization Development Journal*, 14(3), p. 25–29.
77 Bird, A. & Dunbar, R. 1991. 'Getting the job done over there: Improving expatriate productivity', *National Productivity Review*, 10(2), p. 145–156.
78 Domsch, M. & Lichtenberger, B. 1991.'Managing the global manager: Predeparture training and development for German expatriates in China and Brazil', *Journal of Management Development*, 10(7), p. 41–52.
79 Dowling, et al., p. 123–126.
80 Auteri, E. & Tesion, V. 1990. 'The internationalisation of management at Fiat', *Journal of Management Development*, 9(6), p. 6–16.
81 Feldman, D.C. & Tompson, H.B. 1992. 'Career management issues facing expatriates', *Journal of International Business Studies*, 23(2), p. 271–293.
82 Weiss, J.W. & Bloom, S. 1990. 'Managing in China: Expatriate experiences and training recommendations', *Business Horizons*, 33(3), p. 23–29.
83 Feldman & Thompson, op. cit., p. 357.
84 Feldman & Thompson, op. cit., p. 357.
85 Auteri & Tesion, op. cit., p. 9.
86 Feldman & Thompson, op. cit., p. 357.
87 Auteri & Tesion, op. cit., p 9.
88 Feldman & Thompson, op. cit., p 358.
89 Feldman & Thompson, op. cit., p. 359.
90 Material for this case was taken from:
Tannenbaum, J.A. 1990. 'Franchisers see a future in East Bloc', *Wall Street Journal*, 5 June, p. B1.
Toll, E.E. 1988. 'Hasabburgonya, Tejturmix and Big Mac to go', *Journal of Commerce*, 24 August, p. 1A.
Dreyfuss, T.A. 1988. 'Negotiating the Kremlin maze', *Business Month*, Vol. 132, November, pp. 55–63.
Schodolski, V.J. 1990. 'Moscovites stand in line for a "Beeg Mek attack', *Chicago Tribune*, 1 February, Sec. 1, pp. 1–2.
Keller, B. 1990. 'Of famous arches, Beeg Meks, and rubles', *New York Times*, 28 January. p. A1+.
'McDonald's', *The Economist*, Vol. 313, No. 7629, 18 November. 1989, p. 34.
Gumbel, P.1990. 'Muscovites queue up at American icon', *Wall Street Journal*, 1 February. p.A12.
Blackman, A. 1990. 'Moscow's Big Mac attack', *Time*, 5 February. p. 51.
Hertzfeld, J.M. 1991. 'Joint ventures: Saving the Soviets from Perestroika', *Harvard Business Review*, Vol. 69, No. 1, January-February, pp. 80–91.
Bohlen, C. 1993. 'How do you spell Big Mac in Russian?' *New York Times*, 25 May, p. B1.
Essig, B. 1993. 'Russia's economy shows an appetite for U.S. fast food', *Wall Street Journal*, 26 February. p. B2.
Vikhanski, O. and Puffer, S. 'Management education and employee training at Moscow McDonald's', *European Management Journal*, March 1993, pp. 102–107.
McDonald's 1995 Annual Report, various pages.
Snegirjov, V. 1991. 'The hero of capitalist labour',

Pravda, 31July.

Goldberg, C. 1991. 'Perestroika pioneer makes "Beeg Meks" work in Moscow', *Los Angeles Times*, 6 August.

'Russia investment: McDonald's unveils 5th Moscow restaurant', *Economist Intelligence Unit Views Wire*, 11 September, 1995. Available: NEXIS Library: General News: News: Curnws; and McDonald's fact sheets and video.

8 Strategic international human resource management

Key issues

- The SIHRM model
- Expatriate selection
- Training, management development and career planning
- Performance management, international compensation and benefits
- Designing a compensation strategy for multinationals

8.1 Introduction

Firms use four basic strategies to enter and compete in the international arena, namely an international strategy, a multidomestic strategy, a global strategy, and a transnational strategy. These strategies provide the frame of reference for Chapter 9, where the international marketing strategy will be discussed.

The appropriateness of each strategy varies with the extent of pressure for cost reductions and local responsiveness.[1] A short description of these four strategies[2] will provide the platform for the rest of this chapter's focused discussion on strategic international human resource management.

- **International strategy**. This strategy implies that firms try to build global capacity by transferring skills, products, and services to foreign markets where the local competitors lack those skills and products and are not able to provide those services. These firms tend to centralise product development activities at the home base but to decentralise the manufacturing and marketing functions to the major countries where they operate. However, the marketing and product strategies are still tightly controlled by the head office as part of its low-cost focus.
- **Multidomestic strategy**. Firms that pursue a multidomestic strategy focus on local responsiveness and also on transferring skills and products to the foreign markets in which they do business. This strategy differs from the first because these firms customise their product portfolios and marketing strategies to the different local market conditions. The establishment of customised production, marketing, and research and design (R&D) facilities in the foreign countries is a distinct characteristic of firms with a multidomestic strategy, with a resultant high cost structure. The control from head office over these activities is considerably less than in international firms.
- **Global strategy**. This strategy implies that production, research and design functions and marketing activities are strategically located in a few selected countries. Unlike multidomestic firms, global firms focus on marketing standardised products and ser-

vices worldwide in order to benefit from the economies of scale and lower cost embedded in this strategy. The resulting lower cost allows for aggressive global marketing.

- **Transnational strategy**. This strategy differs from the other three strategies in that the flow of skills, products, and services is not just from the home base to the foreign markets, but also from the foreign markets back to the home base of the firm. The underlying philosophy is that skills, products, and competencies do not reside in one particular location. This two-way flow of competencies will add value to the transnational company's knowledge base, R&D capacity, and ability to produce differentiated products and services. This strategy results in greater localised responsiveness but also higher costs. It is also very difficult to maintain high organisational effectiveness.

An essential component in implementing the strategy of a company that is internationalising, or has reached a multinational stage, is Strategic International Human Resource Management (SIHRM).[3] The interdependence of strategy, structure, and staffing in a multidomestic, multinational company or enterprise drives such a company to continually evaluate the fit of its SIHRM with its international strategy and the evolving headquarters and subsidiaries' structures.[4]

SIHRM has been defined as 'human resource management issues, functions, and policies and practices that result from the activities of multinational enterprises and that impact the international concerns and goals of those enterprises'.[5] The way in which SIHRM has developed as a field is related to the emergence of multinational corporations and understanding of the contexts in which they operate. Barnevik[6] notes that 'Unilever's development into one of the great transnationals has not been achieved by applying any particular theory. It has instead come through a messy evolution of trial and error, but with some consistent practices: emphasis on training high quality managers and linking decentralised units through a common corporate culture'. However, the theories of both multinational corporations and SIHRM are still evolving and being refined.

Appropriately skilled managers, who have developed a global mindset (as discussed in Chapter 7), will be the essential ingredient in ensuring that their companies can become internationally competitive. Naisbitt in Rhinesmith[7] points out that managers need to reconceptualise their role in the global economy and redefine the skills needed by managers of global organisations. Mendenhall, Punnett, and Ricks[8] emphasise that global thinking means that managers understand the varied environments that may be encountered around the world, the complexity associated with operating across national boundaries, the impact of ethical issues cross-nationally and cross-culturally, and how international strategic and operations management differs from domestic management.

Strategy and structure are important, but are not sufficient conditions for global success. Managers ensure the *implementation* of a global strategy and structure in a way that means the difference between success and failure in global operations. At the same time, all functional activities of a successful global corporation must be strategically linked. For this to happen, there must be a clear strategy – related to a clear customer need, mission, and set of corporate values – which is understood by all managers. It is useless to build a global corporate culture, infrastructure, and globally-oriented work-force in a corporation which is not clear about its destiny.[9,10]

International managers need to think about the forces that drive the company for which they are (or may be) working, to become global.[11] They need to question the extent to which their company is evolving into a global enterprise – the further it has evolved in the internationalisation process, the more important it is for them to have a knowledge of SIHRM.

8.2 The SIHRM model[12]

In the ever-growing competitive process of globalisation it is becoming critical to develop and manage multinational enterprises more effectively by using international human resource management and linkage with the strategic needs in the larger organisational context.[13]

Should companies fail to gain strategic control of their world-wide operations and manage them in a globally co-ordinated manner, they will not succeed in the international forum.

The reasons for developing SIHRM are that human resource management at any level is important to strategic implementation; major strategic components of multinational enterprises have a significant influence on international management issues, and there is a wide variety of factors that make the relationship between MNEs and SIHRM complex. These factors make the study of SIHRM challenging as well as important.

Schuler et al.[14] created an integrative framework of strategic international human resource management that is anchored in the strategic components of MNEs, namely their *interunit* linkages and internal operations. Interunit linkage describes first how subsidiaries or units of MNEs are to be differentiated, and secondly how they are to be integrated, controlled, and co-ordinated. Questions of differentiation and integration are important because they influence the effectiveness of the firm. The key to strategic management is coping with change, which requires flexibility and continual adaptation to achieve a fit between the firm's changing internal and external environments. The concepts of fit and flexibility need to be clarified in relationship to SIHRM. These are not necessarily opposites and their relationship to each other will vary, depending on the specific nature of the MNE and its external environment. The issues associated with differentiating and integrating the subsidiaries of a MNE represent a major influence on SIHRM issues, functions, policies and practices, and are therefore regarded as strategic.

Internal operations are concerned with the internal operations of subsidiaries. In addition to working together, each subsidiary has to work within the confines of its local environment, host country laws, politics, culture, economy, and society. It has to be operated as effectively as possible relative to the competitive strategy of the MNE and the subsidiary itself.

The integrative framework of Schuler et al. in Exhibit 8.1 (p. 233) contains three major components of SIHRM: issues, functions, and policies and practices. All three components must be included because they are influenced by an MNE's strategic activities and because they, in turn, influence its concerns and goals. These three components of SIHRM are part of the whole and are influenced by factors inside (endogenous) and outside (exogenous) the MNE. All these factors impinge upon the MNE's management of its human resources, as well as its effort to be locally responsive and adaptable, and also globally co-ordinated and controlled.[15]

Although the subsidiaries of an MNE might be separated across several nations, it is still a single enterprise. Globalisation creates a demand for sharing and exchanging information among the managers in subsidiaries since the flow of information is an important strategic function. Global assignments for managers can serve to gather and distribute complex information between subsidiaries. In addition, relationships that are established between managers and staff internationally, facilitate the development of trust and the exchange of information over longer periods of time[16]

Human resource policies and practices must be consistent with the needs of the business to achieve competitiveness. They should also be flexible and facilitate the transfer of learning across units. The larger context for formulating human resource practice consists of human resource philosophy and policies. When such policies and practices are consciously and

Exhibit 8.1: Integrative framework for Strategic International Human Resource Management

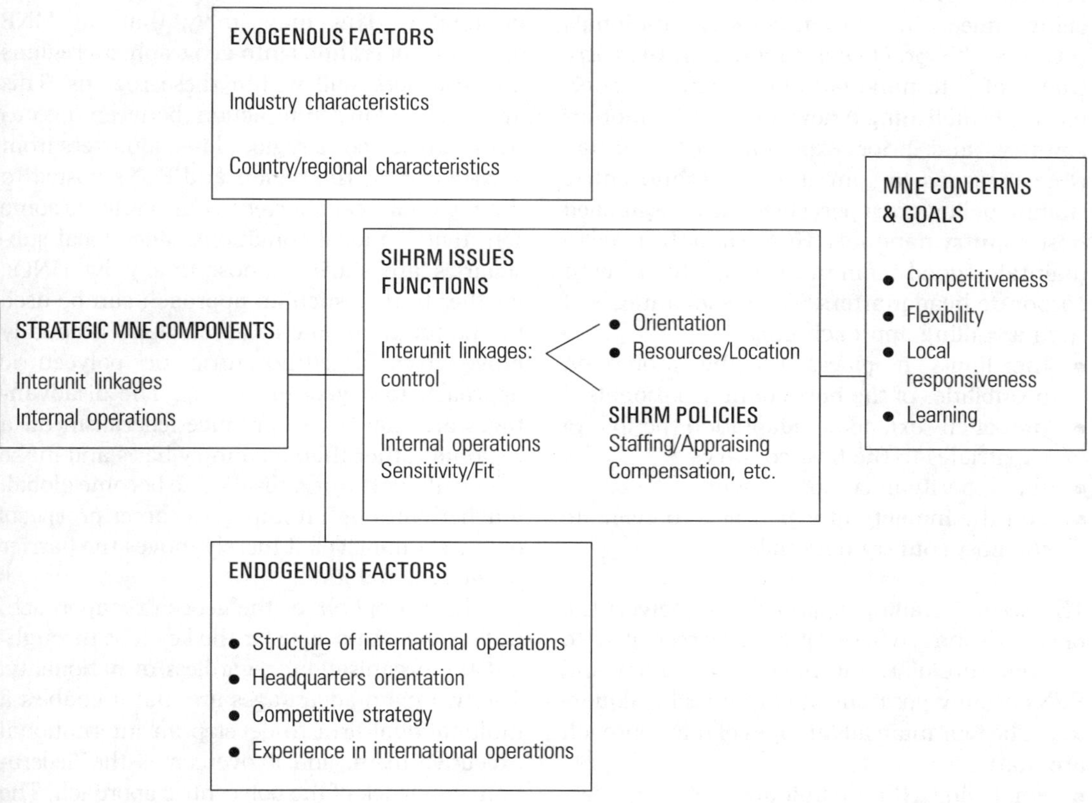

SOURCE: Adapted from Schuler et al. 1993

systematically linked to the strategic business needs of the MNE, they are regarded as SIHRM activities which then give rise to more specific SIHRM practices to be implemented at the subsidiary level. These latter practices will consequently influence or even determine the behaviour of individuals. The development of policies to be used as umbrellas for the practices within subsidiaries, facilitates the attainment of the main objective of interunit linkages. However, this may be easier said than done, particularly if the subsidiaries have dramatically different local environments or are using different competitive strategies with diverse technologies. Success in this regard enables the MNE to control the diversity of the operation while at the same time attaining the goals of competitiveness, flexibility, and transfer of learning.

Each local subsidiary remains a part of the MNE, but it must also fit in with the local environment and local human resource practices. However, it must take aspects beyond the local culture into account in order to be effective and still retain some global responsiveness.[17]

8.3 Expatriate selection

8.3.1 Staffing policies

Multinationals have a choice of four staffing options.[18,19]

The first option is the ethnocentric approach where all the key positions are being filled by parent-country nationals (PCNs). This practice is common in the early stages of internationalisation, when a company is establishing a new business in another country, and prior experience is essential. Other reasons for pursuing an ethnocentric staffing policy are a perceived lack of qualified host-country nationals (HCNs) and the need to maintain good communication links with corporate headquarters. The disadvantages of such a staffing approach are:

- the limits it places on the promotion possibilities of the host-country nationals;
- the often extended adaptation period of expatriates to the host country;
- the disparity in compensation;
- and the inability of expatriates to evaluate the host-country nationals.

The second staffing approach, or polycentric option, is one where HCNs are recruited to manage subsidiaries in their own country and PCNs occupy positions at corporate headquarters. The four main advantages of this approach are that:

- employing HCNs eliminates language barriers;
- HNCs have a more comprehensive understanding of the local sociocultural, political, and economic environments;
- employing HNCs allows multinationals to take a lower profile in sensitive political situations;
- HNCs are less expensive, and there tends to be continuity in the management of foreign subsidiaries.

The major difficulty is to bridge the gap between local national subsidiary managers and the parent-country managers. A second problem concerns the career paths of HCN managers since they have limited opportunities to gain experience outside their own country and cannot progress beyond the senior positions in their own subsidiary.

The third approach to international staffing is a regional policy with regard to executive nationality. This may imply that an MNE divides its operations into geographical regions and transfers staff within these regions. This approach allows interaction between executives transferred to regional headquarters from subsidiaries in the region and PCNs posted to the regional headquarters. It also reflects some sensitivity to local conditions, since local subsidiaries are staffed almost totally by HNCs. Further to this, such an approach can be used by the multinational as a vehicle to gradually move from a ethnocentric or polycentric approach to a geocentric one. The disadvantages are that it can produce federalism on a regional rather than a country basis and make it difficult for the organisation to become global. Further, although it improves career prospects on a national level, it merely moves the barrier to the regional level.

The last option, or the geocentric approach, utilises the best people for the key jobs throughout the organisation, regardless of nationality. The two main advantages are that it enables a multinational firm to develop an international executive team, and it overcomes the 'federation' drawback of the polycentric approach. The disadvantages are that the host governments want a large number of their citizens employed and will make use of immigration controls in order to force HCN employment if enough people and adequate skills are available. This approach can be very expensive because of increased training and relocation costs.[20]

BHP Steel staffing strategy

BHP is an Australian company that became a multinational mining conglomerate. In most Asian countries in which BHP operates, a condition of entry is that the foreign country Asianise their work-forces as quickly as possible. To integrate this condition within its SIHRM strategy, BHP follows a staffing procedure that is dependent on the phase of the project. During the start-up phase the Australian home office human resources manager recruits staff and seeks a local successor. BHP does not depend on joint venture partners to provide staff but appoints people directly. Usually the project manager and the chief financial officer are BHP employees and many BHP short- term assignees (PCNs) are used in the start-up phase.

During the next phase of operations there are still some BHP staff from Australia or New Zealand who are appointed either as expatriates for two to three years or as short-term employees working on specific projects for a few months. However, more local employees (HCNs), especially younger graduates, are appointed. For example, BHP has an Asian graduate programme based in Singapore. A more recent trend is to appoint specialists and third-country nationals from the Asian region.

Lend Lease staffing strategy

Lend Lease is another listed Australian financial services and property management company that internationalises by means of joint ventures in the USA and Asian countries. In contrast to the BHP strategy, Lend Lease is less formalised and does not have a central human resource (HR) department. The HR functions are carried out by a number of departments. It had to develop a policy on expatriate assignments in collaboration with Global Interface to guide its recent moves into Asia. A list of potential candidates for overseas assignments was generated but the opportunities are currently limited to financial and corporate services positions. The approach used for appointing staff from Australia was adapted for Asian conditions because Asian joint venture partners expected more senior Australian managers to work with their senior executives. Asian counterparts emphasised that an appropriate match of cultural skills must be a criterion for selection and not only Lend Lease's guidelines for the best operatives in Australia.

In Jakarta, Lend Lease depended on their joint venture partners to provide local appointees with the aim of nationalising the majority of staff positions over a five-year period. In this and other Asian countries, there may be an unacceptably high staff turnover due to the poaching of staff by other companies. The strategy is to recruit country nationals while they are studying at Australian universities and have the graduates work for a year in Australian operations before they are employed in their country of origin.

SOURCE: Adapted from Kramar, McGraw & Schuler.[21]

8.3.2 Expatriate sources and human resource planning

Briscoe[22] describes the different types of employees that a multinational company can recruit as PCNs, such as the Australian employees of BHP, host-country nationals, such as the Papua New Guinea (PNG) nationals working in a BHP mine in PNG, and third-country nationals, such as an Indonesian working in the BHP mine in PNG.

As labour mobility and temporary assignments become more prevalent, different types of employees who cannot be classified as PCNs, HCNs, or TCNs, are emerging. These groups can be described as 'inpatriates', 'permanent expatriates', and 'international cadres'.[23] All the sources of employees should be explored and the Internet is becoming a valuable tool to analyse recruitment practices of companies worldwide.

In many developing countries, such as those in Africa or Asia, the host country insists on the development of their nationals. Since there may be a shortage of suitably qualified or experienced nationals, this will have a training and development implication. A multinational company has to decide to what extent it will appoint host country nationals and what proportion of international experience is needed on the management team. International competition between MNEs exert pressure on them to develop larger numbers of managers with international experience and global mindsets. Succession planning in MNEs often includes a requirement that an executive has to have worked in a few foreign subsidiaries.

The difficult task of managing expatriates is often the key responsibility of an international human resource manager. Expatriates are moving from the home country to subsidiaries, as well as from country to country. The MNE may decide to follow a division-by-division process of globalisation, which means that a programme of expatriation will follow this process. The company has to formulate policies on the extent, duration, and focus of this programme.

The positive contributions that expatriation can make to the company are numerous. Expatriates build global relationships between subsidiaries and can foster a common corporate identity and business culture between them as well. They can increase the volume and efficiency of international knowledge, technology, and innovation transfers throughout a company. They should upgrade the skill levels in international subsidiaries, mentor the local managers, and facilitate the transfer of technology to the subsidiaries. International experience is seen as important in executive promotion since it helps expatriates gain insight into the functioning of their international competitors. Expatriates gain experience in working in culturally diverse environments that enhance their tolerance of ambiguity.

Briscoe[24] notes that the use of expatriates can follow a distinctive pattern. Initially the company recruits managers with international expertise from external sources, or buys expertise from consulting firms while training its own executives. There is a high use of expatriates from the home office in the initial phases of internationalisation as they move to establish offices in a new foreign location. Expatriation then declines for a period, as the company trains local managers in the countries and upgrades their skills. The number of expatriates again increases as the company grows into a globally integrated operation and expatriates move from one subsidiary to another. Transnational companies report declining use of expatriates from the home office, as they have developed a core of international cadres from which they can draw local and foreign managers.

8.3.3 Selection and preparation

The concept of culture shock refers to the reaction of expatriates to entering a new, unpredictable, and therefore uncertain environment. During the first six months in a new culture, expatriates feel that other people's behaviour does not make sense and that their own behaviour fails to produce expected results. Frustration builds up because the expatriates and their families do not understand the culture, its rituals, or how to get basic things done, especially if they cannot speak the host country's language. Non-working wives, especially, may experience boredom, loneliness, or aimlessness if they are unable to join local associations or make friends. Constant travel by the working spouse deprives the family of his/her presence, leading to a pattern of 'absent husbands and isolated wives'.[26] Many of the expatriate families have teenage children who fear not being able to adapt to schools and make new friends in a strange culture.

The failure of expatriates has traditionally been defined as an early return from the foreign assignment. The rate of return for American expatriates ranges from 10% to 80%, depending on the company or industry, with a median of 20% to 30%, whereas the failure rates for Japanese and European expatriates are substantially lower. However, characteristics such as poor quality of performance in a foreign assignment, little acceptance of the expatriate by local employees, and an inability to adjust to culture shock, are now also viewed as failures. The severity of failure is compounded by factors such as a lack of training for the assignment or an unwillingness on the part of the parent company to provide adequate support.

As knowledge about the reasons for expatriate failure increased, more international companies urgently reviewed their recruitment and selection procedures. Most companies in the 1990s selected expatriates based on their technical competence,[27] but current practices emphasise personal competencies such as communication skills, negotiating ability, organisational and cultural sensitivity, ability to manage cross-functional and cross-cultural teams, and tolerance of ambiguity.

Black, Gregersen, and Mendenhall[28] formulated a global assignment 'best practices cycle' to accomplish short- and long-term strategic objectives of selecting and preparing effective expatriates with technical and cross-cultural skills to prevent the high cost of expatriate failure, which incorporated the following:

- **Identifying the position:** A position description is designed to establish the extent of technical and cross-cultural skills needed. The larger the physical distance between the countries, the more critical the selection and pre-departure orientation; and a hiring team consisting of a senior manager of the division, the hiring manager, and the HR director is formed.
- **Determining the candidates' qualifications:** In addition to technical and cross-cultural qualifications, previous overseas background and experience and specific behavioural dimensions are determined.
- **Screening:** Initial screening according to the criteria is done in the human resources department in consultation with senior management, and the best candidates are presented to the hiring division and senior management.
- **Scheduling of interviews:** Multiple interviews are conducted by the HR department and the staff of the hiring division, but also by other expatriates if they are available.
- **Interviews and tests:** A core list of 28 dimensions was developed by Worldvision International for expatriate selection, but specific dimensions are selected for each assignment. Interviewers concentrate on selected dimensions and write evaluations of the candidates; and candidates are given psychological tests to determine their potential to adapt to new situations and cultures.
- **Evaluations of interviews and tests:** All the information about the candidate is reviewed and at this stage the spouse is interviewed and required to complete the psychological tests.
- **Recommendations:** The HR department compiles reports to senior management and the hiring division about possible candidates.
- **Approval:** The hiring team discusses the recommendation and decides on approval, and the HR department recommends compensation and benefits to the hiring department; further administrative processes are completed.
- **Appointment:** A letter of appointment is presented to the successful candidates.
- **Training and pre-departure preparation:** The family is given the necessary training.
- **Support:** The expatriate and his/her family is supported during the contract period; performance is evaluated.
- **Repatriation:** The expatriate is assigned a sponsor and the HR network ensures successful reintegration.

8.3.4 Dual career couples

Adler[29] describes the loss of the structure and continuity that the spouses experience when their partners accept an international assignment. This source of dissatisfaction and the family's inability to adjust to a foreign environment are some of the most important factors resulting in failure and early return for expatriates.

Companies need to make a distinction between the pressures that single-career couples face and those of a dual-career couple. The fact that there are fewer women expatriates is because of bias and stereotyping in the parent country and company about the foreign acceptance of women in managerial roles, rather than actual prejudice in the host country or subsidiary. Recent research[30] has developed the concepts of a 'trailing spouse' or 'spousal equivalent unit' to indicate the inclusion of both genders as spouses.

The majority of dual-career expatriates expressed dissatisfaction with the lack of support, especially for spouse and family, provided by multinational corporations during their international experience.[31] Dual-career couples recommend that the MNEs should:

- provide employment opportunities for the trailing spouse or assist him/her to find a position in the foreign country;
- assist the couple to obtain work permits and other government requirements to work in a foreign country;
- include commuting allowances and time for being together for the dual-career couples separated by relocation;
- encourage continued executive education during the foreign assignment;
- provide adequate social support (informational, instrumental, emotional, and appraisal) to facilitate the adjustment in the foreign country as well as during repatriation.

8.3.5 Hiring HCNs and TCNs

Most MNEs appoint local nationals in positions below senior management level, but in regions where there is movement of employees between countries, third-country nationals (TCNs) are chosen. Basic education systems and training levels can vary between states in a country or between regions. Offices or factories are often located in border areas or free trade zones to gain access to staff and infrastructure in two countries simultaneously. Companies need to take into account how the gap between the suppliers of labour and the demand for labour will affect them.

In Africa, for example, South Africa is faced with a massive influx of illegal immigrants from neighbouring countries seeking employment and education. Since these TCNs are not unionised and are prepared to work for different rates, they are appointed in positions that HCNs are vacating to move up the corporate ladder.

Case studies about McDonald's operations worldwide describe how the company integrates its respect for the local cultural traditions with its global HR practices (see Chapter 7). Host-country nationals with an ability to become customer-focused, and who have the right attitude, are selected. Applicants who pass the initial screening are invited to work in a temporary capacity to enable the company to evaluate their performance. McDonald's is committed to staffing locally and promoting from within the company, but can deploy its human resources globally. Extensive training enables the company to address local concerns but keep global standards.

8.3.6 Compliance with local laws

A constant dilemma for the MNE is the decision of whether to apply parent-country laws, values, and management practices to their foreign subsidiaries. They need to avoid an ethnocentric approach in favour of a regiocentric or geocentric approach. In the McDonald's case in Chapter 7 the company has specific technical standards and customer service guidelines to which it adheres, but it is sensitive to local labour laws and the necessity for training. In general, expatriates and their families are expected to comply with local laws and customs.

Foreign MNEs in Australia are also expected to conform to Australian labour laws, even if they come from countries with an authoritarian approach to unions or management practices. A further issue in dealing with inpatriates is whether they comply, for example, with Australian immigration laws. Immigration regulations dealing with family migration was tightened in 1997 and this may have a further effect on third-country nationals being employed in Australian companies. Briscoe[32] mentions a number of Japanese firms that have transgressed USA labour laws.

8.4 Training, management development and career planning

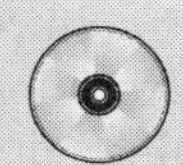

Compact disc

1 Mr Hamzah Bakar of Petronas in Malaysia gives his views on the importance of training people effectively for the 'Global Village'.

Pre-departure training is a key strategy to ensure the effective adaptation of expatriates and their families. The development and training of an international cadre of executives with global mindsets, and the training of HCNs and TCNs are part of this process.

Not only must expatriates be able to work with different legal and financial systems, but they must also operate in markets with diverse cultures, values, and social systems. Although cross-cultural training of expatriates and negotiators is seen to be crucial to international business contracts between companies, more attention is given to language training.[33,34]

8.4.1 Training of expatriates

An erroneous assumption is that management practices in one culture will be acceptable in all cultures. The way that a multinational is doing business in Australia may not be acceptable in Britain, South Africa, or the USA, despite the fact that a common language (English) is spoken and there may be certain cultural similarities (individualism).

Briscoe's[35] model for multinational management deals with the process of objective formulation, problem recognition, development objectives, assessment of development needs, development methods, intermediate and desired results, and re-entry training. The key issues are to identify the training needs of the expatriate and his/her family and then design a programme that addresses those needs. Another issue is that the training methods should be matched to the purpose of the assignment and training need, and the programme should be constantly evaluated and adapted.

Most sources provide a list of topics to be included, suggestions for training methods, and case studies to be used in a multinational's programme.[36,37] They may recommend, for example, that the expatriate family study Internet sources in their own free time. The debate in MNEs is whether the pre-departure training prepares the expatriate family adequately for the realities of the new environment. The Shell company found three-day and six-day pre-departure training programmes reduced their return rates significantly.

8.4.2 Cross-cultural training

Initial efforts at models for cross-cultural training included information or fact-oriented training, cultural awareness training, interaction training, cognitive behaviour modification, attribution training, and experiential learning. A theoretical framework should be used to design cross-cultural training. This will ensure that there is a significant relationship between cross-cultural training and cross-cultural performance in an MNE. These models suggest that learning takes place both by being reinforced and by imitating the behaviour of others, as well as by making associations between behaviour and its consequences. Expatriates therefore need to:

- pay attention to cross-cultural differences between home and host country;
- have the opportunity to experiment with the required behaviours;
- build cognitive maps about acceptable practices and remember the correct behaviours or speech patterns;
- reproduce the behaviours in appropriate situations, and
- receive incentives when they perform in an acceptable way.

In Exhibit 8.2, Black et al. provide a model of the modelling processes, rigour, and training methods underlying cross-cultural training. An international HR manager may choose to implement symbolic processing in training by giving the expatriates models of behaviour to observe in films, demonstrations, or role modelling. If the company decides to use participative modelling, the expatriates will describe verbally what they will do in a negotiation situation or physically engage in an actual or simulated cross-cultural negotiation. Eating rice with chopsticks will involve both mental and physical processes and will be more rigorous than merely watching a film demonstrating the skill.

The international HR manager needs to establish how novel the foreign culture and assignment is to the expatriate, and how often he/she would have to engage in face-to-face, long-term, two-way cross-cultural interactions to determine the intensity and rigour of his/her training. Not only should the expatriate family receive cross-cultural training, but also returnees.[38] Human resource managers should develop an expertise in cross-cultural training so that they can present in-house training programmes. Such training should be considered a necessity and not a luxury.

Chi-sum Li,[39] in studying the strategic design of cross-cultural training programmes in Australia and America, concludes that the degree of human resource management corporate strategy (HRM-CS) integration affects the approaches to and methods of cross-cultural training. In Phase 1 of the HRM-CS integration, the design of cross-cultural training programmes is based predominantly on cognitive methods. In Phase 2, the design is based on both cognitive and affective methods, with the emphasis on the former, while in Phase 3, the design is primarily cognitive- and affective-oriented, with limited application of behavioural/experiential methods. In Phase 4, the design is based on behavioural and experiential methods, but cognitive and affective methods are used when necessary.

Tung[40] recommends that training in cross-cultural communication should enable a person to progress from unconscious incompetence to unconscious competence. An example of unconscious incompetence would be if an expatriate unintentionally insults a Korean colleague by likening Koreans to the Japanese. A person who is consciously incompetent will hesitate while seeking suitable terminology in a business negotiation. Conscious competence is reached when the person is aware of the

Exhibit 8.2: Selection of cross-cultural training methods

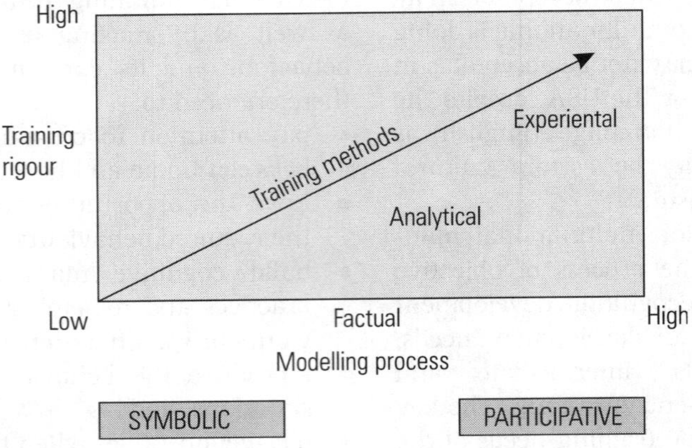

SOURCE: Black, et al. 1991.

differences between national cultures and analyses situations before communicating. In the unconscious competence phases the person has become bilingual as well as bicultural.

BHP training strategy

The BHP human resources manager trains his local successor during the start-up phase. The core of 500 BHP expatriates have received training during each offshore assignment. BHP provides operational training to national employees (who are locally educated personnel). The 20 Asian graduates from the Asian graduate programme in Singapore undertake further Global Leadership programmes in Australia.

SOURCE: Adapted from Kramar, Mcgraw & Schuler, 1997.

8.4.3 Career management – a South African example

The reader may have developed an interest in pursuing an international career. Adler[41] provides guidance in establishing the requirements of a global manager by including a survey. The survey assists potential international managers to analyse how prepared they are for the assignment, what their career plans are, what reasons they have for accepting or rejecting international assignments, and what their expectations are with regard to expatriate success. Additional issues are the level of internationalisation of their company, the psychic distance between their own and the physical host country and the support that their company will provide during their term of office.

The ten factors that may influence the subjects' adjustment as well as their willingness to accept an international assignment are:

- an inadequate financial package;
- feelings of isolation and loneliness;
- immigration/employment laws and host country restrictions;
- disruption of children's education;
- elderly relatives;
- fear of losing influence/visibility at corporate centre;
- the assignment is too long;
- the host country is hostile to foreigners, making it dangerous;
- there is too much travel involved, and
- spouse/partner is reluctant to give up his/her own career.

A South African study[42] tested the survey on MBA students at a large university. The sample consisted of 84% male and 16% female managers. They were mostly Afrikaans-speaking, but 51% spoke other African and European languages. The majority (68%) were married with children (48%) and most were in the age range of 30-39 years. Most had business degrees or engineering undergraduate degrees.

There was a significant difference between Afrikaans-speaking and other language speaking managers in the sample. Afrikaans-speaking subjects were not that keen to pursue an international career after receiving their MBA degrees, because English was a second language for them and they were comfortable in South Africa. However, their spouses were willing to give up their own career aspirations so that the Afrikaans-speaking manager could pursue an international career. Managers were wary of the impact of extensive travel on their marital relationships.

There were differences between managers younger than 30 and those who were older than 30, since the latter tend to have children who might not be so accepting of their parent's international assignment. Managers with children wanted their children to be educated in their home language and anticipated that their international assignment would be in a country where there were different languages. Many of the managers preferred to have their children educated in a school system with which they were familiar. Managers who were willing to consider international careers, focused on the extent to which their overseas financial packages would allow them to send their children to good schools to get a sound education. They were concerned about the ease with which their children would make friends from different cultures. A further familial factor was that managers with elderly relatives would not accept an international assignment. They thought that it would be difficult for their relatives to be exposed to a new culture and a new way of life, or were concerned about the care of elderly relatives left behind in the home country.

There were differences between subjects who have commercial or engineering degrees and those who have other degrees. The engineers were more interested in accepting future international careers, since some employers offered the opportunity for overseas contract work. The engineering managers might experience difficulties during repatriation after lengthy overseas exposure. They noted that they were less likely to accept an assignment in a hostile and unstable country.

There were also differences between students who feared isolation and loneliness in the host country and those who had no problem with it. Managers who do not fear isolation are usually extroverted and are able to integrate with other people and cultures. Those who fear isolation are not usually familiar with other cultures and have had no previous exposure to different people. Another fear was that managers might become 'invisible' to the corporate centre or be overlooked for promotion when they were in the host culture. Thus, these subjects preferred to stay in their home country where they felt safe and were 'visible'. Managers differed in their perception of immigration laws and some used it as a reason for not accepting an international assignment.

8.4.4 International management development

Adler and Israeli[43] argue that the option of limiting senior or international management to one gender has become an archaic luxury that no company can afford. Young American male and female managers express an equal interest in accepting international assignments.[44] This research indicates that women succeed as global managers because they are seen as foreigners who happen to be women and not as women who happen to be foreigners. This reaction is called the 'Gaijin' syndrome – in countries in which women play a traditional role, foreign women are treated with the respect accorded to male expatriate managers.

Adler and Israeli[45] dispel many myths about women in international management based on their research of women in MNEs in different countries. Some of the advantages that women experience in Asian countries are that they are highly visible and therefore find it easier to network with foreign clients. The female expatriate's staff assumes that the company would only risk sending an exceptional person to a foreign posting and therefore expect her to be a high achiever. Female expatriate managers can usually afford household help to manage the multiple roles of homebuilder, professional, and wife. One of the disadvantages was that women were not allowed to visit remote sites for fear of their safety.

As the MNE builds up a cadre of international managers, the company transfers this expertise to the development of its local managers in the parent company and in the subsidiaries. In IBM, Shell, Phillips, and Unilever so much priority is given to the identification and developing of management talent, that it has become a board responsibility.

The common elements in management development that have evolved in a number of MNEs are:

- the early identification of individuals with executive potential through assessment or monitoring strategies;
- recruiting at elite universities or the use of in-house apprenticeships;
- assignments leading to increasing levels of managerial responsibility to evaluate performance;
- close monitoring of the candidates to manage their job assignments to ensure exposure to a variety of experiences;

- ensuring that mobility creates informal networks between peers that assist with problem-solving on international projects.

8.5 Performance management, international compensation and benefits

The international human resource manager is responsible for a number of functions and activities, such as international compensation and performance appraisals, which require a broader global perspective. The compensation and evaluation practices change as the employee mix of parent-and host-country nationals changes over time and in different locations around the world. These managers will be getting greater exposure to complex problems, such as calculating remuneration packages differently in a number of countries. The international human resource manager will be coping with external, political, legal, and economic influences in numerous countries with different cultures.

8.5.1 Performance evaluation

The performance evaluation system plays a role in individual job assignments, developmental plans, cross-cultural and other training, as well as in pay increases and benefits of expatriates. Expatriates, however, argue that they suffer from a lack of recognition for their contributions.

There are numerous common problems associated with performance appraisal in an international context. The choice of evaluator may be controversial since it includes aspects about whether he/she is from the host or home country and what contact the evaluator has had with the expatriate. There may be differences between home country and host-country perceptions of performance and evaluation. There could be an inadequate establishment, clarification, and negotiation of objectives between headquarters and subsidiary, or inadequate understanding between home and host country of each other's culture and business practices with regard to performance appraisal. Performance deficiencies may be caused by environmental or task variables or personality factors. There may be difficulties in long-distance communication between headquarters and subsidiary during the evaluation process. The MNE needs to focus on global strategy and not only on regional or subsidiary performance. Data obtained from subsidiaries may not be comparable because of differences in market conditions, volatility in the international environment, separation by distance, and time zone differences.[46]

The effect of these problems is that the parent company may choose to set financial performance goals for the subsidiary, but does not give any guidelines on how individual performance should be evaluated to achieve results. Dowling et al.[47] recommend that the appraisal of the senior manager should be similar to that of a general manager in a strategic business unit in the parent country. The regional general manager should therefore evaluate the subsidiary's chief executive by using a form similar to that used for parent-country managers. Collecting data in this way will be more applicable across subsidiaries in that specific region. A further recommendation is that a set of parallel accounts, adjusted for differences in financial indicators such as exchange rate fluctuations, should be kept for comparison between regions or subsidiaries.

The subsidiary's chief executive officer (CEO), who is the immediate supervisor of the individual or the home-country manager, usually conducts the appraisal of other expatriate employees. Multinational managers may find that cultural acceptability of performance appraisal influences their evaluation of HCNs and TCNs. Therefore it is desirable to have HCNs and TCNs assist the multinational managers in designing a culturally sensitive performance appraisal system in a particular country, while maintaining global standards.

The following guidelines for appraising an expatriate's performance are provided by Black, Mendenhal and Oddoul:[48]

- Headquarters should provide a breakdown of the difficulty level of the assignment and include factors such as operational language used in the firm, cultural distance between the countries, and acknowledgement of factors influencing the expatriate's performance;
- More attention should be given to the on-site manager's appraisal of the expatriate than to evaluations by managers in the parent country, but consultation between the managers should also take place;
- The parent company's performance criteria may have to be modified to fit the overseas position and site characteristics, and include the expatriate's insights as part of the evaluation.

8.5.2 International compensation and benefits

The design of compensation systems is one of the critical responsibilities of an international HR manager, and the task of formulating policies that cater for the diversity of international operations is complex. Pay and benefits for expatriates who are serving in many different countries need to be developed. The multinational manager will have to cope with subsidiary work-forces in more than one country and manage employees from numerous countries. He/she has to understand the approaches to levels of pay and benefits in various countries and be able to deal with problems of multiple currencies, exchange and inflation rates, tax systems, and diverse cost of living standards.

A key issue is how the company deals with these pressures to have a compensation policy that will be consistent and fair to both expatriates and local employees. An effectively designed policy has to meet a number of objectives, such as selection of employees from both the home and host countries to form a cadre of people who are qualified and willing to be transferred between affiliates. Furthermore, the compensation system should be viewed as consistent and reasonable by local and overseas employees, and offer competitive compensation while minimising costs.[49]

A multinational company has to bear the issues of cost and comparability in mind. Some surveys (Briscoe, 1995) confirm that expatriates are often dissatisfied with their compensation packages and that constant comparisons should take place between the host-country nationals and expatriates, expatriates working for different multinationals, and expatriates and their 'stay-at-home' colleagues. Because of the perceived inequities, the expatriates and home- or host-country nationals demand correction, which again escalates costs.

Compensation of Nestle expatriates

Nestle is sending project managers from South Africa to Australia for periods of two to three years. In South Africa their pensions (superannuation), housing loans, and medical benefits are kept up to date and their furniture is stored. In Australia their children's school fees are paid, apartments or houses are rented, relocation allowances may be paid, and a car provided, while the salary is adjusted for cost of living expenses.

Further questions are the extent to which compensation and benefits should conform to the headquarters' practices, or whether they should conform to practices in the overseas location. For example, if all engineers of a company worldwide are paid according to a standard scale, it simplifies the complexity of different pay systems in countries and reduces inequities, but it does not take into account that it is much more expensive to stay in Hong Kong than in Pretoria or Adelaide. If the expatriates who lived in Hong Kong are returned to Pretoria or Adelaide, their pay scales are usually cut to readjust, and this causes further dissatisfaction.

8.5.3 Approaches to compensation for expatriates

Although there are various approaches to compensation for expatriates, only two will be discussed in this chapter, namely negotiation and the balance sheet approach.

Negotiation approach: At the start of the internationalisation process, a few expatriates are sent overseas to gain market share, transfer technology, and set up and manage the overseas offices. An ad hoc approach is usually followed since a unique compensation and benefit package is designed for each expatriate. As the internationalisation process expands and the company has more than 20 expatriates in various locations, it will be developing a more systematic approach to minimise the inconsistencies in the ad hoc approach.

Balance sheet approach: Expatriates should not be any worse off for accepting an overseas assignment, and they need to be provided with incentives for accepting the assignment while still containing the costs to the company. The balance sheet approach (Exhibit 8.3) is applied when expatriates are moved from the parent company to an overseas location. If individuals are moved between foreign subsidiaries or from the overseas subsidiary back to headquarters, more levels of complexity are added.[50]

The senior employee's current compensation is the basis for the calculation and two components (incentives and equalisation adjustments) are added. Incentive components may range from housing allowances or relocation expenses to displacement allowances for being in uncomfortable environments or unfamiliar countries, to education for children and education allowances for the expatriate, settling-in expenses, or pre-departure language training. Equalisation adjustments can include cost of living and inflation adjustments, tax equalisation allowances, employee benefits adjustments, health insurance or social security payments and a variety of other forms. Since the **base pay** is an important starting point, the company has to decide if it will be using parent-country salaries (for example, South Africa), an international standard, a regional standard such as the European community, host-country standards, or the salaries of other managers in the host location (e.g. Australia).

8.5.4 Cost factors

A further debate revolves around **the type and amount of incentives** that should be given. The 'overseas premium' used to average about 25% of base pay but this has since been reduced to

Exhibit 8.3: International compensation: Balance sheet approach

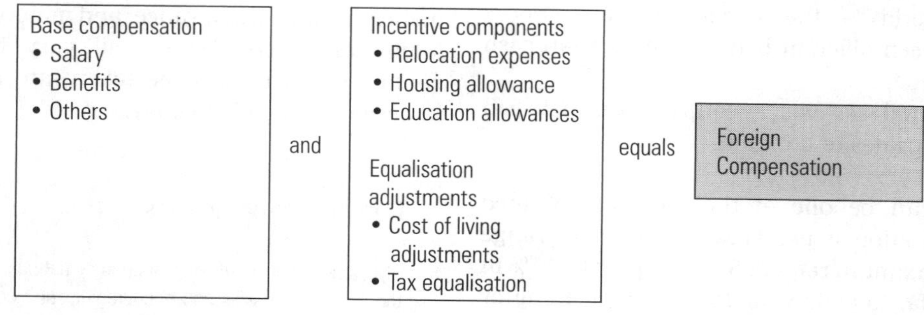

OURCE: Briscoe, 1995. p. 113.

15%[51] and premiums for 'hardship' can add an additional 5% to 25% to the base pay. Some multinationals are beginning to argue that, in a global economy, the stress of dislocation is minimised and that such high premiums need not be paid.

A **cost of living adjustment (COLA)** is usually provided and it will be necessary to consult the cost of living data for locals around the world to calculate the adjustments according to family size and income. For example, an American going to Munich in Germany may need up to 50% COLA above what was needed in a typical American town. The incentives and adjustments can cost a multinational company US$150 000 per expatriate location, and rent for an expatriate family can cost up to US$100 000 per year in Hong Kong.[52] The high cost of maintaining appropriate compensation packages has led many companies such as Colgate-Palmolive, Digital Equipment, General Motors, and General Electric to cut back on PCN assignments as far as possible. A compensation score card between Germany, Japan, and the USA provided by Deresky,[53] illustrates the comparative costs of locating a manager to these countries.

To manage the high costs of relocation, multinationals are using the following approaches:

- localisation – expatriates are paid comparably to local nationals with some supplements;
- lump sum – expatriates have to decide how to spend a lump sum on housing, travel, etc;
- cafeteria – the expatriate can choose between different benefits rather than cash income;
- regional systems – equity exists between expatriates in a region.

Taxes can be one of the most complicated compensation issues because they can range from maximum rates of 56% in Spain to 47% in Australia, to as low as 25% in Hong Kong or 11% in Switzerland. In some cases the expatriate is expected to take care of his/her own taxes in both countries, unless the company follows a tax equalisation approach and withholds the income from a tax obligation in the home country and then pays all the taxes in the host country. With a tax protection approach, the company pays the expatriate any excess of foreign income tax over the tax of the home country, thereby protecting him/her against higher foreign taxes. Multinational managers need to establish whether their country taxes all the income of its citizens, regardless of where they live, or if there are foreign-earned income exclusions or tax credits that may apply. For example, the USA has income tax and social security treaties with a number of countries so that tax exemption is granted to expatriates on a short-term assignment.

8.6 Designing a compensation strategy for multinationals

Multinational companies need to gather reliable data from different locations worldwide about each country's wage rates and salary scales based on valid salary surveys, as well as comparable data on the cost of living expenses within each country. In addition they need to establish whether employee benefits make up a significant portion of the pay package – in some countries the government mandates health care or retirement pensions, whereas in the USA this is left to the discretion of the company. The differences in vacation requirements, pension plans, stock options or employee share-ownership plans, insurance, and maternity and family or carers' leave, will vary between countries and need to be taken into account in designing a global policy.

Compensation policies

BHP found that identifying in-country nationals with the appropriate skills and encouraging their continuing performance has been problematic and costly.

There is a high rate of turnover among staff, especially in the buoyant Asian economies. On the one hand, there is blatant poaching of staff by competitors, while on the other hand staff come to expect high levels of training and participation in BHP Employee Share Schemes. Feedback indicates that many multinationals are vulnerable to poaching of upwardly mobile graduates after the yearly bonus payments. Often national staff are more highly educated than staff in the home country, which again leads to higher expectations for compensation among national staff. Furthermore, BHP is finding it difficult to standardise inter-Asian regional location allowances. There has been a wide variation in the offering of location allowances to regional Asian employees and those offered to international staff.

SOURCE: Adapted from Kramar et al., 1997.

8.7 Summary

The effectiveness of a multinational corporation's managers in foreign subsidiaries is crucial to the success of the headquarters' strategies for global expansion or operation. The cadre of expatriates and local staff are expected to initiate and maintain professional relationships between the home and host country to facilitate the viability of global operations. It is expected that expatriates and local nationals will be proactive in initiating opportunities and will get recognition from headquarters for any successes.

However, this presupposes that the multinational company has a clear strategy for global expansion and is implementing the principles of strategic international human resources management. In most of the sources and examples it is clear that both global strategy and SIHRM are evolving fields, and practical implementation of theoretical principles is gradually emerging.

Case Study

Global human resource management at Coca-Cola

Coca-Cola is one of the most successful MNEs in the world today. Although Coca-Cola's headquarters is in Atlanta, Georgia, USA, the soft-drink giant is more than simply an American-based company with some operations overseas. It's a truly global enterprise. Nearly 80% of the company's operating income comes from its businesses outside the United States. These businesses range from wholly-owned subsidiaries and bottling companies to independent bottling and distribution centres that license its products – mainly soft drinks. The company also manufactures and markets juice and juice-drink products.

The businesses that produce, market, and distribute these products span the globe. Coca-Cola manages them through 25 operating divisions making up six regional groups: North America, the European Union, the Pacific region, the Northeast Europe/-Middle East (NEME) group, Africa, and Latin America. Each of these groups has a president, accountable for the businesses in his/her area. In other words, each region, although a part of the bigger system, is its own entity. As Michael J. Semrau, assistant vice president and director of international human resources, says: 'The Coca-Cola Company just happens to be headquartered in Atlanta. It could just as feasibly be headquartered in any of the other locations (where we do business) and it probably wouldn't make a difference.'

The regions and businesses are linked together by a shared mindset to think globally and act locally, a philosophy that defines a global enterprise, according to Vladimir Pucik, director of international programmes at the Centre for Advanced Human Resources Studies at Cornell University. 'If you look at a global company from a business perspective, the emphasis is on a combination of global integration and local responsiveness,' Pucik says. Drawing a parallel with human resources, Pucik says that its role is to get all the different functional capabilities – such as selection criteria, training processes, and performance assessments – to reinforce the way people can think globally and act locally.

That's exactly what HR at Coca-Cola strives to do. 'Coca-Cola always has been known as a multi-local company,' says Semrau. It's like a family: each business, like each family member, has its own unique qualities and can stand on its own, but benefits from being connected to the group, and just like a family, the businesses have a certain bond. 'The common thread running through Coca-Cola is its willingness to allow the locations to be different, to conduct the business in ways that are appropriate for the market in which they're operating,' says Jeff Peeters, who is currently director of HR for corporate finance and human resources in Atlanta.

Peeters refers to the global human resources practitioners as 'custodians for international equity', who make decisions on such issues as benefits, compensation and training based on corporate philosophies.

Essentially, corporate HR functions by providing the philosophy around human issues while allowing local businesses to apply those philosophies as they see fit for their region. For example, rather than having a standard salary policy for all of its businesses, Coca-Cola has a salary philosophy which is for its total compensation packages, so that its businesses are competitive with the best companies in their markets. 'We focus on the end product – the means to get there might be different in one part of the world versus another,' Semrau says.

Differences in laws and cultures also play a role. For example, Peeters says that the openness that people in the United States have about salaries, doesn't exist in Europe. 'In Europe we don't discuss salaries. That's something between you and your employer, and you will never breach that level of trust. They would find it insulting to have to disclose their salary, and they would find it insulting if you disclose their salaries because they consider that to be something very personal.' On the other hand, you can talk about their family backgrounds, their ages, and so on, without a problem. In fact, they get offended if you aren't interested in their family backgrounds. In the United States, such inquiries would be in violation of the law. 'So certain policies that are perfectly legitimate in the United States, if they aren't applied with the right level of judgement, will offend people in other countries,' Peeters says.

> Central support enables international HR at Coca-Cola to act locally while thinking globally.

Although they're fairly independent, human resources professionals around the world receive support from a core HR staff in Atlanta. One of the support systems available is an HR orientation, held twice a year in Atlanta for international staffers and once a year for those working at headquarters. The two-week orientation is for people who have recently joined Coca-Cola as HR representatives, or for longer-term associates who can benefit. Its purpose is to give an overview of the company's HR perspective. 'We try to blend a business overview with a human resources overview,' Peeters says, 'so we talk about the business, we talk about how the business translates in HR policies and what the practices are that follow from those policies.'

Participants in the programme leave with a much broader view of what the company is doing, not only in HR but in finance, marketing, and other aspects of the business. They also learn about HR philosophies, as well as programmes and policies already created that can be adopted.

In addition to the orientation, Peeters says that the company is planning to roll out a more advanced development programme for HR professionals early next year. It will be targeted specifically at those who aren't quite at a director level but have shown the potential for getting there. Its goal will be to build skills, rather than to establish a knowledge base that the orientation strives to do. 'We have noticed that HR as a profession evolves quickly,' Peeters says.

Also, the market-place changes, theories change, and Coca-Cola accordingly revises policies and practices and tools to cope with these changes. For example, a thrust within the company right now is for managers to become better coaches. 'We can't automatically assume that HR knows how to teach these skills,' Peeters says. The development programme will therefore offer courses on these types of skills on an as-needed basis.

Another support tool for human resources practitioners in the Coca-Cola system is the HR development committee. The company started using the development-committee model 10 years ago within the finance division. Today, almost every functional area of the company has one. The role of the committees is to identify talent within their particular functions and then take the necessary steps to ensure that talent achieves its potential. They also look at openings within their accountability to ensure that they're moving people who have the right skills into the right positions. 'The goal is to make sure that we have the right competencies in the organisation to help us meet our business objectives on an ongoing basis,' Semrau says.

Nancy Schemaria, director of staffing, facilitates the HR development committee which examines all the positions open in human resources during every meeting and evaluates possible candidates. The main focus of the committee is on placing key talent – from mid-management to senior level positions – but because HR is a relatively small function, the placements can run the gamut.

Another task of the development committee is to identify key technical or professional skills for positions in their organisation. The HR development committee identified key experiences or job knowledge in 10 areas that people in HR need. They are: facilitation skills, an understanding of global business and HR trends, organisation design, HR functional knowledge, employee relations, industrial relations, learning and development, performance development, selection and staffing, and total compensation.

In addition to these, the company has core foundation skills that Coca-Cola personnel need. These are a combination of capabilities and skills that the company uses to evaluate any associate in the organisation. For example, foundation skills for managerial people include coaching skills, leadership capabilities, and the ability to think creatively. 'They're quite generic, almost attitudinal,' Peeters says.

Adds Shemaria: 'What you end up with is a comprehensive set of both the general business skills and the function specific skills, and by putting them together, we get a complete picture of what somebody needs to be able to do the job.'

Along with developing key competencies, the HR development committee conducts talent assessments. It slices the organisation either horizontally or vertically to look at a portion of the function. It then determines what skills are required of the positions in the group, evaluates the skills and talents of the people in those positions, and implements strategies to close any gaps.

For example, the committee will encourage and provide managers in that function with the tools to do development planning for their associates. 'We play an influencing leadership role for which we may develop some assessment tools, develop the technical competencies and skills, and get those distributed throughout human resources as tools for all managers in human resources to use,' Shemaria says. 'But the role of the development committee isn't to watch over what the managers do. They still need to be managing, coaching, and gathering feedback, separate from the development committee.'

Essentially what the HR development committee does is to reinforce HR's mission within its own ranks. That mission, says Semrau, is to 'work with all of the associates in the system to enable them to develop their full potential to exceed the expectations of customers, consumers, and shareholders'. Quite straightforward, but nonetheless lofty, considering the extent of Coca-Cola's human resources. However, with staff in Australia and Morocco sharing the same mindset and receiving the same support as those in Italy and the United States, it's a goal that's certainly attainable.

SOURCE: Anfuso, D. 1994. HR unites the world of Coca-Cola. *Personnel Journal*, Novemer, pp 112–120.

? Questions

1 To what extent has Coca-Cola implemented the model of the development of multinational management?

2 To what extent do you think Coca-Cola has implemented the modelling processes and training methods underlying cross-cultural training?

3 Do you think Coca-Cola has succeeded in building a core of 'global managers'? Explain your answer in detail.

4 Is it possible for all staff around the world to be in the same 'global mindset'?

Endnotes

1 Hill, C.W.L. 1997. *International business: Competing in the global marketplace.* 2nd ed. Washington: McGraw-Hill, p. 368

2 Based on Bartlett, C.A. & Ghosal, S. 1989. *Managing across borders.* Boston: Harvard Business School Press.

3 Schuler, R., Dowling, P. & De Cieri, H. 1993. 'An integrative framework of strategic international human resources management'. *Journal of Management,* 19 (2), pp. 419–59.

4 Bartlett, C.A. & Ghosal, S. 1995. *Transnational management.* New York: Irwin.

5 Schuler et al., op. cit., p. 420.

6 Barnevick, P. 1994. Preface. *Harvard Business Review.* 'Global strategies : Insights from the world's leading thinkers'. Boston: Harvard Business School Publishing.

7 Rhinesmith, S.H. 1993. *Globalisation: Six keys to success in a changing world.* New York: Irwin.

8 Mendenhall, M., Punnett, B.J. & Ricks, D. 1995. *Global management.* Oxford: Blackwell Publishers.

9 Adler, N. 1997. *International dimensions of organisational behaviour.* 3rd ed. Boston: PWS-Kent Publishing Company.

10 Enderwick, P. & Akoorie, M. 1996. *Fast forward: New Zealand business in world markets.* Auckland: Longman Paul Limited.

11 Kanter, R. 1994. 'Afterword: What thinking globally really means'. In *Harvard Business Review.* 1994. *Global strategies: Insights from the world's leading thinkers.* Boston: Harvard Business School Publishing.

12 Schuler et al., op. cit., p. 424.

13 Cox, J.W., De Cieri, H. & Fenwick, M. 1998. 'The mapping of strategic international human resource management: Theory development or intellectual imperialism?' Working paper 36/98, Monash University, Faculty of Business & Economics p. 1–23.

14 Schuler et al., op. cit., p. 425.

15 Schuler et al., op. cit., p, 426.

16 Black, J.S., Mendenhall, M. & Oddou, G. 1991. 'Towards a comprehensive model of international adjustment: An integration of multiple theoretical perspectives'. *Academy of Management Review,* Vol. 16, pp. 291–317.

17 Schuler et al., op. cit., p. 434.

18 Cox et al., op. cit., p. 3.

19 Deresky, H. 1997. *International management.* Reading, Massachusetts: Addison-Wesley Longman.

20 Dowling, P.J., Schuler, R.S. & Welch, D.E.1994. *International dimensions of human resource management.* Belmont, CA: Wadsworth.

21 Kramar, R., McGraw, P. & Schuler, R.S. 1997. *Human resources management in Australia.* Melbourne: Longman Publishers.

22 Briscoe, D.R. 1995. *International human resource management.* Englewood-Cliffs: Prentice Hall.

23 Briscoe, op. cit., p. 46.

24 Briscoe, op. cit., p. 277.

25 Stuart, K.D. 1992. 'Teens play a role in moves overseas'. *Personnel Journal,* March, p.72–78.

26 Briscoe, op. cit., p. 57.

27 McEnery, J. & DesHarnais, G. 1990. 'Culture shock'. *Training and Development* Journal, April, pp. 43–47.

28 Black, S., Gregersen, H.B. & Mendenhall, M.E. 1992. *Global assignments.* San Francisco: Jossey-Bass Publications, pp. 284–293.

29 Adler, op. cit. pp. 263–280.

30 Cox et al., p. 5.

31 Harvey, M. 1997. 'Dual-career expatriates: Expectations, adjustment and satisfaction with international relocation'. *Journal of International Business Studies,* 28(3), pp. 627–658.

32 Briscoe, op. cit., p. 73.

33 Black, S.J. & Mendenhall, M. 1991. 'A practical but theory-based framework for selecting cross-cultural training methods'. In Mendenhall, M. & Oddou, G. 1991. *International Human Resource Management.* Boston: PWS-Kent.

34 McEnery, J. & Harnais, D., op. cit., p. 46.

35 Briscoe, op. cit., p. 87.

36 Briscoe, op. cit., p. 88.

37 Deresky, op cit., pp. 294–295.

38 Black, S., Gregersen, H.B. & Mendenhall, M.E. 1992. *Global assignments.* San Francisco: Jossey-Bass Publications, Chapter 11.

39 Chi-sum Li in Cox et al., op. cit., p. 6.

40 Tung, R.L. 1992. 'Managing cross-national and intranational diversity'. Paper presented at the 52nd Academy of Management meeting, Las Vegas.

41 Adler, op cit., Chapter 10.

42 Nel, P. 1997. 'Acculturation and adjustment of the expatriate manager and his spouse'. Unpublished Honours thesis. Pretoria: University of Pretoria.

43 Adler, N.J. & Israeli, D.N. 1994. *Competitive frontiers: Women managers in a global economy.* Cambridge, Massachusetts: Basil Blackwell.

44 Adler, op. cit., p. 309.

45 Adler & Izraeli, op. cit., p. 7.

46 Briscoe, op. cit., p. 102.

47 Dowling et al., op. cit., p.104.

48 Black, Mendenhall & Odou, op. cit., pp. 165–182.

49 Black, Gregersen & Mendenhall op. cit., p. 201–214.

50 Deresky, op. cit., p. 301.

51 Briscoe, op. cit., p. 114.

52 Briscoe, op. cit., p. 118.

53 Deresky, op. cit., pp. 300–302.

9 Global marketing strategy

Key issues

- Globalisation of markets
- Strategic importance of international marketing
- The environment and cultural dimensions of international marketing
- The organisation and structure of international marketing
- International market assessment
- Market entry strategies
- International marketing strategy

9.1 Introduction

Marketing, a key ingredient in the success of any international enterprise, is the subject of this chapter. In the previous chapter we looked at the various types of international strategies that firms can use in pursuing their business goals. These strategies are aligned to actions that will lower the costs of value creation and/or differentiate the firm's products and services to meet diverse customer needs in pursuing their primary goal of optimal profitability in an extremely competitive international marketplace.[1] As discussed in Chapter 8, the first imperative of lowering the costs of value creation essentially requires that standardised products be marketed worldwide to consumers who basically have similar tastes and preferences, which can be achieved by following a **global strategy**. The second imperative of differentiating the firm's products and services to respond to and accommodate local conditions, preferences, and tastes, although at inherently higher costs, is achieved by following a **multidomestic strategy**.[2]

The international firm's products and services, and the strategy of the firm, whether global or multidomestic, provide the overall frame of reference within which its international marketing strategy will have to be developed and implemented. The marketing strategy, in turn, is based on and includes the four crucially important elements of the international firm's **marketing mix**, which are the product strategy, distribution strategy, promotion and communications strategy, and pricing strategy. The firm's overall strategic approach will therefore determine how, and to what extent, it is necessary to vary its marketing mix for different countries.

It is against this background that the international marketing function, international marketing management, and international marketing strategy, have to take place. This unquestionably requires the international marketing manager to know and understand the current diverse markets of his/her company, as well as potential future markets. He/she should also have the appropriate conceptual, interpersonal, and analytical skills for effective marketing management and decision-making in a global context.

In this chapter we accordingly first explore the concept of globalisation of markets and the strategic importance of international marketing. This is followed by a look at the international marketing environment and the cultural dimensions of international marketing before focusing on the basic approach to international market assessment and the identification of markets. Modes of entry into international markets are considered next, and the chapter ends with a discussion of the management of the marketing mix of the international firm and, accordingly, the firm's product, distribution, promotion and communications, and pricing strategies.

9.2 Globalisation of markets

In his seminal article 'The Globalisation of Markets', which appeared in 1983, Theodore Levitt argued that the world was seen to be rapidly moving towards a state of standardised products and **global markets** because of disappearing differences in national preferences and tastes. Levitt contended that:

> A powerful force drives the world toward a converging commonality, and that force is technology. It has proletarianised communication, transport, and travel. The result is a new commercial reality – the emergence of global markets for standardised consumer products on a previously unimagined scale of magnitude. ... Gone are accustomed differences in national or regional preferences. ... The globalisation of markets is at hand. With that, the multinational commercial world nears its end, and so does the multinational corporation. The multinational corporation operates in a number of countries and adjusts its products and practices to each – at high relative costs. The global corporation operates with resolute consistency – at low relative cost – as if the entire world were a single entity; it sells the same thing in the same way everywhere.[3]

As noted in Chapter 1, a number of noteworthy developments such as technological improvements in transportation and communication, declining barriers to trade, internationalisation of economic and financial systems, the collapse of communism, deregulation, regional integration, changing demographics, and changes in consumer expectations have, in a way, contributed to an accelerating trend in globalisation in at least some industries and products.[4] Examples of the latter are Coca-Cola, McDonald's hamburgers, Nike shoes, and Levi's jeans. Notwithstanding these developments, however, Levitt's predictions with regard to globalisation have yet to be realised, even after some 20 years.

In Chapter 1 (Section 1.4) it was explained that firms expand internationally mainly to allow them to increase their profitability in ways not available to purely domestic enterprises. These ways include:

- earning a greater return by deploying their distinctive skills, or core competencies, in the global market;
- realising location economies by dispersing particular value-creating activities to foreign locations where they can be performed most efficiently;
- realising greater experience curve economies, which reduce the costs of value creation.[5]

The latter two reasons, in particular, refer to the potential benefits of large production volumes, economies of scale, lower unit costs, and accordingly, standardised products, to serve predominantly uniform international or global markets.

Furthermore, companies choosing to expand for the above reasons have realised that to compete successfully, increasing their world-wide resource bases is a precondition for long-term growth and profitability.

In this regard, Keegan states emphatically that:

> A company that fails to go global is in danger of losing its domestic business to competitors with lower costs, greater experience, better products and, in a nutshell, more value for the customer. ... In most industries it is clear that the companies that will survive and prosper in the next century will be global enterprises. Companies that do not face the challenges and opportunities of going global will be absorbed by more dynamic enterprises if they are lucky; the others will simply disappear in the wake of the more dynamic competitors.[6]

Also based on the arguments advanced in Chapter 1, we accept the trend towards globalisation and that companies which

- establish a worldwide presence;
- standardise operations world-wide in one or more of the company's functional areas; and
- integrate their operations worldwide

are contributing to the globalisation of production and markets.[7]

It is for reasons like these that international and global marketing is indispensable for international enterprises to realise their full potential, and to grow and prosper.

9.3 Strategic importance of international marketing

In the previous section we discussed the phenomenon of **globalisation** and indicated that globalisation has generally increased competition worldwide, which in turn emphasises the importance of the international firm's strategic marketing initiatives in order to remain competitive. Before elaborating on the strategic importance of international marketing, however, we need to define the relevant marketing concepts.

Griffin and Pustay define **marketing** generically as

> the process of planning and executing the conception, pricing, promotion and distribution of ideas, goods, and services to create exchanges that satisfy individual and organisational objectives.[8]

Accordingly,

> **international marketing** is the extension of these activities across national boundaries.

Firms expanding into new markets in foreign countries must, *inter alia*, deal with differing political, cultural, and legal systems, and with unfamiliar economic and competitive conditions, advertising media, and distribution channels.

When firms enter the international market, the marketing environment becomes exceedingly more complex, and there are also more levels at which marketing can be approached. These levels for international marketing include the following:

- **domestic marketing**, as previously defined;
- **international marketing**, which now includes foreign markets and more environmental variables compared to a domestic setting;
- **global marketing**, which involves even larger, and more complex, international operations, as well as the co-ordination, integration, and control of a whole series of marketing programmes and activities in a substantially global network of synergistic operations.[9]

Keegan accordingly defines **global marketing** as the process of focusing the resources (people, money, and physical assets) and objectives of an organisation on global market opportunities and threats.[10]

The increasing complexity of **international marketing**, which distinguishes it from domestic marketing, is illustrated by the following example. At the one extreme, the extent of a firm's international marketing involvement will be confined to an agreement with a domestic or a foreign agent, who will generally take overall responsibility for the pricing, promotion, distribution, and foreign market development of the firm's products. At the other extreme, we have large-scale enterprises such as the Ford Motor Company, with its integrated network of manufacturing facilities world-wide and extensive operations in about 150 country markets.[11]

Seen in combination, the extent of international trade and the size of the global market-place provide a good indication of the importance of international marketing. In 1998, international trade in merchandise amounted to US$ 5,5 trillion, and trade in services to some US$1 trillion.[12] As far as population size is concerned, the world economy comprises more than 250 nations with a total population of around 5,8 billion people.[13] The regional composition of the global population in 1995 and as projected for 2050 is presented in Exhibit 9.1.

Continuing economic integration and, in particular, the formation of trading blocs, preferential trading areas, and free trade areas as discussed in Chapter 2 (Sections 2.5 and 2.6), will further contribute to expanded regional and global markets and increased international trade for the reasons given in the chapter. These developments, as well as those which were discussed in Section 9.2, serve to confirm the increasing importance of international marketing and provide the framework against which a firm's international marketing strategy will need to be developed and implemented.

9.4 The environment and cultural dimensions of international marketing

9.4.1 The environment of international marketing

Apart from the significant political, economic, cultural, legal, and technological environmental changes which were highlighted in Chapters 3 to 6, a number of factors and forces within these broad categories impact more directly on the market-place and consequently on the

Exhibit 9.1: Regional breakdown of global population

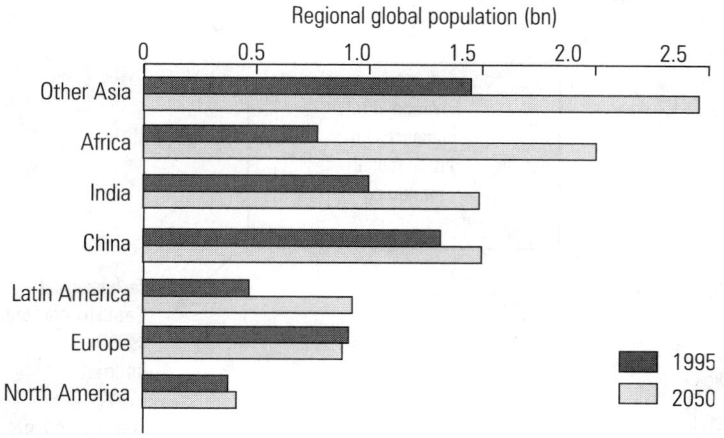

SOURCE: Population Division, Department of Economic and Social Affairs, United Nations Secretariat, *World Population Prospects. The 1996 Revision,* United Nations, New York, in Doole, I. & Lowe, R. 1999. *International marketing strategy,* 2nd ed. London: International Thomson Business Press, p. 15.

firm's marketing function. These environmental influences, which have a more direct bearing on international marketing and with which the international marketing manager has to cope, appear in Exhibit 9.2.

In the discussion that follows, we look at one set of influences in the group of social/cultural factors in Exhibit 9.2, namely the global shifts in population and other demographic changes, since these influences impact directly on the overall market-place and, therefore, on the function of international marketing management. The preferential treatment of these influences should not be taken to mean that the others in Exhibit 9.2, and even the broader environmental issues, are less important. Although this discussion will be limited to these influences, and to the consideration of cultural dimensions later on, the entire spectrum of factors, issues, and influences with regard to all relevant factors, need to be considered in the firm's overall environmental scanning system.

Starting with a macro-perspective, it is important that marketing management should know to what extent continents vary in **population size** and **population growth**. World-wide, Asia has almost three-fifths of the world's population, while Africa has the most rapidly growing population. The regional distribution of world population in Exhibit 9.1 (p. 255), which also shows the expected population size of these regions by 2050 and from which expected population growth rates up to 2050 can be derived, provides invaluable information for the international marketer.

From an international marketing perspective, population growth signals expanding future markets for a firm's products and markets. A precondition for this to happen is that the quality of life in general, and income levels in particular, of individuals in the regions and

Exhibit 9.2: The environmental influences on international marketing

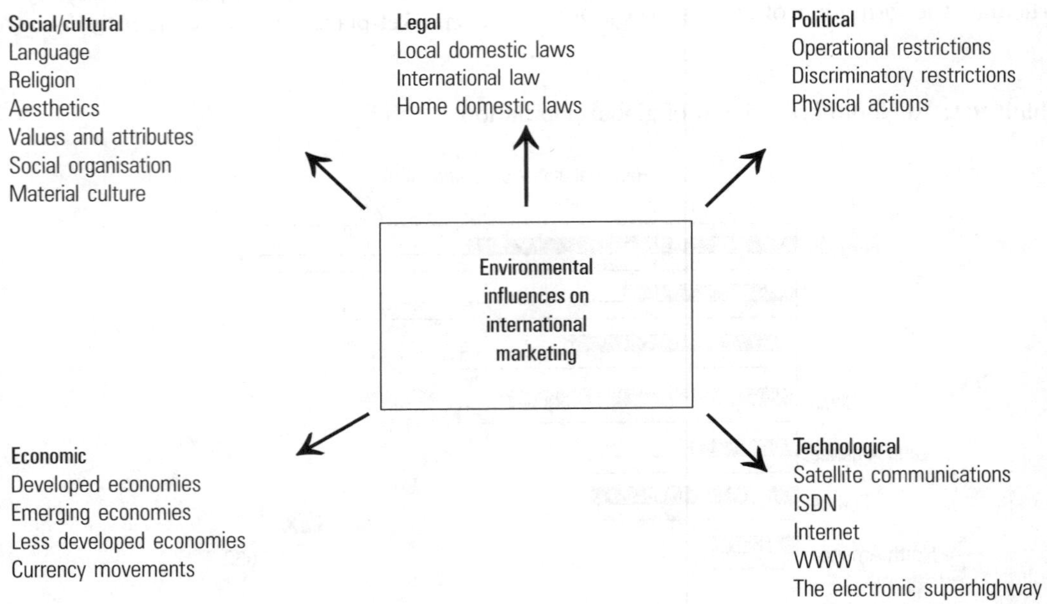

SOURCE: Doole, I. & Lowe, R. 1999. *International marketing strategy.* 2nd ed. London: International Thomson Business Press, p. 11.

Exhibit 9.3: Top and bottom countries for GNP/capita (1995) and average growth rates of GNP/capita and population (1985–1995)

Ranking	Country*	1995 GNP/Capita (current US$)	1995 Population (millions)	Annual growth rates (percentage) GNP/Capita†	Annual growth rates (percentage) Population
1	Luxembourg	$41,210	0,4	1,0%	1,1%
2	Switzerland	40,630	7,0	0,2	0,8
3	Japan	39,640	125,2	2,9	0,4
4	Norway	31,940	4,4	1,6	0,5
5	Denmark	29,890	5,2	1,5	0,2
6	Germany	27,510	81,9	n.a.	0,5
7	United States	26,980	263,1	1,4	0,9
8	Austria	26,890	8,1	1,9	0,6
9	Singapore	26,730	3,0	6,2	1,8
10	France	24,990	58,1	1,5	0,5
11	Iceland	24,950	0,3	0,3	1,1
12	Belgium	24,710	10,1	2,2	0,3
13	Netherlands	24,000	15,5	1,8	0,6
14	Sweden	23,750	8,8	–0,1	0,6
15	Hong Kong	22,990	6,2	4,8	1,3
16	Finland	20,580	5,1	–0,2	0,4
17	Canada	19,380	29,6	0,4	1,3
18	Italy	19,020	57,2	1,7	0,1
19	Australia	18,720	18,1	1,4	1,4
20	United Kingdom	18,700	58,5	1,4	0,3
21	United Arab Emirates	17,400	2,5	–3,5	5,8
22	Kuwait	17,390	1,7	0,9	–0,3
23	Israel	15,920	5,5	2,5	2,7
24	Ireland	14,710	3,6	5,2	0,1
25	New Zealand	14,340	3,6	0,6	1,0
26	Spain	13,580	39,2	2,6	0,2
27	Bahamas	11,940	0,3	–1,0	1,7
141	Togo	310	4,1	–2,8	3,0
142	Kenya	280	26,7	0,1	2,9
143	Cambodia	270	10,0	2,0	3,0
144	Nigeria	260	111,3	1,2	2,9
145	Yemen, Rep. of	260	15,3	n.a.	4,2
146	Mali	250	9,8	0,6	2,8
147	Haiti	250	7,2	–5,2	2,0
148	Guinea-Bissau	250	1,1	1,8	1,9
149	Bangladesh	240	119,8	2,1	2,0
150	Uganda	240	19,2	2,8	3,0
151	Vietnam	240	73,5	4,2	2,2
152	Burkina Faso	230	10,4	–0,1	2,8
153	Madagascar	230	13,7	–2,0	3,1
154	Niger	220	9,0	–2,1	3,2
155	Nepal	200	21,5	2,4	2,5
156	Chad	180	6,4	0,5	2,5
157	Sierra Leone	180	4,2	–3,4	1,6
158	Rwanda	180	6,4	–5,0	0,6
159	Malawi	170	9,8	–0,7	3,1
160	Burundi	160	6,3	–1,3	2,8
161	Zaire	120	43,8	–8,5	3,2
162	Tanzania	120	29,6	0,9	3,1
163	Ethiopia	100	56,4	–0,5	2,6
164	Mozambique	80	16,2	3,6	1,8

NOTES: n.a. = not available

* Only 164 countries for which data were reported to the World Bank are listed.

† GNP/capita growth rates are real.

SOURCE: *World Development Report*, 1997 (Washington, DC: World Bank, 1997), pp. 6–7, 34–36, in Ball, D.A. & McCulloch, W.H. 1999. *International business*, 7th ed. Burr Ridge, Illinois: McGraw-Hill, p. 62.

countries concerned, increase at a faster rate than the growth in population. In the case of certain low-priced, mass-produced products which are mass-consumed, such as soft drinks, cigarettes, and soap, population size alone could serve as an indication of potential consumption. The inherently important marketing reality, however, is that for products not related to the above categories, larger numbers of people alone do not necessarily constitute expanding international markets which will be profitable – unless they are accompanied by sufficiently high and sustainable economic growth.[14]

Consequently, it is imperative that for the identification and evaluation of marketing opportunities in other countries, population growth and GNP growth rates should be considered simultaneously. As indicated before, where GNP growth occurs at a faster rate than the growth in population, markets are most probably expanding, whereas the converse may indicate stagnating or contracting markets. Exhibit 9.3 (p. 257) provides a number of interesting examples of countries that reflect situations like these.

Although few of the top countries had negative GNP per capita growth rates, a country like Zaire in the bottom group, with a negative annual growth rate in GNP per capita of -8,5% and an annual population growth rate of 3,2 %, illustrates the lack of market potential referred to above.

Where market segmentation on the basis of age is of extreme importance in domestic marketing strategy, it becomes even more so in international marketing. The reason for this is that the distribution of age groups varies significantly between countries and, furthermore, does not remain static, because birth and fertility rates are generally higher in developing countries than in developed countries. Furthermore, youthful populations of developing countries are larger than those in developed countries, a fact which has far-reaching implications in targeting markets for a firm's products.[15] This is apart from other factors such as culture, which reflect different local preferences and tastes in different countries.

Exhibit 9.4 (p. 259) illustrates the population distribution by age and gender for developed and developing nations respectively, as well as the expected increase or decrease for each category between 1996 and 2020.

While providing invaluable information for international marketing purposes, these exhibits not only serve to confirm the extreme complexity of international marketing, but also underline its strategic importance in ensuring the sustainable growth and profitability of international companies in increasingly competitive global markets.

Referring to the environmental influences on international marketing as shown in Exhibit 9.2 (p. 256), the focus has been on the increasing importance of population and demographic influences in international marketing. The marketing manager should identify all the relevant environmental factors pertaining to the company's specific situation and assess the implications of each factor or influence in that situation. This implies the evaluation of all the influences in the economic, sociocultural, legal, political and technological groups of environmental factors in Exhibit 9.2. In view of the importance of the cultural dimension in international marketing, this factor is discussed in the following section.

9.4.2 Cultural dimensions of international marketing

The concept of **culture** was defined and the **cultural environment** of international business extensively discussed in Chapter 3. Social and cultural differences between countries could have far-reaching implications for international business in general, and international management in particular. The way in which international management perceives, understands, and approaches culture in international business operations could often mean the difference between success and failure in a specific situation, which has been vividly illustrated in the case of Parris-Rogers International in Chapter 3. This section will briefly consider how culture, as

Exhibit 9.4: Population by age and sex – 1996 and 2020 (millions)

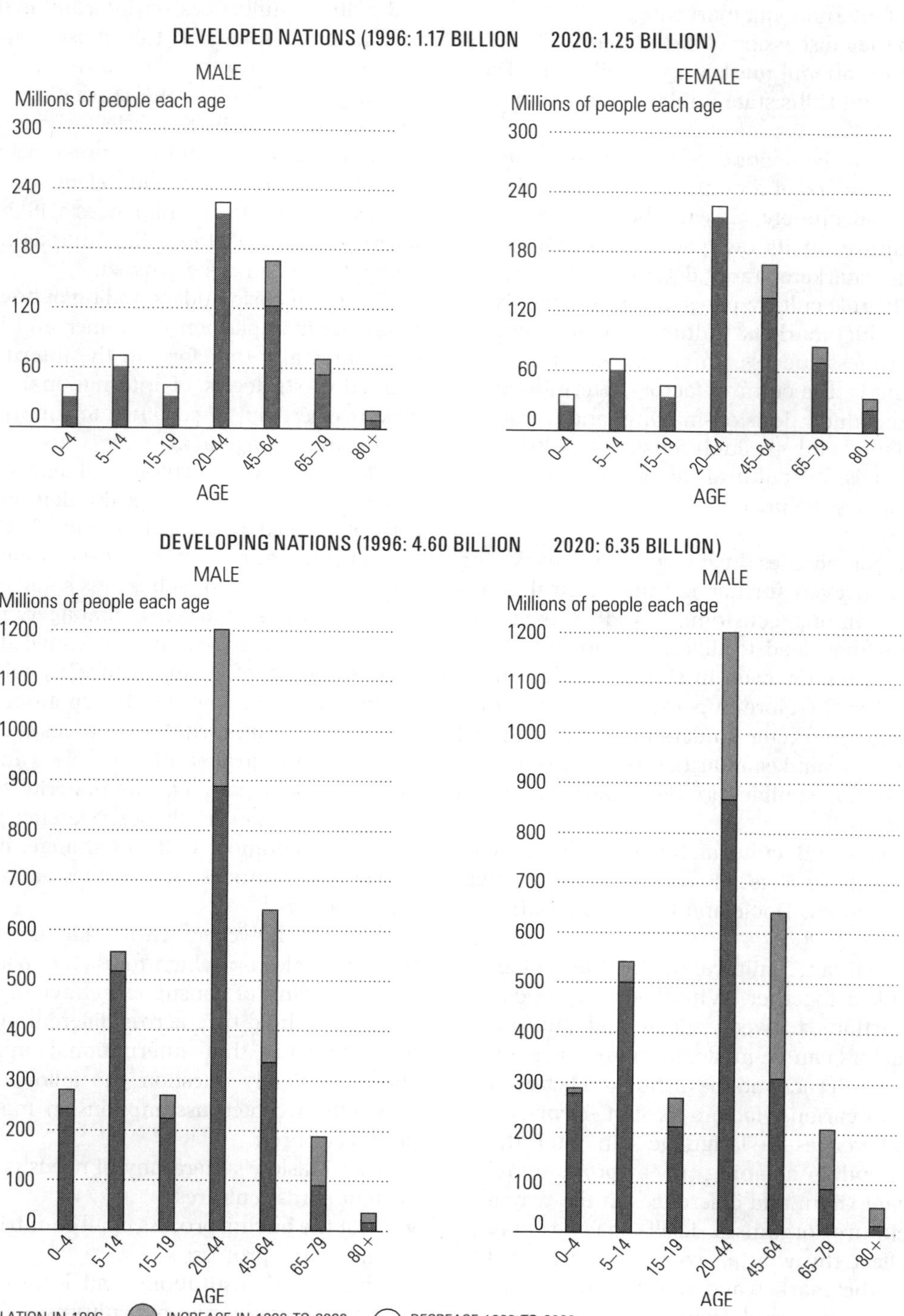

SOURCE: Based on U.S. Bureau of Census projections, www.census.gov/lpc/ored/wp96/wp96a1.pdf (7 December 1997), in Ball & McCulloch, op. cit., p. 217.

an environmental variable, relates to the function of international marketing.

In their discussion of the influence of culture on international marketing Mühlbacher, Dahringer and Leihs state fundamentally that

> ... all behaviour occurs within the framework of a culture. Thus, in order to adequately assess the impact of culture on its own business activities, any marketer must determine the specific role culture plays in the company's product markets. Culture may influence business success via consumer culture, that is, the cultural factors determining consumer decision-making and behaviour, and through business culture, that is, all cultural factors influencing business behaviour.[16]

What complicates the international marketing situation even further is that cultural differences among customer and stakeholder groups may lead to differences in perception and behaviour, even in similar product markets. It is therefore imperative that the international marketer understands the cultural differences and similarities that exist in the search for similar product markets across countries.[17]

Social and cultural factors influence virtually all aspects of consumer and buyer behaviour. As Doole and Lowe point out:

> Social and cultural factors are often linked together. While meaningful distinctions between social and cultural factors can be made, in many ways the two interact and the distinction between the various factors is not clear-cut. Differences in language can alter the intended meaning of a promotional campaign, and differences in the way a culture organises itself socially may affect the way a product is positioned in the market and the benefits a consumer may seek from that product.[18]

Since it is not possible to discuss all the social and cultural influences on international marketing, only some of the most important influences of consumer and buyer behaviour as a key ingredient in the marketing process will be looked at in this brief overview, and given that cultural and consumer behaviour can also influence the four elements of the marketing mix, these influences will be considered where the individual marketing mix elements as such are discussed.

Clearly, a basic understanding of how these components impact on consumer and buying behaviour, and therefore on the international marketing strategies of international companies, is of crucial importance to international marketing management.

The way in which culture influences buying behaviour and the consumer decision process is aptly illustrated in Exhibit 9.5 (p. 261), fully realising that the process is, in reality, much more complex in international business situations.

International marketing managers need to analyse culture, based on their knowledge and understanding of what culture is, what the cultural environment for international business looks like, and what the sources of cultural values are. Cultural analysis involves an examination of such variables as material culture, language, religion, aesthetics, reference groups, cultural adaptation, cultural change, cultural universals, attitudes and values, and social organisations.[19]

Usunier, however, warns that the theoretical principles on which marketers base their understanding of consumer behaviour do not necessarily hold true across different cultures, and contends that international marketers should critically question the following four generally accepted assumptions in marketing across cultures:

- that Maslow's hierarchy of needs is consistent across cultures;
- that the buying process in all countries is an individual process;
- that social institutions and local conventions are similar across cultures;

Exhibit 9.5: Cultural influences on buyer behaviour

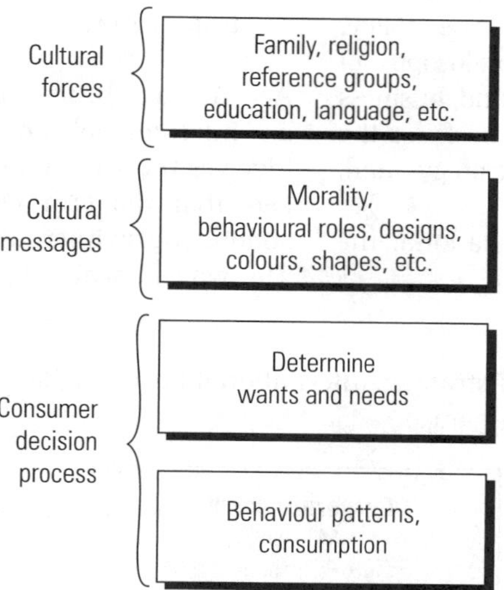

SOURCE: Chee, H. & Harris, R. 1998. *Global marketing strategy.* London: Financial Times/Pitman Publishing. p. 140.

- that the consumer buying process is consistent across cultures.[20]

It is accepted that the foregoing discussion, at best, only touched on certain aspects of consumer behaviour as a key ingredient in the cultural context of marketing, and that a complete picture has in no way been given.

Previous discussions and the complex set of largely integrated cultural variables once more underline the complexities, as well as the challenges, facing the international marketing manager when considering appropriate strategies for a number of culturally diverse foreign markets when seeking competitive advantage.

9.5 The organisation and structure of international marketing

Once a firm decides to enter the international market, it must formulate international and global marketing strategies consistent with its overall corporate policy and strategy. We now look at the **organisation** and **structure** of international marketing, the assessment of international markets, and market entry modes, before discussing how the marketing strategy for an international enterprise evolves and is developed on the basis of the key elements of product strategy, distribution strategy, promotion and communications strategy, and pricing strategy in Section 9.8.

International firms often organise their market activities as a separate, self-contained function within the enterprise. From basic business principles we know that the marketing function affects, and is in turn affected by, all other organisational functions such as financial management, accounting, operations management, human resource management, and purchasing and logistics management. These interrelationships require that all the international marketing activities comply and are in harmony with the corporate policy, corporate strategy, and the business strategy, including business unit strategies of the company.[21] This hierarchical relationship to ensure the co-ordinated pursuance of its mission and goals by a multinational company, is illustrated in Exhibit 9.6. The company's **international business plan** starts with the development of a corporate policy, which includes the mission and philosophy of the company corporate strategy and business unit strategy, and then forms the basis for the development of a marketing strategy and, finally, a marketing plan.

Having decided to become international, the firm needs to decide:

- which international markets to select, and
- what type of international marketing entry strategy to use.

Accordingly, the first step in the development of an international or global market strategy involves the selection of the international markets that the firm would wish to serve, by conducting an international market assessment. The way in which to assess the international

Exhibit 9.6: Hierarchical levels of strategic international business plan development: from corporate policy to the marketing plan

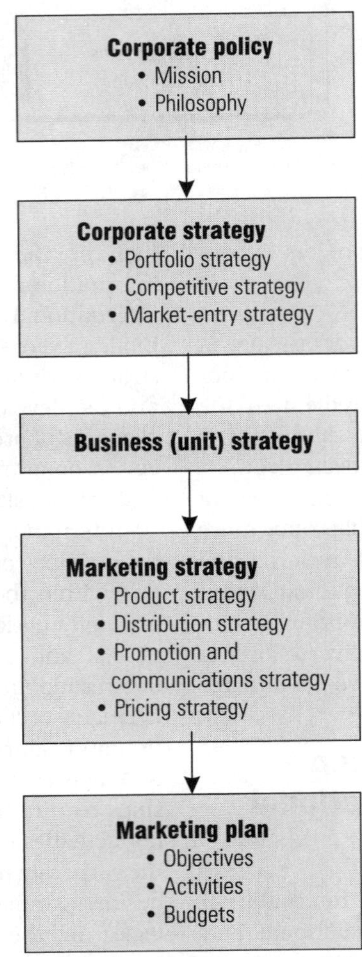

SOURCE: Adapted from Mühlbacher, H., Dahringer, L. & Leihs, H. 1999. *International marketing.* 2nd ed. London: International Thomson Business Press, p. 827.

market will be explored in Section 9.6, and the various market entry modes in Section 9.7.

9.6 International market assessment

Rugman and Hodgetts state that:

> international marketing strategy starts with international market assessment, an evaluation of the goods and services that the multinational enterprise can sell in the global marketplace.[22]

When expanding internationally, companies must decide which markets should be served, and where production should be located to serve these markets. According to Daniels and Radebaugh, many service industries such as hotels, retailing, and construction, must locate their facilities near the customers in foreign markets. In other industries, such as car manufacturing, production and sales may be located in different countries; an example being Ford serving the Italian market with cars primarily produced in its German facilities.[23]

Whether a company is considering whether to expand internationally by selling more of its existing products or by adding new products to its product line, or a combination of these two approaches, it still has to decide where to operate in terms of marketing and production, and also what portion of its production and marketing operations to locate and execute within each of the countries in which it envisages becoming involved.[24] Even though it is faced with situations as described above, the company's decision-making process generally has to conform to and support the company's overall corporate policy, corporate strategy, and business strategies, as previously mentioned.

To enable companies to decide how and where to expand internationally, all promising opportunities and options in this regard are evaluated by means of **international market assessment**, a process which involves a number of analytical screening steps to identify viable international markets for the company's products and services.[25] Care should be taken, however, not to overlook possible promising opportunities such as the markets in some of the emerging economies,[26] but at the same time to avoid unnecessary costs of evaluating too many options.

9.6.1 Initial screening: basic need and potential

The object of this initial screening step is to establish, without too much cost and trouble, whether there is a potential need for the company's existing and/or new products and services. This step will assess issues such as the trade and import policies of government, the types of products being imported, possible excess capacity in the industries concerned, and basic demographic factors such as population variables for the countries being investigated. There should be significantly fewer countries to be further assessed after this initial screening.

9.6.2 Second screening: financial and economic conditions

In the second screening step, the aim is to further reduce the list of prospective countries by eliminating those that do not meet certain predetermined financial and economic criteria. Investment decisions are made on the basis of expected opportunities as determined by expected revenues less costs, and taking into account risk factors that could prevent the opportunities being realised. In this step we consider opportunities, while risks will be evaluated in the third screening step.

Financial assessment criteria include interest rate levels, inflation rates, expected returns on investment, the availability of credit, exchange rate regimes, and spending habits of consumers.

Economic indicators and considerations as indications of the relative market strengths of the geographic areas targeted for potential international operations, include market size, market identity and market growth.

- **Market size**. Daniels and Radebaugh maintain that expectations of large market and sales growth are probably the major attraction of a potential location for expanding operations.[27] One indicator of note is the relative size of each of the markets as a percentage of the total world market. Past, current, and projected sales data on a country-by-country basis, GNP per capita, growth rates of income classes, and level of industrialisation, also provide useful data. As mentioned before, some of the developing countries, especially those in Asia, could develop into exceedingly attractive markets in future, where countries like Taiwan, Indonesia, and Thailand are expected to be among the top 15 countries based on GDP, while China is expected to surpass the United States economy by the year 2020. Even more significant is the fact that the developing countries' share of world output will increase from around 44% in 1990 to just more than 60% by 2020. The corresponding decrease for the rich industrial countries in this respect will be from 56 % in 1990 down to below 40% by 2020. A new triad comprising North America, Europe, and East Asia, is foreseen.[28]
- **Market intensity**. The importance of market intensity as indicator is that it reflects the relative purchasing power in a country, compared to other countries, indicating potential for marketing success, at least in certain industries.
- **Market growth** can be correlated with growth in annual sales, preferably on an industry basis, and country by country. The importance of population and income per capita as two important determinants of the demand for goods and services, and the fact that a large and growing market is a location-specific advantage, form part of the assessment in this second screening step, which should further eliminate a number of prospective countries.

For the economic assessment in this step, certain quantitative techniques like trend analysis and regression analysis can be used.

9.6.3 Third screening: political and legal forces

In this screening step, political and legal forces that could influence the attractiveness of a potential foreign market are identified. Among others, these forces include entry barriers in the form of import restrictions, restraints on local ownership of businesses, production quotas, the limitation on repatriation of profits and royalties, the stability of government, the absence of – or only limited protection of – property rights with regard to patents, trademarks, and copyrights, and the prevalence of pirating and counterfeit operations. Some of the required information in this step may be difficult to obtain, or unreliable. This part of the overall assessment clearly also evaluates certain potential and real risks on a country-by-country basis, using techniques such as grids and matrices, the most popular being the **opportunity-risk matrix** and the **country attractiveness – company strength matrix**. Daniels and Radebaugh point out that by using an opportunity-risk matrix, a company can:

- decide on appropriate indicators and weigh them;
- evaluate each country on the basis of the weighted indicators;
- plot the data to illustrate relative country placements based on a combined consideration of opportunity and risk for each country.[29]

Once again, relevant data to construct the matrix may be difficult to obtain, especially in so far as the projected or future values are concerned. It is advisable to make use of professional expertise in considering the use of this matrix.

The country attractiveness – company strength matrix serves to highlight, on a country-by-country basis, the fit of a company's product to the country concerned. Since it is not always possible to base this type of matrix entirely on objective data, and for other explanatory reasons, the results of the matrix must be interpreted with caution and preferably only used as a guideline for decision-making.

Countries that have survived the third screening are accordingly assessed further in the following step.

9.6.4 Fourth screening: sociocultural forces

Having dealt extensively with social and cultural forces in Chapter 3, and subsequently in Section 9.4, it should be clear that this screening step considers all identifiable social norms and values of a specific country, and assesses the potential influences thereof, should the company decide on operations in that country. Work habits and employment practices vary from one country to another, as do social customs, which could affect the adaptation and effectiveness of expatriate personnel if the decision is made to locate operations in a specific country, as discussed in Chapter 8. Of importance to such a decision would possibly be the degree of expected fit between company culture and that of the country.

9.6.5 Fifth screening: competitive environment

This last screening step focuses almost exclusively on competitive situations and forces prevailing in those selected countries which have survived the first four screening steps. As Rugman and Hodgetts point out, a final decision on whether to establish operations in a specific country will be based on the extent of the competition in each of the countries, and in the specific industry or industries of importance to the company.[30] Given the competitive levels in the various countries, companies will have to decide whether they are prepared to enter strong competitive markets, being aware of the consequences that such a decision will have, or to avoid competitive situations such as these. Because companies differ, each company is likely to base its decision on its own unique circumstances, taking into account the results obtained from the entire screening process.

9.6.6 Final selection

Assessment findings will normally be supplemented by information gained from professionals in the field, on-site visits, and interviews with government officials and trade representatives. The company will then decide as to whether or not it should locate its production and/or marketing operations in one or more foreign countries. In the case of a positive decision, much of the information that was gathered, and the analysis done for the international market assessment, will serve as invaluable external information for the development of the company's marketing strategy and operations in the target country or countries. In the following section we discuss the market entry options available to the international firm.

9.7 Market entry strategies

9.7.1 Overview

In Section 9.6 international market assessment was considered as an evaluation process for the selection of foreign markets for the firm. The alternative **modes of entry** that firms can follow to serve foreign markets, which include exporting, licensing, or franchising to foreign firms, turnkey projects, joint ventures with foreign firms, and setting up wholly-owned subsidiaries in a foreign country, will now be reviewed.[31]

The **market entry decision** often represents the first step for most small and medium-sized enterprises wanting to expand internationally. For established companies in the international arena, however, the challenge lies in how to exploit opportunities in their existing international markets effectively and, even more important, how to enter new and emerging markets.[32]

The complexity of the market entry decision becomes clear when we realise that, with each market entry mode, there are advantages and disadvantages, the extent of which is determined by factors such as trade barriers, transport costs, political risks, economic risks, and firm strategy. Furthermore, each mode of entry is associated with varying degrees of company control over operations, and has varying degrees of risk. For example, companies that decide on a licensing arrangement with a foreign firm, will generally have little or no influence on issues such as product development, provision, and pricing in the licensee's market, but at the same time will experience relatively low risk. Conversely, deciding to establish a wholly-owned subsidiary in a foreign country will give the company a high degree of control in terms of operating and marketing decisions, but will involve significantly higher costs and risks when compared to the licensing alternative.[33] The largely linear relationship between a firm's level of control and the degree of risk associated with reference to a number of entry modes is illustrated in Exhibit 9.7.

Because of these complexities, differences between countries, and the dynamic nature of international markets, it is almost inconceivable that a firm will adopt one specific entry mode for all its foreign markets. The choice of market entry mode consequently involves a fundamental and critical decision in the context of the firm's international marketing function. Not only will the entry strategy that is decided on influence the firm's existing marketing programme, it will also have an effect on the way in which vital company resources are to be deployed.

According to Doole and Lowe, firms consider criteria such as the following when selecting an appropriate market entry mode:

- the company's objectives and expectations relating to the size and value of the anticipated international business;
- the skill, abilities, and attitudes of the company management towards international marketing;

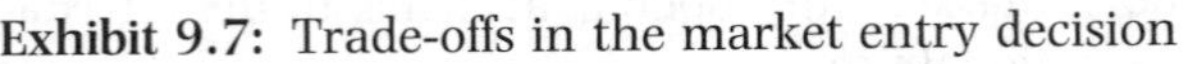
Exhibit 9.7: Trade-offs in the market entry decision

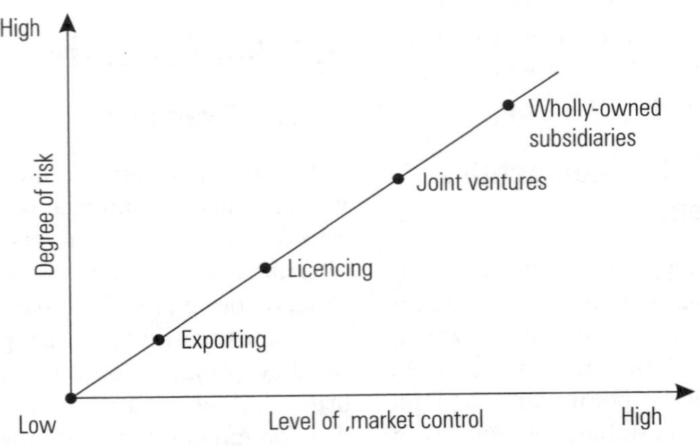

SOURCE: Adapted from Chee & Harris, op. cit. p. 292.

- the company's existing foreign market involvement;
- the size of the company's financial resources;
- the nature and power of the competition in the prospective market(s).[34]

With regard to the increasing importance worldwide of strategic alliances, Hill explains that although companies have various motives for entering into strategic alliance agreements with competitors or potential competitors, these motives often include market access, and that, in this sense, we regard a strategic alliance as a mode of entry. But the term 'strategic alliance' is often used loosely to describe a range of arrangements between actual and potential competitors, including licensing arrangements, joint ventures, and cross-shareholding deals.[35] Strategic alliances are accordingly referred to here only as modes of entry, since they are dealt with comprehensively in Chapter 11.

The various alternative market entry modes available to the firm are now examined and the factors that determine the optimal entry mode are considered in conclusion.

9.7.2 Alternative market entry modes

In this section we briefly discuss exporting, turnkey projects, licensing, franchising and joint ventures, as well as the establishment of wholly-owned subsidiaries in foreign countries, as alternative modes of market entry for an international firm.

(a) Exporting

The simplest and least expensive way for a firm to sell its products overseas is by **exporting**, and it has a choice between indirect and direct exporting methods. **Indirect exporting** involves the sale of a firm's products in foreign markets through an export agent who is based in its home market. In **direct exporting**, the firm sells its products directly to an importer or buyer in a foreign market without an intermediary being involved in the process. In direct exporting the firm is also actively involved in the export process, which requires greater expense, attention to detail, and commitment of more of its resources than in indirect exporting. However, it has more control over the process, compared to indirect exporting. Both indirect and direct exporting normally constitute the first step in a firm's international operations, particularly for small and medium-sized enterprises. However, such enterprises generally progress to the other modes of entry as they gain experience in serving foreign markets. Whether indirect or direct, exporting as a mode of entry has specific advantages and disadvantages.

The advantages of exporting are that it requires a minimum of financial commitment (indirect exporting in particular), it is relatively easy to initiate, experts in international marketing who know the markets for the firm's products are involved, and the risk on the part of the manufacturing firm as such is relatively low. Other advantages are that it avoids the high cost of establishing manufacturing operations in the host country, and it can help the firm to realise experience curve and location economies by locating and producing in an optimal location and exporting large volumes from there. This was how Sony became dominant in the TV market and Matsushita in the VCR market.[36]

Disadvantages of indirect exporting, in particular, are that the firm does not have control over the marketing of its products in foreign markets, and middlemen often also represent numerous other clients, which means that at best the marketing of its products receives divided attention. Middlemen may also suddenly decide to terminate their relationship with the firm. From the firm's perspective, a serious disadvantage with long-term implications is that its own managerial and marketing staff do not gain the necessary experience because they are not involved in the exporting process.

While these disadvantages also apply to direct exporting to a greater or lesser degree, other disadvantages of exporting are that high transport costs can make it uneconomical, particularly in the case of bulk products with a high volume-to-value ratio, such as cement, sugar, and bulk pharmaceutical products.

Further disadvantages of this mode of entry are that exporting from the firm's home base may not be the best option if other lower-cost locations for manufacturing are available abroad, especially for firms following a global or a transnational strategy. Many American firms have moved manufacturing operations for clothing to countries like Indonesia, the Philippines, and Thailand, where labour costs are low and economies of scale for worldwide exports easily achieved. Existing tariff barriers in target countries can also make exports uneconomical. Threats of imposing barriers to trade by the USA government were the primary reason why a company like Honda established manufacturing facilities in the United States. Lastly, where the firm appoints a marketing agent in the host country to sell its products there, the agent's involvement in also having to sell competitors' products may prove to be a major drawback in such an exporting operation.

(b) Turnkey projects

In **turnkey projects**, contractors generally design, construct, and commission large industrial and infrastructure-related projects. A turnkey agreement normally includes the training of staff for the project. On a specified date the 'key' to a project is handed over to the client, which then ends the contractor's involvement in it. Chemical plants, petroleum refineries, hydro-electric schemes, toll roads, and airports are examples of turnkey projects. A turnkey project is characterised by a limited life, but is regarded as a mode of entry since it involves the exporting of design and process technology to foreign countries.

Advantages of turnkey projects include earning substantial income for the companies concerned and valuable foreign exchange for the home country, the fact that it might be the only means of selling the firm's expertise where the governments of host countries limit foreign direct investment (FDI), or where the nationalisation or expropriation of assets are possibilities.

The three main disadvantages of turnkey projects are the absence of a long-term interest in the foreign countries concerned – especially if they are promising prospective markets, the fact that the client itself could become a major international competitor of the firm, and finally that the firm's process technology is divulged and it could lose its competitive advantage as a result.

(c) Licensing

According to Hill:

> A licensing agreement is an arrangement whereby a licensor grants the rights to intangible property to another entity (the licensee) for a specified period of time, and in return, the licensor receives a royalty fee from the licensee.[37]

One advantage of international **licensing** is that the licensor in the home country generally does not have to bear the development costs and risks of entering a foreign market. Licensing is often the only option for firms which lack the capital to establish overseas operations. It is also a viable option for a firm which is unwilling to commit large financial resources to politically risky and unstable markets.

In countries with barriers to foreign investment, licensing might be the only alternative to the establishment of operations in these countries. Licensing is also an option where a firm has marketable intellectual property, but does not want to develop this itself. Examples are where AT&T invented the transistor circuit and licensed the manufacturing of the technology to a number of companies, including Texas Instruments, and where Coca-Cola has licensed its famous trademark to clothing manufacturers for designs on T-shirts and sweaters.[38]

Three major disadvantages of licensing are that:

- the firm has no control over manufacturing, marketing, and strategies in the foreign firm

as far as experience curve and location economies are concerned, because licensees typically decide on and set up their own manufacturing facilities;
- licensing prevents the firm from optimally co-ordinating its activities across countries;
- firms can lose control of their know-how and core competence and, consequently, their competitive advantage.

The classical case where the American firm RCA licensed its colour-TV technology to a number of Japanese companies, including Sony and Matsushita, and the latter used and improved on it to enter the USA market and secured a bigger market share than the one for the RCA brand, illustrates the danger inherent in licensing.[39]

(d) Franchising

Although very similar to licensing, **franchising** involves longer-term commitments than licensing, where the franchisor sells intangible property such as a trademark to the franchisee and obtains the latter's contractual undertaking to comply strictly with all the rules on how to conduct its business. An excellent example of this is McDonald's restaurants, where operations are highly standardised. A franchisor will often provide training to the franchisee's staff and assist in operating the business. Franchisors normally receive an initial payment and a royalty fee based on some percentage of the franchisee's sales income. While manufacturing enterprises primarily use licensing to gain entry to foreign markets, service firms use franchising.

The main advantage of franchising as a mode of entry is similar to that of licensing, since the franchisor has to bear little or no costs and risks. With franchising as an entry mode, a service firm can rapidly develop a franchise network of firms in foreign markets that could be very profitable.

Some of the disadvantages of international franchises as a mode of market entry include:
- the difficulty of maintaining quality control across countries;
- customers and even prospective customers may be driven away by a bad experience;
- geographical distance from the franchisor's home country which may make it difficult to detect poor quality and inefficient operations;
- the sheer number of franchisees, as in the case of McDonald's and Kentucky Fried Chicken, which can complicate quality and other types of control across countries.

Establishing a master franchisee through a joint venture to take responsibility for looking after franchisees in a certain region, has alleviated the above problems to a certain degree.

(e) Joint ventures

An **international joint venture** is a business collaboration between companies based in two or more countries who share ownership in an enterprise established jointly for the production and/or distribution of goods and services.[40] Joint ventures have long been a popular method of foreign market entry. Typically, the two parties to a joint venture each hold a 50% ownership stake, but the ratio can vary, depending on the specific circumstances. The larger a joint venture shareholding, the greater the control or influence of that company with regard to joint operations.

Hill quotes an example where the Fuji-Xerox joint venture was formed, because Xerox was prohibited from doing business in the Japanese market through the establishment of a wholly-owned subsidiary, because of Japan's barriers to investment at that stage. Accordingly, Xerox set up the joint venture with Fuji-Xerox and licensed its know-how to the joint venture.[41]

Joint ventures have a number of advantages. Firstly, they may be the only available option for foreign market entry and setting up business in another country in cases where industries are regarded as politically sensitive, such as the petroleum, aircraft-manufacturing, transportation, and utility industries, and/or st-government policy precludes for- ct investment and therefore the establishment of wholly-owned subsidiaries. Secondly, where a firm's resources are limited and its core competence not amenable to licensing, a greater number of international markets can be entered through joint ventures than through wholly-owned subsidiaries, even when these are permitted. Thirdly, multinational companies can form joint ventures with enterprises in developing countries without much capital outlay from the side of the multinational, but it traditionally provides the technological know-how in exchange for part-equity ownership in such enterprises. The same argument for a joint venture could be considered where an enterprise in a developing country is in need of managerial rather than technological know-how.

Fourthly, joint ventures are also beneficial where the local companies can provide the foreign partner with raw materials. Fifthly, a firm can benefit from a local partner's knowledge of the host country's market and competitive conditions, culture, language, and political, legal, and economic systems. Lastly, when the development costs and risks of opening a foreign market are high, these costs and risks can be shared with a joint venture partner.[42]

Some disadvantages associated with joint ventures include the risks that the company runs of giving away its core competence or technological know-how to the joint venture partner, and that the joint venture dilutes the company's influence and control over other subsidiaries, especially with regard to decisions to exploit the advantage of experience curve and location economies where global or transnational strategies are concerned. Lastly, joint ventures with shared ownership arrangements have the potential for conflict, especially with regard to control. However, international joint ventures, including the various forms of strategic alliances associated with these, remain effective market entry modes in international business.

The big experiment

Les Baxter, chief executive of MB Technologies, believes that the Internet is central to the paradigm shift with regard to the way in which business is done, and that this paradigm shift will be complete three to four years from now.

MB Tech recently acquired a 50% stake in Live Technology for R30 million from Paradigm Interactive Media with a view to a listing on Nasdaq within a year. LiveTech has become one of the top 100 Internet companies in the United States, and is the only group outside the USA that has achieved this status. One of its divisions, LiveBuilder, provides inexpensive ways for designing websites for e-commerce purposes to corporate Internet users. LiveTech has identified a market niche for the quick design and establishment of websites. In May 1999, LiveTech had 152 000 subscribers, and aims for 400 000 by the end of 1999. According to Baxter, there were 5 million websites at this time, and these were expected to increase to 1 trillion by 2003. Currently Internet traffic doubles every 10 days, and Internet advertising every year. Notwithstanding the intense competition, LiveTech and MB Tech have tremendous potential, which has largely, if not exclusively, been made possible by MB Tech forming an international joint venture.

SOURCE: Peter Pittendrigh, *Finansies & Tegniek*, 14 May 1999, p. 64 (translated).

(f) Wholly-owned subsidiaries

In a **wholly-owned subsidiary** in a foreign country, the parent international company owns 100% of the shareholding. Where this is not the case, we are dealing with a joint venture. Wholly-owned subsidiaries in other countries can be established in the following two ways:

- setting up a new operation in the foreign country;
- acquiring an established firm in the industry concerned.

Wholly-owned subsidiaries have three distinct advantages. Firstly, a wholly-owned subsidiary is the preferred mode of entry when the risk of losing know-how and technological expertise is high, such as in the semi-conductor and pharmaceutical industries. Secondly, this mode provides for effective control over and co-ordination with subsidiaries in a global network of companies. Thirdly, a wholly-owned subsidiary may be the preferred option to capitalise on experience curve and location economies, especially where global and transnational strategies are pursued.

The one major disadvantage of a wholly-owned subsidiary is that it is the most costly and riskiest form of foreign market entry, but the one with the highest level of control. The cost and benefits of all factors concerned should be carefully weighed and evaluated when considering this mode of entry.

9.7.3 Selecting a market entry mode

The choice of entry mode is probably the single most important decision that the firm will make in deciding to expand into foreign markets. Having identified the most important market entry modes, it is obvious from the major advantages and disadvantages associated with each of these, that the firm wishing to enter the international market-place is faced with numerous trade-offs in deciding on an appropriate mode of entry, for the following reasons:

Each entry mode differs in:

- the degree of control that the company has over strategic and operational decision-making with regard to its international operations;
- the degree of risk involved in its foreign operations, wherein the firm distinguishes between systemic risk (the extent of political, economic, legal, and financial risks) and dissemination risk (probability of loss of know-how related to core competences);
- the resource commitment related to the amount of the firm's resources invested in foreign operations, including capital, physical assets, training of staff, and foreign marketing costs.[43]

As we have seen in Exhibit 9.7 (p. 266), the firm's degree of control over foreign operations generally ranges from low for exporting to high for wholly-owned subsidiaries. However, as far as the risks associated with these modes of entry are concerned, it is of extreme significance for the firm to realise that:

- systemic risk generally is low for exporting, licensing, franchising, and turnkey projects, but high for wholly-owned subsidiaries; and
- dissemination risk is low for exporting and wholly-owned subsidiaries, medium for franchising and turnkey projects, and high for licensing.[44]

Resource commitments are highest for wholly-owned subsidiaries.

Research has shown that more than 25 different variables derived from theoretical perspectives such as the transactions cost theory, the industrial organisation theory, the theory of the multinational enterprise, and the strategic management theory, have been identified to provide a deeper understanding of the entry mode decision. However, the research findings on the significance of the impact of these variables on the choice of entry mode, have been conflicting.

Phatak has developed an extremely useful five-dimensional framework, which incorporates 17 of the most significant variables, to assess the potential merits of a particular entry mode related to a specific situation and entry mode decision.[45]

The five dimensions in the comprehensive framework for entry mode choice are the capability of the firm, industry factors, location-specific factors, venture specific factors, and strategic factors, and are illustrated in Exhibit 9.8 (p. 272) with the corresponding variables for each dimension.

Although this valuable framework serves to reduce the possibilities that could be relevant in entry mode decisions to a manageable few, there can be no illusions with regard to the complexity of this decision.

Realising that the relevance of all these dimensions and their variables cannot be considered here, a brief discussion of two important issues for market entry decisions, namely core competencies and pressures for cost reductions, will follow.

(a) Core competencies and entry mode

We have seen that firms expand internationally to earn greater profits, primarily by transferring their products, services, and skills derived from their core competencies, to foreign markets, generally when they follow an international strategy. To see how the transfer of competencies affect the entry mode decision, two types of core competencies will be considered – those based on technological know-how, and those based on management know-how.

Where technological know-how is involved, and dissemination risk a possibility, licensing and joint venture arrangements should be avoided as far as possible, and wholly-owned subsidiaries, although more expensive, might be a far better option. These are not rigid rules, and each situation will have to be assessed on its own merits. Dissemination risk can be reduced, or even eliminated, where strategic alliances are appropriately structured. Where a

Exhibit 9.8: A comprehensive framework for entry mode choice

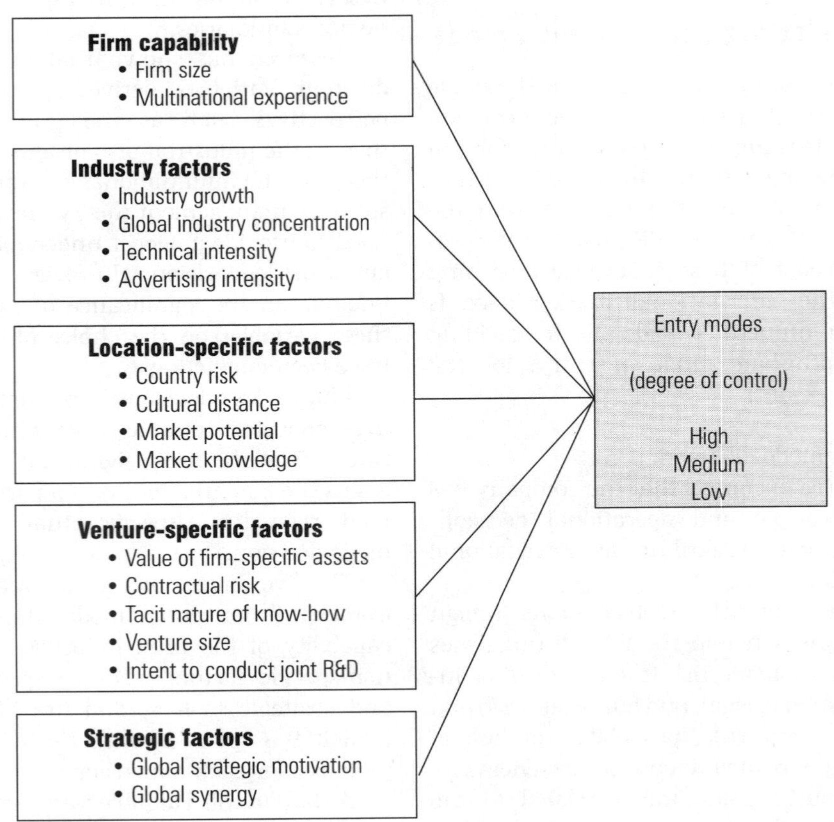

SOURCE: Photak, A.V. 1997. *International management: Concepts and cases.* Cincinatti, Ohio: South Western College Publishing, p. 273.

firm's aim is to avoid foreign firms developing their own technology and becoming competitors, licensing might be preferable. However, wholly-owned subsidiaries will generally be the best choice of entry.[46]

Management know-how appears to be the primary core competence and competitive advantage of service firms such as McDonald's, Kentucky Fried Chicken, Avis, and Holiday Inns. The implications of the risk of disseminating managerial know-how are not significant, since the most valuable asset here is the brand name, which is generally protected internationally by trade-marks. Accordingly franchising, and also licensing and wholly-owned subsidiaries, are popular market entry modes for most service firms. However, the environmental, country, and market factors in each foreign market will have to be evaluated, especially in relation to the possibilities of systemic risk.[47]

(b) Pressures for cost reductions and entry mode

As far as pressures for cost reduction in foreign markets are concerned, the greater these pressures, the more certain combinations of exporting and wholly-owned subsidiaries will be preferred as mode of entry, especially where global and transnational strategies are pursued. Experience curve and location economies will favour the establishment of wholly-owned subsidiaries in optimal, low-labour and other low-cost locations, capitalising on the economies of scale, and using indirect or direct exporting, or a combination of these, to distribute products globally from these optimal locations.[48]

Aberdare Cables

In 1996, Aberdare Cables, a major manufacturer of power and telecommunications cables in South Africa, was a recipient of the Excellence in Exports award of the National Productivity Institute of South Africa. Aberdare's success was based on competitiveness in the face of intense competition in South Africa from foreign traders, optimal use of appropriate technology, and an international orientation.

Robert Venter, Chief Executive of Aberdare Cables, stated that the local cable manufacturing industry had not been intimidated by the invasion of foreign traders. Aberdare competed aggressively against imports lured by a buoyant local market and the lifting of trade restrictions. This had been made possible by advanced cable technology and sustained efforts to maintain consistently high levels of quality and productivity which match international standards. 'We have benchmarked ourselves against the best in the world, introduced basic adult education and multi-skilling training modules and these are showing real benefits at plant level,' Venter said.

He conceded, however, that local cable users had been tempted by aggressively-priced imports. He questioned the ability of off-shore manufacturers to produce quality products consistently and to provide technical back-up services in South Africa. Venter stressed that close customer contact is a fundamental marketing requirement to ensure success in this competitive environment, and pointed out that local manufacturers have the advantage of understanding the needs of local customers better than off-shore manufacturers.

More than 10% of Aberdare's total production turnover is exported and an improvement to 15% is expected in the short term.

The company has developed a long-term strategy to increase exports. Some two years ago it established a cable-manufacturing facility in Portugal. The factory, trading as Alcobre Condutores Electricos, had increased its turnover by 42% since it was acquired and Aberdare was using it as a stepping-stone to penetrate the southern European and northern African markets. With the Portuguese link-up, Aberdare has also benefited from increased exports to Angola and Mozambique. It would seem that exporting, but possibly more important, the establishment of an operation in Portugal, opened the door to international markets and greater profitability for Aberdare Cables.

SOURCE *Productivity SA*, Vol. 22, No. 3, May/June 1996, p. 12.

9.8 International marketing strategy

9.8.1 The marketing mix and strategies for international firms

A firm's international or global marketing strategy must be consistent with its corporate strategy and based on the firm's international marketing mix strategy, which comprises the individual product, distribution, promotion and communications, as well as pricing strategies. Since marketing is the link between the firm and its markets, marketing strategy is vital for the success of the firm. The process of international market assessment as a meaningful approach for selecting foreign markets was discussed in Section 9.6, and the various modes of entry into international markets that firms can use, were considered in Section 9.7.

Next, the international markets which the firm has decided to enter have to be segmented to enable it to focus its marketing activities on effectively serving the needs of those markets. **International or global market segmentation** therefore aims at identifying prospective customers with potentially similar preferences and buying behaviour at national, sub-national, or regional levels. The selected market segments are then targeted for specific marketing strategies and actions. The main advantages of segmentation are that it:

- allows for appropriate and efficient resource allocation;
- facilitates the evaluation of opportunities and competition;
- allows improved focusing on marketing strategies and product positioning;
- enables fine-tuning of the overall marketing mix strategy.[49]

Market segmentation bases traditionally include geographical, political, cultural, and economic variables for international markets, as well as bases such as psychographics, demographics, and personal behaviour. The market segmentation process identifies groups of consumers with similar needs and wants, while market targeting involves identification of the segmented groups with the best potential, and selecting one or more of them. It stands to reason that the international marketing manager will have to select the most appropriate segmentation basis or bases to suit a specific situation.

A firm may consider a number of strategy options in its international marketing approach. These include:

- geographical market expansion strategies;
- generic strategies.

(a) Geographical market expansion strategies

Based on the firm's evaluation of international market opportunities and taking into account its available resources for entering international markets, the scope and approach of this important step has to be defined in terms of how many markets to enter simultaneously, or whether a single market should be entered initially to establish a base, from which the company can proceed to expand its future international marketing activities. Depending on specific circumstances in each situation, the firm can follow any of three strategies:

- **Market concentration strategies**, which involve selecting a limited number of markets, and concentrating the necessary resources and commitment to serving those markets effectively;
- **Market diversification strategies**, which focus on a much larger number of international markets with a more or less equal distribution of company and marketing resources across all the markets concerned;
- **Combination of geographical strategies**, which include any combination of the first two strategies.

Basically, where some markets are stable and growth rates relatively high, firms would be inclined to follow a concentration strategy. Where a global demand for a firm's products has been established, a geographical market diversification strategy might prove more effective. In considering the merits of these alternative strategic approaches, it is assumed that the decisions with regard to products and services to be marketed have already been made. Specific product strategies as part of the marketing mix strategy of the firm are discussed later (Section 9.8.2).

(b) Generic strategies

Generic strategies are market-based strategic alternatives where competitive advantage is sought by exploiting the firm's internal strengths in its response to opportunities in the business environment. Here the primary focus is on external, industry-market factors as the main drivers of the firm's competitive strategies.[50]

Michael Porter's work on competitive strategy and competitive advantage during more than two decades has become generally accepted as the conceptual frame of reference where competitive strategy in general, and generic strategies in particular, are concerned. His two basic generic competitive strategies are:

- **cost leadership strategies**, based on lower product costs than those of competitors; and
- **differentiation strategies**, where a firm's product offerings differ substantially from those of competitors in terms of superior features and attributes, and for which customers would be willing to pay more as a result of actual or perceived superior value.

In the application of these two generic strategies, they can apply to a broad or extensive market segment, or to a small segment or market niche. The latter implies a focus strategy of either of the two generic strategies, providing the following four strategy alternatives:

- broad cost leadership;
- broad differentiation;
- focused low cost; and
- focused differentiation.

A cost leadership strategy implies standardised products, primarily aimed at price-sensitive consumers and based on mass production to benefit from economies of scale and experience curve economies to obtain low unit product costs. Differentiation strategies involve unique products and services with attributes and features that differ substantially from those of competitors and which provide a competitive advantage to a firm by way of:

- allowing a premium price to be charged to price-insensitive buyers;
- obtaining customer loyalty through the differentiated features;
- experiencing increased sales as new customers are attracted to the differentiated products and services.[51]

(c) Relationship between corporate strategy, generic strategies, and the marketing mix

Given the firm's existing products and services, the international marketing manager must appreciate:

- the important relationship between the corporate strategy and business strategies of the firm on the one hand; and
- how the alternative generic strategies of differentiation and cost leadership, whether broad or focused, can align with the marketing mix strategy, on the other hand. These important relationships are illustrated in Exhibit 9.9 (p. 276), where only generic strategies are included by way of example.

Of importance to the international firm is how the product, place or distribution, promotion, and pricing strategies should be aligned in the firm's overall international marketing strategy, while considering relevant key decision-making factors such as those listed in Exhibit 9.9. Because of its strategic importance here, we only consider the key factor of standardisation versus customisation.

Exhibit 9.9: Relationship between business strategies, generic strategies and the marketing mix

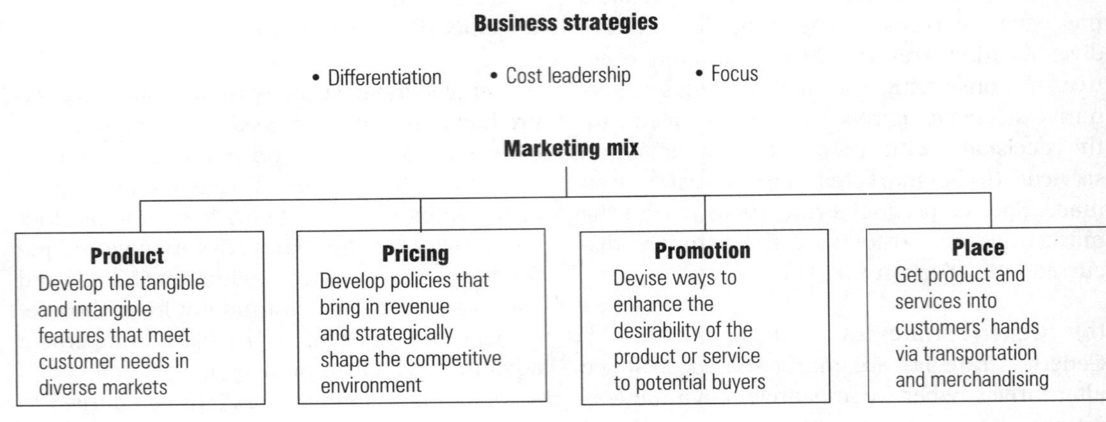

SOURCE: Griffin, R.W. & Pustay, M.W. 1998. *International business.* 2nd ed. Reading, Massachusetts: Addison Wesley Longman, p. 587.

In deciding whether to standardise the firm's marketing mix, there are three basic approaches:

- an **ethnocentric approach**, which is marketing the firm's products internationally the same way as domestically;
- a **polycentric approach**, which involves customisation of the marketing mix to comply with the specific needs of each of the firm's foreign markets;
- a **geocentric approach**, which implies a standardised marketing mix for all international markets that are served, based on largely uniform needs of customers across all foreign markets.[52]

The most important factors that have to be considered in deciding whether the marketing mix should be standardised or customised, and for which markets, are summarised in Exhibit 9.10 (p. 277).

The importance of the standardisation versus customisation decisions is that they basically determine the overall strategy the firm should follow, the alternatives being an 'international strategy', a 'multidomestic strategy', a 'global strategy', a 'transnational strategy', or any combination of these. The rationale for these strategies, as well as their characteristics, were discussed in Chapter 8.

The international marketing manager next has to address the following four issues:

- how to develop the firm's products;
- how to distribute those products internationally;
- how to promote those products in the various international markets;
- how to effectively price those products in the international market-place.

We now examine the strategic elements of the marketing mix for an international firm – the

Exhibit 9.10: Advantages and disadvantages of standardised and customised international marketing

STANDARDISED INTERNATIONAL MARKETING	
Advantages	**Disadvantages**
1 Reduces marketing costs	1 Ignores different conditions of product use
2 Facilitates centralized control of marketing	2 Ignores local legal differences
3 Promotes efficiency in R&D	3 Ignores differences in buyer behaviour patterns
4 Results in economies of scale in production	4 Inhibits local marketing initiatives
5 Reflects the trend toward a single global market place	5 Ignores other differences in individual markets
CUSTOMISED INTERNATIONAL MARKETING	
Advantages	**Disadvantages**
1 Reflects different conditions of product use	1 Increases marketing costs
2 Acknowledges local legal differences	2 Inhibits centralized control of marketing
3 Accounts for differences in buyer behaviour patterns	3 Creates inefficiency in R&D
4 Promotes local marketing initiatives	4 Reduces economies of scale in production
5 Accounts for other differences in individual markets	5 Ignores the trend toward a single global market place

SOURCE: Griffin & Pustay, op. cit., p. 590.

product, distribution, promotion, and pricing strategies.

9.8.2 International product strategy

In international marketing, as in domestic marketing, success depends largely on satisfying the demands of the market. However, the diverse needs of customers around the world and the intense competition which characterises international and global markets require the international marketing manager to be aware of and acutely sensitive to varying consumer needs across countries, regions, and markets, and to have the knowledge, skills, insight, and attitude to execute this demanding and complex task effectively and efficiently.

The **product** is at the centre of the firm's marketing strategy in international markets, and international marketers need to be precise about the core benefits that the product will provide to consumers. A product can be viewed as a bundle of attributes which satisfy consumer needs. As Chee and Harris aptly state:

> Consumers do not buy product features, they buy satisfaction.[53]

Products can be **tangible** (physical products), or **intangible** (services), and are not limited to goods and services, but can include ideas, information, skills, people, organisations, and places. The term 'product' can therefore refer to non-physical as well as physical aspects, and Kotler and Armstrong make a distinction between the concepts of core product, actual product, and the augmented product.

- The **core product** involves the core benefit that the consumer obtains when buying a product – a BMW car is a very efficient, high-quality, tasteful, status symbol;

- The **actual product** comprises the features, brand, quality, styling, and packaging – for the BMW car it is the brand name, the high-quality engineering and outer design, and stylish features;
- The **augmented product** consists of attributes such as installation, pre-delivery service and after-sales service, warranty, delivery, and credit facilities – the product level that many global companies effectively use to obtain a competitive advantage in the market-place. All three different levels collectively constitute the total product offering.[54]

Products can be classified in various ways, depending on the purpose or objective for the need for classification. Although it is customary to divide products into consumer and industrial goods, for international marketing the distinction between local products, international products, and global products is more important.

- **Local products** are considered to have potential only in a particular and limited local market. A local brand of beer produced by a local brewery is an example in this category.
- **International products** are considered to have the potential to be marketed in other international markets – a product that is developed for one national market and then sold in other international markets as such, with little or no modification. Perfume, cosmetics, and standard jewellery are examples in this category.
- **Global products** are designed for the international market and incorporate all necessary differences into one design of the product. Motives for considering global products involve high R&D costs, shorter product life cycles and the intense global competition. TV cabinets which allow installation of the electronic equipment of any of the international systems without the need to change the cabinet, are an example here. Of significance, however, is the fact that the global product design is such that it can still be adapted to meet unique national market needs.

Because of the increasing competitiveness in global markets, the criterion for success in international marketing has gradually changed from satisfying the identified needs of diverse consumers around the world to satisfying those needs better than competitors, which poses an enormous challenge to international marketers to be increasingly innovative, creative, and cost-effective. At least some of these requirements for success in international marketing are reflected in the profile on BMW's ambitions.

BMW's ambitions

BMW, the Munich-based German multinational enterprise, has reshaped its product policy for Africa. BMW's Marketing and Public Relations Manager, Jean Michel Juchet, is infatuated with Africa and its potential, but is also acutely aware of the problems that they face in Africa, stating that:

> BMW is not a company which takes risks without fully assessing the pros and cons of the situation.

BMW has its own subsidiary in South Africa and has been involved in this country for more than 30 years. It recently trebled its production facilities at Rosslyn, outside Pretoria, which will enable it to increase its output from 13 000 units to 40 000 units in the year 2000. This is only one of BMW's three plants, the other two being in Munich, Germany, and in Spartanburg, South Carolina, in the United States. In all other international locations, cars are merely assembled. The South African subsidiary exports BMW cars to Asia, Australia, and South America, as well as to right-hand drive countries in South and East Africa and the Indian Ocean.

At the core of BMW's strategy for Africa is the acquisition of Rover in the UK four years ago, incorporating Land Rover, Rover and Mini vehicles. As Juchet states:

> Land Rover has always been and remains the quality leader in four-wheel drive vehicles in the

world, but when it was part of the Rover group it never received the market share it deserved.

With regard to product development in the past, Land Rover tended to be too sophisticated for Third-World countries, was not very challenging in its communication and marketing, and a price differential of up to 30% between Land Rover and other four-wheel drive vehicles – instead of from 5% to 10% – undoubtedly affected its competitiveness.

These adverse trends are being addressed in BMW's overall product strategy for Africa, which includes the continued sales of the British-made Land Rover, and the introduction of the popular South African-made Defender in BMW's markets in Africa. BMW already has distribution and service facility networks in more than 16 African countries. Its targets, for example, are 200 four-wheel drive vehicles in Ghana and 300 to 400 in Nigeria in the year 2000. Although the Rover and Mini will be redesigned and marketed from 2001, it is with the Land Rover – alongside the BMW car – that the company is determined to establish a higher profile on the African Continent.

SOURCE: Paris, Richard. 1999. 'BMW's ambitions', *Business in Africa'*, Vol.7, No.4, July/August, pp. 50-52

If consumer needs were the same the world over, a firm could sell the same product worldwide to all consumers. However, we know that, in reality, consumer needs, preferences, and tastes vary from country to country, mainly because of differences in culture, levels of economic development, and product and technical standards across countries. The extent to which products and services have to be modified to meet the needs of international customers also depends on the type of product. Rugman and Hodgetts provide a range of possibilities which include typical products that require little or no modification, those that require a moderate amount of modification, and those which have to be modified extensively to meet international requirements.[55] These examples are summarised in Exhibit 9.11.

In the following discussion we will consider culture, levels of economic development, and product and technical standards in relation to their importance in developing appropriate product policies and strategies for diverse international markets.

Exhibit 9.11: Selected examples of product modification in the international arena

Little if any modification required	Moderate amount of modification required	Extensive modification required
Heavy equipment	Automobiles	High-style consumer goods
Electronic watches	Clothing	Cosmetics
Notebook computers	Appliances	Prepackaged foods
Chemical processes	Pharmaceuticals	Education products
Writing implements	Aircraft	Advertising
Cameras	Athletic running shoes	Packaging
Tennis rackets	Television sets	Restaurant meals
Cigarettes	Beer	Health services
		Cultural products
		Consumer distribution

SOURCE: Rugman, A.M. & Hodgetts, R.M. 1995. *International Business.* New York: McGraw-Hill, p. 300.

(a) Cultural differences

The cultural environments facing international business were discussed in Chapter 3, and the environment and cultural dimensions of international marketing in Section 9.4. From these discussions it is apparent that cultures differ from one another in respect of a host of dimensions, including social structure, language, religion, education, economic philosophy, and political philosophy.[56] To effectively satisfy the needs of international consumers, it is obvious that these differences between countries must first be recognised and the implications which they have for marketing should be incorporated into the firm's product policy and strategy. Examples in this regard include:

- the poor sales of 'hamburgers' in Islamic countries, where the consumption of ham is forbidden by Islamic Law;
- where Coca-Cola in Japan added 'Georgia', a cold coffee in a can, and 'Aquarius', a tonic drink, to supplement its normal range of products, to satisfy traditional Japanese tastes in beverages;
- where Coca-Cola has furthermore had success in marketing a low-calorie version in diet-conscious America under the name of Diet Coke, and in other countries under the name of Coca-Cola Light.[57]

Although preferences and tastes in respect of some consumer products have converged globally to some extent, the need to respond to local preferences is still very significant. The astute marketer must know when and how to respond to either globalisation (standardisation) or responsiveness in devising product strategies for the firm's international markets.

(b) Economic differences

In Chapter 5 the importance of the level of economic development of a country in relation to its overall quality of life, consumer needs, and expenditure patterns was explained. One of the implications for the international marketer is that firms in economically developed countries, such as the United States and Germany, are inclined to incorporate a number of performance attributes (at the actual, and especially the augmented, levels referred to previously) which are not usually in demand from customers in less developed economies, who may not have the material means to purchase such products if survival, and not an improved standard of living, is their first priority. In the case of consumer durable products, reliability rather than appearance might be the most important product attribute.

Consumers in economically developed countries, enjoying relatively high income levels and living standards, are willing to pay more for products with additional features and attributes that will satisfy their higher-level needs. This is the case where people value time, and especially leisure time, and are prepared to pay more for product features that will save time and contribute to greater convenience, such as ready-to-consume frozen foods, automatic washing machines, dishwashers, liquidisers, electronically-operated remote garage-door activators, and Internet home-banking facilities. Consumers in this category will generally not feel attracted to low-cost standardised global products where economic cost is the imperative. A fundamental knowledge of the issues and dimensions of the international economic environment, and how these issues and dimensions impact on the buying behaviour of consumers in countries at different levels of economic development, is vividly apparent from the box, 'Tracking the World's Rich'. Once again, this information is indispensable to the international marketer in product policy and strategy decisions.

Tracking the world's rich – they're still getting richer

According to the annual Merrill Lynch and Gemini Consulting *World Wealth Report*, the divide between rich and poor generally seems to be increasing. In the report it is stated that high net worth individuals –

now known as HNWIs – managed to increase their wealth by 5% in 1997, despite market turbulence, and they also managed a 12% increase in 1998.

The survey suggests that even the Asian rich managed to weather the crisis, as a large proportion of their assets was in offshore vehicles. American and European stock markets had bounced back by the end of 1998. This was where the rich had the bulk of their liquid assets, regardless of their official domiciles, so their wealth was protected.

The rich may be getting richer, but the demographics are changing. Another Merrill Lynch study suggests an increasing demand by women for financial services. The study confirms that more women are remaining unmarried and more are choosing to marry later. The percentage of wealthy businesswomen is increasing. In the UK, Dresdner Bank of Germany reports that more than half of its rich private clients are women.

SOURCE: *Financial Mail*, 28 May 1999, p. 18.

(c) Product and technical standards

Having entered the new millennium, and given all the technological and other developments in recent decades, it is amazing how different product and technical standards between countries, often mandated by governments, still largely defy the standardisation of products, mass-marketing, and globalisation.

The effects of differences in technical standards across countries pose a real challenge in terms of a firm's international or global product policy. Hill quotes the case of video equipment manufactured for sale in the United States that cannot be used in the UK, France, or Germany, because of different technical standards for frequencies and television signals.[58] Because of differences in electricity power supply in various countries, electrical appliances cannot be used without a transforming device. For example, the electricity output in the United States is 110 volts, but in European countries and South Africa it is in the 220-240 volt range. Differences in product and technical standards require international marketers to liaise extremely closely with their product development and design functions with regard to products for international markets.

9.8.3 International distribution strategy

Effective distribution systems are required if products intended to satisfy consumer needs are to be available in the right place at the right time. In international markets, where so many variables can affect the effective distribution of products and services, competitive pressures have added to the importance of developing competitive distribution channels to ensure place utility. The distribution channel decision is critical because it affects all aspects of international marketing strategy.[59]

Some international companies own their own distribution systems, and sell direct to customers, but, in the majority of cases, international companies rely on other companies to act as intermediaries in the distribution channel. Especially as far as this last alternative is concerned, the most important issues that the international marketing manager will need to consider in developing an effective distribution system, include the following:

- how to select foreign country intermediaries;
- how to build enduring relationships with intermediaries;
- how to deal with the varying types of wholesaling and retailing infrastructure across international markets;
- how to maximise new and innovative forms of distribution;
- how to manage the means and logistics of physically distributing products across foreign markets.[60]

The following insert aptly illustrates how innovative distribution systems can improve efficiency, cost-effectiveness and customer service.

Logistics logic

Companies used to have to exercise extraordinary foresight in their ordering habits – trying to figure out what people would want to buy and how much, weeks or months before the goods were actually delivered. Now, it is possible to monitor sales and fine-tune ordering, using logistics software and the Internet. Heineken, for example, uses the Internet to provide continually updated information to distributors, who can increase or decrease their orders and obtain an instant response from the supplier.

When the temperature rises in Miami, Florida, while Malibu in California is facing an unseasonable cold snap, Heineken can reroute shipments quickly, or even adjust production schedules. Before using the on-line system, distributors had to wait from 10 to 12 weeks to get their orders filled, meaning that they had to either risk overstocking or running out of stock and losing sales.

SOURCE: 'Logistics logic', Forbes, 7 April 1997, in *Marketing Mix*, Vol.15, No.4, May 1997, p.21.

The structure of a typical international distribution system that illustrates the position of a wholesaler and retailer in the overall distribution channel is outlined in Exhibit 9.12.

In a domestic setting, the manufacturer can sell direct to the wholesaler, the retailer, or the consumer. The manufacturer outside the country can basically follow the same distribution route, but can also sell to an import agent, who would then act as an intermediary in getting the final product to the wholesaler, retailer, or consumer.

According to Hill, there are three main differences that characterise the distribution systems in foreign countries. These are retail concentration, channel length, and channel exclusivity.[61]

(a) Retail concentration in international distribution

Retail systems in different countries are characterised by being either highly concentrated or

Exhibit 9.12: A typical distribution system

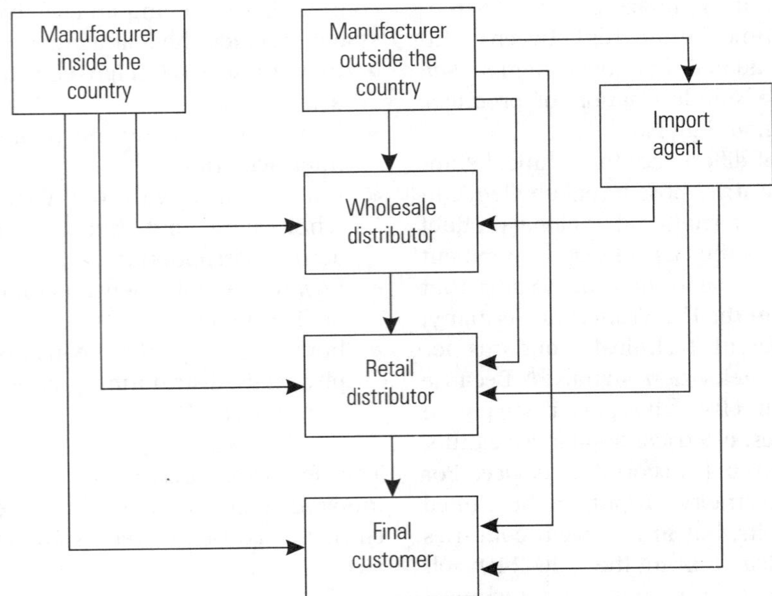

SOURCE: Hill, C.W.L. 1998. *International business.* 2nd ed. Burr Ridge, Illinois: McGraw-Hill Irwin, p. 493.

fragmented. In **concentrated systems**, a relatively small number of retailers, each with a relatively large share of the market, will dominate the retail sector. In such situations, manufacturers have relatively little negotiation power over retailers. In contrast, a **fragmented system** is characterised by many retailers, where no single retailer or group of retailers hold or account for a major share of the overall retail market. Low concentration ratios of retail ownership give manufacturers more negotiating power.

Factors that have contributed largely to retail concentration in specific countries include:

- availability of transport and the mobility of consumers, such as in the United States, where large shopping complexes form an important link in the distribution channel;
- the increasing importance of home convenience appliances, such as refrigerators, evidenced in most developed countries, that to a large extent eliminate frequent, small-quantity purchases.

In countries characterised by high urban population densities and urban centres, such as Japan, the retail sector is relatively more fragmented. Developing countries, which have a lack of transportation and consequently low mobility of consumers, also tend towards fragmented retail sectors.

With regard to these differences between developing and developed countries, Doole and Lowe have identified the four stages of traditional, intermediary, structured, and advanced retailing structures around the world, and indicate how the expansion of international activity of retailers worldwide has resulted in the development of four different types of international retailers: the hypermarket, the power retailers, the niche retailer, and the designer-brand retailer.[62]

Bearing in mind that the majority of consumers worldwide buy from retailers, the importance of evaluating the appropriateness of the various types of retail operations prevalent in foreign markets as part of the overall distribution channel, serves to confirm the importance of this decision for the international marketing manager.

(b) Length of distribution channels

Channel length refers to the number of intermediaries between the producer or manufacturer and the consumer.[63] As is evident from Exhibit 9.12 (p. 282), selling direct to the consumer is the shortest channel. Although the number of intermediaries ultimately determine channel length, research has shown that one of the most important determinants of channel length is the degree of fragmentation of the retail system because of the increase in number of wholesalers in these circumstances. It is obvious that the greater the number of retailers in a specific market, the more expensive it would be for a manufacturer to sell direct to all of them, and, therefore, wholesalers fulfil an important marketing role. In countries with concentrated retail systems, channels tend to be relatively short, as is the case in the United States, Great Britain, and Germany, where manufacturers generally deal direct with retailers.

The international marketing manager will have to take into account the characteristics of the country where the firm's foreign markets are, as well as numerous other factors, as inputs to the development of viable distribution channel strategies.

(c) Exclusivity of international distribution channels

Exclusivity refers to the ease, or otherwise, with which producers gain access to existing distribution channels, a factor which has been proven to vary from country to country. The main reason for this is that long-standing relationships have been developed between manufacturers, wholesalers, and retailers. In these circumstances, wholesalers and retailers give preference to stocking the products of well-known manufacturers. These types of relationships have made it extremely difficult for foreign, and especially United States, producers and distributors to get a foothold in Japanese markets, for example. The international marketing manager must be aware of these possibilities when contemplating international distribution channels for the firm.

(d) Selection of a distribution channel

The basic issue that any international firm has to face is whether it will sell direct to consumers or make use of intermediaries to market its products in foreign markets. The answer to this question will indicate the factors that the international marketing manager may need to consider in selecting the optimal distribution channel for the company. Advantages and disadvantages, as well as all relevant costs and benefits – which will vary from country to country – have to be evaluated for each possibility.[64]

We have seen that **retail concentration**, **channel length**, and **channel exclusivity** could influence the suitability of an international distribution system. An important implication here is that the longer the distribution channel, the higher the final price to the consumer will generally be, which could have dire consequences where products in foreign markets compete on the basis of price.

From earlier discussions, however, it was evident that in countries with fragmented retail systems, longer distribution channels are preferred, and vice versa. With longer distribution channels, producers have a greater chance of access to traditionally exclusive channels through intermediation of export agents in the firm's foreign markets. Direct mail order selling has seemed to work in certain instances where market channel exclusivity posed problems for international companies. Ultimately, a decision will have to be taken on the **mode or means of transport** such as air, sea, rail, road, and other combinations or variations of these. Based on the most important considerations in this section, it is generally accepted that the selection of a distribution channel remains an important international marketing decision.

9.8.4 International promotion and communications strategy

Communicating the attributes, features, and utility of a product or service to potential customers, is a vital link in the international marketing process and a strategically important element in the company's marketing mix. The **communication means** available to the firm include direct selling, sales promotion, direct marketing, advertising and public relations. The choice of communication channel or means defines the international firm's communications strategy to a certain extent.[65]

The primary objective of international marketing communication is to persuade customers that the company's products and services will satisfy their needs. This is achieved by attempting to influence each stage of the buying process and therefore the buying behaviour of the potential customer. Research has shown that these stages in the buying process generally include:

- awareness of the firm, its products and services, and its reputation;
- interest in the products and services, since they may be suited to the consumers' needs and worthy of consideration for potential purchase;
- desire to buy the product or service in preference to that of the competition, after consumers have become better informed about its performance; and
- action by the consumer in overcoming any remaining reservations or barriers and purchasing the product or service.[66]

Marketing communication messages have to be developed for each stage of the process, which is extremely difficult in international markets in particular, mainly because of the geographical and cultural separation of the company from its foreign market-places and prospective customers.

The key to success in **international promotion** depends on the integration of the various promotional tools, such as personal selling and word of mouth, advertising, sales promotion, and public relations in a cost-effective way by using the communication methods that will have the greatest impact on customers. According to Doole and Lowe, the choice of the actual mix of communication methods depends on a number of issues inherently associated with the purchasing situation, such as:

- the market area and industry sector;
- whether it is consumer, institutional, or business-to-business marketing;
- the customer segment to be targeted;
- the participants in the purchasing process, their requirements, and the best methods to reach and influence them;
- the country or region, the culture, the communication infrastructure, and the preferred methods of communicating;
- the resources made available by the organisation and the level of involvement and control it wishes to have over the communication process.[67]

The importance of accurately identifying the market and customer segment to be targeted in the communications and promotion strategy is vividly illustrated in the following insert that relates to the United States, but should also be of importance to the South African marketing manager whose company is involved in the American market.

Learning to love the middle-aged

Social critic and historian Theodore Roszak has disdain for the fascination advertisers have for youth culture (and youth dollars). He contends that such advertisers are 'living in ignorance of the central demographic fact of the 21st century: The young are a vanishing breed. The future lies with the old'. In 1998, Americans over the age of 50 made up the fastest-growing segment of society, and their share of the national wealth vastly exceeded that of their children and grandchildren. Roszak quotes *American Demographic*'s contributing editor, Cheryl Russell, who says: 'In future, American business has got to learn to love the middle-aged'. And Roszak points out: 'America's next older generation will be the best educated, most widely travelled, most professionally trained, most politically savvy, and most culturally creative generation this country has ever produced.'

SOURCE: Roszak, T. 1998. 'Birth of an old generation', *Civilization*, October/November. http://www.civ-mag.com. In *Marketing Mix*, Vol.17, No.3, March 1999, p. 24

The extent to which the different promotional methods must be adapted to be effective in international markets, is the critical issue in the co-ordination and planning of the international marketing communications strategy of the international firm. With these aspects in mind, the barriers to international communication will be briefly considered, and also the determinants for effective communications strategy for particular countries, followed by an overview of global advertising.

(a) Barriers to effective international communication

Hill identifies the following three potential barriers to effective international communication, namely **cultural barriers**, **source effects**, and **noise levels**. Based on our knowledge of cultural differences across countries, it is easy to appreciate that cultural barriers could pose problems in communicating across cultures. In order to address this problem, Hill confirms the value of developing cross-cultural literacy within the company, including its foreign operations, in so far as cultural ignorance and biases could be harmful to the company's international communication, both internally and externally.[68]

For this purpose, local inputs, such as local advertising agents, should be included in developing marketing messages. Because of inherent cultural differences across countries, the marketing manager must be aware of and sensitive to cultural dimensions in devising sales promotion and advertising initiatives.

Problems can also arise where customers evaluate messages based on the image or status of the sender – the so-called source effect.[69] This effect could be serious for international companies that experience subjectivity towards or a bias against firms of foreign origin. Where there is an adverse bias, this can be eliminated or decreased in marketing communication and advertising, but where impressions are favourable, the firm could reinforce this favourable image to its own advantage in its marketing communications.

Noise levels simply refer to the increasingly congested global communication situation where the sheer volume of competing messages could minimise the effectiveness of the firm's communication, promotion, and advertising efforts. Although this phenomenon varies between countries, marketers should be aware of the adverse effect it could have on well-intentioned promotional campaigns.

(b) Push versus pull strategies in communication

It appears that the options which are available for the generic marketing communication strategy are dependent on the extent to which push or pull strategies can, and should, be used. **Push strategies** involve the promotion of products and services to wholesalers and retailers, using promotional methods to force the products or services down the distribution channel, such as personal selling, discounts, and special offers. **Pull strategies**, on the other hand, refer to communication with the final consumers to attract them to the retailer to purchase the company's products or services. Mass advertising and sales promotions are the appropriate marketing communication methods in this case.[70]

It is important for the international marketer to know how to use these two optional strategies to the best effect. The implications of geographical and cultural distance between the company and its foreign markets could mean that pull strategies would be difficult to effect, but that push strategies, using the correct promotional methods, would be preferable. Also, the question of whether the retail systems in particular countries are fragmented or concentrated, will have to be similarly evaluated in terms of the implications in each case. Finally, having decided on whether to use push or pull strategies, the dimensions of an **international marketing communication implementation strategy** include:

- the message to be communicated;
- the target audience at which the message is to be directed;
- the media to be used to convey the message; and
- the way in which the impact of the message will be measured.[71]

Pull strategies are generally favoured for consumer goods in larger markets to benefit from mass advertising. **Push strategies** are more prevalent in the marketing of industrial goods, where personal selling, building relationships, and providing various types of advice and service, are important. This situation could apply generally in less developed countries where consumer sophistication is relatively low compared to developed countries.

Another factor to consider is media availability, since pull strategies rely on ready access to advertising media, both print and electronic. In developing countries, especially, where advertising possibilities are limited, pull strategies are severely constrained. According to Hill, push strategies are preferred:

- for industrial products and/or complex products;
- when distribution channels are short;
- when few electronic or print media are available.

Pull strategies are preferred:

- for consumer goods;
- when distribution channels are long;
- when sufficient print and electronic media are available to convey marketing messages.[72]

(c) Global advertising

Global advertising implies full standardisation of the advertising message for markets worldwide. The advantages of global advertising are that it is extremely cost-effective, a once-off creative effort is used to its fullest extent and, lastly, because many brand names have become global, a global advertising and communication effort makes a great deal of sense.[73]

Forces opposing standardised, global advertising include cultural factors which differ across countries and require customisation or localisation of the promotional message, and regulatory restrictions on advertising which may prevent the worldwide use of certain advertisements. International companies are increasingly adapting their advertising to their markets, which involves globalising those elements which are feasible and would enhance the promotion of global brand names, and customising the message where local responsiveness is required.

In closing, communication through electronic networks in general, and the Internet in particular, has had a permanent, enduring change in the way in which business is done, both locally and internationally, and this trend will continue into the future. The Internet has forever altered the landscape of retailing business, and dynamic companies are wholeheartedly embracing the benfits it brings – especially where e-commerce involves doing business electronically using the Internet – through buying and selling on-line, both locally and globally.

9.8.5 International pricing strategy

International pricing strategy is a critical element of the firm's international marketing mix, because many products and services compete on the basis of price, and pricing policies affect the extent of a firm's income and profits. Chee and Harris have identified the main determinants of the international firm's prices and, therefore, its pricing policy and strategy.[74] These determinants have been divided into three subgroups, as illustrated in Exhibit 9.13 (p. 288).

It is clear from these environmental, market, and company internal factors that pricing the firm's products for international markets involves an extremely complex decision.

In discussing pricing strategy, we will examine the aspects of standard price policy, price discrimination or market pricing, and strategic pricing.

(a) Standard price policy

International firms that adopt a geocentric marketing approach will follow a **standard pricing policy** by charging the same price for all their products and services regardless of the countries in which they are sold. Certain high-value, easily-transported products like computer memory chips, or commodities such as oil and coal, where prices are largely determined by supply and demand in the world market irrespective of countries where it will be sold, generally follow a standard pricing policy.[75]

(b) Price discrimination

In an international context, **price discrimination**, also referred to as **market pricing**, means charging different prices for the same product in different countries. It is widely accepted that price discrimination often allows international companies to maximise their profits.

The following two conditions must prevail for price discrimination to be effective. First, the demand and/or cost conditions must be different in each of the countries in which the firm sells its products or services. These conditions, in effect, mean different price elasticities of demand in different countries, where price elasticity of demand is a measure of how the demand for a product responds to changes in its price. Demand is considered to be elastic when a small change in price leads to a large change in demand, and as inelastic when a large change in price leads to a small change in demand. In markets where demand for a product is inelastic, the firm can set higher prices without any significant adverse effects on

Exhibit 9.13: Factors affecting global pricing decisions

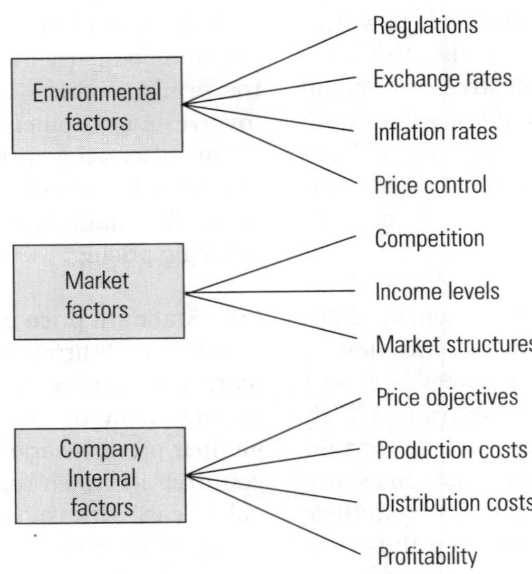

SOURCE: Chee & Harris, op. cit., p. 483.

demand, to maximise income and profits. These conditions of different demand and/or cost are normally met, since, in most countries, there are differences in the general levels of income, competitive conditions, standards of living, and tax regimes. Of these, income levels and competitive conditions are the most important. Countries with low income levels are generally more price-elastic, their consumers more price-conscious, and the spending power on luxury items is relatively low – arguments that would apply to most developing economies. As far as the extent of competition is concerned, generally the stronger the competition, the greater the elasticity of demand due to competitive forces, and the greater the bargaining power of consumers and the lower the switching costs between products. Consequently, prices cannot be increased at will under these circumstances. However, in a country, region, or market where there are few competitors, firms can generally achieve exceptional income and profits.[76]

The second condition for price discrimination or market pricing is that it must be possible for the firm to keep its various national markets separate. Where this is not possible and prices vary greatly from country to country, individuals and organisations may engage in arbitrage by buying the firm's products at a low price in one country and selling it at higher prices in another country, which defeats the purpose of a price discrimination policy, and prevents the firm from attaining its profit targets.[77]

The presence of factors such as transportation costs, tariffs, transaction costs, and infrastructure, make arbitrage unlikely in most cases, thus allowing firms to pursue a polycentric marketing approach and a price discrimination policy. Of critical importance, however, is that the marketing manager should have a profound knowledge of the various countries, regions and markets in which his firm is active, and of how to develop optimal pricing policies for all these markets.

(c) Strategic pricing

Two modes of **strategic pricing**, referred to as **predatory pricing** and **experience curve pricing**, are also used in international marketing. Predatory pricing involves initially low prices to eliminate competition, and ultimately increasing price levels as competitors withdraw from the market. For this approach to succeed, the international firm must have other profitable ventures that can support its low price operations in the market in which predatory pricing is applied. Hill mentions the example of Matsushita using this approach to get a foothold in the United States TV market, relying on high profits in its home market in Japan to see it through the period of predatory pricing.[78]

Experience curve pricing is followed in industries where firms can ultimately benefit from economies of scale and the learning curve. Aggressive low pricing helps to increase volumes with the aim of substantial profits later on when unit costs decrease significantly as a result of the above-mentioned economies. International firms opting for this pricing strategy have to have a long-term vision, and the international marketing manager should once again be aware of all the marketing implications for the firm when this pricing policy is followed.

9.8.6 Managing the international marketing mix

To be successful in international markets, it is of critical importance that the marketing manager should know which and to what extent each of the four marketing mix elements must be standardised, and which customised, in relation to the firm's products and services in each of the foreign markets it serves. As we have seen, the most important environmental factors influencing this decision include:

- political, legal, cultural, and economic conditions across countries;
- competitive conditions in international markets;
- the international regulatory environment;
- international market structures – industrial or consumer.

It is in this international business environment that the international marketing manager has to decide on the extent to which the firm's marketing mix should be standardised or customised by following one or a combination of the following three approaches:

- an **ethnocentric approach** – marketing products and services internationally in the same way as it is done domestically;
- a **polycentric approach** – customising the marketing mix to meet the specific needs of each foreign market being served;
- a **geocentric approach** – analysing the needs of customers worldwide and adopting a standard marketing mix for all markets served.[79]

9.9 Summary

The international firm's products and services, and its strategy, provide the overall frame of reference for the development and implementation of its international marketing strategy. Furthermore, the international firm's marketing function should be organised and structured in such a way that it facilitates the development of a marketing strategy that will support the overall corporate strategy of the firm, in a dynamic, rapidly changing, and increasingly competitive international business environment.

Once firms decide to become international, they need to select the markets they wish to enter, and then decide on appropriate international market entry strategies to service those markets in the most efficient way. International marketing strategy starts with international market assessment which provides fundamental guidelines for selecting, segmenting, and targeting international markets. A crucial decision for international marketing management involves the extent to which its products should be standardised or customised for each of its global markets, and, consequently, the generic strategy to be followed for each market. These decisions are based on the marketing mix of the international firm and the extent to which product, distribution, promotion, and pricing strategies have to be adapted to provide the optimal marketing mix as a basis for the firm's overall marketing strategy. All the above issues were explored, as well as the firm's strategic choice in its decision to follow an ethnocentric, polycentric, or geocentric approach in its marketing strategy – the key ingredient for success in today's highly volatile and competitive international markets.

Case study

How has the Nando's franchise fared?

Based on the discussion on franchising in Chapter 9 and against the background provided by the Appendix, one of the recent exciting international franchises that originated in South Africa – Nando's – will be discussed along the following lines:

- its local expansion by means of franchising;
- its motives to become international, and
- its current status in highly competitive domestic and international markets.

Nando's was founded by Robert Brozin and Fernando Duarte in 1987. The origin and culture of the organisation is aptly captured in the following passage:

> 'It was in the small suburb of Rosettenville, Johannesburg, in a humble eatery called Chickenland that a dream was destined to become a reality in a few short years. There, in the heart of the local Portuguese community, chicken was prepared and enjoyed according to a centuries old, Portuguese tradition – the delicioso and well-kept secret of that tightly-knit community. But Portuguese hospitality being what it is, the secret proved to be one that had to be shared. Fernando Duarte, a member of the community, introduced his close and long-time friend Robert Brozin to Chickenland. When Robert tasted the traditional Portuguese-style chicken he had his first taste of what was to become his sonho (dream) – the dream of sharing something this good with the whole world. Fernando and Robert became partners and, embracing all aspects of its Portuguese heritage, Nando's was born in September 1987. Today, the Nando's restaurant chain is a major success story, with stores stretching all the way from Rosettenville to Cape Town, Canada, and Australia.' (Quoted from www.nandos.co.za)

Based on its rapid success in marketing a variety of spicy, grilled chicken products in the Portuguese tradition through an extensive franchising network in South Africa, Nando's was well positioned for international growth, which had became a reality by the early 1990s.

Nando's pursued a highly effective marketing strategy which accounted for its phenomenal growth since 1987. By the time Nando's was listed on the Johannesburg Stock Exchange in 1997, it already had 37 stores in eight countries, and by 1998, 52 stores in 12 countries, including the UK, Canada, Australia, Portugal, Israel, Mauritius, Botswana, and Zimbabwe. In terms of its group structure in 1998, Nando's had a 30% profit participation in its foreign operations, Nando's International, which houses the royalty-receiving interests of international operations. However, the fact that the operations of Nando's Group Holdings were limited to South Africa could be regarded as a serious restriction for any dynamic company such as Nando's.

Nando's had learnt through experience the difficulties of succeeding in the global marketplace, especially as far as differences in sourcing and input costs, logistics, quality, and cultures, were concerned – factors which all contributed to initial store losses. However, as the management team moved up the learning curve, performance improved.

With regard to its international operations, Nando's has been doing well in the UK (London), Canada (Vancouver), Australia, and in Africa. With three new stores in Malaysia, two in Saudi Arabia, and one to be opened in Egypt, the international prospects appear optimistic, despite the recent downturn in earnings of the group in 1999.

In a bid to change the way the world thinks about chicken, Nando's 'has made marketing everything' – from the quality and taste of their products, packaging, store decor, employee dress, approach to health and hygiene, and advertising – creating opportunities to entice customers and enchant them with the taste of Portugal. Nando's unique products are not expensive, and compete on a number of factors other than price, notably a fun and enjoyable eating experience. The following quotation in a way conveys the unique attributes of Nando's marketing approach.

> 'The rest of the world does their marketing according to the '4 P's' – Well, wouldn't you know it, at Nando's we have five of them!
> Our People – Nandocas (we've already mentioned them) set Nando's far apart in our industry and we wouldn't have it any other way!
> Our Product – You only have to experiperience our chicken to know you've discovered something exceptional!
> Our Place – 'Home from home' just the way the familia (so now you're learning Portuguese!) likes it!
> Our Personality – Proud and passionate about who we are and what we do. Don't ever make the mistake of thinking of us as chicken!
> Our Promotion – The more exciting and adventurous, the better. But you know, as the jarretas (old people) say about the praia (beach) ... it's easy to sell something everyone wants!'

Nando's nandocas reflect an illustrious diversity of character and talent, and each one embodies the Nando creed of pride, passion, courage, integrity, and a sense of family values. At the same time, equality, development of skills, job-creation, and culture are not neglected.

A key ingredient in Nando's success has been its enthusiastic and entrepreneurial management team. Building on the success in the domestic market since its inception in 1987, Nando's realised that the key motives to expand internationally were to open new markets and enhance its profitability. This could be achieved by:

- transferring Nando's core competencies and unique product offerings to international markets with the opportunity of earning greater returns on investment;
- realising location economies;
- realising experience curve economies.

Accordingly, Nando's decision to expand internationally was based on its belief that its core competence, and therefore its competitive advantage, inherent in its unique products, combined with its brand name, innovative and customised advertising, and other skills, would increase its market, income and profitability – core competencies which competitors cannot easily match or imitate.

Notwithstanding its earlier successes and market expansion, Nando's financial performance has come under pressure during the last financial year. Marcia Klein reported in May 1999 that, in the wake of its disappointing results for the year to March, the question had arisen as to whether Nando's is doing an about-turn on a previous decision to convert all its franchises to company-owned stores. In line with its profit warning, Nando's Group Holdings reported a 2,5% drop in headline earnings to 6,68c a share and also indicated that it had embarked on a fundamental restructuring which would include the conversion of 15 of its current 140 stores into franchises, with more to follow.

Chairman Robert Brozin says directors reviewed the strategic focus after an analysis of international quick-service restaurant models. 'We took a view that we had to change something fundamentally, and we have decided to franchise some of our existing store base as well as new opportunities.' This seems to fly in the face of the decision, just prior to Nando's listing, to buy back all of its joint-venture stores and make them company-owned. At the time directors wanted to consolidate.

But Brozin says there is no change in policy: franchising will be introduced only on a steady, limited basis. He says the asset base will be enhanced by franchising some of the stores. 'Also, we feel that we will attract a new pool of people wishing to come into the group.' Brozin says franchising will increase shareholder return by improving the risk-return profile of the earnings stream. 'A franchise element will generate additional corporate earnings without the requirement of incremental group investment.' MD Brian Sacks says the core of the Nando's business will remain company-owned and he expects that Nando's will maintain a 60/40 balance.

The May 1999 announcement shows that while revenue grew 13% to R283 million, operating income was 12% down at R28 million. Higher interest rates put margins under severe pressure. Directors say results were hit by high interest rates. A decline in consumer spending was compounded by Nando's having to continue with 12 costly store openings in the second half without commensurate profits. Nando's incurred store closure costs of R3,8 million and brand development costs of R400 000 for its Tasca restaurants.

Higher interest rates and increased borrowings saw net finance costs more than double to R6,1 million. Brozin says directors decided, at the beginning of the financial year, to go ahead with 23 store openings, based on the assumption that interest rates would decline. Although there has been a dip in earnings, Brozin says the business remains sound. Nando's has received wide acceptance in the black market – about 80% of its sales are in this sector.

Shareholders might be forgiven for asking when Nando's will start to benefit from the 30% profit participation of Nando's International. Brozin says: 'We have had quite a good year internationally. We've got the footprint right and we have profitable stores. Now we can roll out our expansion', referring also to the three new stores in Malaysia and two in Saudi Arabia, and the first store to be opened in Egypt soon. Financial director Les Perlman says that over R120 million has been invested in the international operations during the past 18 months. 'The South African company could never have supported local and international development if it had to call on that country's shareholders to do so in view of the development involved,' he says. Although he is clearly very disappointed about the results, he says directors 'are bullish about the future. We have made some fundamental changes and in the meantime are not trading badly, although business is erratic.'

? Questions

1 In entering the international market, did Nando's choose the correct options, viewed from a long-term perspective? Were there any viable alternatives available to Nando's in this regard?

2 Taking into account international economic, political, market, and competitive conditions, what are the strategic options available to Nando's for the future? Which option or options seem to hold the most promise? (Access the Internet for information on, *inter alia*, the company, as well as the international environments, for information relevant to this issue.)

Sources

Pietrzak, Dominika, 'The strategy of international business – A case study on Nando's', Unpublished Research Report, Department of Business Management, University of Pretoria, 1998.

www.nandos.co.za; www.nandos.co.uk

Klein, Marica, 'Nando's denies it's doing a duck on franchise policy', *Sunday Times Business Times*, 30 May 1999, p. 4.

Endnotes

1 Hill, C.W.L. 1998. *International business.* 2nd ed. Burr Ridge, Illinois: McGraw-Hill Irwin, p. 358.
2 Hill, op. cit, p. 489.
3 Levitt, T. 1983. 'The globalisation of markets', *Harvard Business Review,* May-June, pp. 92–102.
4 Berry, B.J.L. ,Conkling, E.C. & Ray, D.M. 1997. *The global economy in transition.* 2nd ed. Upper Saddle River, New Jersey: Prentice Hall, p. 1.
5 Hill, op. cit, p. 359.
6 Keegan, W.J. 1995, *Global marketing management.* 5th ed. Upper Saddle River, New Jersey: Prentice Hall, pp. 3–4.
7 Ball, D.A. & McCulloch, W.H. 1999. *International business.* 7th ed. Burr Ridge, Illinois:McGraw-Hill, Irwin, p. 3.
8 Griffin, R.W. & Pustay, M.W. 1999. *International business.* 2nd ed. Reading, Massachusetts: Addison Wesley Longman, p. 584.
9 Doole, I. & Lowe, R. 1999. *International marketing strategy.* 2nd ed. London: International Thomson Business Press, p. 9.
10 Keegan, op. cit., p. 3.
11 Doole & Lowe, op. cit., p. 9.
12 Doole & Lowe, op. cit., p. 39.
13 Doole & Lowe, op. cit., pp. 6 and 39.
14 Ball & McCulloch, op. cit., p. 216.
15 Berry et al., op. cit., p. 79.
16 Mühlbacher, H., Daringer, L. & Leihs, H. 1999. *International marketing.* 2nd ed. London: International Thomson Business Press, pp. 171–172.
17 Ibid.
18 Doole & Lowe, op. cit., p. 78.
19 Chee, H. & Harris, R. 1998. *Global marketing strategy.* London: Financial Times Pitman Publishing, p. 140.
20 Usunier, J.C. 1996. *Marketing across cultures.* 2nd ed. Upper Saddle River, New Jersey: Prentice Hall, p. 110.
21 Mühlbacher et al., op. cit., pp. 825–827.
22 Rugman, A.M. & Hodgetts, R.M. 1995. *International business.* New York: McGraw-Hill, p. 296.
23 Daniëls, J.D. & Radebaugh, L.H. 1998. *International business.* 8th ed, Reading, Massachusetts: Addison Wesley Longman, p. 525.
24 Daniëls & Radebaugh, op. cit., p. 526.
25 Rugman & Hodgetts, op. cit., p. 296–299. The discussion is largely based on the excellent approach of Rugman and Hodgetts. For the process of international marketing research see, *inter alia,* Daniëls & Radebaugh, op. cit., Chapter 13; Doole & Lowe, op. cit., Chapter 4; Chee & Harris, op. cit., Chapter 8; and Mühlbacher et al., op. cit., Chapters 6 to 8.
26 Grose, T.K. 1997 'Ten risky businesses', *Time,* 7 July, p. 60.
27 Daniëls & Radebaugh, op. cit., p. 528–30.
28 Ibid.
29 Daniëls & Radebaugh, op. cit., pp. 546–51.
30 Rugman & Hodgetts, op. cit., pp. 298–299.
31 Hill, op. cit., p. 404.
32 Doole & Lowe, op. cit., p. 311.
33 Chee & Harris, op. cit., p. 292.
34 Doole & Lowe, op. cit., p. 312.
35 Hill, op. cit., p. 404–405.
36 Ibid.
37 Contractor, F.J. 1982. 'The role of licensing in international strategy', *Columbia Journal of World Business,* Winter, pp. 73–83.
38 Hill, op. cit., p. 404–405.
39 Ibid.
Phatak, A.V. 1997. *International management: concepts and cases.* Cincinnati, Ohio: South Western College Publishing, pp. 254–55.
40 Phatak, op. cit., p. 262.
41 Hill, op. cit., p. 407.
42 Hill, op. cit., p. 410;
Phatak, op. cit., p. 264.
43 Phatak, op. cit., p. 269.
44 Hill, op. cit., p. 407.
Phatak, op. cit., p. 269–70.
45 Phatak, op. cit., pp. 272–275.
46 Hill, op. cit., p. 414–15.
47 Ibid.
48 Ibid.
49 Chee & Harris, op. cit., p. 224.
50 Chee & Harris, op. cit., pp. 236-237;
Czinkota, M.R, & Ronkainen, I.A. 1998. *International marketing.* 5th ed. New York: Dryden Press, pp. 495–507.
51 Chee & Harris, op. cit., pp. 239–40.
52 Griffin & Pustay, op. cit., pp. 586–87.
Yudelson, J. 1999. 'Adapting McCarthy's four P's for the twenty-first century', *Journal of Marketing Education,* Vol. 21, No. 1, April, pp. 60–67. (This contains an excellent exposition of the elements of the marketing mix.)
53 Chee & Harris, op. cit., p. 372.
54 Kotler, P. & Armstrong, G. 1994. *Principles of marketing.* 6th ed. Englewood Cliffs, New Jersey: Prentice Hall p. 119, in Chee & Harris, op. cit., pp. 370–71.
55 Rugman & Hodgetts, op. cit., pp. 299–300.
56 Hill, op. cit., pp. 68–69 & 491.
57 Hill, op. cit., pp. 491–492.
Griffin & Pustay, op. cit., pp. 592–593.
58 Hill, op. cit., p. 593.
59 Doole & Lowe, op. cit., p. 462–463.
60 Ibid, adapted.
61 Hill, op. cit., p. 494.
62 Doole & Lowe, op. cit., pp. 480–85.

63 Hill, op. cit., pp. 494–504.
64 Hill, op. cit., p. 495–96.
65 Ibid.
66 Doole & Lowe, op. cit., p. 430–31.
67 Ibid.
68 Hill, op. cit., p. 496–97.
69 Ibid.
70 Doole & Lowe, op. cit., p. 429–429.
71 Ibid.
72 Hill, op. cit., p. 498.
73 Grimes, A. & Doole, I. 1998. 'Exploring the relationship between colour and international branding: A cross-cultural comparison of the UK and Taiwan', *Journal of Marketing Management*, Vol. 14, No. 7, pp. 799–817.
74 Chee & Harris, op. cit., p. 483.
75 Griffin & Pustay, op. cit., p . 595.
76 Hill, op. cit., p. 501–504.
Griffin & Pustay, op. cit., p. 596–97.
77 Griffin & Pustay, op. cit., p. 597.
78 Hill, op. cit., p. 504.
79 Griffin & Pustay, op. cit., pp. 587–589.

Appendix

Franchising as a mode of international market entry: a South African perspective

Overview of franchising

Franchising, often regarded as simply the duplication of convenience stores and fast-food outlets, could hold the key to South Africa's unemployment problem, and contribute substantially to the acceleration of economic growth, writes Justin Palmer in the *Sunday Times Business Times*, during June 1999.

It is estimated that for every franchise opened, 15 people are directly employed. However, in the USA research has shown that true job-creation benefits lie outside the franchise itself. For every new franchise, 32 jobs are created and maintained, not by the franchise but because of it.

The entry of McDonald's into South Africa illustrates this. Since opening, this company has employed about 4 500 people. It has also created jobs for companies involved in building the restaurants and supplying signage, packaging, printing, furniture, and ingredients. Even more important in the South African – and indeed the southern African – context is that franchising also enables and facilitates skills transfer at a time when a skills shortage remains one of the main stumbling blocks to job creation in South Africa, as well as in its neighbouring countries.

Franchising currently accounts for 9% of GDP in South Africa. In Australia this figure is 25% and industry experts hope that South [illegible] can reach a similar figure within the [illegible]rs.

Because of these benefits, the government is working closely with South Africa's franchising watchdog, the Franchising Association of SA (FASA), to promote franchising and align it with the country's Gear (growth, employment, and redistribution) policy.

An impediment is the availability of money to finance franchises. Nic Louw, executive director of FASA, concedes that financing is a problem. Steps are being taken to counter this, starting with a trend away from franchises that require high start-up capital, toward low-cost franchises requiring less than R100 000 to start. With banks often accepting a lower deposit for a franchise, a significant portion of the remaining cost can then be financed.

The Department of Trade and Industry (DTI), through its investment arm, Khula Finance, is also looking at creative ways to assist previously disadvantaged entrepreneurs, referred to by the department as 'emerging entrepreneurs'. One way to do so is by introducing franchise support consultants into each province to help people draw up business plans. The DTI is also hoping to set up an Emerging Entrepreneur Franchise Fund (EEFF) to which emerging entrepreneurs will have access. The fund will be a joint venture between government and the private sector.

Although the benefits of franchising are apparent, the pitfalls are perhaps less so. Louw cautions that many people regard franchising as an investment, when in fact it is a job, often requiring longer hours and harder work than if you were working for a boss. The benefit, though, is that you are your own boss.

However, the media have been full of stories recently about franchise relationships gone wrong – Seeff and London Pie among them.

How should individuals interested in a franchise ensure that they don't end up with a dog?

A good starting point is to check whether the franchisor (the person selling the franchise) is registered with FASA. The requirements for joining this organisation are stringent, and the banks are more likely to provide finance if these requirements have been met. Louw estimates that only about 5% of all applicants make the grade.

First, the company must have a pilot operation which has been in business for at least one year. Next, it needs to draw up several separate documents. The first is a disclosure document providing a detailed description of the company and outlining the fees payable by the franchisee (the person buying the franchise) to the franchisor. The franchisee can expect to pay three kinds of fees – an upfront fee covering the cost of setting up, an ongoing management services fee (often referred to as a royalty), and a fee for advertising. The company will also need to submit an agreement defining the relationship between franchisor and franchisee. This is a legal contract. The third document to be submitted is a training/operations manual which outlines business operations.

Franchising has slowed down in recent months, but FASA says that this could be related to the general downturn in the economy.

According to Dr Willie Marais, franchise and business consultant, there has been a perceived shifting of power with regard to franchises in recent years. Marais states that it is becoming increasingly prevalent in South Africa that once you have signed a franchise contract, you become a slave, which has been the experience of many people who have bought franchises. In his view, the most recent winning recipe for franchisors, especially in the USA, is to involve franchisees more in the larger organisation, and to listen to them. During the most recent convention of the International Franchise Association in Miami, Florida, it became apparent that the powerbase in the industry is beginning to shift. It has now become the decade of the franchisee, and everything no longer revolves around the franchisor.

Marais states that a few groups in South Africa are beginning to listen to their franchisees, but not nearly to the same extent as in the USA. 'It is important that both parties in the industry realise that communication channels must be created. The franchisor must create an opportunity where his or her franchisees can air their views, and provide an insight into their problems,' says Marais.

The basic mistake that most South African companies make is that they do not realise that the businesspersons to whom they have sold franchises are their real clients, and not the customers out there. Another problem is that many companies are only involved in selling franchises. They are so focused on expansion that they neglect their existing franchise-holders and do not do nearly enough to improve the franchise concept and product.

Does this mean that you must stay away from franchises? Marais disagrees. It is a brilliant way of doing business, because you can repeat a proven success recipe. But what prospective purchasers of franchises should first do is to establish how the franchise company does business. Are the franchisees left to themselves after the contract has been signed, do they undergo training, and have they had exposure to the company's systems and methods? Or is there continued support and development of the franchise? Are franchisees listened to with regard to their problems and ideas? One way to find out is by contacting a number of existing franchisees.

Before people invest their savings or nest-egg in a franchise, it is advisable that they first of all obtain expert advice from consultants and FASA.

In terms of where the opportunities in franchising are, Douw van der Walt reports that the United States is still regarded as the land of opportunities, and that people first and foremost look to that country for new ideas. Since the decision to go into business should be based on long-term considerations, it has become critically important to identify the existing as well as potential growth areas in franchising. As of May 1999, it appeared that top of the list of franchise ideas in the USA were business-to-business services, such as printing, courier services, and bookkeeping services. Second were food service enterprises, followed by computer-related services, speciality stores, and sports and leisure services – in that order.

Based on recent research in South Africa, opportunities are in business-to-business services (as in the USA), photographic printing and development, and personal services (mainly beauty, hair care, and related services). It would seem that franchising in food services has lost its glamour and has slipped down the order. Marais, however, maintains that food services still provide viable options in South Africa, and so do speciality stores – especially in the baby product lines. Training and development in business and communication skills, and in computer literacy, have emerged as growth areas. A predominantly American concept which has, however, not yet taken on in South Africa, is that of a store-within-a-store. Making retail store space selectively available to franchisees could augment the revenue of larger chain stores. However, the use of franchising 'warehouses', such as in sports equipment and recreational services, appears to be gaining ground in South Africa.

In the context of internationalisation, and given the appropriate product or service, franchising from one's home country has become an excellent way of exploring and entering international markets. We have seen in this chapter that franchising has many advantages as a mode of market entry and a system for international marketing. It is often preferable to outright exports or the use of marketing agents in foreign countries, because the franchisor will have more direct control over quality and the operations.

A growing number of franchisors have taken advantage of opportunities to expand their franchise systems outside South Africa. Expansion into international markets, however, does demand extra preparation and efforts on the part of the franchisor, but the rewards are often substantial.

As we have seen, there are several business, legal, and other practical issues to consider when deciding to enter international markets. In particular, the economic, political, and cultural environments of those countries and regions that have been targeted for international business should be thoroughly investigated.

There are five basic strategies/methods in international franchising which can be followed – each with its own benefits and risks. The methods of expanding a franchise internationally include a master franchise arrangement in the host country, joint venturing, or direct investment. The last option could include a company-owned operation, direct franchising, or licensing.

Basically, in a master franchise arrangement, the franchisor selects and appoints a master franchisee in the target country. This franchisee will usually have the exclusive rights for the whole country, assume the role of franchisor, and may choose either to appoint sub-franchisees or to open all the outlets itself.

In joint venturing the franchisor joins local citizens in the target country in setting up production and/or market locations. The franchisor will need to negotiate what share he/she wishes to take up and how the operation should be financed. The joint venture operation (normally a company) will become the sub-franchisor of the franchisor's system, and help the franchisor to establish the franchise in the target country on a shared basis.

As far as direct investment is concerned, in company-owned operations the franchisor establishes a company-owned network of outlets in the target country, often by way of a branch operation or through the establishment of subsidiary companies. In direct franchising the franchisor enters into direct franchise agreements with individual franchisees in the target country and provides the necessary back-up and continuing support.

Licensing, one of the most common methods of international franchising, involves an agreement between the franchisor and a licensee (franchisee) as to the right to use a product, service, trade mark, trade secret, patent, or other valuable item, in return for a royalty fee. Licensing enables the franchisor to enter the foreign market at little or no risk.

Sources

Palmer, Justin, 'Franchising a fast route to job creation', *Sunday Times Business Times*, Section 3, 20 June 1999, p. 1.

Van der Walt, Douw, 'Dis waar die geleenthede is', *Finansies & Tegniek*, 14 Mei 1999, p. 47 (translated).

Van der Walt, Douw, 'Verskuiwing van mag met franchises', *Finansies & Tegniek*, 14 Mei 1999, p. 46 (translated).

Nieman, G. 1998, *The franchise option – How to franchise your business*. Kenwyn: Juta & Co, pp. 141–146.

International financial management and strategy

Key issues

- Activities and scope of international financial management
- The goal of international financial management
- International working capital and global money management
- Foreign exchange risk management
- International investment analysis and capital budgeting
- International financing decisions

10.1 Introduction

The global economic environment discussed in Chapter 5 and the dynamics of the foreign exchange market described in Chapter 6 provide the frame of reference for a discussion of the key areas of international financial management in this chapter. These areas include the management of global cash flows, foreign exchange risk management, international investment analysis and capital budgeting, and international financing.

The world economy and international business have become increasingly globalised, primarily due to declining trade and investment barriers, advances in technology, the increasing standardisation of products, and the accelerated movement toward free enterprise – all of which have contributed to the greater mobility of resources. As a result of the continued expansion of markets, operations, structures, and sourcing of international firms, effective financial management has not only become increasingly more important, but also significantly more complex.

In the process of internationalisation, a firm generally begins by importing supplies from foreign manufacturers, or by exporting its products to one or more foreign countries. In time, as new opportunities are identified internationally, the firm extends its operations into foreign countries through some kind of co-operative arrangement with host-country organisations. Eventually, it establishes a subsidiary in a foreign country by the acquisition of an existing firm or establishing a new subsidiary enterprise. A fundamental understanding of the requirements of financial management in each of these stages is of crucial importance as the firm evolves into a large MNE with numerous foreign subsidiaries. Despite the importance of traditional financial management approaches and methods, it is clear that international involvement brings new complexities, opportunities and risks beyond those generally found in domestic operations.

It is generally accepted that the following factors or issues tend to make **international financial management** unique and more complex, but also more challenging:

- differences in social, political and legal environments between countries;
- different currencies and, therefore, different foreign exchange exposures between countries;
- differences in tax regimes and varying degrees of exchange controls between countries;
- unique institutional factors, such as the Eurocurrency Market, the Eurobond Market, other international trade financing and credit guarantee instruments, and institutions that impact differently on different countries.[1]

In this chapter the focus will accordingly be on international financial management by first considering the activities, scope, and goals relevant to this kind of management. International working capital management and the important issue of efficient global money management will then be discussed. The various types of foreign exchange exposure and the strategies for managing foreign exchange risk are identified. International investment and capital budgeting decisions, as well as the issues that complicate these decisions in international business, are then explored. The chapter ends with a discussion of the sources of international finance and international financing decisions.

10.2 Activities and scope of international financial management

The activities of financial management relate to the following three major areas of decision-making;[2]

- **Investment or capital budgeting** – analysing, planning, and managing the firm's long-term investments;
- **Financing or capital structure** – identifying the optimal sources of long-term capital and the most favourable combination of debt and equity to maintain an optimum capital structure for the firm;
- **Working capital management** – planning and managing the levels and composition of the short-term or current assets and current liabilities of the firm.

Inherent in the first two decision areas is the so-called profit appropriation or dividend policy decision, which involves elements of both the investment and financing decisions of the firm. All the above-mentioned decisions generally require sound and continuous financial planning and control. In an international setting, however, these traditional financial management activities are executed in a relatively more uncertain, dynamic, and complex business environment, which also requires new approaches, methods, and skills on the part of the financial manager.

According to Madura, international financial management is not only important for large multinational enterprises, but often even more so in the case of small and medium-sized enterprises.[3] For example, 75% of all American firms that export have fewer than 100 employees. Surprisingly enough, international finance is possibly even important to firms that have no intention of engaging in international business, for the following reasons:

- These firms must know how their foreign competitors will be affected by movements in exchange rates, foreign interest rates, and inflation rates, as well as foreign labour costs, since changes in these factors can affect a foreign competitor's cost of production and pricing policies.
- They must also understand how domestic competitors who obtain foreign supplies and/or foreign financing will be affected by changes in economic conditions in foreign countries. These competitors could reduce their prices in the home market, without reducing their profit margins, by capitalising on opportunities in foreign markets and increasing their market share at the expense of domestic firms.[4]

Effective financial management can be a source of competitive advantage for the multinational enterprise. Hill confirms that competitive advantage is gained when a firm decreases the cost of value creation and/or adds value for the customer without increasing the cost of achieving it, compared to its competitors. It is, therefore, essential that the international financial manager should scrutinise the entire value chain of the firm in order to reduce costs and/or add value for the customer through improved service and quality. More specifically, a competitive cost advantage could be attained for the international firm if astute international financial managers are successful in doing the following:

- reducing the firm's cost of capital by financing from low-cost/low-risk international financial sources;
- eliminating or reducing foreign exchange losses;
- optimising global cash flows by methods such as multilateral netting, judicious transfer pricing, and centralised reserves;
- minimising the firm's tax burden;
- minimising the firm's exposure to unnecessarily risky situations;
- analysing potential foreign investment opportunities comprehensively and meticulously .[5]

Exhibit 10.1 illustrates the relationship between the international macro-environment (which

Exhibit 10.1: Relationship between the international macro-environment and managerial decision-making in multinational business finance

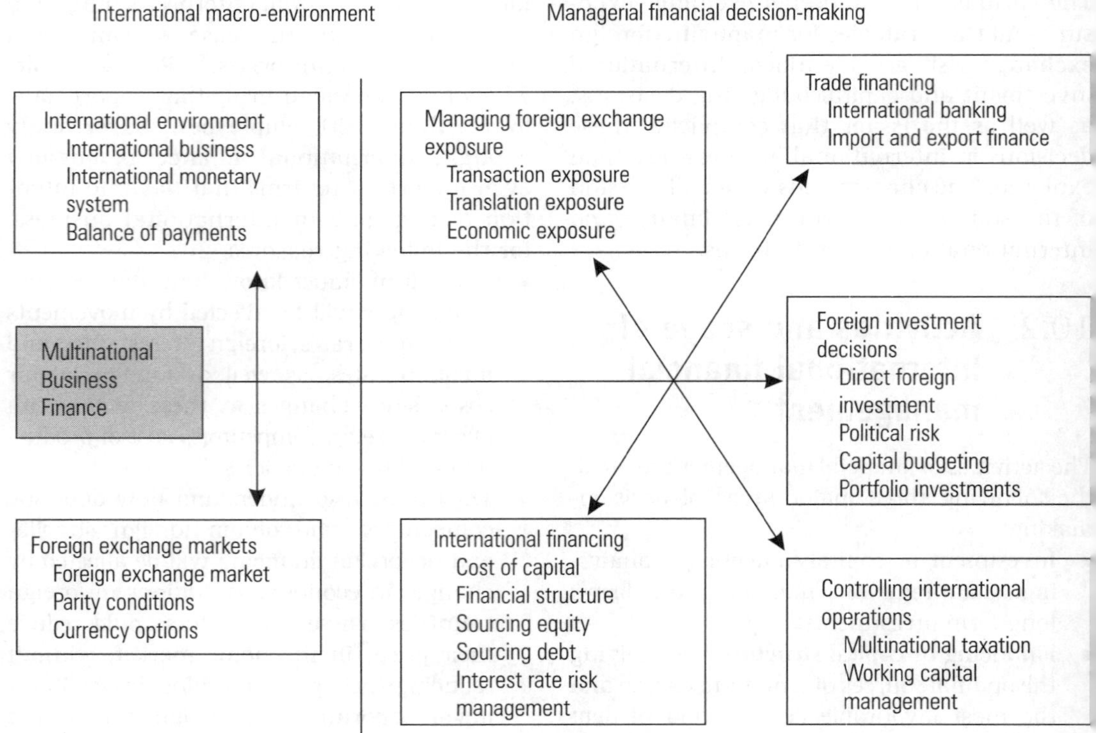

SOURCE: Adapted from Eiteman, D.K., Stonehill, A.I., & Moffett, M.H. 1995. *Multinational business finance.* 7th ed. Reading, Massachusetts: Addison-Wesley, p. 7

includes the foreign exchange market) and the managerial decision-making areas in the function of multinational business finance.

Eiteman et al. summarise the scope of international financial management and the need for a clear goal in this regard as follows:

> Financial management, even in a domestic environment, is one of those curious combinations of mathematical precision ... and the prime source of all random behaviour: human behaviour. When the financial management activities must stretch across geographic, cultural, political, and jurisdictional boundaries, the attention needed to organisation and goals is critical.[6]

Most of the aspects related to the international macro-environment in Exhibit 10.1 were discussed in Chapters 5 and 6. This chapter will consider global money management, foreign exchange risk, and international investment and financing decisions. There will be no further discussion on international trade financing.

10.3 The goal of international financial management

With the Anglo-American approach, **maximising shareholder wealth** is accepted as the goal of management. However, although this goal could probably be regarded as realistic in both theory and practice in Anglo-American markets, it is not necessarily realistic anywhere else.[7]

It seems that managers in other countries place more emphasis on long-term performance than American managers. The implication of this for the multinational enterprise based in the USA is that, in its foreign subsidiaries, managers who have not come from the USA may make decisions which could be inconsistent with the Anglo-American approach of maximising shareholder wealth – not that this is necessarily detrimental to the long-term performance of the MNE.[8]

Apart from the traditional **agency problem** – the conflict that arises where the owners or shareholders of a company differ from their managers as far as the goals of the company are concerned – it is possible that managers of foreign subsidiaries who have been raised in different cultures, may not adhere to uniform company goals for cultural reasons, or may make decisions to maximise the value of their own subsidiaries. Moreover, where a decentralised management style, as opposed to centralised management, is followed in the MNE, adherence to uniform corporate goals may not be ideal.

When the goal of financial managers of MNEs is to **maximise the value of their firms** rather than shareholder wealth, this has to be achieved under various limitations, such as the following:

- environmental constraints;
- regulatory constraints;
- ethical constraints.[9]

The way in which, or the extent to which, any one or more of these constraints impact on the cash flows of a foreign subsidiary and, even more importantly, on the remitted cash flows to the parent company, will affect the value of the firm and constitute one of the primary concerns of international financial management.

Two models of the goal of management which are relevant here are:

- the shareholder wealth maximisation model;
- the corporate wealth maximisation model.

According to Eiteman et al., the shareholder wealth maximisation model (maximising shareholder return, which is seen as the sum of capital gains and dividends for a given level of risk) is based on the concept of efficient markets, with risk, according to portfolio theory, defined as systematic risk only. This model is also based on the one-share-one-vote rule that is followed in Anglo-American markets. In contrast, the corporate wealth maximisation model, which characterises European and Japanese equity markets, stresses the maximisation of corporate wealth, where shareholders (owners) constitute only one of many of the company's interest groups (such as management, labour, the community, suppliers, creditors, and at times even the government), and is based on a long-term perspective. Corporate wealth furthermore includes aspects such as technological, market, and human resources (intellectual capital). Lastly, this model is based on total risk, and is not concerned about efficient markets. These equity markets are not characterised by the one-share-one-vote rule but are based on inherent 'loyalty' on the part of interest groups, which implies that management is not easily displaced.[10]

While the authors adhere to the Anglo-American approach of the shareholder wealth maximisation model, they are fully aware that the goal of management could be different due to 'culturally determined' norms in the context of international business. However, the overall consideration in finance, whether domestic or international, is that it focuses on cash flows.

Since international business or cross-border activities introduce different political, legal, or social settings, different markets, different interest and inflation rates, different tax regimes, but most importantly, different currencies, the challenges for international financial management are:

- how best to manage the firm's financial resources under these diverse, dynamic, and competitive conditions;
- how best to protect the firm from actual or potential political, economic, and financial risks, including foreign exchange risk.

10.4 International working capital and global money management

Based on the goal of shareholder wealth maximisation, the objectives of international financial management include the effective management of the firm's global cash flows, its foreign exchange risk, its investments by means of fundamental capital budgeting approaches, and its capital structure.

Although the responsibility for these activities derives from the parent company in the home country, the implications of such activities and responsibilities permeate the entire multinational enterprise, including the operations of foreign subsidiaries in remote locations. Decisions related to some of the above objectives, such as managing the firm's global cash flows, are made on a day-to-day basis, whereas decisions related to some of the other objectives, such as long-term foreign investment and financing decisions, are made only periodically.

The effective management of international working capital – current assets and liabilities – is a continuous process. In addition, the current assets such as debtors accounts or accounts receivable, inventories, cash, and marketable securities, as well as current liabilities, including trade credit and short-term funding, all impact on the international firm's cash flows on a continuous basis. Accordingly, the next section will focus on the management of the firm's global cash flows and effective global money management.

10.4.1 Global money management

Managing global cash flows and effective global money management include:

- minimising cash balances;
- reducing transaction costs;
- centralising depositories;
- making optimal use of internal funds;
- positioning funds optimally;
- multilateral netting.[11]

Since these issues together constitute one of the key areas in international financial management, each of these activities will be considered briefly in the context of international business.

(a) Minimising cash balances

During any given period, a firm must hold certain cash balances, but keep these balances as low as possible without jeopardising the continuity of the firm.[12]

When firms hold cash in excess of these minimum requirements, they incur an opportunity cost – the interest or return lost on the best available investment opportunity for the firm. However, in order to minimise cash balances and at the same time ensure adequate liquidity, it is necessary to first know why cash is needed, and then how much to hold. Traditionally, three motives determine the cash and liquidity levels of any firm:

- **the transactions motive** – the need to hold cash to satisfy normal payments (accounts and notes) with regard to the firm's ongoing operations;
- **the precautionary motive** – the need to hold cash as a safety margin to serve as a financial reserve;
- **the speculative motive** – the need to hold cash to take advantage of unique and financially beneficial opportunities.[13]

Firms obviously keep a certain amount of cash on hand, especially to satisfy the transactions motive and for contingency purposes, while the remainder of the cash is invested in short-term, low-interest-bearing, marketable securities that allow immediate withdrawal. Thus, the higher the cash and short-term investments, the lower the overall rate of return to the firm.

In the context of international business, the multinational company with numerous subsidiaries is also faced with this dilemma – unlimited liquidity, but very low returns, or limited liquidity and higher returns – but of a far more complex nature. Centralised management of total global cash reserves, as opposed to allowing each subsidiary to decide how to determine and manage its own cash reserves, could substantially reduce the amount of low-interest-bearing liquid funds a company needs to hold, and thereby improve its overall return on investment. This centralised depository approach is discussed below.

(b) Reducing transaction costs

Transaction costs basically involve the commission paid as fees to foreign exchange dealers each time a foreign exchange transaction takes place, and often also include a transfer fee for moving cash from one location to another. These costs attributable to intrafirm transactions and transfers could be substantial for multinational enterprises with networks of foreign subsidiaries in different countries. Multilateral netting is an approach that MNEs can use to great advantage to reduce transaction costs related to foreign exchange dealings. Multilateral netting is discussed further on.

(c) Centralising depositories

Centralised pooling of cash reserves gives firms larger amounts to deposit, and they earn higher rates of return on such amounts, especially if they are located in major financial centres. By pooling cash reserves, multinational enterprises can also reduce the total amount of overall cash-holding.

(d) Making optimal use of internal funds

Multinational enterprises use a number of techniques to transfer funds between countries, which include dividend remittances, royalty payments, licensing fees, transfer prices, and fronting loans.

When MNEs want to expand their international operations, the obvious source of additional funds is the firm's net working capital – the difference between current assets and current liabilities. For example, should South African Breweries (SAB) wish to expand their operations in Hungary, the capital required for this purpose could possibly be derived from funds generated internally by the ongoing operations of the Hungarian subsidiary. Other means of internal funding include a loan from a local Hungarian bank, based on formal or informal guarantees by the parent company or from one of SAB's other foreign subsidiaries, such as in Ireland. A third possibility involves the parent company increasing its equity investment in the subsidiary. These different options are illustrated in Exhibit 10.2. The financing decisions and specific sources of internal funds for the multinational enterprise are discussed in greater detail in Section 10.7.1.

Which one of these options is the most beneficial? Firstly, bear in mind that the objective is the optimal use of internal financial resources in support of the goal of the firm. The answer to this question will therefore depend on numerous factors, such as the following:

- Government regulations with regard to intercompany lending (South Africa/Ireland to Hungary). According to Rugman and Hodgetts, profitable subsidiaries in countries where tax rates are high, are quite willing to lend money at low interest rates to other subsidiaries in need of funds for expansion. From the point of view of the lending subsidiaries, high interest payments would have been heavily taxed on interest receipts. The borrowing subsidiary, with low interest payments, can augment its cash position for expansion purposes. By doing this, MNEs ensure the optimal use of internal funds in financing expansion, while at the same time minimising tax liability. However, to prevent multinational enterprises from capitalising on tax situations such as the above, governments in many countries have introduced minimum interest rates allowable on cross-border intracompany loans in their international tax laws and regulations.
- Where governments limit a parent company's ability to receive royalties, licensing fees, or management fees from foreign subsidiaries in return for the use of technological or managerial know-how, the parent MNE loses a great deal of its freedom in obtaining funds from subsidiary operations for use in other areas of operations.[14]

(e) Positioning funds optimally

To the extent that home- and host-government regulatory and policy measures allow the largely unrestricted transfer of funds, multinational enterprises can use any one or more of the commonly known funds positioning techniques with the object of optimal resource utilisation. These techniques include **transfer pricing**, **tax havens**, and **fronting loans**, which are discussed briefly below.

Transfer pricing: It is common practice in multinational business enterprises to transfer goods and services between the parent company and foreign subsidiaries, as well as between foreign subsidiaries individually. According to Hill, these transfers are likely to be prevalent in MNEs following global and transnational strategies as a result of highly

Exhibit 10.2: Internal sources and flows of funds in a multinational enterprise

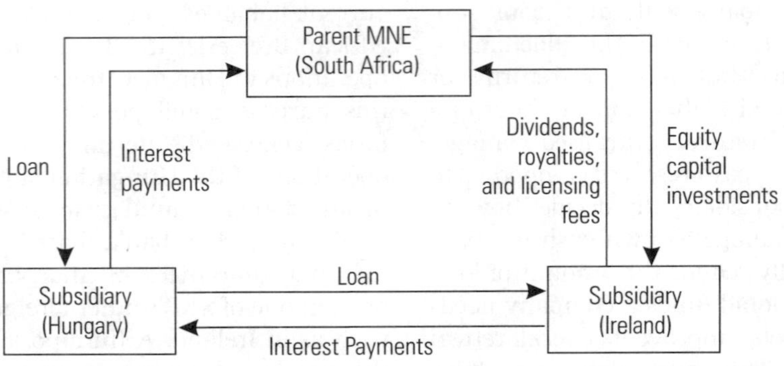

SOURCE: Adapted from Rugman, A.M., & Hodgetts, R.M. 1995. *International business.* New York: McGraw-Hill, p. 387.

dispersed value creation activities in optimal locations worldwide. The **transfer price** is the internal price at which goods and services are transferred between entities within the multinational enterprise.[15]

Bearing in mind that funds can be moved between the parent company and a foreign subsidiary, or between different subsidiaries, transfer prices can be used to effectively position funds within the multinational enterprise, once again with a view to optimising financial resources within the firm. The way in which this is achieved is explained as follows. Funds can be moved out of country A by setting high **transfer prices** for the goods and services which are supplied **to** the subsidiary in country A, and setting **low transfer prices** for the goods and services which are sourced **from** the subsidiary in country A (relatively large funds outflow; relatively low funds inflow). Funds can be moved to a specific country by doing the opposite. For example, funds can be moved into country B by setting **high transfer prices** for goods and services which are obtained **from** the subsidiary in country B, and setting **low transfer prices** for goods and services supplied **to** the subsidiary in country B (relatively large funds inflow; relatively low funds outflow).

Benefits of transfer pricing for multinational enterprises could include:

- reducing the firm's tax liabilities by using transfer prices to move earnings from a country with a high tax rate to one with a low tax rate;
- using transfer prices to remove funds from a country where a currency devaluation is expected, thus reducing the firm's foreign exchange exposure;
- using transfer prices to move funds from a subsidiary to a parent company or to a tax haven where host-government policies restrict or block financial transfers from subsidiaries in the form of dividends;
- using transfer prices to reduce the import duties to be paid by the firm where *ad valorem* tariffs (expressed as a percentage of value) are applicable. Low transfer prices imply a lower value for goods and services and, consequently, lower import duties.[16]

Although the manipulation of transfer prices has obvious benefits, there are also inherent problems associated with this practice, and few governments are favourably disposed towards transfer pricing.[17] To illustrate the funds positioning and tax implications of transfer prices shown in Exhibit 10.3, assume countries A and B with low and high corporate tax rates of 40% and 50% respectively. The subsidiary in country A sells merchandise to the subsidiary in country B. In the first scenario, this intra-company transaction takes place at an **arm's length price** – the price a buyer will pay for merchandise in a market under conditions of

Exhibit 10.3: Shifting profits by transfer pricing

	'Arm's-length' price		Transfer price	
	Country A	Country B	Country A	Country B
Sales	£60 000	£72 000	£72 000	£72 000
Cost of sales	48 000	60 000	48 000	72 000
Operating profit	12 000	12 000	24 000	0
Tax	4 800	6 000	9 600	0
Net profit after tax	£ 7 200	£ 6 000	£14 400	£ 0

SOURCE: Adapted from Rugman & Hodgetts, op. cit., p. 388.

perfect competition. The merchandise which cost £48 000 to produce, is sold for £60 000 to the subsidiary in country B, where a 20% mark-up is added, with both subsidiaries making a profit of £12 000. Given the tax rates of 40% and 50%, the profits of the respective subsidiaries are £7 200 in country A and £6 000 in country B.

The second scenario illustrates a transfer price arrangement, with the objectives of maximising profits in the country with a low tax rate, minimising the MNE's overall tax liability, and maximising its total profit after tax. As shown in Exhibit 10.3, the transfer price is set at £12 000 above the arm's length price of £60 000, which results in an operating profit of £24 000 for the subsidiary in country A. Because subsidiary B has to sell in a competitive market, a cost of sales amounting to £72 000 leaves no room for profit. In this example, even though the subsidiary in country B realises no profit, the end result is that with transfer prices, a total profit of £14 400 is realised (instead of £13 200), and the overall tax liability is reduced to £9 600 (compared to £10 800 previously).

This example illustrates that transfer prices allow the reduction of taxes and the maximisation of profits, and enable the firm to concentrate cash in specific locations such as country A.

However, the practice of transfer pricing also has inherent problems, such as the following:

- where transfer prices are used to reduce taxes and import duties, governments do not take kindly to the loss of potential tax revenue and duties;
- where transfer prices are used to circumvent government restrictions on funds flows, such as restrictions on dividend remittances from the host country, manipulative measures are frowned upon;
- where the management incentives for subsidiaries are based on performance, the fact that financial statements are based on transfer prices, such as for the subsidiary in country B, as shown in Exhibit 10.3, defeats the purpose or objective of performance evaluation;
- the transfer price approach does not encourage efficient performance by the seller where prices are manipulated, as in the case of the subsidiary in country A in the second scenario.[18]

Because of the adverse effect of arbitrary transfer pricing on tax revenues and import duties, many governments have been revising their tax laws in recent years in an attempt to eliminate price manipulation for purposes of evading tax and import duties.

Transfer pricing

PriceWaterhouseCoopers wrote in May 1999 that a recent draft practice note had been issued by the Commissioner of Inland Revenue which deals specifically with Sections 31(1) and 31(2) of the South African Income Tax Act. The practice note is modelled on transfer pricing legislation in New Zealand and Australia, and states that some provisions may change and further provisions added in the final version.

Section 31 was introduced into the South African Income Tax Act in 1995 in anticipation of the relaxation of exchange controls in South Africa and the resultant adverse effect on the South African tax base. According to the Commissioner, each transfer pricing case will be decided on its own merits, taking into account the taxpayer's business strategies and commercial judgement with regard to the application of the arm's-length-price principle. It is furthermore clear that South African taxpayers will have to accumulate comparable data from Europe or the USA, and provide supporting documentation to prove credible transfer pricing policies between related parties. The South African Revenue Services (SARS) will have wide-ranging investigative and other powers in transfer pricing cases where tax risks might be deemed to apply. According to PriceWaterhouse Coopers, it is in the taxpayer's best interest in the event of any dispute to discharge its burden of proof by:

- developing an appropriate transfer price policy;
- determining an arm's-length amount as required by Section 31 of the Act; and
- voluntarily producing documentation to support the taxpayer's analysis.

SOURCE: Summarised from PriceWaterhouseCoopers, *Synopsis*, May 1999, pp.10–11.

Tax havens: International firms can also use **tax havens** such as Bermuda, the Bahamas, Jersey, Guernsey, and the Isle of Man, to minimise their tax liability. Tax havens such as these, which have a low or non-existent income tax rate, can be used by international business firms to either avoid or defer income taxes.

This is normally achieved by establishing a wholly-owned, non-operating subsidiary in the tax haven, which owns the ordinary shares of the MNE's operating foreign subsidiaries. Consequently, all transfers of funds from the foreign subsidiary to the parent company are channelled through the tax haven subsidiary. The tax on the foreign source income by the parent company's home government can then be deferred until such time as the dividend is declared and paid over to the parent company by this tax haven subsidiary.

Such a tax deferral can also contribute to the firm's optimal use of financial resources since, in theory, the deferral can be for an indefinite period if, for example, foreign operations elsewhere require new financing. This is then provided by the tax haven subsidiary. Tax regulations in the USA, however, preclude multinational companies based in that country from deferring taxes as described above.[19]

Fronting loans: A **fronting loan** is described as a parent-to-subsidiary loan that is channelled through a financial intermediary, which is usually a large international bank.[20]

In direct intrafirm loans, the parent company makes the loan direct to the foreign subsidiary, which later repays the loan. In fronting loans, the parent company deposits the loan amount in an international bank, which then lends the same amount to the borrowing foreign subsidiary. From the bank's point of view, the loan is risk-free because of the 100% collateral in the form of the parent company's deposit. The bank, in effect, 'fronts' for the parent company, which also accounts for the name of this type of loan.[21]

Fronting loans could be considered where the potential for political risk in a foreign country may deter a company from engaging in a direct foreign investment, especially where the possibilities of nationalisation or expropriation of assets cannot be ignored. In such instances governments would be more likely to allow local subsidiaries in the host country to repay the loan to a large international bank in a neutral country, than allow the subsidiary to repay the loan direct to the parent company. A second reason for using fronting loans is that these could have tax advantages.

To explain the working, as well as the tax advantages, of a fronting loan, as illustrated in Exhibit 10.4 (p. 310), assume that a tax haven subsidiary in Jersey, that is wholly owned by the parent company in the USA, deposits $2 million in an intermediary London-based international bank at 7% interest. The bank, in turn, lends the $2 million to the operating subsidiary in Italy at 8% interest. The company tax rate in Italy is 50%.

The interest payments, adjusted for tax effects, will be as follows:

- The Italian operating subsidiary pays $160 000 interest to the bank in London. The net after-tax cost of interest to the Italian subsidiary is $80 000.
- The bank receives $160 000, retains $20 000 for its services, and pays $140 000 interest on the deposit of the tax haven subsidiary.
- The tax haven subsidiary now receives $140 000 interest on its deposit, tax free.

The net effect is that the Italian operating subsidiary obtains the $2 million loan, and that at the year-end, $140 000 in cash is moved

Exhibit 10.4: Funds flow and tax aspects of a fronting loan.

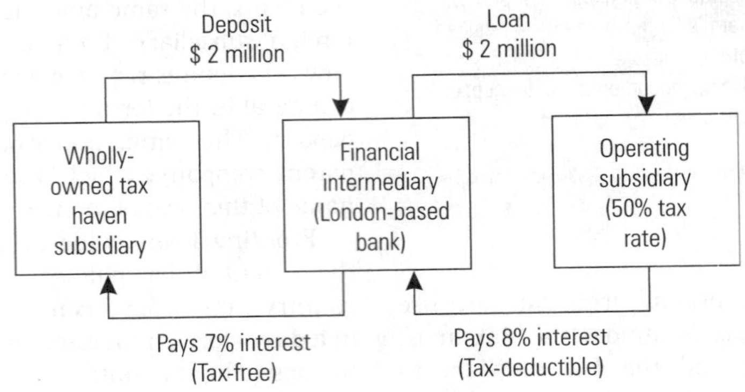

SOURCE: Adapted from Eiteman et al., op. cit., p. 612.

from the Italian subsidiary to the tax haven subsidiary. Since the after-tax cost of interest to the Italian subsidiary is only $80 000, it has been possible to move an additional $60 000 (a tax saving of $80 000 minus $20 000 bank service fee) out of Italy by virtue of the tax advantages inherent in the operation of the fronting loan in this example.

If the tax haven subsidiary had made a direct loan to the operating subsidiary, there is a possibility that the host government (Italy) may not have allowed the interest on the loan as a tax-deductible expense on the basis that it could be considered a dividend to the parent disguised as an interest payment.

This is a simple example to illustrate that fronting loans can be used for the optimal positioning of funds internationally and to obtain tax advantages where local and other considerations allow this.[22] Different countries have different tax regimes and tax laws. Accordingly it should be kept in mind that all relevant tax implications need to be considered in international investment, financing, and operating decisions. An Appendix on international tax issues and tax havens appears on p. 336.

(f) Multilateral netting

Where the subsidiaries of a multinational enterprise are involved in intracompany business, each subsidiary would generally owe money to one or more of the other subsidiaries, and in turn be owed money by one or more of them. In such cases, multilateral netting allows multinational enterprises to reduce the transaction costs that arise when a large number of transactions take place on a continuous basis between the firm's subsidiaries in the course of their business. These transaction costs generally comprise the commissions on foreign exchange transactions that have to be paid to foreign exchange dealers, and the fees that have to be paid to banks for the transfer of funds between subsidiaries in different locations.[23]

The process of multilateral netting involves determining the net amount of money owed to subsidiaries which has arisen from continuous intracompany transactions. By computing the net amounts owed to each subsidiary, the number of payments and the associated costs can be reduced substantially. Exhibit 10.5 (p. 311) illustrates four subsidiaries of a multinational enterprise that have amounts due to them, as well as amounts payable by them to each of the other subsidiaries.

The net cash flow positions resulting from multilateral netting appear in Exhibit 10.6 (p. 311).

Based on these net amounts owing and receivable, settlement can be made direct

Exhibit 10.5: Intracompany cash flows between subsidiaries ($'000)

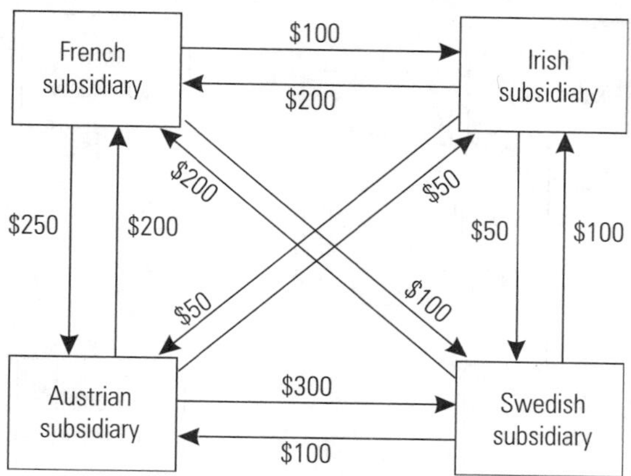

SOURCE: Adapted from Rugman & Hodgetts, op. cit., p. 391.

Exhibit 10.6: Net cash positions of subsidiaries

Subsidiary	Total receivables	Total payables	Net position
French	$600 000	$450 000	$150 000
Irish	250 000	300 000	–50 000
Austrian	400 000	550 000	–150 000
Swedish	450 000	400 000	50 000

SOURCE: Adapted from Rugman & Hodgetts, op. cit., p. 392.

between subsidiaries, although this can still be cumbersome. For this reason, many multinational companies introduce a centralised clearing account[24] to which money owed by subsidiaries is paid (in this case, the Irish and Austrian subsidiaries), and from which the other subsidiaries are paid (the French and Swedish subsidiaries), as indicated in Exhibit 10.7 (p. 312).

As a general rule, clearing transactions take place periodically, which enhances the intracompany flow of funds and significantly reduces transaction costs.

Other reasons for using multilateral netting are that subsidiaries which are owed money have faster access to their funds; the parent company can identify subsidiaries with cash surpluses, which assists in positioning international funds optimally; and the cost of the conversion of foreign exchange is minimised as a result of using a central clearing account facility.

A number of problems which arise in multilateral netting are that many governments allow it only for trade transactions and not generally for the positioning of funds, and the reluctance of subsidiary managers to keep the central clearing account manager fully informed could adversely effect the smooth running of the system.

On balance, multilateral netting can be of great value to MNEs in managing their global cash flows. However, the discussion of the

Exhibit 10.7: Centralised multilateral netting ($'000)

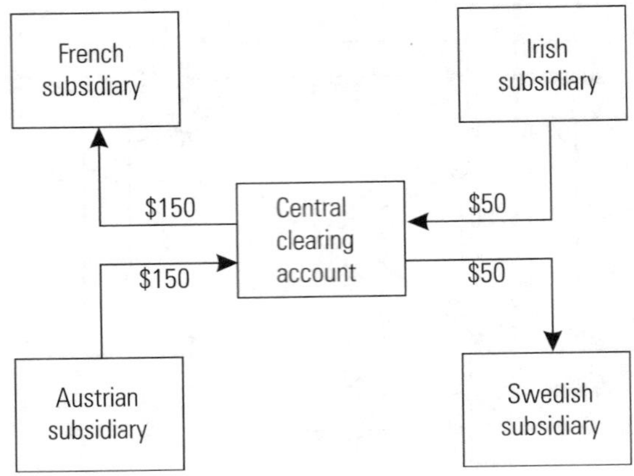

SOURCE: Adapted from Rugman & Hodgetts, op. cit., p. 392.

various approaches to global money management has not taken into account the crucially important fact of fluctuating international currencies and, therefore, the exchange rate implications when using the above money management methods and techniques. Since global cash flows of necessity relate to the movement of funds across borders, the implications of foreign exchange risk are of the utmost importance, also for global money management, and this topic is addressed in the following section.

10.5 Foreign exchange risk management

10.5.1 Introduction

The nature of foreign exchange risk and the characteristics of the foreign exchange market were discussed in Chapter 6. The way in which exchange rates are determined, the way in which changes in exchange rates can affect the profitability of international trade and investments, and how firms can use forward exchange contracts and currency swaps to insure themselves against foreign exchange risk to some degree, also came under the spotlight.

This section will focus on foreign exchange risk management, based on the information in Chapter 6 and an understanding of foreign exchange risk in general. Three types of foreign exchange exposure will first be identified – transaction exposure, translation exposure, and economic exposure. In conclusion, there will be a discussion of the various methods, tactics, and strategies to reduce or eliminate foreign exchange risk – a key area in international financial management.

10.5.2 Types of foreign exchange exposure

According to Stonehill and Eiteman, 'exposure' is a measure of foreign exchange risk.[25] Multinational financial managers have to contend with and manage the three different types of exposure continuously, each of which measures a different kind of foreign exchange risk. These are transaction exposure, translation exposure and economic exposure.

(a) Transaction exposure

The degree to which the value of future cash transactions can be affected by exchange rate fluctuations is referred to as **transaction exposure.**[26] More specifically, transaction exposure measures potential gains or losses on the future settlement of outstanding obligations that are denominated in a foreign currency.

The most common outstanding obligations include the foreign exchange to be received for exports or paid for imports, the purchase on credit of services from foreign sources, and what has been obtained through borrowing or lending in foreign currencies.

To illustrate the implications of transaction exposure for an international firm, we assume that a South African company has decided to purchase 100 video cameras from a manufacturer in the United States for $50 000, and agrees to pay for the cameras in 90 days in US dollars (assuming a current exchange rate of R6 to the US dollar). The transaction risk in this case would be the risk that the US dollar would strengthen against the rand. If the South African company pays for the order immediately, it will remit R300 000 to the American manufacturer. However, if the South African company waits for 90 days and the exchange rate at that point in time is R6,35 to the US dollar, the company would still pay $50 000 dollars, but the cost in rand would now be R317 500 ($50 000 x 6,35). This is higher than the R300 000 that would have been paid, had the US dollar not strengthened against the rand by 5,83% over the 90-day period. The implication for the South African company is that a potentially profitable transaction could be turned into an unprofitable one.

From the other perspective, if a South African company sells 10 000 leather camera cases to the firm in the USA for R240 000 (at an exchange rate of R6 to the US dollar), the consignment could cost $40 000 if the American firm decides to pay immediately. Since this firm will pay in US dollars, the amount that the South African company receives in 90 days will change if the rand-US dollar exchange rate has changed from 6,00 to 6,35 during the 90-day period. Whereas the value of the consignment was $40 000 (R240 000) originally, the South African company receives R254 000 after 90 days ($40 000 x 6,35), with a gain of R14 000.

This example illustrates that in international sales and purchases there is transaction exposure on the part of both the buyer and the seller.[27] Obviously, had the US dollar weakened against the rand to R5,65 over the 90-day period, the South African company would have suffered a foreign exchange loss of R14 000.

(b) Translation exposure

The exposure of the consolidated financial statements of a multinational enterprise to exchange rate fluctuations is known as **translation exposure**.[28] This is sometimes referred to as accounting exposure.

Translation exposure basically arises because parent companies must consolidate the financial statements of all its foreign subsidiaries into the parent company statement. The financial statements of subsidiaries are usually prepared in terms of the foreign currency of the host country and must be 'translated', or restated, in home currency terms to allow its components to be added to the account balances of the parent firm. Where exchange rates change, which is generally the case under floating exchange rate systems, the value of account balances, as measured in the home currency, will also change, and could produce either a gain or a loss relative to the translation of the prior period.[29] Depending on the home country accounting rules and regulations in effect at the time, the translation gain or loss is treated in one of the following two ways:

- it will be added to or subtracted from the net income in the income statement, or
- it will be carried over to the shareholders' equity section in the balance sheet.

Since 1981, the rules of the Financial Accounting Standards Board (FASB) in the United States have required translation of foreign currency financial statements by the current rate method, a procedure that has since been adopted by a number of other countries as well.[30] According to the current rate method, all balance sheet assets and liabilities are translated at the rate of exchange in effect on the date of the balance sheet. Income statement accounts, including depreciation and cost of goods sold, are normally translated by using either the actual exchange rate on the dates the various incomes, expenses, gains, and losses were incurred, or an appropriately weighted average exchange rate for the reporting period concerned. Dividends are translated at the exchange rate on date of payment. Equity accounts are all translated using the historical exchange rate in force at the time the accounts were first introduced in the balance sheet.

It is important to note that gains or losses caused by translation adjustments are not included in the calculation of consolidated net income – these are reported in a separate equity reserve account.

This general outline of the translation procedures serves to illustrate their technical and complex nature, especially where the large multinational enterprise is concerned. However, the implications of translation exposure for the international firm are even more important from a management perspective.

Although the accounting gains or losses as a result of translation are said to be unrealised, Hill contends that they are not unimportant.[31] An example of translation exposure for a home country MNE is when the currency of the host country (where its foreign subsidiary is located) weakens in relation to the home-country currency. For example, when the Zimbabwean dollar weakens by 10% in relation to the South African rand, the value of the Zimbabwean subsidiary's Zim dollar account at the local Zimbabwean bank would also decline when translated into rand in the financial statement consolidation process. In this case, if the deposit was equal to R100 000 before the decline of the local currency, the deposit would be worth R90 000 in translation. Although this does not affect the local deposit or its purchasing power in Zimbabwe in the short term, the decline has the following serious implications:

- The ability of the Zimbabwean dollar to purchase imports from countries with stronger currencies would be adversely affected.
- The total rand value of the parent company's equity reported in the consolidated balance sheet would be reduced.
- The 'perceived' lower equity would raise the apparent leverage (debt ratio) of the company, which could raise its cost of borrowing and access to capital market funding.
- The perceived negative effect on the company's earnings as a result of translation could lead to a decrease in its share price on stock markets, and hence on the value of the company.[32]

(c) Economic exposure

The degree to which a firm's present value of future cash flows can be influenced by exchange rate fluctuations is referred to as **economic exposure** to exchange rates.[33] More specifically, economic exposure is the potential for change in the present value of future cash flows because of an unexpected change in exchange rates.

Economic exposure differs from transaction and translation exposure in two important respects. First, it is a subjective concept that is not easily identified or measured. Second, because of its long-term implications compared to transaction and translation exposure, which are basically short term, recognising and dealing with economic exposure are vastly more important.[34]

Economic exposure is a complex phenomenon and covers a wide spectrum of diverse risks, from the pricing of products, sourcing of supplies, future sales potential, and cost trends in foreign markets, to the geographical location of foreign investments. It is important to understand that economic exposure differs fundamentally from transaction exposure since the latter is exclusively concerned with the effect of changes in exchange rates on individual transactions.[35]

A major problem is that the causes or potential causes of either beneficial or adverse future trends are normally not readily apparent. These include the trends in exchange rates, and developments in countries where a company's subsidiaries are located. According to Stonehill and Eiteman, the potential effect of an event or trend on future cash flows might be apparent but prior to or at the time that such an event occurs, that effect can be estimated only with difficulty.[36]

10.5.3 Strategies and tactics for managing foreign exchange risk

The previous section explained how the foreign exchange risk for the South African importer arose as a result of the declining rand-US dollar exchange rate, but did not indicate how this risk may have been reduced or eliminated by means of appropriate foreign exchange risk management strategies. A brief discussion of the tactics and strategies to reduce or eliminate foreign exchange risk will now follow.

(a) Managing transaction and translation exposure

International firms can use several tactics and strategies to minimise the risk of loss as a result of adverse changes in exchange rates. These include operating financial strategies, forward exchange contracts, currency swaps, and currency options, each one of which is briefly discussed.

Operating financial strategies: The objective of **operating financial strategies** is to minimise the effect of changing exchange rates on the local firm's profitability.

In economies with high inflation, where currencies are expected to depreciate and prices to rise, local subsidiaries will:

- collect their debts as quickly as possible;
- concentrate and encourage cash sales relative to credit sales;
- delay, as far as possible, paying obligations denominated in local currency;
- pay all debts that are denominated in strong currencies as quickly as possible;
- take the opportunity to buy fixed assets that are most likely to have a beneficial effect on cash flows in inflationary conditions.

Firms can, furthermore, use **lead and lag strategies** to protect their cash flows.

- **Lead strategies** involve the collection of foreign currency debts before they fall due, if their currency is expected to depreciate, and to remit foreign currency payables before they are due, if their currency is expected to appreciate.
- **Lag strategies** involve delaying the collection of foreign currency debts, if their currency is expected to appreciate, and delaying payables in foreign currency, if their currency is expected to depreciate.

Although lead and lag strategies make economic sense, some of the problems which could occur include the firm's control over terms of payment and its bargaining position, and government-imposed limits on leads and lags, such as setting a limit of 180 days for the receipt of export payments or for payments for imports.[37]

As far as inventory decisions are concerned, inventories in final products will be kept at a minimum when inflationary prices are rising, to capitalise on increasing prices. With imported inventory, subsidiaries will attempt to increase stocks before the local currency weakens and makes imports more costly. The general rule is to make purchases in a weak currency and sales in a strong currency.

These operating financial strategies enable international firms, and also the foreign subsidiaries of multinational enterprises, to minimise some of the foreign exchange risks in the short-term proactively.

Hedging strategies: Where a hedge is a form of protection against an adverse movement of an exchange rate, operating financial strategies could, in that sense, be regarded as **hedging strategies**. However, forward exchange contracts, currency swaps, and currency options are generally regarded as hedging instruments.

(b) Forward exchange contracts

Forward exchange rates and forward exchange contracts were defined and discussed in Chapter 6 (Section 6.4.1).

A **forward exchange contract** is a legally binding agreement between an international firm and a bank for the delivery of foreign currency at a specified exchange rate on a predetermined future date.[38] The purpose of a foreign exchange contract is to minimise the risk related to foreign exchange fluctuations.

As an example,[39] assume that a South African manufacturer sells stainless steel equipment to a Japanese company for 10 million yen, with payment due in 90 days. The assumed spot exchange rate is 20 yen to the rand, and the value of the contract R500 000 (10 000 000/20). However, who knows what the exchange rate will be in 90 days?

If the South African firm obtains a quote, and enters into a forward contract for 22 yen to the rand, based on forward rate quotations indicating a weakening of the yen, it is willing to accept an amount of R454 545,45 (10 000 000/22) with certainty in 90 days in exchange for the 10 million yen to be paid by the Japanese firm. If, during the 90-day period, the yen weakens beyond 22 yen to the rand, the South African company would have eliminated the potential loss at an exchange rate weaker than 22 yen to the rand. Should the exchange rate happen to be 22 yen to the rand at 90 days, the South African company has in effect 'given up' R45 454,55 (R500 000 – R454 545,45) for the guarantee. What would have happened if the yen had appreciated to 18 yen to the rand after 90 days? In such a case, the company would still receive R454 545,45, but could have received R555 555,56 if it had not hedged its position (10 000 000/18). It has therefore given up R101 101,11 (R555 555,56 – R454 545,45). However, it must be remembered that the purpose of the forward exchange contract was to minimise the possible effect of unfavourable exchange rate fluctuations.

Currency swaps: Currency swaps as a type of forward exchange contract were explained in Chapter 6 (Section 6.4.2), with a practical example of how a currency swap operates. Although a currency swap resembles a back-to-back loan, it does not appear on a firm's balance sheet.[40]

In the United States, a currency swap is treated as a foreign exchange transaction rather than as debt, and the obligation to reverse the swap at some later date as a forward exchange contract. According to Eiteman et al., forward contracts can be matched against assets, but they are entered in the footnotes rather than in the firm's balance sheet as such. What is important here for financial management, is that this avoids both operating and translation exposures, which means that neither a long-term receivable nor a long-term debt is created on the balance sheet.[41]

Currency options: A foreign currency option is a contract giving the option purchaser (the buyer) the right, but not the obligation, to buy or sell a given amount of foreign exchange at a fixed price unit for a specified time period (until the expiry date).[42]

Currency options provide more flexibility than forward exchange contracts because the buyer is not obliged to exercise the option. Moreover, the buyer of an option cannot lose more than the amount paid for the option. With regard to the example of forward exchange contracts, let us now assume that the South African seller decides to protect the value of the 10 million yen. This can be achieved by purchasing an option to deliver 10 million yen for rand at a predetermined exchange rate, say, 22 yen to the rand, in 90 days, at the payment of an option cost of R20 000 for this right. Whatever happens to the rand-yen exchange rate over the ensuing 90-day period, the South African company can turn the 10 million yen over to the seller of the option, who will then have to give the company R454 545,45 (10 000 000/22). The advantage in such a case is that the company will only exercise this option if the value of the yen in 90 days depreciates more than the anticipated rate of 22 yen to the rand, and will return less than the previous amount. However, should the yen appreciate to a level of 20 to the rand, the currency would be worth

R500 000 (10 000 000/20), and the firm accordingly would not exercise the option. On the other hand, had the yen depreciated to 24 per rand, the 10 million yen would be worth only R416 666,67 (10 000 000/24), in which case the firm would exercise the option. Bear in mind that, whether or not the firm decides to exercise the option, it has to pay the cost of the option, namely R20 000, which will reduce its income on the transaction by this amount. Given the uncertainty in the exchange market and the potential for significant losses, firms appear to regard the option cost as a realistic price for knowing for certain what they will receive.

The above tactics and techniques can help the firm to minimise the adverse effects of transaction exposure in particular. Other tactics that could be considered to reduce transaction and translation exposure in some cases, include:

- manipulating transfer prices to move funds out of countries where a decline in currency values is expected;
- using local debt financing to hedge against foreign exchange risk;
- accelerating dividend payments from subsidiaries based in countries with weak currencies;
- adjusting capital budgeting techniques to reflect potential foreign exchange risk.[43]

Translation exposure can be reduced by using a balance sheet hedge. According to Griffin and Pustay, a balance sheet hedge is created when an international firm matches its assets denominated in a given currency with its liabilities denominated in that same currency.[44] It is important to note that this balancing occurs on a currency-by-currency basis, and not a subsidiary-by-subsidiary basis. Having discussed some of the consequences of translation exposure, as well as the technical complexity in dealing with it effectively, multinational companies should strive to reduce the extent of translations in order to lessen the exposure when consolidating their financial statements. This can be achieved to a certain extent through balance sheet hedging as described above, where asset and liability items denominated in specific currencies are netted out, resulting in lower amounts to be translated and possibly also fewer items that need to be considered.

(b) Reducing economic exposure

Because of its long-term nature and the difficulty of the timely recognition of economic exposure, it is clear that reducing economic exposure requires strategic choices, which often lie outside the domain of financial management, when attempting to identify why, how, and when unanticipated exchange rate fluctuations may affect a firm's future sales, profitability, and cash flows.

Strategies to reduce economic exposure include the distribution of the firm's facilities and productive assets to various international locations. This will reduce the effects of adverse changes in exchange rates on the multinational company when compared to the exposure of single locations. The decision of some Japanese car manufacturers to establish manufacturing facilities in the United States and Western Europe during the mid-1980s to remain competitive in the face of the rising value of the yen against other major currencies (US dollar, Deutschmark and pound sterling) is an example of this strategic approach to reduce economic exposure.[45]

Where economic exposure is concerned, it is especially important to monitor the underlying factors and trends that influence exchange rates and give rise to exchange rate fluctuations carefully and continually. This requires monitoring the trends in the following:

- interest and inflation rates in those countries where the firm's subsidiaries are located, or with whom the firm and its subsidiaries are involved in international trade; purchasing power parity; and balance of payments performance;
- major cost items such as labour, raw materials, and other resources;
- productivity.

To sum up, the international financial manager has to scrutinise and monitor all those factors that could affect the firm's international cash flows and hence its present value.

10.5.4 Policy guidelines for managing foreign exchange risk

The characteristics and dynamics of the foreign exchange market as outlined in Chapter 6, and the foregoing discussion of the types of foreign exchange exposure and how they could be managed, confirm the need for multinational enterprises to develop sound mechanisms and policies which would allow the use of the above-mentioned tactics and strategies to minimise the firm's foreign exchange exposure. In this regard, Hill proposes the following considerations which could serve as a basis for such policy guidelines:

- the establishment of a centralised exchange control facility to devise company-wide ways of protecting resources against foreign exchange exposure, comprising a flexible mix of appropriate tactics and strategies for subsidiaries;
- making a clear distinction between transaction, translation, and economic exposure, and developing creative strategies for dealing with economic exposure in particular;
- emphasising the need to forecast future exchange rate movements – despite the difficulty involved in doing so – to effectively manage all three types of foreign exchange exposure. Short-term as well as long-term exchange rate forecasts are indispensable, whether obtained in-house or from external experts;
- establishing sound reporting systems to allow the managers of centralised exchange control facilities (as proposed above) and of central clearing accounts (as in multilateral netting), for example, to monitor the firm's exposure positions on a regular and company-wide basis. This would, in turn, also benefit the managers of foreign subsidiaries;
- producing foreign exchange exposure reports on a monthly basis, or for other reporting periods, depending on the unique situation of the firm, to indicate how cash flows and balance sheet items might be affected by forecasted exchange rate fluctuations, as a basis for the development of hedging and other appropriate strategies.[46]

From these discussions of the three types of exchange exposure and their implications for the profitability, growth, and survival of the international firm, it is clear why foreign exchange risk management is a crucially important area in international financial management.

10.6 International investment analysis and capital budgeting

10.6.1 International investment

Chapter 1 (Section 1.6) discussed **foreign investments** and distinguished between foreign portfolio investment and foreign direct investment. **Foreign portfolio investment** is investment by individuals, firms, or public institutions, in foreign financial instruments such as shares of foreign companies or government bonds in international capital markets. **Foreign direct investment** (FDI) takes place when a firm invests directly in facilities by way of a joint venture, buying an existing enterprise, or establishing a new enterprise in another country to produce and/or market a product. This section will deal with the second type of foreign investment, which is approached from the perspective of international management.

International firms engage in foreign investments for a number of reasons. These are viewed as being part of a firm's long-term strategy to expand its markets by capturing new foreign markets, expanding existing foreign markets, or both. The motivation for foreign investments includes capitalising on new foreign market opportunities and/or responding to emerging problems in the firm's domestic markets, one of which could be the saturation of the local market. Based on theoretical considerations, foreign direct investment will be preferred to exporting and licensing in cases where high transportation costs and barriers to trade will detract from exporting as an alternative to service foreign markets, and where the firm's technology and know-how is not amenable to licensing. In addition, foreign investment will be preferred to licensing if the firm needs to have tight control over foreign operations.

Given these considerations, it is evident that a firm will have to consider a large number of economic, political, and strategic factors, as well as the relevant potential benefits, costs, and risks if it decides to invest abroad. The analysis of foreign investments therefore makes it necessary for the international financial manager to consider all relevant factors that could in any way impact on the net cash flows expected from the potential investment, and to quantify the various benefits, costs, and risks that are associated with such an investment. Capital budgeting techniques provide the framework and the methodology to evaluate foreign investment projects.

10.6.2 Capital budgeting[47]

Multinational enterprises evaluate foreign investment projects by means of **capital budgeting**, which compares the benefits, costs, and risks of the projects. Since this type of investment usually requires large initial amounts, and once investment decisions have been taken they cannot easily be reversed without substantial financial losses to the company, the importance of sound foreign investment decisions in an increasingly competitive global environment is obvious.

Capital budgeting for foreign projects uses the same theoretical framework as domestic capital budgeting. This means estimating the useful economic life of the project, estimating all relevant after-tax net cash flows during its expected lifespan, discounting these net cash flows to present values using an appropriate discount rate, and calculating the **net present value (NPV)** for the project. The appropriate discount rate for this purpose is usually the firm's weighted average cost of capital or the project's required rate of return. Alternatively, when using the **internal rate of return (IRR)** approach, we calculate the internal rate of return that equates the present value of the net cash outflows to the present value of net cash inflows of the project.

While capital budgeting is not particularly straightforward in practice, it is considerably more complex in analysing foreign investment projects compared to purely domestic projects, for reasons which include the following:

- A distinction must be made between **cash flows to the project** and **cash flows to the parent company**, since a different view of value emanates from each of these two types of cash flow.
- Cash flows to the parent company often depend on the form or source of financing for the project. In such cases, **operating cash flows** (payments for purchases of products or services for the project from the parent company; royalties, and license fees) cannot be clearly separated from **financial cash flows** (dividends, loan repayments, and interest payments), as is the case in domestic capital budgeting.
- The remittance of funds to the parent company must be recognised explicitly because of differing tax systems between countries, as well as political or legal constraints which could affect the international movement of funds.
- Differing rates of inflation between countries could affect competitive position, and consequently the extent and value of cash flows over time.
- Unanticipated foreign exchange rate changes (foreign exchange risk) affect the

value to the parent company of local project cash flows, and accordingly have to be kept in mind in the capital budgeting analysis.

- Capital structure decisions and calculation of the cost of capital (as the discount rate), especially where host country subsidised loans are used for project financing, are complicated.
- Political risk which arises from adverse political events could have a negative effect on the availability and extent of expected cash flows from a project.[48]

The ensuing discussion will explore the implications of some of these complications when analysing international investment projects.

(a) Parent and project cash flows

As mentioned above, a complexity in capital budgeting that is a direct consequence of the international dimension when foreign investment projects are analysed, is whether cash flows should be analysed from a project (subsidiary or host-country) perspective, or from a parent company (head office or home-country) perspective. As will become clear, cash flows to the parent company are not necessarily the same as cash flows to the project.

Although it is necessary to analyse a foreign project from a local or host-country viewpoint to determine its performance relative to other competing local projects in terms of return on investment, there are sound arguments as to why foreign investment projects should be analysed from a parent company viewpoint. The reasons why the parent company is primarily interested in the cash flows it will receive, are:

- Subsidiaries (project) may not be able to remit all their cash flows to the parent company, because cash flows may be blocked by the host-country government, they may be taxed at an unfavourable rate, or part of the cash flows generated by the project may have to be reinvested in the host country.
- Cash flows to the parent company ultimately form the basis for dividend payments to parent-company shareholders, for reinvestment at home or in other foreign countries, and for the repayment of company debt.

While noting the convincing evidence that cash flows and the capital budgeting process should be approached from a parent-company point of view, it must be remembered that most of the project's cash flows to the parent company are financial rather than operating cash flows. By including these financial cash flows in our analysis, we deviate from the basic assumption in domestic capital budgeting, namely that operating and financial cash flows should not be mixed. In this regard, Eiteman et al. explain that where, for example, cash flows from a foreign project are blocked from repatriation by a host government, they are not available to the parent company to pay dividends or to repay corporate debt. Therefore, from the perspective of the parent company, and especially shareholders (owners), such blocked cash flows do not contribute to the current value of the parent company. It is, however, extremely important to understand that the manner and form in which project cash flows are remitted to the parent company will largely determine the tax liabilities of the foreign project itself, which will, in turn, affect the project's net cash flows available for remittance to the parent company.[49]

These rather intricate parent company-project cash flow relationships, as well as the foreign tax implications of the two types of cash flow (operating and financial), are summarised in Exhibit 10.8 (p. 321).

The process of remitting cash flow earnings from a subsidiary to a parent company is illustrated in Exhibit 10.9 (p. 322).

Research has shown that most multinational enterprises evaluate foreign investment projects from the points of view of both parent company and project.

Exhibit 10.8: Parent valuation of foreign investment projects: Cash flows derived from the project and impact on foreign tax liability

Cash flows	Derivation of cash flow	Impact on foreign tax liability
Dividends (financial cash flow)	Distributed profits arise only from a foreign project with positive net income in the period	No impact on foreign tax liability because dividends are distributed after tax, but there may be a dividend withholding tax
Intrafirm debt (financial cash flow)	Principal and interest payments flow back to the parent as scheduled in the loan agreement	Interest payments on debt (both intra- and extra-firm) are deductible expenses of the project and therefore lower foreign tax liability
Intrafirm sales (operational cash flow)	Purchases of product or services from the parent firm arise from the operating needs of the project	Intrafirm purchases or transfers are an operating cost of the foreign project and therefore lower foreign tax liability
Royalties and license fees (operational cash flow)	Royalties and other license fees are normally calculated as a percentage of the project's sales revenue or volume	Royalties and license fees are expenses of the foreign project and therefore lower foreign tax liability

SOURCE: Eiteman et al., op. cit., p. 528.

(b) Adjusting for risk in capital budgeting

In the analysis of potential international investment opportunities, all relevant political and economic risks associated with a project – especially the additional risk that stems from its foreign location – need to be considered. From the perspective of international financial management, the potential impact of these risks on the cash flows expected from the project have to be assessed in the capital budgeting process. This requires the identification of the relevant political and economic risks, and obtaining information regarding these risks for consideration in the investment evaluation process.[50]

Political risk: The political environment of international business was discussed in Chapter 4, and political risk referred to in Chapter 7 (Section 7.2), where **political risk** was broadly defined as the likelihood that undesirable political developments and events in a country could adversely affect a country's business environment and consequently the profitability, growth, and survival of business enterprises. Typically, political risks of relevance to foreign investments include the imposition of foreign trade and investment barriers, exchange controls, regulations blocking the remittance of earnings to parent companies, new tax regimes, and increased tax rates. In extreme cases, expropriation of assets and the nationalisation of industries pose serious threats to subsidiaries of multinational enterprises, in particular.

As indicated in Chapter 7, country risk profiles and other risk analyses are available for purposes of identifying and quantifying the effects of potential risks for capital budgeting purposes. Although it is conceded that the meaningful forecasting of political risk remains an elusive objective, all possible attempts should be made to obtain objective and relevant information in this regard when considering potential investments.

Economic risk: The economic environment of international business that was discussed in Chapter 5, and the foreign exchange market and international capital markets described in Chapter 6, provide the international financial

Exhibit 10.9: Process of remitting subsidiary earnings to parent

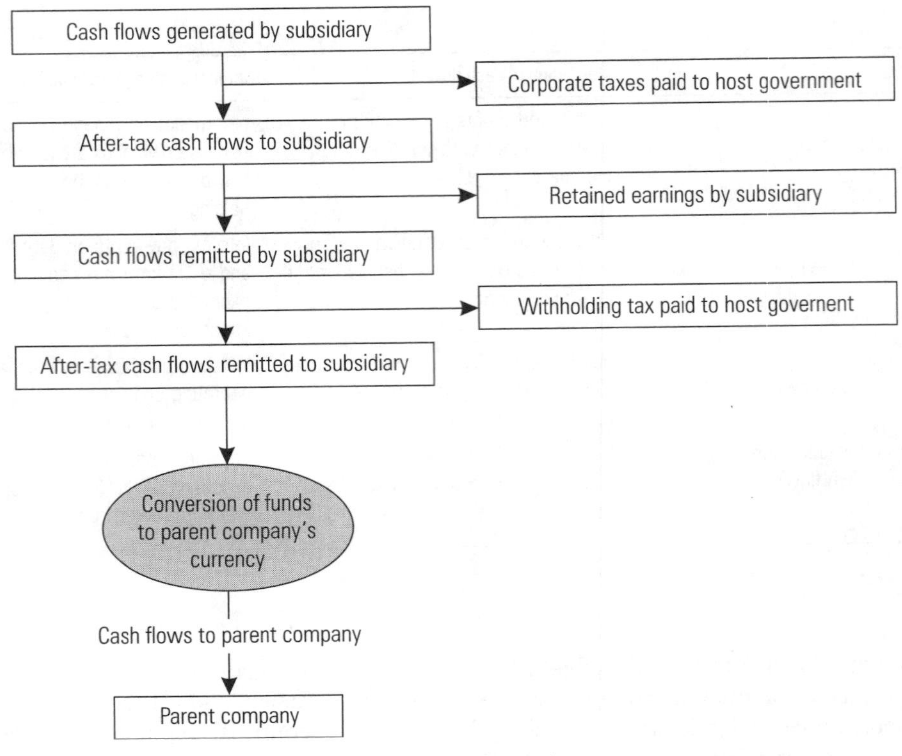

SOURCE: Madura, J. 1998. *International financial management.* 5th ed. Cincinnati, Ohio: South Western College Publishing, p. 513.

framework within which the multinational enterprise has to operate. **Economic risk** is related to the extent of possible mismanagement of a country's economy that could adversely affect the profitability, growth, and survival of business enterprises in that country. The injudicious expansion of a country's money supply has been identified as a major concern relative to foreign economies.

As was evident from Chapter 6, inflation eventually leads to depreciation in the value of a country's currency in the foreign exchange market, with serious consequences for foreign investments in that country. Reliable information on macro-economic trends, including interest rates, inflation rates, balance of payments data, and long-term exchange rate forecasts, have to be evaluated with a view to their possible impact on cash flows expected from projects in that country.

(c) Approaches to risk adjustment

The additional risk that stems from the location of a foreign project can be dealt with in one of the two following ways:

- First, to treat all foreign risk as a single issue by increasing the discount rate applicable to foreign projects relative to the rate used for domestic projects. This will reflect the increased risk due to political, foreign exchange, and other relevant risk factors.
- Second, to adjust all cash flow forecasts selectively during the estimated lifespan of the project to reflect foreign risks.

Because of inherent shortcomings in the first approach of using a higher, risk-adjusted discount rate during the entire life of the project, the second approach of adjusting project cash flows to accommodate risk is preferred. Criticism levelled against the first approach of adjusting the discount rate includes the following:

- First, that the nature and intensity of political and economic risks are likely to change during the life of the project, the effects of which will not be adequately reflected by merely using a uniform, higher discount rate over the total project life.
- Second, using a uniformly higher discount rate during the expected lifespan of the project, penalises early project cash flows heavily, while not penalising distant cash flows sufficiently.
- Third, changes in exchange rates will affect future cash flows primarily as a result of operating exposure. However, the direction of the effect could either increase or decrease net cash flows, depending on where products are sold, and from where inputs are sourced. A uniformly increased discount rate understandably cannot adequately reflect such potential effects.

As Eiteman et al. aptly state:

> Combining all risks into a single discount rate discards much information about the uncertainties of the future.[51]

The complexity of capital budgeting in the multinational enterprise is clearly illustrated in the outline presented by Madura and shown in Exhibit 10.10. Apart from the benefit of identifying the elements of a comprehensive, integrated capital budgeting framework, the relationship between these elements that eventually results in capital budgeting decisions is extremely important in understanding the international capital budgeting process.

To sum up, the capital budgeting analysis requires extensive information inputs, which

Exhibit 10.10: Elements and relationships in the multinational capital budgeting process

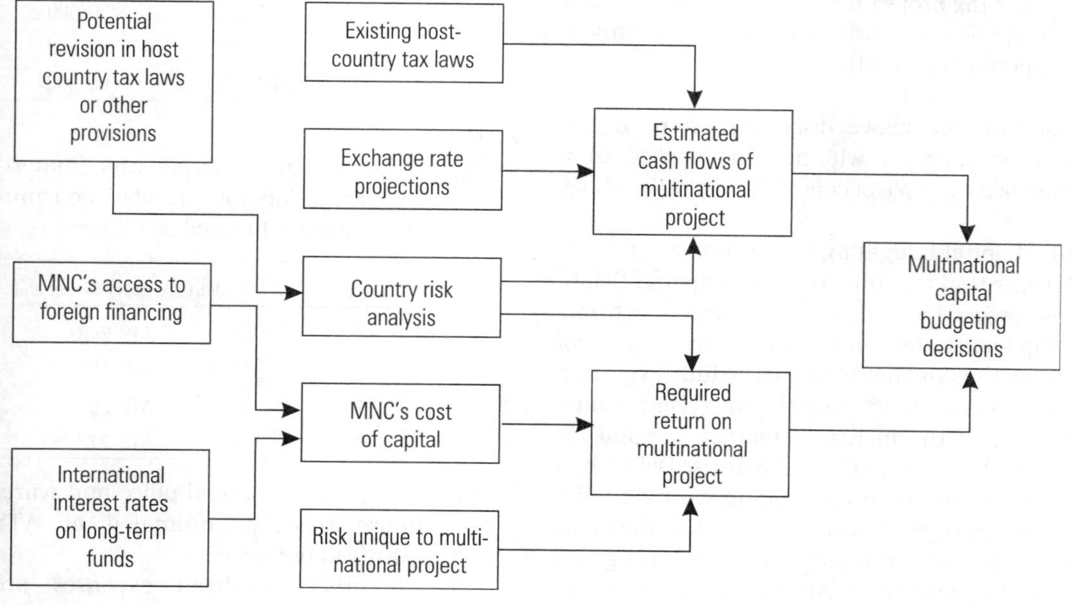

SOURCE: Madura, op. cit., p. 487.

include information and forecasts related to the following economic, financial, and risk characteristics related to the project in the context of its foreign location:

- initial investment (which could occur over several years);
- working capital requirements (with an indication of whether and to what extent it will be recovered when the project is terminated);
- project life;
- product and/or service price information;
- variable costs related to the project;
- project fixed costs;
- salvage value on termination of the project which could be a net cash inflow or a net cash outflow;
- tax implications related to aspects such as operating income, depreciation and amortisation, and salvage values;
- inflation;
- exchange rates and exchange rate forecasts;
- fund transfer restrictions;
- cost of capital or required rate of return (adjusted for foreign risks where the risk-adjusted discount rate is used);
- after-tax project net cash flows (adjusted for risk if the cash flow risk adjustment approach is used).

Based on the above discussion, some of the relevant concepts will now be applied to a simplified example of capital budgeting analysis.

(d) Capital budgeting application [52]

Assume that a South African company, Delphi Enterprises Limited, manufactures electronic components for industrial process control equipment, and has been successfully exporting these products to Austria in recent years. Because of the increased market demand for this product in Austria, and because Delphi had for some time been considering working independently of its Austrian distributor, the company is now thinking of establishing an operating facility in Austria to manufacture and market the product. The relevant information for a capital budgeting analysis has been obtained from various internal as well as external sources, including a number of government departments in Austria, and is summarised below.

- **Initial investment.** It has been estimated that an amount of 10 million Austrian schillings (ATS), which includes the requirements for working capital, would be needed as an initial investment. Assuming a spot rate of R0,50 per Austrian schilling, the South African company's equity investment would currently be R5 million.
- **Project life.** The project life is estimated at four years, after which the Austrian government will take over the plant for a predetermined amount in accordance with certain elements of their industrial policy.
- **Demand and product price.** Based on previous experience and recent market research data, the following price and demand schedules have been developed:

Year	Price per unit (Austrian currency)	Demand in Austria (units)
1	ATS 350	40 000
2	ATS 367	50 000
3	ATS 386	70 000
4	ATS 405	90 000

- Costs.
  (a) Total variable costs per unit (materials, direct labour, variable consumables) were estimated as follows:

Year	Variable cost (VC) per unit
1	ATS 240
2	ATS 252
3	ATS 265
4	ATS 278

  (b) Leasing of additional office and warehouse space is estimated at ATS 500 000 per year.
  (c) All other overhead expenses are expected to be ATS 800 000 per year.

- **Exchange rates.** The spot exchange rate of the Austrian schilling is R0,50. Delphi regards this spot as the best forecast for the exchange rate in future, which would be R0,50 for all future periods – an extreme oversimplification.
- **Host-country taxes on income earned by the Austrian subsidiary.** The Austrian tax rate on income is assumed to be 30%, and the withholding tax on dividends, interest, and royalties remitted to Delphi in South Africa 10%, 0% and 20% respectively.
- **South African tax rate on income earned by the Austrian subsidiary.** The South African Revenue Service will grant a tax credit on taxes paid in Austria, which means that the above remittances – in this case, dividends – will not be taxed further in South Africa (SA tax rate 30%).
- **Cash flows from Austrian subsidiary to South Africa parent company.** The Austrian authorities will not restrict any cash flows sent to the parent company apart from the withholding taxes referred to above. The plan is that the subsidiary will send all net cash flow earnings received as dividend to the parent company at the end of each year.
- **Depreciation.** The Austrian authorities will allow depreciation of the cost of plant and equipment to a maximum of ATS 1 million per year, which rate will be used by the subsidiary.
- **Salvage value.** The Austrian government will make a payment of ATS 6 million to the parent company when it takes ownership at the end of the fourth year. No capital gains tax or withholding taxes are applicable in this case.
- **Cost of capital or required rate of return (discount rate).** Delphi requires a 15% rate of return on projects of this kind, which includes an adjustment for risk.

The capital budgeting analysis uses the following approach. The evaluation is done from the perspective of the parent company since it finances the entire subsidiary, receives all net cash flows at each year-end, and will also receive the amount of ATS 6 million from the Austrian authorities when Delphi terminates its operation in Austria after four years. The cash flows in rand will, therefore, be of importance to Delphi. If the present value of all relevant cash inflows exceeds the present value of all relevant cash outflows, the potential investment should be of benefit to Delphi and contribute to the maximisation of shareholder wealth. The analysis of this potential investment appears in Exhibit 10.11 (p. 326).

The first step in the cash flow analysis is to use the price and demand data to estimate total income (lines 1 to 3). Next, all expenses are calculated to estimate total expenses (lines 4 to 9). Earnings before interest and taxes are calculated in the next step (line 10) by subtracting total expenses from total revenues (interest is not applicable to this example). Host-government taxes (line 11) are deducted from before-tax earnings to determine earnings after tax (line 12). To calculate after-tax cash flow, depreciation is added back to after-tax earnings (line 13). This also constitutes remitted funds and line 14 therefore remains unchanged. All cash flows can be sent to the parent since the initial investment made provision for the subsidiary's ongoing working capital requirements. The 10% withholding tax on dividends is now subtracted (line 15), resulting in the net amount to be remitted to the parent (line 16). The salvage value appears in line 17. The funds to be remitted are converted to rand at the ruling exchange rate for each of the four years (line 18) and the parent company's cash flow from the subsidiary appears in line 19. Bear in mind that the annual cash flows received from the Austrian subsidiary are not taxed in South Africa, since the tax paid in Austria would offset any South African tax liability.

Although we could use any of the accepted capital budgeting techniques, the Net Present Value is chosen, which mathematically is as follows:

$$NPV = -\sum_{t=0}^{n} \frac{C_t}{(1+k)^t} + \sum_{t=1}^{n} \frac{CF_t}{(1+k)^t} + \frac{SV_n}{(1+k)^n}$$

where

C_t = Initial investment at time t

CF_t = After tax net cash flow during period t

SV_n = Salvage value at the end of year n

k = Required rate of return (discount rate)

n = Expected life of the project (number of periods)

The present value of net cash flows for each period (or year) is calculated, using a discount

Exhibit 10.11: Capital bugeting analysis: Delphi Enterprises Limited

	Year 0	Year 1	Year 2	Year 3	Year 4
1. Demand (units)		40 000	50 000	70 000	90 000
2. Price per unit (ATS)		350	367	386	405
3. Total revenue = (1) x (2) (ATS)		14 000 000	18 350 000	27 020 000	36 450 000
4. Variable cost per unit (ATS)		240	252	265	278
5. Total variable cost = (1) x (4) (ATS)		9 600 000	12 600 000	18 550 000	25 020 000
6. Annual lease expense (ATS)		500 000	500 000	500 000	500 000
7. Other fixed annual expenses (ATS)		800 000	800 000	800 000	800 000
8. Noncash expense (depreciation) (ATS)		1 000 000	1 000 000	1 000 000	1 000 000
9. Total expenses = (5) + (6) + (7) + (8) (ATS)		11 900 000	14 900 000	20 850 000	27 320 000
10. Before-tax earnings of subsidiary = (3) – (9) (ATS)		2 100 000	3 450 000	6 170 000	9 130 000
11. Host government tax (30%)(ATS)		630 000	1 035 000	1 851 000	2 739 000
12. After-tax earnings of subsidiary (ATS)		1 470 000	2 415 000	4 319 000	6 391 000
13. Net cash flow to subsidiary = (12) + (8) (ATS)		2 470 000	3 415 000	5 319 000	7 391 000
14. ATS remitted by subsidiary (100% of CF)		2 470 000	3 415 000	5 319 000	7 391 000
15. Withholding tax on remitted funds (10%) (ATS)		247 000	341 500	531 900	739 100
16. ATS remitted after withholding taxes		2 223 000	3 073 500	4 787 100	6 651 900
17. Salvage value					6 000 000
18. Exchange rate of ATS		R 0,50	R 0,50	R 0,50	R 0,50
19. Cash flows to parent (R)		1 111 500	1 536 750	2 393 550	6 325 950
20. PV of parent cash flows (15% discount rate*) (R)		967 005	1 161 783	1 574 956	3 618 443
21. Initial investment by parent (R)	5 000 000				
22. Cumulative NPV (R)		–4 032 995	– 2 871 212	–1 296 256	+2 322 187

* Year 0, 1,000; year 1, 0,870; year 2, 0,756; year 3, 0,658; year 4, 0,5720.

SOURCE: Madura, op. cit., p. 519, adapted.

rate of 15% (line 20). The cumulative NPV is calculated (line 22) by subtracting the initial investment (line 21), while adding successive present values of net cash flows. The critical end result of the entire capital budgeting analysis is the last figure of R2 322 187, a positive NPV for the project.

Since the NPV is positive, the project is acceptable, provided that all relevant information has been incorporated into the analysis. The NPV is a significant informational input for a final strategic decision as to whether or not to go ahead with the project. Because of the deliberate and exceedingly simplified nature of this example to illustrate the principles involved in international capital budgeting, the following observations and questions will help to illustrate the actual complexity of international capital budgeting:

- Working capital has been integrated into the initial investment – usually it is treated separately, with an indication of the extent to which it is expected to be recovered when the project is terminated.
- In the example, the product price and the variable costs were escalated by 5% annually, with no indication of whether this is owing to inflation. There is no further information on inflation in either South Africa or in Austria, which could adversely affect some forecasts and, in particular, the application of the International Fisher effect.
- There is no indication of whether raw materials and other resources are obtained outside Austria, in which case it would have exchange rate implications.
- Moreover, Austria is deemed to be the only market. There is no indication of any export possibilities from Austria. The question of whether these will be to the EU and/or to other countries could have exchange rate effects on export receipts and, ultimately, on cash flows.
- There is no information on financing alternatives. The project is financed by an equity investment from the South African parent company. The effects (interest, loan repayments, tax liability) of debt financing from South Africa, Austria, or some third country on cash flows remitted to the parent company would have to be evaluated. What would the optimal financing decision be in this case? Is entering into a joint venture with an Austrian firm an option? Or selling the subsidiary at market value in the open market? Would a profit or a loss be realised? What could the tax implications be in either of these cases? These are all possiblities to be considered.
- The possibility that the current ruling of 10% withholding tax on remitted earnings could change in future must be kept in mind.
- Where the adjustment of cash flows to reflect risk is the preferred approach, in this case a risk-adjusted discount rate was used for the sake of simplicity. How difficult would it be to adjust cash flows for risk during the lifespan of the project? What additional information would be required?
- Is there any argument for the South African company to consider establishing a tax haven subsidiary? What purpose would it serve?

These are just some of many possible questions that could be relevant to the above example. Foreign investments are generally of a much more complicated nature, and would significantly increase the overall complexity of the capital budgeting process. All this seems to support the relatively complex process illustrated in Exhibit 10.10 (p. 323).

Some of the international financing aspects which were referred to in passing are discussed in the next section.

10.7 International financing decisions[53]

The multinational enterprise can finance profitable foreign investments from either internal or external sources. The firm must first consider the forms and sources of finance and, second, the capital structure to be achieved through an optimal combination of debt and equity capital that would minimise its cost of capital. Bear in mind that the cost of capital, if used as the discount rate, is of vital importance in capital budgeting decisions, which also confirms the intricate relationship between investment and financing decisions.

10.7.1 Sources of funds

Sources of funds which are available to finance foreign subsidiaries and international investment projects generally include:

- internal sources of funds which, in turn, could comprise funds generated internally by the foreign subsidiaries and funds from within the corporate family;
- external sources of funds from outside the corporate family. [54]

(a) Internal sources of funds

Internal sources of funds and investment capital, and the various possibilities of internal financing for a multinational company, are illustrated in Exhibit 10.12.

An obvious source of investment capital for multinational enterprises is the cash flows generated internally within the firm. For financing foreign subsidiaries, these include net cash flows from profitable operations and non-cash expense items such as depreciation, and can be substantial.

The parent company could use the cash flows from any subsidiary, subject to possible legal and regulatory constraints, to finance any investment opportunity within the multinational network of subsidiaries. Generally, the parent company receives these cash flows by way of dividend payments from subsidiaries. These funds can then be used to finance investment projects in other subsidiaries through loans, equity investments, or a combi-

Exhibit 10.12: Internal sources of capital for multinational enterprises

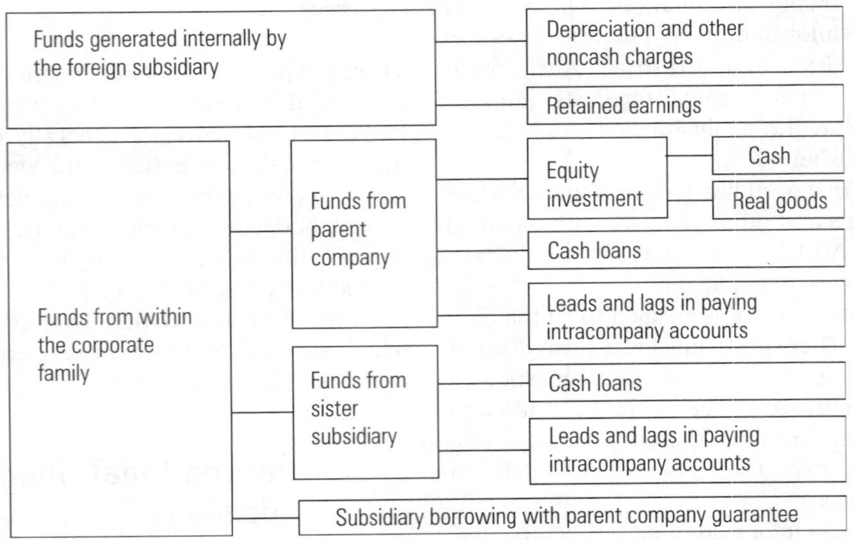

SOURCE: Eiteman, et. al., op. cit., p. 316, adapted.

nation of these. However, a subsidiary can also make a loan to a second subsidiary direct, as indicated in Exhibit 10.12.

Although the legal constraints have already been discussed, it is useful to repeat those that may affect a parent company's ability to move funds between subsidiaries, and between subsidiaries and itself. If a subsidiary is not wholly owned by the parent company, the other stakeholders or shareholders – for example, in a joint venture – could have different views from a subsidiary perspective as to how its cash flows could best be utilised. However, this is not a problem if subsidiaries are wholly owned. In addition, the governments in some host countries may block the intracompany transfer of funds, such as by imposing restrictions on the repatriation of dividends. As a third alternative, parent companies could obtain funds from subsidiaries through licence fees, fees for the use of company know-how or a trademark, or by charging management or administrative fees. Another alternative for moving funds between subsidiaries is by means of transfer prices for intracompany transfers and transactions. The way in which transfer prices work was discussed in Section 10.4.

The possibilities of moving funds internationally, referred to above, present the multinational enterprise with both opportunities and problems. The legal, operational, and management issues, as well as the tax implications (also summarised in Exhibit 10.8 on p. 321) related to these alternatives, must be thoroughly evaluated for the best decisions in all relevant situations. (For taxes, see Appendix, p. 336.)

However, it must be kept in mind that internal financing sources do have a cost, generally an opportunity cost, and that this, as well as the extent of internal financing as a proportion of the total financing of a project, will impact on the financial structure related to the project, and also its cost of capital. The next section will deal with external sources of financing and the discussion concludes with a brief look at financial structure.

(b) External sources of funds

Many alternative sources of funds external to the multinational company are available to finance foreign subsidiaries and investment projects. The main categories of these sources are summarised in Exhibit 10.13.

The major external sources include:

Exhibit 10.13: Potential external sources of capital for multinational enterprises

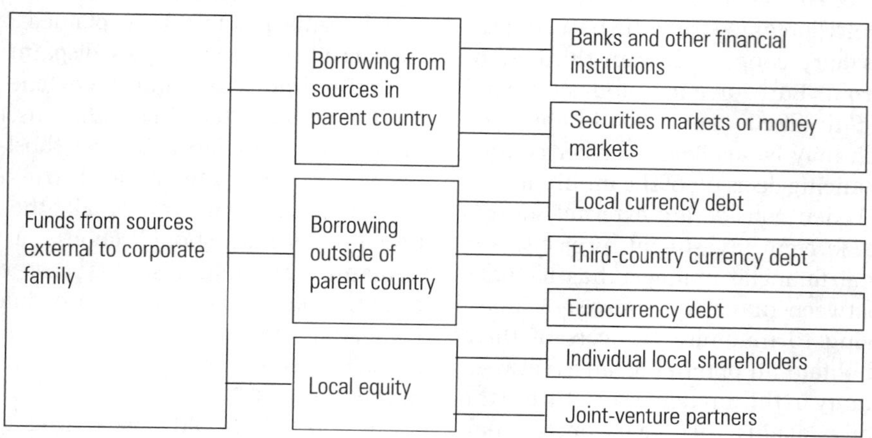

SOURCE: Eiteman et al., op. cit., p. 316.

- borrowing from sources in the home country of the parent company, mainly from banks and other financial institutions, and from securities or money markets;
- borrowing from outside the parent company's home country, which can include local currency (host-country) loans, third-country (not home or host-country) loans, and Eurocurrency loans;
- obtaining local (host-country) equity, from individual shareholders in the host country, or from joint-venture partners where the subsidiary is not wholly owned.

Access to international sources of funds gives multinational firms greater availability of capital than their domestic counterparts, and also the potential for a lower cost of capital. In this regard, the Eurocurrency market and the Eurobond market are the most important international sources of funds. Investment banks and securities firms in the international financial markets continually monitor international capital markets and assist clients to obtain foreign loans and listings on the international stock exchanges.

It is obvious that the decision with regard to external sources and forms of financing is a major one, considering the number of ways in which home-country and/or host-country loans can be obtained and combined with internal equity, obtained from the host country of the subsidiary concerned, from third countries or from Eurocurrency and Eurobond markets. Subsidised and low-interest-rate loans which may be available, further complicate the financing decision of the multinational company. When considering external sources to finance foreign investment projects, the international financial manager has to make a choice between numerous sources of funds, while striving to minimise the cost of these funds, and obtain an optimal balance between debt and equity in the financing structure of the project. Once again, the legal, operational, regulatory, tax, and risk implications of each alternative have to be taken into account when considering external sources of financing in the international context.

10.7.2 Financial structure and cost of capital

International financing decisions, much the same as for domestic financing decisions, should also be based on a financial structure that minimises the cost of capital.

However, in deciding to finance foreign operations or investment projects, the international financial manager has to consider a number of issues simultaneously in striving for an optimal financial structure. These issues include:

- minimising the cost of external funds after adjusting for foreign exchange risk and political risk;
- selecting internal financing sources that will minimise political risk and tax liabilities worldwide;
- minimising the multinational enterprise's worldwide consolidated cost of capital;
- the optimal positioning of funds within the multinational parent company and all its subsidiaries (as discussed in Section 10.4.1).

Research has shown that optimal financial structures based on debt-equity ratios differ significantly from one country to another, which could possibly be explained by factors such as different tax regimes, disparate cultural norms and practices, and the extent to which multinational enterprises either use uniform guidelines or conform to local (host-country) norms with regard to financial structures.

According to Eitman et al., the multinational enterprise should choose a financial structure that minimises its cost of capital from the perspective of the consolidated parent company, and the financial structure of each subsidiary is relevant only to the extent that it affects this goal.[55]

In short, it would appear that the multinational enterprise should choose a financial structure that minimises its own consolidated cost of capital, rather than that of a foreign subsidiary, despite a great variety of diverse practices in this regard which prevail in the international business environment.

10.8 Summary

The important function of international financial management was the subject of discussion in this chapter. The activities, scope, and goals of international financial management provided the background for examining global money management as a critically important element in the management of international working capital.

The important topics of foreign exchange risk management and international capital budgeting were explored from an international management perspective. The different types of foreign exchange exposure were identified, and approaches to the management of transaction exposure, translation exposure, and economic exposure were outlined. The complexities of capital budgeting in the multinational enterprise were highlighted, and guidelines provided for a systematic, integrated approach to the analysis and evaluation of foreign investment projects. Finally, the financing of international operations and projects, based on the important interrelationship between the investment and financing decisions in the international enterprise, was considered briefly.

Case Study

The Sentrachem experience

Sentrachem has been through some very exciting and troubled periods during the last couple of years, including the dramatic fall in its share price in 1996 and the sudden take-over by Dow Chemical Company.

Sentrachem can be described as an umbrella company, which included the following businesses in 1996:

- Karbochem (synthetic rubber)
- NCP (HTH pool chemicals)
- Safripol (polyethylene and polypropylene)
- Sanachem (insecticides, fungicides, and herbicides)
- Delta G Scientific (agrochemicals and bulk pharmaceuticals)
- Hampshire (chelates, nitrides, polymers, and naphthalene)
- Sentrachem International Holdings, which is an international chemical trading subsidiary.

Sentrachem's majority shareholder at the end of 1996 was Sanlam, and the managing director, Dr John Job, was responsible for leading Sentrachem out of its overprotective and import days toward a company that has become market-focused, with a growing offshore presence This was reached through exporting and acquiring offshore businesses.

Karbochem, Safripol, and NCP produced mainly for the domestic market while Sanachem produced for the broader international market. This was, to a certain extent, due to the fact that Sentrachem had acquired Hampshire, a chemical company based in the USA. Together with Sanachem, they established a worldwide marketing edge for glyphosate (the world's most widely used herbicide).

With the falling rand, Hampshire was a sure profit producer. The company boosted local exports to 25% of South African sales and accounted for 20% of the total group sales and operating profit. In the 1996 book-year Hampshire's operating profit rose by 61% as a result of the falling rand.

The operations of Agricura were re-engineered and the sales force and numerous depots were replaced with franchises, dealerships, and agencies. Karbochem's costs were significantly reduced as a result of restructuring, which resulted in the creation of four divisions. The whole idea was to improve market orientation and penetration.

Sentrachem was also involved in a couple of joint ventures, one of the largest being a R510-million agreement concluded with Bayer. Together they produce cost-effective chrome chemicals at a site owned by Karbochem in Newcastle – a site hailed for its size and world-class qualities. About 80% of the chemicals were destined for export, which helped South Africa become self-sufficient in the production of these chemicals.

Safripol's polypropylene plant was commissioned to increase capacity and the materials produced were destined for export, depending on local demand.

Before the Dow takeover, Sentrachem had not exactly earned acclaim from its shareholders. Among other things, one of its subsidiaries, Sanachem, was involved in major foreign exchange losses and other write-offs, sending Sentrachem through a painful restructuring process with the resignation of Robert Maingard (Sanachem's deputy chairman) and Norman Kennedy (the financial director). Maingard's resignation came four days before losses of R117 million from ill-judged foreign exchange contracts were made public, after which it was announced that R144 million had been allocated to patch up the leaking ship that was Sanachem. They were also restructuring, and trying to service a R1-billion debt-restructuring programme. Sentrachem's share price fell from 1 750 cents in the beginning of 1996 to around 700 cents in the middle of 1997.

Although Sentrachem had gone further than any of its competitors in restructuring its businesses, its shareholders had reaped no benefit. Job restructured the company to widen the geographical spread, increase production, and bring a balanced exposure to different markets.

One of Sentrachem's downfalls was its increasing debt/equity ratio, which grew from 1:0,12 in 1994 to 1:0,50 in 1996. The company claimed that this was caused partly by a write-off of R568 million in goodwill during its acquisition phase, whereas the annual capital expenditure had amounted to between R350 and R400 million during previous years. Furthermore, the group's gearing ratio was at about 120%, which was much higher than its target of 30%.

The falling rand played havoc with Sentrachem's margins and pricing arrangements, even though it brought about an increase in Hampshire's profits. The drop in international chemical prices added to the problem, which also accelerated the US dollar liability on the Hampshire acquisition. Shareholders and investors had a right to be concerned about Sentrachem's financial position. Earnings per share (EPS) were propped up at times through the utilisation of deferred taxes.

In December 1996 Sentrachem made public the fact that it had made major foreign exchange losses through its subsidiary, Sanachem. As a result, the share price dropped by 230 cents within a week. Sentrachem did not need to publicise the losses at that particular time, but decided to 'come clean and take the knock now'. The alternative was to try and trade out of the position over the full 18 months, but this approach would have allowed the losses to dip into the earnings until the contracts were completed. The company took the knock by closing out the position on an existing forward contract. The share prices fell on account of these losses, which also led to a 60% decrease in earnings per share the following year.

Sentrachem's apparent lack of financial control over Sanachem appeared to be a major part of the problem; the board had not known that Sanachem had concluded the forward contracts. Sanachem had evidently been given more autonomy than the other group divisions because of its success.

Sentrachem had a great deal of explaining to do since none of these problems had been addressed in their financial reports released in September 1996, nor did the report disclose that Sanachem had largely managed its own currency risk.

Experts put forward several views with regard to the viability of the forward contracts. On the one hand, the view was that investors buy shares in exporting companies because of the foreign exchange exposure, and hedging against this defeated the purpose. On the other hand, it was agreed that one of the main reasons for exporting is the declining rand, although this is not necessarily the case every year. This is why it is accepted practice to lock in an exchange rate which is favourable at the time, although pre-emptive hedging is considered to be somewhat similar to gambling. In effect, this is what Sanachem did, which was contrary to the group's policy. (Pre-emptive hedging occurs when a forward contract is taken out on sales that may occur in the future.) The general view is that only current export commitments should be hedged.

This was not Sanachem's only headache, however. A basic problem was that the company had relied too much on the General Export Incentive Scheme (GEIS). After it had risen from nowhere to become a world leader in agrochemical products, it had pursued market share at all costs. With the GEIS falling away in July 1996, all margins virtually disappeared.

Since the Dow takeover, Sentrachem has moved rapidly to offer R400 million to take control of the Safripol joint venture with Hoechst. This is a state-of-the-art, if small, polymer plant.

Most businesses within the Sentrachem group found a natural home with Dow, which organises its business along international product lines. In the past few months, Dow has invested R100 million in a herbicide plant and moved its African and Middle East headquarters from Europe to Johannesburg.

The old Sentrachem agricultural operations have been neatly packaged into Dow's agrosciences division, and the South African operations will become Dow's global producer of tebuthiuron, a herbicide.

Sentrachem's operation in the USA, housed in Hampshire Chemicals, was an obvious fit with Dow's speciality chemical operations, and was seen by many analysts as a real prize for Dow in the operation.

Through Dow, Sentrachem has again become a well-established global company, using various strategies in different parts of the world where they are involved. Sentrachem under Dow has the means and manpower to carry out these strategies successfully, therefore helping Dow to fulfil its mission 'to be the most productive, best value growth chemical company in the world'.

? Questions

1 From an international financial management perspective, how would you assess Sanachem's greater autonomy, compared to other Sentrachem subsidiaries, with regard to foreign exchange dealings?
2 Should Sanachem have been allowed to manage it own foreign exchange exposure?
3 Should a multinational company's board of directors be informed about the kind of flexibility referred to in (1) above?
4 Based on the limited information available with regard to this case, how should a multinational company like Sentrachem approach the management of foreign exchange exposure?
5 What are the chances that control over foreign exchange dealings and the management of foreign exchange exposure would have changed after the takeover by Dow?

NOTE: Access the Internet for more recent information with regard to this case.

Sources

Bennit, J. 1999. 'There's profit in a clean back yard', *Sunday Times Business Times*, 25 April.

Barnard, E.W. & Van den Bout, A. 1999. 'Analysis of the internationalisation and strategies of Sentrachem'. Unpublished Research Report, Department of Business Management, University of Pretoria.

Harris, S. 1995. 'Sharing up again'. *Financial Mail*, 21 July, p. 93.

Gleason, D. 1996. 'Sentrachem. Catalytic reaction needed for the share'. *Finance Week*, 28 November, pp. 42, 46-47.

Harris, S. 1996.'Sentrachem: Forex nightmare'. *Financial Mail*, 6 December, p. 88. Lawlor, P. 1996. 'To hedge or not to hedge?' *Finance Week*, 5 December, pp.25-26.

Lawlor, P. 1996. 'When companies misread the currency'. *Finance Week*, 12 December, pp. 23-24.

Friedland, R. 1997. 'Dow rides to the rescue'. *Financial Mail*, 8 August, pp. 66-67. Kruger, I. 1997. 'Hou jou Sentrachem-aandele'. *Finansies en Tegniek*, 22 August, p. 70.

Lundin, J. 1997. 'Crown jewels head for auction block'. *Financial Mail*, 16 May, pp. 63-64.

Endnotes

1 Stonehill, A.I. & Eiteman, D.K. 1987. *Finance – An international perspective.* Homewood, Illinois: Irwin, p.1.
Hill, C.W.L., 1998. *International Business.* 2nd ed. Burr Ridge, Illinois: McGraw-Hill Irwin, p. 564.
2 Ross, S.A., Westerfield, R.W. & Jordan, B.D. 1993. *Fundamentals of corporate finance.* Burr Ridge, Illinois: Irwin, pp. 6–8.
Eiteman, D.K., Stonehill, A.I. & Moffett, M.H. 1995. *Multinational business finance.*7th ed. Reading, Massachusetts: Addison-Wesley, p. 6.
3 Madura, J. 1998. *International financial management.* 5th ed. Cincinnati, Ohio: South Western College Publishing, p. 4.
4 Ibid.
5 Hill, op.cit., pp. 564–65.
6 Baker, JC. 1998. *International finance.* Upper Saddle River, New Jersey: Prentice Hall, p. 9.
Madura, op.cit., p. 5.
Eiteman et.al., op.cit., p. 5.
7 Eiteman, et al., op.cit., pp. 10–11. Anglo-American is defined to mean the United States, United Kingdom, Canada, Australia and New Zealand. Because of its historical ties with Britain and the British Commonwealth, South Africa could be added to this group of countries.
8 Madura, op.cit., p. 7.
9 Madura, op.cit., pp. 5–7.
10 Eiteman, et al., op.cit., pp. 11–12.
11 Rugman, A.M. & Hodgetts, R.M. 1995. *International Business.* New York: McGraw-Hill, p.386.
12 Hill, op.cit., p. 574.
13 Ross, S.A., Westerfield, R.W., Jordan, B.D. & Firer, C. 1996. *Fundamentals of corporate finance.* 1st South African edition. London: Irwin, pp. 508–509.
14 Rugman & Hodgetts, op.cit., p. 387.
15 Hill, op.cit., p. 578.
16 Kelly, J. 1995. 'Administrators prepare for a more efficient future', *Financial Times Survey*: World Taxation, 24 February, p. 9.
Crow, S. & Sauls, E. 1994. 'Setting the right transfer price', *Management Accounting*, December, pp. 41–47.
17 Rugman & Hodgetts, op.cit., pp. 388–389, from which the framework for the example has been adapted.
18 Hill, op.cit., pp. 578–580.
Rugman & Hodgetts, op.cit., pp. 388–389.
Baker, op.cit., pp. 476–480.
19 Baker, op.cit., pp. 474–476.
Hill, op.cit., p. 576.
20 Eiteman et al., op.cit., p. 611–612.
21 Ibid.
22 Hill, op.cit., pp. 580–581.
23 Hill, op.cit., p. 583.
24 Rugman & Hodgetts, op.cit., pp. 391–392.
25 Stonehill & Eiteman, op.cit., p. 33.
26 Madura, op.cit., p. 295.
27 Rugman & Hodgetts, op.cit., pp. 395–396, from which the framework for the example has been adapted.
28 Madura, op.cit., p. 312.
29 Stonehill & Eiteman, op.cit., pp. 34–35.
30 Eiteman et al., op.cit., pp. 252–253.
31 Hill, op.cit., p. 585.
32 Madura, op.cit., pp. 312–315.
33 Madura, op.cit., p. 304.
34 Stonehill & Eiteman, op.cit., pp. 43–44.
35 Hill, op.cit., p. 585.
36 Stonehill & Eiteman, op.cit., p. 45.
37 Rugman & Hodgetts, op.cit., p. 397.
Hill, op.cit., p. 586.
38 Rugman & Hodgetts, op.cit., pp. 398–399.
39 Ibid.
40 Eiteman et al., op.cit., pp. 238–241, where the authors define a back-to-back loan as the involvement of two business firms in separate countries arranging to borrow each other's currency for a specific period of time, with the return of the currencies on an agreed upon time.
41 Ibid.
42 Eiteman et al., op.cit., p. 147.
43 Hill, op.cit., p. 586.
44 Griffin, R.W. & Pustay, M.W. 1999. *International Business.* 2nd ed. Reading, Massachusetts: Addison-Wesley, p. 671.
45 Hill, op.cit., p. 586.
46 Hill, op.cit., pp. 587–588.
47 This section draws on the works of Ross et al., (1st South African edition), op.cit., pp. 615–620, Eiteman et al., op.cit., Chapter 19; Rugman & Hodgetts, op.cit., pp. 400–404; Madura, op.cit., Chapter 17; Hill, op.cit., pp. 568–572; Griffin & Pustay, op.cit., pp. 680–682.
48 Eiteman et al., op.cit., pp. 526–527.
49 Ibid.
50 Eiteman et al., op.cit., p. 530.
51 Ibid.
52 Madura, op.cit., pp. 517–520, from which the format for the example has been adapted. Tax information does not necessarily relate to actual tax data in the Appendix.
53 Griffin & Pustay, op.cit., pp. 683–686.
54 Eiteman et al., op.cit., p. 315.
55 Eiteman et al., op.cit., pp. 317–319.

Appendix

International tax issues

Non-resident withholding taxes

The following directives regarding withholding taxes apply to interest, dividend and royalty receipts by external or foreign companies in South Africa.

Interest and dividend receipts or accruals by an external or foreign company in South Africa are not subject to withholding taxes.

Where an external or foreign company derives royalties or similar payments for the use in South Africa of any patent, design, trademark, copyright or right or property of a similar nature, 30% of the gross royalty or similar payment is deemed to be taxable income.

The normal South African company tax rate of 30% is applied to the deemed taxable royalty income, with the effect that 9% (30% of 30%) of the gross royalty is taxed **in the absence of a double tax agreement** between South Africa and the country concerned.

The person liable to make the payment of the royalty or similar payment must withhold tax at a rate of 12% of such amount, and make an advance payment to the local Receiver of Revenue. The recipient, (external or foreign company) is not relieved of the responsibility of filing an annual tax return, and the withholding tax can be claimed on assessment against the tax payable.

Double taxation agreements and tax havens

In order to prevent taxation of the same income in two or more countries, South Africa had entered into double taxation agreements with 41 countries by 1999.

The table on p. 337 illustrates the withholding taxes on dividends, interest and royalties paid to some of the countries with which South Africa has a double tax agreement.

The table on p. 338 illustrates income tax rates and withholding taxes on dividends, interest and royalties paid to South African firms in some of the major countries.

The following table (p. 339) reflects the countries with which South Africa has double taxation agreements.

A list of countries that South Africans can utilise as 'tax havens' for international investment and financial purposes appears in the table on p. 339.

Crossborder transactions

The implications of international taxation should be considered whenever a business or personal transaction involves parties or activities in more than one country.

The manner in which the tax systems of different countries interact poses both tax opportunities and pitfalls for the taxpayer entering into crossborder transactions.

Recipient	Dividends	Interest (note 1)	Royalties (note 2)
• No double taxation agreement	Nil	Nil	12%
• Double taxation agreement			
Austria	Nil	Nil	Nil
Botswana	Nil	Nil (note 3)	12%
Canada	Nil	Nil (note 4)	6% or 10% (note 5)
France	Nil	Nil	Nil or 12% (note 6)
Germany	Nil	Nil (note7)	Nil or 12% (note 6)
India	Nil	Nil (note 4)	10%
Ireland	Nil	Nil	Nil
Japan	Nil	Nil (note 4)	10%
Namibia	Nil	Nil	Nil or 12% (note 6)
Netherlands	Nil	Nil (note 4)	Nil
Singapore	Nil	Nil	5%
Sweden	Nil	Nil	Nil or 12% (note 6)
Switzerland	Nil	Nil (note 3)	Nil
Taiwan	Nil	Nil (note 4)	10%
United Kingdom	Nil	Nil (note 7)	Nil or 12% (note 6)
United States of America	Nil	Nil	Nil
Zimbabwe	Nil	Nil	Nil or 12% (note 6)

NOTES:

1. There is no withholding tax on interest. Where the true source of interest is South Africa, the recipient is liable for normal tax, but this may be limited to a rate specified or exempted in terms of the double taxation agreement.
2. Companies may have to render annual tax returns of income and pay tax at normal rates, with credit being given for the withholding tax deducted.
3. Maximum rate of tax is limited to 15%.
4. Maximum rate of tax limited to 10%.
5. Maximum rate of normal tax limited to 6% or 10%, depending on nature of royalty.
6. Must be subject to tax in the hands of the recipient in the country of residence; otherwise 12% withholding tax applies.
7. Maximum rate of normal tax is limited to 10%, provided the interest is subject to tax in recipient's country of residence.

Country	Income Tax Rate (note 1)	Withholding Tax Rate imposed on income earned by South African firms in host countries		
		Dividends	Interest	Royalties
Australia	36%	30%	10%	30%
Brazil	25%	Nil	15%	15%
Canada	38%	5% or 15% (note 2)	10%	6% or 10%
France	33,33%	5% to 15% (note 3)	Nil	Nil
Germany	45%	7.5% (note 4)	10%	Nil
Japan	37.5%	5% or 15% (note 5)	10%	10%
New Zealand	33%	30% (note 6)	15% (note 7)	15%
South Africa	30%	–	–	–
Taiwan	25%	5% or 15% (note 8)	10%	10%
United Kingdom	31%	Nil	10%	Nil
United States of America	35%	5% or 15% (note 9)	Nil	Nil

NOTES:
1. The tax rates may vary depending on the nature of the company, taxable income and other incentives, which can significantly reduce the tax liability. More details on the tax rates should be obtained when considering international investment.
2. The lower rate applies where the beneficial owner of the dividend is a company that owns/controls a specified interest in the paying company.
3. 5% for parent companies (10% shareholding required to be a parent company) and 15% for non-parent companies.
4. No withholding tax on shareholder holding directly/indirectly at least 25% of the paying German company's shares.
5. 5% for substantial holdings and 15% for portfolio.
6. The rate on all fully imputed dividends is 15%.
7. No withholding tax is imposed where the recipient of the interest has a fixed establishment in New Zealand.
8. 5% for companies with at least 10% shareholding.
9. 5% for companies which own at least 10% of the outstanding voting shares of the payer company, and 15% for portfolio shares.

SOURCE: Compiled by PriceWaterhouseCoopers, Pretoria, September 1999, and reproduced with their permission.

Following the relaxation of exchange controls from 1 July 1997, certain provisions relating to the taxation of foreign source investment and certain trading income were promulgated.

Accordingly, the strategy for South Africa has changed in that it should focus mainly on trading profits or investment income that is associated with a substantive business activity carried on through foreign permanent establishments.

The following provisions are relevant to international transactions:

- transfer pricing;
- thin capitalisation;
- foreign investment income (taxation on the basis of residence of the taxpayer as opposed to the source of the income.)

Countries with which South Africa has double taxation agreements.

Austria	Egypt	Ireland	Mauritius	Singapore
Belgium	Finland	Italy	Namibia	Swaziland
Botswana	France	Israel	Netherlands	Sweden
Canada	Germany	Japan	Norway	Switzerland
Croatia	Hungary	Korea	Pakistan	Thailand
Cyprus	India	Lesotho	Poland	United Kingdom
Czech Republic	Indonesia	Malawi	Republic of China	USA
Denmark	Iran	Malta	Romania	Zambia
				Zimbabwe

Countries that South Africans can utilise as tax havens*.

Barbados	Dubai	Malta
Bermuda	Gibraltar	Mauritius
British Virgin Islands	Ireland	The Netherlands
Cayman Islands	Isle of Man	The Netherlands Antilles
Channel Islands: Jersey	Liechtenstein	Switzerland
	Madeira	

* The above is intended to serve as a guideline only. Professional advice should preferably be obtained before considering investment internationally.

PART IV

Southern Africa and Africa: international co-operation and future perspectives

Global collaboration and strategic alliances

Key issues

- Modes of entry into foreign markets
- Defining strategic alliances
- The importance of strategic alliances in South Africa
- Strategic alliances profile of South African companies
- Strategic alliance linkages by South African companies
- Motivations for entering into strategic alliances
- Success of strategic alliances
- Factors to be considered when forming strategic alliances

11.1 **Introduction**

It has already been mentioned in Chapters 1 and 2 that successful businesses of the future will treat the entire world as their domain in terms of meeting their supply and demand requirements, and that in such a globalised market, the domestic company will not be sustainably competitive. The opening of new markets to South African businesses, together with new technology in communication and transport, has resulted in a major expansion of international trade and investment. In the last part of this book we will focus on global collaboration and the importance of the emerging regional market in Southern Africa.

Companies are forming international strategic alliances in response to global demands and many South African companies, especially those which are research and development-intensive, are considering alliances with foreign partners and companies for the following reasons, among others:

- to seek out new markets as a way of sustaining or increasing growth in sales and profits;
- to achieve lower development, research, and marketing costs;
- to share resources;
- to access natural resource deposits in other countries;
- to do business in a more politically stable environment;
- to learn new skills from competitors.

If South African companies are to compete successfully in the global market-place, it is important that they should become involved in the globalisation process as soon as possible and develop strategic alliances as a means of becoming internationalised.

11.2 Modes of entry into foreign markets

There are various modes of entering foreign markets. The six most often used are exporting, licensing, joint ventures, franchising, turnkey operations, and setting up a wholly-owned subsidiary in the foreign country or countries. Exhibit 11.1 gives a logical layout of the advantages and disadvantages of these six entry modes. In this chapter there will be a discussion of some of these as being critical factors in forming strategic alliances, but the focus will be on the co-operative arrangements between two or more local and/or global firms that can affect their competitive positioning.

11.3 Defining strategic alliances

A strategic alliance is defined as a particular mode of interorganisational relationship in which the partners make substantial investments in developing a long-term collaborative effort and a common orientation towards their individual and mutual goals.[1] These alliances are described as partnerships in which closer connections evolve between separate organisations.[2] In many cases, the linkages between the two companies are so strong that the boundaries become indistinct, and it is often difficult to discern where one organisation ends and the other begins.[3]

Exhibit 11.1: Advantages and disadvantages of entry modes

Entry Mode	Advantage	Disadvantage
Exporting	Ability to realise location and experience curve economies	High transport costs Trade barriers Problems with local marketing agents
Turnkey contracts	Ability to earn returns from process technology skills in countries where FDI is restricted	Creating efficient competitors Lack of long-term market presence
Licensing	Low development costs and risks	Lack of control over technology Inability to realise location and experience curve economies Inability to engage in global strategic co-ordination
Franchising	Low development costs and risks	Lack of control over quality Inability to engage in global strategic co-ordination
Joint ventures	Access to local partner's knowledge Sharing development costs and risks Politically acceptable	Lack of control over technology Inability to engage in global strategic co-ordination Inability to realise location and experience economies
ʼ/holly owned subsidiaries	Protection of technology Ability to engage in global strategic co-ordination Ability to realise location and experience economies	High costs and risks

ʼernational business: competing in the global marketplace*. Washington: McGraw-Hill, p. 410.

343

Strategic alliances embody a future-oriented relationship forged between two or more independent companies in which each attempts to use the strengths of the other as leverage to achieve mutually beneficial goals. The alliance does not have to be based on a singular superordinate goal that drives the relationship.[4] However, there must be perceptual congruity or consensus with regard to the goals of each member. In other words, consensus about domain is more important than a shared unifying focus. Hennart[6] suggests that firms typically engage in joint ventures to achieve objectives such as:

- to take advantage of economies of scale and diversifying risk;
- to overcome entry barriers to new markets;
- to pool complementary knowledge.

Lorange and Roos introduce a new theoretical perspective by looking at the continuous scale between strategic alliances; on the one hand we have 'transactions on a free market (market) and, on the other, total internalisation (hierarchy)'.[7]

Alliances have been defined as collaborative projects implemented by firms operating in the same industry. Although they co-operate with one another, the partner firms in such alliances usually retain their strategic autonomy.[8]

There is a whole range of strategic alliances, including purchasing agreements, marketing/distribution agreements, shared research and development (R&D) efforts, cross licensing, co-operative agreements, and equity-based relationships.

In this chapter a strategic alliance is defined as a co-operative arrangement between two or more local and/or global firms that can affect the competitive positioning of either participant in the market segment in which they set out to compete.

11.4 The importance of strategic alliances in South Africa

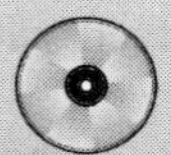

Compact disc

1 Mr Jan de Bruyn of the IDC elaborates on the importance of strategic alliances and the Mozal project in Mozambique

Hough[9] did extensive research into the formation of strategic alliances by South African companies. Companies listed in the importers and exporters registers of the Bureau of Market Research at Unisa were used as the population for this study.[10] A randomised stratified sample of 1 800 companies was drawn proportionally from two of the nine Standard Industrial Classification (SIC) sections, namely the manufacturing, and the wholesale and retail sections. The rest of this chapter is based largely on this empirical research.

Exhibit 11.2 gives an indication of South African companies which are involved in

Exhibit 11.2: Strategic alliances by South African companies

Research method	Strategic alliance group		Non-alliance group
Questionnaire survey	Involvement in local or foreign strategic alliance	Consider forming a local or foreign strategic alliance	Not involved in any strategic alliance
	39%	9%	52%

strategic alliances, or are considering forming strategic alliances.

Thirty-nine per cent of South African companies which responded to the research survey are involved in either a local or foreign strategic alliance (the *strategic alliance group)* while 9% are considering forming such an alliance. Fifty-two per cent are not linked to any local or overseas alliance. From an analysis of the strategic alliance group (SAG) it becomes clear that more than 50% of these alliances are with South African companies (Exhibit 11.3). More than 40% are with overseas companies, although 73% of the group are involved with both local and overseas alliances.

Exhibit 11.4 (p. 347) illustrates the percentages of companies involved in strategic alliances based on categories of turnover/employees.

The turnovers of 50,3 % of the companies in the exhibit are less than R10 million, and in the majority of cases they have less than 100 employees.

11.5 Strategic alliances profile of South African companies

Exhibit 11.5 (p. 347) provides details about the types of alliances being formed with local and overseas partners (details of companies involved in alliances or considering forming alliances were correlated).

The choice of strategic alliances is influenced by a variety of factors, such as legal requirements, access to technology, fixed costs, experience, competition, risks, control aspects, product complexity, international expansion of the enterprise, and the degree of similarity between countries in respect of language and culture.

Exhibit 11.3: Local and overseas strategic alliances by SA companies

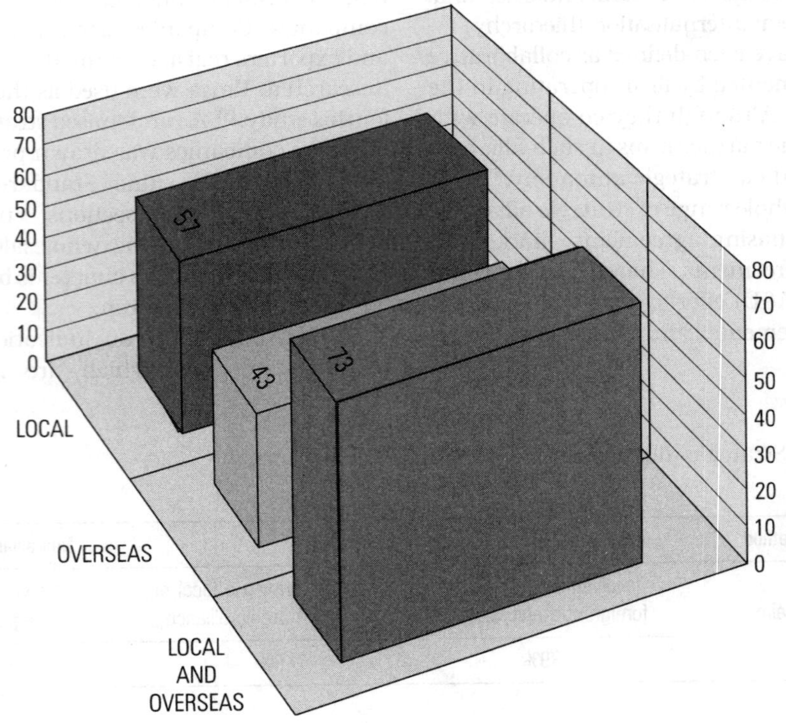

Exhibit 11.4: Strategic alliances by South African companies based on turnover and number of employees

Strategic alliance group	Percentage
Turnover of less than R2 million	18,6%
Turnover of less than R10 million	50,3%
Turnover of more than R10 million	49,7%
Less than 100 employees	65,4%
Less than 600 employees	85,4%
More than 1000 employees	12,4%

Exhibit 11.5: Strategic alliance profile of South African companies

Types of alliances formed	Total (SA and overseas)	South African alliance	Overseas alliance
Joint ventures	36%	19%	25%
Marketing/distribution agreements	76%	41%	56%
Co-operative agreements	30%	16%	19%
Research and development agreements	24%	10%	17%
Informal alliances	34%	20%	19%
Cross-licensing	14%	4%	12%
Equity alliances	7%	4%	4%

It is overwhelmingly clear from Exhibit 11.5 that South African businesses choose marketing and/or distribution agreements when doing business with partners. Joint ventures and informal alliances are also popular, but cross-licensing and equity alliances are mostly avoided. Research and development partnerships comprise only 24% of the alliances formed.

Most alliances are based on marketing and/or distribution agreements with local and overseas partners. More than 50% of all alliance business with overseas partners takes place through marketing and/or distribution agreements, followed by joint ventures, co-operative agreements, and informal alliances. Businesses are also more positive about becoming involved in research and development agreements with overseas partners than with local organisations. The alliance pattern with local partners follows very much the same path, with marketing and/or distribution agreements in first place, followed by informal alliances, joint ventures, and co-operative agreements.

11.6 Strategic alliance linkages by South African companies

Exhibit 11.6 (p. 348) shows the percentages of South African companies involved in alliance

Exhibit 11.6: Strategic alliances linkages by South African companies

Strategic alliance group	Local and overseas
Resource supply	39%
Product manufacturing	51%
Processing	12%
Services	34%
Other	8%

linkages in terms of resource supply, product manufacturing, processing, and services.

Product manufacturing is by far the most popular alliance activity, followed by supply of resources, and service-oriented linkages. The processing of raw materials is still relatively underdeveloped as a driving force for entering into an alliance as far as South African companies are concerned.

> **South Africa can do it!**
>
> South African companies have the ability to compete successfully in the global market-place if they become involved in the globalisation process and develop strategic business partnerships as a vehicle for becoming internationalised and operating more competitively and productively.

11.7 Motivations for entering into strategic alliances

According to Zajac, the four main motivations for engaging in joint venture alliances were:[11]

- to acquire a means of distribution and pre-empt competitors (35%);
- to gain access to new technology and diversify into new businesses (25%);
- to obtain economies of scale and achieve vertical integration (20%);
- to overcome legal/regulatory barriers (20%).

The alliance can result in greater access to raw materials, markets, technology, capital, and other forms of expertise that allow the firm to make better-informed decisions. For example, IBM's pending partnership with Siemens is intended to help IBM establish the foothold in the PBX market that it failed to gain with its acquisition of Rohm.[12] The formation of alliances is also facilitated by internal and external behavioural and economic factors.[13, 14, 15]

The following question was asked to determine motivations for South African companies entering into strategic alliances: 'To what extent does/did your company consider the following ten factors when deciding on strategic alliances? 0 = to no extent; 1 = to a very small extent; 2 = to a small extent; 3 = to a large extent; 4 = to a very large extent.' Responses on a scale of 0 to 4 were converted into percentages.

Exhibit 11.7 (p. 349) shows the relative importance of these strategic factors to South African companies when entering into an alliance.

The most important factor that companies consider is seeking out new markets as a way of sustaining growth in sales and profits. The second most important factor when entering into local and overseas alliances is to create wider and deeper product lines. The impor-

Exhibit 11.7: Motivation for strategic alliance entry by South African companies

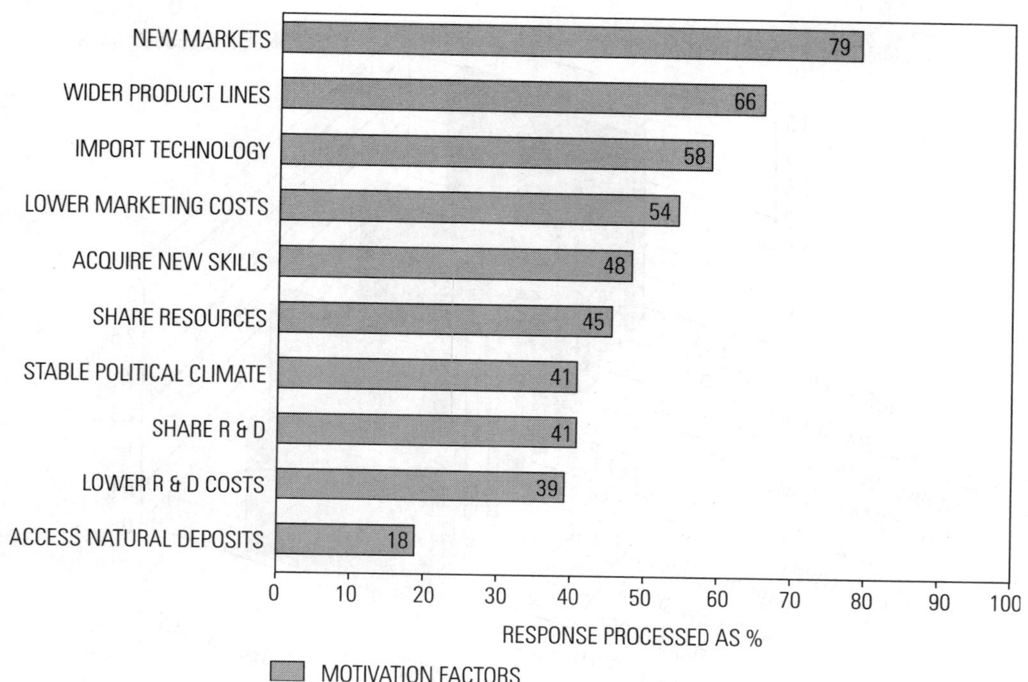

tance of these two factors corresponds with factors listed by Zajac,[16] Kuzmicki,[17] and Pilafidis.[18]

A factor analysis was done on the results of the above question, the results of which are illustrated in Exhibit 11.8 (p. 350). The two main driving forces for entry into an alliance were identified, namely the profit-driven factor, and the technology and research-driven motive. The frequency values on which the factor analysis is based are shown as a response on a scale of 0 to 5.

It can be established from Exhibit 11.8 that considerations such as seeking new markets to increase sales, creating wider and deeper product lines, and reducing marketing and distribution cost, rate high on the profit factor. With regard to the technology/research and development factor, decisions on the importation of technology, whether to share research and development results or acquire new skills from local and international relationships, were the most important considerations for entering into an alliance.

11.8 Success of strategic alliances

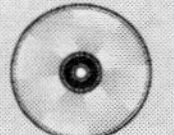

Compact disc

2 Mr André la Grange of Nedbank spells out the different stakeholders in joint ventures between government, labour, and business.

After extensive research and analysis on strategic alliances, Brouthers, Brouthers, and Wilk-

Exhibit 11.8: Factor analysis of motivation for strategic alliances

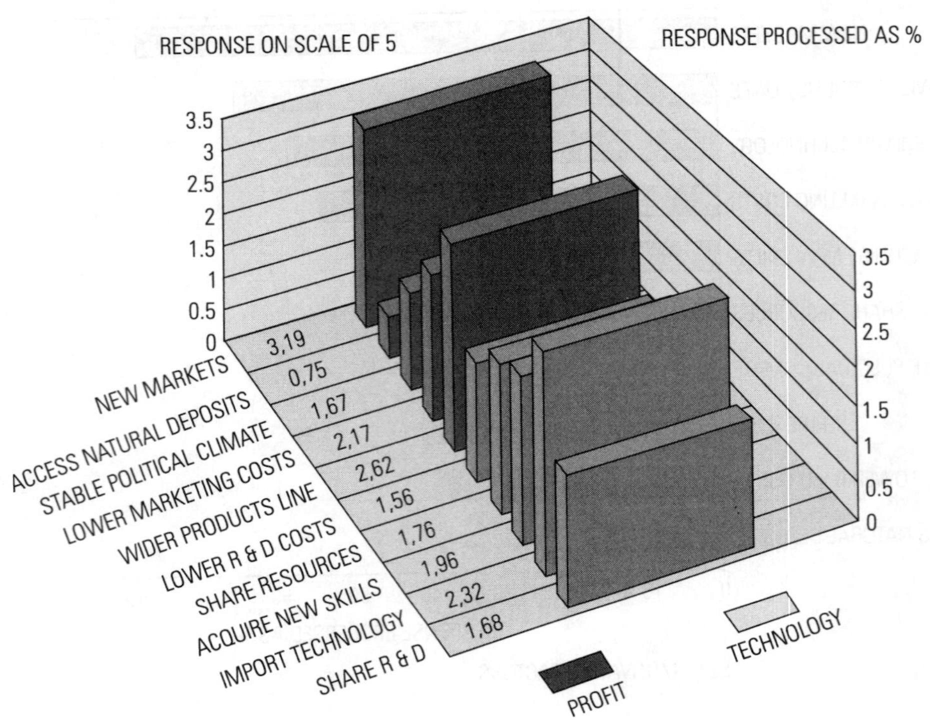

Exhibit 11.9: The 4 C's of successful international strategic alliances

inson[19] arrived at the 4 Cs of successful international strategic alliances, namely complementary skills, co-operative cultures, compatible goals, and commensurate levels of risk (see Exhibit 11.9 on p. 350).

The following question was asked to determine how South African managers perceived the success of their strategic alliances: 'To what extent do you consider the formed alliance as a success?' Their response is illustrated in Exhibit 11.10.

Exhibit 11.10: Perception of the success of strategic alliances

0 = to no extent	2,3%
1 = to a very small extent	3,5%
2 = to a small extent	15,6%
3 = to a large extent	55,5%
4 = to a very large extent	23,1%

South African businesses appear to be very happy with their strategic alliances. Almost 80% of the respondents regard their alliances as a success to a large or very large extent, while only 2,3% feel that their alliances are not at all successful.

11.9 Factors to be considered when forming strategic alliances

Various factors have to be considered when planning to form a relationship or alliance with any business partner. Maintaining the relationship is also a decisive factor in making the partnership succeed. Japan's Toshiba Corporation is one of the world's most successful companies when it comes to forming and maintaining strategic relationships. Despite its own technological and manufacturing expertise, Toshiba knows that it cannot rely solely on its own resources in the global world of digital electronics. This company is currently engaged in more than two dozen major partnerships and joint ventures and has yet to experience an ugly falling-out. Toshiba's success is attributed mainly to the following factors:[20]

- The alliances are constructed in such a way that the roles and rights of each partner are clearly defined from the very beginning;
- Senior management plays an active role in each relationship;
- Toshiba is completely open about all its different relationships;
- Every aspect of the relationship is streamlined and accelerated;
- Partners are carefully chosen.

Exhibit 11.11 (p. 352) provides an analysis of the factors which South African managers regard as crucial when considering forming strategic alliances with local or overseas partners.

Ensuring the partner's credibility is seen as the most important factor when forming a relationship, followed by an analysis of the benefits and advantages of the prospective partnership. During interviews with managers responsible for international business, the importance of trust and openness was emphasised. Jones, as quoted by Wolff, puts it very eloquently: 'No alliance can survive without trust.'[21]

Retaining the management responsibility, focusing on the overall value added, and possibly developing new products in the partnership, are also seen as crucial when considering alliances. Discussing performance standards, checking the tax, financial, and legal issues, holding periodic meetings to monitor progress, and avoiding complete dependency on the alliance partner, are high on the agenda of companies which are considering alliances with local or overseas partners.

Aspects which are of the least concern to South African management when deciding on the formation of strategic alliances, are:

- establishing inter-firm teams to oversee partnerships;

Exhibit 11.11: Factors to be considered when entering strategic alliances

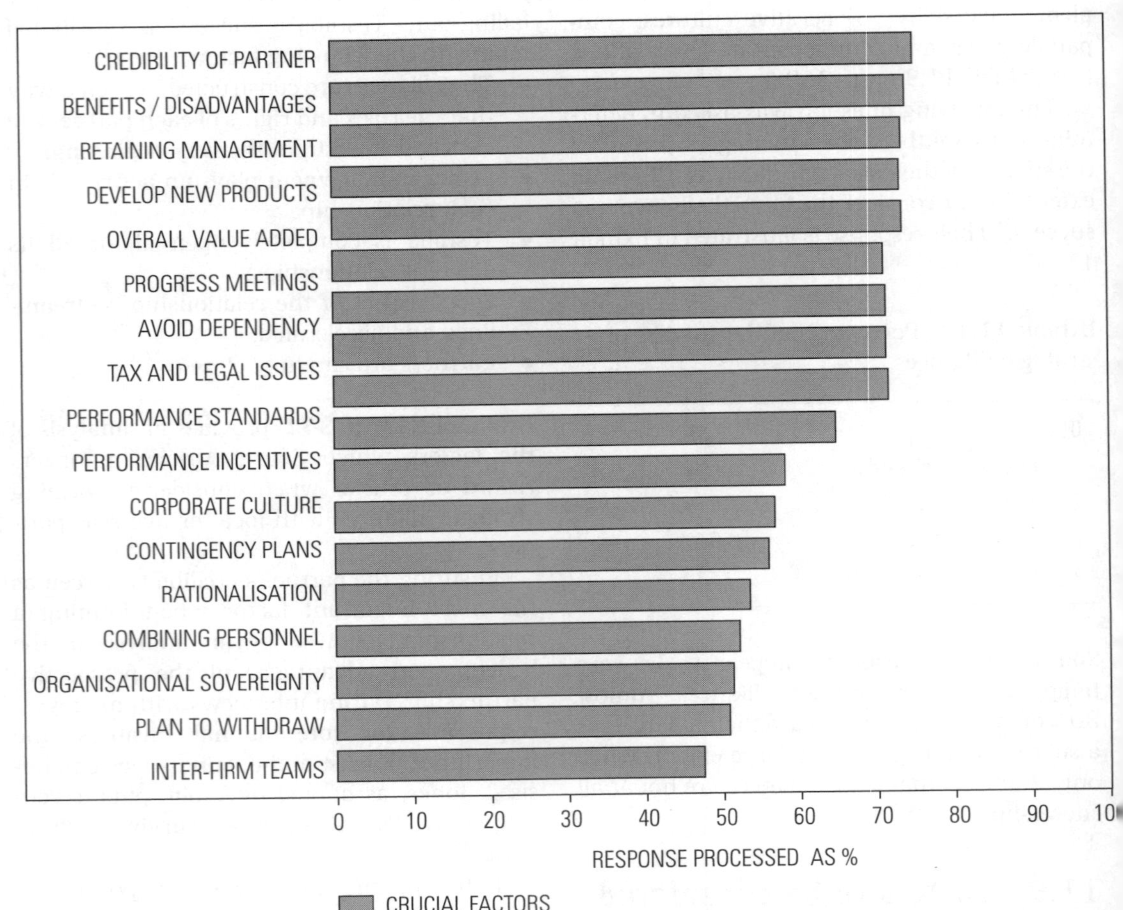

- planning ahead for when and how to withdraw;
- negotiating the boundaries of organisational sovereignty;
- combining personnel from both partners.

11.10 Summary

Successful businesses of the future should be able to treat the entire world as their domain in terms of meeting their supply and demand requirements, especially in view of the fact that in such a globalised market, the domestic company will not be sustainably competitive.

The opening of new markets to South African businesses, together with new technology in communication and transport, have resulted in a major expansion of international trade and investment.

A strategic alliance has been defined as a co-operative arrangement between two or more local and/or global firms that can affect the competitive positioning of either participant in the market segment in which they set out to compete.

Thirty-nine per cent of South African companies which responded to a research survey are involved in a local or foreign strategic alliance, while 9% are considering forming such an alliance.

South African businesses overwhelmingly choose marketing and/or distribution agreements when doing business with partners. Joint ventures and informal alliances are also popular, while they are hesitant about cross-licensing and equity alliances. Research and development partnerships account for only 24% of the alliances.

Most South African alliances are based on marketing and/or distribution agreements with local and overseas partners, while joint ventures, co-operative agreements, and informal alliances are also popular.

The most important factor that South African companies consider when forming alliances is that they need to seek out new markets as a way of sustaining growth in sales and profits.

South African businesses seem to be very happy with their strategic alliances because 80% of them regard their alliances as successful to a large or very large extent.

Case Study

Schwinn in a joint venture with Csepel Bicycle

Joint ventures with host-country firms have many features that make them an attractive means of entering a foreign market, but they also have pitfalls. Consider the case of Schwinn, the American bicycle manufacturer, which set up a joint venture with the Csepel Bicycle Works of Hungary in 1989 to manufacture bicycles for sale in Eastern Europe. Schwinn chose to work with Csepel because the Hungarian enterprise had a good reputation, as well as access to relatively inexpensive, skilled labour.

The joint venture, Schwinn-Csepel, was capitalised at $2,1 million, with Schwinn contributing 51% and Csepel 49%. Negotiations over the structure of the venture proved to be time-consuming and tedious – they took well over a year – because there were no uniform procedures for setting up joint ventures in Hungary. Joint-venture laws changed several times during the negotiations, and they have changed several times since. Nobody – neither lawyers, government officials, nor company officials – could keep track of what had to be done to conform to Hungary's confused and rapidly-changing joint-venture laws.

Since the venture was formally incorporated in June 1989, further regulatory changes have played havoc with its plans. The joint-venture agreement called for Schwinn to import component parts from the United States, assemble bicycles in Hungary, and then sell them throughout Eastern Europe. However, just as Schwinn-Csepel was starting production, the budget-conscious Hungarian government changed import taxes. Import taxes on component parts were levied that included a 15% import duty, a 25% value-added tax (VAT), and a 2% handling charge.

With nearly 300 different component parts coming in each day and no computers in the customs office, Schwinn-Csepel had to establish a five-person department to calculate import taxes. Moreover, although the VAT on re-exported bikes is refunded, six months may pass before this occurs. In effect, Schwinn-Csepel is making an interest-free loan to the Hungarian government that amounts to millions of dollars.

The venture has also been plagued by unexpected productivity problems. Productivity is significantly lower than at Schwinn's North American plants; the percentage of defects is higher and workers are apathetic. Worse still, the venture inherited a management problem. Many of the managers of the former Csepel Bicycle Works, although not all ex-communist, are products of the old communist system. Traditions of secrecy and favouritism, and a lack of attention to productivity and profitability, have persisted.

Despite these problems, the venture is beginning to make headway. About 250 000 bicycles were sold in 1991, half of those in Hungary. The company has built a dealer network of 55 shops, whose owners guarantee servicing and spare parts – unheard-of in the old days of communist rule. There is no other Western competition, and competing bicycles built by other Eastern European firms are poorly built and relatively expensive.

Consequently, Schwinn-Csepel's managers in the USA still believe their venture will succeed, but they warn other firms contemplating similar moves into the Eastern European market that they should expect the unexpected.

SOURCE: 'A bicycle made by two', 1991, *The Economist*, June 8, p. 73.

Questions

1 Define the joint venture between Schwinn and Csepel Bicycle Works in your own words.

2 Identify the main benefits of the Schwinn-Csepel alliance.
3 What risk is Schwinn taking by entering into this joint venture with Csepel? What risk is Csepel Bicycle Works running?
4 Indicate the factors that influence the working relationship between the companies.
5 Do you think this relationship will last very long?

Endnotes

1 Johanson, J. & Mattson, J. 1991. 'Strategic adaptation of firms to the European single market – a network approach'. In Mattson, L-G. & Styme, B. (eds.) *Corporate and industry strategies for Europe*. Amsterdam: Elsevier Publishers.

2 Kanter, R. M. 1988. 'The new alliances: How strategic partnerships are reshaping American business'. In Sawyer, H. (ed.) *Business in a contemporary world*. New York: University Press of America.

3 Spekman, R.E. & Sawhney, K.1990. 'Toward a conceptual understanding of the antecedents of strategic alliances'. Working paper. Cambridge, Massachusetts: Marketing Science Institute.

4 Spekman & Sawhney, ibid.

5 Salmond, D. J.1987. 'When and why buyers and suppliers collaborate: A resource dependence and efficiency view'. Unpublished doctoral dissertation, University of Maryland, USA.

6 Hennart, J.F. 1987. 'A transaction costs theory of equity joint ventures'. *Strategic Management Journal*, 9.

7 Lorange, P. & Roos, J.1993. *Strategic alliances: Formation, implementation and evolution*. London: Blackwell.

8 Lorange & Roos, ibid.

9 Hough, J. 1997. 'Creating strategic alliances in the global village: the South African case'. AIB conference. Monterrey, Mexico

10 Bureau of Market Research. 1992. *A guide to the BMR registers*. Research Report No. 190. Pretoria: University of South Africa.

11 Zajac, E. 1990. 'CEOs' views on strategic alliances'. Paper presented at the Marketing Sciences Conference on managing Long-Run Relationships, Boston.

12 Spekman & Sawhney, op cit.

13 Hutt, M.D., Mokwa, M.P. & Shapiro, S.J.1986. 'The politics of marketing: Analyzing the parallel political marketplace'. *Journal of Marketing*, 5 January.

14 Contractor, F.J. & Lorange, P.1988. 'Competition vs. Co-operation: A benefit/cost framework for choosing between fully-owned investments and co-operative relationships'. *Management International Review*, 28 (Special Issue).

15 Johnston, R., & Lawrence, P.R. 1988. 'Beyond vertical integration – the rise of the value-adding partnership'. *Harvard Business Review*, July-Aug., pp. 94–101.

16 Zajac, op cit.

17 Kuzmicki, J.F. 1993. *Strategic alliances: an investigation of environmental and industry traits conducive to the formation of none-equity alliances*. Unpublished doctoral dissertation. University of Alabama, USA.

18 Pilafidis, E. J. 1994. *Effective structuring and managing of intercompany relationships: case studies in domestic strategic alliances*. Unpublished doctoral dissertation. Claremont Graduate School, USA.

19 Brouthers, K.D., Brouthers, L.E. & Wilkinson, T.J. 1995. 'Strategic alliances: choose your partners. *Long Range Planning*, 28 (3).

20 Schlender, B.R. 1993. 'How Toshiba makes alliances work'. *Fortune International*, October 4.

21 Wolff, M. F. 1994. 'Building trust in alliances'. *Research Technology Management*. 37(3).

Southern Africa – an emerging regional market

Key issues

- Southern Africa as an emerging regional market
- Globalisation as the context of regional integration and development
- Research into strategic issues facing the southern African region
- Key factors affecting foreign direct investment flows into the southern African region
- Identification of business sectors which reflect high growth opportunities in southern Africa
- Perceptions on regional competitiveness
- Factors enhancing competitiveness
- Competitiveness in South Africa's manufacturing industries
- Strategies to develop southern Africa as a global player

12.1 Introduction

There is growing realisation in southern Africa that sustained economic growth will be achieved only if firms in the region begin to think globally. This chapter focuses on this reality and identifies the latest (1999/2000) business and political developments which hold great potential for foreign investors in southern Africa.

It is a fact that southern Africa is emerging as a region of potential importance to these investors because governments have made significant changes over the last five years. However, much of the outside world is not fully aware of these changes. Positive changes include reduction of the role of the State in the economy and relaxation of foreign exchange control.

But southern Africa still has a long way to go if it is to rival the front-runners in the race for foreign capital. In 1995, the 12 countries belonging to the Southern African Development Community (SADC) attracted US$90 million average per country. In the same year New Zealand drew $2,5 bn, Hungary $4,5 bn and Singapore $7 bn.

The main objectives of this chapter are to describe southern Africa as an emerging market, identify the strategic issues facing firms in the region during the next few years, determine the key factors affecting current foreign direct investment flows into these countries, and address perceptions on strategic alliances and competitiveness.

Business and political leaders in southern Africa were identified as the key focus of this research. The Investment Promotion Agencies in selected countries also assisted in collating information to ensure representative data from a wide range of industries in this region. It should be noted that almost one-third of the respondents identified themselves as representing the fishing/agriculture, manufacturing, and banking industries.

12.2 Southern Africa as an emerging regional market[1]

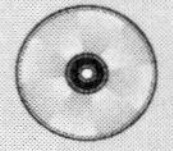

Compact disc

1 Dr Chris Stals of the Reserve Bank speculates about co-operation in the SADC.

With the imminent creation of a large integrated market of currently (1999) 190 million people and a combined Gross Domestic Product of over US$150 billion, southern Africa is an emerging market which will attract substantial domestic, regional, and foreign investment. Continuous flows of investments and sustained growth and development will, however, depend on the ability of industries in the SADC to compete within the domestic, regional, and international markets.

The Declaration and Treaty establishing the SADC were signed at the Summit of Heads of State or Government on 17 August 1992 in Windhoek, Namibia. Member states are Angola, Botswana, Democratic Republic of Congo (DRC), Lesotho, Malawi, Mauritius, Mozambique, Namibia, Seychelles, South Africa, Swaziland, Tanzania, Zambia, and Zimbabwe. Each member state has the responsibility for co-ordinating a sector or sectors on behalf of the others.

The macro-economic situation in the region has improved significantly and the opening up of the markets has also created new opportunities for investors, both domestic and international. The SADC achieved GDP growth of 6,6% in 1996, higher than Africa's average growth of 5%, and surpassing that of the industrialised countries of 4%. Southern Africa is, therefore, one of the most active emerging markets in the developing world. The SADC is viewed as the region with the greatest potential to spearhead the new African Renaissance. This renaissance is about renewal and regeneration, and about creating space for people to express and develop their talents; it embraces tolerance and mutual support, and harnesses the collective energies of member states to achieve a common vision. Other important factors that have contributed to this emerging market are discussed under separate headings below.

Political stability, peace, and security

The SADC has enjoyed relative peace and stability since the 1990s, which has provided an environment conducive to trade and investment. It is important that the SADC should consolidate and continue to pursue measures which promote peace and stability.

A window of opportunity

'The importance of bringing those who command investment resources together with South Africa and its member governments is not merely to provide the former with a window of opportunity. It lies rather in its contribution to the forging of a partnership that goes to the heart of our vision for southern Africa.'

Nelson Mandela, World Economic Forum, Africa Summit, Harare, May 1997

Transformation to market-based economies

All member states have undertaken major economic reforms by embracing market-based economies, with the private sector playing a leading role. The reforms that have been undertaken include privatisation of state-owned enterprises, relaxation of some exchange control restrictions, and freedom from many import restrictions. The short-term social impact of the reforms should be addressed through strategic government programmes.

Resource endowment

The region is richly endowed with abundant agricultural, mineral, and human resources. The availability of these resources in the region can be turned into a competitive edge, given the environment that is being created. More investments should be directed toward the beneficiation of the region's resources, especially in manufactured products, which would lead to the diversification of exports.

Good infrastructure

There is a relatively good infrastructure in the SADC that is a prerequisite for an emerging regional market and investment destination. The region has made substantial investments in telecommunications, railways, ports, and road transport systems. The transformation of the transport corridors into development corridors is a landmark in the SADC's long-term development strategy. The development corridors such as Beira, Maputo, and Walvis Bay, are all intended to open investment opportunities for both domestic and foreign private investors.

Tourism potential

The service sector is one of the sectors where opportunities are enormous, especially in tourism. This is one of the fastest-growing sectors in the region, which also tends to be labour-intensive. The SADC has many centres of tourist attraction which should be developed and marketed.

Development of capital and money markets

The region has established a viable financial sector that has witnessed the creation of stock markets. Of the 16 stock exchanges in Africa, eight of them are in southern Africa – the oldest of which is the Johannesburg Stock Exchange. There has been such remarkable activity on the stock exchanges that some of them are rated highly as the emerging capital markets in developing countries. The capital and money markets are assisted by fewer restrictions on current account transactions, but there are still exchange control restrictions on the capital account which remain a sore point to investors. Member states are urged to remove all capital account exchange control restrictions to allow the free flow of investment capital.

It is therefore evident from the above that the region has all the ingredients of an emerging market and is an attractive destination for investment. Southern Africa could be the boom region of the 21st century.

12.3 Globalisation as the context of regional integration and development

The SADC strategy for integration and development of the region should be seen in the context of globalisation. The world is gripped in a new process of globalisation as reflected in the growth of world trade, unification of capital markets, and the internationalisation of production and distribution networks, and the mega-revolution in information, communications, and technology. Globalisation presents both opportunities and challenges for developing countries, and especially for Africa and the southern African region.

The economies in the region continue to be confined to the export of primary commodities, especially from the agricultural and mining sectors. While the volume of exports has increased substantially, their value has declined drastically. These economies are thus participating in the global market from a weak and disadvantaged position.

The ability of investment capital to seek out the most efficient markets, and for producers and consumers to access the most competitive sources, exposes the vulnerability of southern African economies to being made dumping grounds for multinational corporations. Infant manufacturing industries are subjected to stiff competition and run the risk of being wiped out.

Globalisation in its present form exacerbates the inequable nature of the international market. Increased capital mobility across borders, aided by advanced telecommunication technology, brings with it the risk of destabilising capital flows and gives rise to balance of payments problems and exchange rate volatility. Furthermore, the low level of development of SADC economies in terms of technology, infrastructure, and technical and managerial skills, increases the risk of being marginalised.

The real challenge for the SADC is to develop structures and adopt appropriate policies which will transform the region's productive capacity into manufactured products for export. This would be sustainably competitive at regional level, and would give the region the latitude to launch itself effectively on to the global market.

Notwithstanding the above challenges, there are substantial benefits to be derived from globalisation. These benefits can be noticed in increasing trade, which gives consumers access to a wider choice of low-cost, high-quality goods and services. Producers would also have access to advanced technology that facilitates more efficient and effective use of resources, as well as to world markets, as perceived at the conclusion of the Uruguay Round of the General Agreement on Tariffs and Trade (GATT), and the establishment of the World Trade Organisation (WTO). This gave the SADC countries the opportunity to exploit the available opportunities and comparative advantages.

The fact that the WTO allows greater market openness at regional level at a faster pace than at the global level is in itself an opportunity for expanding production, improving productivity, and enhancing competitiveness in regional trade. This has the potential to increase employment in tradeable goods industries. The expansion of the manufacturing and related sectors opens new employment opportunities in non-tradeable and service sectors. The movement of labour across national boundaries reduces production bottlenecks, thus raising the supply response of the economy. It has been observed that in the industrialised countries, openness to foreign expertise, advanced technology and know-how, and management techniques have also had positive effects on production and marketing efficiency.

Is regional integration an answer to challenges of globalisation?

The region should, therefore, face up to the challenges and exploit the available opportunities. However, southern Africa can only compete effectively if all the countries in the region work together as a group. This is why regional integration is a prelude to globalisation. The trend towards regional integration is clearly reflected in the rising number of economic groupings during the last three decades, such as MERCOSUR, CARICOM, IOR, COMESA, ASEAN, NAFTA, and ANDEAN, to mention a few (refer back to Chapter 2). The importance of large regional markets as a basis for increasing trade flows and building up capacities to produce export products, cannot be over-emphasised. Regional integration is an important instrument for enhancing competition since it offers national economies opportunities for reduced tariff levels, larger markets, and economies of scale in the production of goods and services. Such regional competition will also spur on the adoption of new and advanced technology and management techniques, which will improve the quality of output. Regional trade and capital flows across borders are important for underpinning export growth.

12.4 Research into strategic issues facing the southern African region[2]

Business and political leaders in southern Africa were identified as the key focus of this research. The Investment Promotion Agencies in selected countries also assisted in collating information to ensure representative data from a wide range of industries in this region.

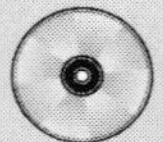

Compact disc

2 The strategic issues facing southern Africa are explained in this clip.

The assessment of the respondents shown in Exhibit 12.1 indicates the high level of concern about **political stability**, as well as the enhancement of **global competitiveness**. A significant effort is also needed to attract **foreign direct investment** into the region.

Management expertise and training and development were identified as other areas of strategic importance. This reflects the relative scarcity of skills which prevents beneficiation and the adding of value to the abundant resources of this region.

Strategic issues

In addition to the above aspects, the importance of the following strategic issues was also highlighted by African respondents:

- information technology
- privatisation
- bilateral trade agreements

There is a growing realisation that countries in the region have abundant natural resources to spur on this opportunity for growth and development. These strategic issues pose tremendous challenges to the economies of southern African countries. Primary concerns and focus areas include:

- shedding the image of turmoil and poverty;
- showing serious commitment to fight crime and corruption;
- rewarding global competitive companies;
- encouraging the training of quality labour.

12.5 Key factors affecting foreign direct investment flows into the southern African region

Exhibit 12.2 (p. 362) shows the key factors affecting foreign direct investment. Political stability, as well as combating crime and ensuring safety, were rated the highest. Foreign direct investment, in particular, has played an important role in stimulating economic growth in developing countries, through the

- transfer of modern technology and production techniques;

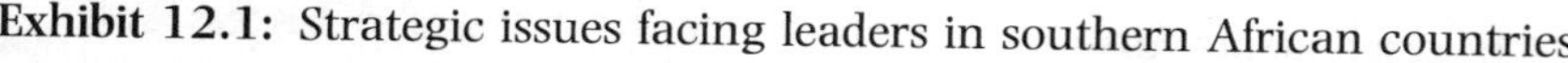
Exhibit 12.1: Strategic issues facing leaders in southern African countries

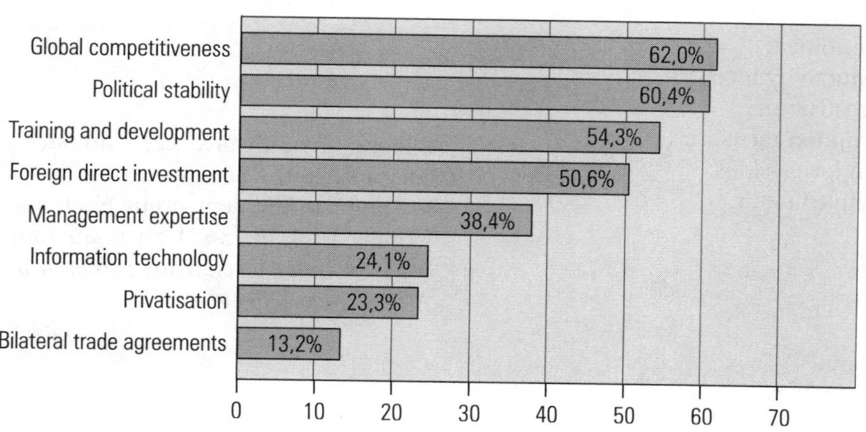

Exhibit 12.2: Key factors affecting FDI flows into southern African countries

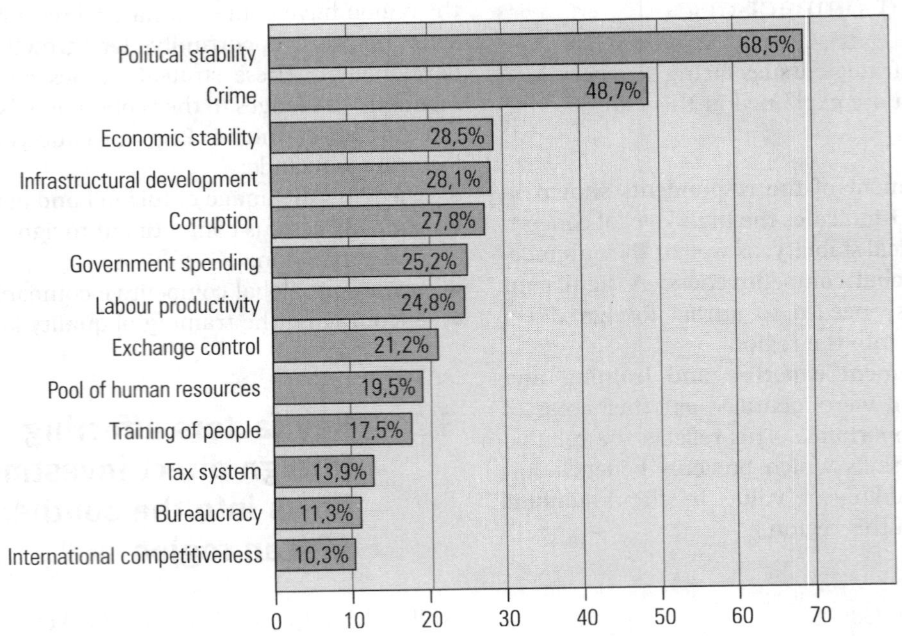

- transfer of skills, management expertise, and high-level training;
- enhancement of access to international sources of finance; and
- facilitation of access to global markets.

The other factors which respondents mentioned were:

- stable economies;
- high productivity levels;
- good infrastructure;
- anti-corruption measures;
- education levels/skills;
- cost-effective labour.

Stumbling-blocks to investment

Many countries in this region have seen little private, domestic capital formation for 20 years; banking and financial services are underdeveloped; aspirant local entrepreneurs lack sophisticated business skills; statistical information is often inadequate, while low levels of skills and productivity fail to attract foreign investment.

Billions of rand have been invested in South Africa since the achievement of political stability and the first democratic elections in 1994. Exhibit 12.3 (p. 363) gives an indication of some of these foreign investments into South Africa since 1994:

Exhibit 12.3: Top ten foreign investors in South Africa since 1994

Investor	Country	R-billion
SBC Communications	USA	3,3
Telekom Malaysia	Malaysia	2,2
Coca-Cola	USA	2,1
Petronas	Malaysia	1,9
Caltex	USA	1,2
BMW	Germany	1,1
Shell	UK	0,9
Nestlé	Switzerland	0,6
Goodyear	USA	0,6
British Petroleum	UK	0,5

SOURCE: *Sunday Times, Business Times,* 16 November 1997.

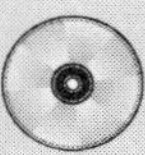

Compact disc

3 President Mbeki analyses the advantages of business opportunities in the SADC and specifically the benefits of the Delta Plant in South Africa.

12.6 Identification of business sectors which reflect high growth opportunities in southern Africa

The tourism, agricultural, and manufacturing industries were identified by business and political leaders as the business sectors which reflect high growth opportunities (Exhibit 12.4 on p. 364). Almost 50% of the respondents indicated that tourism is the major industry with the potential of creating new job opportunities and bringing foreign investment into the region, while more than 30% linked the manufacturing, agricultural, and mining industries with high growth potential.

The growth rate of tourism in Mauritius for 1996, for example, was 16%, while the growth rates for manufacturing and agriculture were 6,3% and 4,3%, respectively.

Focus on Mauritius – where exports have made a difference

Dwarfed in size by even the smallest of its fellow winners, Mauritius may be tiny, but if measured in terms of economic growth and political stability, it is a veritable giant. About the size of the city of Houston in the United States, Mauritius has no diamonds, no gold and no known oil reserves. What this spunky multicultural Indian Ocean nation of one million people does have, though, is an educated and hard-working populace guided by an enlightened democratic government and sound economic policies. Having had seven free and fair elections since independence 25 years ago, the nation was also ranked first as the most competitive country in a report prepared by the Harvard Institute of International Development.

During the past decade and a half, Mauritius has grown at the rate of 5,5% to 6,5% per annum, and has also demonstrated its commitment to regional integration by its membership of the Commonwealth, COMESA, the SADC, and the IOR-ARC (see Chapter 2).

Once a monocultural economy, dependent on sugar for its livelihood, Mauritius now derives the bulk of its income from a dynamic tourist and textile industry. Mauritius imports yarn, makes up garments, and exports the finished goods to major retail organisations such as The Gap in the USA. At the forefront of textile technology, this island nation is the number one apparel manufacturer in Africa. Mauritius is also exporting capital and know-how to other would-be clothing manufacturers such as neighbouring Madagascar. In the 1990s, Mauritius had an unemployment rate of 33%; today it is importing labour from Madagascar and China.

SOURCE: 'Focus on Mauritius', *Business in Africa*, Vol. 7, No. 4, July/August, 1999, p.44.

Exhibit 12.4 (p. 364) also reflects the high value that leaders place on fast-emerging industries such as **financial services and infor-**

Exhibit 12.4: Key industries in southern Africa

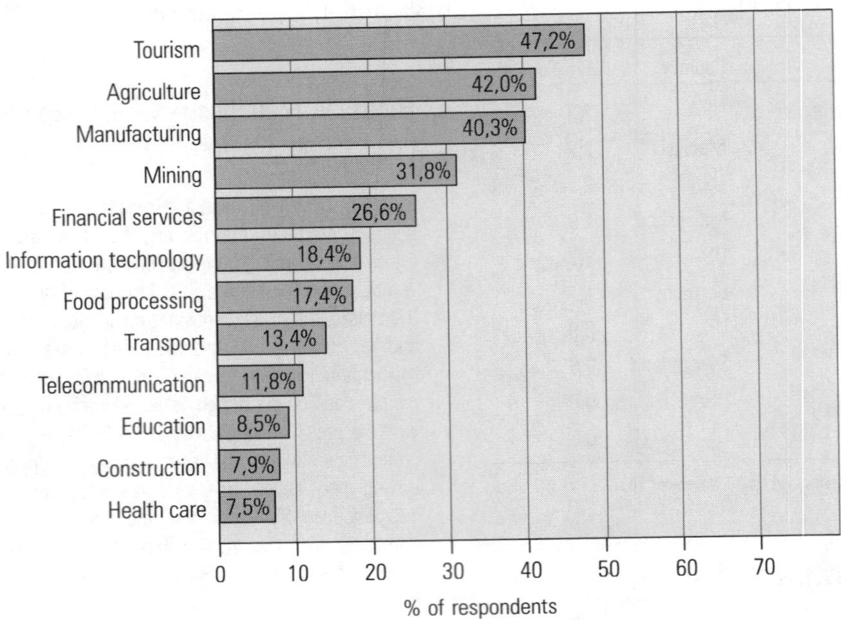

mation technology. The focus placed on food processing, transport, telecommunication, and education, was expected.

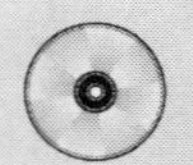

Compact disc

4 Professor Jeffrey Sachs of Harvard University identifies 'competitive weaknesses' in South Africa.

12.7 Perceptions on regional competitiveness

The competitive position of the SADC region and individual member states still leaves a lot to be desired. In the 1997 Global Competitiveness Report,[3] only South Africa was ranked, at number 43, out of 53 countries surveyed. This means that all the southern African countries first have to take a serious look at what is transpiring within their borders, in order to build up their capacities to enhance competitiveness.

But what is competitiveness? It is the capacity of economies to achieve rapid economic growth.

Why is competitiveness such a major discussion point for business and political leaders in southern Africa? Almost every conference has a theme or sub-theme about global and/or regional competitiveness! The answer is clear – high sustained economic growth is the foundation for the fundamental improvement of the quality of life of people in southern Africa.

Much has been said about company or industry competitiveness versus country or national competitiveness. The fact is that companies are heavily influenced by their national and international environments, and the economic growth rates in their individual countries. The authors have made no attempt to establish or rank the southern African countries in terms of their relative competitiveness. However, the qualitative perceptions of decision-makers on competitive issues in southern Africa, and the strong and weak 'links' in competitiveness, were identified.

Respondents were required to assess their own country's competitiveness in terms of people and population characteristics, level of science and technology, management competence, infrastructural development, finance issues, government efficiency, level of internationalisation, and domestic economic features. Exhibit 12.5 gives some examples of these factors of competitiveness. An assessment of 1 is a strong factor, while an assessment of 7 indicates a relatively weak competitive link.

Exhibit 12.6 indicates the perceptions on competitiveness in southern African countries on how eight given factors are linked. According to this exhibit, the government and the people factors are the weakest links in the region, while infrastructure and finance issues (such as cost of capital, rate of return, avail-

Exhibit 12.5: Examples of factors of competitiveness (See IMD, 1997)

1 **Domestic economy:** for example, capital formation, cost of living, value added, private consumption, economic forecasts.
2 **Internalisation:** for example, trade performance, exports, imports, national protectionism, foreign direct investments, cultural openness
3 **Government:** for example, national debt, government expenditures, state involvement in economy, government efficiency and transparency, fiscal policies, social political stability
4 **Finance:** for example, cost of capital, rate of return, availability of finance, stock markets, financial services
5 **Infrastructure:** for example, energy self-sufficiency, technological infrastructure, transport infrastructure, environment
6 **Management:** for example, productivity, labour costs, compensation level, corporate performance, management efficiency
7 **Science and technology:** for example, research and development resources, scientific research, patents, technology management
8 **People:** for example, population characteristics, labour force skills, employment, educational systems and structures, quality of life

Exhibit 12.6: Perceptions on competitiveness in selected southern African countries (1 = strong link; 7 = weak link)

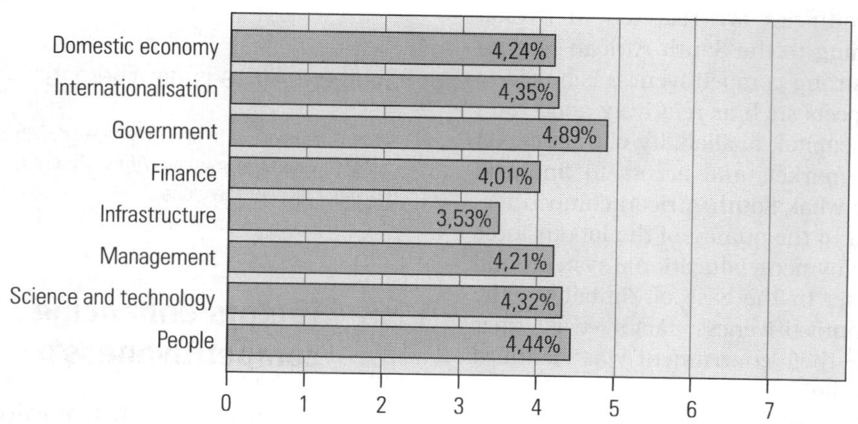

Exhibit 12.7: Perceptions of respondents from specific countries on competitive links with respect to their own countries

	Domestic economy	Internatio-nalisation	Govern-ment	Finance	Infrastruc-ture	Manage-ment	Science & technology	People
Botswana			✔			✗		
Malawi			✗		✔			
Mauritius		✔	✗					
Mozambique	✗							✔
Namibia			✔			✗		
South Africa				✔				✗
Swaziland			✗			✔		
Tanzania							✗	✔
Zambia					✗			✔
Zimbabwe			✗					✔

✔ = perceptions of respondents from a specific country on the strongest 'competitive link' with respect to competitiveness for their own country

✔ = percentage of respondents from a specific country on the weakest 'competitive link' with respect to competitiveness for their own country

ability of finance, stock markets, and financial services) are viewed as having relatively strong competitive links.

The perceptions of respondents from specific countries on 'competitive links' with respect to their own countries are reflected in Exhibit 12.7. According to the South African respondents, their strong competitiveness is linked to financing aspects such as relatively good rates of return on capital, availability of finance, an active stock market, and access to financial services. The weak South African competitiveness is linked to the quality of the labour force skills, unemployment, educational systems and structures, etc. In the case of Zimbabwe, the strongest competitiveness factor was their people, while their government was identified as the 'weak' link.

Perhaps somewhat surprisingly, Exhibit 12.7 shows that the government factor was the weak link in 4 out of the 10 countries in this report, while the people factor was identified as the strong factor also in 4 out of the 10 countries (not in the case of the aforementioned countries).

> **Southern Africa is no different!**
>
> There is no mystery to relatively slow growth or non-competitiveness in southern Africa. The reasons are the same all over the globe.

12.8 Factors enhancing competitiveness[4]

There are a number of factors that will enhance competitiveness in southern Africa and which have to be addressed because of their critical nature. The main ones are discussed under separate headings below.

Market-based economic policies

An open economy empowers the people and allows international transactions in capital inflows, goods, and services, as well as in the movement of expertise with new management techniques which improve production capacity and enhance productivity. Macro-economic stability, embodied in low inflation, appropriate, stable, and predictable real exchange rates and prudent fiscal stance, is essential for expanding economic domestic activity and is a precondition for benefiting from sustained private capital flows. Member states have adopted open-market economic policies. There is also some degree of economic convergence, which augurs well for improving the competitive position of the region.

Roles of government and the legal framework

Legal and political institutions that lay the foundation for supporting a modern, competitive market economy, including the rule of law and protection of property rights, play an important role in building investor confidence. It is gratifying to note that in the SADC we can boast of having transparent and independent judicial systems which are supported by accountable political systems that uphold the rule of law and respect the basic principles of democracy and human rights.

Financial and capital markets

There is a two-way relationship between the financial and productive sectors of the economy. The financial sector's contribution to economic growth lies in the central role it plays in mobilising savings and allocating these resources efficiently to the most productive uses and investments in the economic sector. It is gratifying to observe genuine efforts by governments in the region to restructure and resuscitate the financial sector for enhanced economic performance. The financial sector reforms have brought about an increase in such vital capital market institutions as stock exchanges, stock-broking firms, and issuing houses.

Quality and efficiency of infrastructure

The provision of a low-cost and efficient infrastructure is essential for enhancing competitiveness, especially for landlocked member states. In the SADC, the basic infrastructure is in place. With regard to telecommunications, while the interconnections to international countries appear to be good, the cost to the consumer is still very high. Given that telecommunication has become the key to development, especially for export marketing and importation of machinery and equipment, the need for cost-effective systems cannot be overemphasised.

Modern technology

Man has managed to survive the ravages and calamities of this world through being innovative and improving upon existing technology. Technological changes bring with them the hope that their productive potential can be harnessed to raise the living standards of the region's citizens and eradicate absolute poverty. The absorption and diffusion of new technologies play an important role in transforming the region's productivity levels, production capacities and capabilities, and economic performance, in the same way as technology has created the prosperity of the industrialised world. Regrettably, total spending on research and development (R&D) is very insignificant and yet it is one of the crucial factors for improving productivity and competitiveness. Available statistics indicate that Third World countries, including the SADC, spend less than 2% of their budgets on R&D, as compared to more than 10% in the developed world. There is, therefore, a need to mobilise more resources from government and to bring in the private sector to fund R&D, in order to improve the region's competitive edge.

Human capital

Human capital is another critical factor for promoting competitiveness since it provides the required knowledge, skills, attitudes, and capacities for the development of competitive strategies, product development, quality control, corporate financial operations, marketing, and human resource development. Furthermore, human resource and skills development facilitates the adoption, absorption, and diffusion of new technology. The requisite skills and an ability to learn quickly are needed. As a region, substantial investment in human resource development and training has been made, but this has to be a continuous process as new ways of doing business are developed.

Productivity improvement

Productivity is a decisive factor for the success of the SADC's integration agenda as the region tries to make itself competitive in the fast globalisation of the world economy. High productivity levels are crucial for attracting foreign direct investment, which is a source of new technology, and managerial skills for the enhancement of the competitive edge of southern African export products.

It is clear from the above factors that the SADC cannot allow itself to be marginalised. The region has to liberalise further, embrace new technology, manage the macro-economic policies with prudence, open the markets, and use the market information tool for establishing niche markets in which its export products are competitive.

12.9 Competitiveness in South Africa's manufacturing industries

Exhibit 12.8 (p. 369) shows the competitiveness of South Africa's manufacturing industries based on labour costs (wages) and the level of technology. It is clear that there is a direct link between the level of technology needed to perform a certain function and the level of wage that is attached to the corresponding competency. For example, a high level of competency in technology attracts relatively high wages in the aerospace and computer industries, while people employed in the relatively low technology industries, such as food and wood products, attract comparatively low wages.

12.10 Strategies to develop southern Africa as a global player

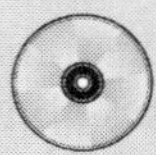

Compact disc

5 Mr Trevor Manuel spells out the South African government's views on policy management, inflation, monetary policy, and competitiveness in southern Africa.

The results of the above survey (Sections 12.4 – 12.7) constitute a broad-scale view of southern African leaders on issues such as foreign direct investment, global competitiveness, political stability, training and development, and the availability of management expertise, which will remain on the political and business agendas for the next few years. In general, these decision-makers are confident that they can tackle these issues and make a positive contribution to the region. The general feeling is: 'If any one country fails, the region as a whole will fail as well.'

However, if southern Africa is serious about entering the 21st century poised to develop into a deregulated and competitive global region, various strategies (some of them radical) will have to be put in place sooner rather than later. Ten strategies which could achieve this goal are:

- enhancing the overall competitiveness of key industries in the region by, *inter alia,*

Exhibit 12.8: South Africa's manufacturing industries competitiveness

Wage	Level of Technology			
	High	Medium	Low	Total
High	Aerospace: computers & office equipment; pharmaceuticals	Scientific instruments; communications equipment & semiconductors	Electrical machinery	
	1,7%	2,0%	3,7%	7,4%
Medium	Chemicals excluding drugs; motor vehicles	Rubber & plastics; non-ferrous metals; non-electrical machinery	Other transport equipment; other manufacturing	
	10,5%	13,3%	1,3%	25,1%
Low	Petroleum refining	Paper & printing; non-metallic mineral products; iron & steel; metal products; shipbuilding	Food, beverages & tobacco; textile, apparel & leather; wood products	
	13,8%	30,2%	23,6%	67,5%
TOTAL	25,9%	45,5%	28,6%	100,0%

SOURCE: Liebenberg, K. 1996. Productivity Focus. NPI.

integrating the regional transport infrastructure, power grids, and port facilities;

- actively encouraging the shift to beneficiated, manufactured exports;
- increasing the speed of liberalising and deregulating the economic activities by public-private partnerships, commercialisation, privatisation, and private sector development;
- promoting the increased use of technology and the efficiency of the economies in the global markets;
- introducing more investor-friendly promotion packages to attract high-class multinational companies;
- encouraging companies and industries to add value to their products and services by entering into increased strategic alliances and joint ventures with world-class companies;
- convincing trade unions of the importance of increased labour productivity and freer labour markets;
- abolishing exchange controls and eliminating internal barriers such as protectionism and industry-specific subsidies;
- combining efforts to fight crime and corruption effectively;
- convincing the private sector of the importance of increased on-the-job training.

Today's world-class governments and companies have found ways to create and sustain their competitive advantage. They have applied technology, developed superior internal capabilities, and marshalled talents from diverse stakeholders, suppliers, customers, competitors, and alliance partners. Through their actions they are constantly redefining the shape of competitiveness.

12.11 **Summary**

Southern Africa is emerging as a region of potential importance to foreign investors because governments have made significant changes during the last five years. However, much of the outside world is not fully aware of these changes.

Positive changes include reducing the role of the State in the economy and relaxing foreign exchange control.

Continuous flows of investments and sustained growth and development will depend on the ability of industries in the SADC to compete within the domestic, regional, and international markets.

The SADC has enjoyed relative peace and stability since the 1990s, which has provided an environment conducive to trade and investment. It is important that SADC consolidates and continues to pursue measures which promote peace and stability.

The real challenge for SADC countries is to develop structures and adopt appropriate policies which will transform the region's productive capacity into manufactured products for export. This would be sustainably competitive at regional level, and give the region the latitude to effectively launch itself on to the global market.

Political stability, crime, economic stability, productivity, infrastructure, corruption, levels of education, and skills were identified as factors affecting FDI into southern Africa, either negatively or positively.

Tourism, agriculture, and the manufacturing industries were identified by business and political leaders as the business sectors which reflect the highest growth opportunities in southern Africa. Emerging industries, such as financial services, information technology, food processing, transport, and telecommunication, were also ranked as growth industries.

Ten strategies were identified which will increase southern Africa's development into a deregulated and competitive global region.

Endnotes

1 Southern African Development Community. 1998. *Official SADC trade, industry and investment review.* Southern African Marketing Co. (Pty) Ltd.

2 Deloitte & Touche. 1998. *Strategic trends and foreign direct investment in Southern Africa.* Researched by Johan Hough and Brian Naicker. In co-operation with the World Economic Forum.

3 *Global competitiveness report.* 1997. Geneva, Switzerland: World Economic Forum.

4 Southern African Development Community, ibid.

Index